PURPOSE AND PROCESS: A READER FOR WRITERS

STEPHEN REID

Colorado State University

PRENTICE HALL, Englewood Cliffs, New Jersey 07632

Library of Congress Cataloging-in-Publication Data

Purpose and process : a reader for writers / [edited by] Stephen Reid.
    p. cm.
  Includes index.
  ISBN 0-13-742552-X
  1. College readers.   2. English language—Rhetoric.   I. Reid,
Stephen.
  PE1417.P855   1991
  808'.0427—dc20   90-48894
                            CIP

Editorial/production supervision
  and interior design: *Mark Tobey*
Cover art: *Marblehead © 1990 Thomas McKnight*
Cover design: *Ben Santora*
Prepress buyer: *Herb Klein*
Manufacturing buyer: *David Dickey*

© 1991 by Prentice-Hall, Inc.
A Division of Simon & Schuster
Englewood Cliffs, New Jersey 07632

Printed in the United States of America
10 9 8 7 6 5 4 3 2 1

ISBN   0-13-742552-X

Prentice-Hall International (UK) Limited, *London*
Prentice-Hall of Australia Pty. Limited, *Sydney*
Prentice-Hall Canada Inc., *Toronto*
Prentice-Hall Hispanoamericana, S.A., *Mexico*
Prentice-Hall of India Private Limited, *New Delhi*
Prentice-Hall of Japan, Inc., *Tokyo*
Simon & Schuster Asia Pte. Ltd., *Singapore*
Editora Prentice-Hall do Brasil, Ltda., *Rio de Janeiro*

CONTENTS

Annotated Essay. Arlene Pfeiffer, a 17-year-old honor student, student council president, and unwed mother, is kicked out of the honor society after giving birth to a daughter, Jessica. Is the school board guilty of hypocrisy?

Contents

2

WRITING: PURPOSES AND PROCESSES   73

3

OBSERVING 141

6
EXPLAINING 347

7

EVALUATING 421

8

PROBLEM SOLVING 489

9

ARGUING   565

PREFACE

"The writer may write to inform, to explain, to entertain, to persuade," Donald Murray says, "but whatever the purpose there should be, first of all, the satisfaction of the writer's own learning." Learning, discovery, excitement, relevance, ownership: These words describe the writer's impetus for writing. Without human curiosity and desire, rhetoric collapses into mere terminology. By giving primacy to the writer's purposes and processes for reading and writing, *Purpose and Process: A Reader for Writers* encourages writers to take control of their reading and writing of texts.

Three basic assumptions form the structure of *Purpose and Process*. First, rhetorical readers should be organized by purpose, not by strategy. *Purpose and Process* follows the sequence of purposes set forth in *The Prentice Hall Guide for College Writers*. In both texts, the writer's purpose (to explain, evaluate, argue, or explore a subject for a specific audience in a defined context) is the ultimate guide. Strategies (definition, comparison-contrast, classification) are subordinated to the writer's purpose(s). Strategies help the writer invent and shape ideas, but they rarely control the writing situation. Writers should be encouraged to choose *among* strategies to achieve a purpose for a given audience. Just as writers select an appropriate voice or choose a formal or informal style, they should choose rhetorical strategies that are tailored to the rhetorical situation.

Second, teaching the skills of critical reading and "reading with a writer's eye" should begin by tapping the writer's own ideas, attitudes, and experiences. *Purpose and Process* uses prereading journal assignments, reader-response activities, and collaborative annotations of texts as means to achieve skill in critical reading and effective writing. The traditional reading/writing model asks students to read the essays and *then* write. This anthology asks students to write and talk before and during reading in order to make read.ng and writing more successful. Prereading and collaborative response are as crucial to the reading process as prewriting and group activities are to the writing process.

Finally, diversity in an anthology requires more than a list of minority authors and multi-cultural readings. It requires sharing multiple perspectives as the classroom community reads and creates texts. It requires a diversity of topics, including familiar campus topics as well as those that are culturally distant. It requires more emphasis on student writing, from both traditional and non-traditional students. *Purpose and Process* includes the "professional" minority voices; it also emphasizes the student's voice and experience. The sixteen prize-winning student essays generated by *The Prentice Hall Contest for College Writers* ensure that students' voices are heard.

The following are key features of *Purpose and Process: A Reader for Writers:*

Introductory Chapters on Reading and Writing. Since writers need to understand basic approaches to reading and writing, Chapters One and Two introduce students to critical reading and textual annotation and to the various purposes and processes for writing. Essays in these chapters by professional and student writers illustrate individual approaches to reading and writing.

Purposes for Writing. *Purpose and Process* follows a logical sequence of purposes. Chapters Three through Five (Observing, Remembering, and Investigating) model the descriptive, narrative, and research skills students need in order to write their essays. Chapters Six through Nine (Explaining, Evaluating, Problem Solving, and Arguing) illustrate how professional and student writers write expository and argumentative prose for a variety of audiences.

Processes for Writing. Writing processes vary from one writer to the next and from one situation to the next. Processes are dependent upon the writer's culture and experience, the purpose, the audience, and the writing situation. *Purpose and Process* focuses on basic writing elements (collecting, shaping, drafting, revising) and gives examples of the individual writing processes of eight student writers.

Critical Reading and Text Annotation. The first reading selection in chapters Three through Nine contains examples of responses to a Prereading Journal Entry and a collaborative annotation of a professional essay. Both prereading journals and annotations are modeled by actual student examples.

Essay Review Questions. Following each student and professional essay are four categories of study questions: Questions about Meaning, Questions about Purpose and Strategy, Questions about Audience and Language, and Questions for Discussion and Writing. These questions, however, are designed to supplement rather than direct or preempt the students' own readings.

Thematic Clusters of Essays. *Purpose and Process* contains ten clusters of essay subjects: Contemporary Issues, The Environment, Popular Culture, The Woman's Perspective, Cultural Diversity, Friends and Family, Education, College

Life, Reading, and Writing. See the alternate Thematic Table of Contents at the end of this book for a list of essays.

Annotated Instructor's Edition. Teaching tips, discussion activities, and answers to questions are integrated into the margins of the Annotated Instructor's Edition. Teachers of students whose essays are included in the anthology also offer information and advice for class activities and assignments.

ACKNOWLEDGMENTS

Special thanks are due to writing instructors at the following schools who encouraged their students to submit entries and who selected the prize-winning essays submitted to *The Prentice Hall Contest for College Writers*:

Belleville Area College, Ann Bennette

Colorado State University, Stephen Reid

Ohio University, Heidi Barcus

Oklahoma State University, Richard Batteiger

University of Central Florida, Gerald Schiffhorst

University of Southwestern Louisiana, Mary Ann Wilson

The hundreds of students who submitted their best essays to *The Prentice Hall Contest for College Writers* deserve a special note of thanks. Their drafts and essays taught me once more that writing is a wonderful, frustrating, creative, tedious, imaginative, and liberating activity.

The following professors gave valuable feedback on ideas for the text, suggestions about apparatus, and advice about specific essays: Patricia Harkin, University of Akron; Peggy Jolly, University of Alabama at Birmingham; Susan J. Miller, Sante Fe Community College; Sylvia T. Miner, Mount Wachesett Community College; and Jean Murphy, Pierce College.

The talented professionals at Prentice Hall deserve far more than a few words tucked away in an acknowledgments paragraph: Phil Miller, for his continued support and expertise; Kate Morgan, for her wise counsel and editorial savvy; Tracy Augustine, for her amazing energy and organization; and Mark Tobey and Ann Knitel for their editorial direction.

Finally, my family of writers has given unwavering encouragement and support: Gus and Loren, Shelley and Michael, and Joy.

Stephen Reid
Colorado State University

1

READING: PURPOSES AND PROCESSES

Every page is a pasture, and we are let out to graze like hungry herds.

—William Gass, author of *Omensetter's Luck*

No one else can read a literary work for us. The benefits of literature can emerge only from creative activity on the part of the reader.

—Louise Rosenblatt, author of *Literature as Exploration*

Bit by bit, one thing at a time . . . the learner learns through reading *like a writer to* write *like a writer.*

—Frank Smith, author of "Essays into Literacy"

You *can* improve your writing without reading a book of essays, but here is what you would be missing:

Imitation is a powerful learning strategy. We learn to cook partly by being in the kitchen and watching our parents or friends put together a meal. We learn how to drive a car partly by observing how others drive. Learning to write essays works the same way. We learn to write, in part, by reading essays written for various purposes and audiences. Notice one key difference, however. We don't learn to cook if we just sit in the kitchen and eat. We have to watch from the cook's point of view; we have to pay attention to what the cook is doing and not be distracted by the wonderful smells coming out of the oven. To learn to drive, we have to imagine ourselves in the driver's seat, doing what the driver does, making decisions and choices. In learning to write, we cannot read passively, hoping just to be entertained or informed. We must learn to read actively, to read with a writer's eye.

Collections of essays offer hundreds of ideas to write about. Faced with an assignment, most of us panic. Why? Basically, because we don't have anything to write about. At first, no ideas come to us. Nada. Nothing. Second, when topics do spring to mind (sports, dating, studying, vacations, family, friends), they seem too trivial for a "real" essay. Third, we don't really feel like authorities on anything. (Isn't that, after all, the purpose of college, to let us learn from people who do know?). This collection of essays will help you discover ideas to write about. It will show you that a seemingly trivial subject can become worth writing about. And it will show you how to draw on your powers of observation, memory, and reading to become knowledgeable on your subject.

The processes of reading and writing support each other. If your goal is to become a better writer and thinker, critical reading will help you write more effectively. As you become a more attentive reader of others' essays, you will read and revise your own writing more effectively. Conversely, writing helps you become a more attentive and critical reader. Your first few examinations in college undoubtedly taught you the best way to study for a test. Open the book, read the chapters, and then take the test, right? Wrong. To make sure you know the material, you should be able to *close* the book and still write out the main ideas—and your reactions—in your own words. Learning to read critically, to annotate what you read, and to share your reactions with others will help you synthesize and recall key ideas. Writing is crucial to the reading and learning process; active reading supports the writing process.

Student essays reveal the composing strategies behind the printed page. Seeing how other writers choose a subject, collect information, organize their ideas, and revise their essays will help you compose essays. What situation or context prompted a particular essay? What personal experience motivated the author to write? What was the original purpose? Who was the intended audience? Where did this writer get the examples and information? How did this writer organize the information clearly and logically? How did this writer revise and edit? Seeing the composing processes behind the printed product will help you write more confidently and effectively.

READING IS NOT A SPECTATOR SPORT

To read more effectively, you may need to break some old habits.

The Television Habit. Television is arguably the most powerful communication medium in the world. Because it is so colorful, so fast paced, and so immediate, it entrances and transfixes us. It invites us to become an advertiser's dream: an unthinking, uncritical consumer. You don't need to quit watching television, but you do need to quit watching passively. *You need to break the passive consumer habit, the couch potato trance that television promotes.* Good readers, readers learning to be better writers, readers learning to appreciate and discriminate, read *actively.* Good readers use the built-in "instant replay" feature of all written texts: They *reread* to engage the text and annotate key features. Good readers also *discuss* what they have read with other readers. Television programs us to be passive; reading invites us to be active—and interactive.

The High School Textbook Habit.   Because most high schools do not require you to buy and own books, they discourage active reading. You are told not to "mark up" your books. The books are not yours; you must return them at the end of the term. Imagine a coach tossing you a volleyball in gym class and saying, "Now don't hit this too hard. Don't get it dirty. This volleyball is the property of Washington High School." Just as you have to use a volleyball to play the game, you have to use books to learn from them. You need to break the this-book-is-not-my-property habit. *Good readers learn how to **own** books,* to like or hate them, to underline key ideas, to write in the margin, to scribble in the pages, to argue with friends about the ideas. Books need pencils and pens to come alive. Books are not really read until they are **re**read and marked up. Good reading must be active and interactive.

The Yellow Highlighter Habit.   The first technique most readers learn is to highlight key passages, usually in bright yellow, red, or pink. Although highlighting is better than totally passive reading, too often readers use it as a crutch. They highlight a whole page in neon yellow, hoping that they will remember more. In fact, research shows that you will remember and learn more *if you can connect what you read to what you already know:* "I remember when I felt like that" or "This was the point Professor Brown made in class" or "I really disagree with this." If there is no connection, go ahead and write, "I don't understand any of this!" or "What's the point?" or "Ask about this in class." Written comments in the margin are more effective than highlighting in promoting active, critical reading.

SOME MYTHS ABOUT READING

As you change your habits, you need to reexamine some of your assumptions about reading.

Myth: The best way to read a textbook or an essay is to begin on page one and read straight through until you reach the end.

Reality: The shortest distance between two points is not always a straight line. Your reading will be more effective if you begin by browsing and skimming, getting a feel for the whole essay, chapter, or text. Look at the table of contents, note chapter titles, and skim beginnings of paragraphs. Look for the big picture. Don't let individual trees keep you from seeing the whole forest.

Myth: Textbooks and essays have hidden in them a single, unambiguous message put there by the author.

Reality: Writers do try to communicate some information or idea clearly in their writing, but their actual language may not communicate their intended meaning. Writers cannot transfer ideas directly into their readers' brains. Writers have to construct meaning as they write, knowing that each reader will react slightly differently. *The words on the page have meaning only when a reader gives them meaning.

Myth: The reader "decodes" the meaning that the writer puts in the text.

Reality: The text helps readers make meaning, but because readers attach slightly different meanings to individual words or sentences, and because readers connect this language to their own personal and cultural experiences, each reading is unique. To illustrate this point, compare your answer to the following riddle with a classmate's answer: In an automobile accident, a man is killed and his young son is critically injured. The man's son is rushed to a hospital. As the boy is wheeled into the emergency room, the doctor on duty looks at the boy and says, "My God, it's my son!" What was the relationship of the doctor to the injured boy?

Myth: Writers are great, learned people whose authority and wisdom you should bow down to and gratefully accept.

Reality: Writers may be intelligent or wise, but readers should not humble themselves before the "Great One" or uncritically "worship" the text. Readers must learn to test writers' ideas, question their facts, check up on their information, and challenge their assumptions or conclusions. (That applies to this text, too. For practice, challenge the sentence above with the asterisk.)

Myth: Reading is a solitary, private activity in which readers try to comprehend written texts.

Reality: Although people do read by themselves, the reading process is not complete until readers *compare* their understanding with other readers. In this class, discussing each essay, sharing annotations of essays, and listening to each other's ideas complement the solitary stage of the reading process.

PURPOSES FOR READING

If you are reading this chapter critically, you should have some questions or objections. "Not all reading is alike—I read the comics in a newspaper just for pleasure—what's wrong with that?" "I read the news on the front page just for relaxation and information—that's different from reading a college textbook." You're right. There are, in fact, many purposes for reading. Here are some:

Relaxing and being entertained

Gathering information

Understanding new ideas

Analyzing a problem and possible solutions

Evaluating a product, service, or performance

Agreeing or disagreeing with an argument

Exploring an idea or feeling

When you are reading for relaxation or entertainment, you may just want to be a couch potato, relaxing and enjoying a story or the comics or an essay. In fact, much writing has entertainment value—humorous anecdotes, original viewpoints, imaginative comparisons, or shocking statistics—designed to get our attention and interest. Most college courses, however, emphasize critical, interactive reading. Reading information, explanations, evaluations, policy recommendations or arguments—and then summarizing, responding, and asking questions—is the focus of many courses. *This course focuses on one particular type of critical reading: How to read with a writer's eye.* How to learn more about the craft of writing and thinking by studying the processes and products of other writers. (Critical reading of other writers' essays is only part of the reading/writing process. Another crucial part, learning how to read and revise your own writing *with a reader's eye,* is discussed in the next chapter.)

PROCESSES FOR CRITICAL READING

The following are four stages, or dimensions, of a critical reading process. Most good readers agree that they use these strategies, but they also acknowledge that critical reading is a very individual process. Each reader is unique. Each reader has different expectations, different reading habits or learning styles, and different goals for reading. With that important qualification in mind, practice these strategies on Ellen Goodman's essay, "Honor Society Hypocrisy," which is reprinted at the end of this section. See which of these strategies works best for you on that essay.

Prereading

The first strategy for critical reading is prereading—what you do before you actually begin reading an essay. Your basic purpose: to get the "big picture" of the subject and author before you read a particular essay.

1. **Write down what you already think or know about the topic.** You will learn and remember more about

the essay if you jot down any experiences you've had that are similar or record what you think about a controversial topic *before* you read the essay. Use the Prereading Journal Topic as a prompt for five minutes of freewriting.

2. **Read about the author and the context for this essay.** Who is the author? Why did the writer choose this topic? What prompted the essay? What does the title suggest to you? Who was the original audience for the essay? In what book or magazine was this essay printed? What else has this writer written?

First Reading

During the first reading, read through to the end, noting your reactions and response. Read for enjoyment. Read to satisfy your curiosity. Read for ideas and information that are important to *you*. Imagine you are a reader of the magazine, newspaper, or book in which this essay first appeared.

1. **Get a pencil or pen in your hand.** If you like to play with colors, use a green pen for your first reading. The pen shouldn't slow you down much, but it will enable you to note your important first reactions.

2. **Make quick marks in the margin to record your reactions.** If you like or are surprised by a passage, put a "!" in the margin next to the sentence. If some passage confuses you, put a "?" in the margin. If you don't like something or completely disagree, use a big "X." Put a wavy line under phrases or sentences you find important, striking, or original. Underline any words you want to look up later. Don't let these quick marks interrupt your reading, however.

3. **At the end of your first reading, record your overall reaction to this essay.** Write in your own words the dominant impression, main idea, thesis, or claim that the essay makes.

Annotated Reading

During your second reading, take the time to write out your reactions in the margin. Then shift gears and begin reading with a writer's eye: Note in the margins the writer's strategies and techniques.

1. **First, write out your reactions more fully in the margin.** If you put a "!" in the margin, explain in the margin what surprised you. If you disagreed, explain what you meant by your "X." If you agree with everything the author says, practice *reading against the text:* Note statements in the essay that you could reasonably disagree with.

2. **Read from the writer's point of view.** What is the purpose of this essay? What is its main idea or thesis? Who is the audience? What writing strategies did the writer use in this essay? *Bracket at least one sentence or passage illustrating each one of the key features for that particular piece of writing.* For argumentative essays, such as Ellen Goodman's column, these features include (a) an introduction that sets the context or background of the argument, (b) a statement or a claim about a controversy, (c) a countering of opposing arguments, (d) some evidence or analysis in support of the writer's claim, and (e) a rational, reasonable tone. Label each of these features in the margins next to the brackets.

3. **Note key features of organization, diction, and style in the margin.** Use roman numerals (I, II, III, IV) to indicate major divisions in the essay. Look up definitions of any underlined words. Comment in the margin on any especially vivid, forceful, memorable, or confusing sentences. Note any figurative language (simile, image, metaphor), historical or literary allusions, or use of irony.

Collaborative Reading

In a small group or in your class as a whole, discuss your annotations and then prepare a collectively annotated version of the essay.

1. **Share your Prewriting Journal responses.** What experiences or attitudes toward this subject did your group or class have in common? What differences did you have? How did the essay change your initial attitudes?

2. **Compare your annotations.** What did other readers notice that you didn't? What did you notice that others didn't?

3. **Compile a collaboratively annotated version of the essay.** The group or class should agree on the best or most representative marginal comments. One person should then write down the annotations agreed on by the majority of the group or class. (Minority opinions or reactions should also be noted.)

4. **The group or class should then write out at least one question they still have about the essay.** Questions may be about any aspect of the essay.

5. **Finally, read the questions in the text following each essay.** Use these questions to supplement your group's critical reading of the essay: Which of these questions have you already answered? Which questions suggest a new idea to your group or class?

TESTING YOUR CRITICAL READING PROCESS

The sample essay that follows is reprinted twice. Use the unannotated version for your practice. First write on *one* of the Prereading Journal Topics in your journal or notebook for five minutes. Then follow the instructions for critical reading: Do a first reading and an annotated reading. Annotate right in the margins of your book.

When you have finished, compare your annotations to the group annotations that accompany the second reprinting of this essay. You'll quickly see that while you may agree with some of these notes, you will undoubtedly disagree at other points, have different reactions, or make different connections. Your reading should use the same process, but it should *not* have identical annotations.

Honor Society Hypocrisy

ELLEN GOODMAN

(1941–   )

PREREADING JOURNAL TOPICS

If you know a teenager who became pregnant during high school, write about her situation. How old was she? Did she want to have the baby? Did she think about abortion? How did the experience affect her schoolwork? How did her experience affect you?

or

Answer the following question: How should pregnant teenagers in high school be treated by the school administration? (Should they be allowed to compete in athletics? Should they be allowed to join clubs? Should they be allowed to be in an honor society? Should schools be required to provide daycare?) Explain.

Ellen Goodman is a Pulitzer Prize-winning columnist whose essays and editorials appear in more than 200 newspapers. Her columns have been published in The Boston Globe, McCall's, *the* Village Voice, *and* Harper's Bazaar. *The titles of her essays show her range of interests:* "AIDS II: The New Lepers?" "Virtue and the Long Distance Runner," "Notes from an Antilawn Snob," *and* "In the Heartland of the Missles." *Some of her most provocative columns, however, are about women. Whether she is writing about Barbara Bush or Raisa Gorbachev, about abortion or divorce, she shows her blue-collar approach to feminism: Real people, for Ellen Goodman, are always more important than abstract issues.*

In "Honor Society Hypocrisy," Goodman recounts a fight in the education arena: Arlene Pfeiffer versus the school board of Marion Center, Pennsylvania. From the title, you can probably guess who wins.

But Goodman makes us wonder, "Are all of us really a part of this problem?"

If they ever give a college board test for students of 1 hypocrisy, I am sure that the teenagers of Marion Center, Pa., will score way up in the 700s. Teenagers are always the great hypocrisy spotters in our culture. But in the past few months, they've had a lot of extra practice in this small rural town.

The central characters of the case that has put Marion 2 Center on the sociological map include 17-year-old Arlene Pfeiffer, her five-month-old daughter, Jessica, the school board and the National Honor Society.

Arlene, a high school senior, was class president for 3 three years, student council president last year and a member of the honor society since tenth grade. But in August, she gave birth to Jessica and decided to keep her. In November, Arlene was kicked out of the honor society by her high school. In January the school board agreed to her removal. Now Arlene is taking her case to the Human Relations Commission and the Equal Employment Opportunity Commission.

What is at issue is not her grades—they have remained 4 high—but two other qualities the honor society demands: "leadership and character." The question is whether an unwed mother had lost her "character," whether she would "lead" others in the wrong direction.

It is easy to follow the trail of hypocrisy in this move 5 against Arlene, easy as a multiple choice questionnaire. To begin with, the school didn't strip Arlene of her honor society epaulets because she had sex but because she "got caught." About 37 percent of 16-year-old teenagers in this country have had intercourse. Arlene was judged to have less character than those who didn't get pregnant.

Then too, if Arlene had not had her baby, she would 6 surely have kept her membership. A little less than half of the teen pregnancies end in abortion. So she was judged to have less character than a girl who chose abortion.

Perhaps it would even have been alright if Arlene had 7 given her baby up for adoption. Or if she had married. No one, for that matter, had ever questioned the character of an unwed teenage father.

Indeed, it is difficult to identify exactly what part of 8 Arlene's behavior—sex, pregnancy, motherhood, singleness, none of the above—the school wants to punish. This speaks to the confusion of the adults in this situation.

It may well be that these adults—teachers and board 9 members—are suffering from simple hypocrisy. Surely the teenagers in town see it that way. But there may also be a more deeply rooted ambivalence that centers around the word "leadership."

A generation ago, unwed pregnancy produced a shot- 10 gun marriage, an illegal abortion, or a six-month stay out of town. A decade ago, a pregnant teenager could be barred altogether from school.

Now those of us who shepherd kids through the high- 11 risk years know that early parenthood is still the surest, most direct route to a diminished future. But we are told that some of the young mothers who have kept their babies were inspired by fairy tales of Hollywood love-children. Many of us now share an underlying anxiety that if we make unwed motherhood appear acceptable, we may make it more possible, and then more likely. If we pin a medal on Arlene Pfeiffer, does she become a role model?

"They said," recalls Arlene Pfeiffer, "that by 'leader- 12 ship' I might lead others to do it—to get pregnant. But I don't go around saying 'stand in line and get pregnant.' " Nor do girls follow the leader into pregnancy.

For all our anxiety, we have no evidence to prove that 13 lifting a sanction produces a bumper crop of babies. On the contrary, we know that teenagers don't get pregnant because they want to. Study after study after study has concluded that they simply take chances.

The saga of Arlene Pfeiffer, who mothers by night 14 and gathers honor grades by day, who lives at home with parental support and child care, is an exception. If we are afraid of lauding her success, it is largely because of our own failures. We've done a poor job of discouraging early sexual activity. A poor job at getting teenagers to take more responsibility. A poor job at communicating the real handicaps of early childbearing.

As for Arlene, she is pursuing fairness through all the 15 flak of hypocrisy and ambivalence in Marion Center, Pa. I think she's giving the adults a lesson in "character" and "leadership."

HONOR SOCIETY HYPOCRISY

If they ever give a college board test for students of hypocrisy, I am sure that the teenagers of Marion Center, Pa., will score way up in the 700s. Teenagers are always the great hypocrisy spotters in our culture, but in the past few months, they've had a lot of extra practice in this small rural town.

I. Lead-in and introduction 1

The central characters of this case that has put Marion Center on the sociological map include 17-year-old Arlene Pfeiffer, her five-month-old daughter, Jessica, the school board and the National Honor Society.

Good lead — this got my interest. Author sets up situation. 2

Arlene, a high school senior, was class president for three years, student council president last year and a member of the honor society since tenth grade. But in August, she gave birth to Jessica and decided to keep her. In November, Arlene was kicked out of the honor society by her high school. In January the school board agreed to her removal. Now Arlene is taking her case to the Human Relations Commission and the Equal Employment Opportunity Commission.

3

I How can they do that? she should?

What is at issue is not her grades—they have remained high—but other qualities the honor society demands: "leadership and character." The question is whether an unwed mother had lost her "character," whether she would "lead" others in the wrong direction.

II. the central question of the essay. good question 4

14

It is easy to follow the trail of hypocrisy in this move against Arlene, easy as a multiple choice questionnaire. To begin with, the school didn't strip Arlene of her honor society epaulets because she had sex but because she "got caught." About 37 percent of 16-year-old teenagers in this country have had intercourse. Arlene was judged to have less character than those who didn't get pregnant.

5

Exactly!

x Source of these statistics?

Then too, if Arlene had not had her baby, she would surely have kept her membership. A little less than half of the teen pregnancies end in abortion.

6

Perhaps it would even have been alright if Arlene had given her baby up for adoption. Or if she had married. No one, for that matter, had ever questioned the character of an unwed teenage father.

7

Yes – Double standard here

Indeed, it is difficult to identify exactly what part of Arlene's behavior—sex, pregnancy, motherhood, singleness, none of the above— the school wants to punish. This speaks to the confusion of the adults in this situation.

8

It may well be that these adults—teachers and board members—are suffering from simple hypocrisy. Surely the teenagers in town see it that way. But there may also be a more deeply rooted ambivalence that centers around the word "leadership."

9

III. Refuting opposition – the adults hypocrisy

A generation ago, unwed pregnancy produced a shotgun marriage, an illegal abortion, or a six-month stay out of town. A decade ago, a pregnant teenager could be barred altogether from school.

10

these were all the wrong solutions.

Now those of us who shepherd kids through the high-risk years know that early parenthood is still the surest, most direct route to a diminished future. But we are told that some of the young mothers who have kept their babies were inspired by fairy tales of Hollywood love-children. Many of us now share an underlying

11

! this is true!

But not all of us! who is us?

anxiety that if we make unwed motherhood appear acceptable, we may make it more possible, and then more likely. If we pin a medal on Arlene Pfeiffer, does she become a role model?

Good question!

"They said," recalls Arlene Pfeiffer, "that by 'leadership' I might lead others to do it—to get pregnant. But I don't go around saying 'stand in line and get pregnant.' " Nor do girls follow the leader into pregnancy.

12

For all our anxiety, we have no evidence to prove that lifting a sanction produces a bumper crop of babies. On the contrary, we know that teenagers don't get pregnant because they want to. Study after study after study has concluded that they simply take chances.

nice reasonable tone here

13

What are these studies?

The saga of Arlene Pfeiffer, who mothers by night and gathers honor grades by day, who lives at home with parental support and child care, is an exception. If we are afraid of lauding her success, it is largely because of our own failures. We've done a poor job of discouraging early sexual activity. A poor job at getting teenagers to take more responsibility. A poor job at communicating the real handicaps of early childbearing.

IV. Conclusion

14

nice reversal of blame

As for Arlene, she is pursuing fairness through all the flak of hypocrisy and ambivalence in Marion Center, Pa. I think she's giving the adults a lesson in "character" and "leadership."

Here is Goodman's main idea or thesis

15

Audience: Seems to be more directed at adults and the school board.

Purpose: To persuade us that Arlene's "problem" is as much ours as it is hers.

How to Mark a Book

MORTIMER ADLER
(1902–   )

PREREADING JOURNAL ENTRY

Open another textbook you are currently reading. Turn to a chapter or passage you have already read. Describe, briefly, anything you have written in the text—marginal notes, highlighted passages, or underlined words. Does your method of reading (either with many annotations or with few or none) help you learn and remember? Explain, referring to *specific passages* in your text.

It is ironic that Mortimer Adler, the father of the Great Books Program and promoter of Aristotle and the classics, was a high school dropout. He did attend Columbia University, but he did not receive his B.A. because he refused to take a required swimming test. Adler did, however, eventually receive a Ph.D., become an editor for the Encyclopedia Britannica, *and write dozens of books on philosophy and education, including* How to Read a Book: The Art of Getting a Liberal Education *(1940), and* The Great Ideas: A Syntopicon of Great Books of the Western World *(1952).*

For Mortimer Adler, reading the great books does not mean buying expensive, leather-bound volumes to display behind glass doors. Reading means consuming, as you consume a steak, to "get it into your bloodstream." In "How to Mark a Book," Adler proposes a radical method for reading the classics. "Marking up a book," he claims, "is not an act of mutilation but of love." Read his essay and see if you agree with his method of paying "your respects to the author."

You know you have to read "between the lines" to get 1
the most out of anything. I want to persuade you to do
something equally important in the course of your reading.

I want to persuade you to "write between the lines." Unless you do, you are not likely to do the most efficient kind of reading.

I contend, quite bluntly, that marking up a book is 2 not an act of mutilation but of love.

You shouldn't mark up a book which isn't yours. 3 Librarians (or your friends) who lend you books expect you to keep them clean, and you should. If you decide that I am right about the usefulness of marking books, you will have to buy them. Most of the world's great books are available today, in reprint editions, at less than a dollar.

There are two ways in which you can own a book. The 4 first is the property right you establish by paying for it, just as you pay for clothes and furniture. But this act of purchase is only the prelude to possession. Full ownership comes only when you have made it a part of yourself, and the best way to make yourself a part of it is by writing in it. An illustration may make the point clear. You buy a beefsteak and transfer it from the butcher's icebox to your own. But you do not own the beefsteak in the most important sense until you consume it and get it into your bloodstream. I am arguing that books, too, must be absorbed in your bloodstream to do you any good.

Confusion about what it means to *own* a book leads 5 people to a false reverence for paper, binding, and type— a respect for the physical thing—the craft of the printer rather than the genius of the author. They forget that it is possible for a man to acquire the idea, to possess the beauty, which a great book contains, without staking his claim by pasting his bookplate inside the cover. Having a fine library doesn't prove that its owner has a mind enriched by books; it proves nothing more than that he, his father, or his wife, was rich enough to buy them.

There are three kinds of book owners. The first has 6 all the standard sets and best-sellers—unread, untouched. (This deluded individual owns woodpulp and ink, not books.) The second has a great many books—a few of them read through, most of them dipped into, but all of them as clean and shiny as the day they were bought.

(This person would probably like to make books his own, but is restrained by a false respect for their physical appearance.) The third has a few books or many—everyone of them dog-eared and dilapidated, shaken and loosened by continual use, marked and scribbled in from front to back. (This man owns books.)

Is it false respect, you may ask, to preserve intact and 7 unblemished a beautifully printed book, an elegantly bound edition? Of course not. I'd no more scribble all over a first edition of *Paradise Lost* than I'd give my baby a set of crayons and an original Rembrandt! I wouldn't mark up a painting or a statue. Its soul, so to speak, is inseparable from its body. And the beauty of a rare edition or of a richly manufactured volume is like that of a painting or a statue.

But the soul of a book *can* be separated from its body. 8 A book is more like the score of a piece of music than it is like a painting. No great musician confuses a symphony with the printed sheets of music. Arturo Toscanini reveres Brahms, but Toscanini's score of the C-minor Symphony is so thoroughly marked up that no one but the maestro himself can read it. The reason why a great conductor makes notations on his musical scores—marks them up again and again each time he returns to study them—is the reason why you should mark your books. If your respect for magnificent binding or typography gets in the way, buy yourself a cheap edition and pay your respects to the author.

Why is marking up a book indispensable to reading? 9 First, it keeps you awake. (And I don't mean merely conscious; I mean wide awake.) In the second place, reading, if it is active, is thinking, and thinking tends to express itself in words, spoken or written. The marked book is usually the thought-through book. Finally, writing helps you remember the thoughts you had, or the thoughts the author expressed. Let me develop these three points.

If reading is to accomplish anything more than passing 10 time, it must be active. You can't let your eyes glide across the lines of a book and come up with an understanding of what you have read. Now an ordinary piece of light fiction, like say, *Gone With the Wind,* doesn't require the most active kind of reading. The books you read for pleasure can be read in a state of relaxation, and nothing is lost. But a great book, rich in ideas and beauty, a book that raises and tries to answer great fundamental questions, demands the most active reading of which you are capable. You don't absorb the ideas of John Dewey[1] the way you absorb the crooning of Mr. Vallee.[2] You have to reach for them. That you cannot do while you're asleep.

If, when you've finished reading a book, the pages are 11 filled with your notes, you know that you read actively. The most famous *active* reader of great books I know is President Hutchins, of the University of Chicago. He also has the hardest schedule of business activities of any man I know. He invariably reads with a pencil, and sometimes, when he picks up a book and pencil in the evening, he finds himself, instead of making intelligent notes, drawing what he calls "caviar factories" on the margins. When that happens, he puts the book down. He knows he's too tired to read, and he's just wasting time.

But, you may ask, why is writing necessary? Well, the 12 physical act of writing, with your own hand, brings words and sentences more sharply before your mind and preserves them better in your memory. To set down your reaction to important words and sentences you have read, and the questions they have raised in your mind, is to preserve those reactions and sharpen those questions.

Even if you wrote on a scratch pad, and threw the 13 paper away when you had finished writing, your grasp of the book would be surer. But you don't have to throw the paper away. The margins (top and bottom, as well as side), the end-papers, the very space between the lines, are all

---

[1] John Dewey (1859–1952) was an educator who believed in learning through experimentation.

[2] Rudy Vallee was a popular singer of the 1920s.

available. They aren't sacred. And, best of all, your marks and notes become an integral part of the book and stay there forever. You can pick up the book the following week or year, and there are all your points of agreement, disagreement, doubt, and inquiry. It's like resuming an interrupted conversation with the advantage of being able to pick up where you left off.

And that is exactly what reading a book should be: a 14 conversation between you and the author. Presumably he knows more about the subject than you do; naturally, you'll have the proper humility as you approach him. But don't let anybody tell you that a reader is supposed to be solely on the receiving end. Understanding is a two-way operation; learning doesn't consist in being an empty receptacle. The learner has to question himself and question the teacher. He even has to argue with the teacher, once he understands what the teacher is saying. And marking a book is literally an expression of your differences, or agreements of opinion, with the author.

There are all kinds of devices for marking a book 15 intelligently and fruitfully. Here's the way I do it:

1. *Underlining:* of major points, of important or   16
   forceful statements.

2. *Vertical lines at the margin:* to emphasize a state-   17
   ment already underlined.

3. *Star, asterisk, or other doo-dad at the margin:* to be   18
   used sparingly, to emphasize the ten or twenty
   most important statements in the book. (You
   may want to fold the bottom corner of each
   page on which you use such marks. It won't
   hurt the sturdy paper on which most modern
   books are printed, and you will be able to take
   the book off the shelf at any time and, by
   opening it at the folded-corner page, refresh
   your recollection of the book.)

4. *Numbers in the margin:* to indicate the sequence   19
   of points the author makes in developing a
   single argument.

5. *Numbers of other pages in the margin:* to indicate   20
   where else in the book the author made points
   relevant to the point marked; to tie up the ideas
   in a book, which, though they may be separated
   by many pages, belong together.

6. *Circling of key words or phrases.*   21

7. *Writing in the margin, or at the top or bottom of the*   22
   page, for the sake of: recording questions (and
   perhaps answers) which a passage raised in your
   mind; reducing a complicated discussion to a
   simple statement; recording the sequence of
   major points right through the books. I use the
   end-papers at the back of the book to make a
   personal index of the author's points in the
   order of their appearance.

The front end-papers are, to me, the most important. 23
Some people reserve them for a fancy bookplate. I reserve
them for fancy thinking. After I have finished reading
the book and making my personal index on the back end-
papers, I turn to the front and try to outline the book,
not page by page, or point by point (I've already done
that at the back), but as an integrated structure, with a
basic unity and an order of parts. This outline is, to me,
the measure of my understanding of the work.

If you're a die-hard anti-book-marker, you may object 24
that the margins, the space between the lines, and the
end-papers don't give you room enough. All right. How
about using a scratch pad slightly smaller than the page-
size of the book—so that the edges of the sheets won't
protrude? Make your index, outlines, and even your notes
on the pad, and then insert these sheets permanently
inside the front and back covers of the book.

Or, you may say that this business of marking books 25
is going to slow up your reading. It probably will. That's
one of the reasons for doing it. Most of us have been
taken in by the notion that speed of reading is a measure
of our intelligence. There is no such thing as the right

speed for intelligent reading. Some things should be read quickly and effortlessly, and some should be read slowly and even laboriously. The sign of intelligence in reading is the ability to read different things differently according to their worth. In the case of good books, the point is not to see how many of them you can get through, but rather how many can get through you—how many you can make your own. A few friends are better than a thousand acquaintances. If this be your aim, as it should be, you will not be impatient if it takes more time and effort to read a great book than it does a newspaper.

You may have one final objection to marking books. 26 You can't lend them to your friends because nobody else can read them without being distracted by your notes. Furthermore, you won't want to lend them because a marked copy is a kind of intellectual diary, and lending it is almost like giving your mind away.

If your friend wishes to read your *Plutarch's Lives,* 27 *Shakespeare,* or *The Federalist Papers,* tell him gently but firmly to buy a copy. You will lend him your car or your coat—but your books are as much a part of you as your head or your heart.

QUESTIONS ON MEANING

1. Adler says that "marking a book is literally an expression of your differences, or agreements of opinion, with the author." Find one statement in the essay you agree with. (What in your experience makes you agree with Adler?) Find one statement you disagree with. (Explain why you disagree.)

2. Compare Adler's method of reading with the process for reading outlined in this chapter. What points does Adler make that this chapter does not? What methods does this chapter suggest that Adler omits?

QUESTIONS ON PURPOSE AND STRATEGY

1. Find one sentence that best expresses Adler's overall purpose for writing this essay. Is his purpose to entertain you, to give you new information, to explain something, or to persuade you? Does he attempt more than one purpose? Explain.

2. Adler enjoys making comparisons and giving illustrations. Find two examples of each strategy. Do his comparisons and illustrations make his essay more convincing? Explain.

3. In this essay, Adler asks questions and then answers them for the reader. What questions does he pose? What are his answers? Explain how his questions and answers are an organizing or shaping strategy.

QUESTIONS ON AUDIENCE AND LANGUAGE

1. Who is Adler's intended audience? Who would voluntarily buy a book entitled, *How to Read a Book: The Art of Getting a Liberal Education?* Who might be assigned to read it? Who would benefit from reading it?

2. What words or sentences reveal that Adler loves the classics and is a literary high-brow? What passages show that he can write informally, in simple vocabulary and sentences, so that anyone can grasp his main point? How, then, would you describe Adler's character and voice, as revealed in this essay?

QUESTIONS FOR DISCUSSION AND WRITING

1. Reread your Prereading Journal Entry. What advice would Adler give you about your reading strategies? What advice would you give him?

2. Interview a class member about his or her reading strategies. Ask this person to show you a textbook with his or her annotations. What advice would Adler give to this student? What advice does this student have for Adler?

3. Look through your shelves for one of your favorite books— one that you've read more than once. Write an essay explaining *what you learned about reading* when you read this book. What was your purpose in reading? Did you follow any parts of Adler's method? Did that add to your enjoyment or understanding?

How Teachers Make Children Hate Reading

JOHN HOLT
(1923–1985)

PREREADING JOURNAL ENTRY

Referring to specific classes you have taken in high school or college, describe one assignment you remember from an English class that made you enjoy reading *or* describe one assignment that made you dislike reading. What made that assignment enjoyable or not—the assignment or the book itself?

"Unfortunately," says John Holt, "we English teachers are easily hung up on this matter of understanding. Why should children understand everything they read? Why should anyone? Does anyone?" John Holt made a career out of asking such questions and proposing answers. After *teaching children for ten years in various school systems, Holt wrote* How Children Fail *(1964),* How Children Learn *(1967),* Instead of Education *(1976), and dozens of other books and articles dedicated to reforming (or bypassing) America's educational system.*

In "How Teachers Make Children Hate Reading," John Holt picks up his recurrent theme that school too often makes children hate learning. Children will read more (and learn more), he claims, if they are not drilled on meaning or forced to look up words in a dictionary. As you read, ask yourself: Would you have learned from a teacher like John Holt when you were in the fifth grade? Would his teaching methods work in a high school or a college English class?

When I was teaching English at the Colorado Rocky 1
Mountain School, I used to ask my students the kinds of questions that English teachers usually ask about reading

assignments—questions designed to bring out the points
that *I* had decided *they* should know. They, on their part,
would try to get me to give them hints and clues as to
what I wanted. It was a game of wits. I never gave my
students an opportunity to say what they really thought
about a book.

I gave vocabulary drills and quizzes too. I told my 2
students that every time they came upon a word in their
book they did not understand, they were to look it up in
the dictionary. I even devised special kinds of vocabulary
tests, allowing them to use their books to see how the
words were used. But looking back, I realize that these
tests, along with many of my methods, were foolish.

My sister was the first person who made me question 3
my conventional ideas about teaching English. She had a
son in the seventh grade in a fairly good public school.
His teacher had asked the class to read Cooper's *The
Deerslayer.* The choice was bad enough in itself; whether
looking at man or nature, Cooper was superficial, inac-
curate and sentimental, and his writing is ponderous and
ornate. But to make matters worse, this teacher had
decided to give the book the microscope and x-ray treatment. He made the students look up and memorize not
only the definitions but the derivations of every big word
that came along—and there were plenty. Every chapter
was followed by close questioning and testing to make
sure the students "understood" everything.

Being then, as I said, conventional, I began to defend 4
the teacher, who was a good friend of mine, against my
sister's criticisms. The argument soon grew hot. What was
wrong with making sure that children understood everything they read? My sister answered that until this year
her boy had always loved reading, and had read a lot on
his own; now he had stopped. (He was not really to start
again for many years.)

Still I persisted. If children didn't look up the words 5
they didn't know, how would they ever learn them? My
sister said, "Don't be silly! when you were little you had a

huge vocabulary, and were always reading very grown-up books. When did you ever look up a word in a dictionary?"

She had me. I don't know that we had a dictionary at home; if we did, I didn't use it. I don't use one today. In my life I doubt that I have looked up as many as fifty words, perhaps not even half that.

Since then I have talked about this with a number of teachers. More than once I have said, "According to tests, educated and literate people like you have a vocabulary of about twenty-five thousand words. How many of these did you learn by looking them up in a dictionary?" They usually are startled. Few claim to have looked up even as many as a thousand. How did they learn the rest?

They learned them just as they learned to talk—by meeting words over and over again, in different contexts, until they saw how they fitted.

Unfortunately, we English teachers are easily hung up on this matter of understanding. Why should children understand everything they read? Why should anyone? Does anyone? I don't, and I never did. I was always reading books that teachers would have said were "too hard" for me, books full of words I didn't know. That's how I got to be a good reader. When about ten, I read all the D'Artagnan stories and loved them. It didn't trouble me in the least that I didn't know why France was at war with England or who was quarreling with whom in the French court or why the Musketeers should always be at odds with Cardinal Richelieu's men. I didn't even know who the Cardinal was, except that he was a dangerous and powerful man that my friends had to watch out for. This was all I needed to know.

Having said this, I will now say that I think a big, unabridged dictionary is a fine thing to have in any home or classroom. No book is more fun to browse around in— *if* you're not made to. Children, depending on their age, will find many pleasant and interesting things to do with a big dictionary. They can look up funny-sounding words, which they like, or long words, which they like, or forbidden words, which they like best of all. At a certain age, and particularly with a little encouragement from parents or teachers, they may become very interested in where words came from and when they came into the language and how their meanings have changed over the years. But exploring for the fun of it is very different from looking up words out of your reading because you're going to get into trouble with your teacher if you don't.

While teaching fifth grade two years or so after the 11 argument with my sister, I began to think again about reading. The children in my class were supposed to fill out a card—just the title and author and a one-sentence summary—for every book they read. I was not running a competition to see which child could read the most books, a competition that almost always leads to cheating. I just wanted to know what the children were reading. After a while it became clear that many of these very bright kids, from highly literate and even literary backgrounds, read very few books and deeply disliked reading. Why should this be?

At this time I was coming to realize, as I described in 12 my book *How Children Fail*, that for most children school was a place of danger, and their main business in school was staying out of danger as much as possible. I now began to see also that books were among the most dangerous things in school.

From the very beginning of school we make books 13 and reading a constant source of possible failure and public humiliation. When children are little we make them read aloud, before the teacher and other children, so that we can be sure they "know" all the words they are reading. This means that when they don't know a word, they are going to make a mistake, right in front of everyone. Instantly they are made to realize that they have done something wrong. Perhaps some of the other children will begin to wave their hands and say, "Ooooh! O-o-o-oh!" Perhaps they will just giggle, or nudge each other, or make a face. Perhaps the teacher will say, "Are you sure?" or ask someone else what he thinks. Or perhaps, if the teacher is kindly, she will just smile a sweet, sad smile—often one of the most painful punishments a child can suffer in school. In any case, the child who has made the mistake knows he has made it, and feels foolish, stupid, and ashamed, just as any of us would in his shoes.

Before long many children associate books and reading 14 with mistakes, real or feared, and penalties and humiliation. This may not seem sensible, but it is natural. Mark Twain once said that a cat that sat on a hot stove lid would never sit on one again—but it would never sit on a cold one either. As true of children as of cats. If they, so to speak, sit on a hot book a few times, if books cause them humiliation and pain, they are likely to decide that the safest thing to do is to leave all books alone.

After having taught fifth-grade classes for four years 15 I felt quite sure of this theory. In my next class were many children who had had great trouble with schoolwork, particularly reading. I decided to try at all costs to rid them of their fear and dislike of books, and to get them to read oftener and more adventurously.

One day soon after school had started, I said to them, 16 "Now I'm going to say something about reading that you have probably never heard a teacher say before. I would like you to read a lot of books this year, but I want you to read them only for pleasure. I am not going to ask you questions to find out whether you understand the books or not. If you understand enough of a book to enjoy it and want to go on reading it, that's enough for me. Also I'm not going to ask you what words mean.

"Finally," I said, "I don't want you to feel that just 17 because you start a book, you have to finish it. Give an author thirty or forty pages or so to get his story going. Then if you don't like the characters and don't care what happens to them, close the book, put it away, and get another. I don't care whether the books are easy or hard, short or long, as long as you enjoy them. Furthermore I'm putting all this in a letter to your parents, so they won't feel they have to quiz and heckle you about books at home."

The children sat stunned and silent. Was this a teacher 18 talking? One girl, who had just come to us from a school where she had had a very hard time, and who proved to be one of the most interesting, lively, and intelligent children I have ever known, looked at me steadily for a long time after I had finished. Then, still looking at me, she said slowly and solemnly, "Mr. Holt, do you really mean that?" I said just as solemnly, "I mean every word of it."

Apparently she decided to believe me. The first book 19 she read was Dr. Seuss's *How the Grinch Stole Christmas*, not a hard book even for most third graders. For a while she read a number of books on this level. Perhaps she was clearing up some confusion about reading that her teachers, in their hurry to get her up to "grade level," had never given her enough time to clear up. After she had been in the class six weeks or so and we had become good friends, I very tentatively suggested that, since she was a skillful rider and loved horses, she might like to read *National Velvet*. I made my sell as soft as possible, saying only that it was about a girl who loved and rode horses, and that if she didn't like it, she could put it back. She tried it, and though she must have found it quite a bit harder than what she had been reading, finished it and liked it very much.

During the spring she really astonished me, however. 20 One day, in one of our many free periods, she was reading at her desk. From a glimpse of the illustrations I thought I knew what the book was. I said to myself, "It can't be," and went to take a closer look. Sure enough, she was reading *Moby Dick*, in the edition with woodcuts by Rockwell Kent. When I came close to her desk she looked up. I said, "Are you really reading that?" She said she was. I said, "Do you like it?" She said, "Oh, yes, it's neat!" I said, "Don't you find parts of it rather heavy going?" She answered, "Oh, sure, but I just skip over those parts and go on to the next good part."

This is exactly what reading should be and in school 21 so seldom is—an exciting, joyous adventure. Find something, dive into it, take the good parts, skip the bad parts, get what you can out of it, go on to something else. How different is our mean-spirited, picky insistence that every child get every last little scrap of "understanding" that can be dug out of a book.

QUESTIONS ON MEANING

1. List the teaching methods that Holt claims make children hate reading. Then list the methods Holt recommends to make reading an "exciting, joyous adventure."

2. How do children learn new words, according to Holt, if not from dictionaries?

QUESTIONS ON PURPOSE AND STRATEGY

1. Is Holt's purpose to propose a solution to a problem, to answer opposing arguments, or both? Explain, referring to specific sentences.

2. Holt's primary strategy is to persuade readers by showing how he changed his own teaching philosophy. He attempts to convert us, in other words, by showing how he was converted. In which paragraphs is this strategy most obvious?

3. Holt uses dialogue as a recurring strategy. How many times does Holt quote himself or someone else? Choose *one* of these exchanges and explain how it effectively supports his purpose.

QUESTIONS ON AUDIENCE AND LANGUAGE

1. Who is Holt's audience? Children in elementary school? Students in high school or in college? Parents of children in school? English teachers? Administrators of schools? Some combination of the above? Explain, citing specific sentences from the essay.

2. If we changed the title of this essay to "How to Make Children Love Reading," how would that affect readers?

3. Holt uses an analogy, comparing children to cats sitting on a stove, to show why children hate reading. Is this analogy effective? Is it fair? (If you are embarrassed in class, do you stop learning or do you try harder?)

QUESTIONS FOR DISCUSSION AND WRITING

1. Is it fair to say that Holt believes we learn only when we enjoy what we are studying or learning? Do you agree with that assumption?

2. Near the beginning of this essay, Holt makes a confession: "Looking back, I realize that these tests, along with many of my methods, were foolish." Describe your best reading experience in an English class. As clearly as you can remember, what exactly was the assignment, and what role did your teacher play?

3. This textbook recommends two different strategies for reading. The first asks you to read and annotate an essay on your own. The second asks you to answer questions such as this one following each reading. Which method do you find more effective? Explain. Would Holt recommend either of these methods? Why or why not?

The Library Card

RICHARD WRIGHT

(1908–1960)

PREREADING JOURNAL ENTRY

Describe one piece of writing—a letter, book, essay, short story, newspaper article, or poem—that greatly affected you when you read it. What was the work, what was happening in your life at that time, and how did it affect you?

"That night in my rented room, while letting the hot water run over my can of pork and beans in the sink, I opened [Mencken's] A Book of Prefaces and began to read. I was jarred and shocked by the style. . . . I pictured the man as a raging demon, slashing with his pen, consumed with hate, denouncing everything American. . . ."

Thus Richard Wright describes the beginning of his self-education through reading. Soon he joined the Communist Party and wrote Uncle Tom's Children *(1938), four stories inspired by the life of a black communist in Chicago. Then he wrote* Native Son *(1940), the powerful and violent story of Bigger Thomas. In 1945, he wrote* Black Boy, *the autobiography from which this story is taken.*

"The Library Card" appears near the end of Black Boy, *but is only the opening chapter in Wright's life-long struggle against racial prejudice and oppression. Literature for Wright was not a pleasant afternoon's escape, but a potential force for his own liberation. "Could words be weapons?" Wright wonders. Considering the effect of books on Wright or the effect Wright's books have had on generations of readers, this chapter might easily be subtitled, "Words as Weapons."*

One morning I arrived early at work and went into 1
the bank lobby where the Negro porter was mopping. I

stood at a counter and picked up the Memphis *Commercial Appeal* and began my free reading of the press. I came finally to the editorial page and saw an article dealing with one H. L. Mencken. I knew by hearsay that he was the editor of the *American Mercury*, but aside from that I knew nothing about him. The article was a furious denunciation of Mencken, concluding with one hot, short sentence: Mencken is a fool.

I wondered what on earth this Mencken had done to 2 call down upon him the scorn of the South. The only people I had ever heard denounced in the South were Negroes, and this man was not a Negro. Then what ideas did Mencken hold that made a newspaper like the *Commercial Appeal* castigate him publicly? Undoubtedly he must be advocating ideas that the South did not like. Were there, then, people other than Negroes who criticized the South? I knew that during the Civil War the South had hated northern whites, but I had not encountered such hate during my life. Knowing no more of Mencken than I did at that moment, I felt a vague sympathy for him. Had not the South, which had assigned me the role of a non-man, cast at him its hardest words?

Now, how could I find out about this Mencken? There 3 was a huge library near the riverfront, but I knew that Negroes were not allowed to patronize its shelves any more than they were the parks and playgrounds of the city. I had gone into the library several times to get books for the white men on the job. Which of them would now help me to get books? And how could I read them without causing concern to the white men with whom I worked? I had so far been successful in hiding my thoughts and feelings from them, but I knew that I would create hostility if I went about this business of reading in a clumsy way.

I weighed the personalities of the men on the job. 4 There was Don, a Jew; but I distrusted him. His position was not much better than mine and I knew that he was uneasy and insecure; he had always treated me in an offhand, bantering way that barely concealed his contempt. I was afraid to ask him to help me to get books;

his frantic desire to demonstrate a racial solidarity with the whites against Negroes might make him betray me.

Then how about the boss? No, he was a Baptist and I 5 had the suspicion that he would not be quite able to comprehend why a black boy would want to read Mencken. There were other white men on the job whose attitudes showed clearly that they were Kluxers or sympathizers, and they were out of the question.

There remained only one man whose attitude did not 6 fit into an anti-Negro category, for I had heard the white men refer to him as a "Pope lover." He was an Irish Catholic and was hated by the white Southerners. I knew that he read books, because I had got him volumes from the library several times. Since he, too, was an object of hatred, I felt that he might refuse me but would hardly betray me. I hesitated, weighing and balancing the imponderable realities.

One morning I paused before the Catholic fellow's 7 desk.

"I want to ask you a favor," I whispered to him.   8

"What is it?"   9

"I want to read. I can't get books from the library. I 10 wonder if you'd let me use your card?"

He looked at me suspiciously.   11

"My card is full most of the time," he said.   12

"I see," I said and waited, posing my question silently. 13

"You're not trying to get me into trouble, are you, 14 boy?" he asked, staring at me.

"Oh, no, sir."   15

"What book do you want?"   16

"A book by H. L. Mencken."   17

"Which one?"   18

"I don't know. Has he written more than one?"   19

"He has written several."   20

"I didn't know that."   21

"What makes you want to read Mencken?"   22

"Oh, I just saw his name in the newspaper," I said.   23

"It's good of you to want to read," he said. "But you 24 ought to read the right things."

I said nothing. Would he want to supervise my read- 25
ing?

"Let me think," he said. "I'll figure out something." 26

I turned from him and he called me back. He stared 27
at me quizzically.

"Richard, don't mention this to the other white men," 28
he said.

"I understand," I said. "I won't say a word." 29

A few days later he called me to him. 30

"I've got a card in my wife's name," he said. "Here's 31
mine."

"Thank you, sir." 32

"Do you think you can manage it?" 33

"I'll manage fine," I said. 34

"If they suspect you, you'll get in trouble," he said. 35

"I'll write the same kind of notes to the library that 36
you wrote when you sent me for books," I told him. "I'll
sign your name."

He laughed. 37

"Go ahead. Let me see what you get," he said. 38

That afternoon I addressed myself to forging a note. 39
Now, what were the names of books written by H. L.
Mencken? I did not know any of them. I finally wrote
what I thought would be a foolproof note: *Dear Madam:
Will you please let this nigger boy*—I used the word "nigger"
to make the librarian feel that I could not possibly be the
author of the note—*have some books by H. L. Mencken?* I
forged the white man's name.

I entered the library as I had always done when on 40
errands for whites, but I felt that I would somehow slip
up and betray myself. I doffed my hat, stood a respectful
distance from the desk, looked as unbookish as possible,
and waited for the white patrons to be taken care of.
When the desk was clear of people, I still waited. The
white librarian looked at me.

"What do you want, boy?" 41

As though I did not possess the power of speech, I 42
stepped forward and simply handed her the forged note,
not parting my lips.

"What books by Mencken does he want?" she asked. 43

"I don't know, ma'am," I said, avoiding her eyes. 44

"Who gave you this card?" 45

"Mr. Falk," I said. 46

"Where is he?" 47

"He's at work, at the M— Optical Company," I said. 48 "I've been in here for him before."

"I remember," the woman said. "But he never wrote 49 notes like this."

Oh, God, she's suspicious. Perhaps she would not let 50 me have the books? If she had turned her back at that moment, I would have ducked out the door and never gone back. Then I thought of a bold idea.

"You can call him up, ma'am," I said, my heart 51 pounding.

"You're not using these books, are you?" she asked 52 pointedly.

"Oh, no, ma'am. I can't read." 53

"I don't know what he wants by Mencken," she said 54 under her breath.

I knew now that I had won; she was thinking of other 55 things and the race question had gone out of her mind. She went to the shelves. Once or twice she looked over her shoulder at me, as though she was still doubtful. Finally she came forward with two books in her hand.

"I'm sending him two books," she said. "But tell Mr. 56 Falk to come in next time, or send me the names of the books he wants. I don't know what he wants to read."

I said nothing. She stamped the card and handed me 57 the books. Not daring to glance at them, I went out of the library, fearing that the woman would call me back for further questioning. A block away from the library I opened one of the books and read a title: *A Book of Prefaces*. I was nearing my nineteenth birthday and I did not know how to pronounce the word "preface." I thumbed the pages and saw strange words and strange names. I shook my head, disappointed. I looked at the other book; it was called *Prejudices*. I knew what that word meant; I had heard it all my life. And right off I was on guard against

Mencken's books. Why would a man want to call a book *Prejudices?* The word was so stained with all my memories of racial hate that I could not conceive of anybody using it for a title. Perhaps I had made a mistake about Mencken? A man who had prejudices must be wrong.

When I showed the books to Mr. Falk, he looked at 58 me and frowned.

"That librarian might telephone you," I warned him. 59

"That's all right," he said. "But when you're through 60 reading those books, I want you to tell me what you get out of them."

That night in my rented room, while letting the hot 61 water run over my can of pork and beans in the sink, I opened *A Book of Prefaces* and began to read. I was jarred and shocked by the style, the clear, clean, sweeping sentences. Why did he write like that? And how did one write like that? I pictured the man as a raging demon, slashing with his pen, consumed with hate, denouncing everything American, extolling everything European or German, laughing at the weaknesses of people, mocking God, authority. What was this? I stood up, trying to realize what reality lay behind the meaning of the words . . . Yes, this man was fighting, fighting with words. He was using words as a weapon, using them as one would use a club. Could words be weapons? Well, yes, for here they were. Then, maybe, perhaps, I could use them as a weapon? No. It frightened me. I read on and what amazed me was not what he said, but how on earth anybody had the courage to say it.

Occasionally I glanced up to reassure myself that I 62 was alone in the room. Who were these men about whom Mencken was talking so passionately? Who was Anatole France? Joseph Conrad? Sinclair Lewis, Sherwood Anderson, Dostoevski, George Moore, Gustave Flaubert, Maupassant, Tolstoy, Frank Harris, Mark Twain, Thomas Hardy, Arnold Bennett, Stephen Crane, Zola, Norris, Gorky, Bergson, Ibsen, Balzac, Bernard Shaw, Dumas, Poe, Thomas Mann, O. Henry, Dreiser, H. G. Wells, Gogol, T. S. Eliot, Gide, Baudelaire, Edgar Lee Masters,

Stendhal, Turgenev, Huneker, Nietzsche, and scores of others? Were these men real? Did they exist or had they existed? And how did one pronounce their names?

I ran across many words whose meanings I did not 63 know, and I either looked them up in a dictionary or, before I had a chance to do that, encountered the word in a context that made its meaning clear. But what strange world was this? I concluded the book with the conviction that I had somehow overlooked something terribly important in life. I had once tried to write, had once reveled in feeling, had let my crude imagination roam, but the impulse to dream had been slowly beaten out of me by experience. Now it surged up again and I hungered for books, new ways of looking and seeing. It was not a matter of believing or disbelieving what I read, but of feeling something new, of being affected by something that made the look of the world different.

As dawn broke I ate my pork and beans, feeling dopey, 64 sleepy. I went to work, but the mood of the book would not die; it lingered, coloring everything I saw, heard, did. I now felt that I knew what the white men were feeling. Merely because I had read a book that had spoken of how they lived and thought, I identified myself with that book. I felt vaguely guilty. Would I, filled with bookish notions, act in a manner that would make the whites dislike me?

I forged more notes and my trips to the library became 65 frequent. Reading grew into a passion. My first serious novel was Sinclair Lewis's *Main Street*. It made me see my boss, Mr. Gerald, and identify him as an American type. I would smile when I saw him lugging his golf bags into the office. I had always felt a vast distance separating me from the boss, and now I felt closer to him, though still distant. I felt now that I knew him, that I could feel the very limits of his narrow life. And this had happened because I had read a novel about a mythical man called George F. Babbitt.

The plots and stories in the novels did not interest me 66 so much as the point of view revealed. I gave myself over to each novel without reserve, without trying to criticize it; it was enough for me to see and feel something different. And for me, everything was something differ- ent. Reading was like a drug, a dope. The novels created moods in which I lived for days. But I could not conquer my sense of guilt, my feeling that the white men around me knew that I was changing, that I had begun to regard them differently.

Whenever I brought a book to the job, I wrapped it 67 in newspaper—a habit that was to persist for years in other cities and under other circumstances. But some of the white men pried into my packages when I was absent and they questioned me.

"Boy, what are you reading those books for?"   68

"Oh, I don't know, sir."   69

"That's deep stuff you're reading, boy."   70

"I'm just killing time, sir."   71

"You'll addle your brains if you don't watch out."   72

I read Dreiser's *Jennie Gerhardt* and *Sister Carrie* and 73 they revived in me a vivid sense of my mother's suffering; I was overwhelmed. I grew silent, wondering about the life around me. It would have been impossible for me to have told anyone what I derived from these novels, for it was nothing less than a sense of life itself. All my life had shaped me for the realism, the naturalism of the modern novel, and I could not read enough of them.

Steeped in new moods and ideas, I bought a ream of 74 paper and tried to write; but nothing would come, or what did come was flat beyond telling. I discovered that more than desire and feeling were necessary to write and I dropped the idea. Yet I still wondered how it was possible to know people sufficiently to write about them? Could I ever learn about life and people? To me, with my vast ignorance, my Jim Crow station in life, it seemed a task impossible of achievement. I now knew what being a Negro meant. I could endure the hunger. I had learned to live with hate. But to feel that there were feelings denied me, that the very breath of life itself was beyond my reach, that more than anything else hurt, wounded me. I had a new hunger.

In buoying me up, reading also cast me down, made 75 me see what was possible, what I had missed. My tension returned, new, terrible, bitter, surging, almost too great to be contained. I no longer *felt* that the world about me was hostile, killing; I *knew* it. A million times I asked myself what I could do to save myself, and there were no answers. I seemed forever condemned, ringed by walls.

I did not discuss my reading with Mr. Falk, who had 76 lent me his library card; it would have meant talking about myself and that would have been too painful. I smiled each day, fighting desperately to maintain my old behavior, to keep my disposition seemingly sunny. But some of the white men discerned that I had begun to brood.

"Wake up there, boy!" Mr. Olin said one day. 77

"Sir!" I answered for the lack of a better word. 78

"You act like you've stolen something," he said. 79

I laughed in the way I knew he expected me to laugh, 80 but I resolved to be more conscious of myself, to watch my every act, to guard and hide the new knowledge that was dawning within me.

If I went north, would it be possible for me to build 81 a new life then? But how could a man build a life upon vague, unformed yearnings? I wanted to write and I did not even know the English language. I bought English grammars and found them dull. I felt that I was getting a better sense of the language from novels than from grammars. I read hard, discarding a writer as soon as I felt that I had grasped his point of view. At night the printed page stood before my eyes in sleep.

Mrs. Moss, my landlady, asked me one Sunday morn- 82 ing: "Son, what is this you keep on reading?"

"Oh, nothing. Just novels." 83

"What you get out of 'em?" 84

"I'm just killing time," I said. 85

"I hope you know your own mind," she said in a tone 86 which implied that she doubted if I had a mind.

I knew of no Negroes who read the books I liked and 87 I wondered if any Negroes ever thought of them. I knew that there were Negro doctors, lawyers, newspapermen, but I never saw any of them. When I read a Negro newspaper I never caught the faintest echo of my preoccupation in its pages. I felt trapped and occasionally, for a few days, I would stop reading. But a vague hunger would come over me for books, books that opened up new avenues of feeling and seeing, and again I would forge another note to the white librarian. Again I would read and wonder as only the naïve and unlettered can read and wonder, feeling that I carried a secret, criminal burden about with me each day.

That winter my mother and brother came and we set 88 up housekeeping, buying furniture on the installment plan, being cheated and yet knowing no way to avoid it. I began to eat warm food and to my surprise found that regular meals enabled me to read faster. I may have lived through many illnesses and survived them, never suspecting that I was ill. My brother obtained a job and we began to save toward the trip north, plotting our time, setting tentative dates for departure. I told none of the white men on the job that I was planning to go north; I knew that the moment they felt I was thinking of the North they would change toward me. It would have made them feel that I did not like the life I was living, and because my life was completely conditioned by what they said or did, it would have been tantamount to challenging them.

I could calculate my chances for life in the South as a 89 Negro fairly clearly now.

I could fight the southern whites by organizing with 90 other Negroes, as my grandfather had done. But I knew that I could never win that way; there were many whites and there were but few blacks. They were strong and we were weak. Outright black rebellion could never win. If I fought openly I would die and I did not want to die. News of lynchings were frequent.

I could submit and live the life of a genial slave, but 91 that was impossible. All of my life had shaped me to live by my own feelings and thoughts. I could make up to Bess and marry her and inherit the house. But that, too, would be the life of a slave; if I did that, I would crush to death something within me, and I would hate myself as much as I knew the whites already hated those who had submitted. Neither could I ever willingly present myself to be kicked, as Shorty had done. I would rather have died than do that.

I could drain off my restlessness by fighting with 92 Shorty and Harrison. I had seen many Negroes solve the problem of being black by transferring their hatred of themselves to others with a black skin and fighting them. I would have to be cold to do that, and I was not cold and I could never be.

I could, of course, forget what I had read, thrust the 93 whites out of my mind, forget them; and find release from anxiety and longing in sex and alcohol. But the memory of how my father had conducted himself made that course repugnant. If I did not want others to violate my life, how could I voluntarily violate it myself?

I had no hope whatever of being a professional man. 94 Not only had I been so conditioned that I did not desire it, but the fulfillment of such an ambition was beyond my capabilities. Well-to-do Negroes lived in a world that was almost as alien to me as the world inhabited by whites.

What, then, was there? I held my life in my mind, in 95 my consciousness each day, feeling at times that I would stumble and drop it, spill it forever. My reading had created a vast sense of distance between me and the world in which I lived and tried to make a living, and that sense of distance was increasing each day. My days and nights were one long, quiet, continuously contained dream of terror, tension, and anxiety. I wondered how long I could bear it.

QUESTIONS ON MEANING

1. What specific incidents in the narrator's account *show* the racial bondage and oppression from which he is trying to escape?

2. The narrator says that he is less intrigued by the plots and stories in the novels he reads than by the "point of view" revealed. What does he mean?

3. Describe the effects that reading has on the narrator.

QUESTIONS ON PURPOSE AND STRATEGY

1. Is Wright's purpose to narrate events in his own life? To explain how reading affected him? To persuade us of the evils of racial prejudice? All of the above? Refer to specific passages that illustrate each of Wright's main purposes.

2. Wright dramatizes key events from his life by describing specific scenes, complete with action and dialogue. Label and number the actual scenes that Wright recreates.

3. Narratives (including autobiography) thrive on conflict between characters and on showing the contrast between the ideal world and the real world. Which of the scenes you labeled in question 2 show conflict between characters, and which show contrast between the ideal and the real?

QUESTIONS ON AUDIENCE AND LANGUAGE

1. Who is Richard Wright's audience for his autobiography? Blacks, whites, children, young people, parents, educators? Who would *not* be interested in this selection?

2. Where does Wright use the language of a young man to recreate key events and experiences? Where does Wright seem to be older, more reflective, and more certain of his beliefs?

QUESTIONS FOR DISCUSSION AND WRITING

1. Compare Wright's strategies for reading with John Holt's proposals. Is the young narrator doing what Holt recommends?

2. At the end of this passage, Wright chooses to leave his job and girlfriend and head for the North. In what ways will this "liberation" make his life easier? In what ways will it be more difficult?

3. Wright describes a world of racial segregation in the 1920s and 1930s. Based on your experience, what has changed in the past sixty years? What has not changed?

Television and Reading

MARIE WINN

(1937–   )

PREREADING JOURNAL ENTRY

Describe one of your childhood experiences watching television. What was your favorite program? When did you watch it? How often did you see it? What was your reaction?

Are we a nation of television addicts, hooked on sitcoms, sports, and news programs? Has television reduced the quality of family life? Does television decrease children's interest in books and their ability to read? Marie Winn raises these questions in her best-known book, The Plug-In Drug: Television, Children, and the Family *(1977). Born in Czechoslovakia, Winn graduated from Radcliffe College and studied at Columbia University. She has written articles for the* Village Voice *and* The New York Times Magazine *and has published two other books that reflect her interest in children and television:* Children without Childhood *(1983) and* Unplugging the Plug-In Drug *(1987).*

In this selection from The Plug-In Drug, *Marie Winn explains how the reading process differs from television viewing and then argues that television viewing adversely affects reading: Television encourages children to be passive, it saps their powers of concentration, and it controls the pace of the program.*

Until the television era young children's access to 1 symbolic representations of reality was limited. Unable to read, they entered the world of fantasy primarily by way of stories told to them or read to them from a book. But rarely did such "literary" experiences take up a significant proportion of a child's waking time; even when a willing reader or storyteller was available, an hour or so a day was more time than most children spent ensconced in the imagination of others. And when pre-television children *did* enter those imaginary worlds, they always had a grown-up escort along to interpret, explain, and comfort, if need be. Before learning to read, it was difficult for a child to enter the fantasy world alone.

For this reason the impact of television was undoubt- 2 edly greater on preschoolers and prereaders than on any other group. By means of television, very young children were able to enter and spend sizable portions of their waking time in a secondary world of incorporeal people and intangible things, unaccompanied, in too many cases, by an adult guide or comforter. School-age children fell into a different category. Because they could read, they had other opportunities to leave reality behind. For these children television was merely *another* imaginary world.

But since reading, once the school child's major im- 3 aginative experience, has now been seriously eclipsed by television, the television experience must be compared with the reading experience to try to discover whether they are, indeed, similar activities fulfilling similar needs in a child's life.

WHAT HAPPENS WHEN YOU READ

It is not enough to compare television watching and 4 reading from the viewpoint of quality. Although the quality of the material available in each medium varies enormously, from junky books and shoddy programs to literary masterpieces and fine, thoughtful television shows, the *nature* of the two experiences is different and that difference significantly affects the impact of the material taken in.

Few people besides linguistics students and teachers 5 of reading are aware of the complex mental manipulations involved in the reading process. Shortly after learning to read, a person assimilates the process so completely that the words in books seem to acquire an existence almost equal to the objects or acts they represent. It requires a fresh look at a printed page to recognize that those symbols that we call letters of the alphabet are completely abstract shapes bearing no inherent "meaning" of their own. Look at an "o," for instance, or a "k." The "o" is a curved figure; the "k" is an intersection of three straight lines. Yet it is hard to divorce their familiar figures from the sounds, though there is nothing "o-ish" about an "o" or "k-ish" about a "k." A reader unfamiliar with the Russian alphabet will find it easy to look at the symbol "III" and see it as an abstract shape; a Russian reader will find it harder to detach that symbol from its sound, *shch*. And even when trying to consider "k" as an abstract symbol, we cannot see it without the feeling of a "k" sound somewhere between the throat and the ears, a silent pronunciation of "k" that occurs the instant we see the letter.

That is the beginning of reading: we learn to transform 6 abstract figures into sounds, and groups of symbols into the combined sounds that make up the words of our language. As the mind transforms the abstract symbols into sounds and the sounds into words, it "hears" the words, as it were, and thereby invests them with meanings previously learned in the spoken language. Invariably, as the skill of reading develops, the meaning of each word begins to seem to dwell within those symbols that make up the word. The word "dog," for instance, comes to bear some relationship with the real animal. Indeed, the word "dog" seems to *be* a dog in a certain sense, to possess some of the qualities of a dog. But it is only as a result of a swift and complex series of mental activities that the word "dog" is transformed from a series of meaningless squiggles into an idea of something real. This process goes on smoothly and continuously as we read, and yet it becomes no less complex. The brain must carry out all the steps of decoding and investing with meaning each time we read; but it becomes more adept at it as the skill develops, so that we lose the sense of struggling with symbols and meanings that children have when they first learn to read.

But not merely does the mind *hear* words in the process 7 of reading; it is important to remember that reading involves images as well. For when the reader sees the word "dog" and understands the idea of "dog," an image representing a dog is conjured up as well. The precise nature of this "reading image" is little understood, nor is there agreement about what relation it bears to visual images taken in directly by the eyes. Nevertheless images necessarily color our reading, else we would perceive no meaning, merely empty words. The great difference between these "reading images" and the images we take in when viewing television is this: we *create* our own images when reading, based upon our own life experiences and reflecting our own individual needs, while we must accept what we receive when watching television images. This aspect of reading, which might be called "creative" in the narrow sense of the word, is present during all reading experiences, regardless of *what* is being read. When we read it is almost as if we were creating our own, small, inner television program. The result is a nourishing experience for the imagination. As Bruno Bettelheim notes, "Television captures the imagination but does not liberate it. A good book at once stimulates and frees the mind."

Television images do not go through a complex sym- 8 bolic transformation. The mind does not have to decode and manipulate during the television experience. Perhaps this is a reason why the visual images received directly from a television set are strong, stronger, it appears, than the images conjured up mentally while reading. But ultimately they satisfy less. A ten-year-old child reports on the effects of seeing television dramatizations of books he has previously read: "The TV people leave a stronger impression. Once you've seen a character on TV, he'll always look like that in your mind, even if you made a different picture of him in your mind before, when you read the book yourself." And yet, as the same child reports, "the thing about a book is that you have so much freedom. You can make each character look exactly the way you

49

want him to look. You're more in control of things when you read a book than when you see something on TV."

It may be that television-bred children's reduced op- 9 portunities to indulge in this "inner picture-making" accounts for the curious inability of so many children today to adjust to nonvisual experiences. This is commonly reported by experienced teachers who bridge the gap between the pretelevision and the television eras.

"When I read them a story without showing them 10 pictures, the children always complain—'I can't see.' Their attention flags," reports a first-grade teacher. "They'll begin to talk or wander off. I have to really work to develop their visualizing skills. I tell them that there's nothing to see, that the story is coming out of my mouth, and that they can make their own pictures in their 'mind's eye.' They get better at visualizing, with practice. But children never needed to learn how to visualize before television, it seems to me."

Viewing vs. Reading: Concentration

Because reading demands complex mental manipulations, 11 a reader is required to concentrate far more than a television viewer. An audio expert notes that "with the electronic media it is openness [that counts]. Openness permits auditory and visual stimuli more direct access to the brain . . . someone who is taught to concentrate will fail to perceive many patterns of information conveyed by the electronic stimuli."

It may be that a predisposition toward concentration, 12 acquired, perhaps, through one's reading experiences, makes one an inadequate television watcher. But it seems far more likely that the reverse situation obtains: that a predisposition toward "openness" (which may be understood to mean the opposite of focal concentration), acquired through years and years of television viewing, has influenced adversely viewers' ability to concentrate, to read, to write clearly—in short, to demonstrate any of the verbal skills a literate society requires.

Pace

A comparison between reading and viewing may be made 13
in respect to the pace of each experience, and the relative
control we have over that pace, for the pace may influence
the ways we use the material received in each experience.
In addition, the pace of each experience may determine
how much it intrudes upon other aspects of our life.

When we read, clearly, we can control the pace. We 14
may read as slowly or as rapidly as we can or wish to read.
If we do not understand something, we may stop and
reread it, or go in search of elucidation before continuing.
If what we read is moving, we may put down the book
for a few moments and cope with our emotions without
fear of losing anything.

When we view, the pace of the television program 15
cannot be controlled; only its beginning and end are
within our control by clicking the knob on and off. We
cannot slow down a delightful program or speed up a
dreary one. We cannot "turn back" if a word or phrase is
not understood. The program moves inexorably forward,
and what is lost or misunderstood remains so.

Nor can we readily transform the material we see on 16
television into a form that might suit our particular
emotional needs, as we invariably do with material we
read. The images move too quickly. We cannot use our
own imagination to invest the people and events portrayed
on television with the personal meanings that would help
us understand and resolve relationships and conflicts in
our own life; we are under the power of the imagination
of the show's creators. In the television experience the
eyes and ears are overwhelmed with the immediacy of
sights and sounds. They flash from the television set just
fast enough for the eyes and ears to take them in before
moving on quickly to the new pictures and sounds . . . so
as *not to lose the thread.*

Not to lose the thread . . . it is this need, occasioned 17
by the irreversible direction and relentless velocity of the
television experience, that not only limits the workings of

the viewer's imagination, but also causes television to intrude into human affairs far more than reading experiences can ever do. If someone enters the room while we're watching television—a friend, a relative, a child, someone, perhaps, we have not seen for some time—we must continue to watch or else we'll lose the thread. The greetings must wait, for the television program will not. A book, of course, can be set aside, with a pang of regret, perhaps, but with no sense of permanent loss.

A grandparent describes a situation that is, by all 18 reports, not uncommon:

"Sometimes when I come to visit the girls, I'll walk 19 into their room and they're watching a TV program. Well, I know they love me, but it makes me feel *bad* when I tell them hello, and they say, without even looking up, 'Wait a minute . . . we have to see the end of this program.' It hurts me to have them care more about that machine and those little pictures than about being glad to see me. I know that they probably can't help it, but still. . . ."

Can they help it? Ultimately, when we watch television 20 our power to release ourselves from viewing in order to attend to human demands that come up is not altogether a function of the pace of the program. After all, we might *choose* to operate according to human priorities, rather than electronic dictatorship. We might quickly decide "to hell with this program" and simply stop watching when a friend enters the room or a child needs attention.

We might . . . but the hypnotic power of television 21 makes it difficult to shift our attention away, makes us desperate not to lose the thread of the program. . . .

In this comparison of reading and television viewing 22 a picture begins to emerge that quite confirms the commonly held notion that reading is somehow "better" than television viewing. Reading involves a complex form of mental activity, trains the mind in concentration skills, develops the powers of imagination and inner visualization; the flexibility of its pace lends itself to a better and deeper comprehension of the material communicated. Reading engrosses, but does not hypnotize or seduce the reader from his human responsibilities. Reading is a two-way process: the reader can also write; television viewing is a one-way street: the viewer cannot create television images. And books are ever available, ever controllable. Television controls.

QUESTIONS ON MEANING

1. In her explanation of the reading process, Marie Winn shows how reading is different from watching television. What are the main parts of the reading process? How is this process different from television viewing?

2. Winn makes two related points about "concentration" and "pace." What claims does she make here?

QUESTIONS ON PURPOSE AND STRATEGY

1. Winn has three distinct purposes in this essay: to explain how children learn to read, to explain how that process differs from television viewing, and to persuade us that television viewing can have harmful effects. Find paragraphs that support each of these three purposes. Which of these purposes represent her ultimate goal?

2. Winn uses comparison as an organizing strategy when she explains the differences between reading and television watching. What is the *purpose* of this comparison?

3. As evidence to support her claim, Winn uses testimonies from experts, reports from research, and quotations from children and grandmothers. Skim the essay again and label, in the margin, examples of these types of evidence.

QUESTIONS ON AUDIENCE AND LANGUAGE

1. Describe Winn's expectations about her audience. Does she think her readers will quickly agree with her? Does she assume they are unaware of television's effects? Does she assume that they will disagree with her? Find at

least three sentences that suggest Winn's expectations about her audience.

2. Where is Winn's language most technical and difficult? Where are her descriptions simple and easy to understand?

QUESTIONS FOR DISCUSSION AND WRITING

1. Without looking back at the essay, describe the passage or point that you remember most clearly. Then find the passage and reread it. What made that passage memorable? (Is your most memorable point different from those of your classmates? Why?)

2. Informally survey your classmates about their television watching and reading habits. Is there a correlation between students who say they watch television heavily and those who say they have trouble reading? Or are good readers also likely to be television addicts?

3. Brainstorm counterarguments to Winn's thesis. Are there occasions when you watch television actively and reactively? Do videotapes allow you to control the pace of programs? In what ways does television viewing promote reading? When have television programs prompted you to read further on a topic or encouraged you to read a book? Write a letter of response to Winn, based on your arguments.

Dyslexia

EILEEN SIMPSON

PREREADING JOURNAL ENTRY

Remember an experience in school when you had difficulty
learning some concept, process, or activity. Perhaps it was
in math, English, art, or physical education. Describe *one
incident* when you were embarrassed by your performance.

Deare Uncel
   The Dr. was hear today and exqmimimed us we are booth
feeling well. I hope to hear from yoU soon the mail cames
hear twiceaday. It is very nirl here we eat well and sleep
well

                    Your loving nice.

*Eileen Simpson, at age nine, wrote this letter. She did not know at the
time that she—along with 23 million other Americans—suffered from
a developmental disorder known as dyslexia. In spite of her disorder—
and the humiliation of being semiliterate—she went on to become a
psychotherapist and novelist. She has published short stories in* The
Southern Review, *the* Transatlantic Review, *and* The Denver
Quarterly. *Her novel,* The Maze *(1975), was followed by an autobiographical account of her struggle with dyslexia,* Reversals: A Personal Account of Victory over Dyslexia *(1979).*

   The following selection contains four passages from Reversals. *Part
I chronicles Simpson's early frustrations in school; Part II defines dyslexia; Part III outlines methods she used to overcome her dyslexia; and
Part IV describes her "cured" condition when she wrote* Reversals. *The
principal characters in her narrative are herself, her sister Marie, her
teacher Miss Henderson, and her guardian Aunt Agnes.*

I.

Since I had said nothing at home about my daily agony [1] in 4A[2], my first month's report card came as a disagreeable surprise. Not having heard from Mr. Snyder or from my teacher again, Aunt Agnes had taken it that, my shyness overcome, I was now catching up to the public school level. Of my earlier academic difficulties, she had had no inkling. The transfer from the Dobbs Ferry School had not mentioned my erratic performance in oral reading. From Farmingdale there had been only the comment that I had satisfactorily completed the work of third grade.

Miss Henderson's report was blunt: "Failure" in read- [2] ing. There was an asterisk after this grade directing the eye to a covering letter in which Miss Henderson threatened that if I did not practice reading aloud at home every evening and show *marked* improvement, there was not the slightest chance that I would be promoted at the end of the year to fifth grade.

Aunt Agnes had recently asked us to call her Auntie, [3] to mark her role as guardian and distinguish her from our other aunts (for although we had neither parent, our mother having died when I was two months old and our father when I was five, we had a large family—a maternal grandmother, a host of aunts, uncles, great aunts and great uncles, cousins and cousins-once-removed). It was as guardian that she studied the report card, looked from it to the letter and back again in perplexity and disbelief. She took off her spectacles, which pinched the flesh of her nose, and put them into a little black box with a lid that snapped shut.

Auntie congratulated Marie on her string of A's, signed [4] her card, and dismissed her. She took up my card again and held it against her lips. She blew a hissing noise against its edge. This meant that she was dangerously vexed but uncertain what course of action to take. "Tsssssss."

It made the sound of steam about to blow the lid off [5] a pot.

"Tssssss." She waved the card at me. "What is the [6] meaning of this?"

What could I say? When she pressed me, I offered 7 the excuse that Miss Henderson's reader was "too hard."

Auntie took out her glasses and pinched them onto 8 her nose again. "Bring it to me."

Miss Henderson's power over me was not in her 9 tongue, though I shrank from its lashes, but in the way she used my classmates as spectators at the side show in which I was the freak. Auntie needed no outside assistance. In her person and in her manner, she was Authority. The command to bring my book to her was the moment of truth.

On the way to my room I flirted with saying I'd left 10 my reader in school. But Auntie would find another book, one that might be even harder.

"Let me hear the lesson you've prepared for tomor- 11 row," she said when I stood before her, my reader in hand.

With no idea how to prepare a lesson, I had this 12 evening, as every other evening, sat looking at the book with unfocused eyes. It would not do to say this, I knew. Instead I read the lesson we had been over in class that day. Ordinarily memory would have taken me a certain way, but in Miss Henderson's class I was so apprehensive waiting for my turn to come, and so miserable after it, that I wasn't able to listen while the others read. Reading to Auntie I found that my memory of the day's lesson ran out after the first few words.

"Continue," Auntie urged. 13

Clearly she was not going to prompt me or help me 14 sound out the next word. She expected me to read until I reached a natural stopping place. So I read. That is to say I repeated my daily performance. I clutched at recognizable words, guessed at others, and invented what I thought would make a suitable connective. As I went along, and Auntie made no corrections, my spirits lifted. I had the impression that I *was* reading, just as I had had when I'd recited from memory at Dobbs Ferry, or had followed the lead of the class at Farmingdale.

A clap of thunder brought my improvisation to an 15

end. *"What is this gibberish?* I can't believe my ears. *Do you hear what you're saying?"*

I didn't say so, but no, I didn't hear. I never heard 16 what I was saying when I read. I was too busy translating what I saw on the page into what I thought everyone else saw.

"Anyone would think you were holding the book *upside* 17 *down."* Auntie grabbed the book from my hand. No, I had been holding it properly. Ominously echoing Miss Henderson she asked, "What's this word?"

Now that the bubble had burst, and I understood that 18 whatever I had been doing it could not be called reading, I knew I had no chance of success if I tried to say what a word was.

"What's this word?" Auntie pointed to another. *"How* 19 *is it possible? You seem to know nothing. Do you even know the alphabet?"*

Auntie sounded scared. The terror in her voice fright- 20 ened me more than anything previously had done.

"Stop crying. Now listen to me. And listen carefully. 21 From now on you're to bring me your book every evening after dinner, do you hear?" As Auntie signed my report card, she added, "I'm going to write a note for you to take to Miss Henderson. I'll tell her that *I* will see to it that you learn to read. *And no nonsense about it."*

Three o'clock, when school was dismissed, was no 22 longer a moment of liberation. After Auntie took over the role of teacher, going home was as much to be dreaded as going to school. Following a brief play period, I went to my room to prepare for the evening lesson. Or, since I had no idea how to prepare, what I did was worry. And as I worried, a going-to-the-doctor feeling grabbed hold of me, squeezing my heart and my stomach. I ate dinner listlessly. As soon as I could, I excused myself and went to my room, hoping to be forgotten. The command to appear before Auntie was not long in coming.

"The sooner we get to the lesson, the sooner it will be 23 over" was Auntie's usual opening remark.

Reluctant to make the first mistake, I delayed as long 24

as possible. I had difficulty finding the place. I had forgotten my handkerchief (which I was sure to have need of), and had to go back to my room to get it.

"Why are you stalling? You seem determined to try 25 my patience."

Miss Henderson and now Auntie: There seemed to 26 be nothing I could do to please either of them. How, in the past, had it been so easy, so effortless to be a favorite? With a feeling of impending doom I would begin. I might get halfway through the first sentence before Auntie would say in a dry, controlled voice, "In the context the word cannot possibly be 'saw.' 'The man saw going home.' Does that make sense to you? It must be 'was.' "

I'd repeat, "The man was going home." In the next 27 sentence, or the one after, meeting the word again, I'd hesitate.

The lessons continued, Auntie grimly determined, I 28 increasingly despairing. She shouted, I cried, the others hid. The night I read "off" for "of" for the third time (as in, "He was off the same family as the old man"), Auntie exploded. She flew out of the chair, grabbed the book from my hand, and hurled it at my head. When it hit me, we were both astonished and shaken.

The following evening Auntie came to the lesson with 29 a fresh resolve. She made a "saintly effort" to correct and repeat with no rise in inflection. By the time she dismissed me she looked pale and drawn, as do athletes who have overextended themselves. The strain was so great she couldn't keep it up. As time went on the lessons had less and less to do with reading. They became skirmishes in a war of nerves, each side, knowing how dangerous an engagement could be, straining for control—Auntie with her temper, I with my "idiotic errors" and ungovernable tears.

Before each lesson I told myself to go slowly. Slowly, 30 slowly. I tried to make my eyes move in an orderly way along the line. By sub-vocalization, I studied to get the words right before pronouncing them aloud. Above all, I admonished myself to keep calm, to fight the panic, opaque as fog, numbing as ether, which rolled in and settled on my brain.

II.

Dyslexia (from the Greek, *dys*, faulty, + *lexis*, speech, 31 cognate with the Latin *legere*, to read), developmental or specific dyslexia as it's technically called, the disorder I suffered from, is the inability of otherwise normal children to read. Children whose intelligence is below average, whose vision or hearing is defective, who have not had proper schooling, or who are too emotionally disturbed or brain-damaged to profit from it belong in other diagnostic categories. They, too, may be unable to learn to read, but they cannot properly be called dyslexics.

For more than seventy years the essential nature of 32 the affliction has been hotly disputed by psychologists, neurologists, and educators. It is generally agreed, however, that it is the result of a neurophysiological flaw in the brain's ability to process language. It is probably inherited, although some experts are reluctant to say this because they fear people will equate "inherited" with "untreatable." Treatable it certainly is: not a disease to be cured, but a malfunction that requires retraining.

Reading is the most complex skill a child entering 33 school is asked to develop. What makes it complex, in part, is that letters are less constant than objects. A car seen from a distance, close to, from above, or below, or in a mirror still looks like a car even though the optical image changes. The letters of the alphabet are more whimsical. Take the letter *b*. Turned upside down it becomes a *p*. Looked at in a mirror, it becomes a *d*. Capitalized, it becomes something quite different, a *B*. The *M* upside down is a *W*. The *E* flipped over becomes Ǝ. This reversed *E* is familiar to mothers of normal children who have just begun to go to school. The earliest examples of art work they bring home often have I LOVƎ YOU written on them.

Dyslexics differ from other children in that they read, 34 spell, and write letters upside down and turned around far more frequently and for a much longer time. In what seems like a capricious manner, they also add letters, syllables, and words, or, just as capriciously, delete them. With palindromic words (was–saw, on–no), it is the order of the letters rather than the orientation they change. The new word makes sense, but not the sense intended. Then there are other words where the changed order—"sorty" for story—does not make sense at all.

The inability to recognize that g, g, and G are the same letter, the inability to maintain the orientation of the letters, to retain the order in which they appear, and to follow a line of text without jumping above or below it— all the results of the flaw—can make of an orderly page of words a dish of alphabet soup. [35]

Also essential for reading is the ability to store words in memory and to retrieve them. This very particular kind of memory dyslexics lack. So, too, do they lack the ability to hear what the eye sees, and to see what they hear. If the eye sees "off," the ear must hear "off" and not "of," or "for." If the ear hears "saw," the eye must see that it looks like "saw" on the page and not "was." Lacking these skills, a sentence or paragraph becomes a coded message to which the dyslexic can't find the key. [36]

It is only a slight exaggeration to say that those who learned to read without difficulty can best understand the labor reading is for a dyslexic by turning a page of text upside down and trying to decipher it. [37]

While the literature is replete with illustrations of the way these children write and spell, there are surprisingly few examples of how they read. One, used for propaganda purposes to alert the public to the vulnerability of dyslexics in a literate society, is a sign warning that behind it are guard dogs trained to kill. The dyslexic reads: [38]

Wurring
Guard God
Patoly

for

Warning
Guard Dog
Patrol

and, of course, remains ignorant of the danger.

Looking for a more commonplace example, and hop- 39 ing to recapture the way I must have read in fourth grade, I recently observed dyslexic children at the Educational Therapy Clinic in Princeton, through the courtesy of Elizabeth Travers, the director. The first child I saw, eight-year-old Anna (whose red hair and brown eyes reminded me of myself at that age), had just come to the Clinic and was learning the alphabet. Given the story of "Little Red Riding Hood," which is at the second grade level, she began confidently enough, repeating the title from memory, then came to a dead stop. With much coaxing throughout, she read as follows:

> Grandma you a top. Grandma [looks over at picture of Red Riding Hood]. Red Riding Hood [long pause, presses index finger into the paper. Looks at me for help. I urge: Go ahead] the a [puts head close to the page, nose almost touching] on Grandma

for

> Once upon a time there was a little girl who had a red coat with a red hood. Etc.

"Grandma" was obviously a memory from having 40 heard the story read aloud. Had I needed a reminder of how maddening my silences must have been to Miss Henderson, and how much patience is required to teach these children, Anna, who took almost ten minutes to read these few lines, furnished it. The main difference between Anna and me at that age is that Anna clearly felt no need to invent. She was perplexed, but not anxious, and seemed to have infinite tolerance for her long silences.

Toby, a nine-year-old boy with superior intelligence, 41

had a year of tutoring behind him and could have managed "Little Red Riding Hood" with ease. His text was taken from the *Reader's Digest's Reading Skill Builder*, Grade IV. He read:

> A kangaroo likes as if he had but truck together warm. His saw neck and head do not ... [Here Toby sighed with fatigue] seem to feel happy back. They and tried and so every a tiger likes Moses and shoots from lonesome day and shouts and long shore animals. And each farm play with five friends ...

He broke off with the complaint, "This is too hard. Do I have to read any more?"
His text was:

> A kangaroo looks as if he had been put together wrong. His small neck and head do not seem to fit with his heavy back legs and thick tail. Soft eyes, a twinkly little nose and short front legs seem strange on such a large strong animal. And each front paw has five fingers, like a man's hand.

That evening when I read aloud to Auntie for the first time, I probably began as Toby did, my memory of the classroom lesson keeping me close to the text. When memory ran out, and Auntie did not correct my errors, I began to invent. When she still didn't stop me, I may well have begun to improvise in the manner of this patient—anything to keep going and keep up the myth that I was reading—until Auntie brought the "gibberish" to a halt.

III.

Auntie had no intention of giving up on me. She had told my new teachers that contrary to the evidence I presented I was not stupid. They tended to believe her, for I didn't look dull-witted, and tried to think of ways to help me. Unfortunately, up-to-date as they were, they had not heard of Orton, who was at that time working close by at the Neurological Institute of Columbia Presbyterian Medical Center. Nor had they heard of Anna Gillingham who, not far from Convent Avenue, at the Ethical Culture School, was experimenting with remedial techniques.

These techniques she perfected when she joined Orton's staff. With Bessie W. Stillman she wrote, some years later, what became the classic instruction manual, *Remedial Reading*.

The Gillingham-Stillman system, and the many varia- 46 tions on it developed since, recognizes that what dyslexics need is not to have more of the same kind of training—be it the "whole-word" method, which came into fashion in the mid-twenties, or a combination of new and old, "whole-word" and phonetics—that children have in the classroom. Dyslexics need different training. For them each stage in the process of learning to read must be broken down into many small steps: each step taught slowly and thoroughly, the learning reinforced by engaging as many sense organs as possible—ear, eye, touch, and with it the musculature of the fingers and arms—in what is called tri-modal reinforcement.

Instead of having had me read aloud the same passage 47 in a story until I made no errors, a remedial teacher would have recognized that I needed to begin at the beginning, with the alphabet. Using objects—an apple, a bottle, a china cat—I would have been taught to associate *a* with apple, *b* with bottle, *c* with cat, all the way to *z* with a glass zebra. I would have held the objects, heard the teacher say the *a*, heard and felt my speech organs repeat it after her. I would have written the *a*, learning the feel of it with my fingers and arms, would have traced a cut-out *a*, or an *a* made in sandpaper. I would also have drawn an apple. The teacher's attentiveness would have kept a pupil like me, who had the attention span of a six-year-old for this kind of lesson, from associating the stick of gum with the letter *j*, or the jack with the letter *g*. At no time would I have been permitted to guess—or, more important, to make an error, for what is learned incorrectly must be relearned. Careful structuring of the material presented would have guaranteed me success. Even a limited success, such as this, would have begun the difficult process of rebuilding my self-confidence and overcoming my resistance to the written word.

Because no two dyslexics are alike, the symptoms and 48 degree of severity differing widely among them, remediation must be tailored to suit individual needs. I had two strengths many dyslexics lack. I was not hyperactive, and my writing was legible and produced without effort. Had my letters been difficult to read, or produced laboriously (dysgraphia), I would have had to be retrained, through finger and arm exercises, before being allowed to go on to cursive letter forms and connectives.

No matter how much training I had had in spelling I, 49 like most dyslexics, would probably never have become a good speller. As Orton said, and remedial teachers have since confirmed, poor spelling cannot be cured. It can be improved, however, vastly improved, by thorough training in phonetics and the learning of spelling rules, like the very useful "*i* before *e*."

Since spelling and intelligence are so inextricably 50 linked in the minds of the educated public that they use a person's spelling as a rough-and-ready test of his intelligence (a linkage no efforts by psychologists are likely to break), the importance of teaching spelling cannot be overestimated. Dyslexics resist writing because they are reluctant to project an image of themselves which they feel does not do their intelligence justice. Also, they are aware that nothing is easier to ridicule than incorrect spelling.

Knowing how little chance I had of writing, without 51 error, the kind of thank-you note that would have expressed my genuine feelings about a gift, I resorted to a safe (or almost safe) and wooden formula:

> Deare Aunt or Uncle So and So,
>   Thank you for the _____. It is just what I wanted. I hope you and Aunt (or Uncle So and So) are well. Marie and I are both fine.
> > Your loving ("i before e," etc.)
> > niece,

Even so, rarely did my note pass the censor. As often as not, Auntie returned it with the "dear" or some other word corrected, and the instruction to rewrite it before it was sent out. Had I learned the rule that in words with *ea,* the silent *a* usually signals that the *e* is long, I would have known that there is no need for a final *e* on "dear" and would not have wasted time speculating about whether to put it on or leave it off.

IV.

For years now I have "passed." Were it not for the 52 periodic threats of exposure—anyone who passes learns to live with them—I would almost have forgotten what it was like to live in the limbo of illiteracy. But in order to write this book under my own name, I had to fight the old shame and the new fear of being patronized: I suffered a relapse. My symptoms returned full-blown, providing me with a sharp reminder of what life had been like before I was "cured." There are undoubtedly details of the early years that I have forgotten. Others that remain repressed. Everything that I remember I have set down, as I remember it.

QUESTIONS ON MEANING

1. Based on Eileen Simpson's account, how do parents and teachers react to dyslexic children? What are their "reasons" that these children have trouble reading?

2. According to Simpson, what does the term *dyslexia* mean? How does it affect reading and writing?

3. What reading strategies does Simpson recommend to help dyslexic readers?

QUESTIONS ON PURPOSE AND STRATEGY

1. Where does Simpson apparently intend to move us emotionally? Where does she try to inform us reasonably and analytically? (Should writers be both emotional and rational if their purpose is to persuade us?)

2. In part II, Simpson explains dyslexia. Find one sentence

illustrating each of the following strategies: definition of a term; use of comparison; and example of dyslexic reading or writing.

QUESTIONS ON AUDIENCE AND LANGUAGE

1. Who would be most interested in reading this selection—or Simpson's book?
2. Locate two examples of Simpson's use of technical language. Is this language appropriate or too difficult for her audience?

QUESTIONS FOR DISCUSSION AND WRITING

1. Reconsider your Prereading Journal Entry. Explain as clearly as possible the nature of your problem and suggest how, in retrospect, your "disorder" might have been cured or prevented.
2. Simpson explains how a dyslexic might easily misread a warning sign:

Warning

Guard Dog

Patrol

Find examples in your own neighborhood or campus of signs that, misread, might endanger a dyslexic. What warning labels on products might go unheeded? What other perils might go unnoticed?
3. Even when people do not have dyslexia, they may acquire information or learn in different ways. Some people learn visually, through reading or watching. Some learn auditorily, by listening. Other people learn by talking about what they are learning. Still others learn by doing something. Interview one of your classmates and compare his or her favorite learning style(s) with your own.

The Inspirational Bookworm

MARNIE ARNOLD

(1971–   )

PREREADING JOURNAL ENTRY

Write a journal entry about the books you remember reading in grade school. Did you have a favorite author? Did you read at home or mostly at school? Did you have a teacher, parent, or friend who encouraged you to read?

Marnie Arnold, a student taught by Catherine Schutz at the University of Central Florida, writes about her third grade teacher in Mt. Laurel, New Jersey, who inspired her to read. Motivated by Mrs. Veston's enthusiasm and her "Bookworm" contest, Arnold read constantly during class, at recess, and in the evenings. Her prizes for winning the contest were the praise of her teacher, a six-inch trophy of a winged woman, and a lifelong love of reading.

If you ask a student at almost any level of education 1 to make a list of his or her extracurricular activities, I'll bet reading will be at the bottom of the list. In fact, it may not appear at all. Given free time, students will do almost anything before sitting down to read a good book. There are a number of theories that experts give to explain why students don't enjoy reading. Some say that television, radio, and movies are replacing books. Others blame the lack of parental encouragement in many households. Still others believe that forcing students to read Shakespeare has a negative effect on their attitudes towards reading. These experts can give all the reasons they can think of, but I know the real reason why students don't enjoy reading: They didn't have Kathy Veston as a third grade teacher.

Mrs. Veston was my third grade teacher at Parkway 2 Elementary School in Mt. Laurel, New Jersey. I loved everything about her, and I tried to be exactly like her. I copied the way she walked, the way she talked, and even the way she chewed on her thumb nail whenever something bothered her. Gaining Mrs. Veston's approval became my ultimate goal in life.

When Mrs. Veston came up with the idea of a reading 3 contest, I was thrilled. She had just given me the perfect opportunity to impress her. I was even more thrilled to learn that the winner of this contest would receive an engraved trophy. The thought of winning a prize sparked the rest of my classmates' interest and motivated them to participate, no matter how "anti-reading" they were.

Mrs. Veston called her contest "Bookworm" and the 4 object was simple: whoever read the most books in one month would be the winner. Each book had a certain value according to its length, print size, and level of difficulty. The value was represented by circles, approximately three inches in diameter, cut from colored construction paper. *Beezus and Ramona,* for example, received three circles while *Stuart Little* only received one circle. Every student started with one circle with his or her name printed on it, which symbolized the head of the worm. The circles that represented each book were stapled to the head, end to end, to form a chain: the body of the worm.

All of the worms were taped up on the wall in one 5 long row so we could watch each other's progress. A fierce sense of competition arose, giving us even more incentive. We read during every possible moment, even when we were supposed to be doing our math. Each day my classmates and I added more and more circles to our worms. Like ivy, our colorful bookworms slowly began to cover the wall, creeping toward the floor.

Determined to win that trophy and Mrs. Veston's 6 approval, I worked even harder than my classmates. I read during recess while everyone else played on the swings. I read in the evenings instead of watching television. My efforts were rewarded as my worm began to grow longer than the rest. Soon, it reached the floor, and I added a second head to my worm—a privilege I shared with only two others in my class.

The excitement grew as the month progressed. We 7 were so caught up in the contest that no one realized that we were actually learning something. We were learning things like fluency, vocabulary, plot, and comprehension. The most important thing we learned, however, was that reading could be fun. We didn't think about the far-reaching effects this contest was having on us because we were too busy having fun.

With the end of the month came the time to count 8 the bookworms. Mrs. Veston tallied the parts of each of the worms and announced the name of the winner. I felt a tremendous amount of pride as I heard her call my name: I had won! With weak knees, I made my way to the front of the room to receive my prize and a hug from my idol.

I stared at the trophy in awe. On a beautiful marble 9 base stood a winged woman, her arms raised upward, holding a torch in her left hand. The figure was a shiny, gold color that sparkled like glitter. Engraved in a gold plate across the front of the base were the words:

MARNIE ARNOLD
1ST PLACE READING
3RD GRADE

The hard work I had put into the Bookworm Contest had been well worth it. I had pleased Mrs. Veston and, at the same time, had won the most beautiful trophy in the world.

Nine years later, before I moved out of my house to 10 go to college, I cleaned out my closet. While rummaging through some old boxes full of forgotten items, I came across my trophy from third grade. I was amazed at how unimpressive it now was. It stood barely six inches high on a small, chipped marble base that lacked luster. The gold paint had dulled over the years and had begun to peel. Yet even though its appearance had changed, the trophy's meaning remains the same. It symbolizes hard work, the desire to win, and, most of all, the discovery of a wonderful source of entertainment, information, and creativity. To those of you who didn't have Kathy Veston for a third grade teacher, I extend my sympathies, for you might never enjoy one of life's greatest resources.

QUESTIONS ON MEANING

1. According to Arnold, what motivated her to read?
2. What does the trophy of the winged woman mean to Arnold?

QUESTIONS ON PURPOSE AND STRATEGY

1. What sentence(s) best express Arnold's purpose for writing her essay?
2. Arnold concludes her essay by recalling how, nine years later, she discovered her tarnished and rather unimpressive third grade trophy. Does this paragraph make an effective conclusion? Should this paragraph be revised? Explain.

QUESTIONS ON AUDIENCE AND LANGUAGE

1. What sentence(s) in the first paragraph suggest Arnold's audience?
2. Parallelism in sentences is achieved by repeating the structure of a clause or phrase two or more times, as in "I came, I saw, I conquered," or "I ran down the hallway and dashed up the stairs." Where does Arnold use parallelism? Explain why these sentences are or are not effective.

QUESTIONS FOR DISCUSSION AND WRITING

1. Arnold says that the students in her class "were so caught up in the contest that no one realized that we were actually learning something." Based on your own experience, was the contest essential to inspiring students to read and learn? Would a teacher's enthusiasm by itself inspire students? Would the books themselves motivate third grade students to read and learn?

2. Assume that you are John Holt or Marie Winn. How might you use Arnold's experience to support your own theories about reading? Write one paragraph on Arnold's experience that you would add to your essay in this chapter.

2
WRITING: PURPOSES AND PROCESSES

A writer is a reader moved to emulation.

> —Saul Bellow, author of *Henderson the Rain King*

The writer may write to inform, to explain, to entertain, to persuade, but whatever the purpose there should be, first of all, the satisfaction of the writer's own learning. . . .

> —Donald Murray, Pulitzer Prize-winning author

The writing process is not linear, moving smoothly in one direction from start to finish. It is messy, recursive, convoluted, and uneven. Writers write, plan, revise, anticipate, and review throughout the writing process. . . .

> —Maxine Hairston, teacher and author of books about writing

In "The Act of Writing" (reprinted in this chapter), William Zinsser states: "Writing is a deeply personal process, full of mystery and surprise. No two people go about it in exactly the same way. . . . There is no 'right' method. Any method that will do the job is the right method for you."

Do you agree with that statement? Since critical reading is active, responsive reading, let's cross-examine Zinsser on this point. (Zinsser is not here to defend himself, so you ask the questions and I'll give Zinsser's responses.)

> **You:** I don't know that writing is always "deeply personal." What if I'm just making a grocery list? What's so "deeply personal" about that?
>
> **Zinsser (me):** OK. You win that one. I just meant that the *way* we write is not mechanical or governed by inflexible rules. It depends on who we are. It depends on the situation—who our audience is, what we're trying to say, and how we want to say it.
>
> **You:** I'll agree that writing, especially in a class, is mysterious. I never know what's right and what's wrong. Usually when I do something I like, the teacher dislikes it—and vice versa. To me, that's the "mystery" in writing.
>
> **Zinsser (me):** I should be clearer. I was talking about the mystery of how we write, not the mystery of how people react to what we've written. But you're right. Both reading and writing are trial-and-error processes. Each is an art, not a mathematical equation.
>
> **You:** What bothers me most is that there is no one right method. You say that everybody writes differently, as though that should comfort me. Frankly, it makes me uneasy. How can I learn if there is no "right" way?
>
> **Zinsser (me):** I think I overemphasized the point. Most writers do agree on some general guidelines: Don't believe that you always have to start at the beginning and write to the end. Start anywhere. Just start. Have a plan as you begin writing, an outline or a direction or a strategy, but be willing to change if you get a better idea. Don't worry about spelling and grammar when you're writing a first draft. Focus on getting your ideas down. When you lose the thread of what you're writing, reread what you've written up to that point. Those are guidelines or methods that many writers follow.

You: How about this: If there is no one "right" method of writing, why are there textbooks on writing?

Me: I'll take this one. Good writing textbooks help you discover and practice appropriate options. You should read several kinds of writing. You should practice writing for a variety of audiences and purposes. You should practice several different invention activities, such as freewriting, clustering, branching, questioning, summarizing, and interviewing. Different strategies will work for different writers and situations, so learn to use what works best for you. Learning to write is learning to diagnose and then solve problems in your writing.

THE WRITING SITUATION

To write effectively, you must consider your writing situation. Effective writing depends on your **purpose** and on the main idea or claim you're making. It depends on your **audience** and on your readers' expectations about the **kind of writing** you're doing. It depends on you as a **writer.** It depends on the **strategies** you're using. The answers to specific questions ("When can I use first person in an essay?" "How detailed should this example be?" "How long should this essay be?" or "Should I use contractions?") depend on you, your purpose, your audience, and what you are trying to write.

PURPOSES FOR WRITING

First think about purposes for writing that relate to you as a writer. You should benefit, directly or indirectly, from everything you write. You may write a journal just to **express** your feelings and thoughts. You may write a funny note to a friend, just to **entertain** yourself. You may take notes in a biology lab or during a field trip to help you see or **observe** something more clearly. You write shopping lists or class notes to help you **remember.** You may also write a story about some event in your life to help you remember. You may read a newspaper or a book, see a film or a television news program, or interview another person to **investigate** and **learn** something new. In each of these cases, writing helps you learn, remember, observe, or discover something new, something that pleases or benefits you. Without those benefits, few writers would want to write anything.

Now think about purposes for writing that relate to your audience. When writers wish to share what they have learned with a specific audience, they have several options. They can write primarily to **inform** their readers about some idea, issue, or event they have read about or investigated. They may wish to **explain** what something is, how it happened, or why it happened. They might want to **persuade** their audience to believe or do something by evaluating a person, product, service, or a piece of literature, film, or art. They might persuade their readers that a serious problem should be solved in a certain way. They might persuade their readers by arguing for or against a certain issue or claim. Finally, they could merely **explore** a difficult idea or dilemma without claiming to understand it fully or without recommending an answer or a solution.

In actual practice, most writers have **multiple purposes** for writing. They may begin by carefully observing a new film, by investigating what film critics have to say about the film, and by remembering other similar films they have seen. They begin, in short, by learning about their topic. Then they may want to inform their audience about the film, to report what the critics are saying. Or they may want to explain the special effects in the film. Or they may want to evaluate the film. Or they may want to persuade others to see the film—or not to see it. They may, in fact, want to combine several of these purposes.

Remember: Choosing or knowing your purpose(s) will help you decide how to write. How you begin a paper, how you organize it, what kind of evidence you use, what kind of writing style is appropriate—the answers to all of these questions depend on your purpose(s). Teachers and student editors in your class can help you revise your paper only if they know your intended purpose. Purpose (along with the audience and the context) helps guide the whole writing process.

AUDIENCE ANALYSIS

The next important element in the writing situation is the intended audience. On some occasions, your essay defines how your readers are likely to respond. If you're writing an autobiographical essay, for example, readers may meet you on your own terms. On other occasions, however, you must accommodate your audience by knowing who they are, what they are likely to believe or know, and what they are expecting. You don't want to bore your readers with information they already have. You don't want to antagonize your readers if you hope that they will accept your proposal. You don't want to use technical language they might not know. (Or you do want to use technical language for experts in the field.) On each writing occasion, analyze your audience by considering the following:

1. **Audience profile.** Who is your intended reader? First decide on the size and interests of your audience. Is it a single person? Is it a small, well-defined group, such as your family? Is it a larger group with well-defined interests, such as the employees in your company? Is it a large, more diverse audience, such as members of your class or readers of *Rolling Stone* magazine? Is it extremely broad and diverse, such as the readers of *The New York Times?* Then describe your readers as accurately as possible. Do they have identifiable roles (businesspeople who read *Forbes* magazine)? Can you identify their age, sex, economic status, ethnic background, or occupational category? All of this information becomes a profile of your intended audience that will help you write.

2. **Audience-subject relationship.** Consider what your audience *knows* about your intended subject. If they are experts, you may want to review the basics

quickly and move right to the important issues. If they are novices, you will have to explain more of the background and avoid technical language. What is your audience's *attitude* toward your position? Are they sympathetic to your ideas or are they more skeptical or even hostile? If they are hostile, you obviously need to establish yourself as a reasonable, caring person who shares some of their ideas and attitudes.

3. **Audience-writer relationship.** Consider your relationship with your audience. Do you know each other? Are you writing for your employer or are you the employer? Are you peers—students in the same class or employees in the same company? Who controls the issue you are writing about? If your reader is in power, you will need to be tactful in your criticism and suggestions. If you are in power, you may want to avoid sounding too autocratic.

4. **Writer's role.** Finally, consider your own perspective or role. You may want to tailor this perspective to your audience. If you are trying to persuade an audience of economists that recycling can pay for itself, you could assume a formal role, citing facts, figures, and statistics. But if you are writing to ordinary citizens, you might be more persuasive if you related how you rode on a trash truck for a day in order to describe trash that people should be recycling.

KINDS OF WRITING

How you write also depends on your audience's expectations about the kind of writing you are doing. A grocery list, an office memorandum, an informal essay, a short story or poem, an interview, a news article, a legal brief, a letter, an advertisement—these are distinctly different kinds of writing. Each kind of writing creates **expectations** for a certain community of readers about purpose and form. We expect grocery lists to inform us through key words rather than complete sentences. We expect news-paper articles to inform us through relatively short sentences and paragraphs. We expect advertisements to persuade us by means of exaggerated claims and appealing images and language. We expect informal essays to inform or persuade us (or explore an idea) by means of well-developed paragraphs, some organizing or shaping strategy(s), and appropriate language.

THE WRITER'S VOICE

Who you are can also guide your writing. Your "voice," **the personality that you project through your writing,** can attract your reader's interest, win your reader's patience as you explain a difficult subject, or defuse your reader's hostility as you argue your point. Writers may use colloquial language to project themselves as relaxed, informal, and conversational. Writers may use direct, candid language to project a no-nonsense approach to the subject. They may write in a humorous or ironic tone to show that they, too, recognize absurdities in life. A writer's voice often guides and controls a piece of writing.

STRATEGIES FOR WRITING

Frequently, a strategy for organizing or developing a topic may control a piece of writing. *Typically, strategies are means or methods of carrying out your purpose.* Strategies are ways of thinking and at the same time ways of organizing your writing. If you are writing an autobiographical essay, **chronological order** will probably be a strategy you will follow. If you are explaining why you've chosen a certain major to a friend, you may give specific **examples** of the classes you find most interesting. In a history class, if you are explaining how *glasnost* led to the opening of Eastern Europe, you may want to **define** *glasnost,* explain the steps in the **process** that led to the dismantling of the Berlin wall, and explain the **effects** of Gorbachev's policies on

East German leaders. If you are evaluating a current film, you may want to **compare and contrast** the film to other recent films of the same type. Chronological order, example, definition, process analysis, comparison and contrast, and cause-and-effect analysis are strategies that can guide your writing.

PROCESSES FOR WRITING

Many writers divide their writing process into stages or dimensions. After assessing their writing situation, they go through four interrelated activities: **collecting** ideas and information, **shaping** or organizing their ideas, **drafting** the piece of writing, and **revising** and editing a final version.

Assessing the Writing Situation

Initially, you should assess the writing situation. Can you decide on a purpose, audience, and topic that interests you? Is this an assignment for a teacher or an employer? Who is the audience? What is or should be the purpose for the writing? What role or voice would be appropriate? Remember: Even an excellent piece of writing can fail if it is not responsive to the assignment or the intended audience.

Collecting

Collecting involves gathering and recording impressions, images, detailed observations, personal examples, ideas, facts, statistics, and quotations that are relevant to your purpose and audience. Three primary strategies for collecting are **observing** people, places, and events, **remembering** events from your own life, and **investigating** ideas and information in books and through interviews. In this reader, essays and assignments in chapters 3, 4, and 5 help you practice these collecting skills.

Shaping

Shaping involves ordering and organizing ideas and information into sentences and paragraphs. A clear organization helps readers understand new ideas, see relationships between ideas and examples, and helps to persuade readers to believe your claim. The essays in this text illustrate how a writer's **thesis or claim** (the main point or idea) works with specific organizational and developmental **strategies** (comparison/contrast, definition, example, process analysis, cause-and-effect analysis, and so forth) to create an essay that flows smoothly and predictably for the reader.

Drafting

Throughout their writing process, most writers are continually writing, taking notes, brainstorming, or drafting a sample paragraph. At some point, however, they sense that they are ready to write out a first version, or assemble various ideas, pieces, and sentences into some whole. The result is a first, or rough, draft. Most writers agree that when this point arrives, they like to plunge ahead, keeping the pencil or word processor moving, sustaining as much momentum as possible. When they become stuck, they reread what they have already written or check their notes, but then they keep moving while the ideas are flowing. The drafting stage is usually not the time to interrupt the train of thought to correct spelling or revise awkwardly worded sentences.

Revising

Revision literally means "re-seeing." When writers revise, they are looking at their writing again, usually from the point of view of their intended audience. Revision includes major changes in content, organization, purpose, audience, or writer's role. Is my organization clear or should I reorganize? Am I just stating or asserting a point without enough examples to show my readers? Have I made transitions between major points or ideas? Are my sentences clear? Revision may require recollecting ideas or information, changing or improving your organization, or writing for a different audience or purpose. Revision also includes editing: fixing spelling, improving awkward sentences, changing word choice, changing punctuation, and correcting mechanics. Writers learn how to revise by rereading their own writing, by reading passages aloud, by listening to the advice of other readers, and by writing alternate versions of a passage and comparing them to the original.

A Reminder about Writing Process(es)

Three points of caution. First, no one process exists for all writers. Writers vary these stages or dimensions according to the writing task at hand. Second, the stages in the writing process are recursive: Typically, writers collect some information, do some initial shaping, draft a paragraph, go back and collect some more information, revise a portion, change their organization, collect additional information, and so forth. Finally, some writers prefer to describe their process in terms of dimensions, since a single idea may affect several stages simultaneously. For example, a shaping strategy (such as comparison/contrast) may provide an organization, suggest some examples for the writer to collect, and indicate how the writer should revise his or her draft.

PURPOSE AND PROCESS: ONE WRITER'S ESSAY

Below are writing process materials, a draft, and the final version of an essay by student writer Nicolle Mircos. Notice how Mircos discovers her idea in a journal entry and then uses her clustering exercise to collect ideas and focus her subject. Compare her first draft to the final draft to see how she shaped and revised her essay. Finally, read her Postscript to her final essay. How do her comments reveal her purpose for writing, her intended audience, and her writing process? Does she successfully convey her experience and her main idea to you?

My Sister, Kari

NICOLLE MIRCOS

(1969–   )

PREREADING JOURNAL ENTRY

Select one moment in your past that changed your life or showed how your life had already changed. What was the event? What were you like before it and afterwards?

STUDENT JOURNAL RESPONSE

My sister is retarded, but I never knew until finally one day while I was being mean to her my father told me. I knew she was different, but I didn't know why, so I was really mean and hateful to her. After he told me, I was only about 9, but I still felt awful and sorry. After that other people made me mad when they were mean to her. I still get mad at her, but I understand why.

   Nicolle Mircos, a student taught by Margaret Sweany at Colorado State University, writes about her disabled younger sister. "Whenever I try to picture the past," Mircos says, "my sister Kari and the discovery of her musical ability comes to mind." Embarrassed by her sister's disability, Mircos one day overhears her sister playing a Neil Diamond song at the piano. As Mircos describes, that moment completely changes their relationship.

Clustering Exercise

Rough Draft

"Shut up!" I yelled at my older sister,
Kari. "Mom doesn't really like you!" We
were having the third argument of that
week. With these words; I turned and ran,

not wanting to see the tears fall that were

making her eyes glisten and her black

mascara run down her cheeks. I hated to see

her cry because deep down, I still loved

her, even though I now knew the truth about

her.

I was only eight years old, but going on

forty. At that time I believed that there

wasn't anything I couldn't understand. So,

when my mother explained to me that my

sister was mentally retarded because of

problems at birth, I pretended to

understand. In actuality, I was confused,

shocked and hurt. ~~At~~ first, ~~I thought~~ God

My *reaction was that*

was punishing my parents for something

they'd done. ~~T~~hen I thought he was

punishing me, ~~L~~ater I ~~decided~~ that he only

realized *was*

punish~~ing~~ Kari. Why, did not know.

I was the one w/out an older sister to

teach me about make-up, fashions and

Since the day my mother had explained it

to me, I found myself fighting a lot more

with ~~her~~. She was fifteen, but had the mind

Kari

of a nine year old and I knew how to use

     get her to do chores that I didn't feel like doing.

that to ~~my advantage now. I was embarrassed~~

I never invited friends home, the fear of her saying some-

~~to bring friends home with me, afraid that~~

thing to embarras me was too great. I understand now

~~they would notice and say something.~~ *how selfish*

                                                        I really was.

For a long time, I would sneak into her

doorway and just watch every move she made.

                      revealed

I guess I was trying to see if she ~~really~~

2 heads, or maybe 3 eyes when she was alone

~~was different than everyone else. The~~

$_S$urprising*ly enough* ~~thing was that~~ she ~~was~~ *did* not, ~~She~~ *on the*

outside she was normal, it was inside that her

~~sat and listened to records a lot, like any~~

circuits were crossed. Most of the time she spent

~~other fifteen year old.~~ *her days listening to the*

                         radio.

One day was different. She listened to

    The music sprayed from the radio

records. ⌄like normal, but then suddenly got

up and walked straight past me. I followed

    as quickly as possible

her⌃downstairs and to the piano. Suddenly,

I was shocked to hear the music from her

records being played perfectly on the

piano. We both played the piano, but I

practiced many long hours using music, she

had none. I spent many hours with the

metronome learning to count and to play

rhythms right, she had none. I approached

her cautiously not really knowing if I

would see a whole new light on her face or

maybe the face of Frankenstein's monster

staring me in the eyes. ~~Surprisingly~~ To my surprise

~~enough~~, she turned to reveal the same face

I had made ~~fun of~~ damp with tears just hours ago. She was

smiling, my ~~face~~ expression hadn't changed:

It was a look of utter amazement. I sat down and began to play a game with

her. Covering her eyes I played a note and

asked her to name it. Several times we

tried this in all ranges of the keyboard,

she never failed to name the correct one.

~~she never missed one~~. On top of all the

other talents, I determined she also had perfect pitch.

This was something I was not born with and would never have. It

can not be learned or taught.

It was at that moment that I saw her situation

with new light. I realized that God had

given her a gift to help overcome what he

had taken away from her. She would never

have a boyfriend or go to the prom, but she

could listen to the radio and play

flawlessly. I sat down with her and she

taught me to use my ear and simple left

hand chords to play ~~anything~~ simple songs without music ;

I taught her to read notes. Even though she

could not tell me the monetary value of a

quarter, she could instantly play a B—flat

when it appeared on a page, or name one when she heard it play.

From that day on, we learned together. I

taught her note values and names and she

explained how to create accompaniment to

right hand melodies. I didn't create fights with

her anymore. And I am no longer embarrassed

to bring friends to meet her. If someone

makes fun of her (while I am around,) I am

the first to defend her while standing

proudly at her side.

Final Draft

"Shut up!" I yelled at my older sister, Kari. "Mom doesn't really like you!" This was the third argument of the week. With these words I turned and ran, not wanting to see the tears fall, making her eyes glisten and her black mascara run down her cheeks. I hated to see her cry. Deep down I still loved her, even though I now knew the truth about her.

I was only eight years old, but going on forty. There wasn't anything I couldn't understand. So, when my mother explained to me that my sister was mentally retarded because of problems at birth, I pretended to understand. In actuality, I was confused, shocked, and hurt. At first, I thought God was punishing my parents for some mistake they'd committed. Then, I thought he was punishing me. I lost the older sister to teach me about make-up, boys, and fashions. Later, I decided that he only punished Kari. Why, I did not know.

But the day my mother explained this deficiency to me, I found myself fighting a lot more with Kari. She was fifteen but had the mind of a nine-year-old. I knew how to use that to get her to do chores that I didn't feel like doing. I never invited friends home: The fear of her saying something to embarrass me loomed too great. For a long time, I would sneak into her doorway and just watch every move she made. Often, I would go unnoticed. She was usually oblivious to the outside world. Most of the time she spent her days listening to the radio, almost motionless. I guess I tried to see if she would reveal two heads or maybe three eyes when alone. Surprisingly to me, she did not. On the outside she was normal; inside her circuits were crossed.

One day was different. The familiar sounds of music spilled from the radio, but then without warning, she got up and walked straight past me. I followed her as quickly and as quietly as possible downstairs as she led me to the piano. Astoundingly, music spilled from the keys that, until now, only my fingers had touched. I use the term *music* loosely here because at first, my mind was too garbled to make sense of anything. Each note seemed to have no bearing on any other. A few moments passed before my mind could make sense of notes and actually recognize that she was playing a song from the radio: Neil Diamond's "Hello Again." All at once, it seemed my ear heard each note before its sound wave had even left the piano string. All at once, my preconceived notions of her dropped into a pit deeper than the darkest pit in the ocean. I played the piano, but I practiced many long hours using music. She had no music and practiced none. I spent many hours with the metronome learning to count and to play rhythms right, she spent none. I approached her cautiously, not really knowing if I would see a whole new light on her face or maybe the face of Frankenstein's monster staring me in the eyes. To my surprise, she turned to reveal the same face I had made dampen with tears just hours ago. She turned to reveal a smile. My look of utter amazement remained for several moments before also slipping into a smile.

I sat down and began to play a game with her. Covering her eyes, I played a note and asked her to name it. Several times we tried this in all ranges of the keyboard; she never failed. Then, I determined that she also had perfect pitch, something I was not born with and would never have. This gift cannot be learned or taught. This moment I saw her with new light. God had given her a gift to help overcome what he had taken away from her. She would never have a boyfriend or go to the prom, but she could listen to the radio and play what she'd heard flawlessly. I sat down with her, and she taught me to use my ear and simple left-hand chords to play easy songs without music, and I taught her to read notes. Even though she could not tell me the monetary value of a quarter, she could instantly play a B-flat when it appeared on a page or name one when she heard it played.

From that day on, we learned together. I taught her note values and names. She explained how to create accompaniment to right-hand melodies. I didn't start fights with her anymore. I was no longer embar-

rassed to bring friends to meet her. I still fight with
her as all sisters will, but they are no longer fictitiously
based on my part. Now, it's difficult to imagine the
past when I didn't want to look at her face, afraid that
her looks would sting or that her condition would
prove contagious. It's difficult because now we are
friends, musical partners in a sense. If someone makes
fun of her while I am around, I am the first to defend
her while standing proudly at her side.

Postscript: Remembering Essay

1. Explain who your audience is and why you think
   they'll find this paper interesting or useful.

My audience is anyone who has not necessarily known someone with a problem, but who has had trouble just being around someone who does. It shows how selfish and mean a "normal" person can be to someone less fortunate and hopefully will teach a lesson about treating people nice. Sometimes it takes a special talent, like perfect pitch, for a person to realize underneath God made everyone the same.

2. What dominant impression do you want to leave
   with your reader?

First, I want them to see how selfish I was by not wanting people to meet her and starting fights. Then I hope I created a visual enough scene at the piano to show that I have overcome all of that.

3. List one or two sentences from your essay that make
   a connection between your memory and the
   present. How do they connect?

It was at that moment – at the piano – that I saw her in a new light : This means that everything I saw in her before had been transformed into my present feeling of love and admiration for her talent.

4. Collecting and shaping: Which strategies helped you to remember incidents more quickly and clearly? Which strategies helped you most to focus and organize your essay? What problems were you unable to solve?

The journal writings, especially the one about the memory of a song. I also got a lot out of the grouping and clustering exercise. I hope that I put enough sensitivity and warmth into the piano scene.

5. Drafting and revising: What problems did you run into during the actual drafting of your essay? Where did you go back and reshape or redraft portions? Where did your workshop advice help most?

My biggest problem was how to put my true feelings into words that would be sensitive enough for this situation. I changed a lot in the actual body of the essay, especially in the piano scene, to try and make things more vivid.

6. Was your writing process effective for this essay? Why or why not? Assuming that you had the same amount of time to work on this essay, what would you do differently? What would you do the same?

Yes, it helped to bring back the memories of that day a lot more clearly. I would like more time to work in the groups on certain problems. It is always the best help to hear what someone else thinks should be different.

7. What do you like best about your essay? What

would you change if you had another day to work
on this assignment?

I would try to work a lot more on the part about the girls
at the piano. It was so hard for me to get this across. I
hope I have done it sufficiently. As for the opening and
concluding paragraphs, they came easily to me and I
rather like them.

Why I Write

GEORGE ORWELL

(1903–1950)

PREREADING JOURNAL ENTRY

What hobby or activity do you enjoy or excel at? Write for five minutes, explaining the *reasons why* you engage in this activity. Do you do it because it entertains you? Because others may admire your skill? Because it helps others? Because you enjoy the finished product?

"I had the lonely child's habit of making up stories and holding conversations with imaginary persons," George Orwell writes. "I think from the very start my literary ambitions were mixed up with the feeling of being isolated and undervalued." George Orwell, a pen name for Eric Blair, was born in India and grew up in England. His penchant for making up imaginary persons is most evident in his classic satires of Stalinism and totalitarianism in Animal Farm *(1945) and* 1984 *(1949), but other novels and collections of essays show his investigative and political style.* Down and Out in Paris and London *(1933) describes the effects of poverty.* Shooting an Elephant and Other Essays *(1950) draws on his Indian experiences.* Homage to Catalonia *(1938) grew out of his involvement in the Spanish Civil War. In "Why I Write," Orwell remembers his early literary ambitions in order to explain his motives for writing. Orwell's essay helps us understand the relationship between* motives *for writing (egotism, desire to create art, historical or political impulse) and* purposes *for writing (to express feelings, to inform, to persuade).*

From a very early age, perhaps the age of five or six, 1 I knew that when I grew up I should be a writer. Between the ages of about seventeen and twenty-four I tried to abandon this idea, but I did so with the consciousness that I was outraging my true nature and that sooner or later I should have to settle down and write books.

I was the middle child of three, but there was a gap 2 of five years on either side, and I barely saw my father before I was eight. For this and other reasons I was somewhat lonely, and I soon developed disagreeable mannerisms which made me unpopular throughout my schooldays. I had the lonely child's habit of making up stories and holding conversations with imaginary persons, and I think from the very start my literary ambitions were mixed up with the feeling of being isolated and undervalued. I knew that I had a facility with words and a power of facing unpleasant facts, and I felt that this created a sort of private world in which I could get my own back for my failure in everyday life. Nevertheless the volume of serious—*i.e.* seriously intended—writing which I produced all through my childhood and boyhood would not amount to half a dozen pages. I wrote my first poem at the age of four or five, my mother taking it down to dictation. I cannot remember anything about it except that it was about a tiger and the tiger had "chair-like teeth"—a good enough phrase, but I fancy the poem was a plagiarism of Blake's "Tiger, Tiger." At eleven, when the war of 1914–18 broke out, I wrote a patriotic poem which was printed in the local newspaper, as was another, two years later, on the death of Kitchener. From time to time, when I was a bit older, I wrote bad and usually unfinished "nature poems" in the Georgian style. I also, about twice, attempted a short story which was a ghastly failure. That was the total of the would-be serious work that I actually set down on paper during all those years.

However, throughout this time I did in a sense engage 3 in literary activities. To begin with there was the made-to-order stuff which I produced quickly, easily and without much pleasure to myself. Apart from school work, I wrote *vers d'occasion*, semi-comic poems which I could turn out at what now seems to me astonishing speed—at fourteen I wrote a whole rhyming play, in imitation of Aristophanes, in about a week—and helped to edit school magazines, both printed and in manuscript. These magazines were the most pitiful burlesque stuff that you could imagine, and I took far less trouble with them than I now would with the cheapest journalism. But side by side with all this, for fifteen years or more, I was carrying out a literary exercise of a quite different kind: this was the making up of a continuous "story" about myself, a sort of diary existing only in the mind. I believe this is a common habit of children and adolescents. As a very small child I used to imagine that I was, say, Robin Hood, and picture myself as the hero of thrilling adventures, but quite soon my "story" ceased to be narcissistic in a crude way and became more and more a mere description of what I was doing and the things I saw. For minutes at a time this kind of thing would be running through my head: "He pushed the door open and entered the room. A yellow beam of sunlight, filtering through the muslin curtains, slanted on to the table, where a matchbox, half open, lay beside the inkpot. With his right hand in his pocket he moved across to the window. Down in the street a tortoiseshell cat was chasing a dead leaf," etc., etc. This habit continued till I was about twenty-five, right through my nonliterary years. Although I had to search, and did search, for the right words, I seemed to be making this descriptive effort almost against my will, under a kind of compulsion from outside. The "story" must, I suppose, have reflected the styles of the various writers I admired at different ages, but so far as I remember it always had the same meticulous descriptive quality.

When I was about sixteen I suddenly discovered the 4 joy of mere words, *i.e.* the sounds and associations of words. The lines from *Paradise Lost*—

> So hee with difficulty and labour hard
> Moved on: with difficulty and labour hee,

which do not now seem to me so very wonderful, sent shivers down my backbone; and the spelling "hee" for "he" was an added pleasure. As for the need to describe things, I knew all about it already. So it is clear what kind of books I wanted to write, in so far as I could be said to want to write books at that time. I wanted to write enormous naturalistic novels with unhappy endings, full of detailed descriptions and arresting similes, and also full of purple passages in which words were used partly for the sake of their sound. And in fact my first completed novel, *Burmese Days,* which I wrote when I was thirty but projected much earlier, is rather that kind of book.

I give all this background information because I do 5 not think one can assess a writer's motives without knowing something of his early development. His subject matter will be determined by the age he lives in—at least this is true in tumultuous, revolutionary ages like our own—but before he ever begins to write he will have acquired an emotional attitude from which he will never completely escape. It is his job, no doubt, to discipline his temperament and avoid getting stuck at some immature stage, or in some perverse mood: but if he escapes from his early influences altogether, he will have killed his impulse to write. Putting aside the need to earn a living, I think there are four great motives for writing, at any rate for writing prose. They exist in different degrees in every writer, and in any one writer the proportions will vary from time to time, according to the atmosphere in which he is living. They are:

1. Sheer egoism. Desire to seem clever, to be talked about, to be remembered after death, to get your own back on grownups who snubbed you in childhood, etc., etc. It is humbug to pretend that this is not a motive, and a strong one. Writers share this characteristic with scientists, artists, politicians, lawyers, soldiers, successful businessmen—in short, with the whole top crust of humanity. The great mass of human beings are not acutely selfish. After the age of about thirty they abandon individual ambition—in many cases, indeed, they almost abandon the sense of being individuals at all—and live chiefly for others, or are simply smothered under drudgery. But

there is also the minority of gifted, willful people who are determined to live their own lives to the end, and writers belong in this class. Serious writers, I should say, are on the whole more vain and self-centered than journalists, though less interested in money.

2. Esthetic enthusiasm. Perception of beauty in the external world, or, on the other hand, in words and their right arrangement. Pleasure in the impact of one sound on another, in the firmness of good prose or the rhythm of a good story. Desire to share an experience which one feels is valuable and ought not to be missed. The esthetic motive is very feeble in a lot of writers, but even a pamphleteer or a writer of textbooks will have pet words and phrases which appeal to him for nonutilitarian reasons; or he may feel strongly about typography, width of margins, etc. Above the level of a railway guide, no book is quite free from esthetic considerations.

3. Historical impulse. Desire to see things as they are, to find out true facts and store them up for the use of posterity.

4. Political purpose—using the word "political" in the widest possible sense. Desire to push the world in a certain direction, to alter other people's idea of the kind of society that they should strive after. Once again, no book is genuinely free from political bias. The opinion that art should have nothing to do with politics is itself a political attitude.

It can be seen how these various impulses must war 6 against one another, and how they must fluctuate from person to person and from time to time. By nature—taking your "nature" to be the state you have attained when you are first adult—I am a person in whom the first three motives would outweigh the fourth. In a peaceful age I might have written ornate or merely descriptive books, and might have remained almost unaware of my political loyalties. As it is I have been forced into becoming a sort of pamphleteer. First I spent five years in an unsuitable profession (the Indian Imperial

Police, in Burma), and then I underwent poverty and the sense of failure. This increased my natural hatred of authority and made me for the first time fully aware of the existence of the working classes, and the job in Burma had given me some understanding of the nature of imperialism: but these experiences were not enough to give me an accurate political orientation. Then came Hitler, the Spanish civil war, etc. By the end of 1935 I had still failed to reach a firm decision. I remember a little poem that I wrote at that date, expressing my dilemma:

> A happy vicar I might have been
> Two hundred years ago,
> To preach upon eternal doom
> And watch my walnuts grow;
>
> But born, alas, in an evil time,
> I missed that pleasant haven,
> For the hair has grown on my upper lip
> And the clergy are all clean-shaven.
>
> And later still the times were good,
> We were so easy to please,
> We rocked our troubled thoughts to sleep
> On the bosoms of the trees.
>
> All ignorant we dared to own
> The joys we now dissemble;
> The greenfinch on the apple bough
> Could make my enemies tremble.
>
> But girls' bellies and apricots,
> Roach in a shaded stream,
> Horses, ducks in flight at dawn,
> All these are a dream.
>
> It is forbidden to dream again;
> We maim our joys or hide them;
> Horses are made of chromium steel
> And little fat men shall ride them.
>
> I am the worm who never turned,
> The eunich without a harem;
> Between the priest and the commissar
> I walk like Eugene Aram;

> And the commissar is telling my fortune
> While the radio plays,
> But the priest has promised an Austin Seven,
> For Duggie always pays.
>
> I dreamed I dwelt in marble halls,
> And woke to find it true;
> I wasn't born for an age like this;
> Was Smith? Was Jones? Were you?

The Spanish war and other events in 1936–7 turned the scale and thereafter I knew where I stood. Every line of serious work that I have written since 1936 has been written, directly or indirectly, *against* totalitarianism and *for* democratic socialism, as I understand it. It seems to me nonsense, in a period like our own, to think that one can avoid writing of such subjects. Everyone writes of them in one guise or another. It is simply a question of which side one takes and what approach one follows. And the more one is conscious of one's political bias, the more chance one has of acting politically without sacrificing one's esthetic and intellectual integrity.

What I have most wanted to do throughout the past ten years is to make political writing into an art. My starting point is always a feeling of partisanship, a sense of injustice. When I sit down to write a book, I do not say to myself, "I am going to produce a work of art." I write it because there is some lie that I want to expose, some fact to which I want to draw attention, and my initial concern is to get a hearing. But I could not do the work of writing a book, or even a long magazine article, if it were not also an esthetic experience. Anyone who cares to examine my work will see that even when it is downright propaganda it contains much that a full-time politician would consider irrelevant. I am not able, and I do not want, completely to abandon the world-view that I acquired in childhood. So long as I remain alive and well I shall continue to feel strongly about prose style, to love the surface of the earth, and to take a pleasure in solid objects and scraps of useless information. It is no use trying to suppress that side of myself. The job is to reconcile my ingrained likes and dislikes with the essentially public, nonindividual activities that this age forces on all of us.

It is not easy. It raises problems of construction and 8 of language, and it raises in a new way the problem of truthfulness. Let me give just one example of the cruder kind of difficulty that arises. My book about the Spanish civil war, *Homage to Catalonia,* is, of course, a frankly political book, but in the main it is written with a certain detachment and regard for form. I did try very hard in it to tell the whole truth without violating my literary instincts. But among other things it contains a long chapter, full of newspaper quotations and the like, defending the Trotskyists who were accused of plotting with Franco. Clearly such a chapter, which after a year or two would lose its interest for any ordinary reader, must ruin the book. A critic whom I respect read me a lecture about it. "Why did you put in all that stuff?" he said. "You've turned what might have been a good book into journalism." What he said was true, but I could not have done otherwise. I happened to know, what very few people in England had been allowed to know, that innocent men were being falsely accused. If I had not been angry about that I should never have written the book.

In one form or another this problem comes up again. 9 The problem of language is subtler and would take too long to discuss. I will only say that of late years I have tried to write less picturesquely and more exactly. In any case I find that by the time you have perfected any style of writing, you have always outgrown it. *Animal Farm* was the first book in which I tried, with full consciousness of what I was doing, to fuse political purpose and artistic purpose into one whole. I have not written a novel for seven years, but I hope to write another fairly soon. It is bound to be a failure, every book is a failure, but I do know with some clarity what kind of book I want to write.

Looking back through the last page or two, I see that 10 I have made it appear as though my motives in writing were wholly public-spirited. I don't want to leave that as the final impression. All writers are vain, selfish and lazy, and at the very bottom of their motives there lies a mystery. Writing a book is a horrible, exhausting struggle, like a long bout of some painful illness. One would never undertake such a thing if one were not driven on by some demon whom one can neither resist nor understand. For all one knows that demon is simply the same instinct that makes a baby squall for attention. And yet it is also true that one can write nothing readable unless one constantly struggles to efface one's own personality. Good prose is like a window pane. I cannot say with certainty which of my motives are the strongest, but I know which of them deserve to be followed. And looking back through my work, I see that it is invariably where I lacked a *political* purpose that I wrote lifeless books and was betrayed into purple passages, sentences without meaning, decorative adjectives and humbug generally.

QUESTIONS ON MEANING

1. What are Orwell's four motives for writing? What dilemma did he face about his motives, and what historical event focused his motives for writing?

2. What political purpose did Orwell settle on, especially after his experiences in the Spanish Civil War? What advantages and disadvantages of writing with a political purpose does Orwell discuss in his example about the writing of *Homage to Catalonia*?

QUESTIONS ON PURPOSE AND STRATEGY

1. Which of Orwell's four motives for writing best explains his purpose in writing this essay?

2. Particularly in the last third of his essay, Orwell implies that one of his purposes in writing this essay is to answer his critics' charge that his writing is too political or too much like propaganda. What sentences show him answering this charge?

3. Orwell organizes his essay into several related parts. In the first part of the essay, he explains his early nature and influences. In the second part, he analyzes writers' motives for writing. How would you describe the last section(s) of the essay? Where does each section begin and end?

QUESTIONS ON AUDIENCE AND LANGUAGE

1. Who is Orwell's audience? The general public? Writers? Readers of his novels? Critics? Defend your choice by citing a key passage or passages.

2. Orwell suggests that "good prose is like a window pane." What does he mean by that statement? Is his own prose "like a window pane"?

QUESTIONS FOR DISCUSSION AND WRITING

1. Near the end of the essay, Orwell exclaims, "If I had not been angry about that [the Spanish Civil War] I should never have written the book." Just two paragraphs later, Orwell says, "And yet it is also true that one can write nothing readable unless one constantly struggles to efface one's own personality." Are these statements contradictory? How can a writer do both at the same time?

2. How do your reasons for pursuing your favorite hobby (see Prereading Journal Entry) compare to Orwell's motives for writing? Do you have a combination of motives, depending on the occasion or your mood? Do you agree that in your hobby as in writing, "these various impulses must war against one another"?

3. Compare Orwell's point about writing with a "political purpose" to Richard Wright's experiences reading Mencken and other writers. What did Wright mean when he said, "The plots and stories in the novels did not interest me so much as the *point of view* revealed"?

4. If Orwell were alive today, what subjects or political causes would he write about?

On Keeping a Notebook

JOAN DIDION

(1934–   )

PREREADING JOURNAL ENTRY

If you have access to your diary, journal, or school note-book from several years ago, reread several passages. Transcribe any interesting passages. What can you reconstruct about who you were then, why you were writing, or what your interests were?

"My first notebook," Joan Didion says, *"was a Big Five Tablet, given to me by my mother with the sensible suggestion that I stop whining and learn to amuse myself by writing down my thoughts."* Didion has *written several award-winning novels, including* Play It as It Lays *(1971),* A Book of Common Prayer *(1977), and* Democracy *(1984), but her reputation as a nonfiction writer is equally strong. Her essays, collected in* Slouching Towards Bethlehem *(1968) and* The White Album *(1979), show her ability to combine precise, journalistic observation with an elegant prose style.*

In "On Keeping a Notebook," Didion distinguishes between a diary and a notebook, and then explains how keeping a notebook involves more than simply recording facts. Since the "facts" may not turn out to be true, the point is to record scenes and images to remember "how it felt to me."

" 'That woman Estelle,' " the note reads, " 'is partly   1
the reason why George Sharp and I are separated today.'
*Dirty crepe-de-Chine wrapper, hotel bar, Wilmington RR, 9:45
A.M. August Monday morning."*
Since the note is in my notebook, it presumably has   2

some meaning to me. I study it for a long while. At first
I have only the most general notion of what I was doing
on an August Monday morning in the bar of the hotel
across from the Pennsylvania Railroad station in Wilmington, Delaware (waiting for a train? missing one? 1960?
1961? why Wilmington?), but I do remember being there.
The woman in the dirty crepe-de-Chine wrapper had
come down from her room for a beer, and the bartender
had heard before the reason why George Sharp and she
were separated today. "Sure," he said, and went on mopping the floor. "You told me." At the other end of the
bar is a girl. She is talking, pointedly, not to the man
beside her but to a cat lying in the triangle of sunlight
cast through the open door. She is wearing a plaid silk
dress from Peck & Peck, and the hem is coming down.

Here is what it is: the girl has been on the Eastern 3
Shore, and now she is going back to the city, leaving the
man beside her, and all she can see ahead are the viscous
summer sidewalks and the 3 A.M. long-distance calls that
will make her lie awake and then sleep drugged through
all the steaming mornings left in August (1960? 1961?).
Because she must go directly from the train to lunch in
New York, she wishes that she had a safety pin for the
hem of the plaid silk dress, and she also wishes that she
could forget about the hem and the lunch and stay in the
cool bar that smells of disinfectant and malt and make
friends with the woman in the crepe-de-Chine wrapper.
She is afflicted by a little self-pity, and she wants to
compare Estelles. That is what that was all about.

Why did I write it down? In order to remember, of 4
course, but exactly what was it I wanted to remember?
How much of it actually happened? Did any of it? Why
do I keep a notebook at all? It is easy to deceive oneself
on all those scores. The impulse to write things down is a
peculiarly compulsive one, inexplicable to those who do
not share it, useful only accidentally, only secondarily, in
the way that any compulsion tries to justify itself. I suppose
that it begins or does not begin in the cradle. Although I
have felt compelled to write things down since I was five

years old, I doubt that my daughter ever will, for she is a singularly blessed and accepting child, delighted with life exactly as life presents itself to her, unafraid to go to sleep and unafraid to wake up. Keepers of private notebooks are a different breed altogether, lonely and resistant rearrangers of things, anxious malcontents, children afflicted apparently at birth with some presentiment of loss.

My first notebook was a Big Five tablet, given to me 5 by my mother with the sensible suggestion that I stop whining and learn to amuse myself by writing down my thoughts. She returned the tablet to me a few years ago; the first entry is an account of a woman who believed herself to be freezing to death in the Arctic night, only to find, when day broke, that she had stumbled onto the Sahara Desert, where she would die of the heat before lunch. I have no idea what turn of a five-year-old's mind could have prompted so insistently "ironic" and exotic a story, but it does reveal a certain predilection for the extreme which has dogged me into adult life; perhaps if I were analytically inclined I would find it a truer story than any I might have told about Donald Johnson's birthday party or the day my cousin Brenda put Kitty Litter in the aquarium.

So the point of my keeping a notebook has never been, 6 nor is it now, to have an accurate factual record of what I have been doing or thinking. That would be a different impulse entirely, an instinct for reality which I sometimes envy but do not possess. At no point have I ever been able successfully to keep a diary; my approach to daily life ranges from the grossly negligent to the merely absent, and on those few occasions when I have tried dutifully to record a day's events, boredom has so overcome me that the results are mysterious at best. What is this business about "shopping, typing piece, dinner with E, depressed"? Shopping for what? Typing what piece? Who is E? Was this "E" depressed, or was I depressed? Who cares?

In fact I have abandoned altogether that kind of 7 pointless entry; instead I tell what some would call lies. "That's simply not true," the members of my family frequently tell me when they come up against my memory of a shared event. "The party was not for you, the spider was *not* a black widow, *it wasn't that way at all*." Very likely they are right, for not only have I always had trouble distinguishing between what happened and what merely might have happened, but I remain unconvinced that the distinction, for my purposes, matters. The cracked crab that I recall having for lunch the day my father came home from Detroit in 1945 must certainly be embroidery, worked into the day's pattern to lend verisimilitude; I was ten years old and would not now remember the cracked crab. The day's events did not turn on cracked crab. And yet it is precisely that fictitious crab that makes me see the afternoon all over again, a home movie run all too often, the father bearing gifts, the child weeping, an exercise in family love and guilt. Or that is what it was to me. Similarly, perhaps it never did snow that August in Vermont; perhaps there never were flurries in the night wind, and maybe no one else felt the ground hardening and summer already dead even as we pretended to bask in it, but that was how it felt to me, and it might as well have snowed, could have snowed, did snow.

How it felt to me: that is getting closer to the truth about 8 a notebook. I sometimes delude myself about why I keep a notebook, imagine that some thrifty virtue derives from preserving everything observed. See enough and write it down, I tell myself and then some morning when the world seems drained of wonder, some day when I am only going through the motions of doing what I am supposed to do, which is write—on that bankrupt morning I will simply open my notebook and there it will be, a forgotten account with accumulated interest, paid passage back to the world out there: dialogue overheard in hotels and elevators and at the hatcheck counter in Pavillon (one middle-aged man shows his hat check to another and says, "That's my old football number"); impressions of Bettina Aptheker and Benjamin Sonnenberg and Teddy ("Mr. Acapulco") Stauffer; careful *aperçus* about tennis bums and failed fashion models and Greek shipping heiresses, one of whom taught me a significant lesson (a lesson I could have learned from F. Scott Fitzgerald, but perhaps we all must meet the very rich for ourselves) by asking, when I arrived to interview her in her orchid-filled sitting room on the second day of a paralyzing New York blizzard, whether it was snowing outside.

I imagine, in other words, that the notebook is about 9 other people. But of course it is not. I have no real business with what one stranger said to another at the hatcheck counter in Pavillon; in fact I suspect that the line "That's my old football number" touched not my own imagination at all, but merely some memory of something once read, probably "The Eighty-Yard Run." Nor is my concern with a woman in a dirty crepe-de-Chine wrapper in a Wilmington bar. My stake is always, of course, in the unmentioned girl in the plaid silk dress. *Remember what it was to be me:* that is always the point.

It is a difficult point to admit. We are brought up in 10 the ethic that others, any others, all others, are by definition more interesting than ourselves; taught to be diffident, just this side of self-effacing. ("You're the least important person in the room and don't forget it," Jessica Mitford's governess would hiss in her ear on the advent of any social occasion; I copied that into my notebook because it is only recently that I have been able to enter a room without hearing some such phrase in my inner ear.) Only the very young and the very old may recount their dreams at breakfast, dwell upon self, interrupt with memories of beach picnics and favorite Liberty lawn dresses and the rainbow trout in a creek near Colorado Springs. The rest of us are expected, rightly, to affect absorption in other people's favorite dresses, other people's trout.

And so we do. But our notebooks give us away, for 11 however dutifully we record what we see around us, the common denominator of all we see is always, transparently, shamelessly, the implacable "I". We are not talking here about the kind of notebook that is patently for public consumption, a structural conceit for binding together a series of graceful *pensées;* we are talking about something private, about bits of the mind's string too short to use, an indiscriminate and erratic assemblage with meaning only for its maker.

And sometimes even the maker has difficulty with the 12 meaning. There does not seem to be, for example, any point in my knowing for the rest of my life that, during 1964, 720 tons of soot fell on every square mile of New York City, yet there it is in my notebook, labeled "FACT." Nor do I really need to remember that Ambrose Bierce liked to spell Leland Stanford's name "£eland $tanford" or that "smart women almost always wear black in Cuba," a fashion hint without much potential for practical application. And does not the relevance of these notes seem marginal at best?:

> In the basement museum of the Inyo County Courthouse 13 in Independence, California, sign pinned to a mandarin coat: "This MANDARIN COAT was often worn by Mrs. Minnie S. Brooks when giving lectures on her TEAPOT COLLECTION."

> Redhead getting out of car in front of Beverly Wilshire Hotel, chinchilla stole, Vuitton bags with tags reading:
>
> MRS LOU FOX
> HOTEL SAHARA
> VEGAS

Well, perhaps not entirely marginal. As a matter of fact, 14 Mrs. Minnie S. Brooks and her MANDARIN COAT pull me back into my own childhood, for although I never knew Mrs. Brooks and did not visit Inyo County until I was thirty, I grew up in just such a world, in houses cluttered with Indian relics and bits of gold ore and ambergris and the souvenirs my Aunt Mercy Farnsworth brought back from the Orient. It is a long way from that world to Mrs. Lou Fox's world where we all live now, and is it not just as well to remember that? Might not Mrs. Minnie S. Brooks help me to remember what I am? Might not Mrs. Lou Fox help me to remember what I am not?

But sometimes the point is harder to discern. What 15 exactly did I have in mind when I noted down that it cost the father of someone I know $650 a month to light the place on the Hudson in which he lived before the Crash? What use was I planning to make of this line by Jimmy Hoffa: "I may have my faults, but being wrong ain't one of them"? And although I think it interesting to know where the girls who travel with the Syndicate have their hair done when they find themselves on the West Coast, will I ever make suitable use of it? Might I not be better off just passing it on to John O'Hara? What is a recipe for sauerkraut doing in my notebook? What kind of magpie keeps this notebook? *"He was born the night the Titanic went down."* That seems a nice enough line, and I even recall who said it, but is it not really a better line in life than it could ever be in fiction?

But of course that is exactly it: not that I should ever 16 use the line, but that I should remember the woman who said it and the afternoon I heard it. We were on her terrace by the sea, and we were finishing the wine left from lunch, trying to get what sun there was, a California winter sun. The woman whose husband was born the night the *Titanic* went down wanted to rent her house, wanted to go back to her children in Paris. I remember wishing that I could afford the house, which cost $1,000 a month. "Someday you will," she said lazily. "Someday it all comes." There in the sun on her terrace it seemed easy to believe in someday but later I had a low-grade afternoon hangover and ran over a black snake on the way to the supermarket and was flooded with inexplicable fear when I heard the checkout clerk explaining to the man ahead of me why she was finally divorcing her husband. "He left me no choice," she said over and over as she punched the register. "He has a little seven-month-old baby by her, he left me no choice." I would like to believe that my dread then was for the human condition, but of course it was for me, because I wanted a baby and did not then have one and because I wanted to own the house that cost $1,000 a month to rent and because I had a hangover.

It all comes back. Perhaps it is difficult to see the value 17
in having one's self back in that kind of mood, but I do
see it; I think we are well advised to keep on nodding
terms with the people we used to be, whether we find
them attractive company or not. Otherwise they turn up
unannounced and surprise us, come hammering on the
mind's door at 4 A.M. of a bad night and demand to know
who deserted them, who betrayed them, who is going to
make amends. We forget all too soon the things we thought
we could never forget. We forget the loves and the
betrayals alike, forget what we whispered and what we
screamed, forget who we were. I have already lost touch
with a couple of people I used to be; one of them, a
seventeen-year-old, presents little threat, although it would
be of some interest to me to know again what it feels like
to sit on a river levee drinking vodka-and-orange-juice
and listening to Les Paul and Mary Ford and their echoes
sing "How High the Moon" on the car radio. (You see I
still have the scenes, but I no longer perceive myself
among those present, no longer could even improvise the
dialogue.) The other one, a twenty-three-year old, bothers
me more. She was always a good deal of trouble, and I
suspect she will reappear when I least want to see her,
skirts too long, shy to the point of aggravation, always the
injured party, full of recriminations and little hurts and
stories I do not want to hear again, at once saddening me
and angering me with her vulnerability and ignorance, an
apparition all the more insistent for being so long banished.

It is a good idea, then, to keep in touch and I suppose 18
that keeping in touch is what notebooks are all about.
And we are all on our own when it comes to keeping
those lines open to ourselves: your notebooks will never
help me, nor mine you. *"So what's new in the whiskey business?"* What could that possibly mean to you? To me it
means a blonde in a Pucci bathing suit sitting with a couple
of fat men by the pool at the Beverly Hills Hotel. Another
man approaches, and they all regard one another in silence
for a while. "So what's new in the whiskey business?" one

of the fat men finally says by way of welcome, and the blonde stands up, arches one foot and dips it in the pool, looking all the while at the cabana where Baby Pignatari is talking on the telephone. That is all there is to that, except that several years later I saw the blonde coming out of Saks Fifth Avenue in New York with her California complexion and a voluminous mink coat. In the harsh wind that day she looked old and irrevocably tired to me, and even the skins in the mink coat were not worked the way they were doing them that year, not the way she would have wanted them done, and there is the point of the story. For a while after that I did not like to look in the mirror, and my eyes would skim the newspapers and pick out only the deaths, the cancer victims, the premature coronaries, the suicides, and I stopped riding the Lexington Avenue IRT because I noticed for the first time that all the strangers I had seen for years—the man with the seeing-eye dog, the spinster who read the classified pages every day, the fat girl who always got off with me at Grand Central—looked older than they once had.

It all comes back. Even that recipe for sauerkraut: 19 even that brings it back. I was on Fire Island when I first made that sauerkraut, and it was raining, and we drank a lot of bourbon and ate the sauerkraut and went to bed at ten, and I listened to the rain and the Atlantic and felt safe. I made the sauerkraut again last night and it did not make me feel any safer, but that is, as they say, another story.

QUESTIONS ON MEANING

1. What are notebooks, according to Didion? What are they *not*?

2. "The impulse to write things down is a peculiarly compulsive one." "*How it felt to me:* that is getting closer to the truth about a notebook." "I think we are well advised to keep on nodding terms with the people we used to be." Which of these sentences best expresses Didion's main point?

3. What does Didion mean when she says that her entries are "what some would call lies"?

QUESTIONS ON PURPOSE AND STRATEGY

1. Didion says that notebooks are about "something private, about bits of the mind's string too short to use, an indiscriminate and erratic assemblage with meaning only for its maker." If her notebooks are not "useful" or have only private meaning, why is Didion sharing them with us?

2. Didion uses a discovery strategy: She asks a question and then guesses at possible answers. (She may, in fact, have already known the answer before she began writing, or she may have discovered the answers as she wrote.) In paragraph four, she asks, "Why did I write it down? . . . Why do I keep a notebook at all?" Reread the essay, looking for her answers. What answer does she "discover" by the end of the essay?

QUESTIONS ON AUDIENCE AND LANGUAGE

1. Who is Didion's audience for this essay? *Based on your own reaction,* is she addressing literary critics and people who have read her essays and novels, or is she addressing people who are interested in learning to write?

2. Didion has said she learned how sentences were put together by recopying passages from Ernest Hemingway and Joseph Conrad. Pick a paragraph from this essay and recopy it. What do you learn about how Didion puts her sentences together?

3. Reread paragraph eight. Count the number of sentences in that paragraph. What does that tell you about Didion's prose style? What effect might this style have on her audience? How does it affect you?

4. List the unfamiliar words and names of famous people you underlined during your reading. Did these unfamiliar words or people interfere with your reading?

QUESTIONS FOR DISCUSSION AND WRITING

1. Didion's essay is similar to Orwell's. She talks about her childhood writing habits to show how her writing relates to her personal development, and she talks about her motives for writing. What different conclusions does Didion reach about the motives that govern her writing?

2. If you keep a notebook or a journal, compare the purpose of your journal with Didion's. Do you make the same kinds of observations? Do you use your journal to help you write essays? Do you record events to "keep in touch with yourself," as Didion does?

The Act of Writing: One Man's Method

WILLIAM ZINSSER

(1922–   )

PREREADING JOURNAL ENTRY

Describe your writing rituals. When you write an essay assignment, what is your favorite environment? Do you have to be isolated in a room, or can you work with a television blaring in the background? What time of day is best? Do you write longhand on a yellow legal pad or compose on a computer? Explain, using an example of a paper you wrote recently, which rituals give you the best results.

"Simplify. Be Clear. Get rid of pomposity in your writing. Above all, be yourself." *This, in brief, is William Zinsser's advice in his best seller,* On Writing Well: An Informal Guide to Writing Non-fiction *(1976). Born in New York City, Zinsser became an editor and film critic for the* New York Herald Tribune, *taught in the English department at Yale, and served as executive editor of the Book-of-the-Month Club. His publications include* Seen Any Good Movies Lately? *(1958),* Pop Goes America *(1966), and* The Lunacy Bloom *(1970).*

In the following selection from Writing with a Word Processor *(1983), Zinsser explains how word processors help him write more clearly. The word processor, Zinsser admits, is the "perfect new toy. I began playing on page 1—editing, cutting and revising—and have been on a rewriting high ever since."*

Writing is a deeply personal process, full of mystery 1
and surprise. No two people go about it in exactly the
same way. We all have little devices to get us started, or
to keep us going, or to remind us of what we think we
want to say, and what works for one person may not work
for anyone else. The main thing is to get something
written—to get the words out of our heads. There is no
"right" method. Any method that will do the job is the
right method for you.

It helps to remember that writing is hard. Most non- 2
writers don't know this; they think that writing is a natural
function, like breathing, that ought to come easy, and
they're puzzled when it doesn't. If you find that writing
is hard, it's because it *is* hard. It's one of the hardest things
that people do. Among other reasons, it's hard because it
requires thinking. You won't write clearly unless you keep
forcing yourself to think clearly. There's no escaping the
question that has to be constantly asked: What do I want
to say next?

So painful is this task that writers go to remarkable 3
lengths to postpone their daily labor. They sharpen their
pencils and change their typewriter ribbon and go out to
the store to buy more paper. Now these sacred rituals, as
[the computer manuals] would say, have been obsoleted.

When I began writing this book on my word processor 4
I didn't have any idea what would happen. Would I be
able to write anything at all? Would it be any good? I was
bringing to the machine what I assumed were wholly
different ways of thinking about writing. The units massed
in front of me looked cold and sterile. Their steady hum
reminded me that they were waiting. They seemed to be
waiting for information, not for writing. Maybe what I
wrote would also be cold and sterile.

I was particularly worried about the absence of paper. 5
I knew that I would only be able to see as many lines as
the screen would hold—twenty lines. How could I review
what I had already written? How could I get a sense of
continuity and flow? With paper it was always possible to
flick through the preceding pages to see where I was

117

coming from—and where I ought to be going. Without paper I would have no such periodic fix. Would this be a major hardship?

The only way to find out was to find out. I took a last 6 look at my unsharpened pencils and went to work.

My particular hang-up as a writer is that I have to get 7 every paragraph as nearly right as possible before I go on to the next paragraph. I'm somewhat like a bricklayer: I build very slowly, not adding a new row until I feel that the foundation is solid enough to hold up the house. I'm the exact opposite of the writer who dashes off his entire first draft, not caring how sloppy it looks or how badly it's written. His only objective at this early stage is to let his creative motor run the full course at full speed; repairs can always be made later. I envy this writer and would like to have his metabolism. But I'm stuck with the one I've got.

I also care how my writing looks while I'm writing it. 8 The visual arrangement is important to me: the shape of the words, of the sentences, of the paragraphs, of the page. I don't like sentences that are dense with long words, or paragraphs that never end. As I write I want to see the design that my piece will have when the reader sees it in type, and I want that design to have a rhythm and a pace that will invite the reader to keep reading. O.K., so I'm a nut. But I'm not alone; the visual component is important to a large number of people who write.

One hang-up we visual people share is that our copy 9 must be neat. My lifelong writing method, for instance, has gone like this. I put a piece of paper in the typewriter and write the first paragraph. Then I take the paper out and edit what I've written. I mark it up horribly, crossing words out and scribbling new ones in the space between the lines. By this time the paragraph has lost its nature and shape for me as a piece of writing. It's a mishmash of typing and handwriting and arrows and balloons and other directional symbols. So I type a clean copy, incorporating the changes, and then I take that piece of paper out of the typewriter and edit it. It's better, but not much better. I go over it with my pencil again, making more changes, which again make it too messy for me to read critically, so I go back to the typewriter for round three. And round four. Not until I'm reasonably satisfied do I proceed to the next paragraph.

This can get pretty tedious, and I have often thought 10 that there must be a better way. Now there is. The word processor is God's gift, or at least science's gift, to the tinkerers and the refiners and the neatness freaks. For me it was obviously the perfect new toy. I began playing on page 1—editing, cutting and revising—and have been on a rewriting high ever since. The burden of the years has been lifted.

Mostly I've been cutting. I would guess that I've cut 11 at least as many words out of this book as the number that remain. Probably half of those words were eliminated because I saw that they were unnecessary—the sentence worked fine without them. This is where the word processor can improve your writing to an extent that you will hardly believe. Learn to recognize what is clutter and to use the DELETE key to prune it out.

How will you know clutter when you see it? Here's a 12 device I used when I was teaching writing at Yale that my students found helpful; it may be a help here. I would put brackets around every component in a student's paper that I didn't think was doing some kind of work. Often it was only one word—for example, the useless preposition that gets appended to so many verbs (order up, free up), or the adverb whose meaning is already in the verb (blare loudly, clench tightly), or the adjective that tells us what we already know (smooth marble, green grass). The brackets might surround the little qualifiers that dilute a writer's authority (a bit, sort of, in a sense), or the countless phrases in which the writer explains what he is about to explain (it might be pointed out, I'm tempted to say). Often my brackets would surround an entire sentence— the sentence that essentially repeats what the previous sentence has said, or tells the reader something that is implicit, or adds a detail that is irrelevant. Most people's writing is littered with phrases that do no new work whatever. Most first drafts, in fact, can be cut by fifty percent without losing anything organic. (Try it; it's a good exercise.)

By bracketing these extra words, instead of crossing 13 them out, I was saying to the student: "I may be wrong, but I think this can go and the meaning of the sentence won't be affected in any way. But *you* decide: read the sentence without the bracketed material and see if it works." In the first half of the term, the students' papers were festooned with my brackets. Whole paragraphs got bracketed. But gradually the students learned to put mental brackets around their many different kinds of clutter, and by the end of the term I was returning papers to them that had hardly any brackets, or none. It was always a satisfying moment. Today many of those students are professional writers. "I still see your brackets," they tell me. "They're following me through life."

You can develop the same eye. Writing is clear and 14 strong to the extent that it has no superfluous parts. (So is art and music and dance and typography and design.) You will really enjoy writing on a word processor when you see your sentences growing in strength, literally before your eyes, as you get rid of the fat. Be thankful for everything that you can throw away.

I was struck by how many phrases and sentences I 15 wrote in this book that I later found I didn't need. Many of them hammered home a point that didn't need hammering because it had already been made. This kind of overwriting happens in almost everybody's first draft, and it's perfectly natural—the act of putting down our thoughts makes us garrulous. Luckily, the act of editing follows the act of writing, and this is where the word processor will bail you out. It intercedes at the point where the game can be won or lost. With its help I cut hundreds of unnecessary words and didn't replace them.

Hundreds of others were discarded because I later 16 thought of a better word—one that caught more precisely or more vividly what I was trying to express. Here, again, a word processor encourages you to play. The English language is rich in words that convey an exact shade of meaning. Don't get stuck with a word that's merely good if you can find one that takes the reader by surprise with its color or aptness or quirkiness. Root around in your dictionary of synonyms and find words that are fresh. Throw them up on the screen and see how they look.

Also learn to play with whole sentences. If a sentence 17 strikes you as awkward or ponderous, move your cursor to the space after the period and write a new sentence that you think is better. Maybe you can make it shorter. Or clearer. Maybe you can make it livelier by turning it into a question or otherwise altering its rhythm. Change the passive verbs into active verbs. (Passive verbs are the death of clarity and vigor.) Try writing two or three new versions of the awkward sentence and then compare them, or write a fourth version that combines the best elements of all three. Sentences come in an infinite variety of shapes and sizes. Find one that pleases you. If it's clear, and if it pleases you and expresses who you are, trust it to please other people. Then delete all the versions that aren't as good. Your shiny new sentence will jump into position and the rest of the paragraph will rearrange itself as quickly and neatly as if you had never pulled it apart.

Another goal that the word processor will help you to 18 achieve is unity. No matter how carefully you write each sentence as you assemble a piece of writing, the final product is bound to have some ragged edges. Is the tone consistent throughout? And the point of view? And the pronoun? And the tense? How about the transitions? Do they pull the reader along, or is the piece jerky and disjointed? A good piece of writing should be harmonious from beginning to end in the voice of the writer and the flow of its logic. But the harmony usually requires some last-minute patching.

I've been writing this book by the bricklayer method, 19 slowly and carefully. That's all very well as far as it goes— at the end of every chapter the individual bricks may look fine. But what about the wall? The only way to check your piece for unity is to go over it one more time from start to finish, preferably reading it aloud. See if you have executed all the decisions that you made before you started writing. . . .

I mention this [in part] because word processors are 20 going to be widely used by people who need to impart technical information: matters of operating procedure in business and banking, science and technology, medicine and health, education and government and dozens of other specialized fields. The information will only be helpful if readers can grasp it quickly and easily. If it's muddy they will get discouraged or angry, or both, and will stop reading.

You can avoid this dreaded fate for your message, 21 whatever it is, by making sure that every sentence is a logical sequel to the one that preceded it. One way to approach this goal is to keep your sentences short. A major reason why technical prose becomes so tangled is that the writer tries to make one sentence do too many jobs. It's a natural hazard of the first draft. But the solution is simple: see that every sentence contains only one thought. The reader can accommodate only one idea at a time. Help him by giving him only one idea at a time. Let him understand A before you proceed to B.

In writing this book I was eager to explain the pro- 22 cedures that I had learned about how word processors work, and I would frequently lump several points together in one sentence. Later, editing what I had written, I asked myself if the procedure would be clear to someone who was puzzling through it for the first time—someone who hadn't struggled to figure the procedure out. Often I felt that it wouldn't be clear. I was giving the reader too much. He was being asked to picture himself taking various steps that were single and sequential, and that's how he deserved to get them.

I therefore divided all troublesome long sentences into 23 two short sentences, or even three. It always gave me great pleasure. Not only is it the fastest way for a writer to get out of a quagmire that there seems to be no getting out of; I also like short sentences for their own sake. There's almost no more beautiful sight than a simple declarative sentence. This book is full of simple declarative sentences that have no punctuation and that carry one simple thought. Without a word processor I wouldn't have chopped as many of them down to their proper size, or done it with so little effort. This is one of the main clarifying jobs that your machine can help you to perform, especially if your writing requires you to guide the reader into territory that is new and bewildering.

Not all my experiences, of course, were rosy. The 24 machine had disadvantages as well as blessings. Often, for instance, I missed not being able to see more than twenty lines at a time—to review what I had written earlier. If I wanted to see more lines I had to "scroll" them back into view.

But even this wasn't as painful as I had thought it 25 would be. I found that I could hold in my head the gist of what I had written and didn't need to keep looking at it. Was this need, in fact, still another writer's hang-up that I could shed? To some extent it was. I discovered, as I had at so many other points in this journey, that various crutches I had always assumed I needed were really not necessary. I made a decision to just throw them away and found that I could still function. The only real hardship occurred when a paragraph broke at the bottom of the screen. This meant that the first lines of the paragraph were on one page and the rest were on the next page, and I had to keep flicking the two pages back and forth to read what I was writing. But again, it wasn't fatal. I learned to live with it and soon took it for granted as an occupational hazard.

The story that I've told in this chapter is personal and 26 idiosyncratic: how the word processor helped one writer to write one book. In many of its details it's everybody's story. All writers have different methods and psychological needs. . . .

QUESTIONS ON MEANING

1. What advantages and disadvantages of writing with a word processor does Zinsser cite? What single advantage does he emphasize?

2. Zinsser says that no two people write the same way. Then he explains his own writing process. What are his particular hang-ups or procedures for writing?

3. List Zinsser's specific bits of advice for cutting the "clutter" out of writing.

QUESTIONS ON PURPOSE AND STRATEGY

1. Describe Zinsser's purpose in this selection. Is he informing you about how word processors work? Is he explaining his own process for writing? Is he explaining how he uses a word processor? Is he persuading you to use a word processor? Is he persuading you to write in simple, clear language? Justify your choice(s) by refering to specific paragraphs.

2. Describe Zinsser's "voice" in this essay. Does his voice help organize, shape, or unify this essay? Explain.

QUESTIONS ON AUDIENCE AND LANGUAGE

1. In another essay, Zinsser writes, "The man snoozing in his chair with an unfinished magazine open on his lap is a man who was being given too much unnecessary trouble by the writer." What are Zinsser's recommendations to avoid giving readers too much trouble?

2. Zinsser claims, "There's almost no more beautiful sight than a simple declarative sentence. This book is full of simple declarative sentences that have no punctuation and that carry one simple thought." Select one paragraph you like from this essay and transcribe it. Are Zinsser's claims correct? Does this paragraph have simple declarative sentences, and do you agree that they are "beautiful" because they are clear and direct?

3. Writing textbooks often recommend reducing the number

of "to be" verbs (*is, are, was, were*) and using more colorful, active verbs. Reread Zinsser's sixteenth paragraph. Does he follow this advice? Should he revise any sentences?

QUESTIONS FOR DISCUSSION AND WRITING

1. Zinsser says that he writes "somewhat like a bricklayer," adding new rows of bricks only when he's confident that the foundation will hold the house. What activities best describe your writing process? Do you write like a runner who stretches and warms up and then sprints for the finish line? Do you write like a miner who "digs deep" for ideas, like a gardener who "plants" ideas and waits for them to "grow," or like a cook who gathers his or her "ingredients" and starts "cooking" ideas? Use a comparison with a familiar activity to explain your writing process.

2. If you frequently use a word processor, brainstorm other advantages and disadvantages of writing on a computer. Write your own essay on "Writing with a Word Processor."

Writing Around Rules

MIKE ROSE

(1944–   )

PREREADING JOURNAL ENTRY

In five minutes, brainstorm as many "rules for writing" as you can. Then reread your list. Put an asterisk next to any rule that could be broken, depending on the writer or the writing situation.

"No one writes effortlessly," Mike Rose suggests. "Our composing is marked by pauses, false starts, gnawing feelings of inadequacy, crumpled paper." When pauses, false starts, and anxiety block a writer, however, the results can be disastrous. Mike Rose was born in Los Angeles, studied at the University of California at Los Angeles, and wrote his dissertation on "writer's block." He has written articles in professional journals, published Writer's Block: The Cognitive Dimension *(1983), and edited a collection of articles,* When a Writer Can't Write: Studies in Writer's Block and Other Composing Process Problems *(1984). Currently, Rose directs the Freshman Writing Program at UCLA.*

In this selection, Rose cites examples of student writers who have problems writing—not because they are especially anxious about writing—but because they follow certain "rules" too rigidly. As you read this essay, see if you recognize yourself in any of these case studies.

I.

Here's Liz, a junior English major, at work on a paper 1 for a college course: she has been given a two-page case study and must analyze it using the ideas contained in a second, brief handout. She has about one hour to complete her assignment. As she reads and rereads the handouts, she scribbles notes to herself in the margins. Liz is doing what most effective writers would do with such materials: paraphrasing the main points in the passages, making connections among them, recording associations to other pertinent knowledge. But a closer look at these interpretive notes reveals something unusual: Liz seems to be editing them as she goes along, cleaning them up as though they were final copy. In one of her notes she jots down the phrase "is saying that not having creative work is the. . . ." She stops, thinks for a moment, and changes "is the" to "causes." (Later on, explaining this change, she'll comment that "you're not supposed to have passive verbs.") She then replaces "is saying" with "says," apparently following her directive about passive voice, but later changes it again, noting that "says" is "too colloquial." Liz pauses after this editing and looks up—she has forgotten what she initially was trying to capture in her writing. "That happens a lot," she says.

Liz was one of the many college students I studied 2 over a two-and-one-half-year period (*Writer's Block: The Cognitive Dimension*). The purpose of my study was to try to gain insight into what causes some young writers to compose with relative fluency and what leads others to experience more than their fair share of blocks, dead-ends, conflicts, and the frustrations of the blank page. What I uncovered was a whole array of problems that I would label as being primarily *cognitive* rather than primarily *emotional* in nature. That is, many students were engaging in self-defeating composing behaviors not because they had some deep-seated fear of revealing their thoughts or of being evaluated or because of some long-standing aversion to writing, but rather because they had somehow learned a number of rules, planning strategies, or assumptions about writing that limited rather than enhanced their composing. We saw Liz lose her train of thought by adhering too rigidly to stylistic rules when she should have been scribbling ideas freely in order to discover material for her essay. Let me offer two further

vignettes that illustrate some of the other cognitive difficulties I uncovered.

    Tyrrell, also a junior English major, says he doesn't 3
like to sketch out any sort of plan or draft of what he's
going to write. He'll think about his topic, but his pen
usually won't touch paper until he begins writing the one,
and only, draft he'll produce. As he writes, he pauses
frequently and at length to make all sorts of decisions
about words, ideas, and rhetorical effects. In short, he
plans his work as he goes along. There's nothing inherently
wrong with writing this way, but where difficult assignments involving complex materials are concerned, it helps
to sketch out a few ideas, some direction, a loose organizational structure before beginning to write. When a
coworker and I studied Tyrrell's composing, we noted the
stylistic flourishes in his essay, but also its lack of direction.
As my colleague noted, "[His] essay bogs down in description and in unexplained abstractions." Perhaps the essay
would have had more direction if Tyrrell had roughed
out a few ideas before composing his one and only draft.
Why didn't he do so? Consider his comment on planning:

> [Planning] is certainly not spontaneous and a lot of the
> times it's not even really what you feel because it becomes
> very mechanical. It's almost like—at least I feel—it's dia-
> bolical, you know, because . . . it'll sacrifice truth and real
> feelings that you have.

Tyrrell assumes that sketching out a plan before writing
somehow violates the spontaneity of composing: to plan
dooms one to write mechanical, unemotional prose. Yet,
while too much planning may sometimes make the actual
writing a joyless task, it is also true that most good writing
is achieved through some kind of prefiguring, most often
involving pen and paper. Such planning does not necessarily subvert spontaneity; in fact, since it reduces the load
on the writer's immediate memory, it might actually free
one to be more spontaneous, to follow the lead of new
ideas as they emerge. Tyrrell's assumption, then, is inac-
curate. By recognizing only this one path to spontaneity,

he is probably limiting his effectiveness as a writer and, ironically, may be reducing his opportunities to be spontaneous.

Gary is an honors senior in biochemistry. When I 4 observed him, he spent over half of his writing time meticulously analyzing each sentence of the assignment's reading passage on one of the handouts. He understood the passage and the assignment well enough but wanted to make sure the passage was sufficiently broken down to be of use when he composed his essay. As Gary conducted this minute analysis, he wrote dozens and dozens of words and phrases across the handouts. He then summarized these words and phrases in a list of six items. He *then* tried to condense all six items into a thesis sentence:

> I have concepts . . . and my task here is to say what is being said about all of those all at once.

Gary's method was, in this case, self-defeating. He worked in too precise a fashion, generating an unwieldy amount of preliminary material, which he didn't seem to be able to rank or thin out—and he was unable to focus his thinking in a single thesis sentence. Gary's interpretive and planning strategies were inappropriately elaborate, and they were inflexible. It was not surprising that when Gary's hour was up, he had managed to write only three disconnected sentences. Not really an essay at all.

But what about the students who weren't stymied, who 5 wrote with relative fluency? They too talked of rules and assumptions and displayed planning strategies. The interesting thing, though, is that their rules were more flexible; that is, a rule seemed to include conditions under which it ought and ought not to be used. The rules weren't absolutes, but rather statements about what one might do in certain writing situations. Their assumptions, as well, were not absolute and they tended to enhance composing, opening up rather than restricting possibilities. And their planning strategies tended to be flexible and appropriate to the task. Fluent writers had their rules, strategies, and assumptions, but they were of a different kind from those of the blocked writers.

What to do? One is tempted to urge the blocked 6 writers to clear their minds of troubling rules, plans, and assumptions. In a few cases, that might not be such a bad idea. But what about Liz's preoccupation with passive constructions? Some degree of concern about casting one's language in the active voice is a good thing. And Gary's precise strategies? It would be hard to imagine good academic writing that isn't preceded by careful analysis of one's materials. Writers need the order and the guidance that rules, strategies, and assumptions provide. The answer to Liz's, Tyrrell's, and Gary's problems, then, lies in altering their approaches to make them more conditional, adaptive, and flexible. Let me explain further. For the sake of convenience, I'll focus on rules, though what I'll say has application to the assumptions we develop and the planning strategies we learn.

II.

Writing is a phenomenally complex learned activity. 7 To write in a way that others can understand we must employ a large and complicated body of conventions. We learn from our parents or earliest teachers that script, in English, goes left to right straight across the page. We learn about letter formation, spelling, sentence structure, and so on. Some of this information we absorb more or less unconsciously through reading, and some of it we learn formally as guidelines, as directives . . . as rules.

And there are all kinds of rules. Some tell us how to 8 format our writing (for example, when to capitalize, how to paragraph, how to footnote). There are grammar rules (for example, "Make a pronoun agree in number with its antecedent"). There are preferences concerning style that are often stated as rules ("Avoid passive voice"). There are usage rules (*"That* always introduces restrictive clauses; *which* can introduce both restrictive and nonrestrictive clauses"). There are rules that tell us how to compose ("Before you begin writing, decide on your thesis and write it down in a single declarative sentence"). The list goes on and on. Some of these rules make sense; others are confusing, questionable, or contradictory. Fortunately, we assimilate a good deal of the information they contain gradually by reading other writers, by writing ourselves, or by simply being around print. Therefore, we can confirm or alter or reject them from experience.

But all too often the rules are turned into absolutes. 9 And that's where the trouble begins. Most rules about writing should not be expressed (in textbooks), stored (in our minds), or enacted (on the page) as absolutes, as mathematical, unvarying directives. True, a few rules apply in virtually all situations (for example, certain formatting rules or capitalization rules). But most rules do not. Writing rules, like any rules about language, have a history and have a time and place. They are highly context-bound.

Should you always, as some textbooks suggest, place 10 your thesis sentence at the beginning of your first paragraph or, as others suggest, work up to it and place it at the end of the paragraph? Well, the answer is that both injunctions are right . . . and wrong. Students writing essay exams would be well-advised to demonstrate their knowledge and direct the reader's attention as soon as possible. But the writer who wants to evoke a mood might offer a series of facts and events that gradually lead up to a thesis sentence. The writing situation, the rhetorical purpose, and the nature of the material one is working with will provide the answer. A single-edged rule cannot.

How about our use of language, usage rules? Certainly 11 there's a right and a wrong here? Again, not quite. First of all, there's a time in one's writing to worry about such things. Concern yourself with questions of usage too early in your composing and you'll end up like Liz, worrying about the minutiae of language while your thought fades to a wisp. Second, the social consequences of following or ignoring such rules vary widely depending on whether you're writing formal or informal prose. Third, usage rules themselves have an evolutionary history: we aren't obliged to follow some of the rules that turn-of-the-century writers had to deal with, and our rules will alter and even disappear as the English language moves on in time. No, there are no absolutes here either.

Well, how about some of the general, commonsense 12 rules about the very act of writing itself? Certainly, rules like "Think before you write" ought to be followed? Again, a qualification is in order. While it certainly is good advice to think through ideas before we record them for others to see, many people, in fact, use writing as a way of thinking. They make major decisions *as* they write. There are times when it's best to put a piece of writing aside and ponder, but there are also times when one ought to keep pen in hand and attempt to resolve a conceptual tangle by sketching out what comes to mind. Both approaches are legitimate.

I'll stop here. I hope I've shown that it's difficult to 13 make hard and fast statements about the structure, the language, or the composing of an essay. Unfortunately, there's a strong push in our culture to make absolute statements about writing, especially where issues of style and usage are concerned. But I hope by now the reader of this essay believes that most rules about writing—about how to do it, about how it should be structured, about what words to use—are not absolute, and should be taught and enacted in a flexible, context-dependent way. Given certain conditions, you follow them; given other conditions you modify or suspend them. A teacher may insist that a young writer follow a particular dictum in order to learn a pattern, but there must come a time when the teacher extends the lesson and explains when the dictum is and isn't appropriate.

QUESTIONS ON MEANING

1. Rose suggests that Liz, Tyrrell, and Gary are too inflexible about "rules" for writing. What rule causes each writer a problem? What is Rose's solution for each writer?

2. Writing rules are "highly context-bound," Rose says. "The writing situation, the rhetorical purpose, and the nature of the material" should all affect rules for writing. Choose one of the "rules" Rose mentions and describe one situation in which writers *should* follow that rule and one situation in which they *should not*.

QUESTIONS ON PURPOSE AND STRATEGY

1. Explain Rose's purpose in this essay.
2. Rose opens with a lengthy example and states his main idea in paragraph two. Should Rose state his main idea sooner? Is Rose violating a "rule" of writing by beginning with a long example?
3. Explain what you learned from this essay. Do you find yourself blocked at any time during your writing process? Did you see any of your writing strategies in Liz, Tyrrell, or Gary? Does Rose convince you that inflexible rules may be causing you a problem?

QUESTIONS ON AUDIENCE AND LANGUAGE

1. Who is Rose's intended reader for this essay? College writers? Writing teachers? Writing researchers? Cite at least two sentences to support your decision.
2. Choose one paragraph from Rose's essay. Rewrite this paragraph, using Zinsser's advice (in "One Man's Method"). Has Rose already eliminated the "clutter," or could Zinsser (or you) tighten and clarify his sentences?

QUESTIONS FOR DISCUSSION AND WRITING

1. In class, list on the chalkboard the rules you generated during your Prereading Journal Entry. Which rules did you place an asterisk by? After reading Rose's article, which rules do you think should have an asterisk?

2. In groups of three, interview your classmates about their problems with writing. Two students should interview the third student; then switch roles. From the interviews, make a list of the most difficult problems your group faces. What solutions can the class as a whole offer to these problems?

Revision and Life: Take It from the Top—Again

NORA EPHRON

(1941–   )

PREREADING JOURNAL ENTRY

Think about a recent discussion or argument you had with family or friends. Did you feel slightly frustrated because you didn't say exactly what you meant? What was the discussion about? What point did other people make? What was your position? If you had a chance to discuss this topic again, what exactly would you say?

Nora Ephron was born into a family of writers. Both her parents were writers and her younger sister, Delia, became an accomplished journalist. Nora Ephron has written articles and columns for McCalls, Cosmopolitan, *and* Esquire. *Her novel* Heartburn *(1983), about her divorce from journalist Carl Bernstein, made her a celebrity, and her screenplay for* Silkwood *(1983) was nominated for an Oscar by the American Academy of Motion Picture Arts and Sciences.*

In "Revision and Life," Ephron writes about her own writing and revising process. Retyping, she explains, is her rather bizarre strategy for "catapulting" her into the paragraph or chapter. In the course of writing a short essay, she often uses 300 to 400 pieces of typing paper. In this essay, she focuses not only on revising her essays, but on how writing novels gives her a chance to "revise" her life.

I have been asked to write something for a textbook   1
that is meant to teach college students something about
writing and revision. I am happy to do this because I

believe in revision. I have also been asked to save the early drafts of whatever I write, presumably to show these students the actual process of revision. This too I am happy to do. On the other hand I suspect that there is just so much you can teach college students about revision; a gift for revision may be a developmental stage—like a 2-year-old's sudden ability to place one block on top of another—that comes along somewhat later, in one's mid-20s, say; most people may not be particularly good at it, or even interested in it, until then.

When I was in college, I revised nothing. I wrote out 2 my papers in longhand, typed them up and turned them in. It would never have crossed my mind that what I had produced was only a first draft and that I had more work to do; the idea was to get to the end, and once you had got to the end you were finished. The same thinking, I might add, applied in life: I went pell-mell through my four years in college without a thought about whether I ought to do anything differently; the idea was to get to the end—to get out of school and become a journalist.

Which I became, in fairly short order. I learned as a 3 journalist to revise on deadline. I learned to write an article a paragraph at a time—and I arrived at the kind of writing and revising I do, which is basically a kind of typing and retyping. I am a great believer in this technique for the simple reason that I type faster than the wind. What I generally do is to start an article and get as far as I can—sometimes no farther in than a sentence or two— before running out of steam, ripping the piece of paper from the typewriter and starting all over again. I type over and over until I have got the beginning of the piece to the point where I am happy with it. I then am ready to plunge into the body of the article itself. This plunge usually requires something known as a transition. I approach a transition by completely retyping the opening of the article leading up to it in the hope that the ferocious speed of my typing will somehow catapult me into the next section of the piece. This does not work—what in fact catapults me into the next section is a concrete thought about what the next section ought to be about—but until I have the thought the typing keeps me busy, and keeps me from feeling something known as blocked.

Typing and retyping as if you know where you're 4 going is a version of what therapists tell you to do when they suggest that you try changing from the outside in— that if you can't master the total commitment to whatever change you want to make, you can at least do all the extraneous things connected with it, which make it that much easier to get there. I was 25 years old the first time a therapist suggested that I try changing from the outside in. In those days, I used to spend quite a lot of time lying awake at night wondering what I should have said earlier in the evening and revising my lines. I mention this not just because it's a way of illustrating that a gift for revision is practically instinctive, but also (once again) because it's possible that a genuine ability at it doesn't really come into play until one is older—or at least older than 25, when it seemed to me that all that was required in my life and my work was the chance to change a few lines.

In my 30's, I began to write essays, one a month for 5 *Esquire* magazine, and I am not exaggerating when I say that in the course of writing a short essay—1,500 words, that's only six double-spaced typewritten pages—I often used 300 or 400 pieces of typing paper, so often did I type and retype and catapult and recatapult myself, sometimes on each retyping moving not even a sentence farther from the spot I had reached the last time through. At the same time, though, I was polishing what I had already written: as I struggled with the middle of the article, I kept putting the beginning through the typewriter; as I approached the ending, the middle got its turn. (This is a kind of polishing that the word processor all but eliminates, which is why I don't use one. Word processors make it possible for a writer to change the sentences that clearly need changing without having to retype the rest, but I believe that you can't always tell whether a sentence needs work until it rises up in revolt against your fingers as you retype it.) By the time I had produced what you might call a first draft—an entire article with a beginning, middle and end—the beginning was in more like 45th draft, the middle in 20th, and the end was almost newborn. For this reason, the beginnings of my essays are considerably better written than the ends, although I like to think no one ever notices this but me.

As I learned the essay form, writing became harder 6 for me. I was finding a personal style, a voice if you will, a way of writing that looked chatty and informal. That wasn't the hard part—the hard part was that having found a voice, I had to work hard month to month not to seem as if I were repeating myself. At this point in this essay it will not surprise you to learn that the same sort of thing was operating in my life. I don't mean that my life had become harder—but that it was becoming clear that I had many more choices than had occurred to me when I was marching through my 20's. I no longer lost sleep over what I should have said. Not that I didn't care—it was just that I had moved to a new plane of late-night anxiety: I now wondered what I should have done. Whole areas of possible revision opened before me. What should I have done instead? What could I have done? What if I hadn't done it the way I did? What if I had a chance to do it over? What if I had a chance to do it over as a different person? These were the sorts of questions that kept me awake and led me into fiction, which at the very least (the level at which I practice it) is a chance to rework the events of your life so that you give the illusion of being the intelligence at the center of it, simultaneously managing to slip in all the lines that occurred to you later. Fiction, I suppose, is the ultimate shot at revision.

Now I am in my 40's and I write screenplays. Screen- 7 plays—if they are made into movies—are essentially collaborations, and movies are not a writer's medium, we all know this, and I don't want to dwell on the craft of screenwriting except insofar as it relates to revision. Because the moment you stop work on a script seems to be determined not by whether you think the draft is good but simply by whether shooting is about to begin: if it is, you get to call your script a final draft; and if it's not, you can always write another revision. This might seem to be a hateful way to live, but the odd thing is that it's somehow comforting; as long as you're revising, the project isn't dead. And by the same token, neither are you.

It was, as it happens, while thinking about all this one 8 recent sleepless night that I figured out how to write this particular essay. I say "recent" in order to give a sense of immediacy and energy to the preceding sentence, but the truth is that I am finishing this article four months after the sleepless night in question, and the letter asking me to write it, from George Miller of the University of Delaware, arrived almost two years ago, so for all I know Mr. Miller has managed to assemble his textbook on revision without me.

Oh, well. That's how it goes when you start thinking 9 about revision. That's the danger of it, in fact. You can spend so much time thinking about how to switch things around that the main event has passed you by. But it doesn't matter. Because by the time you reach middle age, you want more than anything for things not to come to an end; and as long as you're still revising, they don't.

I'm sorry to end so morbidly—dancing as I am around 10 the subject of death—but there are advantages to it. For one thing, I have managed to move fairly effortlessly and logically from the beginning of this piece through the middle and to the end. And for another, I am able to close with an exhortation, something I rarely manage, which is this: Revise now, before it's too late.

QUESTIONS ON MEANING

1. What parallels does Ephron see between revising her writing and revising her life?

2. Ephron says that a "gift for revision may be a developmental stage." What does she mean by this statement?

3. Zinsser says that no two people write in the same way. What is peculiar about Ephron's composing style?

QUESTIONS ON PURPOSE AND STRATEGY

1. What is George Miller's purpose in requesting this essay? What does he hope it will show? How are Ephron's purpose and main idea different from Professor Miller's expectations?

2. Conclusions of essays often create a sense of "closure," of being finished, by picking up some idea, image, or thread from the introduction and recalling it or echoing it. Where in her conclusion does Ephron try this strategy? Does her conclusion give her essay a sense of "being finished" with the topic?

3. This essay follows a *chronological order,* moving from Ephron's writing style and her life in college to her style and life as a journalist and playwright. Locate the major chronological divisions in her article.

QUESTIONS ON AUDIENCE AND LANGUAGE

1. What is the specific audience and occasion for this essay?

2. Ephron says that she gradually found a personal style or voice for her writing, a "way of writing that looked chatty and informal." Find several examples of Ephron's "chatty and informal" voice in this essay. Do you think her voice is effective?

QUESTIONS FOR DISCUSSION AND WRITING

1. Compare Ephron's revising technique with Zinsser's. Do they accomplish the same result with different means?

2. Based on Ephron's and your own experience, do you think college students should be required to revise their essays? Do you have an example of a paper you improved through revision or one that was actually worse in its revised form?

3. Write an essay about some event in your life you would like to "revise." If you had the chance, what would you do and say differently?

3

OBSERVING

It's all a matter of keeping my eyes open. Nature is like one of those line drawings that are puzzles for children: Can you find hidden in the tree a duck, a house, a boy, a bucket, a giraffe, and a boot?

—Annie Dillard, author of *Pilgrim at Tinker Creek*

To say nothing is out here is incorrect; to say the desert is stingy with everything except space and light, stone and earth is closer to the truth.

—William Least Heat Moon, author of *Blue Highways*

Facts are stupid things, until brought into connection with some general law.

—Louis Agassiz, Swiss naturalist

Observing is an initial purpose for many kinds of writing. We observe in order to discover and learn; once we have taught ourselves by close observation, we can explain our subject to others or even persuade them to take a course of action. In every field of study, careful observation triggers the discovery and learning process. In the sciences, researchers design experiments and then carefully observe their data. In business, people record sales figures and observe buying trends. In the humanities, writers carefully observe (read) books, watch dramas, listen to speeches, examine works of art, and chronicle human behavior.

As writers learn about their subjects, they communicate their findings through specific, observed detail that re-creates the subject for their readers. In a sense, observational writing imitates a scientific experiment. The piece of writing creates the data so each reader can conduct the "experiment" for himself or herself. Just as the crucial part of a scientific experiment is the presentation of data, so the essential part of descriptive writing is the re-creation of key sensory detail.

Although specific detail or data is essential for descriptive writing, the observed detail must be related to the writer's purpose. Sometimes writers have a purpose before they begin observing their subject: "I want to describe the effects of acid rain on a forest to show my readers the consequences of burning fossil fuels." Sometimes writers discover their purpose only after carefully observing something that catches their interest: "Describing how freshmen live at the University of Moscow let me discover that young people in different cultures are very much alike." Writers should use detail to make a point or create a dominant impression.

STRATEGIES FOR READING AND WRITING ABOUT OBSERVING

From the writer's point of view, observing techniques help the writer see and learn about the subject by observing repeatedly and describing accurately and vividly. From the reader's point of view, descriptive writing gives the data, the details, the examples, and the who, what, when, and where of the subject so that the reader reaches a conclusion based on evidence.

As you read the observing essays in this chapter (and write your own), look for the following features of writing about observations:

Use of sensory details (sight, sound, smell, touch, taste). These details include actual *dialogue* as well as the *names* of things. In the desert, for example, a writer may find several kinds of cacti: barrel cactus, hedgehog cactus, or prickly pear cactus.

Use of comparisons and images. Writers often describe what something looks *like:* from a high vantage point, roads in the desert may look like *veins* stretched out across the terrain.

Descriptions of what is *not* there. Careful observation requires noticing who or what is *not* present or what is *not* happening. Why are there no large plants in the desert? Why is there no water in this river?

Descriptions of changes in the subject's form or condition. Observing a subject over a period of time may reveal crucial changes that are unapparent at first. A mesa may look static and unchanging, but continued observation reveals that the soil is crumbling and decaying. How fast is it eroding? How has it changed in a hundred years?

Use of a distinct point of view. What writers see or sense depends on who they are, what their purpose is in observing, and what experience they bring to the observation. In the desert, a hitchhiker may hear the sound of a faraway truck in the night; a tourist may hear coyotes howling; an Indian may hear a sacred voice calling from the sky.

Focus on a main idea or dominant impression. All the details in an effective observing essay should add up to a main idea or create a dominant impression.

READING AN OBSERVING ESSAY

As you practice active, critical reading of observing essays, pay attention to individual bits of description, but also look for the big picture. Keep asking yourself: What main point does the writer want these details to make?

Prereading

Get a feel for the writing situation: Who is the author? What is the context, the purpose, and type of essay? The introductory comments in this chapter and the biographical headnote about the author will help orient you. Also explore what you already know about this subject by writing the Prereading Journal Entry at the beginning of each essay.

First Reading

Read the essay quickly, just to get the main idea and to enjoy your reading. If you find an unfamiliar word, underline it to look up later (don't stop to look up these words). If a passage has especially *vivid description,* place a "!" in the margin. If you are *confused* by a sentence, place a "?" in the margin. If you can't *visualize* what the writer is saying, place a "X" in the margin. Highlight or place a wavy line under passages that suggest the *main idea* or dominant impression of the essay. At the end of your first reading, write one sentence describing your *initial impression* of the essay.

Annotated Reading

During your second reading, write your own questions, reactions, and comments in the margin: "This is especially vivid" or "Why is the writer describing this?" Bracket [ ] and *label* key features of observing essays: sensory details, images, changes, what is not there, point of view, and dominant impression. In the margin, list or outline the major parts of the writer's description. Finally, look up definitions of any words you underlined during your first reading or that catch your attention now.

Collaborative Reading

In a small group or in your class as a whole, share and discuss your annotations. Begin by reading each other's prewriting responses. Then share your annotations, noting what other readers noticed that you didn't. Your group or class may focus on one aspect of the essay (the imagery, the style, the point of view, the overall impression) or you may generate questions for further understanding of the whole essay. During (or following) this group discussion, reread key passages to test your understanding of the essay and compare your reactions to what other readers noticed. Check the questions following the essay—do they suggest ideas you haven't considered?

WRITING AN OBSERVING ESSAY

Writing an observing essay is basically a matter of opening your eyes—and the rest of your senses. First teach yourself to see; then use what you've seen to teach your reader. Novice writers mistakenly begin with their conclusions and then they rephrase them several times, as if to emphasize their point:

> There doesn't appear to be much out in the desert. Except for some cactus and dirt, the desert looks pretty empty. Basically, it's just a lot of sand, sun, and nothing. But if you really look there are a whole lot of things that will catch your eye. Actually, the desert has some fascinating stuff.

This writer is merely **telling** the reader. Look at the vague, empty language: "*much,*" "*some* cactus," "*pretty* empty," "*a lot* of sand," "whole *lot* of *things,*" and "*fascinating stuff.*" Instead, a writer should be **showing** the reader, representing and re-creating the desert for the reader. To do that, writers approach their subjects as artists do, paint-brush or pencil in hand, drawing and recording everything they see. William Least Heat Moon's essay in this chapter **shows** the reader the desert near the Pecos River in West Texas:

> For a while, I heard only miles of wind against the Ghost; but after the ringing in my ears stopped, I heard myself breathing, then a bird note, an answering call, another kind of bird song, and another: mockingbird, mourning dove, an enigma. I heard the high zizz of flies the color of gray flannel and the deep buzz of a blue bumblebee. I made a list of nothing in particular:
>
> 1. mockingbird
>
> 2. mourning dove
>
> 3. enigma bird (heard not saw)
>
> 4. gray flies
>
> 5. blue bumblebee
>
> 6. two circling buzzards (not yet boys)
>
> 7. orange ants
>
> 8. black ants
>
> 9. orange-black ants (what's been going on?)

These details do the writer's work. Moon's description of the birds (some seen, some not seen), the flies, and the ants **show** that there is more to the desert than meets the unexperienced eye.

Details are important, but just as important is the overall point the writer discovers or wishes to make. "Facts are stupid things," Louis Agassiz reminds us, "until brought into connection with some general law." **Writers construct and arrange observed details so they add up to some dominant impression.** The dominant impression in Moon's essay is the idea that the desert is not "miles of nothing," but contains a special meaning for the traveler who takes the time to look carefully. Writers make meaning by selecting certain details that they want the reader to "see" and then ordering and arranging these details to focus on a dominant impression.

Choosing a Subject for an Observing Essay

Choose some specific person, place, object, or event as the subject for your observing piece. Observe it repeatedly. Your initial purpose is to use your writing to help you observe, discover, and learn about your subject. When you write your essay from your observing notes, focus on some main idea or dominant impression that the observed details will create for your reader.

Possible subjects for an observing essay:

A public place: airport, bar, library, hotel, shop, park, or street

A place on campus: a science lab, art exhibition, greenhouse, veterinary clinic, research library, campus radio station, gymnasium or stadium, or theater

A personal place: your home, your favorite natural spot, your favorite shop or street, or your dormitory or apartment

People: teachers, students, clerks in stores, artists, police officers, disc jockeys, musicians, other writers, or family and friends

Events: sporting events, concerts, theater, films, or classes

As you brainstorm for possible subjects, remember to choose something that you can reobserve during your writing process. No person, place, or event will be exactly the same on the second observation, but you do need to be able to observe it a second or a third time.

Collecting Details for Your Observing Essay

Observing is a collecting strategy, but some tricks of the trade will help you gather details.

Draw your subject. Even if you are not an artist, a

sketch may help you see more clearly. Pencils make good eyes.

Zoom in for a closer look at your subject. What do you notice when you examine it closely?

Record sounds accurately. If people are talking, record *actual dialogue*. Turn on a tape recorder and notice what it hears that you don't.

Take double entry notes. Draw a line vertically down the middle of a page. On the left-hand side, write observed details: color, size, shape, behavior, sound, taste, touch, smell. On the right-hand side, write your impressions, reactions, feelings, or questions.

Ask yourself questions about what you are observing. What exactly is this—can you *define* it? How much could this subject change and still be recognizable? How does it *compare* to other related people, places, or events? From what *points of view* is it usually seen? Who usually sees it; who rarely sees it?

Discuss your subject with other people. What do *they* notice when they observe it? How is that different from what you see? Reobserve your subject and compare with your first notes.

Look up your subject in reference material. What are the *names* of the details or parts? What is its *history or biography*? Reobserve your subject to see what else you notice, now that you have background information.

Freewrite or cluster on your subject. What is seen depends on who is doing the seeing. What are your *memories* about this subject? What do you *associate* with this subject?

Shaping Your Observing Essay

To help organize your observing notes, consider your purpose and audience. Your purpose is to help your reader see, notice, observe, and learn from your subject, but what do you want them to focus on? Start by thinking or writing about what you learned from your observations.

Then think about your readers. What order, strategy, or sequence would help them "discover" what you found out? Test several of the following strategies on your subject. See which one(s) work best.

Chronological Order. Two common shapes are the natural time order (A, B, and C) a flashback order (B, A, and C). What is the natural time order for the event you observed? In what time order did you *notice* certain details about your subject? Would a flashback order be more effective?

In her essay, "Rules of the Game: Rodeo," Gretel Ehrlich uses a natural time order to organize several paragraphs in her essay. Notice how she sets up her time order and then uses the first sentences of each paragraph to let the reader see her chronology:

> There's a traditional order to the four timed and three rough stock events that make up a rodeo program. Bareback riders are first, then steer wrestlers, team ropers, saddle bronc riders, barrel racers, and finally, the bull riders.

> After Pat Linger came Steve Dunham, J. C. Trujillo, Mickey Young, and the defending champ, Bruce Ford on a horse named Denver. Bareback riders do just that: they ride a horse with no saddle, no halter, no rein. . . .

> Now the steer wrestlers shoot out of the box on their own well-trained horses. . . .

> The team ropers are next. . . .

Spatial Order. Sometimes choosing some logical order—right to left, top to bottom, outside to inside—will help organize your observations.

In Albert Goldman's description of Elvis Presley's dining room, notice how the introductory phrases ("on the left-hand side," "in the center," "above the table," and "at each corner") signal a spatial order:

> On the left-hand side of the entrance hall is the dining room. In the center of the crimson carpet is a large

quadrangle of black marble tiles on which is set a table. . . .
Round the table in great state stand ten tall, ladder-backed
Louis XIV chairs with tufted velour seats. . . . Above the
table hangs a brass Louis XIV chandelier with two tiers of
scrolled candlearms fitted with glass lusters. At each corner
of the room . . . are tall diagonal bric-a-brac cabinets. . . .

Comparison/Contrast. Reread your collecting notes. If
there are striking similarities/differences among parts of
your subject, perhaps a comparison/constrast structure
will organize your details.

Notice how Albert Goldman contrasts his impression
of the front lawn at Graceland and his reaction once he
enters the mansion:

> Prominently displayed on the front lawn is an elaborate
> creche. The stable is a full-scale adobe house strewn with
> straw. Life-sized are the figures of Joseph and Mary, the
> kneeling shepherds and Magi, the lambs and ewes, as well
> as the winged annunciatory angel hovering over the roof
> beam. Real, too, is the cradle in which the infant Jesus
> sleeps.
>
> When you step through the ten-foot oak door and enter
> the house, you stop and stare in amazement. Having just
> come from the contemplation of the tenderest scene in the
> Holy Bible, imagine the shock of finding yourself in a
> whorehouse! Yet there is no other way to describe the
> drawing room of Graceland except to say that it appears to
> have been lifted from some turn-of-the-century bordello
> down in the French Quarter of New Orleans. . . .

Classification. If you are observing people, grouping
them according to types may help. At a fast food place,
you might classify (and then describe) people by occupation: office workers, students, construction workers, and
retired people. You might classify and describe paintings
by type: impressionist, cubist, and surrealist.

Figurative Language. Figurative language and images
can make your description more vivid. In "West Texas,"
William Least Heat Moon relies on figurative language to
create both a visual picture and a feeling for the landscape:

> West of the Pecos, a strangely truncated cone rose from

the valley. In the oblique evening light, its silhouette looked *like a Mayan temple,* so perfect was its symmetry. I stopped again, started climbing, stirring *a panic of lizards* on the way up. From the top, the rubbled land below—*veined with the highway and arroyos,* topographical relief *absorbed in the dusk*— looked *like a roadmap.*

Titles, Introductions, and Conclusions. Titles, like labels, should indicate the contents of the package. In addition, titles may catch the reader's attention through some imaginative language. Look at the titles of the essays in this chapter. "West Texas," "Lenses," "Graceland," and "Freshmen" are merely labels. "Rules of the Game: Rodeo" is a bit more descriptive. Look in the table of contents of this reader. Which titles are more catchy?

Introductions help readers anticipate the subject of the essay. Sometimes they set up the context by answering who, what, where, or when questions. At other times, observing essays begin immediately with some description and let the main idea evolve out of the description.

Conclusions for observing essays often focus on the writer's discovery, the main idea, or the dominant impression. In some cases writers give direct statements of the main idea, but just as often the main idea is implied in the details that the writer selects. An idea, word, or phrase that echos or repeats an idea from the introduction gives an essay a sense of conclusion or closure.

Drafting Your Observing Essay

When you are ready to write a complete draft, begin by *rereading* your collecting notes, focusing on a dominant impression you want the details to create. You may need to reobserve your subject, just to add additional details that support your main idea. If you are not sure about the dominant impression, you may want to start writing, paying attention to what you notice as you write. Once you start writing, try to keep going. Do not stop to look up words—just draw a line and keep going. If you get stuck, go back and reread your collecting notes.

Revising Your Observing Essay

Before your revise, get some feedback from other members of your class. Remember that you should consider their reactions, but do not make changes just because one reader did not like something. Explain your purpose and your audience, and ask your readers to explain *why* they like something, or *why* it should be cut, or *why* you need more details at one place. *You* must make the final decisions. As you revise, keep the following tips in mind.

Reconsider your purpose and audience. Are you doing what you intended? Can you clearly identify your main idea or dominant impression? Have you identified your audience (has it changed since you began writing)?

Identify your point of view. Your dominant impression will probably be related to your point of view: who you are as an observer, what knowledge you bring to your subject, what your attitude toward your subject is.

Consider your vantage point. Do you have a bird's eye view? Are you observing from a low angle? Do you zoom in for a closer look? Would a different vantage point make your observation more vivid or help emphasize your dominant impression?

Check your essay for the key features of observing. Are you using sensory details? Do you include actual dialogue? Do you use the names of things? Have you used comparisons and images to make your description more vivid? Are you describing what is *not* present or *not* happening? Have you described any important changes in your subject's form or condition? Would your essay be improved by using any of these observing techniques?

Edit your essay for clear sentences and appropriate word choice, punctuation, usage, or grammar. When you are relatively satisfied with your observation, re-read it primarily for clarity and appropriateness of language. If possible, have another class member read your essay for possible editing changes.

Postscript for Your Observing Essay

When you've finished your essay, write an entry in your journal describing your writing process. Briefly, answer each of the following questions.

1. On what occasions did you observe your subject?
2. Which collecting strategies worked best?
3. Which shaping strategies helped you organize your essay?
4. What was the main idea or dominant impression your essay created?
5. What did this essay teach you about writing?

West Texas

WILLIAM LEAST HEAT MOON
(1939–   )

PREREADING JOURNAL ENTRY

Freewrite for five minutes on an experience you have had
in a desert or in the country. What were you doing and
what did you notice about the land?

or

Describe an incident when you got out of your car to
look more closely at a place you had been driving through.
Describe the difference between what you saw from your
car and what you noticed when you left your car and
started walking.

STUDENT JOURNAL RESPONSES

I can remember our trip to Death Valley, California in
about 1982. Our car broke down, but luckily we were in
a town. I remember driving at night because of the heat
during the day. We stayed in some cabins, saw a
lizard, rattlesnake, a lynx, and many horses +
wild donkeys. The ground was sandy and there
grew only low bushes — no trees. It was very hot during
the day. We went on nature hikes with rangers
I visited the gift shop, bought a ceramic donkey + still
have it today. At the hotel where the car died, we saw
a monkey + two dingo dogs.

Although I have never been in a true desert climate, I have
visited the Badlands of South Dakota. These strange eroded
mounds of multi-colored clay struck me as reminiscent of what the
terrain on another planet might look like. The landscape presented
a serious of grotesque pinnacles and spires along with weird and
twisted shapes.

William Least Heat Moon wrote Blue Highways: A Journey Into America *(1982) about his travels around America on the "blue" highways, the secondary roads marked in blue on road maps. His account of the places and people in "down home" America quickly became a best seller. As one early reviewer of the book commented, "Some men, when they lose their jobs and their wives, take to drink and go to the dogs. When William Least Heat Moon lost his, he took to the road and . . . wrote a book about his travels in order to find out where he was trying to arrive." Moon traveled in "Ghost Dancing," his van named in memory of the futile ghost dances of the Plains Indians who believed, in the 1890s, that their dances would return the old lands, the Bison, and the Indian warriors fallen in battle.*

"West Texas" is an excerpt from Blue Highways *in which Least Heat Moon tests the hypothesis that "nothing is out there" in the barren waste of Southwest Texas. He stops one evening, somewhere in western Crockett County, just off Texas highway 29, and records what he sees and feels.*

Straight [as a Chief's countenance,] the road lay ahead, curves so long and gradual as to be imperceptible except on the map. For nearly a hundred miles due west of Eldorado, [not a single town.] It was the Texas some people see as barren waste when they cross it, the part they later describe at the motel bar as "nothing." [They say, "There's nothing out there."]

[margin note: Nice image! What is not there. Sets up his main point here. Rest of the essay shows that this is NOT true.] 1

Driving through the miles of nothing, I decided to test the hypothesis and stopped somewhere in western Crockett County on the top of a broad mesa, just off Texas 29. At a distance, the land looked so rocky and dry, a religious man could believe that the First Hand never got around to the creation in here. Still, somebody had decided to string barbed wire around it.

[margin note: Part I: TEST HYPOTHESIS. First Hand: God? Passage has religious theme. Some people will put a fence anywhere!] 2

No plant grew higher than my head. For a

3

while, [I heard only miles of wind against the Ghost;] but after the ringing in my ears stopped, I heard myself breathing, then a bird note, an answering call, another kind of bird song, and another: mockingbird, mourning dove, an enigma. I heard the high zizz of [flies the color of gray flannel] and the deep buzz of a <u>blue</u> bumblebee. I made a list of nothing in particular:

[margin: figurative language]

[margin: Image: grey flannel blue?? thought they were yellow and black.]

1. mockingbird

2. mourning dove

3. enigma bird (heard not saw)

4. gray flies

5. blue bumblebee

[margin: Great List! Sensory Details]

6. two circling buzzards (not yet boys)

7. orange ants

8. black ants

9. orange-black ants (what's going on?)

[margin: Humor is great — very comical. Makes me smile.]

10. three species of spiders

11. opossum skull

12. jackrabbit (chewed on cactus)

13. deer (left scat)

14. coyote (left tracks)

15. small rodent (den full of seed hulls under rock)

16. snake (skin hooked on cactus spine)

17. prickly pear cactus (yellow blossoms)

18. hedgehog cactus (orange blossoms)

19. barrel cactus (red blossoms)

20. devil's pincushion (no blossoms)

21. catclaw (no better name)

[margin: Observing Strategy: <u>Names</u> of cacti and other plants.]

[margin: Devil: religious theme]

22. two species of grass (neither green, both alive)

23. yellow flowers (blossoms smaller than peppercorns)

24. sage (indicates alkali-free soil)

25. mesquite (three-foot plants with eighty-foot roots to reach water that fell as rain two thousand years ago)

? Really ?
Is this true?
Interesting !

26. greasewood (oh, yes)

27. joint fir (steeped stems make Brigham Young tea)

28. earth

29. sky

30. wind (always)

Yes !

That was all the nothing I could identify then, but had I waited until dark when the desert really comes to life, I could have done better. To say nothing is out there is incorrect; to say the desert is stingy with everything except space and light, stone and earth is closer to the truth.

Statement of his main idea or dominant impression.

I drove on. [The low sun turned the mesa rimrock to silhouettes, angular and weird and unearthly; had someone said the far side of Saturn looked just like this, I would have believed him.] The road dropped to the Pecos River, now dammed to such docility I couldn't imagine it formerly demarking the western edge of a rudimentary white civilization. Even the old wagonmen felt the unease of isolation when they had crossed the Pecos, a small but once serious river that has had many names: [Rio de las Vacas (River of Cows—perhaps a reference to bison), Rio Salado (Salty River), Rio Puerco (Dirty River).]

Part II: 4
Driving further and description.
Every sentence in this para-graph could be bracketed !

} Names again

West of the Pecos, [a strangely truncated cone rose from the valley. In the oblique evening light, its silhouette looked like a Mayan temple,

Descriptive details: image 5

Religion :
mesa = altar

157

so perfect was its symmetry.] I stopped again, started climbing, stirring a [panic of lizards] on the way up. From the top, the rubbled land below—[veined with the highway and arroyos,] topographical relief absorbed in the dusk—[looked like a roadmap.]

Great Image: panic of lizards.

The desert, more than any other terrain, shows its age, shows time because so little vegetation covers the ancient erosions of wind and storm. [What appears is tawny grit once stone and stone crumbling to grit.] Everywhere rock, earth's oldest thing. Even desert creatures come from a time older than the woodland animals, and they, in answer to the arduousness, have retained prehistoric coverings of chitin and lapped scale and primitive defenses of spine and stinger, fang and poison, shell and claw.

6

!! I really love this passage. Sensory detail: "grit".

The night, taking up the shadows and details, wiped the face of the desert into a simple, uncluttered blackness until there were only three things: land, wind, stars. I was there too, but my presence I felt more than saw. It was as if I had been reduced to mind, to an edge of consciousness. Men, <u>ascetics,</u> in all eras have gone into deserts to lose themselves—Jesus, <u>Saint Anthony, Saint Basil,</u> and numberless medicine men—maybe because such a losing happens almost as a matter of course here if you avail yourself. <u>The Sioux once chanted, "All over the sky a sacred voice is calling."</u>

Great figurative language

7

Religious theme again. Is Moon going back to his roots here?

<u>Back</u> to the highway, <u>on with</u> the headlamps, <u>down</u> Six Shooter Draw. In the darkness, deer, just shadows in the lights, <u>began moving toward</u> the desert willows in the wet bottoms. Stephen Vincent Benet:

Part II: Description Verbs and prepositions create <u>movement</u> here.

8

When Daniel Boone goes by, at night,
The <u>phantom deer</u> arise
And all lost, wild America
Is burning in their eyes.

? Ghost deer and ghost dancing?

? What do the last two mean? 9

From the top of another high mesa: twelve

miles west in the flat valley floor, the lights of
Fort Stockton blinked white, blue, red, and
yellow in the heat like a mirage. How is it that
desert towns look so fine and big at night? It
must be that little is hidden. The glistering
ahead could have been a golden city of Cibola.
But the reality of Fort Stockton was plywood
and concrete block and the plastic signs of
Holiday Inn and Mobil Oil.

Vivid colors!
Sensory detail

Here's the civilized reality!

Part Conclusion 10

The desert had given me an appetite that
would have made carrion crow stuffed with
saltbush taste good. I found a Mexican cafe of
adobe, with a whitewashed log ceiling, creek-
stone fireplace, and jukebox pumping out ma-
riachi music. It was like a bunkhouse. I ate
burritos, chile rellenos, and pinto beans, all
ladled over with a fine, incendiary sauce the
color of sludge from an old steel drum. At the
next table sat three big, round men: an Indian
wearing a silver headband, a Chicano in a
droopy Pancho Villa mustache, and a Negro in
faded overalls. I thought what a litany of grievances that table could recite. But the more I
looked, the more I believed they were someone's
vision of the West, maybe someone making ads
for Levy's bread, the ads that used to begin,
"You don't have to be Jewish."

I can almost taste this!

? How does this conclusion relate to his main point?

? Does he mean that the land is - should be - open to all?

Initial Impression: I liked this essay. There is so much more to the desert than just "nothing".

QUESTIONS ON MEANING

1. What surprises does the desert hold for Moon? List some of
   the things he probably didn't expect to find in the desert.

2. What main idea does this essay make? What is its dominant
   impression?

QUESTIONS ON PURPOSE AND STRATEGY

1. In your own words, describe Moon's purpose(s) in this essay.
   Why is he describing the desert: to entertain us, to inform
   us about the desert, to persuade us that we should go there,

or to explore his almost religious attraction to the desert? Some or all of the above? Which is his principal purpose?

2. Underline sentences that show the *chronological order* that shapes this essay.

QUESTIONS ON AUDIENCE AND LANGUAGE

1. Analyze Moon's intended audience: What kind of reader would find this essay interesting?

2. Moon mixes naming and literal description with figurative language. Choose one paragraph that you like. What parts are just names and literal descriptions? What parts are figurative language? Should he use more literal description and less figurative language? Or the reverse? Explain.

3. Moon uses a variety of sentence lengths and types. He uses lists. He quotes a poem. Find examples of short sentences. Find examples of longer, more complex sentences. Is his style readable? Is it effective? (Compare it to Zinsser's style— would Zinsser say Moon is "giving the reader too much trouble"?)

QUESTIONS FOR DISCUSSION AND WRITING

1. If you wrote your Prereading Journal Entry about the desert, what did you notice that Moon did not describe? What did he describe that you had not noticed?

2. In the margin of the essay, next to the first paragraph one student wrote: "Passage has a religious theme." Find other passages in this essay that refer or allude to religion. What is Moon saying about the desert, himself, and religion?

Lenses

ANNIE DILLARD

(1945–   )

PREREADING JOURNAL ENTRY

If possible, find or borrow a pair of binoculars. Go to a park or just sit outside somewhere. For three minutes, write down what you see without the binoculars. Then look at one area or object through the binoculars. For three minutes, write down what you see.

Annie Dillard was born in Pittsburgh, Pennsylvania, and received her B.A. and M.A. degrees from Hollins College. She has published a book of poetry, Tickets for a Prayer Wheel *(1974), columns and essays for* Living Wilderness, Harpers, *and the* Atlantic, *and several books including* Holy the Firm *(1978),* Living by Fiction *(1982), and* An American Childhood *(1987). Dillard established her reputation with the Pulitzer Prize-winning book,* Pilgrim at Tinker Creek *(1984), which showcases her extensive reading in the natural sciences and her talent for observing nature.* Pilgrim at Tinker Creek *was based on nearly ten years of observations near Roanoke, Virginia, but was written, Dillard explains, not in the great outdoors, but in a library study carrel, working seven days a week for eight months.*

"Lenses," which appears in Teaching a Stone to Talk *(1982), recounts two parallel experiences from Dillard's life: as a child, looking through a microscope at animals and plants in a single drop of pond water; and later, as an adult, looking through binoculars at a pair of whistling swans flying over a pond.*

You get used to looking through lenses; it is an 1
acquired skill. When you first look through binoculars, for instance, you can't see a thing. You look at the inside

of the barrel; you blink and watch your eyelashes; you play with the focus knob till one eye is purblind.

The microscope is even worse. You are supposed to 2 keep both eyes open as you look through its single eyepiece. I spent my childhood in Pittsburgh trying to master this trick: seeing through one eye, with both eyes open. The microscope also teaches you to move your hands wrong, to shove the glass slide to the right if you are following a creature who is swimming off to the left— as if you were operating a tiller, or backing a trailer, or performing any other of those paradoxical maneuvers which require either sure instincts or a grasp of elementary physics, neither of which I possess.

A child's microscope set comes with a little five-watt 3 lamp. You place this dim light in front of the microscope's mirror; the mirror bounces the light up through the slide, through the magnifying lenses, and into your eye. The only reason you do not see everything in silhouette is that microscopic things are so small they are translucent. The animals and plants in a drop of pond water pass light like pale stained glass; they seem so soaked in water and light that their opacity has leached away.

The translucent strands of algae you see under a 4 microscope—Spirogyra, Oscillatoria, Cladophora—move of their own accord, no one knows how or why. You watch these swaying yellow, green, and brown strands of algae half mesmerized; you sink into the microscope's field forgetful, oblivious, as if it were all a dream of your deepest brain. Occasionally a zippy rotifer comes barreling through, black and white, and in a tremendous hurry.

My rotifers and daphniae and amoebae were in an 5 especially tremendous hurry because they were drying up. I burnt out or broke my little five-watt bulb right away. To replace it, I rigged an old table lamp laid on its side; the table lamp carried a seventy-five-watt bulb. I was about twelve, immortal and invulnerable, and did not know what I was doing; neither did anyone else. My parents let me set up my laboratory in the basement, where they wouldn't have to smell the urine I collected in test tubes and kept in the vain hope it would grow something horrible. So in full, solitary ignorance I spent evenings in the basement staring into a seventy-five-watt bulb magnified three hundred times and focused into my eye. It is a wonder I can see at all. My eyeball itself would start drying up; I blinked and blinked.

But the pond water creatures fared worse. I dropped 6 them on a slide, floated a cover slip over them, and laid the slide on the microscope's stage, which the seventy-five-watt bulb had heated like a grill. At once the drop of pond water started to evaporate. Its edges shrank. The creatures swam among algae in a diminishing pool. I liked this part. The heat worked for me as a centrifuge, to concentrate the biomass. I had about five minutes to watch the members of a very dense population, excited by the heat, go about their business until—as I fancied sadly—they all caught on to their situation and started making out wills.

I was, then, not only watching the much-vaunted 7 wonders in a drop of pond water; I was also, with mingled sadism and sympathy, setting up a limitless series of apocalypses. I set up and staged hundreds of ends-of-the-world and watched, enthralled, as they played themselves out. Over and over again, the last trump sounded, the final scroll unrolled, and the known world drained, dried, and vanished. When all the creatures lay motionless, boiled and fried in the positions they had when the last of their water dried completely, I washed the slide in the sink and started over with a fresh drop. How I loved that deep, wet world where the colored algae waved in the water and the rotifers swam!

But oddly, this is a story about swans. It is not even a 8 story; it is a description of swans. This description of swans includes the sky over a pond, a pair of binoculars, and a mortal adult who had long since moved out of the Pittsburgh basement.

In the Roanoke valley of Virginia, rimmed by the Blue 9 Ridge Mountains to the east and the Allegheny Mountains to the west, is a little semiagricultural area called Daleville.

In Daleville, set among fallow fields and wooded ridges, is Daleville Pond. It is a big pond, maybe ten acres; it holds a lot of sky. I used to haunt the place because I loved it; I still do. In winter it had that airy scruffiness of deciduous lands; you greet the daylight and the open space, and spend the evening picking burrs out of your pants.

One Valentine's Day, in the afternoon, I was crouched 10 among dried reeds at the edge of Daleville Pond. Across the pond from where I crouched was a low forested mountain ridge. In every other direction I saw only sky, sky crossed by the reeds which blew before my face whichever way I turned.

I was looking through binoculars at a pair of whistling 11 swans. Whistling swans! It is impossible to say how excited I was to see whistling swans in Daleville, Virginia. The two were a pair, mated for life, migrating north and west from the Atlantic coast to the high arctic. They had paused to feed at Daleville Pond. I had flushed them, and now they were flying and circling the pond. I crouched in the reeds so they would not be afraid to come back to the water.

Through binoculars I followed the swans, swinging 12 where they flew. All their feathers were white; their eyes were black. Their wingspan was six feet; they were bigger than I was. They flew in unison, one behind the other; they made pass after pass at the pond. I watched them change from white swans in front of the mountain to black swans in front of the sky. In clockwise ellipses they flew, necks long and relaxed, alternately beating their wide wings and gliding.

As I rotated on my heels to keep the black frame of 13 the lenses around them, I lost all sense of space. If I lowered the binoculars I was always amazed to learn in which direction I faced—dazed, the way you emerge awed from a movie and try to reconstruct, bit by bit, a real world, in order to discover where in it you might have parked the car.

I lived in that circle of light, in great speed and utter 14 silence. When the swans passed before the sun they were distant—two black threads, two live stitches. But they kept coming smoothly, and the sky deepened to blue behind them and they took on light. They gathered dimension as they neared, and I could see their ardent, straining eyes. Then I could hear the brittle blur of their wings, the blur which faded as they circled on, and the sky brightened to yellow behind them and the swans flattened and darkened and diminished as they flew. Once I lost them behind the mountain ridge; when they emerged they were flying suddenly very high, and it was like music changing key.

I was lost. The reeds in front of me, swaying and out 15 of focus in the binoculars' circular field, were translucent. The reeds were strands of color passing light like cells in water. They were those yellow and green and brown strands of pond algae I had watched so long in a light-soaked field. My eyes burned; I was watching algae wave in a shrinking drop; they crossed each other and parted wetly. And suddenly into the field swam two whistling swans, two tiny whistling swans. They swam as fast as rotifers: two whistling swans, infinitesimal, beating their tiny wet wings, perfectly formed.

QUESTIONS ON MEANING

1. Dillard's essay is about discovery. What does she learn about the microscopic life in a drop of pond water? What does she learn about the two whistling swans? Why is this essay titled, "Lenses"?

2. Dillard's essay is also about herself. How does she describe herself at twelve years old? Does she think she was cruel as she "boiled and fried" the microscopic life in the pond water? (Do you?) What does she discover later, when she watches the two swans? How has she changed from those early years?

QUESTIONS ON PURPOSE AND STRATEGY

1. What is Dillard's purpose (or purposes) in this essay? Does the essay have a main idea or leave you with a dominant impression? Explain.

2. Comparing and contrasting her two experiences is Dillard's principal shaping strategy in "Lenses." As she explains in the final paragraph, the two swans parallel the "zippy rotifers," and the reeds of the pond recall the strands of algae. *List* all the other parallels (similarities and differences) you can find between her two experiences.

QUESTIONS ON STRATEGY AND LANGUAGE

1. "Lenses" has some technical language, such as the names of algae ("Spirogyra") and the name of microscopic, aquatic animals ("rotifers"). The essay also uses some sophisticated language, such as "purblind" and "apocalypses." How does this language affect Dillard's intended audience? (Did it bother or confuse you as you read the essay?)

2. What examples of figurative language can you find in this essay? Where does this language help you *see* more vividly? Where does it re-create how Dillard *feels?*

QUESTIONS FOR DISCUSSION AND WRITING

1. Effective description helps readers "see" and at the same time helps them remember. Without looking back at the essay, write down the most memorable descriptions from this essay. Compare your notes with those of your classmates. If several people have remembered the same passages, what makes those descriptions so effective?

2. Compare Dillard's essay, "Lenses," with Least Heat Moon's essay, "West Texas." Which essay do you like better, and why? Which uses more interesting observed detail? Which essay uses more vivid or imaginative figurative language? Which writer does a more effective job of bringing themselves into their descriptions?

3. In an interview, Dillard says that "people want to make you into a cult figure because of what they fancy to be your life-style, when the truth is your life is literature! You're writing consciously, off hundreds of index cards. . . . But all this never occurs to people. They think it happens in a dream, that you just sit on a tree stump and take dictation from

some little chipmunk." In "Lenses," what parts come from observation and what parts depend on Dillard's knowledge of biology and botany?

4. Recall an incident in your life in which you saw some person, place, or thing that recalled an earlier scene or incident. Describe the two people, places, or things using Dillard's parallel organization.

Graceland

ALBERT GOLDMAN

(1927–   )

PREREADING JOURNAL ENTRY

Imagine that a month ago, you won a ten million dollar lottery. Today, your architect and interior decorator are coming over to discuss plans for your new house. Choose *one room* in this house and describe how you would like it designed, furnished, and decorated. Begin by drawing a floor plan for this room.

Albert Goldman's most controversial book, Elvis *(1981), begins with a fascinating description of Graceland, Elvis Presley's mansion and shrine in Memphis. Although Elvis's fans revere Graceland as a kind of Buckingham Palace, Goldman says that the gaudy furnishings are better suited to a bordello's madame than rock music's King. "Though it cost a lot of money to fill up Graceland with things that appealed to Elvis Presley," Goldman exclaims, "nothing in the house is worth a dime." Goldman, a former pop music critic for* Life *magazine, attended Carnegie-Mellon University and the University of Chicago and then earned a Ph.D. at Columbia University, where he taught English. His books include* Wagner on Music and Drama *(1964),* Freakshow: The Rocksoulbluesjazzsickjewblackhumorsexpoppsych Gig *(1971),* Ladies and Gentlemen—Lenny Bruce!! *(1974), and* The Lives of John Lennon *(1988).*

In "Graceland," an excerpt from the opening chapter of Elvis, *Goldman guides us through the garish rooms of the King's mansion. Right from the first page, readers know that Goldman is no Robin Leach, puffing the "Lifestyles of the Rich and Famous." Instead, "Graceland" seems more like Edgar Allan Poe's "The Fall of the House of Usher": Goldman uses detailed descriptions of the mansion to reflect Elvis' bizarre character.*

Though the holidays are long past, Graceland looks 1
still like a picture on a Christmas card. The classic colonial
façade, with its towering white columns and pilasters, is
aglow with jewel lights, rose, amethyst and emerald. The
templelike pediment is outlined in pale blue fire. This
same eerie electric aura runs like St. Elmo's fire along the
eaves, zigzags up and down the gables and shimmies down
the drainpipes to the ground. Here it pales beside the
brilliance of a rank of Christmas trees that have been
transformed into cones of ruby, topaz, carnelian and
aquamarine incandescence.

Prominently displayed on the front lawn is an elaborate 2
crèche. The stable is a full-scale adobe house strewn with
straw. Life-sized are the figures of Joseph and Mary, the
kneeling shepherds and Magi, the lambs and ewes, as well
as the winged annunciatory angel hovering over the roof
beam. Real, too, is the cradle in which the infant Jesus
sleeps.

When you step through the ten-foot oak door and 3
enter the house, you stop and stare in amazement. Having
just come from the contemplation of the tenderest scene
in the Holy Bible, imagine the shock of finding yourself
in a *whorehouse!* Yet there is no other way to describe the
drawing room of Graceland except to say that it appears
to have been lifted from some turn-of-the-century bordello
down in the French Quarter of New Orleans. Lulu White
or the Countess Willie Piazza might have contrived this
plushy parlor for the entertainment of Gyp the Blood.
The room is a gaudy mélange of red velour and gilded
tassels, Louis XV furniture and porcelain bric-a-brac, all
informed by the kind of taste that delights in a ceramic
temple d'amour housing a miniature Venus de Milo with
an electrically simulated waterfall cascading over her
naked shoulders.

Looking a little closer, you realize that the old madams 4
of the French Quarter would have been horrified at the
quality of the hangings and furniture at Graceland. They
decorated their sporting houses with magnificent pieces
crafted in Europe, upholstered them in the finest reps

and damasks, laid costly Persian carpets on their floors and hung imposing oil paintings on their walls. Though it cost a lot of money to fill up Graceland with the things that appealed to Elvis Presley, nothing in the house is worth a dime.

Take that fake fireplace that blocks with its companion 5 bookcases (filled with phony leather bindings) the two big windows that should offer a commanding view of the front lawn. This hokey facsimile looks like it was bought at the auction of some bankrupt road company of *East Lynne*. Or consider the Louis Quinze furniture strewn about the parlor. Every piece is elaborately carved and gilded, escutcheoned and cabrioleted; but it's not only fake (Louis XV's upholsterers didn't go in for sectional sofas), it's that dreadful fake antique that Italian gangsters dote on: garish, preposterous, uncomfortable and cheating wherever it can, as in the substitution of velour for velvet. Or look at the real fireplace of white marble that stands against the back wall of the room, obviously innocent of use. It, too, has been flanked not with bookcases but with a great spread of smoked-glass mirror threaded with gold seams. The whole ensemble is crowned with an electric clock inside a three-foot sunburst that looks like someone took an ostrich egg and smashed it against the glass.

The entrance to the adjoining music room is flanked 6 by two tall, broad windows adorned with painted peacocks. Marvelously campy as are these bits of stained glass, they can't hold a candle to the bizarre chamber they frame. In this mad room, King Elvis's obsession with royal red reaches an intensity that makes you gag. Not so much a room as a crimson cocoon, every inch of it is swathed in red satin drapes, portieres, valences and braided ropes. As weird as anything in Edgar Allan Poe, the effect is that of stepping into the auricle of an immense heart. At the center of this king-sized valentine is the crowning touch: a concert grand piano that appears to have been dipped in liquid gold.

The entrance to the next room is blocked by a tall 7

folding screen covered with mirrored glass. Screens and other masking devices abound at Graceland because Gladys and Vernon, Elvis's parents, imbued him with the old hillbilly superstition: Never close up windows or doors. Through this folding looking glass lies one of Elvis's favorite spots, the trophy room. A pop archeologist would find the excavation of this site a satisfying occupation. No part of Graceland was subject to more visions and revisions.

Originally, this room was a patio adjoining the dressing 8 rooms for the outdoor pool. On hot Nilotic nights, Elvis and the Guys (known to the media as the "Memphis Mafia") would sit here cutting the ripe red hearts out of iced watermelons and vying to see who could eat the most. As they consumed this sweet satisfying pap, they would spit the pits out on the ground as Sweetpea, Gladys's Pomeranian, pranced about in the black hail.

In the late sixties, Elvis decided to build a forty-foot 9 room over the patio to house his slot car racecourse. On a huge raised platform, a figure-eight track was laid out, in whose grooves could be fitted expensive scale-model replicas of Ferraris, Maseratis, Lotuses and Porsches. By means of an electric drive system, you could race these little cars around the tracks and up and down inclines at great speeds, which Elvis sought constantly to increase by means of continual improvements in the cars' motors. Manipulating the pistol-grip controls, you could make the cars skid, spin out and crash. It was a grand if costly game, and the Guys enjoyed it enormously.

Like all of Elvis's toys, the slot cars soon lost their 10 charm. One day the track was banished to the attic, where it was stored alongside cartons of old teddy bears, discarded guitars and gilt lamps from the house on Audubon Avenue. Elvis never allowed anything to be cast out of Graceland except human beings. Once an object, no matter how trivial, came into his possession, it remained with him for the rest of his life.

Commencing in the Royal Period, the slot car room 11 became the trophy room. Elvis pushed back the end wall twenty feet to make a chamber fit for a pharaoh's tomb. Then he filled it with gold. He ranked his fifty-three gold records along one wall, like patents of nobility. Against the opposite wall, he piled up, like the offerings before a shrine, a great heap of gold loving cups, gold statuettes and gold tablets. The effect is less that of a trophy case than of the display case of a trophy manufacturer.

The showcase effect is even more pronounced in the 12 center of the room, which is occupied by a set of old-fashioned department store counters, under whose glass tops or stuffed inside storage drawers and cupboards lie an immense profusion of plaques, medals, certificates and scrapbooks received from professional organizations, charities and fan clubs. Like any true sovereign, King Elvis never forgets that all his wealth and power are derived from his subjects. No matter what they offer him, whether it be a huge stuffed animal or a little crocheted doily, he not only keeps the gift but puts it on display.

The oddest feature of the trophy room is the soda 13 fountain that stands in one corner, one of two at Grace-land, the other one being downstairs in the poolroom. Soda fountains and jukeboxes are symbolic objects for fifties rock heroes, no more to be wondered at than the old binnacle in the den of a steamship captain or the pair of crossed sabers on the wall of a retired general. What is disconcerting about this domestic altar is its formica mean-ness. Yet it would be out of character for Elvis to own a handsome old green marble counter with mottled glass lamps and quaint seltzer pulls because Elvis detests every-thing antique with the heartfelt disgust of a real forward-looking American of his generation. Like so many of his kind, he gloats over the spectacle of the wrecking ball bashing down the walls of historic Memphis. In fact, he likes to get into the driver's seat of a bulldozer and smash down old buildings himself. . . .

On the left-hand side of the entrance hall is the dining 14 room. In the center of the crimson carpet is a large quadrangle of black marble tiles on which is set the table: an eight-foot oval of mirrored glass on an ebonized and fluted wooden pedestal. Round the table in great state stand ten tall, ladder-backed Louis XIV chairs with tufted velour seats. They appear to have been drawn up for King Elvis and the Nine Worthies. (When Elvis dines with the Guys, he often jokes about Jesus breaking bread with his disciples. They respond by singing the old hymn, "What a Friend We Have in Jesus," substituting "Elvis" for "Jesus.") Above the table hangs a brass Louis XIV chandelier with two tiers of scrolled candlearms fitted with glass lusters. At each corner of the room, like bumpers on a game board, are tall diagonal bric-a-brac cabinets or chrome-plated étagères crammed with statuettes, vases, jars, boxes, plaques, goblets, ewers, compotes, porringers, shells, cloches, etc., *viz:*

ceramic statuette of a grey poodle

ceramic statuette of a nude girl with perched bird

pair of Portuguese glazed pottery drug jars

five specimens of butterflies in plastic cases

artificial floral bouquet under a glass cloche

two glass bowls with bouquet of black and white feathers

model of 1932 antique radio

ceramic statuette of a trumpeting elephant

Wherever Elvis goes in his travels, he indulges his middle-aged woman's passion for knickknacks, curios and chatz-kahs. A domestic appraiser once remarked that Elvis appeared to have furnished Graceland largely from road-side stands.

A familiar feature of a number of the world's greatest 15 palaces is a room decorated in an exotic style, inspired, perhaps, by the culture of one of the ruler's most remote or colorful provinces. Graceland possesses such a room; indeed, of all the public rooms in the mansion, it is the King's favorite. The den is an addition to the original building, created by enlarging and enclosing a back porch that ran along the entire rear wall. The room looks like Elvis scooped up the setting for one of his Hawaiian movies and brought it home inside a sixty-foot walnut hope chest. You reach the den by going through the kitchen, which is all white formica, walnut paneling and Kitchen-Aid stainless steel, with a couple of oddly feminine touches, like the calico carpeting and the hanging lampshades painted with fruits and vegetables. Entering the den, the first thing that strikes you is a towering statue of the god Tiki, confronting the visitor with outstretched arms holding an empty bowl. Obviously not an ashtray nor an hors d'oeuvre tray nor a place to drop your calling card, this empty basin is a puzzler. In any case, the statue serves to proclaim the room's provenance.

The style of the den could be characterized as Poly- 16 nesian Primitive or Ugh! The decorator divided its sixty-foot length with another of those hinged screens that one finds all over Graceland. This one is composed of huge panels of stressed, stained pine perforated in long spermatozoid scrolls cut in the wood with a chain saw. On the side of the screen opposite that dominated by the figure of Tiki is a seating area focused upon an early-model Advent video projector.

Here, as Elvis watches his favorite football teams or 17 boxing matches with the Guys, he enjoys the full flavor of the Polynesian Primitive. The huge sofa and the pair of oversized armchairs are carved out of the same dark coarse pine as the room divider and upholstered with thick, dark artificial fur. As the chairs have huge pawlike armrests, the impression created by this curious suite is rather like the Three Bears watching TV. This animalistic sofa is also Elvis's favorite downstairs dining spot. Like so many boy-men, he dislikes the formality of table service. Whenever possible, he has his meals served to him here on the cocktail table, a huge slab of boldly grained wood cut out of the crotch of a cypress tree and surfaced with what appears to be about a quarter-inch layer of lustrous polyurethane.

The most impressive feature of the den is the wall 18
behind the TV, which is straight out of the lobby of a
Waikiki Beach resort hotel. Constructed of layers of rough-
cut fieldstone, it has been arranged artfully like a natural
cataract and equipped with pipes and a pumping system
so that a constant stream of soothing water flows down
over the jutting rocks, catching as it falls the colors cast
by the lamps concealed in the ceiling. What more perfect
object of contemplation could be imagined for a man who
is perpetually stoned?

The King's bedchamber is the most bizarre room in 19
the hillbilly palace. The walls are padded and tufted with
button-studded strips of black artificial suede. The crimson carpet covers not only the floor but rises at the foot
of the bed like a red wave, atop which rides an enormous
color TV set. Confronting the bed are two big windows
that overlook the front lawn. Sealed with the same black
upholstery that covers the walls, they are crowned with
gold valences and hung with floor-length crimson drapes,
producing a somberly surrealistic image, like a painting
by Magritte. The space between the windows is filled with
a mirror, which reflects the bed.

What a bed! An immense slab, nine by nine, a double 20
king size, it has a mortuary headboard of black quilted
Naugahide, with a built-in plastic back angle and retract-
able armrests of speckled metal, like the skeletons of those
padded "husbands" beloved of suburban matrons. To one
side is an easel supporting a large photograph of Elvis's
mother; on the other a sepia-toned portrait of Jesus Christ.
Back in the corners of the room crouch big round seats
covered with white fake fur like enormous bunnies.

As in a funeral parlor, the light in this inner sanctum 21
is always dim, supplied by cove lamps that illuminate the
ceiling but produce below only a murky subaqueous
gloaming. The air is chilled, the temperature being driven
down during the hot Memphis summer by powerful
refrigeration units that groan night and day to keep the
King from sweating. The odor of the room is sometimes
fetid, the stink of a Bowery flophouse full of dirty old

men incontinent of their urine and feces. The most grotesque object in this Cave of Morphia, this black and crimson womb, this padded cell, is the King.

QUESTIONS ON MEANING

1. List the rooms in Graceland that Goldman describes. What, according to Goldman, is the most striking feature in each of these rooms?

2. One of Goldman's main ideas is that Elvis is King in a hillbilly palace. Which paragraphs most clearly create this dominant impression?

3. Goldman is definitely not complimentary about Elvis and his tastes. Which sentences or phrases most clearly state or imply Goldman's judgments about Elvis?

QUESTIONS ON PURPOSE AND STRATEGY

1. What is Goldman's purpose in this essay? To minutely describe Graceland? To reveal Elvis's character and tastes through description? To trash the legend of the King?

2. Goldman's overall observing strategy is to give his readers a *tour* of Graceland, moving from one room to the next. In what paragraphs is that most apparent? Occasionally, he stops during the tour to give a short biographical or historical narrative. In what paragraphs are those strategies most apparent?

QUESTIONS ON AUDIENCE AND LANGUAGE

1. Goldman's essay is full of allusions (Lulu White, Countess Willie Piazza), French words ("mélange," "étagères"), and specific, almost technical language ("ewers, compotes, porringers"). What effect does this language have on his intended audience? How did it affect you?

2. Goldman, like Dillard, uses imagery and figurative language. Which images help you visualize a particular room? Which

images seem intended to reveal Goldman's opinion of Graceland and Elvis? Do some effectively do both?

QUESTIONS FOR DISCUSSION AND WRITING

1. If you have been to Graceland, compare your observations with Goldman's account. When you walked in the front door, did you think you were walking into a bordello? Which rooms does he most accurately describe?

2. One critic of Goldman's biography of Elvis points out that "reviewers on both sides of the Atlantic have been quick to point out [that] Goldman's [book] is one of the most vengeful and cannibalistic biographies ever written." Check *Elvis* out of the library and read at least one additional chapter. Do you agree with this statement?

3. Visit a store, restaurant, or public building whose design, furnishings, or decor you find unappealing and tasteless. Use Goldman's method of both describing and judging this place, without overusing judgmental adjectives such as *horrible, tasteless,* or *pretentious.*

Rules of the Game: Rodeo

GRETEL EHRLICH

PREREADING JOURNAL ENTRY

Attend one game or performance of a sport that has multiple events, such as gymnastics, track and field, swimming, frisbee, skiing, or rodeo. Describe the individual participants and activities as well as the overall spectacle for a friend who couldn't attend this event.

"It's May and I've just awakened from a nap, curled against the sagebrush the way my dog taught me to sleep—sheltered from the wind. A front is pulling the huge sky over me, and from the dark a hailstone has hit me on the head. I'm trailing a band of two thousand sheep across a stretch of Wyoming badlands, a fifty-mile trip that takes five days. . . ." Thus begins Gretel Ehrlich's journal of her experiences as a ranch worker in Wyoming, The Solace of Open Spaces *(1985)*. Gretel Ehrlich *was born in California, went to school at Bennington, and attended the* UCLA Film School. *She went to Wyoming in 1976 as part of a documentary film crew and stayed to work and write. Her publications include two volumes of poetry, essays in the* The Atlantic, Harper's, *and the* New York Times, *and a recent book,* Heart Mountain *(1988).*

In "Rules of the Game: Rodeo," Gretel Ehrlich describes the National Finals Rodeo, the "World Series of Professional Rodeo." "A good rodeo," Ehrlich explains, "like a good marriage, or a musical instrument when played to the pitch of perfection, becomes more than what it started out to be. It is effort transformed into effortlessness. . . ."

Instead of honeymooning in Paris, Patagonia, or the 1 Sahara as we had planned, my new husband and I drove through a series of blizzards to Oklahoma City. Each

December the National Finals Rodeo is held in a modern, multistoried colosseum next to buildings that house banks and petroleum companies in a state whose flatness resembles a swimming pool filled not with water but with oil.

The National Finals is the "World Series of Professional 2 Rodeo," where not only the best cowboys but also the most athletic horses and bucking stock compete. All year, rodeo cowboys have been vying for the honor to ride here. They've been to Houston, Las Vegas, Pendleton, Tucson, Cheyenne, San Francisco, Calgary; to as many as eighty rodeos in one season, sometimes making two or three on a day like the Fourth of July, and when the results are tallied up (in money won, not points) the top fifteen riders in each event are invited to Oklahoma City.

We climbed to our peanut gallery seats just as Miss 3 Rodeo America, a lanky brunette swaddled in a lavender pantsuit, gloves, and cowboy hat, loped across the arena. There was a hush in the audience; all the hats swimming down in front of us, like buoys, steadied and turned toward the chutes. "Out of chute number three, Pat Linger, a young cowboy from Miles City, Montana, making his first appearance here on a little horse named Dillinger." And as fast as these words sailed across the colosseum, the first bareback horse bumped into the lights.

There's a traditional order to the four timed and three 4 rough stock events that make up a rodeo program. Bareback riders are first, then steer wrestlers, team ropers, saddle bronc riders, barrel racers, and finally, the bull riders.

After Pat Linger came Steve Dunham, J.C. Trujillo, 5 Mickey Young, and the defending champ, Bruce Ford on a horse named Denver. Bareback riders do just that: they ride a horse with no saddle, no halter, no rein, clutching only a handhold riveted into a girth that goes around the horse's belly. A bareback rider's loose style suggests a drunken, comic bout of lovemaking: he lies back on the horse and, with each jump and jolt, flops delightfully, like a libidinous Raggedy Andy, toes turned out, knees flexed, legs spread and pumping, back arched, the back of his hat bumping the horse's rump as if nodding, "Yes, let's do 'er again." My husband, who rode saddle broncs in amateur rodeos, explains it differently: "It's like riding a runaway bicycle down a steep hill and lying on your back; you can't see where you're going or what's going to happen next."

Now the steer wrestlers shoot out of the box on their 6 own well-trained horses: there is a hazer on the right to keep the steer running straight, the wrestler on the left, and the steer between them. When the wrestler is neck and neck with the animal, he slides sideways out of his saddle as if he'd been stabbed in the ribs and reaches for the horns. He's airborne for a second; then his heels swing into the dirt, and with his arms around the horns, he skids to a stop, twisting the steer's head to one side so the animal loses his balance and falls to the ground. It's a fast-paced game of catch with a thousand-pound ball of horned flesh.

The team ropers are next. Most of them hail from the 7 hilly, oak-strewn valleys of California where dally roping originated.[1] Ropers are the graceful technicians, performing their pas de deux (plus steer) with a precision that begins to resemble a larger clarity—an erudition. Header and heeler come out of the box at the same time, steer between them, but the header acts first: he ropes the horns of the steer, dallies up, turns off, and tries to position the steer for the heeler who's been tagging behind this duo, loop clasped in his armpit as if it were a hen. Then the heeler sets his generous, unsweeping loop free and double-hocks the steer. It's a complicated act which takes about six seconds. Concomitant with this speed and skill is a feminine grace: they don't clutch their stiff loop or throw it at the steer like a bag of dirty laundry the way I do, but hold it gently, delicately, as if it were a hoop of silk. One or two cranks and both arm and loop vault

---

[1] The word dally is a corruption of the Spanish *da la vuelta,* meaning to take a turn, as with a rope around the saddle horn.

forward, one becoming an appendage of the other, as if the tendons and pulse that travel through the wrist had lengthened and spun forward like fishing line until the loop sails down on the twin horns, then up under the hocks like a repeated embrace that tightens at the end before it releases.

The classic event at rodeo is saddle bronc riding. The 8 young men look as serious as academicians: they perch spryly on their high-kicking mounts, their legs flicking forward and back, "charging the point," "going back to the cantle" in a rapid, staccato rhythm. When the horse is at the high point of his buck and the cowboy is stretched out, legs spurring above the horse's shoulder, rein-holding arm straight as a board in front, and free hand lifted behind, horse and man look like a propeller. Even their dismounts can look aeronautical: springing off the back of the horse, they land on their feet with a flourish—hat still on—as if they had been ejected mechanically from a burning plane long before the crash.

Barrel racing is the one women's event. Where the 9 men are tender in their movements, as elegant as if Balanchine had been their coach, the women are prodigies of Wayne Gretsky, all speed, bully, and grit. When they charge into the arena, their hats fly off; they ride brazenly, elbows, knees, feet fluttering, and by the time they've careened around the second of three barrels, the whip they've had clenched between their teeth is passed to a hand, and on the home stretch they urge the horse to the finish line.

Calf ropers are the whiz kids of rodeo: they're expert 10 on the horse and on the ground, and their horses are as quick-witted. The cowboy emerges from the box with a loop in his hand, a piggin' string in his mouth, coils and reins in the other, and a network of slack line strewn so thickly over horse and rider, they look as if they'd run through a tangle of kudzu before arriving in the arena. After roping the calf and jerking the slack in the rope, he jumps off the horse, sprints down the length of nylon, which the horse keeps taut, throws the calf down, and ties three legs together with the piggin' string. It's said of Roy Cooper, the defending calf-roping champion, that "even with pins and metal plates in his arm, he's known for the fastest groundwork in the business; when he springs down his rope to flank the calf, the resulting action is pure rodeo poetry." The six or seven separate movements he makes are so fluid they look like one continual unfolding.

Bull riding is last, and of all the events it's the only 11 one truly dangerous. Bulls are difficult to ride: they're broad-backed, loose-skinned, and powerful. They don't jump balletically the way a horse does; they jerk and spin, and if you fall off, they'll try to gore you with a horn, kick, or trample you. Bull riders are built like the animals they ride: low to the ground and hefty. They're the tough men on the rodeo circuit, and the flirts. Two of the current champs are city men: Charlie Samson is a small, shy black from Watts, and Bobby Del Vecchio, a brash Italian from the Bronx who always throws the audience a kiss after a ride with a Catskill-like showmanship not usually seen here. What a bull rider lacks in technical virtuosity—you won't see the fast spurring action of a saddle bronc rider in this event—he makes up for in personal flamboyance, and because it's a deadlier game they're playing, you can see the belligerence rise up their necks and settle into their faces as the bull starts his first spin. Besides the bull and the cowboy, there are three other men in the ring—the rodeo clowns—who aren't there to make children laugh but to divert the bull from some of his deadlier tricks, and, when the rider bucks off, jump between the two—like secret service men—to save the cowboy's life. . . .

The National Finals run ten nights. Every contestant 12 rides every night, so it is easy to follow their progress and setbacks. One evening we abandoned our rooftop seats and sat behind the chutes to watch the saddle broncs ride. Behind the chutes two cowboys are rubbing rosin—part of their staying power—behind the saddle swells and on their Easter-egg-colored chaps which are pink, blue, and

light green with white fringe. Up above, standing on the
chute rungs, the stock contractors direct horse traffic:
"Velvet Drums" in chute #3, "Angel Sings" in #5, "Rusty"
in #1. Rick Smith, Monty Henson, Bobby Berger, Brad
Gjermudson, Mel Coleman, and friends climb the chutes.
From where I'm sitting, it looks like a field hospital with
five separate operating theaters, the cowboys, like sur-
geons, bent over their patients with sweaty brows and
looks of concern. Horses are being haltered; cowboys are
measuring out the long, braided reins, saddles are set:
one cowboy pulls up on the swells again and again,
repositioning his hornless saddle until it sits just right.
When the chute boss nods to him and says, "Pull 'em up,
boys," the ground crew tightens front and back cinches
on the first horse to go, but very slowly so he won't panic
in the chute as the cowboy eases himself down over the
saddle, not sitting on it, just hovering there. "Okay, you're
on." The chute boss nods to him again. Now he sits on
the saddle, taking the rein in one hand, holding the top
of the chute with the other. He flips the loose bottoms of
his chaps over his shins, puts a foot in each stirrup, takes
a breath, and nods. The chute gate swings open releasing
a flood—not of water, but of flesh, groans, legs kicking.
The horse lunges up and out in the first big jump like a
wave breaking whose crest the cowboy rides, "marking
out the horse," spurs well above the bronc's shoulders. In
that first second under the lights, he finds what will be
the rhythm of the ride. Once again he "charges the point,"
his legs pumping forward, then so far back his heels touch
behind the cantle. For a moment he looks as though he
were kneeling on air, then he's stretched out again, his
whole body taut but released, free hand waving in back
of his head like a palm frond, rein-holding hand thrust
forward: *"En garde!"* he seems to be saying, but he's
airborne; he looks like a wing that has sprouted suddenly
from the horse's broad back. Eight seconds. The whistle
blows. He's covered the horse. Now two gentlemen dressed
in white chaps and satin shirts gallop beside the bucking
horse. The cowboy hands the rein to one and grabs the

waist of the other—the flank strap on the bronc has been undone, so all three horses move at a run—and the pickup man from whom the cowboy is now dangling slows almost to a stop, letting him slide to his feet on the ground.

Rick Smith from Wyoming rides, looking pale and 13 nervous in his white shirt. He's bucked off and so are the brash Monty "Hawkeye" Henson, and Butch Knowles, and Bud Pauley, but with such grace and aplomb, there is no shame. Bobby Berger, an Oklahoma cowboy, wins the go-round with a score of 83.

By the end of the evening we're tired, but in no way 14 as exhausted as these young men who have ridden night after night. "I've never been so sore and had so much fun in my life," one first-time bull rider exclaims breathlessly. When the performance is over we walk across the street to the chic lobby of a hotel chock full of cowboys. Wives hurry through the crowd with freshly ironed shirts for tomorrow's ride, ropers carry their rope bags with them into the coffee shop, which is now filled with contestants, eating mild midnight suppers of scrambled eggs, their numbers hanging crookedly on their backs, their faces powdered with dust, and looking at this late hour prematurely old.

We drive back to the motel, where, the first night, 15 they'd "never heard of us" even though we'd had reservations for a month. "Hey, it's our honeymoon," I told the night clerk and showed him the white ribbons my mother had tied around our duffel bag. He looked embarrassed, then surrendered another latecomer's room.

The rodeo finals in Oklahoma may be a better place 16 to honeymoon than Paris. All week, we've observed some important rules of the game. A good rodeo, like a good marriage, or a musical instrument when played to the pitch of perfection, becomes more than what it started out to be. It is effort transformed into effortlessness; a balance becomes grace, the way love goes deep into friendship.

In the rough stock events such as the one we watched 17 tonight, there is no victory over the horse or bull. The point of the match is not conquest but communion: the rhythm of two beings becoming one. Rodeo is not a sport of opposition; there is no scrimmage line here. No one bears malice—neither the animals, the stock contractors, nor the contestants; no one wants to get hurt. In this match of equal talents, it is only acceptance, surrender, respect, and spiritedness that make for the midair union of cowboy and horse. Not a bad thought when starting out fresh in a marriage.

QUESTIONS ON MEANING

1. According to Ehrlich, what seven events make up a rodeo program? Describe each event. What are the "rules of the game" for each event?
2. How is a rodeo similar to marriage, according to Ehrlich?

QUESTIONS ON PURPOSE AND STRATEGY

1. What are Ehrlich's purposes in this essay? To describe rodeo events? To explain to novices the main events of the sport? To argue that rodeo is a great sport? Explain, referring to specific passages.
2. Which paragraphs are shaped by Ehrlich's *analysis* of the parts of rodeo? Where does *chronological order* organize her paragraphs?
3. Throughout the essay, Ehrlich uses *comparison* as a major observing strategy. Find sentences that show her comparison of rodeoing to each of the following activities: baseball, football, ballet, hockey, lovemaking, riding a bicycle, fishing, flying an airplane, riding a wave, fencing, and playing a musical instrument. Which of these comparisons are similes, introduced by *like, as,* or *as if*?
4. Ehrlich concludes her essay by echoing her introduction. What ties the introduction and the conclusion together? Does her conclusion effectively end the essay?

QUESTIONS ON AUDIENCE AND LANGUAGE

1. Ehrlich's essay is full of rodeo terminology, such as "hazer," "dallies up," "hocks," "cantle," and "piggin' string." Find other examples of this specialized language. If you are not familiar with rodeo, are you still able to understand this essay?

2. One critic of *The Solace of Open Spaces* accuses Ehrlich of occasionally using "fancy pants" language—words such as "concomitant" and "pas de deux." Do you think her vocabulary or her figurative language are too fancy? Where?

QUESTIONS FOR DISCUSSION AND WRITING

1. Is rodeo cruel to animals? What might an animal rights activist say about the sport? How would you respond to their charges? How would Ehrlich respond to their charges?

2. Reobserve the sporting event described in your Prereading Journal Entry. What additional details do you notice? Using some of Ehrlich's strategies, revise and expand your journal entry.

Freshmen

ANDREA LEE

(1953–   )

PREREADING JOURNAL ENTRY

If possible, visit an unfamiliar grade school or high school—preferably during lunch, an assembly, or a sporting event. For half an hour, sit, observe, and take notes. How do these students, their surroundings, and their behavior compare to your own experiences?

In the Foreword to Russian Journal *(1981), Andrea Lee writes, "I came to Russia with my husband, Tom—then a Harvard doctoral candidate in Russian history—as part of a government-sponsored exchange of scholars. . . . The fact that we were young (we were both twenty-five) made meeting people still easier: most young Russians . . . have a devouring curiosity about Westerners their age." Lee, a black writer educated at Harvard, has written articles for the* New Yorker, The New York Times, *and* Vogue, *and has published a novel,* Sarah Phillips *(1984).*

*"Freshmen" describes the matriculation process at Moscow University in a pre-*Glasnost *era. Despite great differences in politics and culture, Andrea Lee reveals that freshmen are still freshmen: anxious about tests, self-conscious about their clothes, and a bit overwhelmed about everything.*

The nights are cold; the apples are ripe on the trees 1
in the university orchard. Today was the first day of
school, and though I slept late and missed the cute and
much-photographed primary schoolers (marching in
starched pinafores, with flowers for the teachers), Tom
and I did catch the opening exercises tonight for freshmen

here at Moscow State. We had seen the build-up to the ceremony over the past month, as entrance exams took place around us. Outside the immense glass-and-steel humanities building, crowds of parents stood staring anxiously up at the windows of the examination rooms. The children of many of them had spent the past six months in intensive "prepping" courses for three days of tests. This is an expensive procedure, especially for provincial families, whose children must come to live in Moscow during the half year. The expense is often worthwhile, however, since these all-day examinations really do determine a student's future career. Three papers are posted on the bulletin board outside the building: a description of the exams; a list of appeal procedures for students who fail; and an employment ad from an automobile factory, addressed specifically to candidates whose appeals are turned down. (These young people don't always face a future of factory work. Russian friends have told me that a common tactic after rejection from Moscow State is to try institutes whose prestige is less and which have fewer applications. Determined students can find a place in these humbler schools, as students of, for instance, forest management or soil chemistry.)

The hundreds of students in the auditorium tonight 2 were the happy winners, survivors of a tough selection system; they seemed like freshmen anywhere. Before the ceremony they straggled into the room, smoking cigarettes, laughing, calling to their friends. A few loners stood gazing at the vast embossed ceiling, obviously overwhelmed by the stupendous size of the building and perhaps as well by the prestige of the institution they were entering. One or two couples strolled in with their arms around each other, but for the most part the sexes stayed in packs, eying each other covertly. By Soviet standards, they were dressed modishly: the girls in bright miniskirts and clumsy platform shoes, the boys in wildly patterned polyester shirts. Among them, a small group stood out in especially naïve clothing: crop-headed boys in tight suits, girls whose tremendous coiled braids were topped with frilly ribbons. These, I guessed, were country kids, in Moscow for the first time. A sophisticated Russian friend had described to me the reaction of these rural students to the university cafeteria: "They all came charging in, wearing these incredible suits—narrow lapels and short trousers. They gawked at everything, and then they started to gobble the food—tough meat and watery soup—as if it was the best thing they'd eaten in their lives." Aside from the provincials, the students made a fairly homogeneous group. I was surprised to find so few representatives of the various Soviet ethnic and racial groups. Most students were clearly Great Russian, the ethnic group that dominates Central European Russia and makes up most of the population of Moscow.

The huge auditorium filled, then quieted, and at seven 3 o'clock the head of the university began to speak. At his first few phrases, I felt stealing irresistibly over me the memory of my own freshman year: the universal confusion; the unexpected liberty; awe; the endlessly proffered, absurd advice, which we ritually ignored. The faraway official, with his plump vest full of medals, was urging the students to uphold the standards of Lenin. He reminded them to follow the principles of the Twenty-fifth Party Congress in their scholarship. He told them that university life itself was an educational experience, that one must be fit in mind as well as body. Two grave, pink-cheeked Komsomol leaders carried in the flag of the Order of Lenin, and the speeches continued. I felt my ears closing, and I guessed that the ears of hundreds of students around me had closed as well. For a few minutes they had all stared up at the platform with the polite forbearance of the young for the pompous old, then the natural life of the crowd took over. Boys elbowed each other and stared at girls; girls put on lipstick and passed notes down the rows to their friends. I could feel the classic freshman sense of universal ogling, and also the question burning in the back of every mind: What will happen tonight? Because what was important was not the ceremony but afterward, when the freshman class had been promised a dance with live music.

The series of long speeches ended with a memorial to 4 the Moscow State University students killed in the Second World War. The freshmen grew quiet as a soldier marched slowly forward with a wreath. I was curious about what they were thinking, these children born in the early sixties, to whom the forlorn hope of crudely armed students in the defense of Moscow could mean little more than an excerpt from a cycle of legends. The young faces around me wore only a strict ceremonial gravity. After a few minutes of silence, a stylishly dressed girl beside me glanced down at her watch and gave a little frown of impatience.

Later Tom and I watched the dance. It was held in 5 the main hall of the dormitory, a dreary marble room whose walls give off a penetrating cold even in the summer. On a small platform in the center, four young men in jeans and suspenders played English and American rock music. Their hair was shoulder-length and their expressions were grim; they pronounced the English words with savage precision. A few girls in miniskirts hovered on the floor below, staring up at the musicians and hurrying to adjust microphones and amplifiers. As the lead singer shook his hair and began to sing "Satisfaction," I had an acute sense of time lag. The music, the setting were those of any small college dance a decade ago in the United States. But there was a naïveté about the crowd which would have been unusual for any group of young Americans. The tiny refreshment stand served only fizzy *limonad,* and we didn't see anyone slip off to drink vodka or beer in a corner. A wall of spectators surrounded the dance floor, where a few shy couples were moving in the strange rhythmless combination of Monkey and Jerk which makes up Russian "pop" dancing. The action, however, was not on the dance floor but among the hovering watchers. Packs of girls and boys approached and fell away from each other, giggling at the near-intersections but never actually meeting. I thought of the formality that seems to govern encounters of sexes in the Soviet Union. Many of my young married Russian friends were introduced by relatives.

So the freshman dance at Moscow State failed as a 6 meeting ground for male and female students. Both sexes listened raptly to the music. Boys roughhoused in corners. Someone upset a tray of *zakuski* (snacks), and the floor was slippery with bologna sandwiches. The band played a slow song, and the few dancers moved heavily and chastely, their heads on the shoulders of their partners. At exactly eleven o'clock a uniformed guard appeared and told the band members to pack up. The dance was over, and in a minute the students had filed obediently away. The freshman class needs its rest, I discovered. Early tomorrow morning they leave on a bus to fulfill another first-year tradition: a month of work in a potato-harvest brigade at a collective farm.

QUESTIONS ON MEANING

1. What does Lee tell us about the Moscow State University's examination system? What happens to the students who pass and those who fail?

2. Based on Lee's perceptions, how are Moscow University freshmen like freshmen in the United States? How are they different? (What sentences reveal that this is pre-*Glasnost* Russia?)

3. What does this essay tell us about Andrea Lee herself?

QUESTIONS ON PURPOSE AND STRATEGY

1. Lee says that the chapters of *Russian Journal* are like "a set of photographs taken by an amateur who is drawn to his subjects by instinct and capricious inclination. . . ." What is the purpose of this entry about freshmen? Is it like the purpose of a photograph? How is Lee's description different from a photograph?

2. Read the opening sentences of the paragraphs. What words or phrases show that Lee uses *chronological order* to shape her essay?

QUESTIONS ON AUDIENCE AND LANGUAGE

1. Who would be interested in reading *Russian Journal?* Tourists? American students? Historians? Would Russians themselves find her account interesting? Should Lee have been worried that government officials might confiscate her manuscript?

2. The first sentence in this essay is in present tense. What effect does the tense have on the reader?

3. Lee's point of view is that of a curious observer. Where is her curiosity most apparent? How do we as readers react to her curiosity?

QUESTIONS FOR DISCUSSION AND WRITING

1. Based on your reading of more recent articles about Russian life and politics, what do you think has changed about the Russia Lee observes? What has not changed?

2. What is observed depends on *who* is observing. Identify each time Lee refers to herself in the essay. Do Lee's references to herself and to her own memories add to or detract from this observing essay?

3. Reread your Prereading Journal Entry. In what senses was visiting this school like a visit to a foreign country or culture? Revisit the school and revise your Prereading Journal Entry to describe both the school and your reactions to it, as Lee does.

Welcome to Willham!

JENNIFER SCHMITT
(1971–   )

PREREADING JOURNAL ENTRY

Visit a public place, restaurant, lobby, business, or mall near where you live. Observe the people and activity at different times of the day. Describe how the personality of the place changes from morning to evening.

Jennifer Schmitt, a mathematics major at Oklahoma State University, wrote her observing essay for Francesca McNease about the social life in the mezzanine in the Willham residence complex. "When we were given the assignment to observe a scene and describe it," Schmitt explains, "the lobby immediately came to mind. The evening I chose was a typical weekend night when people were going out to have fun or just hanging around." She focuses on the nightclerk, Gus, who takes the incoming calls, watches couples come and go, handles the pizza delivery chaos, and wiles away the small hours of the night playing Monopoly. By three o'clock in the morning, the drama at the "mez" winds down, but Schmitt knows the play will reopen the following night with different characters playing the same roles on the same set.

Willham Complex is full of interesting and unique 1 people. The huge mezzanine downstairs in the complex is basically the center of social life within the residence hall. Everyone has to go to the "mez" for some reason, even if it is only to walk out the front doors, and the front desk is the center of all the activity. People are in the "mez" to eat, to study, to meet people, to buy snacks, to watch people, to socialize, to pick up pizza, or to get their mail. There are so many different situations that come up and such a variety of people around, that the mezzanine is never boring to anyone who watches closely.

It is eleven o'clock Friday night, and the desk clerk 2 has been on duty for an hour. He just found out he has to work an extra shift for a clerk who is sick. He is going to be here until six o'clock in the morning. He is not a happy camper. "Willham Complex, this is Gus. May I help you?" He answers the phone in a pleasant voice. At the same time his hands gracefully count out quarters for a red-head getting ready to do her laundry. The coins make a pleasant clinking noise together. He then goes to the phone book and quickly thumbs through the pages to find a number for the person on the other end of the phone line. Immediately after he hangs up, a studious guy wants to check out the key to a study room and two girls want to check in the equipment from the pool table. The phone rings again in the middle of all the chaos. As Gus busies himself with his duties at the desk and looks forward to another seven hours of this, life in the rest of the mezzanine goes on without noticing.

The big-screen television blares the music of MTV 3 from above. The electronic noises from the video games can barely be heard in the background. People walk by on their way out. They are going to clubs, bars, or parties. They have bright, shining eyes from the excitement of it all as they giggle and talk on their way out. The strong smell of perfume and after-shave lingers in the air. There are also people coming back already. Some walk in the doors talking about this movie or that one, so I guess that is probably where they have been. Couples come in holding hands, and head up to their rooms together. One couple comes in not even looking at one another. They stalk toward one of the patio tables and begin "discussing" their relationship. As the two glare at each other, the words fly and the volume grows until the guy gets up and practically throws his chair across the room, then stomps off to his own room. The girl puts her head in her hands and her dark hair falls like a curtain around her face. "Are you all right?" It is Gus. He is worried about her and it shows in the concerned tone in his voice. She smiles shakily, comes over to the desk, and talks to us. She rubs her bare arms against the cool air coming in the doors.

The Pizza Shuttle man, looking harried, comes in with 4 four pizzas, followed immediately by a calm Domino's Pizza man with two pizzas. The smell fills the whole mezzanine. Within minutes two girls in pajamas and with their hair in curlers, one girl in sweats, and three guys in shorts mob the delivery men. Money and pizzas quickly change hands, the pizzas disappear, and the delivery men walk back out the front doors.

The electronic ringing of the phone echoes through 5 the "mez" again. "Willham Complex, this is Gus. May I help you?" Now someone wants a VCR. The television has been turned off or down or something and someone is playing beautifully on one of the pianos upstairs. The sound is almost celestial. The girl who had a fight with her boyfriend finally wanders off to her own room. Another girl wants some quarters and then rushes off to get a Diet Coke. Two guys acting like they know everything and they own the world want to check out the pool table equipment. "They must be freshmen!" comments Gus after they leave.

It is now 12:30 A.M., only five and one half hours until 6 Gus gets off work. Gus calls his neighbor and gets him to bring stuff down from his room. Mike brings down a whole box of grown-up "toys." Gus starts juggling red, yellow, and blue colored balls. He has to be very tired if he has to do that to stay awake. He starts yelling at anyone he knows and gets about six people around the desk. They all get a game of Monopoly going. The television is back on upstairs and someone is cooking popcorn. The smell drifts through the air reminding me of the smell of a movie theater. The cool air rushes in the door every time someone comes in or goes out.

Around 1:30 A.M. people really start coming back from 7 the clubs and parties. Three girls come staggering in laughing and talking just too loudly. One of the girls flips her long, blond hair back over her shoulder, throws herself off balance, and almost falls. Two girls and a guy come in basically sober, but carrying a girl who has passed out. One whole floor of guys went out together tonight. They come in strongly supporting their president so he can walk. If they were not there, he would be on the floor, crawling, if he was moving at all.

By three o'clock everything has basically quieted down. 8 Most people are home in bed or will be soon, if they are coming home at all. The Monopoly game has been over for quite a while and the phone has not rung in almost an hour. Gus still has three hours of work to stay awake for, but he will be all right. I am heading up to sleep, too. The "mez" is nearly deserted except for Gus, two guys watching MTV, and four foreign students from Mexico who cannot speak English. The night has been like a strange play with sets and props and a script. I somehow get the feeling that it has been played out thousands of times before and will be played out many more. It is the same set, the same props, the same words; only the characters are different.

QUESTIONS ON MEANING

1. List everything that the Gus, the night clerk, does in Schmitt's essay.

2. Where is Schmitt when she makes her observations of the mezzanine activities?

QUESTIONS ON PURPOSE AND STRATEGY

1. What does Schmitt learn from her mezzanine observations? Where in the essay does she explain her discovery?

2. In what ways is Gus the focal point of this essay? In what sense is Gus just another character in the play?

QUESTIONS ON AUDIENCE AND LANGUAGE

1. What kind of reader would find this essay interesting?
2. What senses does Schmitt appeal to in her description? Find examples of her sensory detail.

QUESTIONS FOR WRITING AND DISCUSSION

1. Based on Schmitt's essay, write a job description for the night clerk at Willham mezzanine.
2. Reread your prewriting journal entry. If appropriate, choose one of the people you describe and organize your observations around that person, as Schmitt organizes her essay around the night clerk, Gus.

Fetal Pig

ELIZABETH WESTON

(1967–   )

PREREADING JOURNAL ENTRY

Write for five minutes about a class that was initially difficult or traumatic but later became one of your favorite subjects. Explain the causes of your fear. What events changed your attitude?

Elizabeth Weston is a student at Colorado State University majoring in Zoology. She is coeditor of the college yearbook and, encouraged by her teacher Margaret Sweany, hopes to become a "science writer for a news organization, translating scientific discoveries into terms the general public can understand." In "Fetal Pig," Weston selects a subject she describes as "one of the worst but most enlightening experiences" she has had in college. Required by her zoology course to dissect a fetal pig preserved in formaldehyde, Weston musters her courage and enters the fascinating world of biology.

ONE WRITER'S OBSERVING PROCESS

Fetal Pig Sketch

Rough Draft

I remember being a sociology major as a
timid freshman. Now there was logic behind
this choice, I hated science passionately.
I don't know exactly when I began to detest
the subject. All I know is by college I
wanted nothing to do with it.
 Colorado State had other plans for me.
The science requirement was staring me
straight in the face. Like many science
haters, I decided to get the worst over
early. Zoology 110 was my fate. I vividly
recall crying before laboratory after
hearing we had to dissect a fetal pig.
Still I went. There it was in front of me,
a tiny bluish grey baby pig in the fetal
position. Barely developed ears held
tightly to its large head, just above never
opened eyes. That was it, the tears flooded
my vision. I tried to cover it up, but the
instructor spotted me from across the huge,
cold lab. I felt so ridiculous and childish
as he approached, but this scientist
assured me that compassion was a rare but
exceptional trait of a scientist. Suddenly
the formaldehyde didn't make me nauseated,
and the dissection gave me a chance to see
first hand one of the most incredible
things this world offers, life. From that
day forward, my curiosity about life and
the workings of our world has exploded. All
thanks to a scientist with that rare
quality of compassion.

Final Draft

Fetal Pig

I hate science. Every slimy, theoretical, mathematical ı
experiment makes my skin crawl. I'm not certain what

events led to this conclusion, all I know is that I want nothing to do with it. Colorado State had other plans for me. The science requirement was staring me straight in the face, and unfortunately, no amount of whining or pleading seemed to change the minds of advisors. I reluctantly chose Zoology 110 as my fate.

So here I sit slumped over the hard black table top 2 marked for posterity by students long since gone. My emotions pass through every extreme but somehow always avoid that content feeling when you know everything will work out. A slow glance around the room reveals cold stainless steel instruments that belong in a B grade horror movie. A human skeletal replica looms in the far corner as if to remind us of our frailty and to keep a watchful eye to prevent any grotesque acts that might be attempted in the name of black humor. I pull my gaze to the front of the laboratory where a stocky man, wearing a starched lab coat oddly matched with green Converse sneakers, is preparing to speak.

"Today we will dissect the fetal pig." 3

A headline flashes in my mind, "Girl Sickened By 4 Dead Pig Fails College." My heartbeat quickens; I am actually frightened.

Mustering all the courage I can, I timidly reach 5 into the bucket holding the tiny corpses. I hold my breath and turn my head so I won't be asphyxiated by the nauseating formaldehyde fumes. Looking at my motionless rival, I feel sympathy for the never born baby now held in a plastic bag womb. Utilizing my forceps I remove the piglet from the baggie. Its barely formed ears are pinned snugly against its head as if this world was far too loud. Never opened eyes sleep serenely over the snout, the smooth tongue protruding. Uncalcified bones twist painfully, creating distorted limbs too weak to ever support the infant's weight, and the tail is only an accumulation of tissue lacking all resemblance to the characteristically spiraled pig's tail. Curled in fetal position, like a human baby,

I'd believe it was only napping if only the skin weren't so icy and blue.

The innocence of my victim paralyzes me except 6 for the warm tear I feel trickle down my cheek. Another breaks free from the boundary of my eye. Embarrassed, I hurriedly attempt to wipe them away. Too late, the instructor has spotted me. He strides across the room and ends up at my side.

"You know, Elizabeth, compassion is a rare quality 7 in a scientist, but definitely an exceptional one."

His words hang precariously in my mind. Could 8 this be true? I let the thought sink into my head. Now for some reason the formaldehyde isn't quite so mal-odorous and the skin not as clammy and lifeless.

"If you'd prefer you can just watch the dissection." 9 The TA suggests kindly.

"That's okay, I think I'd like to do this."   10

Methodically I cut the thick skin revealing the 11 wonders that reside within. My curiosity peaks with each new discovery. Uninflated lungs ready to fill with air, a perfect miniature heart, tiny kidneys and liver waiting to fulfill their intended functions: the tiny body is miraculous. As the end of the two hour period draws near, I gently place the baby back into the bag and tenderly lay him in the bucket. Aware that I have uncovered something that fascinates me, I smile and turn to see the instructor who nods at me with a grin.

QUESTIONS ON MEANING

1. Where does Weston reveal her original attitude toward science and dissection?

2. What changes her attitude?

QUESTIONS ON PURPOSE AND STRATEGY

1. Is Weston's purpose to describe in detail the fetal pig or to tell you about herself? Explain, referring to specific sentences in the essay.

2. What specific details or images convey Weston's sense of fear and hatred? What specific details communicate her sense of wonder?

3. Should Weston describe her instructor and give their dialogue in a descriptive essay about a fetal pig? Explain.

QUESTIONS ON AUDIENCE AND LANGUAGE

1. Weston begins her essay by describing her hatred of science. Does her introduction make you want to read further? Why or why not?

2. In paragraph 11, should Weston describe in more detail her dissection of the pig? What other details should she give to convey her sense of wonder?

QUESTIONS FOR DISCUSSION AND WRITING

1. Explain how Weston might respond to animal rights activists who suggest that fetal pig dissections are cruel and should be done with computer simulations?

2. Following Weston's model, recall a discovery you made about science, either by yourself or in a science class. Recreate the conditions as closely as possible and observe more closely what is happening. Describe this event, using both your memories and observations.

4

REMEMBERING

To write one's life is to live it twice. . . .

—Patricia Hampl, author of *A Romantic Education*

Memory teaches me what I know of these matters; the boy reminds the adult.

—Richard Rodriguez, author of *Hunger of Memory*

I have a photo of the three of us when I was twelve: my mother, my sister Susie, and I, on a big chintz sofa, each on a separate cushion, leaning away from one another with big spaces in between.

—Nancy Friday, author of *My Mother/My Self*

Remembering, like observing, is an initial purpose for writing and learning as well as a strategy that serves other purposes. Sometimes our initial purpose—remembering—remains our final purpose: We write about our past experiences to share a part of our life with another person. At other times, remembering leads to some larger purpose for our writing: We use specific examples from our personal experience to explain what something is, to propose a solution to a problem, or to explore a difficult question.

Personal experience makes writing effective in two ways. First, it enables the reader to *connect* with the writer and his or her experiences. When it triggers a similar experience, the reader thinks, "Yes, I can identify with that." If the reader hasn't had a similar experience, showing the experience helps the reader visualize and understand: "That hasn't happened to me, but I can see how important it was." Second, specific examples from personal experience act as *evidence* to illustrate a point. In a scientific experiment, researchers prove a point by demonstrating that in 95 out of 100 cases, a vaccine prevented a certain disease. In an essay, writers use personal experience not to prove that something happens in all or most cases, but to *show that it did happen in this one case.* Readers may be convinced if the example fairly represents other similar cases. A writer explaining how drinking causes automobile accidents, for example, needs to give just one vivid illustration to persuade a reader that tragedy can result.

In this chapter, however, the focus is on the autobiographical narrative itself. Each essay tells a brief story, but it focuses on some *main idea* that shows how an experience changed the writer. In the best essays, writers do not *tell* their readers about the events—they *show* the events. They re-create the places, scenes, people, and dialogue so that the story itself reveals that main idea.

STRATEGIES FOR READING AND WRITING ABOUT REMEMBERING

As you read the remembering essays in this chapter and recall events from your own life to write about, keep the following key features in mind.

Use of detailed observation of people, places, and events. Effective remembering essays build on observing strategies. Writers recall *sights, sounds, smells, tactile feelings, tastes.* Writers use actual or re-created *dialogue.* They give actual *names* of people and places—even if they have changed the names in their account.

Creation of specific scenes set at an actual time and place. Instead of describing the outcome of an important event or describing a habitual action ("We used to sit in class a lot and cause trouble"), writers re-create an event by setting it in specific *time* and *space:* In his essay reprinted in this chapter, "Shame," Dick Gregory sets the scene vividly for his readers: "It was on a Thursday. I was sitting in the back of the room, in a seat with a chalk circle drawn around it."

Use of important changes, contrasts, or conflicts. The main idea or dominant impression in autobiographical accounts often grows out of *changes* in people or places, *conflicts* between people, or *contrasts* between the past and the present.

Focus on connections between past events, people, or places and the present. Often in autobiographical accounts, the main point crystallizes when the writer makes *connections* between the past and the present. Writing about his experiences in school, Gregory says, "I guess I would have gotten over Helene by summertime, but something happened in that classroom that made her face hang in front of me for the next twenty-two years."

Creation of a main idea or dominant impression. The details, specific scenes, accounts of changes or conflicts, and connections between past and present should point to a *single main idea* or dominant impression for the passage as a whole.

READING A REMEMBERING ESSAY

Reading other people's accounts of important people, places, and events in their lives may be the most enjoyable kind of reading we do. Everyone likes to see how other people live and discover how their lives are different from ours—and yet the same, too. Curiosity propels us into the story, and the power of the narrative keeps us interested.

After a first or second reading, however, we may want to tell our story, to make it as entertaining, suspenseful, vivid, or dramatic as the account we just read. At this point, we reread the account *with a writer's eye,* looking for those strategies and tricks that make that particular narrative effective. The following strategies will help you understand the craft of story telling.

Prereading

Think about your own life. Do the Prereading Journal Entry. Writing about your own life *before* you read will help you enjoy the passage more and see the author's strategies for writing an autobiographical essay. In addition, read about the author, his or her life, and the time and place the author describes.

First Reading

The first reading should be for your enjoyment. If you come across an unknown word, underline it. If you are puzzled by a passage, put a "?" in the margin. If you read a vivid or interesting passage, put a "!" in the margin, but keep reading. Highlight or place a wavy line under or next to key passages, but don't allow these marks to detract from your enjoyment of the story. *At the end of the first reading, write a sentence describing your initial impression.*

Annotated Reading

As you reread the essay, read to understand what happened. Don't just highlight or underline passages—write your *reactions* and *questions* in the margin: "This scene is especially memorable" or "Why does the writer describe this incident?" Also read with a writer's eye. Bracket [ ] and label the key features of writing about memories. Finally, note in the margin any sentences that seem to give the writer's *main idea* or dominant impression for the passage as a whole. As necessary, look up definitions of any unfamiliar words.

Collaborative Reading

In a small group or in your class as a whole, share your reading experiences and annotations. Trade journal entries and discuss each other's experiences. Then exchange your books and read each other's annotations. Your group or class should discuss the various annotations and then agree on the ones that illustrate *consensus* reactions to the essay. One person in the group or class should record in the margin the best annotations from the group or class. At the bottom of the essay, write out the *main idea or dominant impression* created by the essay. After compiling a collective annotation of the essay, list ideas, questions, and interpretations for further reading or writing about the essay. A group or class recorder should write down at least two such ideas or questions.

WRITING A REMEMBERING ESSAY

Writing a remembering essay requires much more than just remembering. In your mind, memories are vivid sets of pictures. To show these pictures to your reader, however, you must re-create each image and scene, painstakingly, frame by frame. Imagine that you are a Disney cartoonist: You must draw dozens of separate sketches which will then be flipped through in a matter of a second or two, creating the illusion for your readers of a technicolor trip through your past.

As you write about your memories, decide which scenes or sketches should be fully drawn, set in an actual time and place, and which should be presented as habitual actions, blurred and impressionistic. Specific scenes are those that occur only once. They happen on a specific day. They re-create key events by using detailed description and actual dialogue. They may even present the thoughts of the central character.

Use your observing skills to set the scene for specific events. Often, just a detail or two, a specific sight, sound, or smell will give your scene an authentic ring. In "Shame," Gregory describes the chair he sat in with a chalk circle drawn around it. He describes how he was shaking, scared to death. He describes the teacher, opening her book and calling out names alphabetically. Without these details in your sketches, readers will not see a vivid picture.

Finally, keep arranging and rearranging these pictures until they tell a story, focused by some dominant impression, main idea, or central discovery. They may present some conflict—and then resolve it. They may present a question—and then show your answer or discovery. They may show a scene from the past and then contrast that past with the present.

Choosing a Subject for a Remembering Essay

Write an essay about an important person, place, event, scene, or object in your life. Your purpose is to *re-create* key scenes containing some conflict/resolution and, in the process, show *why* these memories are important. Begin by assuming that you are writing down these memories for a family member or good friend.

As you begin writing and planning, look for an angle or a way to **focus** your experience. Your essay will be about yourself, but it may be about only one day, or perhaps only an hour. It may focus on a certain person, a place that is important, or an object. Or, instead of focusing on one thing, look for several experiences linked by a **single thread:** three days at school, two different but really similar friends, or three weird but prophetic dreams. Finally, look for an **uncommon subject** or a **unique point of view** that has the power to surprise your reader.

Collecting Memories and Ideas

Whether or not you have a possible topic, try some of the following collecting strategies. If you already have a topic, these strategies may help you remember more. If you don't have a topic, they may suggest one.

Go to the library and look in a popular magazine issue published when you were five, ten, or fifteen years old. What memories do the articles and even the advertisements evoke?

Draw a sketch of a place, person, or object you're writing about. Or get out a map of a place you've visited and want to remember.

Dig out old pictures of yourself, family, or friends. Write a journal entry about a picture that catches your attention.

If possible, visit a business, a school, a house where you used to live or work. What personal memories does it evoke? Then observe it objectively: What does it probably look like to a stranger?

Interview friends or family members about your topic. What do they remember about these events?

Try brainstorming: Just begin writing about your subject and write nonstop, whatever comes into your mind. Don't worry about whether it really makes sense; just keep writing.

Do a looping exercise: Brainstorm for five minutes. Then stop and reread what you have written. Under-line the sentence or idea that is most interesting. Then write for five more minutes, using that sentence as your starting point. Stop and reread your second brainstorm. Underline the most interesting sentence. Use that sentence as the starting point for your last five-minute brainstorm.

For clustering, start with a clean piece of paper. Write your person, place, or scene in the center of the page and circle it. Draw several inch-long spokes or lines out from that center circle. Draw a circle or oval at the end of each spoke. Then write in these circles whatever ideas, scenes, people, events, objects pop into your mind. Again, draw spokes out from several of these circles and write key words or phrases. Keep this clustering exercise going until you've identified several important scenes, people, places, or ideas. (See Nicolle Mircos's clustering exercise in Chapter 2, page 85.)

Shaping Your Remembering Essay

Several of the following shaping strategies may help you organize your memories. For each strategy, read the examples from the essays in this chapter and then write a few notes showing how each strategy might apply to your topic. After you have made some notes for each of these strategies, decide which one(s) work best for your topic.

Chronological Order. Usually writers follow a natural time order (A, B, and C), but you may wish to try a flashback or inverted order (B, A, and C)

In "Living in Two Cultures," Jeanne Wakatsuki Houston signals her natural time order with occasional phrases at the beginning of paragraphs.

In remembering myself as a small child. . . .
After the war . . . my world drastically changed.
As I passed puberty and grew more interested in boys. . . .
When I met my blond samurai. . . .
When we were first married. . . .
When my mother visited us, as she often did. . . .
How my present attitudes will affect my children . . . remains to be seen.

Conflict/Resolution. Your remembering essay may have one central conflict or it may have several related conflicts, each showing your main idea. These conflicts may be resolved immediately, or resolved only with the passage of time, or only partially resolved. *As you work with your own topic, identify the conflict(s) and resolution(s) contained in your memories.*

In "Drowning 1954," Garrison Keillor reveals his fear of drowning, the central conflict in his story: "The truth was that my cousin's death had instilled in me a terrible fear. . . ." Keillor only partially resolves this conflict when suddenly, almost inexplicably, he learns to swim. But when he thinks of his own son, "his eyes closed tight, and his pale slender body . . . tense as a drawn bow," the old fear surges back in Keillor's mind, and he hears the "Big Snapper" bellowing, "You have fifteen minutes. Get changed."

Comparison/Contrast. At the heart of a remembering essay is a comparison or contrast between the person you were then and the person you are now. Look for similarities or common threads between people, places, things, images, or memories. Look also for those key changes in another person, place, thing, or attitude.

In "Living in Two Cultures," Houston contrasts her old family traditions with the expectations of her Caucasian husband: "When we first married I wondered if I should lay out his socks and underwear every morning like my mother used to do for my father. But my brothers' warning would float up from the past: don't be subservient to Caucasian men or they will take advantage."

Image. Look for key images that may connect or illuminate scenes. Once you've found an image that evokes your feelings or experiences, you may be able to use it several times to organize and shape your essay. In "Shame," Dick Gregory says he is "pregnant with poverty." In "Drowning 1954," Keillor recalls the lifeguard in his image of the "Big Snapper." Used several times, images can shape an entire essay.

Tone and Voice. *Tone* is the writer's attitude toward his or her subject. In a remembering essay, a writer may write with a nostalgic tone, or a bitter tone, or a philosophical, accepting tone. *Voice* is the writer's personality as revealed in the essay. In a remembering essay, writers sometimes use an adult voice, reflecting on their experiences, or sometimes a child's voice. A writer's voice may be emotional, conversational, and colloquial, or it may be impersonal and detached. Tone and voice overlap, but together they help a reader re-create the attitude and personality of the writer.

In "Shame," we occasionally hear the voice of a child in Dick Gregory's account: "The teacher thought I was stupid. Couldn't spell, couldn't read, couldn't do arithmetic. Just stupid." In contrast, Richard Rodriguez's voice in "Gains and Losses" is much more sophisticated: "Again and again in the days following, increasingly angry, I was obliged to hear my mother and father: 'Speak to us *en ingles.*' (*Speak.*) Only then did I determine to learn classroom English."

Dialogue. Wherever possible, *use actual dialogue* to recreate key scenes from your memories. Even if you cannot accurately reproduce conversation from years ago, your remembered dialogue will re-create what was important to you. (When you write dialogue, use quotation marks and indent each time a different character speaks.)

Gregory's dialogue in "Shame" recreates the climax of his story:

> I stood up and raised my hand.
> "What is it now?"
> "You forgot me."
> She turned toward the blackboard. "I don't have time to be playing with you, Richard."
> 'My Daddy said he'd . . .'
> "Sit down, Richard, you're disturbing the class."
> "My Daddy said he'd give . . . fifteen dollars."
> She turned and looked mad. "We are collecting this money for you and your kind, Richard Gregory. If your Daddy can give fifteen dollars you have no business being on relief."

Drafting Your Remembering Essay

After you've collected some possible characters, scenes, or places for your essay and tried several of the shaping strategies, you are ready to write a draft. Begin by re-reading your notes and ideas. If the first five minutes of writing does not seem to be going in the right direction, save what you've written and start again. Once you begin writing, try to keep writing—without stopping to look up spelling or check punctuation. If you get stuck, go back and reread what you have written and pick up the thread.

Revising Your Remembering Essay

Use feedback from your readers to help you revise, but if you are in doubt, trust your own judgment. This essay must be your story, not theirs. However, if they don't get your point or cannot vividly see key scenes, then work more on re-creating those memories on the page. As you revise, keep the following tips in mind.

Reexamine your purpose and audience. Are you doing what you intended? Should you write for a different audience?

Reread your essay for dominant impression or main idea. Did your readers understand why this memory was important for you? You probably don't want a flat statement explaining the "moral" of the story, but the importance of the narrative must be clear.

Look for specific scenes, set in time and place. Avoid just telling about key events. Show them. Check the essay for specific scenes, located in time and space, that use actual dialogue and detailed observation.

Where is the central conflict and resolution? Can it be made clearer for the reader? Is it *shown* (not just told) in the specific scenes?

Have a reader describe the essay's voice and tone. Does your reader's description match what you intended to convey? Should you change any sentences to make your intended voice or tone clearer?

Edit and proofread the essay. Reread the essay for clarity of sentences, spelling, punctuation, grammar, or problems in mechanics.

Postscript for your Remembering Essay

When you've finished your essay, write a journal entry that answers the following questions about your writing process. Hand in this entry with all the drafts of your essay.

1. What idea or collecting strategy helped you decide on your topic?

2. Which of the shaping strategies worked best for your essay? Which strategies didn't work? Why not?

3. What problems did you have during your drafting? What worked out well?

4. What worked best about your writing process? What was just busy work and got in your way?

5. If you had another day to work on this essay, what would you change?

Shame

DICK GREGORY

(1932–   )

PREREADING JOURNAL TOPIC

Freewrite for five minutes about an experience in school that caused you embarrassment, disappointment, or disgrace.

STUDENT JOURNAL RESPONSES

I was in grade school when it happened. We had been studying our "times" tables for a few weeks, and on the day it happened, my teacher told us to get out a pencil and paper. He said we were having a quiz. I had never heard the term before, but I didn't think much about it. After all, I was in fourth grade. Anyway, I was stumped on one of the answers, so I looked! My teacher promptly scolded me for cheating and took my paper. To this day I have a hard time with my "times" tables. I look back on that day with a mixture of feelings. Shame for my actions and anger for the teacher's insensitivity.

I can laugh about this now, but back in eighth grade it wasn't too funny. I was taking a creative writing course and our assignment was to write a short story. I enjoyed playing around with words even then. And creating a brand new, unique world — through creative writing — was one of my favorite pastimes. Anyhow, I wrote this short story about a suicidal adolescent. I liked it. The rest of the students in the class (and the teacher), however, did not. They thought it was a little too weird. The teacher gave me a "B" on the story, and I got steamed. I think I created a scene during class. The entire event was pretty embarrassing. Funny thing, I look back on it now and the story had several flaws, the worst being point of view: It was told in the first person who would eventually commit suicide.

Dick Gregory—track star, civil rights activist, candidate for the mayor of Chicago, and vegetarian activist for the obese—is best known as the first black comedian to perform for white audiences. "Where else in the world but America," *he said of his 1960s Playboy Club performances,* "could I have lived in the worst neighborhoods, attended the worst schools, rode in the back of the bus, and got paid $5,000 a week just for talking about it?" *His books reflect his varied causes: From the* Back of the Bus *(1962),* No More Lies: The Myth and Reality of American History *(1971),* Dick Gregory's Political Primer *(1972), and* Dick Gregory's Natural Diet for Folks Who Eat *(1973).*

"Shame," a selection from Gregory's best-selling Nigger: An Autobiography *(1964), describes an episode from his childhood in St. Louis. "We ain't poor; we're just broke," Gregory's mother used to say, but "Shame" reveals the truth: "Poor is a state of mind you never grow out of." Reproduced in the margin are collaborative annotations by one group of students.*

SHAME

[I never learned hate at home, or shame. I had to go to school for that.] I was about seven years old when I got my first big lesson. I was in love with a little girl named Helene Tucker, a light-complexioned little girl with pigtails and nice manners. She was always clean and she was smart in school. I think I went to school then mostly to look at her. I brushed my hair and even got me a little old handkerchief. [It was a lady's handkerchief, but I didn't want Helene to see me wipe my nose on my hand.] [The pipes were frozen again, there was no water in the house, but I washed my socks and shirt every night. I'd get a pot, and go over to Mister Ben's grocery store, and stick my pot down into his soda machine. Scoop out some chopped ice.] By evening the ice melted to water for washing. I

Gregory's main idea   1

Good, specific details from his memory.

This is written in a younger style and vocabulary.

got sick a lot that winter because the fire would go out at night before the clothes were dry. In the morning I'd put them on, wet or dry, because they were the only clothes I had.

[Everybody's got a Helene Tucker, a symbol of everything you want.] I loved her for her goodness, her cleanness, her popularity. She'd walk down my street and my brothers and sisters would yell,["Here comes Helene,"]and I'd rub my[tennis sneakers on the back of my pants and wish my hair wasn't so nappy and the white folks' shirt fit me better.] I'd run out on the street. If I knew my place and didn't come too close, she'd wink at me and say hello. That was a good feeling.[Sometimes I'd follow her all the way home, and shovel the snow off her walk and try to make friends with her Momma and her aunts. I'd drop money on her stoop late at night on my way back from shining shoes in the taverns.]And she had a Daddy, and he had a good job. He was a paper hanger.

[I guess I would have gotten over Helene by summertime, but something happened in that classroom that made her face hang in front of me for the next twenty-two years.]When I played the drums in high school it was for Helene and when I broke track records in college it was for Helene and when I started standing behind microphones and heard applause I wished Helene could hear it, too. It wasn't until I was twenty-nine years old and married and making money that I finally got her out of my system. Helene was sitting in that classroom when I learned to be ashamed of myself.

[It was on a Thursday. I was sitting in the back of the room, in a seat with a chalk circle drawn around it. The idiot's seat, the trouble-maker's seat.]

[The teacher thought I was stupid. Couldn't spell, couldn't read, couldn't do arithmetic. Just

Shifts here from child to adult. 2

Dialogue and detail.

Show his love for Helene

Connection of past and present. 3

Specific scene! 4

Language mirrors seven-year old's mind. 5

stupid. Teachers were never interested in finding out that you couldn't concentrate because you were so hungry, because you hadn't had any breakfast.] All you could think about was noontime, would it ever come? Maybe you could sneak into the cloakroom and steal a bite of some kid's lunch out of a coat pocket. A bite of something.[Paste. You can't really make a meal of paste, or put it on bread for a sandwich, but sometimes I'd scoop a few spoonfuls out of the paste jar in the back of the room.] Pregnant people get strange tastes.[I was pregnant with poverty. Pregnant with dirt and pregnant with smells that made people turn away, pregnant with cold and pregnant with shoes that were never bought for me, pregnant with five other people in my bed and no Daddy in the next room, and pregnant with hunger.] Paste doesn't taste too bad when you're hungry.

too preachy about his poverty.

Paste: great image

Pregnant: image suggests a burden, not happiness.

    The teacher thought I was a troublemaker. [All she saw from the front of the room was a little black boy who squirmed in his idiot's seat and made noises and poked the kids around him. I guess she couldn't see a kid who made noises because he wanted someone to know he was there.]

6

Adult voice again.

Conflict, too.

    It was on a Thursday, the day before the Negro payday. The eagle always flew on Friday. The teacher was asking each student how much his father would give to the Community chest. On Friday night, each kid would get the money from his father, and on Monday he would bring it to the school.[I decided I was going to buy me a Daddy right then.] I had money in my pocket from shining shoes and selling papers, and whatever Helene Tucker pledged for her Daddy I was going to top it. And I'd hand the money right in. I wasn't going to wait until Monday to buy me a Daddy.

7

I want to know more about Richard's history. Why doesn't he have a daddy?

    I was shaking, scared to death. The teacher

8

opened her book and started calling out names alphabetically.

["Helene Tucker?"

"My daddy said he'd give two dollars and fifty cents."

"That's very nice, Helene. Very, very nice indeed."]

That made me feel pretty good. It wouldn't take too much to top that. I had almost three dollars in dimes and quarters in my pocket. I stuck my hand in my pocket and held onto the money, waiting for her to call my name. But the teacher closed her book after she called everybody else in the class.

[I stood up and raised my hand.

"What is it now?"

"You forgot me."]

She turned toward the blackboard. "I don't have time to be playing with you, Richard."

"My Daddy said he'd . . ."

"Sit down, Richard, you're disturbing the class."

'My Daddy said he'd give . . . fifteen dollars."

She turned around and looked mad. "We are collecting this money for [you and your kind,] Richard Gregory. If your Daddy can give fifteen dollars you have no business being on relief."

"I got it right now, I got it right now, my Daddy gave it to me to turn in today, my Daddy said . . ."

"And furthermore," she said, looking right at me, her nostrils getting big and her lips getting thin and her eyes opening wide, "we know you don't have a Daddy."

Helene Tucker turned around, her eyes full of tears. She felt sorry for me. Then I couldn't see her too well because I was crying, too.

"Sit down, Richard."

Handwritten margin notes:
- Dialogue very effective. Brings the past alive [9] [10]
- [11]
- [12]
- [13]
- Major conflict. [14] [15]
- [16]
- [17]
- [18]
- [19]
- Refers to his being black and on welfare [20]
- [21]
- [22]
- Richard doesn't want his "love" to pity him. [23]
- [24]

And I always thought the teacher kind of liked me. She always picked me to wash the blackboard on Friday, after school. That was a big thrill, it made me feel important. If I didn't wash it, come Monday the school might not function right.

Did the teacher like him or only pity him?   25

"Where are you going, Richard?"   26

I walked out of school that day, and for a long time I didn't go back very often.[There was shame there.]

Identifies shame with school.   27

Main idea: shame is a terrible thing for a child to learn from a teacher and a terrible source of motivation for life.

QUESTIONS ON MEANING

1. Is the source of Richard's shame his poverty, his lack of a father, his "troublemaking" behavior, his teacher, his love for Helene, or some combination? Explain.

2. What passages best reflect the teacher's attitude toward Richard?

QUESTIONS ON PURPOSE AND STRATEGY

1. What are Gregory's purposes in this selection? To describe a traumatic moment from his childhood? To criticize his teacher and the school system? To explain the effects of poverty and racial prejudice? Explain.

2. Which paragraphs show Gregory *re-creating* key events from his past life? Which paragraphs show Gregory describing *typical or habitual* actions in the past? Which paragraphs show Gregory *reflecting* on those events?

3. Are the reflective or "adult" parts of this story told in a different *style* (sentences, vocabulary, voice) than the parts that re-create actual events from Gregory's life? Explain, referring to specific passages.

4. Create a time line for this story. First, list in chronological order all the events referred to or described in the story— including events that occur before the story begins. Where on this time line does Gregory's story open?

QUESTIONS ON AUDIENCE AND LANGUAGE

1. Describe Gregory's intended audience.

2. Gregory frequently uses sentence fragments in this selection: "The idiot's seat, the troublemaker's seat." "Couldn't spell, couldn't read, couldn't do arithmetic. Just stupid." Are sentence fragments appropriate in this essay? What effect do they have on readers?

3. In what year did these events probably take place? What words and references date these events?

QUESTIONS FOR DISCUSSION AND WRITING

1. In "Why I Write," George Orwell says, "Looking back through my work, I see that it is invariably where I lacked a *political* purpose that I wrote lifeless books. . . ." Does Gregory have a political purpose for his essay?

2. Rewrite the key scene in Gregory's class without using dialogue. What does dialogue add that a descriptive account lacks? What can you add in a descriptive account that dialogue doesn't present?

3. Reread your Prereading Journal Entry. Does that incident have a potential political point? Could you use your account to make a larger point about the use of power in families, schools, or society? Revise your journal entry into a longer account about that incident in your life.

Competition

NANCY FRIDAY

(1937–   )

PREREADING JOURNAL ENTRY

Describe one specific incident from your life that shows
how *competition* with siblings, parents, or friends affected
your personality, behavior, or ambition. Be sure to describe
when and where it happened, who the key people were,
and what the short- and long-term effects were.

Nancy Friday wrote her autobiography, My Mother/My Self *(1977),
with a distinctive twist: In the process of re-creating her own life, she
interviewed more than 300 women about their relationships with their
daughters or mothers. Friday discovered that mothers and daughters both
"feel inappropriately guilty—guilty for what they could have done, or
think they should have done or been, and guilty for wanting emotional
independence." Friday's other publications reflect her interest in psychology, sexual fantasies, and family relationships:* My Secret Garden
(1973), Men in Love, Male Sexual Fantasies *(1981), and* Jealousy
(1985).

In "Competition," an excerpt from My Mother/My Self, *Friday
describes how her ambitions and self-identity grew out of the competition
between herself and her sister Susie for her mother's attention and between
all three women for her grandfather's approval. "The competitive drive
that made me so self-sufficient," Friday explains, "was fired by more
than jealousy of my sister. If my mother wasn't going to acknowledge
me, her father would."*

Although I didn't realize it at the time, my mother 1
was getting prettier. My sister was a beauty. My adolescence
was the time of our greatest estrangement.

I have a photo of the three of us when I was twelve: 2 my mother, my sister Susie, and I, on a big chintz sofa, each on a separate cushion, leaning away from one another with big spaces in between. I grew up fired with a sense of family spirit, which I loved and needed, with aunts and uncles and cousins under the omnipotent umbrella of my grandfather. "All for one and one for all," he would say at summer reunions, and no one took it more seriously than I. I would have gone to war for any one of them, and believed they would do the same for me. But within our own little nucleus, the three of us didn't touch much.

Now, when I ask her why, my mother sighs and says 3 she supposes it was because that was how she was raised. I remember shrinking from her Elizabeth Arden night-cream kiss, mumbling from under the blanket that yes, I had brushed my teeth. I had not. I had wet the toothbrush in case she felt it, feeling that would get even with her. For what? The further we all get from childhood, the more physically affectionate we try to be with one another. But we are still shy after all these years.

I was a late bloomer, like my mother. But my mother 4 bloomed so late, or had such a penetrating early frost, that she believed it even less than I would in my turn. When she was a freckled sixteen and sitting shyly on her unfortunate hands, her younger sister was already a famous beauty. That is still the relationship between them. Grandmothers both, in their eyes my aunt is still the sleek-haired belle of the ball, immaculately handsome on a horse. My mother's successes do not count. They will argue at 2:00 A.M. over whether one of my aunt's many beaux ever asked my mother out. My mother could never make up a flattering story about herself. I doubt that she so much as heard the nice things men told her once she had grown into the fine-looking woman who smiles at me in family photos. But she always gives in to my aunt, much I'm sure as she gave in to the old self-image after my father died. He—that one splendidly handsome man— may have picked her out from all the rest, but his death just a few years later must have felt like some punishment for having dared to believe for a moment that her father was wrong: who could possibly want her? She still blushes at a compliment.

I think she was at her prettiest in her early thirties. I 5 was twelve and at my nadir. Her hair had gone a delicate auburn red and she wore it brushed back from her face in soft curls. Seated beside her and Susie, who inherited a raven version of her beautiful hair, I look like an adopted person. But I had already defended myself against my looks. They were unimportant. There was a distance between me and the mirror commensurate with the growing distance between me and my mother and sister. My success with my made-up persona was proof: I didn't need them. My titles at school, my awards and achievements, so bolstered my image of myself that until writing this book I genuinely believed that I grew up feeling sorry for my sister. What chance had she alongside The Great Achiever and Most Popular Girl in the World? I even worked up some guilt about outshining her. Pure survival instinct? My dazzling smile would divert the most critical observer from comparing me to the cute, petite girls with whom I grew up. I switched the contest: don't look at my lank hair, my 5'10", don't notice that my right eye wanders bizarrely (though the eye doctor said it was useless to keep me in glasses); watch me tap dance, watch me win the game, let me make you happy! When I describe myself in those days my mother laughs. "Oh, Nancy, you were such a darling little girl." But I wasn't little any more.

I think my sister, Susie, was born beautiful, a fact that 6 affected my mother and me deeply, though in different ways. I don't think it mattered so much until Susie's adolescence. She turned so lush one ached to look at her. Pictures of Susie then remind me of the young Elizabeth Taylor in *A Place in the Sun*. One has to almost look away from so much beauty. It scared my mother to death. Whatever had gone on between them before came to a head and has never stopped. Their constant friction determined me to get away from this house of women, to be free of women's petty competitions, to live on a bigger scale. I left home eventually but I've never gotten away from feeling how wonderful to be so beautiful your mother can't take her eyes off you, even if only to nag.

I remember an amazing lack of any feeling about my 7 only sibling, with whom I shared a room for years, whose clothes were identical to mine until I was ten. Except for feelings of irritation when she tried to cuddle me when I was four, bursts of anger that erupted into fist fights which I started and won at ten, and after that, indifference, a calculated unawareness that has resulted in a terrible and sad absence of my sister in my life.

My husband says his sister was the only child his father 8 ever paid any attention to: "You have done to Susie what I did to my sister," he says. "You made her invisible." Me, jealous of Susie, who never won a single trophy or had as many friends as I? I must have been insanely jealous.

I only allowed myself to face it twice. Both times 9 happened in that twelfth year, when my usual defenses couldn't take the emotional cross currents of adolescence. When I did slash out it wasn't very glorious, no well-chosen words or contest on the tennis courts. I did it like a thief in the night. Nobody ever guessed it was I who poured the red nail polish down the front of Susie's new white eyelet evening dress the day of her first yacht club dance. When I stole her summer savings and threw her wallet down the sewer, mother blamed Susie for being so careless. I watched my sister accept the criticism with her mother's own resignation, and I felt some relief from the angry emotions that had hold of me.

When Susie went away to boarding school, I made 10 jokes about how glad I was to be rid of her. It was our first separation. Conflicting urges, angers, and envies were coming at me from every direction; I had nothing left over to handle my terrible feelings of loss at her going. It was the summer I was plagued by what I called "my thoughts."

I read every book in the house as a talisman against 11 thinking. I was afraid that if my brain were left idle for even one minute, these "thoughts" would take over. Perhaps I feared they already had. Was my sister's going away the fulfillment of my own murderous wishes against her? I wrote in my first and only diary: "Susie, come home, please come home!!!!!!! I'm sorry, I'm sorry!!!!!!!"

When I outgrew the Nancy Drew books for perfect 12 attendance at Sunday school, and the Girl Scout badges for such merits as selling the most rat poison door to door, I graduated to prizes at the community theater. I won a plastic wake-up radio for the I Speak for Democracy contest. I was captain of the athletic association, president of the student government, and had the lead in the class play, all in the same year. In fact, I wrote the class play. It might have been embarrassing, but no one else wanted these prizes. Scoring home runs and getting straight A's weren't high on the list of priorities among my friends. (The South takes all prizes for raising noncompetitive women.) In the few cases where anyone did give me a run for the money, I had an unbeatable incentive: my grandfather's applause. It was he for whom I ran.

I can't remember ever hearing my grandfather say to 13 my mother, "Well done, Jane." I can't remember my mother ever saying to my sister, "Well done, Susie." And I never gave my mother the chance to say it to me. She was the last to hear of my achievements, and when she did, it was not from me but from her friends. Did she really notice so little that I was leaving her out? Was she so hurt that she pretended not to care? My classmates who won second prize or even no prize at all asked their families to attend the award ceremonies. I, who won first prize, always, did so to the applause of no kin at all. Was I spiting her? I know I was spiting myself. Nothing would have made me happier than to have her there; nothing would induce me to invite her. It is a game I later played with men: "Leave!" I would cry, and when they did, "How could you hurt me so?" I'd implore.

If I deprived her of the chance to praise me, she never 14 criticized me. Criticism was the vehicle by which she could articulate her relationship to my sister. No matter what it was, Susie could never get it right—in my mother's eyes.

It continues that way to this day. Difficult as it is to think of my mother as competitive with anyone, how else could she have felt about her beautiful, ripe fourteen-year-old daughter? My mother was coming into her own mature, full bloom but perhaps that only made her more sensitive to the fact that Susie was simultaneously experiencing the same sexual flush. A year later, my mother remarried. Today, only the geography has changed: the argument begins as soon as they enter the same room. But they are often in the same room. They have never been closer.

How often the dinner table becomes the family battle- 15 ground. When I met Bill he had no table you could sit around in his vast bachelor apartment. The dinner table was where his father waged war; it was the one time the family was together. In Charleston, dinner was served at 2:00. I have this picture of our midday meals: Susie on my right, mother on my left, and me feeling that our cook, Ruth, had set this beautiful table for me alone.

No one else seemed to care about the golden squash, 16 the crisp chicken, the big silver pitcher of iced tea. While I proceeded to eat my way from one end of the table to the other, Susie and mother would begin: "Susie, that lipstick is too dark. . . . Must you pluck your eyebrows? . . . Why did you buy high-heeled, open-toe shoes when I told you to get loafers? . . . Those pointy bras make you look a, like a—" But my mother couldn't say the word. At this point one of them would leave the table in tears, while the other shuddered in despair at the sound of the slammed bedroom door. Meanwhile, I pondered my problem of whose house to play at that afternoon. I would finish both their desserts and be gone before Ruth had cleared the table. Am I exaggerating? Did it only happen once a week? Does it matter?

I was lucky to have escaped those devastating battles. 17 "I never had to worry about Nancy," my mother has always said. "She could always take care of herself." It became true. Only my husband has been allowed to see the extent of my needs. But the competitive drive that made me so self-sufficient was fired by more than jealousy of my sister. If my mother wasn't going to acknowledge me, her father would. If she couldn't succeed in his eyes, I would. It's my best explanation for all those years of trophies and presidencies, for my ability to "reach" my grandfather as my mother never could. I not only won what she had wanted all her life—his praise—I learned with the canniness of the young that this great towering man loved to be loved, to be touched. He couldn't allow himself to reach out first to those he loved most, but he couldn't resist an overture of affection.

I greeted his visits with embraces, took the kisses I 18 had won and sat at his feet like one of his Dalmations, while my sister stood shyly in the background and my mother waited for his criticism. But I was no more aware of competing with my mother than of being jealous of my sister. Two generations of women in my family have struggled for my grandfather's praise. Perhaps I became his favorite because he sensed I needed it most. The price I paid was that I had to beat my mother and my sister. I am still guilty for that.

In the stereotyping of the sexes, men are granted all 19 the competitive drives, women none. The idea of competitive women evokes disturbing images—the darker, dykey side of femininity, or cartoons of "ladies" in high heels, flailing at each other ineffectively with their handbags. An important step has been left out of our socialization: mother raises us to win people's love. She gives us no training in the emotions of rivalry that would lose it for us. With no practical experience in the rules that make competition safe, we fear its ferocity. Never having been taught to win, we do not know how to lose. Women are not raised to compete like gentlemen.

QUESTIONS ON MEANING

1. Describe the *sources* of tension, jealousy, or competition between Nancy and her mother, between Nancy's mother and Susie, and between Nancy and Susie.
2. According to Friday, what were her positive attributes and

achievements as a young woman? What did she think her shortcomings were?

3. How did Friday compete with her mother? How did she compete with her sister? Does she feel guilty for the actions she took? (Should she?)

QUESTIONS ON PURPOSE AND STRATEGY

1. Is Friday's purpose to describe her own adolescence? To confess her jealousy toward her sister and mother? To explain how competition helps to create a sense of identity? To argue that mothers should teach their daughters how to compete? Support your choice(s) with references to specific passages.

2. One of Friday's strategies is to alternate between describing the past and reflecting on its meaning. Reread the essay. Write "DES" in the margin next to a passage that describes the past and "REF" in the margin when Friday reflects on the meaning of her past. Write "DES/REF" if she seems to be doing both at the same time.

QUESTIONS ON AUDIENCE AND LANGUAGE

1. Does Friday address this essay more to daughters or to mothers? Are men likely to be interested in Friday's experiences? Explain.

2. Describe Friday's tone, her attitude toward her subject. Is she objectively interested in the truth? Does she want to confess her misdeeds and receive some measure of forgiveness? Is she angry about her past? Does she still want to attack her sister and mother?

3. Friday uses a sophisticated vocabulary. Did words such as "estrangement," "omnipotent," "nadir," "commensurate," and "persona" detract from or add to your understanding and appreciation of this essay?

QUESTIONS FOR DISCUSSION AND WRITING

1. Imagine that Friday's mother and sister have just read this passage. What might each person say to Friday? How might each of their lives parallel Friday's experiences?

2. In what ways does competitiveness between men differ from Friday's experiences? Is there more or less competition? Does it take the same or different forms?

3. Write your own essay on competition. Drawing on your own experience with your family and in school, decide whether competition has been a healthy or destructive force in your life.

Gains and Losses

RICHARD RODRIGUEZ

(1944–   )

PREREADING JOURNAL ENTRY

Recall an event in your life about which you have mixed emotions: The experience was painful, but it carried some benefits, too. Describe this incident to show what was beneficial and what was painful.

In Hunger of Memory: The Education of Richard Rodriguez *(1982), Richard Rodriguez focuses on a controversial political point. The son of Mexican-American immigrants, Rodriguez learned English in the Sacramento school system, received an M.A. degree from Stanford, and was a Fulbright scholar in London. Instead of accepting one of many teaching offers from prestigious schools, however, Rodriguez chose to leave academic life, arguing that he was benefiting as a minority when the "genuinely disadvantaged," the "people who cannot read or write" were ignored by the system.*

In "Gains and Losses," an excerpt from Hunger of Memory, *Rodriguez claims that bilingual education—allowing students to be taught in their own language—may undermine rather than enhance a child's efforts to learn English. To support this claim, Rodriguez tells his own story: how he entered a Catholic school, learned to read, and eventually excelled in America's "public language." In this selection, Rodriguez chronicles both his gains (his acquisition of English) and his losses (his gradual abandonment of his private language and cultural identity).*

Supporters of bilingual education today imply that 1 students like me miss a great deal by not being taught in their family's language. What they seem not to recognize is that, as a socially disadvantaged child, I considered Spanish to be a private language. What I needed to learn in school was that I had the right—and the obligation— to speak the public language of *los gringos*. The odd truth is that my first-grade classmates could have become bilingual, in the conventional sense of that word, more easily than I. Had they been taught (as upper-middle-class children are often taught early) a second language like Spanish or French, they could have regarded it simply as that: another public language. In my case such bilingualism could not have been so quickly achieved. What I did not believe was that I could speak a single public language.

Without question, it would have pleased me to hear 2 my teachers address me in Spanish when I entered the classroom. I would have felt much less afraid. I would have trusted them and responded with ease. But I would have delayed—for how long postponed?—having to learn the language of public society. I would have evaded—and for how long could I have afforded to delay?—learning the great lesson of school, that I had a public identity.

Fortunately, my teachers were unsentimental about 3 their responsibility. What they understood was that I needed to speak a public language. So their voices would search me out, asking me questions. Each time I'd hear them, I'd look up in surprise to see a nun's face frowning at me. I'd mumble, not really meaning to answer. The nun would persist, 'Richard, stand up. Don't look at the floor. Speak up. Speak to the entire class, not just to me!' But I couldn't believe that the English language was mine to use. (In part, I did not want to believe it.) I continued to mumble. I resisted the teacher's demands. (Did I somehow suspect that once I learned public language my pleasing family life would be changed?) Silent, waiting for the bell to sound, I remained dazed, diffident, afraid.

Because I wrongly imagined that English was intrins- 4 ically a public language and Spanish an intrinsically private one, I easily noted the difference between classroom language and the language of home. At school, words were directed to a general audience of listeners. ('Boys and girls.') Words were meaningfully ordered. And the point was not self-expression alone but to make oneself understood by many others. The teacher quizzed: 'Boys and girls, why do we use that word in this sentence? Could we think of a better word to use there? Would the sentence change its meaning if the words were differently arranged? And wasn't there a better way of saying much the same thing?' (I couldn't say. I wouldn't try to say.)

Three months. Five. Half a year passed. Unsmiling, 5 ever watchful, my teachers noted my silence. They began to connect my behavior with the difficult progress my older sister and brother were making. Until one Saturday morning three nuns arrived at the house to talk to our parents. Stiffly, they sat on the blue living room sofa. From the doorway of another room, spying the visitors, I noted the incongruity—the clash of two worlds, the faces and voices of school intruding upon the familiar setting of home. I overheard one voice gently wondering, 'Do your children speak only Spanish at home, Mrs. Rodriguez?' While another voice added, 'That Richard especially seems so timid and shy.'

That Rich-heard!   6

With great tact the visitors continued, 'Is it possible 7 for you and your husband to encourage your children to practice their English when they are home?' Of course, my parents complied. What would they not do for their children's well-being? And how could they have questioned the Church's authority which those women represented? In an instant, they agreed to give up the language (the sounds) that had revealed and accentuated our family's closeness. The moment after the visitors left, the change was observed. '*Ahora,* speak to us *en inglés,*' my father and mother united to tell us.

At first, it seemed a kind of game. After dinner each 8 night, the family gathered to practice 'our' English. (It was still then *inglés,* a language foreign to us, so we felt drawn as strangers to it.) Laughing, we would try to define words we could not pronounce. We played with strange English sounds, often over-anglicizing our pronunciations.

And we filled the smiling gaps of our sentences with familiar Spanish sounds. But that was cheating, somebody shouted. Everyone laughed. In school, meanwhile, like my brother and sister, I was required to attend a daily tutoring session. I needed a full year of special attention. I also needed my teachers to keep my attention from straying in class by calling out, *Rich-heard*—their English voices slowly prying loose my ties to my other name, its three notes, *Ri-car-do*. Most of all I needed to hear my mother and father speak to me in a moment of seriousness in broken—suddenly heartbreaking—English. The scene was inevitable: One Saturday morning I entered the kitchen where my parents were talking in Spanish. I did not realize that they were talking in Spanish however until, at the moment they saw me, I heard their voices change to speak English. Those *gringo* sounds they uttered startled me. Pushed me away. In that moment of trivial misunderstanding and profound insight, I felt my throat twisted by unsounded grief. I turned quickly and left the room. But I had no place to escape to with Spanish. (The spell was broken.) My brother and sisters were speaking English in another part of the house.

Again and again in the days following, increasingly 9 angry, I was obliged to hear my mother and father: 'Speak to us *en inglés*.' (*Speak.*) Only then did I determine to learn classroom English. Weeks after, it happened: One day in school I raised my hand to volunteer an answer. I spoke out in a loud voice. And I did not think it remarkable when the entire class understood. That day, I moved very far from the disadvantaged child I had been only days earlier. The belief, the calming assurance that I belonged in public, had at last taken hold.

Shortly after, I stopped hearing the high and loud 10 sounds of *los gringos*. A more and more confident speaker of English, I didn't trouble to listen to *how* strangers sounded, speaking to me. And there simply were too many English-speaking people in my day for me to hear American accents anymore. Conversations quickened. Listening to persons who sounded eccentrically pitched voices, I usually noted their sounds for an initial few seconds before I concentrated on *what* they were saying. Conversations became content-full. Transparent. Hearing someone's *tone* of voice—angry or questioning or sarcastic or happy or sad—I didn't distinguish it from the words it expressed. Sound and word were thus tightly wedded. At the end of a day, I was often bemused, always relieved, to realize how 'silent,' though crowded with words, my day in public had been. (This public silence measured and quickened the change in my life.)

At last, seven years old, I came to believe what had been technically true since my birth: I was an American citizen.

But the special feeling of closeness at home was diminished by then. Gone was the desperate, urgent, intense feeling of being at home; rare was the experience of feeling myself individualized by family intimates. We remained a loving family, but one greatly changed. No longer so close; no longer bound tight by the pleasing and troubling knowledge of our public separateness. Neither my older brother nor sister rushed home after school anymore. Nor did I. When I arrived home there would often be neighborhood kids in the house. Or the house would be empty of sounds.

Following the dramatic Americanization of their children, even my parents grew more publicly confident. Especially my mother. She learned the names of all the people on our block. And she decided we needed to have a telephone installed in the house. My father continued to use the word *gringo*. But it was no longer charged with the old bitterness or distrust. (Stripped of any emotional content, the word simply became a name for those Americans not of Hispanic descent.) Hearing him, sometimes, I wasn't sure if he was pronouncing the Spanish word *gringo* or saying gringo in English.

Matching the silence I started hearing in public was a new quiet at home. The family's quiet was partly due to the fact that, as we children learned more and more English, we shared fewer and fewer words with our parents. Sentences needed to be spoken slowly when a child addressed his mother or father. (Often the parent wouldn't understand.) The child would need to repeat himself. (Still the parent misunderstood.) The young voice, frustrated, would end up saying, 'Never mind'—the subject was closed. Dinners would be noisy with the clinking of knives and forks against dishes. My mother would smile softly between her remarks; my father at the other end of the table would chew and chew at his food, while he stared over the heads of his children.

My *mother!* My *father!* After English became my pri- 15 mary language, I no longer knew what words to use in addressing my parents. The old Spanish words (those tender accents of sound) I had used earlier—*mamá* and *papá*—I couldn't use anymore. They would have been too painful reminders of how much had changed in my life. On the other hand, the words I heard neighborhood kids call *their* parents seemed equally unsatisfactory. *Mother* and *Father; Ma, Papa, Pa, Dad, Pop* (how I hated the all-American sound of that last word especially)—all these terms I felt were unsuitable, not really terms of address for *my* parents. As a result, I never used them at home. Whenever I'd speak to my parents, I would try to get their attention with eye contact alone. In public conversations, I'd refer to 'my parents' or 'my mother and father.'

My mother and father, for their part, responded 16 differently, as their children spoke to them less. She grew restless, seemed troubled and anxious at the scarcity of words exchanged in the house. It was she who would question me about my day when I came home from school. She smiled at small talk. She pried at the edges of my sentences to get me to say something more. (What?) She'd join conversations she overheard, but her intrusions often stopped her children's talking. By contrast, my father seemed reconciled to the new quiet. Though his English improved somewhat, he retired into silence. At dinner he spoke very little. One night his children and even his wife helplessly giggled at his garbled English pronunciation of the Catholic Grace before Meals. Thereafter he made his wife recite the prayer at the start of each meal, even on formal occasions, when there were guests in the house. Hers became the public voice of the family. On official business, it was she, not my father, one would usually hear on the phone or in stores, talking to strangers. His children grew so accustomed to his silence that, years later, they would speak routinely of his shyness. (My mother would often try to explain: Both his parents died when he was eight. He was raised by an uncle who treated him like little more than a menial servant. He was never encouraged to speak. He grew up alone. A man of few words.) But my father was not shy, I realized, when I'd watch him speaking Spanish with relatives. Using Spanish, he was quickly effusive. Especially when talking with other men, his voice would spark, flicker, flare alive with sounds. In Spanish, he expressed ideas and feelings he rarely revealed in English. With firm Spanish sounds, he conveyed confidence and authority English would never allow him.

The silence at home, however, was finally more than a literal silence. Fewer words passed between parent and child, but more profound was the silence that resulted from my inattention to sounds. At about the time I no longer bothered to listen with care to the sounds of English in public, I grew careless about listening to the sounds family members made when they spoke. Most of the time I heard someone speaking at home and didn't distinguish his sounds from the words people uttered in public. I didn't even pay much attention to my parents' accented and ungrammatical speech. At least not at home. Only when I was with them in public would I grow alert to their accents. Though, even then, their sounds caused me less and less concern. For I was increasingly confident of my own public identity.

I would have been happier about my public success had I not sometimes recalled what it had been like earlier, when my family had conveyed its intimacy through a set of conveniently private sounds. Sometimes in public, hearing a stranger, I'd hark back to my past. A Mexican farmworker approached me downtown to ask directions to somewhere. '¿Hijito . . . ?' he said. And his voice summoned deep longing. Another time, standing beside my mother in the visiting room of a Carmelite convent, before the dense screen which rendered the nuns shadowy figures, I heard several Spanish-speaking nuns—their busy, singsong overlapping voices—assure us that yes, yes, we were remembered, all our family was remembered in their prayers. (Their voices echoed faraway family sounds.) Another day, a dark-faced old woman—her hand light on my shoulder—steadied herself against me as she boarded a bus. She murmured something I couldn't quite comprehend. Her Spanish voice came near, like the face of a never-before-seen relative in the instant before I was kissed. Her voice, like so many of the Spanish voices I'd hear in public, recalled the golden age of my youth. Hearing Spanish then, I continued to be a careful, if sad, listener to sounds. Hearing a Spanish-speaking family walking behind me, I turned to look. I smiled for an instant, before my glance found the Hispanic-looking faces of strangers in the crowd going by.

QUESTIONS ON MEANING

1. Skim the essay again, circling every occurrence of the word *sound* or *sounds*. How often does it occur? What point is Rodriguez making?

2. How does the title emphasize one meaning of this passage? In acquiring English, what does the narrator gain? What does he lose?

QUESTIONS ON PURPOSE AND STRATEGY

1. Rodriguez describes the sometimes painful process of shifting from his private language to a new public language. But he also seems to be arguing against the concept of bilingual education. Where is each purpose most obvious?

2. Without looking at the essay, describe the scenes you found

most memorable. Then look at the essay. Number the specific scenes (located in a specific time and place) that Rodriguez weaves into his narrative. In which scenes does Rodriguez use actual dialogue? Were the scenes you remembered the specific scenes with dialogue, or not? Explain.

QUESTIONS ON AUDIENCE AND LANGUAGE

1. Is Rodriguez writing to anyone interested in another person's childhood? Is Rodriguez writing primarily to Spanish speakers who have learned English? Is he writing to English speakers to show them how he acquired English? Is he writing for teachers and parents and administrators? Defend your choice(s) by referring to specific passages.

2. Which essay did you like better—Rodriguez's or Gregory's? Why? Compare Rodriguez's style (sentences, vocabulary, voice) to Gregory's style. Which is more formal? Which is more sophisticated? Which is more emotional?

QUESTIONS FOR DISCUSSION AND WRITING

1. Where does Rodriguez describe his feelings from the perspective of a child? Where does he give an outsider's or adult's perspective about his behavior? Should he tell the story just from his perspective?

2. In an interview, Rodriguez explained that he tries to "write about everyday concerns—an educational issue, say, or the problems of the unemployed—but to write about them as powerfully, as richly, as well as I can. My model in this marriage of journalism and literature is, of course, George Orwell." Compare "Why I Write" to "Gains and Losses." In what ways does Rodriguez write like Orwell? Which writer combines journalism and literature most effectively?

3. If you learned a second language as a child, write about your own experiences. How did you acquire English? How did it affect your family life?

Living in Two Cultures

JEANNE WAKATSUKI HOUSTON

(1934–   )

PREREADING JOURNAL ENTRY

We all play multiple roles, behaving one way with our
parents, another way with friends, and a third way with
members of the opposite sex. Describe two or three
different roles that you play, indicating how the roles are
different and for whom you play each role.

---

*Following the bombing of Pearl Harbor on December 7, 1941, many
Japanese-American citizens were sent to prison camps. Although the U.S.
government said that the Japanese were just being "detained" for their
own protection, the widespread fear was that they might become spies or
even fight against the United States. Jeanne Wakatsuki, "interned" with
her family during World War II at Manzanar near Death Valley, described her experiences in* Farewell to Manzanar: A True Story of
Japanese American Experience During and After the World
War II Internment *(1973).*

*"Living in Two Cultures" describes Houston's experiences growing
up in California after the war. The essay shows how the conflict between
the traditional Japanese customs and the "Hakujin" or "All-American"
culture in California created a "double standard" for Houston's self-
image as a Japanese-American female.*

The memories surrounding my awareness of being   1
female fall into two categories: those of the period before
World War II, when the family made up my life, and
those after the war, when I entered puberty and my world
expanded to include the ways and values of my Caucasian

peers. I did not think about my Asian-ness and how it influenced my self-image as a female until I married.

In remembering myself as a small child, I find it hard 2 to separate myself from the entity of the family. I was too young to be given "duties" according to my sex, and I was unaware that this was the organizational basis for operating the family. I took it for granted that everyone just did what had to be done to keep things running smoothly. My five older sisters helped my mother with domestic duties. My four older brothers helped my father in the fishing business. What I vaguely recall about the sensibility surrounding our sex differences was that my sisters and I all liked to please our brothers. More so, we tried to attract positive attention from Papa. A smile or affectionate pat from him was like a gift from heaven. Somehow, we never felt this way about Mama. We took her love for granted. But there was something special about Papa.

I never identified this specialness as being one of the 3 blessings of maleness. After all, I played with my brother Kiyo, two years older than myself, and I never felt there was anything special about him. I could even make him cry. My older brothers were fun-loving, boisterous and very kind to me, especially when I made them laugh with my imitations of Carmen Miranda dancing or of Bonnie Baker singing "Oh, Johnny." But Papa was different. His specialness came not from being male, but from being the authority.

After the war and the closing of the camps, my world 4 drastically changed. The family had disintegrated; my father was no longer godlike, despite my mother's attempt to sustain that pre-war image of him. I was spending most of my time with my new Caucasian friends and learning new values that clashed with those of my parents. It was also time that I assumed the duties girls were supposed to do, like cooking, cleaning the house, washing and ironing clothes. I remember washing and ironing my brothers' shirts, being careful to press the collars correctly, trying not to displease them. I cannot ever remember my brothers performing domestic chores while I lived at home. Yet, even though they may not have been working "out there," as the men were supposed to do, I did not resent it. It would have embarrassed me to see my brothers doing the dishes. Their reciprocation came in a different way. They were very protective of me and made me feel good and important for being a female. If my brother Ray had extra money, he would sometimes buy me a sexy sweater like my Caucasian friends wore, which Mama wouldn't buy for me. My brothers taught me to ride a bicycle and to drive a car, took me to my first dance, and proudly introduced me to their friends.

Although the family had changed, my identity as a 5 female within it did not differ much from my older sisters who grew up before the war. The males and females supported each other but for different reasons. No longer was the survival of the family as a group our primary objective; we cooperated to help each other survive "out there" in the complicated world that had weakened Papa.

We were living in Long Beach then. My brothers 6 encouraged me to run for school office, to try out for majorette and song leader, and to run for queen of various festivities. They were proud that I was breaking social barriers still closed to them. It was acceptable for an Oriental male to excel academically and in sports. But to gain recognition socially in a society that had been fed the stereotyped model of the Asian male as cook, houseboy or crazed kamikaze pilot was almost impossible. The more alluring myth of mystery and exotica that surrounds the Oriental female made it easier, though no less inwardly painful, for me.

Whenever I succeeded in the *Hakujin* world, my broth- 7 ers were supportive, whereas Papa would be disdainful, undetermined by my obvious capitulation to the ways of the West. I wanted to be like my Caucasian friends. Not only did I want to look like them, I wanted to act like them. I tried hard to be outgoing and socially aggressive and to act confidently, like my girlfriends. At home I was careful not to show these personality traits to my father. For him it was bad enough that I did not even look very

Japanese: I was too big, and I walked too assertively. My breasts were large, and besides that I showed them off with those sweaters the *Hakujin* girls wore! My behavior at home was never calm and serene, but around my father I still tried to be as Japanese as I could.

As I passed puberty and grew more interested in boys, 8 I soon became aware that an Oriental female evoked a certain kind of interest from males. I was still too young to understand how or why an Oriental female fascinated Caucasian men, and of course, far too young to see then that it was a form of "not seeing." My brothers would warn me, "Don't trust the *Hakujin* boys. They only want one thing. They'll treat you like a servant and expect you to wait on them hand and foot. They don't know how to be nice to you." My brothers never dated Caucasian girls. In fact, I never really dated Caucasian boys until I went to college. In high school, I used to sneak out to dances and parties where I would meet them. I wouldn't even dare to think what Papa would do if he knew.

What my brothers were saying was that I should not 9 act toward Caucasian males as I did toward them. I must not "wait on them" or allow them to think I would, because they wouldn't understand. In other words, be a Japanese female around Japanese men and act *Hakujin* around Caucasian men. This double identity within a "double standard" resulted not only in a confusion for me of my role or roles as female, but also in who or what I was racially. With the admonitions of my brothers lurking deep in my consciousness, I would try to be aggressive, assertive and "come on strong" toward Caucasian men. I mustn't let them think I was submissive, passive and all-giving like Madame Butterfly.[1] With Asian males I would tone down my natural enthusiasm and settle into patterns

---

[1] Madame Butterfly is the heroine of an American play and an Italian opera. She marries an American lieutenant for love and then commits suicide when he leaves her for an American woman.

instilled in me through the models of my mother and my sisters. I was not comfortable in either role.

Although I was attracted to males who looked like 10 someone in a Coca-Cola ad, I yearned for the expressions of their potency to be like that of Japanese men, like that of my father: unpredictable, dominant, and brilliant—yet sensitive and poetic. I wanted a blond samurai.

When I met my blond samurai, during those college 11 years in San Jose, I was surprised to see how readily my mother accepted the idea of our getting married. My father had passed away, but I was still concerned about her reaction. All of my married brothers and sisters had married Japanese-American mates. I would be the first to marry a Caucasian. "He's a strong man and will protect you. I'm all for it," she said. Her main concern for me was survival. Knowing that my world was the world of the *Hakujin,* she wanted me to be protected, even if it meant marriage to one of them. It was 1957, and interracial couples were a rare sight to see. She felt that my husband-to-be was strong because he was acting against the norms of his culture, perhaps even against his parent's wishes. From her vantage point, where family and group opinion outweighed the individual's, this willingness to oppose them was truly a show of strength.

When we first married I wondered if I should lay out 12 his socks and underwear every morning like my mother used to do for my father. But my brothers' warning would float up from the past: don't be subservient to Caucasian men or they will take advantage. So I compromised and laid them out sporadically, whenever I thought to do it . . . which grew less and less often as the years passed. (Now my husband is lucky if he can even find a clean pair of socks in the house!) His first reaction to this wifely gesture was to be uncomfortably pleased. Then he was puzzled by its sporadic occurrence, which did not seem to coincide as an act of apology or because I wanted something. On the days when I felt I should be a good Japanese wife, I did it. On other days, when I felt American and assertive, I did not.

When my mother visited us, as she often did when 13
she was alive, I had to be on good behavior, much to my
husband's pleasure and surprise. I would jump up from
the table to fill his empty water glass (if she hadn't beat
me to it) or butter his roll. If I didn't notice that his plate
needed refilling, she would kick me under the table and
reprimand me with a disapproving look. Needless to say,
we never had mother-in-law problems. He would often
ask, with hope in his voice, "when is your mother coming
to visit?"

My mother had dutifully served my father throughout 14
their marriage, but I never felt she resented it. I served
my brothers and father and did not resent it. I was made
to feel not only important for performing duties of my
role, but absolutely integral for the functioning of the
family. I realized a very basic difference in attitude between Japanese and American cultures toward serving
another. In my family, to serve another could be uplifting,
a gracious gesture that elevated oneself. For many white
Americans, it seems that serving another is degrading, an
indication of dependency or weakness in character, or a
low place in the social ladder. To be ardently considerate
is to be "self-effacing" or apologetic.

My father used to say, "Serving humanity is the greatest 15
virtue. Giving service of yourself is more worthy than
selling the service or goods of another." He would prefer
that we be maids in someone's home, serving someone
well, than be salesgirls where our function would be to
exchange someone else's goods, handling money. Perhaps
it was his way of rationalizing and giving pride to the
occupations open to us as Orientals. Nevertheless, his
words have stayed with me, giving me spiritual sustenance
at times when I perceived that my willingness to give was
misconstrued as a need to be liked or an act of manipu-
lation to get something.

My husband and I often joke that the reason we have 16
stayed married for so long is that we continually mystify
each other with responses and attitudes that are plainly
due to our different backgrounds. For years I frustrated

him with unpredictable silences and accusing looks. I felt a great reluctance to tell him what I wanted or what needed to be done in the home. I was inwardly furious that I was being put into the position of having to *tell* him what to do. I felt my femaleness, in the Japanese sense, was being degraded. I did not want to be the authority. That would be humiliating for him and for me. He, on the other hand, considering the home to be under my dominion, in the American sense, did not dare to impose on me what he thought I wanted. He wanted me to tell him or make a list, like his parents did in his home.

Entertaining socially was also confusing. Up to recent 17 times, I still hesitated to sit at one head of our rectangular dining table when my husband sat at the other end. It seemed right to be seated next to him, helping him serve the food. Sometimes I did it anyway, but only with our close friends who didn't misread my physical placement as psychological subservience.

At dinner parties I always served the men first, until 18 I noticed the women glaring at me. I became self-conscious about it and would try to remember to serve the women first. Sometimes I would forget and automatically turn to a man. I would catch myself abruptly, dropping a bowl of soup all over him. Then I would have to serve him first anyway, as a gesture of apology. My unconscious Japanese instinct still managed to get what it wanted.

Now I just entertain according to how I feel that day. 19 If my Japanese sensibility is stronger, I act accordingly and feel comfortable. If I feel like going all-American, I can do that, too, and feel comfortable. I have come to accept the cultural hybridness of my personality, to recognize it as a strength and not weakness. Because I am culturally neither pure Japanese nor pure American does not mean I am less of a person. It means I have been enriched with the heritage of both.

How my present attitudes will affect my children in 20 later years remains to be seen. My world is radically different from my mother's world, and all indications point to an even wider difference between our world and our children's. Whereas my family's and part of my struggle was racially based, I do not foresee a similar struggle for our children. Their biracialism is, indeed, a factor in their identity and self-image, but I feel their struggle will be more to sustain human dignity in a world rapidly dehumanizing itself with mechanization and technology. My hope is they have inherited a strong will to survive, that essential trait ethnic minorities in this country have so sharply honed.

QUESTIONS ON MEANING

1. Explain which of the following phrases best expresses the central focus of Houston's essay: "learning new values that clashed with those of my parents," "my self-image as a female," or "the entity of the family." Defend your choice with references to the rest of the essay.

2. Describe how "living in two cultures" led Houston to *change* her traditional Japanese patterns of living. Find examples from her early years as well as from her married life. How does she resolve each conflict?

3. What traditional Japanese trait does Houston think her own children will need in the future?

QUESTIONS ON PURPOSE AND STRATEGY

1. Is Houston's purpose to explain how living in two cultures shaped her life? Does she have a larger "political purpose" or point to make, as Rodriguez does? Explain.

2. Often autobiography encourages readers to reflect on similar incidents in their own lives. Explain how Houston's essay caused you to reflect on something from your own life.

3. Create a time line for Houston's essay. List, in chronological order, all the events described or referred to in the essay. Where does Houston begin her story? Does she use flashback, or do all events occur in chronological order?

QUESTIONS ON AUDIENCE AND LANGUAGE

1. If you liked this essay, explain why you are a good audience for this essay. If you disliked or were bored by this essay, explain why you are an inappropriate reader. If you disliked

this essay, what could Houston have done to get your interest—apart from changing the *subject* of the essay?

2. Cite three passages that illustrate Houston's voice, the sense of personality that comes through her writing. Describe her voice in one word, such as *self-centered, engaging, naive, philosophical,* or *sensible.*

QUESTIONS FOR DISCUSSION AND WRITING

1. Compare Houston's ability to adjust to her two cultures with Rodriguez's experiences with the gringo world. Which writer compromises most comfortably with both worlds? Cite specific passages to support your conclusion.

2. In her essay, Houston says, "I felt a great reluctance to tell him [her husband] what I wanted or what needed to be done in the home. I was inwardly furious that I was being put into the position of having to *tell* him what to do. I felt my femaleness, in the Japanese sense, was being degraded. I did not want to be the authority." Is being angry about having to tell someone what you want a universal emotion? Interview several classmates and see if they—regardless of sex or cultural background—have experienced Houston's frustration.

3. Write an autobiographical essay about you and your family, describing how female and male *expectations and roles* differed. Or describe how your *values* contrasted with those of your parents. Focus on several specific incidents illustrating differing roles or values and showing how you adjusted to those differences.

Drowning 1954

GARRISON KEILLOR

(1942–   )

PREREADING JOURNAL ENTRY

Recall a time when you were afraid of some place, activity, or person. Think of something that frightened you over a period of time, something that invaded even your dreams. Describe how it began, how it affected you, and how you overcame it—or at least outgrew it.

Garrison Keillor is best known for his "Prairie Home Companion" broadcasts which, at the height of their popularity in the 1980s, were carried by hundreds of public radio stations across the country. The centerpiece for the radio variety show was always Keillor's monologue, without notes or script, about the latest news from Lake Wobegon, a fictitious place in Minnesota "where all the women are strong, all the men are good-looking, and all the children are above average." Keillor has written articles and stories for the New Yorker *and the* Atlantic Monthly, *and has published a collection of stories,* Happy to Be Here *(1982) and* Lake Wobegon Days *(1985).*

In "Drowning 1954," from Happy to Be Here, *Keillor describes his nightmares about drowning: "I was dragged deeper and deeper, with my body bursting and my arms and legs flailing against nothing, down and down, until I shot back to the surface and lay in my dark bedroom exhausted, trying to make myself stay awake." As you read his essay, look for a second fear that Keillor encounters, an anxiety just as alarming as his fear of drowning.*

When I was twelve, my cousin Roger drowned in Lake 1 Independence, and my mother enrolled me in a swimming class at the Y.M.C.A. on La Salle Avenue in downtown

Minneapolis. Twice a week for most of June and July, I got on the West River Road bus near our home in Brooklyn Park township, a truck-farming community north of Minneapolis, and rode into the stink and heat of the city, and when I rounded the corner of Ninth Street and La Salle and smelled the chlorine air that the building breathed out, I started to feel afraid. After a week, I couldn't bear to go to swimming class anymore.

Never before had I stood naked among strangers (the 2 rule in the class was no swimming trunks), and it was loathsome to undress and then walk quickly through the cold showers to the pool and sit shivering with my feet dangling in the water (Absolute Silence, No Splashing) and wait for the dread moment. The instructor—a man in his early twenties, who was tanned and had the smooth muscles of a swimmer (he wore trunks)—had us plunge into the pool one at a time, so that he could give us his personal attention. He strode up and down the side of the pool yelling at those of us who couldn't swim, while we thrashed hopelessly beneath him and tried to *look* like swimmers. "You're walking on the bottom!" he would shout. "Get your legs up! What's the matter, you afraid to get your face wet? What's *wrong* with you?" The truth was that my cousin's death had instilled in me a terrible fear, and when I tried to swim and started to sink it felt not so much as if I was sinking but as if something was pulling me down. I panicked, every time. It was just like the dreams of drowning that came to me right after Roger died, in which I was dragged deeper and deeper, with my body bursting and my arms and legs flailing against nothing, down and down, until I shot back to the surface and lay in my dark bedroom exhausted, trying to make myself stay awake.

I tried to quit the swimming class, but my mother 3 wouldn't hear of it, so I continued to board the bus every swimming morning, and then, ashamed of myself and knowing God would punish me for my cowardice and deceit, I hurried across La Salle and past the Y and walked along Hennepin Avenue, past the pinball parlors and bars and shoeshine stands to the old public library, where I viewed the Egyptian mummy and the fossils and a facsimile of the Declaration of Independence. I stayed there until eleven-thirty, when I headed straight for the WCCO radio studio to watch "Good Neighbor Time."

We listened regularly to this show at home—Bob 4 DeHaven, with Wally Olson and His Band, and Ernie Garvin and Burt Hanson and Jeanne Arland—and then to the noontime news, with Cedric Adams, the most famous man in the upper Midwest. It amazed me to sit in the studio audience and watch the little band crowded around the back wall, the engineers in the darkened booth, and the show people gliding up to a microphone for a song, a few words, or an Oxydol commercial. I loved everything except the part of the show in which Bob DeHaven interviewed people in the audience. I was afraid he might pick me, and then my mother, and probably half of Minnesota, would find out that I was scared of water and a liar to boot. The radio stars dazzled me. One day, I squeezed into the WCCO elevator with Cedric Adams and five or six other people. I stood next to him, and a sweet smell of greatness and wealth drifted off from him. I later imagined Cedric Adams swimming in Lake Minnetonka—a powerful whale of happiness and purpose—and I wished that I were like him and the others, but as the weeks wore on I began to see clearly that I was more closely related to the bums and winos and old men who sat around in the library and wandered up and down Hennepin Avenue. I tried to look away and not see them, but they were all around me there, and almost every day some poor ragged creature, filthy drunk at noon, would stagger at me wildly out of a doorway, with his arms stretched out toward me, and I saw a look of fellowship in his eyes: *You are one of us.*

I ran from them, but clearly I was well on my way. 5 Drinking and all the rest of the bum's life would come with time, inevitably. My life was set on its tragic course by a sinful error in youth. This was the dark theme of the fundamentalist Christian tracts in our home: one misstep would lead you down into the life of the infidel. One misstep! A lie, perhaps, or disobedience to your mother. There were countless young men in those tracts who stumbled and fell from the path—*one misstep!*—and were dragged down like drowning men into debauchery, unbelief, and utter damnation. I felt sure that my lie, which was repeated twice a week and whenever my mother asked about my swimming, was sufficient for my downfall. Even as I worked at the deception, I marveled that my fear of water should be greater than my fear of Hell.

I still remember the sadness of wandering in downtown 6 Minneapolis in 1954, wasting my life and losing my soul, and my great relief when the class term ended and I became a kid again around the big white house and garden, the green lawns and cool shady ravine of our lovely suburb. A weekend came when we went to a lake for a family picnic, and my mother, sitting on the beach, asked me to swim for her, but I was able to fool her, even at that little distance, by walking on the bottom and making arm strokes.

When I went to a lake with my friends that summer, 7 or to the Mississippi River a block away, I tried to get the knack of swimming, and one afternoon the next summer I did get it—the crawl and the backstroke and the sidestroke, all in just a couple of weeks. I dived from a dock and opened my eyes underwater and everything. The sad part was that my mother and father couldn't appreciate this wonderful success; to them, I had been a swimmer all along. I felt restored—grateful that I would not be a bum all my life, grateful to God for letting me learn to swim. It was so quick and so simple that I can't remember it today. Probably I just stood in the water and took a little plunge; my feet left the bottom, and that was it.

Now my little boy, who is seven, shows some timidity 8 around water. Every time I see him standing in the shallows, working up nerve to put his head under, I love him more. His eyes are closed tight, and his pale slender body is tense as a drawn bow, ready to spring up instantly should he start to drown. Then I feel it all over again, the way I used to feel. I also feel it when I see people like the imperial swimming instructor at the Y.M.C.A.—powerful people who delight in towering over some little twerp who is struggling and scared, and casting the terrible shadow of their just and perfect selves. The Big Snapper knows who you are, you bastards, and in a little while he is going to come after you with a fury you will not believe and grab you in his giant mouth and pull you under until your brain turns to jelly and your heart almost bursts. You will never recover from this terror. You will relive it every day, as you lose your fine job and your home and the respect of your friends and family. You will remember it every night in your little room at the Mission, and you will need a quart of Petri muscatel to put you to sleep, and when you awake between your yellow-stained sheets your hands will start to shake all over again.

You have fifteen minutes. Get changed.   9

QUESTIONS ON MEANING

1. What specific circumstances help create Keillor's fear of drowning?

2. What does Keillor do to avoid his swimming lessons? What second fear does Keillor develop because he lies to his mother?

QUESTIONS ON PURPOSE AND STRATEGY

1. In addition to sharing his boyhood fear of swimming, what do Keillor's experiences teach us? What main ideas or points does Keillor wish to communicate?

2. List the specific scenes (located in time and space) that Keillor re-creates for his reader. How much of this story is re-created and how much is just told?

3. Next to passages where Keillor talks about his fear of drowning, write "1." Next to passages where Keillor describes his fear of making a "misstep" and becoming a bum, write

"2." Where do these two themes come together? What does that show you about Keillor's strategy for organizing his story?

QUESTIONS ON AUDIENCE AND LANGUAGE

1. What kind of reader would like Keillor's story? Must you have a phobia about swimming to appreciate this story? Do you have to be raised in a fundamentalist Christian home to appreciate this story? Explain.
2. What effect does Keillor create in the last two paragraphs by changing his narrative from the first person "I" to "you"?

QUESTIONS FOR DISCUSSION AND WRITING

1. Which story do you like better: Gregory's "Shame" or Keillor's "Drowning 1954"? Explain which specific themes, strategies, or styles make one story more effective than the other.
2. Keillor "escapes" to the Bob DeHaven show, fascinated by the band, the engineers, and the show people. Explain what you escape to when there's too much pressure.
3. Who is the "Big Snapper" in Keillor's story? Think of examples of "Big Snappers" in your life, those "powerful people who delight in towering over some little twerp who is struggling and scared. . . ." Write your own essay about the "Big Snapper" in your life. ˙

Metamorphosis

PEGGY L. BRELAND

(1951–   )

PREREADING JOURNAL ENTRY

If you've had a friendship or relationship with a person that has recently ended, describe how the relationship ended and how the change has affected you.

In an essay written in Anthony Martinetti's composition class at Southwestern Louisiana State University, Peggy Breland describes the breakup of her marriage: "Out of desperation for a topic," she writes, "I chose the worst thing that ever happened to me. I didn't think it would be of interest to anyone else, and it was difficult, emotionally speaking, to put on paper." Although Breland writes about her divorce from her gun–toting husband, her essay focuses on her own metamorphosis, on her gradual transformation back into herself.

The time was 1982. The place was an old neighbor- 1 hood in Baton Rouge known as "Old Goodwood." The people were an almost traditional family consisting of a mother (me), a father (Donnie), and two little boys. Alfie was thirteen, and athletic. Joey was twelve and a budding young musician.

We lived on a tree-lined street; every front yard had 2 oak trees, so old and tall they formed a canopy over the street. There were big yards and plenty of boys for my sons to play with. Around the corner was a street known as the circle. If you wanted to find your kids, the circle was the first place to look. There was always something going on for the kids to do, and best of all, they had a father. My husband had adopted my boys shortly after we were married. Their own father had deserted them.

I liked being married and expected to grow old and 3 die a married woman. In an age where marriage and family were looked upon as unfashionable and not worth the effort, I ranked marriage right up there with the Nobel prize. I enjoyed being a wife and mother and wouldn't have traded places with anyone. I also worked full time at a large medical clinic, didn't blow my paycheck, and did the yardwork. Actually, I should have been concerned about the fact that while I was doing the yardwork, my husband was playing with his guns and holding down his recliner. It never occurred to me that things were a little out of balance; all I knew was that I loved Donnie and he loved me and that made everything right.

Donnie was tall, handsome, funny, and looking back, 4 crazy? Donnie was liked by everyone. He was a real homebody and I thought, very stable. Donnie had a more than casual interest in guns. He had guns, gun books, gun tools, and gunsmithing equipment all over the house, which drove me crazy. But, at least I knew where he was, unlike my first husband.

I'm a little slow about some things. I didn't worry too 5 much about the M-16 on the porch. You see, Donnie's other interests included terrorists, mercenaries, and sur-vivalists. As a matter of fact, he had a not so secret desire to go off to some godforsaken country and be a mercenary. We used to have coffee on the front porch in the evening after work, and there, in the corner, stood the ever-present M-16. I used to hope the neighbors didn't see it. Sometimes he had a .38 strapped to his ankle. One year, for our second wedding anniversary, he presented me with my very own .357 magnum. How's that for romance?

Donnie's jobs fluctuated between law enforcement and 6 emergency medical services. Once he quit his job with the Sheriff's Department to pursue bounty hunting and private investigation. He and his partner went about it all wrong and didn't make any money, so he had to go back to the ambulance service.

One evening we were out taking a walk. It was late 7 July, warm, and the air was fragrant with the smell of flowers and freshly cut grass. We were talking about everything and nothing, when he turned to me and said, "Oh, by the way, I have a female partner. Her name is Linda."

"No big deal, she has a job to do," I said. He and I 8 worked together for an ambulance service while we were dating, so I understood the job and its demands. I always thought that was the way to hold on to a husband, by being his buddy as well his wife. Right then, I asked him to promise me that if something were to happen between them, that if they ever became more than just partners, to tell me first. He tried to assure me that nothing like that would ever happen.

Three weeks later, Donnie informed me that he wanted 9 a divorce.

"I don't think I'm in love with you anymore," he said. 10

"How long have you felt like this?"   11

"About six months."   12

I couldn't believe what I was hearing. I was the most 13 married person in the world. I'd always said I was living in the wrong time period, and that I belonged back in the forties and fifties when it was fashionable to be a wife and mother. Naturally, I blamed myself for everything. Women tend to do that. "What have I done? What have I not done? I'll change jobs, dye my hair, lose weight. We can move to Australia. Tell me what to do!"

He said, "It's not you, it's me. I can't handle the 14 pressure and responsibility of marriage and a family." A very interesting statement coming from a man who plays with the dog and balances the bank statement once a month. He didn't have to do anything else, but why should he? I did everything for him.

I said, "Who else knows about this?"   15

"Linda knows," he said.   16

"Why does Linda know?"   17

"She's my partner." 18

That night, I arranged for the boys to sleep over with 19 a friend. I had to fix this. We had to talk to somebody. I couldn't go through another divorce. I held his 20 mother in very high regard and thought we should talk to her. So what if he's 6'4" tall and a grown man? She's his mother and mothers can fix anything.

Miss Betty didn't have any more success with him than 21 I did. She, like me, suggested a psychiatrist and a vacation. She talked and I talked and it was pointless. I don't think Donnie was even listening. He wanted out and nothing would change his mind.

We went home to a very quiet, empty house that was 22 normally filled with noise and laughter. Usually, there were little boys in and out and Cub Scout meetings held on the back porch. Donnie was the Cub Scout leader for their troop. Now this house was like a morgue. Quite a change within just a few hours.

I stayed up all night, thinking, crying, and having my 23 first migraine, while in our room, in the king-sized bed that was his grandparent's, Donnie slept. Had I just torn someone's heart out and wrecked his life, I don't think I would have been able to sleep. That should have told me something. Donnie never had any trouble sleeping. Especially during the winter storm of 1982, when the electricity went out and the house was so cold. I'm the one who drove to the store and wrote a rubber check so I could make soup and try to keep everyone warm. I was also the one outside trying to wrap the water pipes so that they wouldn't burst. Well, they did burst, and Donnie still slept.

Right away, my boys started asking questions, and I 24 had to tell them their lives would be changing again. I had to tell them that Donnie and I were separating. Joey started crying.

Alfie just said, "I don't like it but there's nothing I can 25 do about it."

I can still see their faces. So much pain for such little 26 boys. And they were so good. Elderly people in the neighborhood always told me what good boys they were. This was so unfair. Their own father had deserted them. Now they would lose another father.

We always had music in the house. Donnie had been 27 a drummer in a few rock and roll bands. He taught Joey how to play, and Joey lived for music. Alfie played football. This life was good for them. I could look at their school pictures and see happiness and confidence. Before, when we were on our own, I saw fear. Would I see that again?

I won't bore you with anymore details about what a 28 great wife I was and what a sweet deal he was giving up. I reasoned and suggested for three weeks, and, finally, I gave up when he told me he went into bounty hunting with the intention of getting "blown away" as a means of escape. At that point, I gave up.

I didn't want to get out of bed to go to work. I was so 29 embarrassed. The great love affair of the century was all a big joke, and the joke was over. But the girls I worked with did everything they could to console me and were so supportive. Actually, they were just as shocked as I was.

With their help, I eventually stopped crying and started 30 eating again. I'd dropped twenty pounds and looked awful. The girls kept me busy, and I had my boys to look after. I knew that with time, I would get over this. I prayed for strength and for time to pass quickly. And looking back, it did pass quickly, though at the time it seemed to stand still.

It took a long time for the grief to subside and longer 31 still to learn to enjoy my freedom. I learned to enjoy lingering in bed on Sundays with my coffee and the newspaper. Realizing that I didn't have to be Superwoman took a few more years. I learned to enjoy a social life, joined an exercise class, started weightlifting, and even did private investigation part time for extra money. I received a promotion at work and began working for a surgeon.

I ran into Donnie one day, and he was still having his 32 little daydream about saving the world from terrorism. He also had a python and a boa-constrictor as pets. He had married Linda and she liked his snakes, so I guess they were meant for each other.

One day, it hit me. I was relieved to be out of it. I was 33 in my apartment enjoying the fact that it was decorated to my taste and not a single gun, gun book, or gun tool in the whole place, with the exception of my own gun placed discreetly under my bed. For the first time, I was enjoying seeing my things around me, my clothes, my make-up. My bedroom smelled like jasmine instead of gun oil. I was learning to feel as comfortable in a dress shop with my friends as I once felt in a gun store.

QUESTIONS ON MEANING

1. Describe the major characters, including Breland herself, in this essay.

2. What specific scenes, set in time and place, does Breland re-create or show? What events does she tell about or refer to in passing?

QUESTIONS ON PURPOSE AND STRATEGY

1. In your own words, describe the main idea that Breland's essay conveys.

2. Draw a time line for this story. First, list everything that happens, in chronological order, in Breland's life. What is happening when the essay opens? Where else might Breland begin her essay? Would beginning the story at another point on the time line be more or less effective?

QUESTIONS ON AUDIENCE AND LANGUAGE

1. Who is Breland's intended audience? What kind of readers would find her essay interesting or instructive?

2. Describe Breland's voice—her personality as revealed through her language. Find one sentence that expresses that voice. Describe her tone—her attitude toward her subject.

Find one sentence that expresses her tone. How would the main idea of the essay change if she were more emotional, more angry, jealous, or vindictive?

QUESTIONS FOR DISCUSSION AND WRITING

1. Who is most responsible for the breakup between the narrator and Donnie? What does Donnie do or not do to cause the divorce? What does the narrator do or not do to cause the divorce?

2. Reread your Prewriting Journal Entry. Explain how your breakup was similar to or different from Breland's. What did you learn from Breland's experience? What could Breland have learned from yours?

Mine 'Till I Learn Better

WAYNE SCOTT BALLINGER

(1960–   )

PREREADING JOURNAL ENTRY

What was the best present you ever received on your birthday or at Christmas? Describe the actual day, the present you got, your reactions, and the reactions of your family or friends.

Scott Ballinger, a student in Kimberly Miller's writing class at Colorado State University, writes his remembering essay about receiving a motorcycle at age fourteen. "I always enjoyed telling this story just for the drama," he writes, "though I was surprised that the real story was a bit different than I had remembered." In Ballinger's version, just as he is about to take his first ride on his very own bike, his mother, who has never ridden a motorcycle, decides that she wants to ride. The essay describes Ballinger's excitement about his long–awaited first ride and his mother's startling request. Was the outcome ever in doubt?

ONE WRITER'S REMEMBERING PROCESS

Collecting Exercises

Brainstorming: List of Key Scenes/Events

```
Tentative Title: "A Mother of a Ride"

The field available for motorcycle riding

Dad and Bill inspecting the bike

The exchange of money and the walk home
```

The faces of excitement of the adults

My brother wants to ride

Mother wants to ride

Explanation of operation and control

The wreck

My feelings from the wreck

The wait for Grampa to fix the bike

The moralistic lesson

Dialogue Writing for Sample Scene

"Does it go fast?" my brother asked.
"Of course," I scornfully replied to my
obviously dumb brother.
"Can I ride?" He ejected.
"No! Maybe when you're my age." Being
two years older and much wiser, it was the
only reply.

Rough Draft

I imagined the field held fantastic
races, dirt and rock and weeds all flew as
I leaned into the corner kicking the
spinning back tire out as everyone looked
on with awe and want. Then my mind snapped
back when father asked, "Ready?" I nodded
and eyed the cash, clutched in my fourteen
year old, sweaty hand, and fell in behind
my dad's huge frame for the walk.
My hand trembled with excitement at the
exchange of tender. The motorcycle sat,
promising me of adventure and excitement.
Sun splashed from the revolving spokes on
the way home. Rules forming in my head of
care and selfishness that would be acted
upon. Wash it. Check the oil, tires and
chain, and never, never let anyone else
ride it. My father's friend, Bill, was in

the driveway when I proudly strode up. I
could see that he too was excited with my
purchase. "Start 'er up!" Bill said. I was
only too happy to comply with this request.
"Ride slow down the street to see if the
frame isn't sprung." What!? Oh no, a
problem arises already. Sprung? How could
it be sprung, it's new! (New to me but
boughten used.) My guts relaxed when upon
inspection, the bike proved to be tracking
straight. Bill's wife, my brother and
sister and my mother came from the
backyard. "Whoa!" my brother stated. My
sister simply sniffed, turned and went
inside, but my mother, whom I portrayed as
the antagonist of the great BB Gun Debate
of '78, looked on with shining eyes and a
certainly large amount of interest. My face
blank, and mouth agape, I waited for the
horrible, future callings of dismemberment,
decapitation, and death. Her mouth started
to move and out came, "I want to ride it."
Silence hung for eternity, minds trying to
visualize this quiet, happy, careful mother
of three at the controls of this machine of
death. Realizing the . . .

Final Draft

Mine 'Till I Learn Better

My mind snapped back from fantasy when my
father's deep voice questioned,
"Are you ready?"
I nodded and eyed the cash clutched in my fourteen-year-old sweaty hand and fell in behind father's
huge frame for the walk.
My hand trembled with excitement at the exchange
of toy for tender, and my eyes raked the new purchase
with excitement. While Dad and the seller discussed

unimportant things like bill of sale and title, I slipped back into my visions.

Rabbits, cats, snakes, bears, and moose ran with tongues hanging and eyes rolling from the onslaught of knobbed, spinning tires propelled by massive horsepower, pushing the rider ever faster and closer to . . .

"Start er' up!" Bob, my father's friend, requested. Bob's voice broke my fantastic games of chase, but I could see that he too was excited about my purchase, so I quickly complied. I kicked the motorcycle engine over and looked up for faces of approval.

"Ride er' slow down the street, see if the frame isn't sprung."

What!? My bike!? A problem already? Sprung? How could it be sprung? It's new! (New to me but bought used.) My guts and mind relaxed when upon inspection the bike proved to be tracking straight.

"Ride it into the backyard and we'll have a look at it," Pa stated.

I eased out the clutch and my mind went into joyous overture; "Mine, mine, MINE!" screamed my head. I mentally noted previously made rules. One: wash it, oil it, and keep the chain tight. Two: never, never, never let anyone ride it! It was mine and mine alone, built and bought only for me. No more sharing with little brother, whose tantrums always won Mother's favorable decision when I applied my rightful dominance. Ha, the untouchable toy!

Bob's wife Bev, my mother, my little brother and older sister, all walked out of the house into the backyard.

"Whoa!" my brother exclaimed.

My sister, upon a rather snobbish inspection, simply sniffed, turned, and walked back inside. (I knew she was impressed just by the way she stuck her nose in the air. Translation: Jealousy.) My mother, oh no! Mom! The ultra-antagonistic enemy of the great B.B. gun debate of '78, the rival lobbying power sure to downcast any legislative right that would prove to be fun, looked on the scene with shiny eyes and a firm lip. With my face blank and mouth agape, I waited for horrible future callings of dismemberment, decapitation, and death. Then with her mouth moving, forming these words of killjoy, she said:

"I want to ride it."

Silence hung for a short eternity. The minds of the circled group tried to visualize this quiet, happy, careful mother of three at the controls of this machine of death. My mind screamed: "Mine! Rule number two! RULE NUMBER TWO! Never, never let anyone ride the bike!" Quickly though, my joy-seeking and manipulating mind visualized my mother happily putting around the yard, smiling at the innocent fun she was experiencing. Then later, no death chants, no words of mortification, just a pleasant "Have fun" goodbye when future permission was asked to ride away.

"Sure, you bet, Mom. Get on and I'll show you how to work it."

Mother slung her green polyester covered leg over the seat and with eyes fixed straight ahead, she said,

"Okay, I'm ready."

A quick and thoroughly professional fourteen-year-old's introduction to control was made and then the highly complicated concepts of gas/clutch and clutch/brake were added.

"Kick it while the clutch is in and give it some gas," I instructed.

Mother adjusted her diamond studded (false, of course) cat-eyed glasses and let loose with a start kick a mule would have been proud of. The motor caught on the second kick.

"Now ease out the clutch and give it a little gas."

Mom gave her "I'm a little nervous about this" smile and cranked open the throttle. My mind warned "Too much" as Mom suddenly let out the clutch and leaned forward in response to the acceleration. Dad's eyes were widening as his big hands began to rise. My brother's face-swallowing smile hinted toward disappearance and Bev's hand covered what I'm sure was a perfectly formed "O." Mom's polyester pants lost traction with the seat, back went her butt, down went her shoulders, up came her legs, and on came the power.

The bike raised as if it were some screaming monster trying to shake mother's hands from its ears. It was my monster, born of my toils of sweaty, wasted days mowing lawns for perfection-minded, overscrutinizing people always peering out their windows in search for that spot of gas or inevitably missed blade of grass. My rearing and smoking beast, spawned by red, numbed fingers from the cold handle of the snow shovel. All were efforts performed by the call of the bike's purchase price and were now in peril of being wasted. "No! Never let anyone ride it!" screamed my selfish conscious. The front tire raised further as the yard-encircling fence loomed closer. Mother hung on, racing away, out of control. My motorcycle will be wrecked! Visions spilled from my head of bent chrome and oil bleeding from the cracked steel as the slowing spokes signified the ending life of my bike. All hope was lost.

My mother, with peril wracking her body, gave a last-ditch effort and threw her almost vertical body the opposite direction of the leaning, standing bike. Metal met metal and flesh met fence. Mother baseball-slid sideways into the fence and the bike ram-fashionedly butted the steel clothspole. My feelings of concern were split for an instant between the two subjects, mother with her leg under the sharp twists of the chain link fence or my bike lying sideways on the grass, twisted, bent, and broken.

Later, when hearts beat normally, messes were cleaned, and scratches were patched, my mother, with large watery eyes, simply and sincerely said to me,

"I'm sorry I wrecked your motorcycle."

I envisioned my earlier hesitation for choice of concern, smiled, and said,

"Oh, that's okay, Ma."

Then I walked away, knowing it was just a motorcycle.

QUESTIONS ON MEANING

1. Of the original scenes Ballinger listed in his prewriting, which does he retain for his final draft?
2. Between which people are there potential sources of tension or conflict? Which conflicts does Ballinger underplay and which does he emphasize?

QUESTIONS ON PURPOSE AND STRATEGY

1. In your own words, describe the main idea or dominant impression that Ballinger's essay creates.
2. Which of the shaping strategies discussed in this chapter does Ballinger use to organize his essay? Cite at least one sentence or paragraph illustrating each of his primary strategies.

QUESTIONS ON AUDIENCE AND LANGUAGE

1. Who is Ballinger's intended audience? Who would find this essay interesting?
2. In which passages does Ballinger imitate the thoughts and language of a fourteen-year-old boy? Which words or passages seem most adult?
3. Find one sentence in Ballinger's essay that could be revised for clarity or effectiveness. Revise the sentence.

QUESTIONS FOR DISCUSSION AND WRITING

1. Examine the changes Ballinger makes in his final version of the essay. What did you like about the rough draft that Ballinger omits in the revised version? Do you agree with his decision to omit those parts?

2. Reread your Prereading Journal Entry. Re-create one brief scene from those events, using *dialogue* and the narrator's *thoughts* as Ballinger does in his essay.

3. Rewrite one scene from Ballinger's essay from the point of view of the father, the mother, the younger brother, or the sister.

5

INVESTIGATING

Objectivity is not an erasure of emotions, but a firm recognition of their inevitable role and presence.

—Stephen Jay Gould, author of *Ever Since Darwin*

Most non-fiction writers . . . wrote in a century-old British tradition in which it was understood that the narrator shall assume a calm, cultivated and, in fact, genteel voice. . . . When [readers] came upon that pale beige tone, it began to signal to them, unconsciously, that a well-known bore was here again, "the journalist," a pedestrian mind, a phlegmatic spirit, a faded personality. . . . To avoid this I would try anything.

—Tom Wolfe, author of *The Right Stuff*

I went to cover the [Vietnam] war, and the war covered me.

—Michael Herr, author of *Dispatches*

Investigating—along with observing and remembering—is a third initial purpose for writing. Writers investigate in order to learn—through summaries of written accounts, interviews, surveys, and direct observation. Then, they usually **report** what they have learned to their readers. As a result of an investigation, however, a writer's purpose may shift from reporting information to arguing for or against an issue, or to proposing a solution to a problem. For example, writers interested in air pollution may summarize articles on acid rain and interview experts to better inform themselves—and then their readers—about a complex issue. They could even decide to argue for tougher emission controls on automobiles or to propose an international solution to reducing sulphur emissions throughout North America. Although the investigative essays in this chapter illustrate how to gather evidence as you write for a variety of purposes, this chapter focuses just on **investigating** a topic and **reporting** what the writer learns to a specific audience.

Investigative writing should *inform* readers, not take a stand, argue for or against, or editorialize. Its hallmark is objectivity. True objectivity is not possible (or desirable, some would say), but good reporters try to present information accurately to their readers. Objective reporting is a matter of intent, personal integrity, and method. Writers of investigative reports should *intend* to focus not on their own opinions but on other people's ideas, opinions, and arguments. In doing so, however, they may need to acknowledge their own biases or emotions. They should also maintain their *personal integrity* around topics that trigger their own prejudices. Preconceived opinions should not disable writers' intent to "tell it like it is." Finally, writers of investigative reports should use the *methods* of accurate investigating and reporting: checking facts, finding multiple witnesses, quoting accurately, and summarizing surveys and other reports thoroughly and fairly.

Investigative reporting takes a variety of forms. Investigative writers sometimes merely summarize longer written reports or scientific studies, and in that case, their purpose is to condense and highlight the study, usually for a general audience. In a longer investigation, writers may summarize many written sources, conduct their own interviews, gather information from surveys, observe people and events firsthand, and report on their investigations. In that case, they become the principal investigators rather than just summarizers of other studies. In either case, their final purpose is to report their findings to a specific audience.

STRATEGIES FOR READING AND WRITING ABOUT INVESTIGATING

As you read the essays in this chapter, look for the following techniques for gathering information and reporting it to an audience.

A title and "lead" that get the reader's attention and interest. Investigative reporters recognize that readers may flip the page if their report does not have an interesting or succinct title and a lead-in that invites the reader to read the article. Titles such as "Attack of the Killer Cats" or "The Jeaning of America" trigger the reader's curiosity.

Presentation of basic who, what, when, where, why, and how information. Readers expect to find basic information early in the report, and they expect the information to be reliable and accurate.

Summarizing, quoting, or reporting information from oral or written sources. Investigative reporters use interviews, surveys, summaries, paraphrases, and accurate quotations from their sources.

Focus on some key question or questions. Effective investigative writing collects information that relates to a key question: what something means or is, when or how it happened, how or why something happened, or who did it. Are cats decimating the bird population? Is frozen orange juice really "natural"? What goes on behind the scenes at a beauty pageant? The key question becomes the main idea or focus of the report.

Language that is readable, interesting, and accurate. Investigative reports should be easily read and understood by the intended audience. Where appropriate, graphics or diagrams may illustrate important points.

READING AN INVESTIGATIVE ESSAY

Prereading

Begin by writing what you already know about the topic of the article. Whether the article is about blue jeans or oranges, write down what you already know about the subject. You'll find it interesting to compare what you wrote before you read the article with what you learned from the article. Then find out about the author, the occasion for this article, and the audience for which the article was written.

First Reading

Your first reading should be for enjoyment, to satisfy your curiosity about the subject. If some passage confuses you, put a "?" in the margin. If you like a passage or are surprised by the information, put a "!" in the margin. Highlight or put a wavy line under any key passages. Underline any words you want to look up later, but don't let these brief marks interrupt your reading. *At the end of this reading, write the question that this investigative report answers.*

Annotated Reading

For your annotated reading, write your own reactions in the margin: "I didn't know that"; "How did he get that information?"; or "This part is boring." Be sure to read with a writer's eye. Bracket and label key features of investigative reports: title, lead-in, who-what-when-where information, examples of clear or interesting style, and focus of the investigation. In the margin, list or outline the main parts of the report or the key stages in the writer's investigation. As necessary, look up definitions of words.

Collaborative Reading

In your class or small group, share your Prereading Journal entries. What, collectively, did the class or your group already know about the subject? Appoint a recorder to make a collaborative annotation for this essay by compiling the best annotations. At the end of the essay, write the central question that the report addresses. When you have finished the collaborative annotation, write down two questions you or your group still has about the article.

WRITING AN INVESTIGATIVE ESSAY

As you prepare to write an investigative essay, keep three important points in mind.

First, you will be practicing particular **investigative skills,** such as reading and summarizing, interviewing and taking notes, listening and writing down dialogue, or conducting surveys and organizing responses. You will use your skills of observing other people and places and remembering your experiences, but now the focus is on what you learn from *written sources* and from *other people.* Although you may include your own experiences during the investigation, you are the investigator, not the subject of the investigation.

Second, your **primary purpose** is **to report** what you discover to your intended audience. Although you will probably form an opinion about your topic or subject during your investigation, you should *not* editorialize, argue for one side or the other, offer your solutions to problems you discover, or evaluate your subject. Your purpose should be to **inform** your readers about the subject. You should attempt to report objectively, even if that means reporting your own biases or limited perspectives. You may report other people's judgments or opinions, but as the investigator, you should not argue for any particular position or belief.

Third, an investigation requires asking—and then answering—questions that your readers might have about your subject. You will provide answers to basic who, what, when, where, why, and how questions, but your report should **focus on** the answer(s) to a single basic question about a specific subject: How is frozen orange juice made? How did Levi's® jeans originate? Are domestic cats decimating wild populations of small animals and birds?

Choosing a Subject for an Investigative Essay

Your first thought may be that you have to investigate something weird and unknown, like the feeding habits of the aardvark. However, your investigation may be more successful (and much easier) if you investigate some everyday object or phenomenon, or an ordinary person. Look for something interesting, unusual, or surprising in your everyday life.

Investigate some aspect of your favorite hobby: cars, fashion, cooking, scuba diving, photography, listening to records, or watching television. In your library, browse through magazines related to your hobby to get a sense of a possible audience. Interview a friend to find out what he or she would like to know about your hobby. Find some written sources and informed people you could interview about your basic question.

Investigate something related to your business or place of work. How is this business organized? Who is a key person you could interview or profile? Survey your customers on their reactions to your service or product.

In a class you are currently taking, what idea, concept, person, performance, or product could you investigate? Initially, discuss the idea with a classmate. Then informally interview your teacher: What angle or focus does he or she suggest? What other books or sources does this teacher suggest? Try to frame your investigative question.

Review the essays you have read so far in this text. Then make a "curiosity list." What topics discussed in your favorite essays might you investigate?

Collecting Information

Begin by stating your investigative question: For your hobby, it might be, "Are compact discs going to take over the entire record market?" or "Who is Public Enemy and what is its contribution to rap music?" For a class, your question might be, "What marketing strategies has the McDonald's franchise used to retain their market share?" or "Who is John Millington Synge and how did he write his classic play, *Riders to the Sea?*" You will probably modify your central question as you collect information, but you need a focus for your initial investigation.

Once you have a tentative question, try the following collecting strategies.

Ask the reporter's "wh" questions about your topic: Who? What? When? Where? Why? How? (Note: You may ask each "wh" question several times: Who is Public Enemy? Who is the audience for their rap music? What is rap music, exactly? What are its cultural or musical roots?)

Interview people who are knowledgeable on your topic. You may use early interviews to help you focus your investigative question, or you may interview experts after you know more about your topic. For your interview, be sure to make an *appointment*. Prepare for your interview by writing down the *questions* you want to ask. At key points in your interview, try *restating* the point your interviewee has just made: "Are you saying that . . . ?" or "OK. So you believe that . . . ?" During your interview, bring a *tape recorder* and/or take *careful notes*.

Use your library sources. Take an orientation tour of your library. Ask your teacher or reference librarian for sources that might be appropriate for your investigation. *When you find a source, make a photocopy.* In class, you can practice taking information from articles without plagiarizing.

Write a questionnaire if you need to know the attitudes, preferences, or opinions of a group of people. (Be sure to test your questionnaire on friends or members of your class before you distribute it.) If you are investigating the popularity of compact discs versus vinyl records or tapes, you might ask the following types of questions:

Yes/No Questions:
    Do you own a compact disc player?___Yes ___No
    Do you own a record player?   ___Yes ___No
    Do you own a tape player?   ___Yes ___No

Multiple Choice: How many compact discs do you own?

___ 1–5   ___ 6–10   ___ 10–15   ___ Over 15

Ranking Lists: Rank the types of music you prefer to listen to. 1 indicates highest preference; 5 indicates lowest preference.

___ Rock   ___ Jazz   ___ Country
___ Classical   ___ Other (Specify)

Open Question: Which format (records, tapes, or CD) will you choose for your next purchase? Explain why.

Note: If you refer to your informal survey in your report, be sure to *describe your survey* and *avoid excessive claims* about the results. In your report on CDs, for example, you might say, "In an informal survey of thirty students conducted in Durward's cafeteria, twenty-one students said that their next purchase would be tapes rather than CDs. Based on their responses, CDs do not yet dominate the local college market."

Shaping Your Investigative Essay

Test the following shaping strategies to see which one(s) will best organize your information and present it clearly to your readers.

Chronological Order of Your Investigation. Writers often follow the natural chronological order of their investigation. They describe their investigation and what they found, step by step. In "Fast Food for Thought," Norman Atkins organizes parts of his essay by narrating successive steps in his own investigation. Notice how the following sentences from the early paragraphs in the article tell the story of Atkins's investigation:

> Setting out to find Cliff was a weird idea, kind of like embarking on a mission to meet Uncle Ben, Mrs. Butterworth, or Dr. Denton.
> I land in Lincoln, a lackluster, spick-and-span cow town of 175,000. . . .
> I have to admit that I was half expecting to see a bronze likeness of Cliff in the center of town.
> Just then, from out of nowhere appears this kindly looking old man, wearing a bolo tie, a well-worn Ultrasuede jacket, and brown Rockports. . . .

Chronological Order of the History of Your Topic. Investigative writers sometimes organize parts of their report to follow the chronological history of their subject: the key events in the life of an important person or the history of an idea, experiment, political movement, cultural trend, or commercial product. In "The Jeaning of America," Carin Quinn tells the story of Levi Strauss and at the same time narrates the history and development of his famous jeans:

> When a married sister in San Francisco offered to pay his way West in 1850, he jumped at the opportunity, taking with him bolts of canvas he hoped to sell for tenting.
> When Strauss ran out of canvas, he wrote his two brothers to send more.
> Almost from the first, Strauss had his cloth dyed the

distinctive indigo that gave blue jeans their name, but it was
not until the 1870s that he added the copper rivets. . . .

Over the ensuing years the company prospered locally,
and by the time of his death in 1902, Strauss had become
a man of prominence in California.

Process Analysis.   When investigative writers ask *how*
something happens, they often turn to process analysis.
A step-by-step description of some process can easily
organize material in an investigative essay. In "Attack of
the Killer Cats," Leon Jaroff describes the steps that British
researchers Churcher and Lawton took in designing their
study and collecting their data. In "Oranges," John Mc-
Phee describes each stage or step in the process of making
orange juice: culling, scrubbing, juicing, finishing, pas-
teurizing, evaporating, and cutting back.

Analysis of Causes or Effects.   Investigative writers answer
the question "Why?" by describing causes or effects that
relate to their topics. In "Fast Food for Thought," Atkins
spends two pages analyzing *why* Cliff succeeded in his
enterprise: He treats the Notes as perishables; he is
colordeaf; he began just as the GI Bill added thousands
of students to American colleges; and he takes advantage
of educational reform movements.

Additional Shaping Strategies.   Other shaping strategies
may help organize your information. Perhaps you could
use **comparison or contrast** to organize (or help gather)
ideas. In "Pop Goes to College," Anthony De Curtis
contrasts popular culture study with the more traditional
academic classes. You can also use **voice** as a thread to tie
your essay together, as Atkins does in "Fast Food for
Thought." Using first person and continually referring to
his experiences and reactions, Atkins connects the various
parts of his investigation.

Drafting Your Investigative Essay

Before you begin drafting, write your central *investigative
question* at the top of the page. Use this question to keep
you focused as you write. If you have extensive informa-

tion, you may need to make a brief *outline* before you begin writing: What are you going to discuss first, second, next, or last? Decide whether you want to write in *first person,* as Atkins does, or more anonymously, as Carin Quinn and Leon Jaroff do. Finally, check the shaping strategies you think will work, *reread* your material and notes one more time, and start your draft.

Revising Your Investigative Essay

After you have finished a first draft and let it sit for a day or so, you are ready to begin revising. As you revise, keep the following tips in mind.

Compare your essay to your central investigative question. Does your essay answer the question you intended to answer? (You may need to change the question or some parts of the essay to make them fit.)

Check the essay for your purpose. Remember that you should be reporting information to your readers, *not* arguing for or against any particular idea.

Reconsider your audience. If you have a specific magazine in mind, skim through an article similar to yours. Reread your essay. Are you being too technical in places? Do you need to be more specific in other places?

Revise your title or your lead-in. Titles and opening sentences should describe your topic and get your reader's attention. Jot down two additional titles. Do you still like your first choice? Ask your peer readers about your lead-in. Do you have some attention-getting *example, statistic, play on words, quotation* from some expert, or *question* that plays on your reader's curiosity?

Reread your opening paragraphs for answers to "wh" questions. Do you give basic who, what, when, and where information for your readers early in your essay?

Do you have transitions in the opening sentences of

body paragraphs? Look for key words or transitions that signal your organization to your reader. Are there key chronological words? Do key phrases indicate that you are investigating cause or effect? Make sure your shaping strategy is apparent to your readers.

Check the accuracy of your summaries, paraphrases, and direct quotations against your notes or your photocopies. Direct quotations must be accurate, word-for-word transcriptions. Be sure to identify your sources and give proper credit.

Revise and edit sentences to improve clarity and avoid errors. Use your peer readers' reactions and check your handbook to simplify sentences and correct any errors in spelling, punctuation, or inappropriate usage.

Postscript For Your Investigative Essay

When you have finished your essay, answer the following questions about your composing process.

1. What sources of information (your own observation, interviews, surveys, printed articles, books) were most helpful?

2. How did your central investigative question change from your first idea to its final form?

3. Which shaping strategies were most helpful in organizing your essay?

4. What did you learn about investigating techniques as you wrote this essay?

5. What do you like best about your final version? What would you change if you had more time?

Attack of the Killer Cats

LEON JAROFF

PREREADING JOURNAL TOPIC

Freewrite for five minutes about a pet you have—a cat, dog, or other animal. Explain in what ways your pet is domestic and in what ways it is still wild.

STUDENT JOURNAL RESPONSES

My cocker spaniel Angel was in some ways more wild than domesticated. She would, when she wanted to go to sleep, do at least twenty circles, all the while scratching and clawing at the floor or couch, before she actually would lie down. She used to do some pretty strange things, and I believe this preparation was similar to scraping a sleeping place on the ground. She had another strange activity. She would carry around rocks. I'm not sure whether this is instinct or not, but when you tossed a rock, she would pick it up. Once I saw her trying to pick up a rock that must have weighed ten pounds. She would constantly try to sneak rocks into the house, and we had to pry her mouth when she came in the door.

My cat, Karl. What a cat! He truly is more of a person than a cat. First, some background. About three years ago, my roommate's cat had kittens. I kept one of them and named him Karl after Karl Marx. When I moved in with my girlfriend, he ran away. He was gone for over three months and I counted him for dead. But then someone across town called and said they had found him. Since the day he came back, he has been the best pet. He is still wild to a large extent. His most notorious behavior is that he is a bat-catcher. He has brought in a least a half a dozen bats in the last three months. He injures them just enough to pose a slight challenge to his hunting capabilities. I'm always the one who has to kill the thing and throw it away. As far as being domesticated, he shows this when I go to bed at night. As soon as he hears me brushing my teeth, he runs to the bedroom and jumps on the bed. He mandates that I give him an intensive "petting session" before he jumps down off the bed and goes on his way.

Are cats furry and lovable pets, or are they neighborhood killers, decimating the local population of rabbits and songbirds? Do they, in fact, lead a Jekyll and Hyde existence? Leon Jaroff summarizes a scientific study appearing in Natural History *on the predatory habits of domestic cats. A science editor at* Time *since 1984, Leon Jaroff graduated from the University of Michigan, and worked at* Life *and* Time *before becoming managing editor of* Discover *magazine. He has published award-winning articles on earthquakes and black holes.*

In the following Time *magazine article, Jaroff reports on a study by two English scientists who estimate that, in Britain, cats kill some 70 million animals and birds every year. Jaroff's report in* Time *reached millions of readers, and many objected to this portrait of their pets as "killer cats." In fact, 82 percent of the readers who responded to Jaroff's article defended their pets, claiming that the cats were, after all, only following their natural instincts.*

ATTACK OF THE KILLER CATS   *Attention-getting title!*

While fond of his cat, [British biologist Peter Churcher] looked askance at its practice of dragging small mammals and birds into [his Bedfordshire house and devouring them] under the kitchen table "to the sound of crunching bones." One of [Churcher's associates, John Lawton, a   *who* · *where - what* · *graphic image* · *who*   1 professor of community ecology at the University of London,] was similarly impressed by his own cat's predatory pursuits. With the natural curiosity of true scientists, they decided to look further into the depredations of felines. If all the domestic cats in Britain caught as much prey as theirs did, the two men reasoned, they could be having a "very significant" impact on the environment.

Hyperbole? Not at all. Writing [in the July issue] of *Natural History,* Churcher and Lawton estimate that Britain's 5 million house cats wreak an annual toll of some 70 million animals and birds.

In reaching this astonishing conclusion, the intrepid investigators used only the most rigorous scientific methods. Choosing Churcher's small village as their test site, they conducted a feline census and [found that 78 cats resided in the community's 173 houses, "a slightly higher incidence of cat owning than in Britain as a whole."] Owners of 77 of the cats agreed to cooperate. Each was given a supply of consecutively numbered polyethylene bags labeled with his cat's code letter and asked to store whatever was left of any prey his pet brought home.

For a full year the scientists made weekly rounds of the village, collecting bags and identifying the remains. If the cat had consumed the entire catch, the victim was simply recorded as an "unknown." Otherwise, the identification process was simple, the scientists report, although "initially—the study began during the summer months—it was rather smelly." Surprisingly enough, they write, "the villagers were much less squeamish than we had expected." In fact, some went about their assigned task with great gusto, placing their cats' trophies in home freezers to await collection.

Tallying and analyzing their data at the end of a year, the investigators found that the cats

Margin notes:
Investigative question: How do cats affect their enviroment?

when   2

That's alot but is it a problem?   3

Tone: Is Jaroff serious here? More what-the data of the study

How the data was collected.   4

funny! Talks about the cats' victims

| Great line!

the results   5

had claimed almost 1,100 items of prey, 64% consisting of small mammals: mostly wood mice, field voles and common shrews, interspersed with an occasional rabbit, weasel or pipistrelle bat. The remaining victims, all birds, included sparrows, song thrushes, blackbirds and robins.

Shouldn't cats kill mice?

I Didn't know cats killed weasels! [6]

Delving further into the sparrow toll, which accounted for 16% of the total feline catch, the scientists concluded that from a third to a half of all sparrow deaths were attributable to cats. Extrapolating these figures, they estimated that cats kill at least 20 million birds a year in Britain. "Yet," write the authors indignantly, "we are supposed to be a nation of bird lovers, many of whom keep cats but still castigate bird hunters and trappers on the continent of Europe."

Everybody's favorite bird, right?

True: I'm guilty of that.

Impressive as these statistics are, the scientists note, the carnage may be even worse. They cite an American study indicating that house cats bring only about half their victims home.

What does the american study show? [7]

Will cat fanciers find these conclusions unsettling? Evidently not. When the authors' work was published earlier in a scientific journal, including the fact that a few Bedfordshire cats had each contributed as many as 100 items of prey to the study, they received letters from other cat owners boasting of their own pets' prowess. The record, they report, is currently held by a cat from Dorset that dragged in more than 400 little creatures in one year. The scientists are aghast. "These proud owners," they report, "seem quite unperturbed by the slaughter."

We couldn't agree about conclusion. Some liked it, others said what's the point? [8]

Investigative question: Are cats loving pets or are they killing machines that are hazardous to our enviroment?

QUESTIONS ON MEANING

1. What answers does Jaroff provide to the following "wh" questions: *Who* did the study? *Where* and *when* was it conducted? *How* were the data collected? *What* were the results?

2. Each cat owner was "asked to store whatever was left of any prey his pet brought home." What question does this raise about Churcher's and Lawton's estimates that "cats kill at least 20 million birds a year in Britain"?

QUESTIONS ON PURPOSE AND STRATEGY

1. Readers often expect journalists to report information accurately, without judging, editorializing, or sensationalizing. Where does Jaroff appear to be most and least objective in his report?

2. Jaroff's article follows the organization of the original study: introduction to the question, methods for the study, data, and conclusions. Identify these major divisions in Jaroff's report.

QUESTIONS ON AUDIENCE AND LANGUAGE

1. Does Jaroff's title effectively appeal to his intended audience? Write two alternate titles. Would either of them be more appropriate for his audience?

2. Jaroff's article appeared in *Time* magazine. What technical language does Jaroff use that perhaps could be eliminated or explained?

3. Is Jaroff's tone (his attitude toward Lawton's and Churcher's study) serious or slightly humorous? Cite specific sentences or words to support your reaction.

QUESTIONS FOR DISCUSSION AND WRITING

1. According to Jaroff, the English researchers reasoned that cats in Britain "could be having a 'very significant' impact on the environment." Do the researchers (or Jaroff) think this "impact" is good or bad for the environment? Do you agree?

2. Read the "Letters to the Editor" section of a current *Time*

magazine. Following the format of those letters, write *Time*'s editors about your response to this article.

3. Many libraries keep a shelf of new acquisitions—books that have just arrived. Browse through these books. Choose one whose subject interests you and write a short investigative summary, modeled on Jaroff's essay.

The Jeaning of America

CARIN QUINN

PREREADING JOURNAL ENTRY

Levi's jeans are an American legend, a cultural icon or symbol. Brainstorm for a minute or two: List as many other American icons as you can. Choose one that catches your attention. What do you know about its origins? What would you like to find out about it?

Today, there are tough double-kneed jeans for kids, acid-washed jeans for teens, designer jeans for the fashion set, and boot-cut jeans for outdoor workers. But it all began in the 1850s when Levi Strauss, a German immigrant gone West to seek his fortune, sewed up some sturdy canvas pants for a miner. Carin Quinn, who received her Master's degree from California State University in Los Angeles, first published "The Jeaning of America—and the World" in American Heritage.

The story of Levi Strauss's career, and the parallel career of his proletarian pants, is part true grit, part luck, and part legend. The bottom line, Quinn reports, is 83 million pairs of Levi's riveted blue jeans sold every year.

This is the story of a sturdy American symbol which 1 has now spread throughout most of the world. The symbol is not the dollar. It is not even Coca-Cola. It is a simple pair of pants called blue jeans, and what the pants symbolize is what Alexis de Tocqueville called "a manly and legitimate passion for equality. . . ." Blue jeans are favored equally by bureaucrats and cowboys; bankers and deadbeats; fashion designers and beer drinkers. They draw no distinctions and recognize no classes; they are merely American. Yet they are sought after almost everywhere in the world—including Russia, where authorities recently broke up a teen-aged gang that was selling them on the black market for two hundred dollars a pair. They have been around for a long time, and it seems likely that they will outlive even the necktie.

This ubiquitous American symbol was the invention 2 of a Bavarian-born Jew. His name was Levi Strauss.

He was born in Bad Ocheim, Germany, in 1829, and 3 during the European political turmoil of 1848 decided to take his chances in New York, to which his two brothers already had emigrated. Upon arrival, Levi soon found that his two brothers had exaggerated their tales of an easy life in the land of the main chance. They were landowners, they had told him; instead, he found them pushing needles, thread, pots, pans, ribbons, yarn, scissors, and buttons to housewives. For two years he was a lowly peddler, hauling some 180 pounds of sundries door-to-door to eke out a marginal living. When a married sister in San Francisco offered to pay his way West in 1850, he jumped at the opportunity, taking with him bolts of canvas he hoped to sell for tenting.

It was the wrong kind of canvas for that purpose, but 4 while talking with a miner down from the mother lode, he learned that pants—sturdy pants that would stand up to the rigors of the digging—were almost impossible to find. Opportunity beckoned. On the spot, Strauss measured the man's girth and inseam with a piece of string and, for six dollars in gold dust, had [the canvas] tailored into a pair of stiff but rugged pants. The miner was delighted with the result, word got around about "those pants of Levi's," and Strauss was in business. The company has been in business ever since.

When Strauss ran out of canvas, he wrote his two 5 brothers to send more. He received instead a tough, brown cotton cloth made in Nîmes, France—called *serge de Nîmes* and swiftly shortened to "denim" (the word "jeans" derives from Gênes, the French word for Genoa, where a similar cloth was produced). Almost from the first, Strauss had his cloth dyed the distinctive indigo that gave blue jeans their name, but it was not until the 1870s that he added the copper rivets which have long since become a company trademark. The rivets were the idea of a Virginia City, Nevada, tailor, Jacob W. Davis, who added them to pacify a mean-tempered miner called Alkali Ike. Alkali, the story goes, complained that the pockets of his jeans always tore when he stuffed them with ore samples and demanded that Davis do something about it. As a kind of joke, Davis took the pants to a blacksmith and had the pockets riveted; once again, the idea worked so well that word got around; in 1873 Strauss appropriated and patented the gimmick— and hired Davis as a regional manager.

By this time, Strauss had taken both his brothers and 6 two brothers-in-law into the company and was ready for his third San Francisco store. Over the ensuing years the company prospered locally, and by the time of his death in 1902, Strauss had become a man of prominence in California. For three decades thereafter the business remained profitable though small, with sales largely confined to the working people of the West—cowboys, lumberjacks, railroad workers, and the like. Levi's jeans were first introduced to the East, apparently, during the dude-ranch craze of the 1930s, when vacationing Easterners returned and spread the word about the wonderful pants with rivets. Another boost came in World War II, when blue jeans were declared an essential commodity and were sold only to people engaged in defense work. From a company with fifteen salespeople, two plants, and almost no business east of the Mississippi in 1946, the organization grew in thirty years to include a sales force of more than twenty-two thousand, with fifty plants and offices in thirty-five countries. Each year, more than 250,000,000 items of Levi's clothing are sold—including more than 83,000,000 pairs of riveted blue jeans. They have become, through marketing, word of mouth, and demonstrable reliability, the common pants of America. They can be purchased pre-washed, pre-faded, and pre-shrunk for the suitably proletarian look. They adapt themselves to any sort of idiosyncratic use; women slit them at the inseams and convert them into long skirts, men chop them off above the knees and turn them into something to be worn while challenging the surf. Decorations and ornamentations abound.

The pants have become a tradition, and along the way   7
have acquired a history of their own—so much so that the company has opened a museum in San Francisco. There was, for example, the turn-of-the-century trainman who replaced a faulty coupling with a pair of jeans; the Wyoming man who used his jeans as a towrope to haul his car out of a ditch; the Californian who found several pairs in an abandoned mine, wore them, then discovered they were sixty-three years old and still as good as new and turned them over to the Smithsonian as a tribute to their toughness. And then there is the particularly terrifying story of the careless construction worker who dangled fifty-two stories above the street until rescued, his sole support the Levi's belt loop through which his rope was hooked.

QUESTIONS ON MEANING

1. Quinn's main idea is that jeans are an American symbol because they are proletarian. What specific sentences from Quinn's essay support or refute that statement?

2. What questions about Levi Strauss and his jeans does this essay answer? Which of those questions focus on the basic who, what, when, where, how, and why information? Write out the central question for this investigative essay.

3. According to Quinn, did Levi Strauss and his jeans become famous through hard work, good fortune, or both?

QUESTIONS ON PURPOSE AND STRATEGY

1. List several possible purposes for Quinn's essay. Which of these is her main purpose?

2. Which paragraphs discuss jeans? Which paragraphs discuss the life of Levi Strauss? Which paragraphs discuss both? Based on your findings, does this essay focus more on Strauss than on his jeans?

3. Which of the following shaping strategies organizes this essay: comparison/contrast, analysis, chronological order? Defend your choice by citing examples from the text.

QUESTIONS ON AUDIENCE AND LANGUAGE

1. Page through a copy of *American Heritage*, the magazine in which this article appeared. Where in Quinn's essay is she most obviously writing for an *American Heritage* readers?

2. *Etymology* means the study of the history and origin of words. Where does Quinn give us the etymology of a word? Look up this word in your own dictionary. Does it give an etymology?

QUESTIONS FOR DISCUSSION AND WRITING

1. Quinn says Levi's jeans are sturdy, ubiquitous, and proletarian. Could all these words apply to Levi Strauss himself? Explain.

2. Read William Zinsser's essay, "College Pressures" in chapter 6. Explain how Levi Strauss's biography illustrates Zinsser's main point.

3. Go to your library. Ask the reference librarian which resources, in addition to the encyclopedia, would help you find out information about Levi Strauss. Make photocopies of biographical information on Levi Strauss from at least three sources. Is Carin Quinn's information correct? What could she have added? Is it likely that she used any of the sources you found?

4. Write your own investigative essay on some cultural icon in America: the Coke bottle or can, Kleenex® tissue, Campbell's soup label, a baseball, the hot dog, cowboy boots, the bikini, glass high-rise buildings, the flag, the Apple computer, shopping malls, the Ford Mustang or Edsel, and so forth.

Pop Goes to College

ANTHONY DECURTIS

(1951–   )

> **PREREADING JOURNAL ENTRY**
>
> Find a copy of your college catalogue. Look through the
> course listings for course titles focusing on some aspect of
> popular culture: contemporary pop songs, sports, art,
> literature, and psychology. Copy down course descriptions
> of several classes that focus on popular culture.

Anthony DeCurtis is a writer and senior editor at Rolling Stone, *where
he currently edits the record review section. He received his Ph.D. from
Indiana University and has taught in the English department at Emory
University. His retrospective essay on Eric Clapton, "Crossroads," received a 1988 Grammy Award.*

*"Pop Goes to College," DeCurtis says, was "the result of a long-
standing desire to break down the boundaries between popular culture
and so-called high art." In a Western culture class, for example, what
books belong in the "canon," the list of "officially recognized" works?
Academics agree that the canon should include works by women and
minorities, but should it also include artifacts of popular culture? In his
article on the popular-culture program at Bowling Green University,
DeCurtis investigates the question, "Can television sitcoms and rock and
roll peacefully co-exist with modern poetry and Shakespearean drama?"*

It's a luscious, sunny April day in Bowling Green,   1
Ohio, and along Wooster Street, the southern border of
the campus of Bowling Green State University (BGSU),
students are engaged in the time-honored spring rituals
of academic life: catching rays, tossing Frisbees and pump-

ing rock & roll out the open windows of frat houses. Far
from being mere breaks from the rigors of study or ways
to relieve tension as final exams approach, however, these
activities could well be subjects of study at Bowling Green,
"the only institution in the nation with a degree program
in popular culture," as a school brochure proudly states.

Naturally, rock & roll is a mainstay in the curriculum 2
of Bowling Green's Department of Popular Culture; the
department offers a course called Introduction to Popular
Music, which examines "musical styles, trends in popular
music, popular performers and entertainers." It might be
a stretch, but sunbathing and Frisbee tossing could perhaps find a home in another course, Popular Entertain-
ments, which analyzes "circuses, carnivals, parades, vaude-
ville, professional and amateur sports, camping, etc."

At both Bowling Green and other campuses, pop 3
culture is a booming—and increasingly controversial—
academic business. Last March in New Orleans, more than
3000 professors, scholars and students attended the annual joint convention of the Popular Culture Association
and the American Culture Association, both of which are
based in Bowling Green. There the pop culturists, as they
call themselves, heard presentations like "The Reconcili-
ation of Archie and Meathead: *All in the Family*'s Last
Episode," " '*Carpe Diem*' in the Music of Jimmy Buffet"
and "The Tupperware Party and the American Dream."

It has been difficult for such pursuits to gain respect- 4
ability in the ivory tower. Academia is hardly noted for
the speed with which it accepts new fields of study, and
as enrollment in pop-culture courses has risen, scholars
in the field have had to endure the snobbism of their
more conventional colleagues.

In fact, battle lines have been drawn. Perhaps the most 5
significant face-off took place at Stanford, where the
faculty senate, after a rancorous debate, voted earlier this
year to drop a required course called Western Culture,
which had essentially been a yearlong "great books" survey.
In its place is a new course called Cultures, Ideas and
Values, which keeps roughly half of the Western Culture

syllabus but also prescribes a work from "at least one non-European culture" and books by "women, minorities and persons of color." The canon busting at Stanford augurs well for pop-culture advocates.

Ray Browne, the founder and head of Bowling Green's 6 popular-culture program, has been at the forefront of his discipline's battle for credibility for more than twenty years—a struggle he perceives as having ended in victory. A sixty-six-year-old man of unfailing optimism, Browne is like a civil-rights worker who remembers when segregation was the law of the land and who is proud and happy to be alive in a time when equality is legally guaranteed—even if, in practice, such equality is far from a reality.

Browne's cluttered office is in the basement of the 7 popular-culture building—a small brick house located, appropriately enough, just off campus, across Wooster Street. Asked if popular culture is still an embattled field, Browne leans forward and says, "No, no longer. Fifteen years ago, if you'd asked that question, the answer would have been yes. Maybe even five or seven years ago. But not any longer." Browne's certainty is based on his sense of the mood at the convention in New Orleans. "I detected a sense of accomplishment and dignity and complete self-reliance which I had never felt before," he says. "The people there could stand up alongside any academic with the assurance that 'my field is just as important as your field.' "

Not everyone would grant popular-culture studies 8 anywhere near that degree of intellectual status. Even members of Browne's own faculty say that their war is far from won. "I think that it's too early to declare victory," says Jack Santino, an assistant professor in the department. "What we have is a single master's program in a single department in a single university in one state in this country. I don't think that's the top of the mountain."

The climb, however, may begin to get easier. Debate 9 has raged about what exactly the appropriate subjects for college study are. Over the past eight years, the consensus about what belongs in the curriculum has narrowed, for reasons that are political as well as educational. Although the campus upheavals of the Sixties and student demands for "relevance" reshaped college curricula in the Seventies, the Reagan administration swept into power with a far more conservative education policy.

As head of the National Endowment for the Human- 10 ities (NEH) during Reagan's first term, William J. Bennett, who would go on to become the secretary of education, established himself as a leading spokesperson for the "back to basics" movement, which advocates a return to a "core curriculum" based on traditional fields of study and a canon of great works. Considerable anxiety was raised by the 1983 Department of Education study *A Nation at Risk,* which depicted American students as ignorant of the most elementary facts of their nation's history and culture.

If that weren't enough, Allan Bloom's best-selling 11 jeremiad *The Closing of the American Mind* and E. D. Hirsch Jr.'s *Cultural Literacy* heated the argument even more. Bloom's book asserts, among other things, that rock & roll "ruins the imagination of young people and makes it very difficult for them to have a passionate relationship to the art and thought that are the substance of liberal education." Meanwhile, Lynne Cheney, who succeeded Bennett at the NEH, is firmly in agreement with Bennett's vision, and she has used the enormous funding power of her agency to advance further the Reagan administration's agenda.

So it's no surprise that a prominent sign in the pop- 12 culture building at BGSU reads, ALLAN BLOOM AND LYNNE CHENEY WILL BURN IN HELL. Browne sees the Reagan administration's attitude toward popular culture as out of step with what's happening at universities around the country. "The only thing they've done is deny us any kind of federal assistance," he says. "William Bennett and Lynne Cheney are just as intransigent and opposed as they've ever been, but their voices have not been heard. The number of courses is growing."

One reason schools are creating popular-culture 13
courses is that, even in the era of the business major,
students flock to them. "We may be or may not be halfway
decent scholars," says Jack Nachbar, a professor of popular
culture at Bowling Green. "But I think the department as
a whole takes its teaching very seriously." At a time when
many professors regard teaching as an annoying distrac-
tion from the research projects that can win them tenure
and promotion, such dedication is no small attraction to
students. In addition, pop-culture professors are often
more willing to be imaginative in their instructional methods.

When Van Cagle—a young professor at Bowling 14
Green who will be offering popular-culture courses this
year at Tulane University, in New Orleans—was teaching
Dick Hebdige's *Subculture: The Meaning of Style* in his
popular-music class, he decided to take his subject to the
streets. "The assignment for that night," Cagle says, "was
to try to figure out the literal reactions in everyday life
that punks got on the street in London in 1977. I asked
the students to think about the clothing, think about what
it meant and dress that way for the class."

Cagle then led a group of students decked out in 15
spiked hair, leather dresses, handcuffs, chains, safety pins,
red Mohawks and ripped fish-net stockings on a walk
around campus. Cagle himself donned a dog collar, a
leather jacket and a shirt stained with fake blood. The
group elicited quite a response. "Hebdige suggests that
you'll either get the reaction that you're insane, people
will want to draw you back into their own reality and
make you seem normal, or they'll feel very threatened,"
Cagle says. "We had a group of fraternity guys follow us
from the education building to the library, and they were
talking about how much they wanted to kill us. They
thought we were very real. . . . We got the reactions we
needed, and we were able to go back to the class and talk
about it."

At Bowling Green, a school of about 15,000 students, 16

there are currently 20 undergraduates majoring in pop culture, 8 undergraduates minoring in it and 14 graduate students working toward a pop-culture master's degree. Students can also pursue a Ph.D. in American culture with a concentration in popular culture. About 2000 students a year enroll in pop-culture classes, which are cross-listed with disciplines ranging from philosophy to home economics. Many students drift into the classes hoping to fill a humanities requirement with a course that demands little more than flipping on the tube or reading comic books. If they eventually find that these classes can teach them a good deal about the media-saturated world around them and decide to pursue their interest further, they often encounter the same condescending attitudes that afflict their professors.

"I think the main reason the classes are looked upon 17 as a blow-off is that the people who come to them enjoy them," says Brett Henne, a journalism student who has taken a few popular-culture courses. "If you enjoy a class, it doesn't necessarily make it a blow-off. It just means that you're interested in learning."

Popular-culture students tend to be people who are 18 interested in college less as a means of career advancement than as a time of exploration. "College years are such a small percentage of your life—why not enjoy them?" asks Lora Marini, a double major in pop culture and psychology who has just given an energetic report on "death rock"— the Smiths, the Jesus and Mary Chain and Siouxsie and the Banshees—in Cagle's popular-music class. "There are so many people who say they have to graduate in four years. They have to get diplomas so they can go out and get a job. I don't care if I'm here eight years."

Though pop-culture students tend to do no worse 19 than other humanities majors on the job market, some students are hedging their bets. "I'm not a pop-culture major; I'm a communications major," says John McAlea, who is also in a local band called the Exchange. "I'm wading both streams, because I'm taking business classes but I'm also taking pop-culture classes. The reason why I take pop-culture classes is for *me*—I want to know this knowledge."

The traditional academic dogma would seem to say 20 that the knowledge McAlea wants is not worth knowing. If disconcerting numbers of students don't know who T. S. Eliot was or when the Civil War was fought, should they really be permitted to fulfill requirements with a course on detective novels?

"The one thing that I think is important is that we 21 don't necessarily say that T. S. Eliot shouldn't be taught," says Jack Santino. "It's not an either-or situation. I think people should know when the Civil War was and they should know about T. S. Eliot—but they should also be aware that the culture they live in is important and meaningful and operative.

"What we *don't* do is just flip on the television for an 22 hour," Santino adds. "The point is to talk about it in terms of social context, in terms of creation and intentionality and audience—questions that, I would say, have never occurred to most of the students before. That's a legitimate perspective."

The growth of pop-culture studies is also related to 23 another intellectual trend. Many young academics are less interested in establishing the "quality" of a particular book or song or movie than in discovering what it expresses about the society that created it. This approach is closer to sociology than to aesthetics, and it is one thread in the weave of "cultural relativism"—the belief that standards of value are embedded in specific societies and do not translate meaningfully from one culture to another.

"The whole argument of 'Is this great art?' is irrelevant 24 to the framework in which we're studying," says Mickey Stephens, a Ph.D. student in the American-culture program and a guitarist in the Bowling Green band the Sygn, which formerly was known as the Sex Beatles. "The point would be that you can find the same amount of interest in any cultural product. We're not looking for aesthetic values. We're not looking for value judgments. What we're looking for is cultural indicators, how well you can feel the pulse of the culture by analyzing any artifact of the culture at a given time."

But according to Dieter Frank, another Ph.D. candi- 25 date in American culture and Stephens's partner in the Sygn, this cultural relativism, combined with the uncertain standing of popular culture in the academic hierarchy, makes for a credibility crisis in the field. "The last piece that finally defines what exactly it is that we're studying is, in my opinion, missing," he says. "A good example might be the questions for my M.A. exam, the comps I took last week. The questions were basically 'Tell me, what do you think about this program? Is it okay? Do you have suggestions?' There's still this uncertainty. 'Is this the right direction, or is there any direction at all? Do you feel that we're heading somewhere?' "

Whatever the final destination proves to be, popular 26 culture is certain to be part of the academic landscape in the future. The great tradition of Western culture is increasingly seen as a white-male hegemony. As minorities and women achieve a greater say in the definition of that culture, it's inevitable that popular forms of expression— which, because they have been seen as less "serious," have allowed for broader participation—will be viewed as valid fields of study. Also, since the late Fifties, America itself has been a virtual laboratory of popular culture. Anyone who wants to figure out what's been going on in this society for the past thirty years simply must take television, the movies and pop music into account.

And sometimes popular-culture studies can lead to 27 more personal insights. "Studying popular culture helped me find myself," says Rod Hatfield, a Bowling Green undergraduate and a member of a local performance-art band called Elvis Christ. "I was such a fan of pop culture, and I didn't even realize until I began studying it: 'Wow, this stuff applies to *me*—to my haircut, to my clothes.' I think it's a really valid study of society, what America's up to at a particular time."

QUESTIONS ON MEANING

1. DeCurtis says that "the battle lines have been drawn" between studies of classic works and popular works. Who is on each side? What is the controversy about?

2. According to this report, what are typical subjects for popular culture classes? How do popular-culture advocates justify the study of popular culture?

QUESTIONS ON PURPOSE AND STRATEGY

1. What question does this investigative report attempt to answer?

2. Is DeCurtis reporting on the battle or arguing for one side in the controversy?

3. Does DeCurtis use a chronological order to report his findings? Does he contrast opposing points of view? Does he analyze the causes for the increasing interest in popular-culture classes? Does he analyze his findings by discussing faculty response and then student response?

QUESTIONS ON AUDIENCE AND LANGUAGE

1. Who is DeCurtis's audience for this essay? Students? Teachers? Anyone interested in trends in education? Cite specific passages to support your answer.

2. How does DeCurtis characterize Ray Browne, the founder of Bowling Green's popular-culture program? Is it appropriate for DeCurtis's audience to know that Brown is sixty-six years old, that he is like a civil rights worker, and that he "leans forward" when he talks?

3. In this essay, are students who take popular-culture courses portrayed sympathetically or humorously?

QUESTIONS FOR DISCUSSION AND WRITING

1. In the next-to-last paragraph, DeCurtis says: "As minorities and women achieve a greater say in the definition of that culture, it's inevitable that popular forms of expression—

which, because they have been seen as less 'serious,' have allowed for broader participation—will be viewed as valid fields of study." Is DeCurtis implying that minorities and women are capable of creating only popular literature?

2. Reconstruct how DeCurtis probably wrote this essay. What places did he visit? Identify the sources—both printed material and people—he used in writing the essay.

3. Reread several responses given by the teachers and students that DeCurtis interviewed. For each response, what *question* do you think DeCurtis asked?

4. Investigate the status of popular-culture courses at your college and report your findings in an article suitable for your college newspaper.

Fast Food for Thought

NORMAN ATKINS

(1962–   )

> **PREREADING JOURNAL ENTRY**
>
> If you have ever used study guides such as *Cliffs Notes* or *Monarch Notes,* describe your experience. What was the course and what book were you studying? Did you find the guide helpful? Did you also read the book?

Cliffs Notes, *like McDonald's hamburgers or Levi's jeans, has a secure place in American popular culture. Clifton Keith Hillegass and his study guides for literary classics ranging from* The Canterbury Tales *to* The Color Purple *are the subject of Norman Atkins's investigative essay published in* Rolling Stone. *A free-lance writer, Atkins has also published articles in* The Village Voice, *the* Boston Globe, *and the* Washington Post.

In "Fast Food for Thought," Atkins takes us to the headquarters of Cliffs Notes *in Lincoln, Nebraska, introduces us to Cliff and his associates, tells the story of Cliff's life, and explains why these "garish yellow and black study outlines" have sold 60 million copies since they were introduced twenty-eight years ago.*

In those wastrel days of youth, when zoning out in 1 front of "Mannix" reruns stirred me more than *Crime and Punishment,* that fat Russian thing, I felt indebted to Cliffs Notes. Like most of my bonehead classmates, I'd skip the novel and fill up a few blue books with the literary pabulum I'd pilfered from Cliffs. I figured Dostoevski was for losers.

It is positively criminal, but it's true: high school and 2

college students have been getting away with murder by this device for more than a quarter of a century now. But like that Raskolnikov character, one is prone to suffering a fit of remorse later on. It got so terrible for me that I had to incinerate all my old Cliffs Notes, the worst reminders I know of what absolute morosophs we once were.

For as long as I can remember, I imagined that those 3 garish yellow and black study outlines were knocked off by a mad horde of Mr. Chipses sequestered in cells at the foot of the Magic Mountain or the Wuthering Heights. Isn't that what the cliffs in the logo suggested? Actually, I was by nature such an inattentive reader that I didn't even notice that it says right there on the title page that the Notes are published in Lincoln, Nebraska. There are no cliffs: the logo is a visual pun on the name of Cliff. These are *his* notes, of course. Setting out to find Cliff was a weird idea, kind of like embarking on a mission to meet Uncle Ben, Mrs. Butterworth, or Dr. Denton.

I land in Lincoln, a lackluster, spick-and-span cow 4 town of 175,000 that looks as if it were plucked right out of *Babbitt* or *Main Street*. No surprise then that there are Notes for both these Sinclair Lewis novels. Churches call their flocks from every other corner, and when I open the curtains in my room at the Cornhusker Hotel, there's the Back to the Bible/Good News Broadcasting Association right outside my window. Wonder whether they're planning a Note on *Elmer Gantry*, too.

I have to admit I was half expecting to see a bronze 5 likeness of Cliff in the center of town. So I'm somewhat stymied when nobody seems to have heard of him. "Cliff Thone, of Cliff's Smoke Shop?" asks one woman I meet. "You mean the guy who runs Kinko's Copies?" asks a young man. Could it be *my* Cliff is a hoax?

Undaunted, I walk the eight blocks to Cliffs Notes, 6 Inc., which occupies a squat, white, ten-thousand-square-foot warehouse and office building, a sterling example of bland neo-Rotarian architecture. I'm greeted at the door by J. Richard Spellman, the president of Cliffs Notes, who tells me he assumed most of the day-to-day responsibilities of running the company when Chairman Cliff ducked into semiretirement about three years ago. Spellman's speech betrays his accountant's training as he briefs me on the bare essentials:

Did you know that more than 60 million Cliffs Notes 7 have been sold in twenty-eight years, which could mean that roughly one in every four American students has used one? Did you know that Cliffs annually ships out about 5 million Notes a year and rakes in more than $7 million in revenues and completely dominates the book-notes market? Did you know that the best-selling Note is *The Scarlet Letter*, followed closely by *Huckleberry Finn, Hamlet,* and *Macbeth?*

Spellman says company-sponsored surveys show that, 8 my suspicion to the contrary, most students who use the Notes also read the books. "The better the student, the more likely he is to use the Notes." I can tell I'm not going to get anywhere with Spellman. Where is Cliff?

I mosey by the company bulletin board, where a recent 9 *National Lampoon* parody is tacked up. It catches the general public's perception of the Notes better than Spellman's lecture does. Kafka's *Metamorphosis* is condensed thus: "A man turns into a cockroach and his family gets annoyed." Dante's *Inferno* is summed up this way: "A man visits hell and sees a lot of terrible things."

Just then, from out of nowhere appears this kindly 10 looking old man, wearing a bolo tie, a well-worn Ultra-suede jacket, and brown Rockports—a triumph of sartorial function over style. I can tell right away I am face to face with Cliff, the hero and villain of my putative literature education. Actually, he looks like Ike.[1] Even his second wife, Mary, says so. "Same haircut," he admits. On top of his bald dome, he wears a pair of tortoise-shell bifocals. "So he won't lose them," says Connie Brakhahn, the

---

[1] Name of President Dwight David Eisenhower (1890–1969).

advertising director, who's been working here for eight years.

When I tell Cliff how I used his Notes, he gives me a 11 broad corn-eating grin, slaps his knee and says, with hyper-meticulous enunciation, "I can tell I'm dealing with a *sat-is-fied* customer!"

That night, we break steak together, and over the next 12 several days our friendship grows as we zoom across the Nebraska landscape in Cliff's silver Lincoln Continental. The car is the only thing I can find about him that's patently un-Cliff. I'm pleased to report, for instance, that he's an avid reader of *USA Today,* the Cliffs Notes of newspapers. I also detect that Cliff's style has rubbed off on Mary when I see her snap a photo with her pocket Instamatic, a quick-read camera in the spirit of Cliffs.

Maybe someday Cliff will write his memoirs and tell 13 you all this himself. In the meantime, since I don't want to steal his story, let me merely Cliff it.

No matter how you view it, Rising City is neither— 14 just four hundred folks grabbing some sleep near a couple of Nebraska grain elevators. But if ancient Mesopotamia is considered the cradle of Western civilization, Rising City can arguably be called the crib of courses in Western civilization. For it was here, sixty-nine years ago next month, that a rural postman and a housewife delivered unto the world of abbreviated learning one Clifton Keith Hillegass. It should have been apparent thereafter, when *Clifton* was shortened simply to *Cliff,* that truncating texts would become synonymous with his name.

Cliff's childhood was, as Ronald Reagan has described 15 his own, "one of those rare Huck Finn-Tom Sawyer idylls." For the purposes of understanding what prepared him for his life's mission, three chapters in his youth bear special consideration here.

In the first one, we learn how Cliff's nose came to be 16 the shape of the inside of a book. At the age of seven, little Cliff was bedridden for two months after a mastoid operation. In order to pass the time, he practically taught himself how to read, starting with a sappy but advanced novelette called *Pappina.* This is what launched his lifelong romance with letters. As a kid, he'd sneak a flashlight under the covers and pore over Jack Harkaway sports adventures or Robert Louis Stevenson's *Black Arrow,* a story to which he's returned six times. He was also keen on Sir Walter Scott, James Fenimore Cooper, and, especially, Charles Dickens. Unlike Holden Caulfield, the protagonist of *The Catcher in the Rye,* the first contemporary book Cliff Noted, this boy couldn't get enough of "that David Copperfield kind of crap."

Legend has it that before graduating from high school, 17 Cliff read every last volume in the Rising City public library. Ask the librarian from the early thirties to check this fact, and he'll tell you it's 100 percent true. "Every book," says the librarian, who just happens to be Cliff. "Many of them with regret."

In the course of his life, Cliff says, he's read 200 of 18 the more than 225 books for which he's made "keys to the classics" (as he touts them), but he's never gone cover to cover through any of the Notes themselves. "*I* don't need the Notes," he says. "I can read the book."

When I ask him whether he's had a chance to read 19 Gabriel García Márquez's *One Hundred Years of Solitude,* a recent addition to the Cliffs family of titles, he says, "No, but if you recommend it, I will. I read four or five books a week." When I ask him which four or five he read last week, he says, "I just finished something by Michener, but I forgot the name. And a thriller—I'm not good at remembering titles. You'll have to ask Mary."

Cliff employs a very peculiar method of reading, which 20 may account for his somewhat spotty memory. "Back when black literature was *the* thing, and I'm not running down black literature, because some of it is very fine, but there was this one book, and I don't remember the name, but people were having trouble reading it. So I picked it up and did the same thing I usually do with Michener. If it's not a subject I'm familiar with, I turn to page 100 and start there, and then come back to them when I get through. Because his first 100 pages are setting the whole story. And I did the same thing with this book and didn't have any trouble reading it. And I told Gary [Carey, a Cliffs editor], and he tried it that way, and it worked."

In the second chapter, we see how Cliff, like his fellow 21 Midwestern hick Jay Gatsby,[2] got a heavy dose of the Protestant work ethic at an early age. His parents, ultra-conservative Lutherans, sat their self-taught boy down one day when he was seven or eight and asked him to consider his future. The long haul. "My parents told me if I wanted to go to college, I would have to pay for most of it myself," Cliff says. "It seemed fair to me. So I spent a lot of my childhood concerned with how to make money."

He started his college fund by yanking the teats of a 22 couple of Jersey cows and running paper routes. He later worked as a houseboy and as a Woolworth stock boy, putting himself through Midland College, a Podunk Lutheran outfit in Fremont, Nebraska. Actually, at the start of his junior year, he transferred to Colorado State University with the expressed aim of learning forestry. Fortunately for all of us, he cut short this phase of his education and returned to Midland.

The third chapter is not one Cliff himself would 23 connect to the other two, but I believe it is absolutely essential in coming to terms with the history of study aids. In this chapter, we see how Cliff learns to blow off his schoolwork.

In 1937, Cliff entered grad school at the University 24 of Nebraska in Lincoln, preparing for his master's in physics and geology. Understand, up until this point, Clifton was an awkward, shy pencil grind. He managed well in school, but he wasn't exactly a big smash at the hoedowns. "I was a terrible introvert," he says. "All I did was study." But going to school in the Big City, Cliff joined a frat and started hanging with a faster crowd. Lincoln may seem about as exciting as a pet-food store to you or me, but it's a regular sin city Nebraskawise.

---

[2] A character in F. Scott Fitzgerald's novel *The Great Gatsby* (1925).

"My fraternity dad recognized that I didn't understand 25 girls," says Cliff. "So he undertook to make sure that I did."

"He *majored* in girls!" says Mary. Well, keeping the 26 ladies out late, Cliff the swinger had to let something slip, and guess what went first?

You got it—the books. "I think I still hold the record 27 for the most incompletes that any one student ever had at the University of Nebraska in graduate school," Cliff says, with a modicum of pride. To me, this is the most fascinating sentence in the biography of Cliff, because it indicates how he could come to appreciate the unreasonable academic burden placed upon students during their most libidinally demanding years. Now there are those who argue persuasively that Dr. Rock, who midwifed the pill, made the Nookie Revolution biologically possible. But let us not forget that Cliff and his Notes gave kids the free time that made such a lifestyle change feasible.

Following this wild period, Cliff met, courted, and 28 married his first wife, Catherine. He dropped out of school and knocked on the door of a university bookstore. The owner was leaving town and asked Cliff to come back the next week for an interview. But Cliff saw that the store's Greek and Latin sections were a mess, seized the initiative in fixing them up, and was rewarded with a job when the boss got back. For the next twenty years, Cliff hop-scotched the country, bartering and selling used college texts.

One day, during Cliff's middle age, a book-biz buddy, 29 Jack Cole, the publisher of Coles Notes in Canada, suggested Cliff peddle some outlines in America. (Coles Notes, which flopped in America when they were introduced a few years ago, are still getting Canadian students through school today.) Cole even offered to lend Cliff sixteen Shakespeare synopses so he wouldn't have to hire his own writers. In some way, Cliff's whole life had been a preparation for this moment.

He immediately borrowed four thousand dollars, set 30 up shop in the basement of his home, and persuaded his bookstore pals around the country to stock his new product, even though they predicted it would bomb. They were wrong. The first printing of Cliff's Notes—the apostrophe vanished during some redesign years later—sold out. By 1961, he was selling 129,000 a year. In 1964, the company moved out of the basement to a converted supermarket. By the end of that year, Cliff had quit his old job to work on the Notes full time. And by 1965, he was selling more than 2 million Notes a year. And just like that he became the Ray Kroc[3] of study outlines, America's single greatest purveyor of fast food for thought.

Now there had been synopses before. Fraternities were 31 notorious for keeping extensive files of old papers and crib notes for the collective cheating of their members. Same with sororities. Classic Comics and Masterplots summaries were also fairly popular. In the olden days, books from *The Decameron* to *Pinocchio* were published with short synopses of their contents at the start of each chapter. But the origin of Cliffs-style notes goes back further than that. In fact, they can be traced to a fairly esteemed Jewish author named Moses. I have it on the authority of a few rabbis that it is not sacrilegious to consider the five Books of Moses a plot summary of and commentary on the greater knowledge God gave the folks in attendance at Mount Sinai.

So Cliff didn't invent the study note any more than 32 Kroc created the hamburger. But for some odd reason, luck in America tends to seek out run-of-the-mill businessmen. However Cliff was chosen, we see there are four very specific reasons why his enterprise succeeded:

1. *Cliff treats Notes as perishables.* Bookstore managers instantly loved him because he made it policy to always send out their orders the day he received them. From his years in the college-book business,

---

[3] The founder of the McDonald's fast food chain.

he could appreciate that a stock of *Mrs. Dalloway* Notes is as useless as brown bananas once the Virginia Woolf exam is past.

2. *Cliff is colordeaf.* He chose yellow and black, the loudest color combination, because he "wanted to be sure if students were in the bookstore, they would see them." Not much of a problem there. But as Cliff and I drive past an endless row of yellow and black diagonally striped road signs on the Nebraska highway, I see a weird similarity in his color scheme.

"Look at these signs," I say to him. "Don't you see what these colors connote? YIELD! DANGER! WARNING! That's one reason why students have always been so reluctant to bring Cliffs Notes to class. They seem like the kind of thing you don't want your teacher to see you with."

Cliff says, "That never occurred to me." And I'm convinced this insensitivity to color proved to be one hell of a windfall. My theory is that students covet the Notes precisely because they have an aura of forbiddenness to them.

Cliff himself explains how this reverse psychology works. "The best thing that happened to us, from the point of view of sales, was when teachers forbade students to use the Notes. Especially during the early years, students who had never heard of Cliffs Notes immediately thought, 'Hey, I better find out what these are; they must be pretty useful.' It was great advertising."

3. *The GI Bill.* After World War II, Uncle Sam paid soldiers to go to college, filling universities with a new breed of students, serious about learning but not so well trained for the task. The GI Bill, historians now believe, completely changed the character of universities, from elitist enclaves to paragons of populism. And the baby boom pro-

vided a steady stream of students, the more people to purchase Cliffs.

4. *The commies.* This is Cliff's historical perspective: "Don't forget '58 was about the time that we had come through that first Russian situation, where they put that thing in space [*Sputnik,* in 1957], and everybody was really damning the hell out of our educational system. The college profs were really pouring it on, loading the student down with a lot of work. Because they were being told Americans were lagging behind.

"Now you take a student in mechanical engineering, let's say. There's no such thing as an average student, but let's get as close as we can. He was loaded down, and if he was going to let anything slide, it was going to be literature. And this always struck me as being a sad commentary on education, but if there was anything he really didn't like, it was to read. He had no *love* of literature. And I figured if I could make it possible for this student—and others like him, engineers, lawyers, businessmen—if I could get him through college, and he was still on speaking terms with literature, then ten years out of college, he would be willing to do some reading and continue to read.

"And I've had FBI men, doctors, dentists tell me this is what's happened to them. One man had been my dentist five years before he found out I was *the* Cliff of Cliffs Notes, and he said, 'Do you know how many of your books I have? I didn't have time to read in college, but now I do. First thing I do when I pick up a book is go over and pick up the Cliffs Notes, too. They help me read the book just as well as I could in any literature course in college.' "

After listening to this, you begin to see that Cliff sees 33 his successes and failures inextricably bound in the cycles of American schooling. During a speech he delivered to the Newcomen Society when it honored him in October 1985, he practically said you could read educational trends by examining the Cliffs Notes sales charts.

"It was no accident that in the mid-1960s, our sales 34 began to falter," he said. "Students . . . began to demand radical changes in education. . . . They wanted either to grade themselves or else enroll in courses that were graded pass-fail. As a result, everyone in the class got A's. There was no distinction between excellence and mediocrity. . . . It was not until teachers once again took charge of the classrooms, in the mid-1970s, that our sales began to increase once more. From 1980 until the present, sales have grown steadily—parallel to the academic excellence that was lost in the mid-1960s and finally restored to the classroom."

Cliffs was disrupted not only by the educational bedlam 35 of the mid-1960s but by a lawsuit that could have sucked the company dry. Scribner's and Random House sued for copyright infringement, claiming Cliffs quoted too liberally in its summaries. Too bad both suits were settled out of court, because if the publishers could have proved damage—that people were buying Cliffs *instead* of the books—it might have settled the controversy about what the Notes are really used for. But after lawyers dicked around for two years on the Random House suit, Cliff flew to New York, met company head Bennett Cerf, and agreed to pony up about five hundred dollars and cut down on the quoting.

As a result of the suit, Cliff had to change the way the 36 Notes were put together. The company shifted emphasis from brute summaries to thicker commentaries, though the Shakespeares still keep a balance of the two.

There is a vast but poorly kept archive of letters to 37 the company from helpless students God-blessing Cliffs for its revamped and sophisticated study aids. The way the students frame it, Cliff comes off as a populist educator, a twentieth-century Horace Mann who has made Western literature more accessible to the average American student.

Cliff himself is quick to admit that he has never written 38 or edited any Notes and suggests that I visit the office of editor Gary Carey. Informal, articulate, plump, Carey has been editing Cliffs Notes for nearly a decade. He's just returned from a teachers' convention, where one of the hottest-selling Cliffs items was a set of keys designed especially for teachers. Carey says that a growing number of teachers use the Notes themselves. Consulting editor James L. Roberts, who occupies a small desk in Carey's office, points out that a professor he knows forbade his class to use Cliffs only so he could lecture from them.

Carey says that the writers (who are paid a measly 39 fifteen hundred to three thousand dollars for a Note) are often academics who want to trot out five-syllable words and labyrinthine analysis. "I tell writers to take a Polaroid snapshot of their class, especially the student who sits in the middle row, furrows his brow, and looks slightly confused. To take that snapshot and put it on top of their word processor so they'll be reminded of the audience for whom they're writing."

The recently released Note on Alice Walker's novel 40 *The Color Purple* not only is one of the best ever written, says Carey, but illustrates that you don't need a Ph.D. to write these things. After the Note went to press, Carey got a call from the author, Gloria Rose, who said, "I guess I should tell you I'm a sophomore at Georgetown. I'm eighteen." Carey fell out of his chair. *"But you wrote that, right? It wasn't your mother or your aunt."* She said it was her work, and he told her it was "brilliant." "Maybe because she was a student she knew how to handle it," he says.

Or more likely because she was a student of Cliffs. 41 From her two older sisters, Rose had inherited a library of one hundred Notes. "In the fall of 1985," she says, "I was taking a Shakespeare class, and I had a problem with the Elizabethan English. I used about twelve Cliffs Notes for the course. And then I noticed there were no Notes for *The Color Purple,* and I thought a lot of people would benefit from something to make Alice Walker's nonstandard English more accessible. So I asked if I could do the Notes."

Cliffs publishes only three to six new titles a year, and 42 only for books that are widely read and are the subjects of a sufficient body of criticism. The company gets besieged with requests for all sorts of stuff, but Cliff puts his foot down at *Love Story.* And Carey hits his limit at *The Cat Ate My Gymsuit,* a widely taught junior-high-school book about an unpopular girl who triumphs over rotundity. "That would be it," Carey says. "I'd be out looking for a new job." I wonder whether writers of the so-called classics approve of their Cliffs. Chaucer would probably dig the soon-to-be-published Note by the late novelist John Gardner on *The Canterbury Tales.* (It was written but mothballed several years before his death and only recently discovered in the company's files.) But how would Shakespeare feel about his Notes, two of which were written by Cliff's daughter, Linda Hillegass? Gloria Rose is sure Alice Walker wouldn't like the Note on *The Color Purple.* "I've written her three times," says Rose, "and she hasn't written me back." Isaac Asimov, says consulting editor James Roberts, is pleased as punch to be included in the parade of literary all-stars. In Carey's opinion, "Dostoevski would have said, 'Fly, get out of here.' I think Shakespeare would be rolling in the aisles."

Since sixteen of Shakespeare's plays kicked off the 43 Notes, Cliff recently decided to complete the set, even though nobody ever assigns the more obscure plays. "After twenty-five years, we've made good money off Will," he says. "So maybe we owed the old boy a bit."

Driving from Lincoln to Kearney is like starting out 44 on the edge of nowhere and winding up right in the middle of it. Cliff, the self-appointed Nebraska ambassador, tells me interesting facts about his state. "Do you know that the third biggest city in the state is the University of Nebraska football stadium on Saturday?" Of course, you'll find Cliff and Mary on the fifty-yard line of that city, too. When it comes to state sports or art museums or libraries, they're among the grand pooh-bahs of boosters. It's important to them that Cliffs Notes stays in Lincoln.

"As you might imagine," says Cliff, "people keep trying 45 to buy the Notes, and I keep saying no. They fly in, you name 'em. The first one that tried was Simon and Schuster. Random House tried. *Esquire* tried. Viking Penguin has tried. It's gotten to the place now where they say, 'We know you don't want to sell it, but maybe you will someday.' Twenty years ago, someone offered me $25 million. The last time I turned down an offer, someone said, 'Would $50 million interest you?' "

Cliff's family owns eighty percent of the company; the 46 rest is held by employees. The way Cliff has it figured, if one of these major publishers swallows his Notes up, they'll take the Cliffs name and sterling reputation and move it to New York. As we stand by the river behind the house of some good friends of Cliff's in Kearney, watching Canada geese hitting this way station en route to Mexico, I'm reminded of something Cliff told me earlier. Once he went to New York, and a friend treated him to a Betty Grable nightclub show. "I was a big leg man," Cliff said, but not even Grable's gams could lure him away. Unlike the geese, Cliff will never leave Nebraska.

His name, however, already has. Somewhere in that 47 vast space between Ray Kroc and Horace Mann, Cliff will be remembered. If not the man, then surely the myth. For the expression *Cliffs Notes* has already become a part of our language, as a generic expression for "study outlines." The competition, Monarch Notes and Barron's, has never even approached that status. You turn on "The Cosby Show" and there's a whole episode about the prudence of using Cliffs. (Yes, but only along with the book).

Appropriately enough, Bret Easton Ellis, a voice from 48 this generation's den of Philistines, offers a tribute to Cliffs in his novel *Less Than Zero*. "Trent and Daniel are standing by Trent's BMW and Trent's pulling the Cliffs Notes to *As I Lay Dying* out of his glove compartment and hands them to Blair. . . . She fingers the Cliffs Notes but doesn't say anything." No wonder she doesn't have anything to say. I'll lay odds she didn't read the book.

QUESTIONS ON MEANING

1. What information does Atkins give us about *Cliffs Notes*? What are they? Who writes them? Who reads them? Why are they so successful?

2. What does Atkins tell us about Clifton Keith Hillegass? What are the key events in his life? How did he start *Cliffs Notes*? What is his current role in the company?

QUESTIONS ON PURPOSE AND STRATEGY

1. Is Atkins's purpose to inform us about Cliff and his Notes? To explain why the outlines are so successful? To make us feel guilty for using them or to persuade us that *Cliffs Notes* serve a useful function?

2. How does Atkins's attitude toward Cliff and *Cliffs Notes* change during his investigation?

3. Which paragraphs in the essay follow the chronological order of Atkins's investigation? Which paragraphs follow the history of *Cliffs Notes*? Which paragraphs use analysis of causes to explain why the Notes are successful?

QUESTIONS ON AUDIENCE AND LANGUAGE

1. If you could take a snapshot of a representative person in Atkins's intended audience, who would be in this picture?

2. Throughout the essay, Atkins sprinkles colloquial language (that is, informal or spoken language), such as "knocked off," "kind of like," and "mosey by." What effect does such language have on Atkins's intended audience?

QUESTIONS FOR DISCUSSION AND WRITING

1. Read Tom Wolfe's quotation at the beginning of this chapter. Then compare Norman Atkins's voice with Carin Quinn's voice in "The Jeaning of America." Which writer appears to

be following Wolfe's practice? Support your answer by citing passages from each essay.

2. Write a letter to one of your former English teachers explaining why *Cliffs Notes* should be included as official study guides in his or her course.

3. Investigate the history of some local publication: a student newspaper or literary magazine, a guide for new students, or even a brochure for your college. Find out who publishes it, how it began, and what its readers think of it.

Oranges

JOHN McPHEE

(1931–   )

PREREADING JOURNAL ENTRY

If you have worked in a restaurant or fast-food place, choose one particular food and describe how it is prepared. Would you still eat this particular food? If you do not have firsthand experience, interview someone who does. What did this person learn about the preparation of a particular food?

According to one critic, "John McPheeland is a small nation populated almost entirely by canoemakers, basketball players, inspired tinkerers, backyard inventors, restaurateurs, vegetable growers and geologists." Even a selected list of McPhee's books demonstrates his range of interests: A Sense of Where You Are *(1965),* Oranges *(1967),* The Pine Barrens *(1968),* Levels of the Game *(1970),* Wimbledon: A Celebration *(1972),* The Survival of the Bark Canoe *(1975),* Coming into the Country *(1977), and* In Suspect Terrain *(1983). Throughout McPhee's career, from his Princeton schooling to his work as a teacher, editor, and nonfiction writer, his trademark has been an obsession for the authentic detail that thrusts his readers into the heart of the subject.*

To the list of characters in McPheeland should be added the "frozen people" or "citrus men," the processors of America's orange juice. In the following excerpt from Oranges, *McPhee gives us special insight into the process of making that "100% pure" orange juice we enjoy every morning.*

The enormous factories that the frozen people have 1 built more closely resemble oil refineries than auto plants.

The evaporators are tall assemblages of looping pipes, quite similar to the cat-cracking towers that turn crude oil into gasoline. When oranges arrive, in semitrailers, they are poured into giant bins, so that a plant can have a kind of reservoir to draw upon. At Minute Maid's plant in Auburndale, for example, forty bins hold four million oranges, or enough to keep the plant going for half a day. From samples analyzed by technicians who are employed by the State of Florida, the plant manager knows what the juice, sugar, and acid content is of the fruit in each bin, and blends the oranges into the assembly line accordingly, always attempting to achieve as uniform a product as possible. An individual orange obviously means nothing in this process, and the rise of concentrate has brought about a basic change in the system by which oranges are sold.

Growers used to sell oranges as oranges. They now 2 sell "pounds-solids," and modern citrus men seem to use the term in every other sentence they utter. The rise of concentrate has not only changed the landscape and the language; it has, in a sense, turned the orange inside out. Because the concentrate plants are making a product of which the preponderant ingredient is sugar, it is sugar that they buy as raw material. They pay for the number of pounds of solids that come dissolved in the juice in each truckload of oranges, and these solids are almost wholly sugars. Growers now worry more about the number of pounds of sugar they are producing per acre than the quality of the individual oranges on their trees. If the concentrate plants bought oranges by weight alone, growers could plant, say, Hamlins on Rough Lemon in light sand—a scion, rootstock, and soil combination that will produce extremely heavy yields of insipid and watery oranges.

As the fruit starts to move along a concentrate plant's 3 assembly line, it is first culled. In what some citrus people remember as "the old fresh-fruit days," before the Second World War, about forty per cent of all oranges grown in Florida were eliminated at packinghouses and dumped in fields. Florida milk tasted like orangeade. Now, with the exception of the split and rotten fruit, all of Florida's orange crop is used. Moving up a conveyor belt, oranges are scrubbed with detergent before they roll on into juicing machines. There are several kinds of juicing machines, and they are something to see. One is called the Brown Seven Hundred. Seven hundred oranges a minute go into it and are split and reamed on the same kind of rosettes that are in the centers of ordinary kitchen reamers. The rinds that come pelting out the bottom are integral halves, just like the rinds of oranges squeezed in a kitchen. Another machine is the Food Machinery Corporation's FMC In-line Extractor. It has a shining row of aluminum jaws, upper and lower, with shining aluminum teeth. When an orange tumbles in, the upper jaw comes crunching down on it while at the same time the orange is penetrated from below by a perforated steel tube. As the jaws crush the outside, the juice goes through the perforations in the tube and down into the plumbing of the concentrate plant. All in a second, the juice has been removed and the rind has been crushed and shredded beyond recognition.

From either machine, the juice flows on into a thing 4 called the finisher, where seeds, rag, and pulp are removed. The finisher has a big stainless steel screw that steadily drives the juice through a fine-mesh screen. From the finisher, it flows on into holding tanks. Orange juice squeezed at home should be consumed fairly soon after it is expressed, because air reacts with it and before long produces a bitter taste, and the juice has fatty constituents that can become rancid. In the extractors, the finishers, and the troughs of concentrate plants, a good bit of air gets into the juice. Bacilli and other organisms may have started growing in it. So the juice has to be pasteurized. In some plants, this occurs before it is concentrated. In others, pasteurization is part of the vacuum-evaporating process—for example, in the Minute Maid plant in Auburndale, which uses the Thermal Accelerated Short Time Evaporator (T.A.S.T.E.). A great, airy network of bright-red, looping tubes, the Short Time stands about fifty feet high. Old-style evaporators keep one load of juice within them for about an hour, gradually boiling the water out. In the Short Time, juice flows in at one end in a continuous stream and comes out the other end eight minutes later.

Specific gravity, figured according to a special scale 5 for sugar solutions, is the measurement of concentrate. The special scale, worked out by a nineteenth-century German scientist named Adolf F. W. Brix, is read in "degrees Brix." Orange juice as it comes out of oranges is usually about twelve degrees Brix—that is, for every hundred pounds of water there are twelve pounds of sugar. In the Short Time, orange juice passes through seven stages. At each stage, there are sampling valves. The juice at the start is plain, straightforward orange juice but with a notable absence of pulp or juice vesicles. By the third stage, the juice is up to nineteen degrees Brix and has the viscosity and heat of fairly thick hot chocolate. The flavor is rich and the aftertaste is clean. At the fifth stage, the juice is up to forty-six degrees Brix—already thicker than the ultimate product that goes into the six-ounce can—and it has the consistency of cough syrup, with a biting aftertaste. After the seventh stage, the orange juice can be as high as seventy degrees Brix. It is a deep apricot-orange in color. It is thick enough to chew, and its taste actually suggests apricot-flavored gum. Stirred into enough water to take it back to twelve degrees Brix, it tastes like nothing much but sweetened water.

As a season progresses, the sugar-acid ratio of oranges 6 improves. Pineapple oranges, at their peak, are better in this respect than Hamlins at theirs; and Valencias are the best of all. So the concentrators keep big drums of out-of-season concentrate in cold-storage rooms and blend them with in-season concentrates in order to achieve even more uniformity. Advertisements can be misleading, however, when they show four or five kinds of oranges and imply that each can of the advertiser's concentrate contains an exact blend of all of them. It would be all but impossible to achieve that. The blending phase of the process is at best only an educated stab at long-term uniformity, using whatever happens to be on hand in the cold rooms and the fresh-fruit bins. The blending is, moreover, merely a mixing of old and new concentrates, still at sixty degrees Brix and still all but tasteless if reconstituted with water.

The most important moment comes when the cutback 7 is poured in, taking the super-concentrated juice down to forty-five degrees Brix, which MacDowell and his colleagues worked out as a suitable level, because three cans of tap water seemed to be enough to thaw the juice fairly quickly but not so much that the cooling effect of the cold concentrate would be lost in the reconstituted juice. Cutback is mainly fresh orange juice, but it contains additional flavor essences, peel oil, and pulp. Among the components that get boiled away in the evaporator are at least eight hydrocarbons, four esters, fifteen carbonyls, and sixteen kinds of alcohol. The chemistry of orange juice is so subtle and complicated that most identifications are tentative and no one can guess which components form its taste, let alone in what proportion. Some of these essences are recovered in condensation chambers in the evaporators, and they are put back into the juice. The chief flavoring element in cutback is d-limonene, which is the main ingredient of peel oil. The oil cells in the skins of all citrus fruit are ninety per cent d-limonene. It is d-limonene that burns the lips of children sucking oranges. D-limonene reddened the lips of the ladies of the seventeenth-century French court, who bit into limes for the purpose. D-limonene is what makes the leaves of all orange and grapefruit trees smell like lemons when crushed in the hand. D-limonene is what the Martini drinker rubs on the rim of his glass and then drops into his drink in a twist of lemon. The modern Martini drinker has stouter taste buds than his predecessors of the seventeenth century, when people in Europe used to spray a little peel oil on the outside of their wineglasses, in the belief that it was so strong that it would penetrate the glass and impart a restrained flavor to the wine. In the same century, peel oil was widely used in Germany in the manufacture of "preservative plague-lozenges." In the fourteenth century in Ceylon, men who dived into lakes to search the bottom for precious stones first rubbed their bodies with orange-peel oil in order to repel crocodiles and poisonous snakes. Peel oil is flammable. Peel oil is the principal flavoring essence that frozen people put into concentrated orange juice in order to attempt to recover the flavor of fresh orange juice. "We have always had the flavor of fresh oranges to come up against," MacDowell told me. "People who make things like tomato juice and pineapple juice have not had this problem." . . .

Plants that make "chilled juice" are set up as concen- 8 trate plants are, but without the evaporators. Instead, the juice goes into bottles and cartons and is shipped to places as distant as Nome. Tropicana, by far the biggest company in the chilled-juice business, ships twelve thousand quarts of orange juice to Nome each month. People in Los Angeles, surprisingly enough, drink two hundred and forty thousand quarts of Tropicana orange juice a month, and the company's Los Angeles sales are second only to sales in New York.

Tropicana used to ship orange juice by sea from 9 Florida to New York in a glistening white tanker with seven hundred and thirty thousand gallons of juice slurping around in the hold. For guests of the company, the ship had four double staterooms and a gourmet chef. Among freeloaders, it was considered one of the seven wonders of commerce. To sailors of the merchant marine, it was the most attractive billet on the high seas. A typical week consisted of three nights in New York, two nights at sea, and two nights in Florida. There was almost no work to do. There were forty-two men in the crew, some with homes at each end. White as a yacht, the ship would glide impressively past Wall Street and under the bridges of the East River, put forth a stainless-steel tube, and quickly drain its cargo into tanks in Queens.

Tropicana unfortunately found that although this was 10

a stylish way to transport orange juice, it was also uneconomical. The juice now goes by rail, already packed in bottles or cartons. The cartons are being phased out because they admit too much oxygen. Tropicana people are frank in appraisal of their product. "It's the closest thing to freshly squeezed orange juice you can get and not have to do the work yourself," one of the company's executives told me. To maintain the cloud in the juice and keep it from settling, enzymes have to be killed by raising the temperature of the juice to nearly two hundred degrees. Even so, there is some loss of Vitamin C if the juice remains unconsumed too long, just as there is a loss of Vitamin C if concentrate is mixed in advance and allowed to stand for some time.

During the winter, Tropicana freezes surplus orange 11 juice in huge floes and stores it until summer, when it is cracked up, fed into an ice crusher, melted down, and shipped. In this way, the company avoids the more usual practice of chilled-juice shippers, who sell reconstituted concentrate in the summertime, adding dry juice-sacs in order to create the illusion of freshness. The juice-sacs come from California as "barreled washed pulp."

Leftover rinds, rag, pulp, and seeds at chilled-juice 12 and concentrate plants have considerable value of their own. In most years, about fourteen million dollars are returned to the citrus industry through its by-products. Orange wine tastes like a one-for-one mixture of dry vermouth and sauterne. It varies from estate-bottled types like Pool's and Vino del Sol to Florida Fruit Bowl Orange Wine, the *vin ordinaire* of Florida shopping centers, made by National Grape Products of Jacksonville, and sold for ninety-nine cents. Florida winos are said to like the price. Florida Life cordials are made from citrus fruit, as are Consul gin, Surf Side gin, Five Flag gin, Fleet Street gin, and Consul vodka.

Peel oil has been used to make not only paint but 13 varnish as well. It hardens rubber, too, but is more commonly used in perfumes and as a flavor essence for anything that is supposed to taste of orange, from candy to cake-mixes and soft drinks. Carvone, a synthetic spearmint oil which is used to flavor spearmint gum, is made from citrus peel oil. The Coca-Cola Company is one of the world's largest users of peel oil, as anyone knows who happens to have noticed the lemony smell of the d-limonene that clings to the inside of an empty Coke bottle.

A million and a half pounds of polyunsaturated citrus-seed oil is processed and sold each year, for cooking. Hydrogenated orange-seed oil is more like butter, by-products researchers told me, than oleomargarine. Noticing a refrigerator in their laboratory, I asked if they had some on hand. They said they were sorry, but all they had was real butter. Would I care for an English muffin? 14

Looking out a window over an orange grove, one researcher remarked, "We are growing chemicals now, not oranges." Dried juice vesicles, powdered and mixed with water, produce a thick and foamy solution which is used to fight forest fires. Albedecone, a pharmaceutical which stops leaks in blood vessels, is made from hesperidin, a substance in the peels of oranges. But the main use of the leftover rinds is cattle feed, either as molasses made from the peel sugars or as dried shredded meal. Citrus pulp and chopped rinds are dried for dairy feed much in the same way that clothes are dried in a home dryer—in a drum within a drum, whirling. The exhaust vapors perfume the countryside for miles around concentrate plants with a heavy aroma of oranges. The evaporators themselves are odorless. People often assume that they are smelling the making of orange juice when they are actually smelling cattle feed. If the aroma is not as delicate as the odor of blossoms, it is nonetheless superior to the aroma of a tire and rubber plant, a Limburger cheese factory, a pea cannery, a paper mill, or an oil refinery. Actually, the orange atmospheres of the Florida concentrate towns are quite agreeable, and, in my own subjective view, the only town in the United States which outdoes them in this respect is Hershey, Pennsylvania. 15

QUESTIONS ON MEANING

1. List the stages in the preparation of frozen orange juice concentrate. Which of these steps did you expect to find? Which surprised you?

2. What orange juice by-products does McPhee describe? Were you aware of any of these? Which of these have you used, perhaps unknowingly?

QUESTIONS ON PURPOSE AND STRATEGY

1. Is McPhee's purpose to inform us how orange juice is actually made, or does he want to persuade us not to drink frozen orange juice?

2. McPhee divides his essay into three major parts. Part 1 describes the stages in the process of making frozen orange juice concentrate. Part 2 describes the making and transporting of chilled juice. Part 3 lists orange juice by-products and their uses. Identify where each major part begins and ends. (Should McPhee use clearer transitions?)

QUESTIONS ON AUDIENCE AND LANGUAGE

1. Who is McPhee's audience? The average orange juice drinker? A person with a Ph.D. in organic chemistry? Someone in between these two extremes?

2. What magazine(s) might be interested in publishing this article: *Better Homes and Gardens, Organic Gardening, Time, Business Week, Rolling Stone, The New Yorker?* Explain your choice(s).

3. Find two examples of technical language or jargon that McPhee explains and two that he does not. Is there some technical language that he should eliminate, or do you understand what he is talking about even if he doesn't explain what esters and carbonyls are?

QUESTIONS FOR DISCUSSION AND WRITING

1. "Familiarity breeds contempt" may apply also to orange juice. Will you be able to have a glass of orange juice tomorrow without feeling slightly nauseated?

2. What investigative methods (interviews, library research, on-site observation, surveys, etc.) do you think McPhee used in writing this essay?

3. McPhee's critics sometimes argue that he should include a more personal stance in his essays. Choose one paragraph from this essay and rewrite it as Norman Atkins might, using *I* and including personal references.

4. Do your own investigative report on a particular food item served at a local restaurant, fast-food chain, or cafeteria.

There Is a Whole Lot of Shaking Going On!

GERALD FORD

(1952–   )

PREREADING JOURNAL ENTRY

Make a log or list of everything you have read or seen over the past twenty-four to forty-eight hours. From that list, circle three items that you might investigate further— either by reading or by talking to someone.

A student at Belleville Area College, Gerald Ford begins his search for an investigating topic right in front of his nose, in his writing class. As his teacher, Jean Kaufmann, gave the assignment, Ford noticed other students nervously clicking their pens and twisting their hair. Presto— he had a topic: nervous tics or what the psychologists call "Displacement Activities." Ford takes the reader on his search through the library and on the phone for answers to his question, "What are nervous habits and do they help?"

I was a man with a mission. "You have two weeks to 1 come up with an investigative paper," the woman in charge of molding rhetorical abilities challenged her writers-to-be. "Good Luck!"

"My kingdom for a topic," I thought as I drummed 2 my fingers and chewed the end of my Bic pen. "What can I investigate?" I muttered under my breath, tapping my foot as I pulled on the corner of my moustache. I scanned my horizons for some magical clue. As I looked around the classroom at my fellow writers-to-be, I noticed that there was a whole lot of shaking going on.

Feet were tapping, gum was smacking, ink pens were 3 clicking, fingers were flicking, hair was twisted, thumbs drummed, and voices hummed, clothes were preened, and glasses were cleaned. Like a fifty-pound bass on a five-pound line, my topic was waiting to be reeled in. Nervous Habits! They have to be more popular than sex. Everyone I watched had one or two little trademark nervous habits. What are they? Do they help?

I was plastered with a plethora of puzzling possibilities. 4 It was like the dam had broken and a flood of unanswered questions poured forward. I was swept off to the local library in a search for answers.

I first went to the card catalog, just knowing I would 5 find volumes of information on nervous habits, but like the St. Louis Cardinals did too many times last year, I struck out.

Next I looked in the *Encyclopedia of Human Behavior,* 6 which is a huge book that I knew would have all the answers. It didn't, but you will sure look like a serious student if you sit at a table and read it. After several more pitches and strikes, I hit a home run. I found exactly what I was looking for in a book by Desmond Morris titled *Manwatching: A Field Guide to Human Behavior.*

It seems that these little nervous habits we have are 7 clinically referred to as Displacement Activities. They are small, seemingly irrelevant movements made during moments of inner conflict or frustration (Morris 179).

If you find yourself in a social situation, like a cocktail 8 party or wedding reception, take some time to observe the different varieties of Displacement Activities. Because of the various tensions that are often carried into these social events, you will more than likely be treated to a complete spectrum of Displacement Activities. See the bride that constantly smooths her veil, although it was in order to begin with. The groom twists his newly acquired wedding ring. The bride's father appears to be a cool customer, but look at that cigarette he is smoking. He continuously taps it into the ashtray although no ash is present. Caught him! How about the guests who sip their drinks, even though they are not thirsty. Look at the guests who munch food at their tables even though they aren't hungry. These are all common Displacement Activities. We do these things as an avenue to vent our anxieties.

Do these activities help? One thought is that they do 9 help to relieve central nervous energy. An energy surplus that cannot be discharged into its normal channel will then flow over into another channel and discharge itself in an irrelevant activity (Tinbergen 1952). These actions are not unique to humans. Animals have been observed in similar activities in moments of tension. One example of this is that fighting roosters, which are held back from attacking, while also feeling the tendency to flee, will peck the ground displaying displacement eating.

I checked with the St. Anthony's parent hot line, which 10 is a free guidance service, and inquired as to the level of concern I should show to a child who was constantly twisting her hair. The reply I received was that "in itself it is not a problem; however, it can be an indication that other stress problems are present." St. Anthony's suggested close observation and attention for a child showing Displacement Activities.

If you enjoy watching people, I would suggest that 11 this is an area that merits attention. I venture to say that you will be hard pressed to find anyone who does not exhibit an Achilles Heel in the form of one or more Displacement Activities. As for this writer, I will be much more conscious of the little actions and noises around me, but I will undoubtedly continue to chew my Bic pen.

QUESTIONS ON MEANING

1. Ford's central investigating questions are "What are nervous habits?" and "How do they help?" What answers does he give to these questions?

2. List the steps Ford takes in his investigation of his topic. What does he do to gather his information?

QUESTIONS ON PURPOSE AND STRATEGY

1. Ford's purpose is to inform his readers about nervous habits. What questions about nervous habits do you still have after reading his essay?
2. Of the shaping strategies discussed in the "Writing an Investigative Essay" section in this chapter, which does Ford use to organize his essay?

QUESTIONS ON AUDIENCE AND LANGUAGE

1. Describe Ford's intended audience for this essay.
2. Alliteration is the repetition of initial sounds in a sequence of words. Ford uses alliteration of the "m" sound in his first sentence: "I was a man with a mission." Where else in the essay does Ford use alliteration? Is it effective for his audience and topic?
3. In paragraph three, Ford creates an image when he says, "Like a fifty-pound bass on a five-pound line, my topic was waiting to be reeled in." Find two other images in the essay. Which do you find most or least effective, considering the audience and topic?

QUESTIONS FOR DISCUSSION AND WRITING

1. What are Ford's published sources of information? Since he does not have a "Works Cited" page, he should cite his sources in the text of his essay. Which sources does he cite? Which doesn't he cite?
2. In the library, spend thirty minutes investigating Desmond Morris. Ask your reference librarian how to find a biograph-

ical sketch of his life and writings. Look up Desmond Morris in card catalog or on the computer. Check out and page through a book by Morris. Photocopy the title page and an interesting page or two. For another member of your class, describe what you learned during this brief investigation.

The Beauty behind Beauty Pageants

MARY WHITE

PREREADING JOURNAL ENTRY

Think of a job, sport, or hobby you have. What goes on before the performance, during practice, at rehearsals, or at business meetings that the general public may not know about? For other members of your class, explain what happens "behind the scenes."

Mary White, a student in Jimmie Cook's composition class at Oklahoma State University, writes about appearances versus reality at a beauty pageant. After reading several articles and interviewing Lisa Scott, a seventeen-year-old participant, she reports on what goes on behind the scenes—how much money contestants spend on their clothes, how they suffer embarrassment and pain, and how they sacrifice dignity for the chance at a modeling career.

Notes and Article

Purpose: To inform the public of the trauma, pain, and money involved in the pageant. As beautiful and glamorous as pageants appear, not all of the preparation is smiles and roses.
Audience: The general public who sees only the final performance, either live or on television.

Brief Outline:
I. Introduction

II. Learning to be beautiful

III. The clothes

IV. The look

V. The <u>pain</u>

VI. That night

VII. Conclusion

Article: "Let Tom Edison Be the Judge."
<u>U.S. News and World Report</u> 5 June 1989: 13.

Let Tom Edison Be the Judge

Victorians tried to cover them up, feminists tried to dress them down and Stalinists tried to throw them out, but no one can stop those indomitable beauty contests. Last week, even the Soviets succumbed, picking their first Miss U.S.S.R. before thousands of screaming fans.

Forerunners of this *glasnost* glamour girl were chosen 700 years ago from a neighboring empire. Marco Polo reported that Genghis Khan's grandson, Kublai Khan, augmented his love nest by ordering a jury of officers to identify the land's most beautiful girls. Those getting the highest rating—20—were summoned to his court. Meanwhile, European villagers chose the fairest May queen each spring.

The modern beauty pageant would have originated with P. T. Barnum in 1854 had Victorian America not shuddered at the thought of women displaying themselves. Ever the showman, Barnum turned his plan for a parade of beauties into a contest for best portrait. Rehoboth Beach, Del., dared the first Miss United States competition in 1880 (with Thomas Edison judging), and Atlantic City, N.J., caught the wave in 1921, crowning the first Miss America. In the next few decades, the voices of puritanism faded, only to be replaced in the '70s by feminists arguing that, as men's equals, women shouldn't be judged like heifers. But millions of young contestants with Cinderella dreams weren't dissuaded and, with even the prudish Evil Empire now worshiping the female form, they may never be.

Rough Draft

Beauty pageants aren't always what they seem. It seems that being a contestant in a pageant today is as difficult as being a neurosurgeon, and almost as stressful. These women are put through an incredible amount of pain, embarrassment, and schooling, just to make them beautiful. The amount of money spent on dresses alone is enormous, not to mention make-up, hair, and shoes. Recently, I attended a pageant and was astonished to learn that not all of what you see on stage is real.

It is not uncommon for a beauty pageant contestant to attend school to learn proper etiquette for a pageant. "I have been in a pageant class all semester. This is just like a final," said Lisa Scott, contestant of the Carl Albert Junior College Scholarship pageant. "In class they taught us how to walk, how to smile, and how to answer the judges," said Lisa. The class is a "dry run" of the actual pageant. They are given the rules in class as well as a support group of other contestants. "Talent is the most important part. It counts 40% of the points. In class they teach you how to act talented, even if you aren't . . . . Well, in reality, I guess they teach you to act beautiful even if you are not," Lisa smiled.

Everyone knows that clothes are an important part of pageants, but few people realize how difficult it is to find an appropriate pageant dress. "It is hard to find a dress that is beautiful, but not too showy. Or find one that is beautiful, not too showy, and doesn't cost a small fortune. It is even harder to find all of those things in a dress that fits. I got super lucky. All of my dresses were marked down, but they all had to be altered from sizes 11 to 13 to size 1 or 3," Lisa recited. Lisa was correct. She only spent $700 on two dresses, but it is not uncommon for contestants to spend $1500 to $6000 on one dress. Finding the right dress, the right size, and the right price are all obstacles that the viewer never sees.

Another startling fact that the public isn't aware of is the pain associated with being pageant beautiful. When asked about the "pageant pain," Lisa said this: "I am really enjoying the pageant atmosphere, but I haven't been able to feel my left big toe for 3 days now. And I have no skin left under my arms from taping my chest up." Numb toes are common among contestants. Contestants are encouraged to buy tight shoes, or shoes that are too small so they won't slip or the contestant won't take large steps. The raw skin under the arms is even more common. All but one of the contestants in the Carl Albert Junior College pageant had to tape their chests for cleavage. The taping was done with duct tape and medical tape. Pads were placed underneath their breasts to produce a fuller look. Every contestant wore a bustier instead of a regular bra. "It really does make us look better. It is uncomfortable though," Lisa said. Some contestants taped their stomachs and rear ends also. "It (the taping) is all done to give a firmer, more smooth look. Once everyone is taped and dressed, they look completely different." Firm grip is used on the contestants rear ends to keep their swimsuits down. "Firm grip doesn't really hurt, but it is sticky and hard to get off."

Pageant night is the grande finale.
Pageant mothers run around back stage doing
make-up, fixing hair, looking for another
set of pads, doing motherly type things.
The audience sits in the auditorium
watching the stage, waiting for the games
to begin. Backstage, contestants help tape
each other, and utter encouraging words.
They sit in front of mirrors, trying to
cover up bags under their eyes. A pageant
mother runs around with Vaseline so that
the contestants lips won't stick to their
teeth from smiling too much. The hair is
taken out of rollers and the hair dressers
go to work on it.

Final Draft

The Beauty behind Beauty Pageants

Sitting in front of the television or sitting in the 1
audience, all of the pageant contestants look absolutely
breathtaking. Every girl has just the right figure, smile,
poise, and grace it takes to be the next Miss Whatever.
The sad truth is that although the contestants say they
are living a dream, the dream turns out to be more
like a nightmare. It seems that being a contestant in a
pageant today is as difficult as being a successful lawyer
in Washington, D.C., or even as difficult as being a
professional athlete, where the competition is so fierce
to be number one. These women are put through an
incredible amount of schooling, embarrassment, and
pain just to make them beautiful. The money they
spend on one dress alone is enormous, not to mention
the cost of make-up, hair, nails, and shoes. Recently,
I attended a pageant and talked with one of the
contestants. I was astonished to learn that not all of
what I saw on stage was real.

It is not at all uncommon for a contestant to go to 2
school to learn proper pageant etiquette. "I have been

in pageant class all semester. This is just like the final exam," said Lisa Scott, contestant in the Carl Albert Junior College Scholarship Pageant. The pageant is associated with the Miss America Scholarship Pageant. The winner of the CAJC Pageant has the opportunity to participate in the Miss Oklahoma Scholarship Pageant. If the girl should win the title of Miss Oklahoma, she is then off to the Miss America Scholarship Pageant. "In class they taught us how to walk, smile, and answer the questions we are asked by the judges," said Lisa. The class is a dry run of the actual pageant. The contestants are given the rules of the pageant in class as well as the support of their fellow contestants. "Talent is the most important part of the contest; it counts forty percent of the points. In class they teach you how to act talented even if you are not . . . well . . . I guess, truthfully, they teach you to act beautiful even if you aren't," Lisa says as she flashes her pageant smile.

Everyone knows that clothes are an important part 3 of pageant competition. Few people, however, realize how difficult it is to find an appropriate pageant dress. "It is hard to find a dress that is beautiful but not showy. It is even harder to find a dress that is beautiful, not showy and doesn't cost a small fortune. It is just about a miracle to find a dress that is all of those things and fits. I got super lucky. All of my dresses were marked down, but they all had to be altered." Lisa was correct in using the word "lucky." She spent about seven hundred dollars total on her two pageant dresses. It is not uncommon for a contestant to spend anywhere from one thousand to six thousand dollars on just one dress. Finding the right dress, at the right price, and in the right size are all obstacles that the pageant viewer never sees.

Another startling fact about pageants that the 4 general public is not aware of is the pain involved in being beautiful. When asked about pageant pain Lisa said this: "I am really enjoying the pageant atmosphere, but I haven't been able to feel my big toe for three days. I have no skin left under my arms from taping my chest up." Numb toes are fairly common among pageant contestants. Contestants are encouraged to buy shoes that are too small so they will not slip. Having small shoes also cuts down on the size of steps the girl takes. The raw skin is even more common. All but one of the contestants in the Carl Albert Junior College Scholarship Pageant had to tape their chests up for cleavage. The taping was done with duct tape and medical tape. Pads were placed underneath their breasts to produce a fuller look. Every contestant wore bras that gave extra support for their new cleavage. "It really does make us look better; it is uncomfortable though," Lisa said. Some contestants taped their stomachs and their behinds. "It is all done to give a firmer, more smooth look to the contestant. Once everyone is dressed they look completely different." Firm grip is used on the contestants' behinds to keep their swimsuits in place. "Firm grip doesn't hurt but it is sticky and hard to get off." It is apparent that the beauty that is seen on stage is not all real. The beauty seen on stage is an enhancement of what society thinks should be there.

The modern beauty pageant would have originated 5 with P. T. Barnum in 1854 ("Let Tom Edison Be the Judge"). Victorian women, however, shuddered at the thought of displaying themselves publicly ("Let Tom Edison"). Mr. Barnum would not be put off by this and turned his beauty pageant into a "best portrait" contest ("Let Tom Edison"). The best portrait contest is still a part of pageantry today. The contestants are judged on their poise, talent, diction, individual beauty, and on the way they photograph. The First Miss United States Pageant was held in 1880 with Thomas Edison judging ("Let Tom Edison"). The first Miss America Pageant was held in Atlantic City, New Jersey, in 1921.

Since those first pageant nights, the glamour as 6 well as competition has increased. Pageant mothers

run around backstage doing hair, fixing make-up,
looking for mislaid items, and offering words of encouragement. The audience sits in the auditorium
waiting for the games to begin. Backstage the contestants offer suggestions and support to each other.
Contestants sit in front of mirrors trying to cover the
bags under their eyes, hoping that this night will be
the beginning of a great modeling career.

Finally, all preparations are done, and the dresses 7
are on. Everyone is picture perfect. The contestants
move through the parade like they have been doing
this for years. The spotlight falls on the winner and a
sigh is let out among the contestants. Everyone con-
gratulates the winner and wipes away the tears of joy
and disappointment. When asked if she would participate in another pageant Lisa, who placed second
runner-up in the CAJC pageant, said this: "Well . . . a
lot of people have told me tonight that I have a lot of
potential. They have said I need to mature some. I
am only seventeen. With more improvement, I could
really do well in another pageant."

Pageants have been the gateway for many career 8
openings and they have been a source of entertainment
for people for years. Not everyone, however, believes
that pageants serve a worthy purpose. According to
model Kaylan Pickford, "A beauty contest is not a
guarantee of launching you as a model, even if you
win. The whole experience could be very degrading"
("Beauty Pageants" 93). She believes that dignity is the
most important thing when it comes to being beautiful.
It would seem very difficult to be dignified with a
taped chest and Vaseline-coated teeth.

Not everyone's attitudes about pageants are the 9
same. The fact is the public encourages women to be
beautiful no matter what it costs, whether it be money,
pain, or time. Pageants have been enjoyed by millions
over the years. Contestants compete in them year after
year, trying to look just a little better in hopes of
winning the coveted title of Miss. . . .

Works Cited

"Let Tom Edison Be the Judge." *U.S. News and World Report* 5 June 1989: 13.

Pickford, Kaylan. "Beauty Pageants Are Only Skin Deep." *50 Plus* Oct. 1986: 92–93.

Scott, Lisa D. Interview. 28 October 1989.

QUESTIONS ON MEANING

1. List the basic who, what, when, and where information that White gives in her essay.

2. Describe the differences between appearance and reality that White discusses in her essay.

QUESTIONS ON PURPOSE AND STRATEGY

1. Reread White's statement of purpose in her notes. Which parts of her thesis (trauma, pain, money) does her essay most effectively and least effectively show? Cite specific sentences to support your answer.

2. Which shaping strategies (chronological order, process analysis, causal analysis, comparison) does White use to organize her essay? Would another shaping strategy also work?

3. If you were helping White revise her essay, would you advise her to keep paragraph five (on the history of beauty pageants)? Explain.

QUESTIONS ON AUDIENCE AND LANGUAGE

1. Who is White's audience? Write a different lead-in for White's essay that would also appeal to her audience.

2. What sentences, words, and images are most effective in White's essay? What sentences could be revised to describe beauty pageants more clearly or vividly for the audience?

QUESTIONS FOR DISCUSSION AND WRITING

1. Reconstruct how White probably wrote her essay. Where did she go? What did she read? Whom did she interview?

2. If White asked for your help revising this paper, what changes in content would you suggest to make this paper more effective? More of White's own observations behind stage? Interviews with other contestants or mothers? More references to feminists' arguments about beauty contests?

3. Reread the article, "Let Tom Edison Be the Judge." Where does White use information from that article in her essay? Does she cite her source accurately in the text and in her "Works Cited"? Should she use direct quotation marks at any point?

4. Reread your Prereading Journal Entry. If you wanted to write an investigating paper on this topic, how might you proceed? What would you read? Whom might you interview? What might you observe?

6

EXPLAINING

A Japanese-style conversation, however, is not at all like tennis or volleyball. It's like bowling. You wait your turn. And you always know your place in line. It depends on such things as whether you are older or younger, a close friend or a relative stranger to the previous speaker, in a senior or junior position, and so on.

—Nancy Sakamoto, "Conversational Ballgames"

If we refuse to talk "like a lady," we are ridiculed and criticized for being unfeminine. ("She thinks like a man" is, at best, a left-handed compliment.) If we do learn all the fuzzy-headed, unassertive language of our sex, we are ridiculed for being unable to think clearly, unable to take part in a serious discussion, and therefore unfit to hold a position of power.

—Robin Lakoff, "You Are What You Say"

When we want to explain something to a reader, we draw on all our observing, remembering, and investigating skills. Our purpose is to use what we already know (and what we learn during the process of writing) to explain, to our reader, how something happens or should happen, what something is or means, or why something happens. *What, how,* and *why:* These are the words that drive explanatory writing. *What* is the greenhouse effect? *How* does it work? *Why* does a buildup of carbon dioxide in the atmosphere warm our planet? If we keep polluting at the present rate, what will be the effect in twenty years?

Expository writing, or writing that explains, uses a variety of strategies: *analysis* (dividing a subject into its parts to explain the whole), *classification* (grouping ideas, people, or things into similar categories), *comparison and contrast* (noting similarities and differences), *definition* (placing limits on the meaning of a word or idea), *process analysis* (explaining how to do something, or how it happens), and *causal analysis* (explaining the causes or effects of ideas or events). Each of these strategies represents a way of thinking, a way of showing the relationships between ideas, events, or people. Expository writing typically uses several of these strategies to help explain the subject to a reader.

In a sense, expository writing is like doing math problems. Writers must show their work and their thinking, not just give the "answers." Writers explaining what *perestroika* is must *show* examples of *perestroika* at work in the Soviet Union. Writers explaining how to tune an engine must *show* all the steps in the process. Writers explaining the effects of cocaine addiction in teenagers should *show* examples of actual people who have used cocaine. An effective explanation makes a generalization and then supports that main idea with examples, illustrations, facts, or other data. *Showing the specific examples* and then *explaining the relationship between the specific case and the general idea* is the principal task of the expository writer.

STRATEGIES FOR READING AND WRITING ABOUT EXPLAINING

As you read the expository essays in this chapter, look for the following key features of expository writing.

Beginning with an attention-getting title and lead-in. Since readers are busy and easily distracted, expository writing should appeal to their curiosity or self-interest. The lead and/or the title should pique their interest in the subject.

Statement of the thesis or main idea early in the essay. Expository writing should present no mysteries for the reader. The reader should not wonder, "Why is this writer telling me this?" Writers present the thesis early and then demonstrate that idea in the essay.

Definition of key terms or ideas or description of what something is. If one purpose of an essay is to explain what something is, writers use definition and description to explain the subject to their reader. What is a computer "modem" and how did it get its name? What characterizes a Japanese conversation and how is it different from an American conversation?

Analysis of the steps in the process. If one purpose of the essay is to explain some process or show how to do something, writers use process analysis. A writer might explain to school children what happens during photosynthesis (a descriptive process) or explain to novice cooks the best way to cook fried chicken (a prescriptive or how-to process).

Analysis of causes or effects. If one purpose of the essay is to show the relationship between causes and effects, writers use causal analysis to explain their subject. Typically, writers show how an event or a condition has several causes (What are the causes of alcoholism among college students?) or how an event or a condition has multiple effects (How does prejudice in the workplace affect women's salaries?)

Demonstration of main ideas with examples or specific data. The heart of expository writing is the demonstration. Without specific illustrations, firsthand observation, remembered examples, facts, statistical data, or quotations from written sources or interviews, expository writing will not explain anything to its readers.

Use of transitions to show connections between main points. Clarity is a primary goal of exposition, so writers use transitions (*first, second, then, although, moreover, on the one hand, while, after, next, in addition, finally*) to show key relationships to their readers.

READING AN EXPLAINING ESSAY

Prereading

Determine what you already know about the subject *before* you begin reading an essay. If you had to define the idea of a "good friend," what would it be? If you had to explain why you think advertising is deceptive, what would you say? Writing what you already know about the subject of a particular essay will help you connect with the subject. In addition, finding out about the author and the occasion for the essay will help you understand the intended relationship between writer and reader. Is the writer an expert, explaining AIDS to medical students? Is the writer a journalist, informing readers how AIDS is or is not transmitted? Your Prereading Journal Entry and the information about the author and the article will help answer those questions.

First Reading

During your first reading, concentrate on understanding the writer's explanation. If some passage is confusing, place a "?" in the margin. If you like an idea or an example, put a "!" in the margin. If the writer is wrong about some point, put a "X" in the margin. Highlight or put a wavy line under any key passages. Underline words you need to look up later. At the end of your first reading, state in a single sentence the writer's main idea: "This essay explains how television detracts from the quality of family life."

Annotated Reading

For your annotated reading, begin by writing your reactions to the essay. Which passages were the clearest? If a passage was not clear, did you miss something on the first reading or did the writer fail to give a good example or fail to use simple, clear language? Write your reactions in the margin: "I liked this example" or "This idea still isn't clear to me." In addition to writing your reactions, read with a writer's eye. Which explaining techniques were most effective? Least effective? In the margin, bracket [ ] and label key features of expository essays: beginning with a clear title, lead-in, and thesis; use of definition, process analysis, or causal analysis; sufficient use of specific examples and data; and effective use of transitions. As necessary, look up definitions of words that you underlined or that catch your attention now.

Collaborative Reading

In your class or small group, share your Prereading Journal entries. Based on the journal entries, does your class or group represent the intended audience for this essay? Was the writer addressing people more informed on the subject? Less informed? Appoint a recorder to compile typical annotations from the class or group. Annotate one copy of the essay with your collected notes. At the end of the essay, write out a statement of the writer's *thesis*. When you have finished the collective annotations, write at least two questions you or your group has about this essay.

WRITING AN EXPLAINING ESSAY

In an explaining essay, your *purpose* is to explain the what's, how's, and why's of a subject: what something is, how to do something, how something usually happens, and/or why something happens. You are writing to an *audience* that may be interested in the subject or may be indifferent. If the audience is already interested or knowledgeable, you need to show them that you have a certain angle or a special understanding that they may not have considered. If they are indifferent, you should arouse their curiosity and show them why they need to understand the subject.

To succeed with your readers, you must meet their expectations. In expository writing, readers have three key expectations: They expect you to state the **main idea** or thesis, to use **specific support,** and to **organize** your explanation coherently. First, readers are busy and impatient. They want to know the main idea. Their first question is, "Why is the writer telling me this?" By the time they've read for two or three minutes, they expect to know what your point is. Second, your readers want general statements to be supported with specific examples, statistics, quotations, detailed descriptions, images, or brief narratives from your experience. Third, readers appreciate a sense of order, of progression, of organization. They like to see that you first define a term and then explain it, that first you discuss *x* and then compare it to *y;* that you explain that *x* has three key causes or effects, that you show the steps (1, 2, 3, and 4) in the process, or that you explain events in a chronological order.

Finally, don't forget that you are a person explaining something to another person. In an informal essay, your personality or **voice** can make your explanation worth reading. You may use *I* in your essay; you may want to describe why *you* are curious about the subject; you may want to show your readers what (and how) *you learned* about your subject. You will most likely want to share some of your own experience. If your audience can relate to you, they will more easily understand your ideas and explanations.

Choosing a Subject for an Explaining Essay

The questions following the essays in this chapter suggest some ideas for an explaining essay, but here are other possibilities.

Start an **authority list.** In your journal, write down topics that you know about, that you are an authority on. Perhaps a hobby, a subject you have studied, a place you have been, or a person you know could become the subject for your explaining essay.

Reread your **class notes** from your other courses for subjects you could explain. Since you are still studying this subject, you might not feel comfortable writing a technical explanation for your professor, but perhaps a friend who is not taking this class might be your audience. Pick an idea, term, process, phenomena, or event and explain it to your friend.

Find a **specialized magazine** that focuses on one of your favorite subjects or hobbies. There are magazines devoted to cars, fashions, cooking, skiing, sports, interior decorating, gardening, religion, fishing, sewing, vegetarian diets, aerobics—the list is almost endless. Browse through magazine shelves in your bookstore or grocery store. Ask your librarian for magazines that focus on your interests. Look through several issues to find possible topics.

Collecting Ideas and Examples

Use the observing, remembering, and investigating skills you've practiced in the previous chapters. Start by **observing** a place that is relevant to your explaining paper. If you're writing about cars, visit a showroom to get the flavor of a new car place. If you're describing vegetarian diets, go to a restaurant that serves vegetarian food. If you're explaining an idea from your biology class, describe your classroom, or the professor, or the laboratory. Next, write two pages in your journal **remembering** all your experiences with this subject. In your explaining essay, you can then take the best memories and experiences and use them as *specific examples* to support your main idea. Finally, begin **investigating** your subject: Read an article on your topic, interview an expert, or conduct a survey. These collecting skills will help you focus your subject and generate the specific support that your readers expect.

As you work on your subject, ask key questions. The answers to the following questions will suggest additional support you can use, but they will also help you to shape and organize your essay.

To explain **what** something is or means, answer the following questions:
How can you describe it?
What examples of it can you find?
What is it similar to? What is it unlike?
What are its parts? What is its function?
How can it be classified? Is it a type of something?

Which of these questions is most useful to your audience?

To explain **how** to do something or **how** something happens, answer the following questions:
What are necessary conditions or equipment for the process?
What are the key steps in the process?
Do or should the steps occur in a specific sequence?
If any steps or events were omitted, would the outcome change?
Which steps are most important?

Which steps or events does your audience most need to know?

To explain **why** something happens, answer the following questions:
Do several causes (1, 2, 3) lead to one effect?
Does one cause lead to several effects (1, 2, 3)?
What is the order of the causes or effects?

Is there an action or situation that would prevent
an effect?

What causes or effects need clarification for your   .
audience?

Shaping Your Explaining Essay

As you collect ideas and examples and think about shaping
and organizing, *narrow* and *focus* your subject into a topic
suitable for your purpose, audience, and occasion. If
you're writing a short essay about automobile repair for
a friend, do not try to explain how to overhaul a whole
engine. Instead, *narrow* your explanation to a limited
operation, such as setting the engine's timing. If you are
writing about an effective diet, *focus* on some angle appropriate for your audience: a weight loss diet that is not
only low in calories but also good for your heart.

Test the following shaping strategies against your
particular topic. Some of these strategies may suggest an
idea or example to include in your essay, while others
may suggest how to organize your whole essay.

Example.   Most explaining essays can be developed by
example. Remember: An example is one specific incident,
located in time and space, that illustrates your point. Don't
begin your example by saying, "That happened to me
often" or "I used to do that a lot." Instead, describe an
incident that happened at a specific time. Show the scene,
just as you would in a remembering essay. In "Why Don't
We Complain," William F. Buckley shows each example
clearly. He puts the reader into a specific situation, describes the scene and key events, gives his own thoughts,
and even includes dialogue.

It was the very last coach and the only empty seat on
the entire train, so there was no turning back. The problem
was to breathe. Outside, the temperature was below freezing.
Inside the railroad car the temperature must have been
about 85 degrees. . . .

I watched the train conductor appear at the head of the car. "Tickets, all tickets, please!" In a more virile age, I thought, the passengers would seize the conductor and strap him down on a seat over the radiator to share the fate of his patrons. He shuffled down the aisle picking up tickets.... He approached my seat, and I drew a deep breath of resolution. "Conductor," I began, with a considerable edge to my voice....

Definition. Definition can organize a whole essay, but more likely it will help you develop a small part of your essay. Defining key terms and ideas helps you explain your ideas to a specific reader who may not know the terms or concepts you are using. In "You Are What You Say," Robin Lakoff uses definition to explain key ideas and words. At one point, she defines what she means by *euphemism:* "A euphemism is a substitute for a word that has acquired a bad connotation by association with something unpleasant or embarrassing."

Classification. Classification is a process of sorting individual items into the groups, categories, or classes to which they belong. We can classify university students by their major (Music, Engineering, Business, History, English) or by race or culture (Asian, Black, Hispanic, Anglo). We can classify automobiles by price (luxury, moderately priced, inexpensive) or by body type (sports car, sedan, truck, or van). Judith Viorst, in "Friends, Good Friends, and Such Good Friends" classifies her friends primarily by their context or role: convenience friends, special-interest friends, historical friends, crossroads friends, and so forth.

Process Analysis. Process analysis explains how to do something (how to make great fried chicken, or how to study for a class) or how something typically happens (how the electoral college works or how photosynthesis works). Jim Villas's essay, "Fried Chicken," describes the necessary equipment and ingredients for his fried chicken and then gives the steps in preparing, frying, draining, and serving his delicious fried chicken.

Causal Analysis. Analysis and discussion of causes and effects can organize a whole essay. A writer might explain why an airplane crashed by devoting a paragraph to each of the possible causes: bad weather, engine problems, and pilot error. Or the writer might explain how a single cause, such as an air traffic controller's failure to understand a pilot's request, causes the plane to circle the airport, run out of fuel, and eventually crash several miles short of the runway. In "Why Don't We Complain," Buckley uses two examples (the overheated train and the out-of-focus film) to explain the effects of *not* asserting ourselves. Then he uses three examples (the ski shop misunderstanding, the stewardess confrontation, and the editor's testimony) to show the possible negative and positive effects of asserting ourselves. "When our voices are finally mute," Buckley concludes, "when we have finally suppressed the natural instinct to complain, whether the vexation is trivial or grave, we shall have become automatons, incapable of feeling."

Voice. A writer's voice, used with other shaping strategies, can organize an entire essay. Jim Villas explains how to fry chicken, but his voice dominates and thus shapes the essay right from the opening paragraph:

> When it comes to fried chicken, let's not beat around the bush for one second. To know about fried chicken you have to have been weaned and reared on it in the South. Period. . . . Now, I don't know exactly why we Southerners love and eat at least ten times more fried chicken than anyone else, but we do and always have and always will. Maybe we have a hidden craw in our throats or oversize pulley bones or . . . oh, I don't know what we have, and it doesn't matter. What does matter is that we take our fried chicken very seriously. . . .

Introductions. Introductions to explaining essays often have three key features:

> **Lead-in:** An example, statement, definition, statistic, quotation, short narrative, or a description that gets the reader's *interest.*

Thesis: A statement of the writer's main idea; a *promise* to the reader that the essay fulfills.

Essay map: A sentence or phrase that *previews* or *lists* the main subtopics that the writer plans to discuss.

In "Friends, Good Friends, and Such Good Friends," Viorst's first two paragraphs explain what she used to think friendship meant. Her third paragraph gets her readers' attention by focusing on how she has *changed* her definition of friendship.

> In other words, I once would have said that a friend is a friend all the way, but now I believe that's a narrow point of view. For the friendships I have and the friendships I see are conducted at many levels of intensity, serve many different functions, meet different needs and range from those as all-the-way as the friendship of the soul sisters mentioned above to that of the most nonchalant and casual playmates.
>
> Consider these varieties of friendship. . . .

Viorst's thesis and essay map are mixed together. Her thesis is that "friendships are conducted at many levels . . . serve many different functions, [and] meet different needs." Her essay map is contained partly in the thesis (she will discuss levels of intensity, variety of functions, and range of needs) and partly in the final sentence: The "varieties of friendship" sets up the eight kinds of friends she discusses.

Conclusions.   Conclusions connect your main examples and evidence to your thesis. In addition to reemphasizing the thesis, conclusions often wrap up the essay by *echoing* some word, phrase, or idea from the introductory paragraph. At the beginning of her conclusion, Judith Viorst creates for the reader a sense of completeness and closure by echoing the first sentence of her introduction. The added italics indicate repeated words or phrases:

> The best of friends, I still believe, *totally love and support and trust each other, and bare to each other the secrets of their souls,*

and run—no questions asked—to help each other, and tell harsh truths to each other when they must be told.

Drafting Your Explaining Essay

First, reread your prewriting notes. What is your purpose and audience? What examples do you intend to use? Which shaping strategy will work best for your essay? Especially for a long essay, write a brief outline or list of the order of your main points. Some writers prefer to have their lead-in, thesis, and map written before drafting the body of their essay; other writers prefer to compose the introduction last, after they have written the body of the essay.

Revising Your Explaining Essay

When you have finished writing your draft—and have let it sit for a day or so—have another reader review your essay. Be sure to explain your purpose, audience, and the primary shaping strategy you are using. As you revise your essay, take your reader's advice as you review the following checklist.

Compare your thesis sentence with your conclusion. If your conclusion states your main idea more clearly than your thesis, revise your thesis to make it fit your conclusion.

Check your introductory paragraphs. Do you have an interesting *lead-in* to catch your reader's attention? Does your *essay map* preview the main points in the essay?

Have you defined key words for your audience? Definitions may include a *description* of an object, a *comparison* to something similar or different, a description of the object's *purpose or function,* or an *example* of its use.

In a process analysis, explain each step clearly for your reader. Have you described the equipment or ingredients for your process? Make clear to your reader which steps or parts of the sequence are *most* or *least* important.

In a causal analysis, explain how or why each cause contributes to the effect. Are there other possible causes for your effect that your readers will know about? Are there other possible effects of your cause?

Review your essay for overall coherence. Body paragraphs often begin with a *transition* from the previous idea as well as a statement of that paragraph's topic. Check the opening sentences in each body paragraph: Is the main idea of that paragraph clear? Is there a smooth transition from the previous paragraph?

Edit your essay. Revise for clarity of sentences and appropriate word choice, punctuation, usage, and grammar. Correct any spelling errors.

Postscript for Your Explaining Essay

When you finish your essay, answer the following questions. Be sure to hand in this postscript with your completed essay.

1. In your essay, what is your main purpose or purposes? Who is your intended audience?

2. Does your essay explain **what** (definition), **how** (process analysis), **why** (causal analysis), or some combination? Refer to specific paragraphs in your essay to support your answer.

3. What parts or stages in your writing process (getting an idea, collecting, shaping, drafting, revising) caused you the most trouble as you wrote this essay? Which parts were the easiest?

4. What do you like best about your finished product? What do you like least? Cite one paragraph that you like best and one paragraph that you like least.

Conversational Ballgames

NANCY SAKAMOTO

PREREADING JOURNAL TOPIC

Recall the last time you talked with people from another country or culture—either foreigners or Americans from a cultural background different from yours. Write for five minutes, describing your conversation and then explaining what you learned about *their* language or culture, or what you discovered about your *own* language or culture.

STUDENT JOURNAL RESPONSES

My brother was thinking of becoming a Hari Krishna and invited me and my mom to attend one of their feasts at "the temple." We went. We had to sit on the floor, which was OK. We got there early, and as it got closer to the time set for the beginning of the festivities, more and more people came. Soon it was so crowded, we were packed in like slabs of bacon in an Oscar Mayer package. Besides having to contend with so many people, Mom and I were encircled by people from India. I've always thought of Americans as fairly friendly people, but our experience with the Indians led me to believe that Americans are pretty cold fish. The festivities started and even more people crowded in. Then Mom and I noticed we were being used as chair backs. Several people were leaning against us. They didn't seem to care that we were complete strangers. It was getting hotter and hotter and I was getting more and more uncomfortable having so many strange bodies pressed up against me. Then I saw my mom remove an Indian man's hand from her calf. He had been using Mom as a bolster to prop himself up. That was it— I couldn't stand it anymore! We got up and left. I couldn't believe how uncomfortable that made me.

My mom is Japanese -- that makes me ½ Japanese. Last summer my cousins Yoshiko and Yoko visited us from Japan. Talking to them was very interesting. I know Japanese a little bit enough to get by if I were to suddenly become lost in Japan. But nonetheless speaking with my two cousins opened my eyes quite a bit. Japanese is a passive language. So whenever they spoke (Yoko, the younger one could speak a little bit of English), they put it in the passive. That drove me nuts. But then I realized how English must sound to Japanese -- very straightfoward and pushy. Western. Anyway, that experience made me see things in a new light.

Nancy Sakamoto is an American woman married to a Japanese man. Her essay, which originally appeared in Polite Fictions *(1982), indicates that she has lived in both cultures and taught English to Japanese students. Her topic—how conversing in a foreign language requires learning about cultural expectations—is increasingly important as Americans become more aware of dramatic differences in cultures around the world: East European men may kiss each other when they meet; Latins may be late for a meeting without intending insult; Americans' loud voices may seem rude and obnoxious to Asians; and Arabs may converse with their faces only ten inches apart—an uncomfortably close distance for most Americans.*

"Conversational Ballgames" explains how different cultural expectations distinguish North American from Japanese conversations. Ms. Sakamoto compares conversations to different kinds of games. For Americans, talking is like playing tennis or volleyball, whereas for the Japanese, talking is more like bowling. As you read her essay, see if her comparison of the rules of conversation and the rules of a game helps to illustrate different cultural "rules for the game."

CONVERSATIONAL BALLGAMES

After I was married and had lived in Japan for a while, my Japanese gradually improved to the point where I could take part in simple conversations with my husband and his friends

Lead-in:
Personal experience

1

and family. And I began to notice that often, when I joined in, the others would look startled, and the conversational topic would come to a halt. After this happened several times, it became clear to me that I was doing something wrong. But for a long time, I didn't know what it was.

why didn't her husband tell her?

Finally, after listening carefully to many Japanese conversations, I discovered what my problem was. Even though I was speaking Japanese, I was handling the conversation in a western way.

2

[Japanese-style conversations develop quite differently from western-style conversations. And the difference isn't only in the languages.] I realized that just as I kept trying to hold western-style conversations even when I was speaking Japanese, so my English students kept trying to hold Japanese-style conversations even when they were speaking English. We were unconsciously playing entirely different conversational ballgames.

Sakamoto's thesis 3

[A western-style conversation between two people is like a game of tennis. If I introduce a topic, a conversational ball, I expect you to hit it back.] If you agree with me, I don't expect you simply to agree and do nothing more. I expect you to add something—a reason for agreeing, another example, or an elaboration to carry the idea further. But I don't expect you always to agree. I am just as happy if you question me, or challenge me, or completely disagree with me. Whether you agree or disagree, your response will return the ball to me.

analogy is interesting and easy to understand. 4

And then it is my turn again. [I don't serve a new ball from my original starting line. I hit your ball back again from where it has bounded. I carry your idea further, or answer your questions or objections, or challenge or question you.] And so the ball goes back and forth, with each of us doing our best to give it a new twist, an original spin, or a powerful smash.

Continues comparison or analogy— Explains the process. 5

And the more vigorous the action, the more interesting and exciting the game. Of course, if one of us gets angry, it spoils the conversation, just as it spoils a tennis game. But getting excited is not at all the same as getting angry. After all, we are not trying to hit each other. We are trying to hit the ball. So long as we attack only each other's opinions and do not attack each other personally, we don't expect anyone to get hurt. A good conversation is supposed to be interesting and exciting.

6

More exciting for whom?

I can relate to this because I play tennis

If there are more than two people in the conversation, then it is like doubles in tennis, or like volleyball. There's no waiting in line. Whoever is nearest and quickest hits the ball, and if you step back, someone else will hit it. No one stops the game to give you a turn. You're responsible for taking your own turn. But whether it's two players or a group, everyone does his best to keep the ball going, and no one person has the ball for very long.

7

Changes comparison to volleyball — why?

[A Japanese-style conversation, however, is not at all like tennis or volleyball. It's like bowling.] You wait for your turn. And you always know your place in line. It depends on such things as whether you are older or younger, a close friend or a relative stranger to the previous speaker, in a senior or junior position, and so on.

8

Good transition here.

Depends on status or gender, then?

[When your turn comes, you step up to the starting line with your bowling ball, and carefully bowl it.] Everyone else stands back and watches politely, murmuring encouragement. Everyone waits until the ball has reached the end of the alley and watches to see if it knocks down all the pins, or only some of them, or none of them. There is a pause, while everyone registers your score.

9

Process analysis. Interesting description.

Score: that means there is a winner?

Then, after everyone is sure that you have completely finished your turn, the next person in line steps up to the same starting line, with

10

a different ball. He doesn't return your ball, and he does not begin from where your ball stopped. There is no back and forth at all. All the balls run parallel. And there is always a suitable pause between turns.[There is no rush, no excitement, no scramble for the ball.]

So how do the Japanese accomplish anything?

No wonder everyone looked startled when I took part in Japanese conversations. I paid no attention to whose turn it was and kept snatching the ball halfway down the alley and throwing it back at the bowler.[Of course the conversation died. I was playing the wrong game.]

11

Great analogy Shows cause and effect

[This explains why it is almost impossible to get a western-style conversation or discussion going with English students in Japan.]I used to think that the problem was their lack of English language ability. But I finally came to realize that the biggest problem is that they, too, are playing the wrong game.

But writer has NOT given a specific example.

12

Whenever I serve a volleyball, everyone just stands back and watches it fall, with occasional murmurs of encouragement. No one hits it back. Everyone waits until I call on someone to take a turn. And when that person speaks, he doesn't hit my ball back. He serves a new ball. Again, everyone just watches it fall.

Why change from tennis to volleyball?

13

[So I call on someone else. This person does not refer to what the previous speaker has said. He also serves a new ball.]Nobody seems to have paid any attention to what anyone else has said. Everyone begins again from the same starting line, and all the balls run parallel. There is never any back and forth. Everyone is trying to bowl with a volleyball.

Process analysis — descriptive

14

Now that you know about the difference in the conversational ballgames, you may think that all your troubles are over. But if you have been trained all your life to play one game, it is no simple matter to switch to another, even if you know the rules. Knowing the rules is not at all the same thing as playing the game.

15

This is true.

Even now, during a conversation in Japanese I will notice a startled reaction and belatedly realize that once again I have rudely interrupted by instinctively trying to hit back the other person's bowling ball. It is no easier for me to "just listen" during a conversation, than it is for my Japanese students to "just relax" when speaking with foreigners. Now I can truly sympathize with how hard they must find it to try to carry on a western-style conversation.

[handwritten margin note: thesis: the differences between Western and Japanese conversations are due to the different cultures. The Japanese are playing one game and Westerners are playing another.]

[handwritten: 16]

QUESTIONS ON MEANING

1. What sentence best states Sakamoto's thesis for her essay?
2. According to Sakamoto, what games best describe American conversations? What games characterize Japanese conversations?
3. What crucial differences between Japanese conversational games and American conversational games cause the author trouble? What Japanese "rules" did she violate? What American "rules" did her Japanese students fail to follow?

QUESTIONS ON PURPOSE AND STRATEGY

1. Write out Sakamoto's main idea or central question for her essay in a sentence beginning with *Why*. What are her answers to this question? Is her essay analyzing causes and effects? Explain.
2. An analogy is an extended comparison between two ideas, objects, or processes. The purpose of an analogy is to explain something unfamiliar or difficult by reference to something more familiar. What analogies does Sakamoto use in this essay? Do they effectively serve her purpose?

QUESTIONS ON AUDIENCE AND LANGUAGE

1. Describe Sakamoto's intended audience.
2. How might a teacher of a foreign language use the information in Sakamoto's essay?

QUESTIONS FOR DISCUSSION AND WRITING

1. Consider Sakamoto's analogies. Does conversation have rules and expectations, as games do? Is an American conversation really like tennis or volleyball? How is it not like tennis or volleyball? Do the analogies break down at any point?

2. Not all American conversations follow identical rules. Observe and take notes on several different kinds of conversations: your family dinner time conversation; the discussion in one of your classes; the talk between two or three close friends; your telephone conversations; and so forth. Compare and contrast two of these types of conversations to explain how the "rules" are determined by each situation.

Friends, Good Friends, and Such Good Friends

JUDITH VIORST

(1936–   )

PREREADING JOURNAL ENTRY

Judith Viorst suggests that the best of friends don't necessarily agree with each other about everything, but they
are "there" for each other, and they tell "harsh truths to
each other" when the truth must be told. Describe one
incident with a good friend that illustrates Viorst's definition of a best friend.

---

*An author that critics have described as "part Ann Landers, part
Ogden Nash," Judith Viorst writes poetry, children's stories, and essays.
A native of Newark, New Jersey, and a graduate of Rutgers university,
she is currently a contributing editor for* Redbook *magazine. Viorst is
best known for her light verse, as in* When Did I Stop Being Twenty
and Other Injustices *(1987) and* It's Hard to Be Hip over Thirty
and Other Tragedies of Married Life *(1968), and for her children's
stories, such as* I'll Fix Anthony *(1969) and* My Mamma Says There
Aren't Any Zombies, Ghosts, Vampires, Creatures, Demons,
Monsters, Fiends, Goblins, or Things *(1973).*

*"Friends, Good Friends, and Such Good Friends" appeared orig-
inally in* Redbook *magazine. Viorst's essay shows that we have several
different kinds of friends, depending on our varied interests, roles, and
family backgrounds. By classifying her friends into types and sharing
specific examples, Viorst invites us to reflect on and understand our own
friendships—both the people whose friend we are and the people who
are our friends.*

Women are friends, I once would have said, when 1 they totally love and support and trust each other, and bare to each other the secrets of their souls, and run—no questions asked—to help each other, and tell harsh truths to each other (no, you can't wear that dress unless you lose ten pounds first) when harsh truths must be told.

Women are friends, I once would have said, when 2 they share the same affection for Ingmar Bergman, plus train rides, cats, warm rain, charades, Camus, and hate with equal ardor Newark and Brussels sprouts and Lawrence Welk and camping.

In other words, I once would have said that a friend 3 is a friend all the way, but now I believe that's a narrow point of view. For the friendships I have and the friendships I see are conducted at many levels of intensity, serve many different functions, meet different needs and range from those as all-the-way as the friendship of the soul sisters mentioned above to that of the most nonchalant and casual playmates.

Consider these varieties of friendship: 4

1. Convenience friends. These are the women with 5 whom, if our paths weren't crossing all the time, we'd have no particular reason to be friends: a next-door neighbor, a woman in our car pool, the mother of one of our children's closest friends or maybe some mommy with whom we serve juice and cookies each week at the Glenwood Co-op Nursery.

Convenience friends are convenient indeed. They'll 6 lend us their cups and silverware for a party. They'll drive our kids to soccer when we're sick. They'll take us to pick up our car when we need a lift to the garage. They'll even take our cats when we go on vacation. As we will for them.

But we don't, with convenience friends, ever come too 7 close or tell too much; we maintain our public face and emotional distance. "Which means," says Elaine, "that I'll talk about being overweight but not about being depressed. Which means I'll admit being mad but not blind with rage. Which means I might say that we're pinched this month but never that I'm worried sick over money."

But which doesn't mean that there isn't sufficient value 8
to be found in these friendships of mutual aid, in convenience friends.

2. Special-interest friends. These friendships aren't 9
intimate, and they needn't involve kids or silverware or
cats. Their value lies in some interest jointly shared. And
so we may have an office friend or a yoga friend or a
tennis friend or a friend from the Women's Democratic
Club.

"I've got one woman friend," says Joyce, "who likes, 10
as I do, to take psychology courses. Which makes it nice
for me—and nice for her. It's fun to go with someone
you know and it's fun to discuss what you've learned,
driving back from the classes." And for the most part, she
says, that's all they discuss.

"I'd say that what we're doing is *doing* together, not 11
being together," Suzanne says of her Tuesday-doubles
friends. "It's mainly a tennis relationship, but we play
together well. And I guess we all need to have a couple
of playmates."

I agree.   12

My playmate is a shopping friend, a woman of mar- 13
velous taste, a woman who knows exactly *where* to buy
what, and furthermore is a woman who always knows
beyond a doubt what one ought to be buying. I don't have
the time to keep up with what's new in eyeshadow,
hemlines and shoes and whether the smock look is in or
finished already. But since (oh, shame!) I care a lot about
eyeshadow, hemlines and shoes, and since I don't *want* to
wear smocks if the smock look is finished, I'm very glad
to have a shopping friend.

3. Historical friends. We all have a friend who knew 14
us when . . . maybe way back in Miss Meltzer's second
grade, when our family lived in that three-room flat in
Brooklyn, when our dad was out of work for seven months,
when our brother Allie got in that fight where they had
to call the police, when our sister married the endodontist
from Yonkers and when, the morning after we lost our
virginity, she was the first, the only, friend we told.

The years have gone by and we've gone separate ways 15 and we've little in common now, but we're still an intimate part of each other's past. And so whenever we go to Detroit we always go to visit this friend of our girlhood. Who knows how we looked before our teeth were straightened. Who knows how we talked before our voice got un-Brooklyned. Who knows what we ate before we learned about artichokes. And who, by her presence, puts us in touch with an earlier part of ourself, a part of ourself it's important never to lose.

"What this friend means to me and what I mean to 16 her," says Grace, "is having a sister without sibling rivalry. We know the texture of each other's lives. She remembers my grandmother's cabbage soup. I remember the way her uncle played the piano. There's simply no other friend who remembers those things."

4. Crossroads friends. Like historical friends, our 17 crossroads friends are important for *what was*—for the friendship we shared at a crucial, now past, time of life. A time, perhaps, when we roomed in college together; or worked as eager young singles in the Big City together; or went together, as my friend Elizabeth and I did through pregnancy, birth and that scary first year of new motherhood.

Crossroads friends forge powerful links, links strong 18 enough to endure with not much more contact than once-a-year letters at Christmas. And out of respect for those crossroads years, for those dramas and dreams we once shared, we will always be friends.

5. Cross-generational friends. Historical friends and 19 crossroads friends seem to maintain a special kind of intimacy—dormant but always ready to be revived—and though we may rarely meet, whenever we do connect, it's personal and intense. Another kind of intimacy exists in the friendships that form across generations in what one woman calls her daughter-mother and her mother-daughter relationships.

Evelyn's friend is her mother's age—"but I share so 20 much more than I ever could with my mother"—a woman

she talks to of music, of books and of life. "What I get
from her is the benefit of her experience. What she gets—
and enjoys—from me is a youthful perspective. It's a
pleasure for both of us."

I have in my own life a precious friend, a woman of 21
65 who has lived very hard, who is wise, who listens well;
who has been where I am and can help me understand
it; and who represents not only an ultimate ideal mother
to me but also the person I'd like to be when I grow up.

In our daughter role we tend to do more than our 22
share of self-revelation; in our mother role we tend to
receive what's revealed. It's another kind of pleasure—
playing wise mother to a questing younger person. It's
another very lovely kind of friendship.

6. Part-of-a-couple friends. Some of the women we 23
call our friends we never see alone—we see them as part
of a couple at couples' parties. And though we share
interests in many things and respect each other's views,
we aren't moved to deepen the relationship. Whatever the
reason, a lack of time or—and this is more likely—a lack
of chemistry, our friendship remains in the context of a
group. But the fact that our feeling on seeing each other
is always, "I'm *so* glad she's here" and the fact that we
spend half the evening talking together says that this too,
in its own way, counts as a friendship.

(Other part-of-a-couple friends are the friends that 24
came with the marriage, and some of these are friends we
could live without. But sometimes, alas, she married our
husband's best friend; and sometimes, alas, she *is* our
husband's best friend. And so we find ourself dealing
with her, somewhat against our will, in a spirit of what I'll
call *reluctant* friendship.)

7. Men who are friends. I wanted to write just of 25
women friends, but the women I've talked to won't let
me—they say I must mention man-woman friendships
too. For these friendships can be just as close and as dear
as those that we form with women. Listen to Lucy's
description of one such friendship:

"We've found we have things to talk about that are 26

different from what he talks about with my husband and different from what I talk about with his wife. So sometimes we call on the phone or meet for lunch. There are similar intellectual interests—we always pass on to each other the books that we love—but there's also something tender and caring too."

In a couple of crises, Lucy says, "he offered himself, 27 for talking and for helping. And when someone died in his family he wanted me there. The sexual, flirty part of our friendship is very small, but *some*—just enough to make it fun and different." She thinks—and I agree—that the sexual part, though small is always *some*, is always there when a man and a woman are friends.

It's only in the past few years that I've made friends 28 with men, in the sense of a friendship that's *mine*, not just part of two couples. And achieving with them the ease and the trust I've found with women friends has value indeed. Under the dryer at home last week, putting on mascara and rouge, I comfortably sat and talked with a fellow named Peter. Peter, I finally decided, could handle the shock of me minus mascara under the dryer. Because we care for each other. Because we're friends.

8. There are medium friends, and pretty good friends, 29 and very good friends indeed, and these friendships are defined by their level of intimacy. And what we'll reveal at each of these levels of intimacy is calibrated with care. We might tell a medium friend, for example, that yesterday we had a fight with our husband. And we might tell a pretty good friend that this fight with our husband made us so mad that we slept on the couch. And we might tell a very good friend that the reason we got so mad in that fight that we slept on the couch had something to do with that girl who works in his office. But it's only to our very best friends that we're willing to tell all, to tell what's going on with that girl in his office.

The best of friends, I still believe, totally love and 30 support and trust each other, and bare to each other the secrets of their souls, and run—no questions asked—to help each other, and tell harsh truths to each other when they must be told.

But we needn't agree about everything (only 12-year- 31 old girl friends agree about *everything*) to tolerate each other's point of view. To accept without judgment. To give and to take without ever keeping score. And to *be* there, as I am for them and as they are for me, to comfort our sorrows, to celebrate our joys.

QUESTIONS ON MEANING

1. Is the thesis of Viorst's essay most clearly stated in the introduction or in the conclusion?

2. How many different kinds of friends does Viorst describe? Describe or define each type.

3. How are Viorst's seventh and eighth categories different from her first six categories? Does Viorst change her basis of classification?

QUESTIONS ON PURPOSE AND STRATEGY

1. Viorst's purpose is to explain something about friends to her readers. Does she concentrate on explaining *how,* explaining *what,* or explaining *why?* Refer to passages in the article to support your choice(s).

2. To write her article, Viorst apparently interviewed her friends and then used their experiences (along with her own) to illustrate each type of friend. How many different women does Viorst quote? Is her interview strategy appropriate for her subject and purpose?

QUESTIONS ON AUDIENCE AND LANGUAGE

1. From the first sentence, Viorst states that she is discussing friendships between women. What kind of women (age, social standing, cultural and geographical background) does

she discuss? How closely does that match the typical reader of *Redbook*? Would any men be interested in her article?

2. In paragraph fifteen, Viorst writes four sentence fragments in a row, beginning with "Who knows how we looked before our teeth were straightened." Do these sentence fragments make sense? Are they too informal for her audience? What effect do these four parallel fragments have on the reader?

QUESTIONS FOR DISCUSSION AND WRITING

1. Reread your Prereading Journal Entry. In which of Viorst's categories would you place the friend you described? Would your friendship require a different category?

2. How are men's friendships different from Viorst's types? Which of her categories apply also to men? Which do not apply? What new categories of friendships do men have?

3. Write an essay classifying the types of friends you have. Use examples from your own experience, but also interview your friends for their ideas and examples. From these examples, determine your own categories.

Fried Chicken

JIM VILLAS

(1938–   )

PREREADING JOURNAL ENTRY

Describe precisely how to tie your shoe. Go through the
process, slowly, describing each step in the process. Come
to class prepared to read your instructions aloud while
your classmates follow your instructions.

---

*A native of Charlotte, North Carolina, Jim Villas is currently res-
taurant reviewer and food editor for* Town and Country *magazine.
He has written articles for* Gourmet *and* Food & Wine, *and his books
include* American Taste *(1982), an investigation of American cookery,
and* The Town and Country Cookbook *(1985).*

In "Fried Chicken," first published in Esquire *magazine, Villas
transforms the cookbook recipe into an extended commentary on the state
of culinary affairs in America. "There are not many writers around who
are as much fun to read as James Villas," writes one critic. "In his
intensely personal style, he is elegant, quirky, opinionated, precise, and
lyrical." As you read Villas's essay on how to create impeccable fried
chicken from scratch, see if you agree with this judgment.*

When it comes to fried chicken, let's not beat around 1
the bush for one second. To know about fried chicken
you have to have been weaned and reared on it in the
South. Period. The French know absolutely nothing about
it, and Julia Child and James Beard very little. Craig
Claiborne knows plenty. He's from Mississippi. And to set
the record straight before bringing on regional and pos-

sible national holocaust over the correct preparation of this classic dish, let me emphasize and reemphasize the fact that I'm a Southerner, born, bred, and chicken-fried for all times. Now, I don't know exactly why we Southerners love and eat at least ten times more fried chicken than anyone else, but we do and always have and always will. Maybe we have a hidden craw in our throats or oversize pulley bones or . . . oh, I don't know what we have, and it doesn't matter. What does matter is that we take our fried chicken very seriously, having singled it out years ago as not only the most important staple worthy of heated and complex debate but also as the dish that non-Southerners have never really had any knack for. Others just plain down don't *understand* fried chicken, and, to tell the truth, there're lots of Southerners who don't know as much as they think they know. Naturally everybody everywhere in the country is convinced he or she can cook or identify great fried chicken as well as any ornery reb (including all the fancy cookbook writers), but the truth remains that once you've eaten real chicken fried by an expert chicken fryer in the South there are simply no grounds for contest.

As far as I'm concerned, all debate over how to prepare 2 fried chicken has ended forever, for recently I fried up exactly twenty-one and a half chickens (or 215 pieces) using every imaginable technique, piece of equipment, and type of oil for the sole purpose of establishing once and for all the right way to fix great fried chicken. In a minute I'll tell you what's wrong with most of the Kentucky-fried, Maryland-fried, oven-fried, deep-fried, creole-fried, and all those other classified varieties of Southern-fried chicken people like to go on about. But first *my* chicken, which I call simply Fried Chicken and which I guarantee will start you lapping:

Equipment (no substitutes):

A sharp chef's or butcher's knife 12 to 13 in. long

A large wooden cutting board

A small stockpot half-filled with water (for chicken soup)

A large glass salad bowl

A heavy 12–in. cast-iron skillet with lid

Long-handled tweezer tongs

1 roll paper towels

2 brown paper bags

1 empty coffee can

A serving platter

A wire whisk

A home fire extinguisher

Ingredients (to serve 4):

3 cups whole milk

½ fresh lemon

1½ lbs. (3 cups) top-quality shortening

4 tbsp. rendered bacon grease

1 whole freshly killed 3½– to 4–lb. chicken

1½ cups plus 2 tbsp. flour

3 tsp. salt

Freshly ground black pepper

TO PREPARE CHICKEN FOR FRYING

Remove giblets and drop in stockpot with neck. (This is for a good chicken soup to be eaten at another time.) Cut off and pull out any undesirable fat at neck and tail. Placing whole chicken in center of cutting board (breast-side up, neck toward you), grab leg on left firmly, pull outward and down toward board, and begin slashing down through skin toward thigh joint, keeping knife close to thigh. Crack back thigh joint as far as possible, find joint with fingers, then cut straight through to remove (taking care not to pull skin from breast). Turn bird around and repeat procedure on other thigh. To separate thigh from leg, grasp one end in each hand, pull against tension of joint, find joint, and sever. Follow same procedure to remove wings. Cut off wing tips and add to stockpot.

To remove pulley bone (or wishbone to non-South- 4 erners), find protruding knob toward neck end of breast, trace with fingers to locate small indentation just forward of knob, slash horizontally downward across indentation, then begin cutting carefully away from indentation and downward toward neck till forked pulley-bone piece is fully severed. Turn chicken backside up, locate two hidden small pinbones on either side below neck toward middle of back, and cut through skin to expose ends of bones. Put two fingers of each hand into neck cavity and separate breast from back by pulling forcefully till the two pry apart. (If necessary, sever stubborn tendons and skin with knife.) Cut back in half, reserving lower portion (tail end) for frying, and tossing upper portion (rib cage) into stockpot. Place breast skin-side down, ram tip of knife down through center cartilage, and cut breast in half.

(*Hint:* Level cutting edge of knife along cartilage, then 5 slam blade through with heel of hand.)

Rinse the ten pieces of chicken thoroughly under cold 6 running water, dry with paper towels, and salt and pepper lightly. Pour milk into bowl, squeeze lemon into milk, add chicken to soak, cover, and refrigerate at least two hours and preferably overnight.

TO FRY CHICKEN

Remove chicken from refrigerator and allow to return 7 to room temperature (about 70°). While melting the pound and a half of shortening over high heat to measure ½ inch in skillet, pour flour, remaining salt and pepper to taste into paper bag. Remove dark pieces of chicken from milk, drain each momentarily over bowl, drop in paper bag, shake vigorously to coat, and add bacon grease to skillet. When small bubbles appear on surface, reduce heat slightly. Remove dark pieces of chicken from bag one by one, shake off excess flour, and, using tongs, lower gently into fat, skin-side down. Quickly repeat all procedures with white pieces; reserve milk, arrange chicken in skillet so it cooks evenly, reduce heat to medium, and cover. Fry exactly 17 minutes. Lower heat, turn pieces with tongs and fry 17 minutes longer uncovered. With paper towels wipe grease continuously from exposed surfaces as it spatters. Chicken should be almost mahogany brown.

Drain thoroughly on second brown paper bag, transfer 8 to serving platter *without* reheating in oven, and serve hot or at room temperature with any of the following items: mashed potatoes and cream gravy, potato salad, green beans, turnip greens, sliced home-grown tomatoes, stewed okra, fresh cornbread, iced tea, beer, homemade peach ice cream, or watermelon.

TO MAKE CREAM GRAVY

Discard in coffee can all but one tablespoon fat from 9 skillet, making sure not to pour off brown drippings. Over high heat, add two remaining tablespoons flour to fat and stir constantly with wire whisk till roux browns. Gradually pour 1¾ cups reserved milk from bowl and continue stirring till gravy comes to a boil, thickens slightly, and is smooth. Reduce heat, simmer two minutes, and check salt and pepper seasoning. Serve in gravy boat.

Now, that's the right way, the only way, to deal with 10 fried chicken. Crisp, juicy on the inside, full of flavor, not greasy and sloppy, fabulous. Of course one reason my recipe works so well is it's full of important subtleties that are rarely indicated in cookbooks but that help to make the difference between impeccable fried chicken and all the junk served up everywhere today. And just to illustrate this point, I cite a recipe for "Perfect Fried Chicken" that recently appeared in *Ladies' Home Journal.*

1. Rinse cut-up 2½– to 3–lb. broiler-fryer and pat dry.

2. Pour 1 in. vegetable oil in skillet, heat to 375°. Combine ½ cup flour, 2 tsp salt, dash of pepper in a bag. Coat a few pieces at a time.

3. Preheat oven to 250°. Place paper towels in shallow baking pan.

4. Fry thighs and drumsticks, turning occasionally, for 12 minutes until golden. Pierce with fork to see if juices run clear. Remove to baking pan and place in heated oven. Fry remaining pieces for 7 or 8 minutes. Serves four.

Snap! That's it. A real quicky. Fast fried chicken that 11 promises to be perfect. Bull! It tasted like hell, and if you don't believe me, try it yourself. The pitfalls of the recipe are staggering but typical. First of all, nobody in his right mind fries a skinny two-and-a-half-pound chicken for four people, not unless everyone's on some absurd diet or enjoys sucking bones. Second, the recipe takes for granted you're going to buy a plastic-wrapped chicken that's been so hacked and splintered by a meat cleaver that blood from the bones saturates the package. What help is offered if the chicken you happen to have on hand is whole or only partially cut up? Third, what type of skillet, and what size, for heaven's sake? If the pan's too light the chicken will burn on the bottom, and if you pour one full inch of oil in an eight-inch skillet, you'll end up with deep-fried chicken. And as for sticking forks in seared chicken to release those delicious juices, or putting fried chicken in the oven to get it disgustingly soggy, or serving a half-raw thick breast that's cooked only seven or eight minutes—well, I refuse to get overheated.

Without question the most important secret to any 12 great fried chicken is the quality of the chicken itself, and without question most of the three billion pullets marketed annually in the U.S. have about as much flavor as tennis balls. But, after all, what can you expect of battery birds whose feet never touch the dirty filthy earth, whose diet includes weight-building fats, fish flours, and factory-fresh chemicals, and whose life expectancy is a pitiful seven weeks? Tastelessness, that's what, the same disgraceful tastelessness that characterizes the eggs we're forced to consume. How many people in this country remember the rich flavor of a good old barnyard chicken, a nearly extinct species that pecked around the yard for a good fifteen weeks, digested plenty of barley-and-milk mash, bran, grain, and beer, got big and fat, and never sent one solitary soul to the hospital with contamination? I remember, believe you me, and how I pity the millions who, blissfully unconscious of what they missed and sadly addicted to the chicken passed out by Colonel Sanders, will never taste a truly luscious piece of fried chicken unless they're first shown how to get their hands on a real chicken. Of course, what you see in supermarkets are technically real chickens fit for consumption, but anyone who's sunk teeth into a gorgeous, plump barnyard variety (not to mention an inimitable French *poularde de Bresse*) would agree that to compare the scrawny, bland, mass-produced bird with the one God intended us to eat is something more than ludicrous.

I originally intended to tell you how to raise, kill, draw, 13 and prepare your own chickens. Then I came to my senses and faced the reality that unless you were brought up wringing chickens' necks, bleeding them, searching for the craws where food is stored, and pulling out their innards with your hands—well, it can be a pretty nauseating mess that makes you gag if you're not used to it. Besides, there's really no need to slaughter your own chickens, not, that is, if you're willing to take time and make the effort to locate either a good chicken raiser who feeds and exercises his chickens properly (on terra firma) or a reliable merchant who gets his chickens fresh from the farm. They do exist, still, be their number ever so dwindling. If you live in a rural area, simply get to know a farmer who raises chickens, start buying eggs from him and then tell him you'll pay him any amount to kill and prepare for you a nice 3½– to 4–pound pullet. He will, and probably with pride. If you're in a large city, the fastest method is to study the Yellow Pages of the phone book, search under "Poultry—Retail" for the words "Fresh poultry and eggs" or "Custom poultry" or "Strictly kosher poultry," and proceed from there.

Now, if you think I take my fried chicken a little too 14 seriously, you haven't seen anything till you attend the National Chicken Cooking Contest held annually in early summer at different locations throughout the country. Created in 1949, the festival has a Poultry Princess; vintage motorcar displays; a flea market; a ten-feet-by-eight-inch skillet that fries up to seven and a half tons of chicken; ten thousand chicken-loving contestants cooking for cash prizes amounting to over $25,000; and big-name judges who are chosen from among the nation's top newspaper, magazine, and television food editors. It's a big to-do. Of course, I personally have no intention whatsoever of ever entering any chicken contest that's not made up exclusively of Southerners, and of course you understand my principle. This, however, should not necessarily affect your now going to the National and showing the multitudes what real fried chicken is all about. A few years back, a young lady irreverently dipped some chicken in oil flavored with soy sauce, rolled it in crushed chow mein noodles, fried it up, and walked away with top honors and a few grand for her Cock-a-Noodle-Do. Without doubt she was a sweetheart of a gal, but you know, the people who judged that fried chicken need help.

QUESTIONS ON MEANING

1. List the key steps in the process of making Villas's guaranteed perfect fried chicken. How does his procedure differ from the recipe taken from *Ladies' Home Journal*?

2. Other than how to *cook* impeccable fried chicken, what else does Villas describe in his essay?

QUESTIONS ON PURPOSE AND STRATEGY

1. Is Villas's purpose to explain how to make great fried chicken? To argue that only Southerners know how to cook it? To persuade you to buy fresh, homegrown pullets and avoid the Colonel's chicken like the plague? Where in the essay are these (and other) purposes most evident?

2. Describe Villas's voice, his personality as projected through his essay. Is he just a country kind of guy? Is he a patriot or fanatic about the South? Is he egotistical, assertive, or self-indulgent? Is his tone serious or humorous? Find at least one passage that shows Villas's voice or tone.

QUESTIONS ON AUDIENCE AND LANGUAGE

1. Who is Villas's audience? Expert cooks? People who cook or eat fried chicken occasionally? People who are just curious about how good chicken should be made? (How does Villas keep the attention of readers who are not experts but are merely curious?)

2. "When it comes to fried chicken, let's not beat around the bush for one second. To know about fried chicken you have to have been weaned and reared on it in the South. Period." Where else in his essay does Villas talk directly to his audience? What effect does his direct address and use of "you" have on his readers?

3. Villas relies on colloquial language to give his essay a down-home-I'm-talking-to-you-so-pay-attention flavor. In the first paragraph, he uses phrases such as "beat around the bush," "a Southerner, born, bred, and chicken-fried for all times," "had any knack for," and "others just plain down don't *understand* fried chicken." Find other examples of Villas's colloquial language in the essay. Explain why his colloquial language is or is not effective or appropriate.

QUESTIONS FOR DISCUSSION AND WRITING

1. Locate one or two places in Villas's essay where you are confused about his procedure. How should he clarify his explanation so you understand his process?

2. Interview your father, mother, or friend who has a great recipe for a particular food. Write an investigative essay reporting not only on this person's recipe but also on his or her personality. Show how your friend's personality relates to his or her art of cooking.

3. Choose a hobby or activity that you do especially well. Write an essay that explains how to do your activity and also argues that your way is better than the techniques that other so-called experts recommend. Try to entertain your readers with your own voice.

Why Don't We Complain?

WILLIAM F. BUCKLEY, JR.

(1925–   )

PREREADING JOURNAL ENTRY

Describe some recent public occasion when you sat or stood meekly by when something in your immediate surroundings was obviously wrong: the service was non-existent, the room temperature too hot or cold, the food was awful, or whatever. What might you have said, and to whom? Why didn't you speak up?

As founder and editor for the National Review, *host of the television show, "Firing Line," and columnist in dozens of journals, William F. Buckley, Jr. is still America's most articulate defender of conservatism. A Yale graduate, Buckley began his career with an attack on his alma mater's liberal philosophy in* God and Man at Yale: The Superstitions of Academic Freedom *(1951).* Cruising Speed: A Documentary *(1971), a personal account of a typical week's activities, reveals Buckley's varied political and literary interests demonstrated by his espionage novels, which range from* Saving the Queen *(1976) to* Mongoose, R.I.P. *(1988), and his sailing-adventure books, such as* Atlantic High: A Celebration *(1982) and* Racing through Paradise: A Pacific Passage *(1987).*

"Why Don't We Complain," which first appeared in Esquire *magazine, has a clear political message, but it is rooted in examples from Buckley's life. The essay catches our attention by jumping into a specific example from Buckley's life and then gradually explaining why Americans often behave like such sheep and why we should learn to be more assertive in personal and political matters.*

It was the very last coach and the only empty seat on 1 the entire train, so there was no turning back. The problem was to breathe. Outside, the temperature was below freezing. Inside the railroad car the temperature must have been about 85 degrees. I took off my overcoat, and a few minutes later my jacket, and noticed that the car was flecked with the white shirts of the passengers. I soon found my hand moving to loosen my tie. From one end of the car to the other, as we rattled through Westchester County, we sweated; but we did not moan.

I watched the train conductor appear at the head of 2 the car. "Tickets, all tickets, please!" In a more virile age, I thought, the passengers would seize the conductor and strap him down on a seat over the radiator to share the fate of his patrons. He shuffled down the aisle picking up tickets, punching commutation cards. *No one addressed a word to him.* He approached my seat, and I drew a deep breath of resolution. "Conductor," I began with a considerable edge to my voice. . . . Instantly the doleful eyes of my seatmate turned tiredly from his newspaper to fix me with a resentful stare: what question could be so important as to justify my sibilant intrusion into his stupor? I was shaken by those eyes. I am incapable of making a discreet fuss, so I mumbled a question about what time were we due in Stamford (I didn't even ask whether it would be before or after dehydration could be expected to set in), got my reply, and went back to my newspaper and to wiping my brow.

The conductor had nonchalantly walked down the 3 gauntlet of eighty sweating American freemen, and not one of them had asked him to explain why the passengers in that car had been consigned to suffer. There is nothing to be done when the temperature *outdoors* is 85 degrees, and indoors the air conditioner has broken down; obviously when that happens there is nothing to do, except perhaps curse the day that one was born. But when the temperature outdoors is below freezing, it takes a positive act of will on somebody's part to set the temperature *indoors* at 85. Somewhere a valve was turned too far, a furnace overstocked, a thermostat maladjusted: something that could easily be remedied by turning off the heat and allowing the great outdoors to come indoors. All this is so obvious. What is not obvious is what has happened to the American people.

It isn't just the commuters, whom we have come to 4 visualize as a supine breed who have got on to the trick of suspending their sensory faculties twice a day while they submit to the creeping dissolution of the railroad industry. It isn't just they who have given up trying to rectify irrational vexations. It is the American people everywhere.

A few weeks ago at a large movie theater I turned to 5 my wife and said, "The picture is out of focus." "Be quiet," she answered. I obeyed. But a few minutes later I raised the point, again, with mounting impatience. "It will be all right in a minute," she said apprehensively. (She would rather lose her eyesight than be around when I make one of my infrequent scenes.) I waited. It was *just* out of focus—not glaringly out, but out. My vision is 20-20, and I assume that is the vision, adjusted, of most people in the movie house. So, after hectoring my wife throughout the first reel, I finally prevailed upon her to admit that it *was* off, and very annoying. We then settled down, coming to rest on the presumption that: (a) someone connected with the management of the theater must soon notice the blur and make the correction; or (b) that someone seated near the rear of the house would make the complaint in behalf of those of us up front; or (c) that—any minute now—the entire house would explode into catcalls and foot stamping, calling dramatic attention to the irksome distortion.

What happened was nothing. The movie ended, as it 6 had begun, *just* out of focus, and as we trooped out, we stretched our faces in a variety of contortions to accustom the eye to the shock of normal focus.

I think it is safe to say that everybody suffered on that 7 occasion. And I think it is safe to assume that everyone was expecting someone else to take the initiative in going back to speak to the manager. And it is probably true even that if we had supposed the movie would run right through the blurred image, someone surely would have summoned up the purposive indignation to get up out of his seat and file his complaint.

But notice that no one did. And the reason no one 8 did is because we are all increasingly anxious in America to be unobtrusive, we are reluctant to make our voices heard, hesitant about claiming our rights; we are afraid that our cause is unjust, or that if it is not unjust, that it is ambiguous, or if not even that, that it is too trivial to justify the horrors of a confrontation with Authority; we will sit in an oven or endure a racking headache before undertaking a head-on, I'm-here-to-tell-you complaint. That tendency to passive compliance, to a heedless endurance, is something to keep one's eyes on—in sharp focus.

I myself can occasionally summon the courage to 9 complain, but I cannot, as I have intimated, complain softly. My own instinct is so strong to let the thing ride, to forget about it—to expect that someone will take the matter up, when the grievance is collective, in my behalf— that it is only when the provocation is at a very special key, whose vibrations touch simultaneously a complexus of nerves, allergies, and passions, that I catch fire and find the reserves of courage and assertiveness to speak up. When that happens, I get quite carried away. My blood gets hot, my brow wet, I become unbearably and unconscionably sarcastic and bellicose; I am girded for a total showdown.

Why should that be? Why could not I (or anyone else) 10 on that railroad coach have said simply to the conductor, "Sir"—I take that back: that sounds sarcastic—"Conductor, would you be good enough to turn down the heat? I am extremely hot. In fact, I tend to get hot every time the temperature reaches 85 degr—" Strike that last sentence. Just end it with the simple statement that you are extremely hot, and let the conductor infer the cause.

Every New Year's Eve I resolve to do something about 11

the Milquetoast in me and vow to speak up, calmly, for my rights, and for the betterment of our society, on every appropriate occasion. Entering last New Year's Eve, I was fortified in my resolve because that morning at breakfast I had had to ask the waitress three times for a glass of milk. She finally brought it—after I had finished my eggs, which is when I don't want it any more. I did not have the manliness to order her to take the milk back, but settled instead for a cowardly sulk, and ostentatiously refused to drink the milk—though I later paid for it— rather than state plainly to the hostess, as I should have, why I had not drunk it, and would not pay for it.

So by the time the New Year ushered out the Old, 12 riding in on my morning's indignation and stimulated by the gastric juices of resolution that flow so faithfully on New Year's Eve, I rendered my vow. Henceforward I would conquer my shyness, my despicable disposition to supineness. I would speak out like a man against the unnecessary annoyances of our time.

Forty-eight hours later, I was standing in line at the 13 ski repair store in Pico Peak, Vermont. All I needed, to get on with my skiing, was the loan, for one minute, of a small screwdriver, to tighten a loose binding. Behind the counter in the workshop were two men. One was industriously engaged in servicing the complicated requirements of a young lady at the head of the line, and obviously he would be tied up for quite a while. The other—"Jiggs," his workmate called him—was a middle-aged man, who sat in a chair puffing a pipe, exchanging small talk with his working partner. My pulse began its telltale acceleration. The minutes ticked on. I stared at the idle shopkeeper, hoping to shame him into action, but he was impervious to my telepathic reproof and continued his small talk with his friend, brazenly insensitive to the nervous demands of six good men who were raring to ski.

Suddenly my New Year's Eve resolution struck me. It 14 was now or never. I broke from my place in line and marched to the counter. I was going to control myself. I dug my nails into my palms. My effort was only partially successful:

"If you are not too busy," I said icily, "would you mind 15 handing me a screwdriver?"

Work stopped and everyone turned his eyes on me, 16 and I experienced that mortification I always feel when I am the center of centripetal shafts of curiosity, resentment, perplexity.

But the worst was yet to come. "I am sorry, sir," said 17 Jiggs deferentially, moving the pipe from his mouth. "I am not supposed to move. I have just had a heart attack." That was the signal for a great whirring noise that descended from heaven. We looked, stricken, out the window, and it appeared as though a cyclone had suddenly focused on the snowy courtyard between the shop and the ski lift. Suddenly a gigantic army helicopter materialized, and hovered down to a landing. Two men jumped out of the plane carrying a stretcher, tore into the ski shop, and lifted the shopkeeper onto the stretcher. Jiggs bade his companion good-by, was whisked out the door, into the plane, up to the heavens, down—we learned—to a nearby army hospital. I looked up manfully—into a score of man-eating eyes. I put the experience down as a reversal.

As I write this, on an airplane, I have run out of paper 18 and need to reach into my briefcase under my legs for more. I cannot do this until my empty lunch tray is removed from my lap. I arrested the stewardess as she passed empty-handed down the aisle on the way to the kitchen to fetch the lunch trays for the passengers up forward who haven't been served yet. "Would you please take my tray?" "Just a *moment,* sir!" she said, and marched on sternly. Shall I tell her that since she is headed for the kitchen *anyway,* it could not delay the feeding of the other passengers by more than two seconds necessary to stash away my empty tray? Or remind her that not fifteen minutes ago she spoke unctuously into the loudspeaker the words undoubtedly devised by the airline's highly paid public relations counselor: "If there is anything I or Miss

French can do for you to make your trip more enjoyable, *please* let us—" I have run out of paper.

I think the observable reluctance of the majority of 19 Americans to assert themselves in minor matters is related to our increased sense of helplessness in an age of technology and centralized political and economic power. For generations, Americans who were too hot, or too cold, got up and did something about it. Now we call the plumber, or the electrician, or the furnace man. The habit of looking after our own needs obviously had something to do with the assertiveness that characterized the American family familiar to readers of American literature. With the technification of life goes our direct responsibility for our material environment, and we are conditioned to adopt a position of helplessness not only as regards the broken air conditioner, but as regards the overheated train. It takes an expert to fix the former, but not the latter; yet these distinctions, as we withdraw into helplessness, tend to fade away.

Our notorious political apathy is a related phenome- 20 non. Every year, whether the Republican or the Democratic Party is in office, more and more power drains away from the individual to feed vast reservoirs in far-off places; and we have less and less say about the shape of events which shape our future. From this alienation of personal power comes the sense of resignation with which we accept the political dispensations of a powerful government whose hold upon us continues to increase.

An editor of a national weekly news magazine told me 21 a few years ago that as few as a dozen letters of protest against an editorial stance of his magazine was enough to convene a plenipotentiary meeting of the board of editors to review policy. "So few people complain, or make their voices heard," he explained to me, "that we assume a dozen letters represent the inarticulated views of thousands of readers." In the past ten years, he said, the volume of mail has noticeably decreased, even though the circulation of his magazine has risen.

When our voices are finally mute, when we have finally 22

suppressed the natural instinct to complain, whether the vexation is trivial or grave, we shall have become automatons, incapable of feeling. When Premier Khrushchev first came to this country late in 1959, he was primed, we are informed, to experience the bitter resentment of the American people against his tyranny, against his persecutions, against the movement which is responsible for the great number of American deaths in Korea, for billions in taxes every year, and for life everlasting on the brink of disaster; but Khrushchev was pleasantly surprised, and reported back to the Russian people that he had been met with overwhelming cordiality (read: apathy), except, to be sure, for "a few fascists who followed me around with their wretched posters, and should be horse-whipped."

I may be crazy, but I say there would have been lots 23 more posters in a society where train temperatures in the dead of winter are not allowed to climb to 85 degrees without complaint.

QUESTIONS ON MEANING

1. According to Buckley, what are the advantages of a calm, reasonable, and well-timed complaint? Why don't we complain? What are the possible disadvantages?

2. Buckley states his thesis or main idea several times, but each time he makes his point a bit more clearly. Identify the places in the essay where he states the main idea. Where is his statement most explicit?

QUESTIONS ON PURPOSE AND STRATEGY

1. Is Buckley's purpose to inform us about several times he has suffered without complaining? To explain why we don't complain? To explain why we should complain? To argue that if we don't complain, we may allow America's centralized political and economic system to overwhelm us?

2. In supporting his purpose, Buckley uses personal experience to illustrate his cause and effect reasoning. Which personal

examples most effectively illustrate the effects of not complaining? Which illustrate the effects of actual complaints?

QUESTIONS ON AUDIENCE AND LANGUAGE

1. Which paragraphs suggest that Buckley is writing to a general audience that may share his personal frustration? Which paragraphs suggest that Buckley is writing for an audience interested in politics and political action?

2. Find several passages that illustrate Buckley's *voice,* the sense of his personality and character conveyed in this essay. What adjectives would you use to characterize Buckley's voice: *humble, pompous, charming, egotistical, witty, engaging, self-mocking, courteous, serious,* or *pedantic?*

3. Readers often complain that Buckley's writing is extremely sexist. Find examples of language in this essay that stereotypes men's or women's talents or occupations by their gender.

4. The reader doesn't venture more than a few paragraphs into this essay before encountering Buckley's large vocabulary: "my sibilant intrusion," "nonchalantly walked down the gauntlet," and "a supine breed." By the end of the article, Buckley has used the following words—and more: "hectoring," "intimated," "provocation," "complexus," "unconscionably," "bellicose," "girded," "ostentatiously," "supineness," "telepathic," "mortification," "perplexity," and "unctuously." Does this large vocabulary increase your interest, or should Buckley substitute easier synonyms?

QUESTIONS FOR DISCUSSION AND WRITING

1. Often, readers laugh at several points in Buckley's essay. What is the source of the humor? The conditions that try our patience? Buckley's own character that wavers between trying to remain inconspicuous and wanting to vent his rising irritation and anger? What is funny—or not so funny— about this essay?

2. Buckley describes a "reversal" experience, his encounter with

Jiggs in the Vermont ski shop. Does this incident detract from Buckley's overall point, that Americans *should* be more assertive? Does it illustrate when we should not be assertive? What conclusion do we (or Buckley) draw from this episode?

3. Following Judith Viorst's strategy in "Friends, Good Friends, and Such Good Friends," write an essay about types of occasions that call for assertiveness. Interview several friends about their experiences. Include both their examples and your own to illustrate the effects of assertiveness versus nonconfrontation.

You Are What You Say

ROBIN LAKOFF

(1942–   )

PREREADING JOURNAL ENTRY

The following phrases are examples of sexist language: *businessman, lady doctor, career girl,* and *congressman.* Why are these phrases sexist? What substitutes would you use to avoid these stereotypes?

We often hear the cliche, "You are what you eat," but we rarely consider how the words we speak describe (and thus limit) our roles. As a social and cultural linguist, Robin Lakoff has studied how language sometimes nourishes us and sometimes malnourishes us. Lakoff was born in Brooklyn, New York, and received her B.A. from Radcliffe College, her M.A. from Indiana University, and her Ph.D. from Harvard. Since 1972, she has taught in the linguistics department at the University of California, Berkeley. She has written Language and Woman's Place *(1975), and coauthored* Face Value: The Politics of Beauty *(1984).*

"You Are What You Say," which originally appeared in Ms. *magazine before it was included in* Language and Woman's Place, *explains that women face more than a double standard: They face a linguistic double-whammy. Not only does sexist language create reduced expectations and opportunities for women, but women's own language often reinforces the role society expects them to play.*

"Women's language" is that pleasant (dainty?), euphe-   1
mistic, never-aggressive way of talking we learned as little girls. Cultural bias was built into the language we were allowed to speak, the subjects we were allowed to speak about, and the ways we were spoken of. Having learned our linguistic lesson well, we go out in the world, only to

discover that we are communicative cripples—damned if we do, and damned if we don't.

If we refuse to talk "like a lady," we are ridiculed and 2 criticized for being unfeminine. ("She thinks like a man" is, at best, a left-handed compliment.) If we do learn all the fuzzy-headed, unassertive language of our sex, we are ridiculed for being unable to think clearly, unable to take part in a serious discussion, and therefore unfit to hold a position of power.

It doesn't take much of this for a woman to begin 3 feeling she deserves such treatment because of inadequacies in her own intelligence and education.

"Women's language" shows up in all levels of English. 4 For example, women are encouraged and allowed to make far more precise discriminations in naming colors than men do. Words like *mauve, beige, ecru, aquamarine, lavender,* and so on, are unremarkable in a woman's active vocabulary, but largely absent from that of most men. I know of no evidence suggesting that women actually *see* a wider range of colors than men do. It is simply that fine discriminations of this sort are relevant to women's vocabularies, but not to men's; to men, who control most of the interesting affairs of the world, such distinctions are trivial—irrelevant.

In the area of syntax, we find similar gender-related 5 peculiarities of speech. There is one construction, in particular, that women use conversationally far more than men: the tag question. A tag is midway between an outright statement and a yes–no question; it is less assertive than the former, but more confident than the latter.

A *flat statement* indicates confidence in the speaker's 6 knowledge and is fairly certain to be believed; a *question* indicates a lack of knowledge on some point and implies that the gap in the speaker's knowledge can and will be remedied by an answer. For example, if, at a Little League game, I have had my glasses off, I can legitimately ask someone else: "Was the player out at third?" A *tag question,* being intermediate between statement and question, is used when the speaker is stating a claim, but lacks full confidence in the truth of that claim. So if I say, "Is Joan here?" I will probably not be surprised if my respondent answers "no"; but if I say, "Joan is here, isn't she?" instead, chances are I am already biased in favor of a positive answer, wanting only confirmation. I still want a response, but I have enough knowledge (or think I have) to predict that response. A tag question, then, might be thought of as a statement that doesn't demand to be believed by anyone but the speaker, a way of giving leeway, of not forcing the addressee to go along with the views of the speaker.

Another common use of the tag question is in small talk when the speaker is trying to elicit conversation: "Sure is hot here, isn't it?" 7

But in discussing personal feelings or opinions, only the speaker normally has any way of knowing the correct answer. Sentences such as "I have a headache, don't I?" are clearly ridiculous. But there are other examples where it is the speaker's opinions, rather than perceptions, for which corroboration is sought, as in "The situation in Southeast Asia is terrible, isn't it?" 8

While there are, of course, other possible interpretations of a sentence like this, one possibility is that the speaker has a particular answer in mind—"yes" or "no"— but is reluctant to state it baldly. This sort of tag question is much more apt to be used by women than by men in conversation. Why is this the case? 9

The tag question allows a speaker to avoid commitment, and thereby avoid conflict with the addressee. The problem is that, by so doing, speakers may also give the impression of not really being sure of themselves, or looking to the addressee for confirmation of their views. This uncertainty is reinforced in more subliminal ways, too. There is a peculiar sentence intonation-pattern, used almost exclusively by women, as far as I know, which changes a declarative answer into a question. The effect of using the rising inflection typical of a yes–no question is to imply that the speaker is seeking confirmation, even though the speaker is clearly the only one who has the 10 requisite information, which is why the question was put to her in the first place:

(Q) When will dinner be ready?
(A) Oh . . . around six o'clock . . . ?

It is as though the second speaker were saying, "Six o'clock—if that's okay with you, if you agree." The person being addressed is put in the position of having to provide confirmation. One likely consequence of this sort of speech-pattern in a woman is that, often unbeknownst to herself, the speaker builds a reputation of tentativeness, and others will refrain from taking her seriously or trusting her with any real responsibilities, since she "can't make up her mind," and "isn't sure of herself."

Such idiosyncrasies may explain why women's lan- 11 guage sounds much more "polite" than men's. It is polite to leave a decision open, not impose your mind, or views, or claims, on anyone else. So a tag question is a kind of polite statement, in that it does not force agreement or belief on the addressee. In the same way a request is a polite command, in that it does not force obedience on the addressee, but rather suggests something be done as a favor to the speaker. A clearly stated order implies a threat of certain consequences if it is not followed, and— even more impolite—implies that the speaker is in a superior position and able to enforce the order. By couching wishes in the form of a request, on the other hand, a speaker implies that if the request is not carried out, only the speaker will suffer; noncompliance cannot harm the addressee. So the decision is really left up to the addressee. The distinction becomes clear in these examples:

Close the door.

Please close the door.

Will you close the door?

Will you please close the door?

Won't you close the door?

In the same ways as words and speech patterns used 12
by women undermine her image, those used *to describe*
women make matters even worse. Often a word may be
used of both men and women (and perhaps of things as
well); but when it is applied to women, it assumes a special
meaning that, by implication rather than outright assertion, is derogatory to women as a group.

The use of euphemisms has this effect. A euphemism 13
is a substitute for a word that has acquired a bad connotation by association with something unpleasant or embarrassing. But almost as soon as the new word comes
into common usage, it takes on the same old bad connotations, since feelings about the things or people referred
to are not altered by a change of name; thus new euphemisms must be constantly found.

There is one euphemism for *woman* still very much 14
alive. The word, of course, is *lady*. *Lady* has a masculine
counterpart, namely *gentleman,* occasionally shortened to
gent. But for some reason *lady* is very much commoner
than *gent(leman)*.

The decision to use *lady* rather than *woman* or vice 15
versa, may considerably alter the sense of a sentence, as
the following examples show:

(a) A woman (lady) I know is a dean at Berkeley.
(b) A woman (lady) I know makes amazing things out of
shoelaces and old boxes.

The use of *lady* in (a) imparts frivolous, or nonserious, 16
tone to the sentence: the matter under discussion is not
one of great moment. Similarly, in (b), using *lady* here
would suggest that the speaker considered the "amazing
things" not to be serious art, but merely a hobby or an
aberration. If *woman* is used, she might be a serious
sculptor. To say *lady doctor* is very condescending, since
no one ever says *gentleman doctor* or even *man doctor*. For
example, mention in the San Francisco *Chronicle* of January
31, 1972, of Madalyn Murray O'Hair as the *lady atheist*
reduces her position to that of scatterbrained eccentric.

Even *woman atheist* is scarcely defensible: sex is irrelevant to her philosophical position.

Many women argue that, on the other hand, *lady* 17 carries with it overtones recalling the age of chivalry: conferring exalted stature on the person so referred to. This makes the term seem polite at first, but we must also remember that these implications are perilous: they suggest that a "lady" is helpless, and cannot do things by herself.

Lady can also be used to infer frivolousness, as in titles 18 of organizations. Those that have a serious purpose (not merely that of enabling "the ladies" to spend time with one another) cannot use the word *lady* in their titles, but less serious ones may. Compare the *Ladies' Auxiliary* of a men's group, or the *Thursday Evening Ladies' Browning and Garden Society* with *Ladies' Liberation* or *Ladies' Strike for Peace.*

What is curious about this split is that *lady* is in origin 19 a euphemism—a substitute that puts a better face on something people find uncomfortable—for *woman.* What kind of euphemism is it that subtly denigrates the people to whom it refers? Perhaps *lady* functions as a euphemism for *woman* because it does not contain the sexual implications present in *woman:* it is not "embarrassing" in that way. If this is so, we may expect that, in the future, *lady* will replace *woman* as the primary word for the human female, since *woman* will have become too blatantly sexual. That this distinction is already made in some contexts at least is shown in the following examples, where you can try replacing *woman* with *lady:*

(a) She's only twelve, but she's already a woman.
(b) After ten years in jail, Harry wanted to find a woman.
(c) She's my woman, see, so don't mess around with her.

Another common substitute for *woman* is *girl.* One 20 seldom hears a man past the age of adolescence referred to as a boy, save in expressions like "going out with the boys," which are meant to suggest an air of adolescent frivolity and irresponsibility. But women of all ages are "girls": one can have a man—not a boy—Friday, but only a girl—never a woman or even a lady—Friday; women have girlfriends, but men do not—in a nonsexual sense— have boyfriends. It may be that this use of *girl* is euphemistic in the same way the use of *lady* is: in stressing the idea of immaturity, it removes the sexual connotation lurking in *woman*. *Girl* brings to mind irresponsibility: you don't send a girl to do a woman's errand (or even, for that matter, a boy's errand). She is a person who is both too immature and too far from real life to be entrusted with responsibilities or with decisions of any serious or important nature.

Now let's take a pair of words which, in terms of the 21 possible relationships in an earlier society, were simple male–female equivalents, analogous to *bull* : *cow*. Suppose we find that, for independent reasons, society has changed in such a way that the original meanings now are irrelevant. Yet the words have not been discarded, but have acquired new meanings, metaphorically related to their original senses. But suppose these new metaphorical uses are no longer parallel to each other. By seeing where the parallelism breaks down, we discover something about the different roles played by men and women in this culture. One good example of such a divergence through time is found in the pair, *master* : *mistress*. Once used with reference to one's power over servants, these words have become unusable today in their original master-servant sense as the relationship has become less prevalent in our society. But the words are still common.

Unless used with reference to animals, *master* now 22 generally refers to a man who has acquired consummate ability in some field, normally nonsexual. But its feminine counterpart cannot be used this way. It is practically restricted to its sexual sense of "paramour." We start out with two terms, both roughly paraphrasable as "one who has power over another." But the masculine form, once one person is no longer able to have absolute power over another, becomes usable metaphorically in the sense of "having power over *something*." *Master* requires as its object only the name of some activity, something inanimate and abstract. But *mistress* requires a masculine noun in the possessive to precede it. One cannot say: "Rhonda is a mistress." One must be *someone's* mistress. A man is defined by what he does, a woman by her sexuality, that is, in terms of one particular aspect of her relationship to men. It is one thing to be an *old master* like Hans Holbein, and another to be an *old mistress*.

The same is true of the words *spinster* and *bachelor*— 23 gender words for "one who is not married." The resemblance ends with the definition. While *bachelor* is a neuter term, often used as a compliment, *spinster* normally is used pejoratively, with connotations of prissiness, fussiness, and so on. To be a bachelor implies that one has the choice of marrying or not, and this is what makes the idea of a bachelor existence attractive, in the popular literature. He has been pursued and has successfully eluded his pursuers. But a spinster is one who has not been pursued, or at least not seriously. She is old, unwanted goods. The metaphorical connotations of *bachelor* generally suggest sexual freedom; of *spinster,* puritanism or celibacy.

These examples could be multiplied. It is generally 24 considered a *faux pas*, in society, to congratulate a woman on her engagement, while it is correct to congratulate her fiancé. Why is this? The reason seems to be that it is impolite to remind people of things that may be uncomfortable to them. To congratulate a woman on her engagement is really to say, "Thank goodness! You had a close call!" For the man, on the other hand, there was no such danger. His choosing to marry is viewed as a good thing, but not something essential.

The linguistic double standard holds throughout the 25 life of the relationship. After marriage, bachelor and spinster become man and wife, not man and woman. The woman whose husband dies remains "John's widow"; John, however, is never "Mary's widower."

Finally, why is it that salesclerks and others are so 26 quick to call women customers "dear," "honey," and other terms of endearment they really have no business using? A male customer would never put up with it. But women, like children, are supposed to enjoy these endearments, rather than being offended by them.

In more ways than one, it's time to speak up.   27

QUESTIONS ON MEANING

1. What sentence in Lakoff's introductory paragraphs best expresses her thesis?
2. According to Lakoff, what specific words and speech patterns used *by* women and *about* women undermine their self-image?
3. How does Lakoff define the terms *tag question* and *euphemism*? How does she define each of the following pairs of terms: *master* versus *mistress* and *bachelor* versus *spinster*?

QUESTIONS ON PURPOSE AND STRATEGY

1. Is Lakoff's purpose to inform us about sexist language? To explain why certain phrases and words have a derogatory effect on women? To argue that we should avoid using language that unfairly assigns roles or attributes behavior to people on the basis of their sex? Where in the essay is each purpose most apparent?
2. Where in the essay does Lakoff develop her ideas through comparison and contrast? Where does she use examples to illustrate her points? Where does she analyze the causes or effects of language?
3. In her second sentence, Lakoff says, "Cultural bias was built into the language we were allowed to speak, the subjects we were allowed to speak about, and the ways we were spoken of." Is this sentence an essay map? Where does Lakoff develop each of these three points?

QUESTIONS ON AUDIENCE AND LANGUAGE

1. Lakoff's essay was originally published in *Ms.* magazine. Who was her audience? Could or should this essay have been published in *Esquire* or *Playboy*?

2. Describe Lakoff's tone, her attitude toward her subject. Is she calm, reasonable, and analytic? Is she defensive, angry, or emotional? Cite specific passages to support your answer.

QUESTIONS FOR DISCUSSION AND WRITING

1. What are other examples of sexist language? Can sexist language be derogatory to men as well as women?

2. In discussing tag questions, Lakoff says they help explain "why women's language sounds much more polite than men's. It is polite to leave a decision open, not impose your mind, or views, or claims, on anyone else." Is Lakoff advocating that women should be less polite? Why shouldn't men be more polite?

3. At a social gathering where both men and women are present, take notes or use a tape recorder to gather evidence about how people use language to characterize themselves, to stereotype other people (men, women, minorities, young people, old people, students). What conclusions can you draw from your evidence?

4. Describing specific scenes from your own life, explain how your parents, friends, and teachers have or have not created expectations about your behavior or your career based primarily on your gender.

The Yellow Stain

ANDREA SAIKI

(1970–   )

PREREADING JOURNAL ENTRY

Choose one of your bad habits: procrastination, smoking, eating too much, buying unnecessary clothes, lying to your friends, driving too fast, or staying up late. Write one paragraph explaining the bad *physical* effects of your habit and one paragraph explaining its negative *mental* effects.

Andrea Saiki, a student in Carol Forseth's composition class at Colorado State University, decided to write her explaining essay on the effects of smoking on her mental and physical health. "I smoked for four years, from the age of fifteen to the age of nineteen," she writes. "I know how it feels to be addicted to tobacco." Saiki directs her paper to a nonsmoking audience since "often nonsmokers are totally against smokers instead of being on their side and helping them quit." As she explains in her essay, she was able to stop smoking only after her psychological dependency combined with the physical effects—the lingering odor of stale cigarettes, the persistent cough and sore throat, and the yellow stains on her hands— forced her to take control of her life.

In 1979, the World Health Organization's theme was 1 "Smoking or Health: The Choice is Yours." Today it is "Smoking or Health: Choose Health." (qtd. in "The Choice" 27). In 1985, three years before this slogan was written, I made the choice to smoke. I can still hear the instructions my friend Kristin gave me after I had lit my first cigarette. "Suck in and let the smoke go to the lungs," she said. At the time I knew smoking, in the long run, was unhealthy. I had seen advertisements produced by the Heart Association against this deadly habit, and my grandpa had died of a smoking-related disease, lung cancer, that previous year. I didn't realize the injurious effects this first puff would have on my life. After two weeks of smoking, I began to observe serious negative psychological and psychological effects on my health.

Before describing the initial effects of smoking, I want 2 to compare two definitions of smoking. For the non-smoker, the dictionary definition applies: Smoking is the act of drawing in and exhaling tobacco ("Smoke" 1242). In contrast, a smoker's definition suggests why many people smoke and find it so hard to quit. The smoker's definition includes the crackling noise as he or she takes a deep breath from the cigarette and tastes the sweet tobacco on his or her lips. It includes the relaxing feeling of inhaling and slowly exhaling, feeling the cigarette's calming effects. It includes watching airy smoke rush out of the mouth, blending with the lighter smoke already in the air. Finally, the smoker's definition suggests feelings of comfort as he or she reaches for an ashtray to flick the soot-like ashes off the burning end of the cigarette.

Smokers have an enhanced definition of smoking 3 because tobacco causes psychological dependency. I noticed my dependency after just one week of having a cigarette at three o'clock every day after school. I bought a pack of Marlboro Reds and hid them behind a fence at King Soopers, a grocery store half a mile away from my home. I regulated my smoking by having the cigarettes far enough away so that I did not smoke every hour, but close enough so I could drive to have one every day. Two weeks after my first smoking experience, my mother decided not to let me use the car to get my daily cigarette because guests were arriving at three-thirty. Trying to hurt her, I said, "I cannot believe you would be so cruel to me." She looked at me strangely, but I thought nothing of it. The idea of going without a cigarette made me tense and frightened. I would have jumped off a bridge to have that cigarette in my hand and feel my tense muscles loosen as a result.

Another consequence of dependency on cigarettes is 4 that smokers lie to themselves and call their cigarettes their "friend." Heidi, an acquaintance of mine, tried to quit smoking a month ago. "After worrying for a week about my smoking, I dreamed that I died," she said. This scared her enough to try to quit. Every day for a week, I asked her how quitting smoking was coming along. Unfortunately, she broke down and had a cigarette one week after she started to quit smoking. "I had this huge test to study for, and George [her boyfriend] and I got into a big fight. I just had to have a cigarette." Heidi simply rationalized that because the cigarette gave her comfort in a time of stress, it was her "friend." The fear that this cigarette (friend) could cause an early death was nonexistent to Heidi in her time of stress.

In addition to the psychological effects, smoking causes 5 unpleasant signs of physical deterioration. First, a stale smell clings to the smoker's hair and clothes, remaining there until the next washing. My parents knew I smoked because of the foul scent that traveled with me. I was quick to deny the existence of the odor because my sense of smell was limited. When I went shopping to the bakery, people in line would stand aside because of the smell that clung to my hair and clothes. When I bought bread or pastry, I could no longer smell that fresh-baked aroma. My constant smoking made me feel as though I had a cold twenty-four hours a day. Then I noticed a sore, swollen throat, particularly during the mornings. Swallowing was like having a cactus take a journey down my throat. After six months of averaging ten cigarettes a day, my mother commented, "You've been snoring a lot in your sleep, like you have asthma." I knew I did not have asthma, but sometimes I felt as though I did. When I scrambled up bleachers at a basketball game, for example, pushing air in and out of my lungs became a chore. Furthermore, my first visit to the dentist since I started to smoke made me more aware of the yellow stain that was covering my teeth, my fingers, and my life. "You had better lay off that coffee, Andrea," the dentist said. "You are getting huge yellow stains on your teeth!" I knew I had never drunk coffee in my life.

Overall, smoking is a process that causes obvious 6 psychological and physical impairment. Last year on Valentine's day, I chose to quit smoking. Now, I have white teeth and stainless hands. I can run miles without having to stop. I can smell the red carnations my friend gave me. I don't have to wash cigarette smoke out of my hair and clothes. I don't have to scrub yellow stains off my teeth and fingers. I wake up in the morning and can actually taste and enjoy breakfast. I can swallow painlessly. I am no longer driven by my smoking habit, and I no longer lie to myself by calling a cigarette my friend.

Works Cited

"The Choice is Now: Health." *World Health* Jan.–Feb. 1988: 27.
"Smoke." *Webster's New World Dictionary*. 1983 ed.

QUESTIONS ON MEANING

1. What sentence best expresses Saiki's thesis?

2. List the major mental and physical effects of smoking that Saiki describes in her essay.

QUESTIONS ON PURPOSE AND STRATEGY

1. Is Saiki's major purpose to explain the effects of smoking or to persuade her readers to quit smoking? Support your answer by referring to specific sentences or paragraphs.

2. Why does Saiki give two definitions of smoking in paragraph two? What would the essay lose if she omitted these definitions?

QUESTIONS ON AUDIENCE AND LANGUAGE

1. Who is Saiki's intended audience? People who want more information about the negative effects of smoking? People who are still smoking? People who have quit smoking?

2. Where does Saiki use sensory details to describe the effects of smoking?

3. Where does Saiki use parallel sentence structure (sentences that follow a repeated pattern) to describe the effects of smoking? How do these sentences help reinforce her main point?

QUESTIONS FOR DISCUSSION AND WRITING

1. In her conclusion, Saiki describes how her life changed after quitting smoking. Is this relevant to her purpose, or should she conclude by reemphasizing the negative effects of smoking? What words or ideas does she repeat from early parts of the paper to create a sense of closure?

2. Saiki describes the effects of smoking on her life, but what were the probable causes that started her smoking in the first place? She suggests that her friend Kristin was one cause, but what were other probable causes?

3. Following the pattern of Saiki's essay, write about a person or event that has had negative mental and physical effects on your life.

Wine Tasting: How to Fool Some of the People All of the Time

MICHAEL J. JONES

(1965–   )

PREREADING JOURNAL ENTRY

Describe some esoteric activity such as preparing gourmet foods, selecting and serving vintage wines, or appreciating fine art, classical music, or jazz. What should a novice know about this activity? What should they learn to do—or not do?

Michael Jones, an international business major at Colorado State University, decided to write his essay on wine tasting. Rather than describe the process in sophisticated language for the wine aficionado, Jones adds some humor to his essay by creating a fictitious history about the origins of the ritual. As his teacher Emily Golson explains, when she read his paper aloud in class, everyone was smiling. When she asked how many people believed what Jones had written, almost every student raised his or her hand. Although Jones quickly admitted that he invented most of his history of wine tasting, his essay shows how to appreciate wine—without becoming too snobbish about the whole process.

Postscript on The Writing Process

1. How did you decide on this topic?

My topic was somewhat suggested to me by a friend. He suggested that I write about wine making. I refined that to wine tasting.

2. How did you actually write the paper?

I found myself writing this paper under self-imposed deadlines, such as having to have two pages done before dinner, or before classes started. I found this paper very entertaining to write. Although I did need to consult a few friends on the actual techniques of wine tasting, I wrote the paper with a hint of satire. The best place this can be seen is in the history paragraph. The entire history that I have recorded is fictitious and is not intended to parallel any person or event.

3. What did you like best about your paper?

The strength is the introduction to the wine-tasting ritual with an edge of humor applied. This lighthearted approach makes the ritual more accessible to the average reader, instead of just the wine aficionado. I try to use a tone of humor to let people realize that the techniques of wine tasting, though taken very seriously by some, should be a source of entertainment and exploration by the novice.

First Two Paragraphs of Rough Draft

It never fails, you've finally got a date with the person you've been watching all semester. They're coming over for dinner tonight; the lasagna is in the oven, the salad is in the refrigerator, and you're at the liquor store wondering what the difference is between the four different brands of Bardolino wine. They're all red, and have the same amount of wine in each bottle, but the difference in price is as much as eleven dollars. You could be frugal and buy the cheapest bottle, saving enough money for a cheap six-pack and a pizza later in the week, or you could go for broke and buy the most expensive, but with your luck, they won't like it, and you've wasted that extra money, or they won't be able to tell the difference, and again, you can kiss that pizza and beer good-bye. You've wasted ten minutes already, staring at labels printed in Italian (after all, you are having lasagna) and have five minutes to decide before you have to get back to clean the bathroom. You finally give up and choose one of the medium priced bottles, get home, and get everything ready. They show up, you uncork the bottle, and pour the first glass to taste it. You swirl and swish it as if rinsing with a fluoride wash, hopefully impressing this person beyond belief. Do you know what you're doing? Most likely not, but it's all a show, isn't it?

Before we get started, let's take a look at where winetasting got its start. In 1637, in the wine cellar of an influential nobleman's estate outside of Paris, the host and his two guests were inadvertently locked in by a faithful manservant. Jean-Pierre, the nobleman, resigned the three of them to the fact that they were there for the night. Francois and Michelle suggested that they become comfortable and partake of some of the fine wine available. While on their third bottle, and no longer worried about their present situation, or whether or not the world would revolve another inch, they noticed, in their giddy state, the color cast from the wine by the candles, and started comparing the colors with various shades of flowers, or as it became later in the night, the fleshtones of certain women known to them. They also began swishing and swirling the wine about their mouths, at first to remove the particles of beef and cabbage from between their teeth, but later to see who could make the most obnoxious or outrageous noises. One term, the "nose of the wine," was originally derived when Francois, when caught in a fit of laughter with a mouthful of wine, was able to expel wine through his nostril, and give in great detail the experience he got from it. Since then, the actual technique has changed in judging the wine's nose. Weeks later, while reuniting at an elite restaurant in Paris, Francois, Jean-Pierre, and Michelle joyfully engaged in a reenactment of their wining experiments from the estate's cellar. During their meal, they cooed over the color of the wine, again using descriptions from their collective imaginations. And while they swirled, sniffed, and gurgled, the nobles of Paris looked on in amazement at a ritual in which they had not yet been introduced. The aristocrats, being of the elitist mindset, soon adopted the sniff, swirl, and gurgle techniques, and elevated it to a level high above its farcical beginnings.

Final Draft

Wine Tasting: How to Fool
Some of the People
All of the Time

It never fails, you've finally got a date with that certain person you've been watching all semester. They're coming over for dinner tonight. The lasagna is in the oven, the salad is in the refrigerator, and you're at the liquor store wondering what the difference is between the four different brands of Bardolino wine. They're all red and have the same amount of wine in each, but the difference in price is as much as eleven dollars. You could be frugal and buy the cheapest bottle, saving enough money for a cheap six-pack and a pizza later in the week, or you could go for broke and buy the most expensive. But with your luck, they won't know the difference, and your pizza and beer fund is drained. You've wasted ten minutes already, staring at labels printed in Italian (after all, you are having lasagna) and have five minutes to decide before you have to get back to clean the bathroom. You finally give up and choose one of the medium-priced bottles, get home, and get everything ready. They show up, you open the bottle, and pour the first glass to taste it. You swirl and swish it as if rinsing with a fluoride wash, hopefully impressing this person beyond belief. Do you know what you are doing? Most likely not, but it's all a show, isn't it? Well, let's take a look at wine tasting and where it got its start to find out.

In 1637, in the wine cellar of an influential noble- 2 man's estate outside of Paris, the host and his two guests were inadvertently locked in by a faithful man-servant. Jean-Pierre, the nobleman, resigned his guests to the fact that they were there for the night. Francois and Michelle suggested that they become comfortable and partake in some of the fine wine available. While on their third bottle, and no longer worried about their present situation, they noticed, in their giddy state, the color cast from the wine by the candles. At this point, they started comparing the colors with various shades of flowers, or as it became later in the night, the fleshtones of certain women known to them. They also began swishing and swirling the wine about their mouths, at first to remove the particles of beef and cabbage from between their teeth, but later to see who could make the most obnoxious or outrageous noises. One term, the "nose of the wine," was originally derived when Francois, caught in a fit of laughter with a mouthful of wine, was able to expel through his nostrils a noseful of wine, and give in great detail the experience he got from it. Weeks later, while reuniting at an elite restaurant in Paris, Francois, Jean-Pierre, and Michelle joyfully engaged in a reenactment of their wining experiments from the estate's cellar. During their meal, they cooed over the color of the wine, again using descriptions from their collective imaginations. And while they swirled, sniffed, and gurgled, the nobility of Paris looked on in amazement at a ritual to which they had not yet been introduced. The aristocrats, being of the elitist mindset, soon adopted the sniff, swirl, and gurgle technique and elevated it to a level high above its farcical beginnings.

The aristocrats' education—and yours—begins 3 with the uncorking the wine. This involves, simply, removing the cork, but removing it in one piece. Don't try to screw the corkscrew in any spot of the cork and yank that sucker out of there. Instead, position the corkscrew in the middle of the cork, and gently pull the cork straight out of the bottle. If the cork is pulled at an angle, it could possibly break, making you look like an unexperienced clod.

Now that the bottle is open, your first urge may 4 be to sniff the cork. Try to suppress this urge, because I can tell you exactly what it smells like, cork. That's right, a cork smells like a cork, and a wet dog smells like a wet dog. If you must do something with the cork, "inspect" it to see if it is extremely dry, or if it is encrusted with a dried substance. In the case of the former, it is a sign of not having been stored on its side, very typical for lower end wines. And with the latter, it tells you that the cork was not tight, and some of the wine leaked out and dried, which is possible with any wine, and will not hurt it at all.

Before you start "tossing down" a few glasses of 5 wine, give some consideration to the wine itself. It has been cooped-up in the bottle for years, and finally has a chance for some fresh air. What you need to do next is let the wine "breathe," as this will soften, or take away the bitterness of the wine. The traditionalists say to let it stand in the bottle for some time, usually no longer than twenty minutes. Think about it, however.

Letting a whole bottle of wine try to aerate itself through a three-quarters of an inch hole is like breathing through your nose when it's stuffed up from a cold; it's not very efficient. Instead, pour the wine into glasses, half of a glass is usually enough, and let the wine breathe there. It is much more effective, and you can begin drinking it sooner, because there is less wine to breathe and more surface area in contact with the air.

The sniff, swirl, and gurgle technique is by far the 6 funnest part of the predrinking ritual, and it is at this point that you can recover from any minor *faux pas* that you may have made. The actual order is to swirl, then sniff, and lastly to gurgle the wine in your mouth. The swirling of the wine in the glass is to, again, aerate the wine, and also to observe the color of the wine. At this point you can become very creative in describing the wine's color, and use images of the sun setting over the rolling waves of the ocean. Possibly the color would remind you of the flushed cheeks of a young man or woman. However you describe it, use more than just "Yep, it's red all right." The sniffing of the wine is used to determine its "nose" or bouquet. The actual technique has changed since its conception back in 1637. Nowadays, all you need to do is inhale the vapors of the wine through your nose. With this you get the first impression of the wine, whether it will be hearty and strong, or light and sweet. During this, the rolling of the eyes is appropriate; however, too much eye play is theatrical and should be avoided. Again, be creative in describing its bouquet.

The final step in the triad is the gurgling, or 7 swishing of the wine in the mouth. The purpose of this step is to introduce the wine to your tastebuds, which are located on your tongue. So by swishing the wine around your mouth, you are actually moving the wine around your tongue. Remember this, because all too often people get carried away and act as if they are rinsing while at the dentist's office. Also, do not swallow too soon, for it is in the mouth that the wine will be tasted, and in the stomach where it will be felt, and it will reach the stomach soon enough. Enjoy the taste, and the aftertaste of the wine, because that is the reason you chose wine in the first place.

Now that the tasting ritual is completed, you and 8 your guests are ready to enjoy dinner with the marvelous wine that you have chosen. And the purpose of all this that you have gone through? To impress someone, of course. Because by the time you finish the bottle, you won't care what the wine's bouquet was like, or whether or not the color was tantalizing to the eyes. But you are now armed with the knowledge and technique that can charm the shorts off any ritual-fearing person. Even the Maitre d' will look down his nose at you with an air of approval.

QUESTIONS ON MEANING

1. In your own words, state the thesis of this essay. What sentence(s) in the essay best express this thesis?
2. What specific techniques for wine tasting does Jones explain?

QUESTIONS ON PURPOSE AND STRATEGY

1. Jones's purpose is to explain wine tasting and at the same time entertain the reader. Which paragraphs in the essay most successfully accomplish one or both of these purposes?
2. What primary shaping strategy does Jones use to organize his essay? What different processes does Jones explain? What terms related to wine tasting does Jones define?

QUESTIONS ON AUDIENCE AND LANGUAGE

1. In his postscript, Jones says that his "lighthearted approach makes the ritual more accessible to the average reader, instead of just the wine aficionado." Where is Jones most or least successful at addressing his audience?

2. Jones uses words such as "sucker," "funnest," "clod," and "Yep." In the context of this paper and each particular sentence, is this colloquial or conversational language appropriate or effective?

QUESTIONS FOR DISCUSSION AND WRITING

1. Reread paragraph twelve in Zinsser's essay in chapter 2. Assume that you are helping Jones edit clutter out of his sentences. The following sentences could be phrased more concisely (fewer words) without changing the meaning. Revise each sentence, and then decide whether you would recommend that Jones use your revisions.

   The aristocrats, being of the elitist mindset, soon adopted the sniff, swirl, and gurgle technique and elevated it to a level high above its farcical beginnings.

   In the case of the former, it is a sign of not having been stored on its side, very typical for lower end wines.

   Before you start "tossing down" a few glasses of wine, give some consideration to the wine itself.

2. Compare Jones's first two paragraphs of his rough draft with the final version. What major or minor changes did he make? Should he have made more changes?

3. Reread your Prereading Journal Entry. Rewrite one portion of that entry, using a humorous approach to your subject.

7

EVALUATING

There may be no more romantic flight of imagination in modern movies than the drive that Vicki and Batman take, by Batmobile, rocketing through a magical forest. Yet though we're watching a gothic variation of the lonely-superhero theme, we're never allowed to forget our hero's human limitations. He's a touchingly comic fellow. When he's all dressed up in his bat drag, he still thinks it necessary to identify himself by saying, in a confidential tone, "I'm Batman."

—Pauline Kael, "The City Gone Psycho"

What good was the Civil Rights Movement? If it had just given this country Dr. King, a leader of conscience, for once in our lifetime, it would have been enough. If it had just taken black eyes off white television stories, it would have been enough. If it had fed one starving child, it would have been enough.

—Alice Walker, author of *The Color Purple*

We are all critics. Whether we are praising a movie we saw last week or discussing the value of the Civil Rights Movement, dispensing criticism is a national pastime. When we exercise our right to free speech, most of the time we are evaluating a person, product, performance, or work of art.

When we write a formal evaluation, however, the stakes are a bit higher. If we're writing an evaluation of some historical event for a class, our grade may depend on the outcome. If we're evaluating the competition for our employer, our job may depend on careful research. If we're evaluating a political candidate, the future may hinge on our careful judgment. We should learn, therefore, what separates a statement of opinion that may make *us* feel good from an evaluation that will actually persuade *others*.

Formal written evaluations are not mere statements of opinion. First, evaluations contain a careful *description* of the product, performance, or event being evaluated. Readers need to know exactly what thing or event is being evaluated. Second, evaluations usually *consider both good and bad points*. They do not advertise or hype the subject. An evaluation sells the writer's critical judgment by acknowledging virtues and faults—and weighing them in the balance. Third, evaluations persuade a specific audience by using *criteria* (standards of judgment) that experts on the subject agree are important. If filmgoers agree that a good escape film should have an entertaining plot, stereotyped good and bad characters, and an exotic setting, then the writer has three criteria (ideal standards) by which to judge a specific film. Finally, evaluations give *specific evidence* to support the writer's judgments: citations of specific characters, dialogue, or scenes from *Batman;* or references to specific people and events related to the Civil Rights Movement.

As the essays in this chapter illustrate, evaluations vary widely in length, style, and format. Book critiques, television and film reviews, and evaluations of products have slightly different styles and formats that are designed to appeal to their different audiences. A consumer article may be written in simple, direct language, with separate headings for each criterion. A film review, on the other hand, may have a literary style with implied criteria. We determine style and format by knowing our audience and the magazine, newspaper, or book that might publish our evaluation. All evaluations establish criteria, balance strengths and weaknesses, and use supporting evidence, but each uses a particular style to appeal to the intended audience.

STRATEGIES FOR READING AND WRITING ABOUT EVALUATING

Because evaluative writing must both inform and persuade an audience, it uses techniques of observing and explaining. It demonstrates what the product, object, or performance is and then explains its virtues and faults. As you read the essays in this chapter, pay attention to the following techniques for writing evaluations.

Description of the person, product, performance, or work of art. Since most reviews and evaluations are intended for readers who are not familiar with a particular subject, writers usually provide background information: who, what, when, and where. A critique of a film, for example, gives the director and the principal actors, the context of the story and some of the plot, the filming location (perhaps), and may explain when and where the film is currently showing.

Statement of an overall claim about the subject. The claim about the overall value is the thesis of the critique or review. It considers the virtues and faults and renders an overall judgment. The overall claim may be that the film is worth seeing for the special effects, even though the plot is not believable.

Use of criteria for the evaluation. A criterion is a standard of judgment. It is the ideal case, against which the writer measures his or her particular subject.

Thus, for a film, "plot" is not a criterion, but "fast-moving and entertaining plot" is a possible criterion for an adventure film.

Separate judgment for each criterion. If a writer's criteria for judging a family restaurant are pleasant decor, quick service, nutritious food, and moderate prices, then the writer will make a separate judgment in each of these areas. (Remember: Criter*ia* is plural, referring to several standards; criter*ion* is singular, referring to one standard of judgment.)

Each judgment supported with evidence. Writers typically use their own careful observation and description of the subject for evidence, but they may also use the results of interviews and surveys, quotations from authorities, or data from experiments.

Criteria, style, and format adjusted to the particular audience. Writers anticipate which criteria are most acceptable for the subject and the audience, and they present their claims in an appropriate format and style.

READING AN EVALUATIVE ESSAY

As you read the essays in this chapter, use the following strategies for active, critical reading.

Prereading

Begin by writing down what you already know about the subject. The Prereading Journal Entry may suggest a topic. However, if you aren't familiar with that particular product, service, or performance, choose a similar subject and write some notes for an evaluation of it. It's important to record what *you* think before you are influenced by a particular critique or review. Then read the headnotes about the author and the topic for background and context: Understanding the writer's situation, his or her purpose and audience, and some biographical details will make your reading more effective.

First Reading

Read for information and enjoyment, as you would an article you picked up in a magazine. If some passage is confusing, place a "?" in the margin. If you disagree with a criterion or a judgment, place an "X" in the margin. If you especially enjoy some sentence or insight (or are surprised by the information or judgment), put a "!" in the margin. Highlight or put a wavy line under any key passages. Underline any words you want to look up later. *When you finish reading, write the overall claim that the writer makes.*

Annotated Reading

For your critical reading, write your own observations and reactions in the margin: "This is a full description. I can visualize it," "I disagree here," "This evidence is persuasive," or "Why doesn't this writer discuss . . . ?" Also read with a writer's eye, noting key features of writing evaluations. Place brackets around one passage containing *background description,* around the sentence stating the *overall claim,* and around *one criterion,* the writer's *judgment,* and the accompanying *evidence.* Identify each of these key features in the margin. In the margin, list the writer's criteria or outline the critique. As necessary, look up definitions of the words you've underlined.

Collaborative Reading

In your class or small group, share your Prereading Journal Entries. What did other class members think about this subject *before* they read this evaluation? Appoint a recorder to write down your ideas. Then read each other's marginal annotations and compile a jointly annotated version of the essay. Finally, when your group or class has completed a collaborative annotation, write one or two questions that you still have about this review or critique—

questions that you'd like to investigate in a further reading of this essay or that you'd like to discuss in class.

WRITING AN EVALUATING ESSAY

As you write your own evaluation of a product, service, performance, or person, remember the following important tips:

1. Choose a subject you are already relatively knowledgeable about. You don't have to be Bobby Unser to write about cars or Steven Spielberg to write about films, but you should have experience with the subject you are evaluating.

2. To become more expert, have your subject close at hand so you can *reobserve* it as you write. For films or television programs, use a videocassette to review key scenes. For books, essays, art objects, places, and commercial products, reread key passages, reobserve the object, or retest the product. Do not write an evaluation wholly from memory.

3. Review the key features of evaluative writing: You must *describe* the product, service, or performance so your audience knows what you are evaluating. You must state an *overall claim:* What is this subject's overall value? To support your overall claim, you establish *criteria* (standards of value), you make a *judgment* about each separate criterion (meets or doesn't meet the standard), and you give supporting *evidence* for your judgment. Finally, make your criteria and supporting evidence appropriate for your *audience.* Readers of *Film Quarterly*, for example, expect more sophisticated judgments and evidence than do the readers of a local newspaper.

4. Two important items about audience: First, be sure to check your criteria with your potential readers. Will they agree with your criteria for a restaurant, a book or essay, a commercial product, or a per-

formance? Your readers may forgive you if your judgment differs from theirs, but not if you have inappropriate or uninformed criteria for your judgments. Second, remember that you have a "double audience": Some readers will know your product, film, restaurant, book, or event, so they will be reading to compare their reactions with yours. Other readers will know about the subject, but they will *not* have seen this particular product or performance. Keep both of these readers in mind as you write.

Choosing a Subject for an Evaluating Essay

If your instructor has left the topic open, you might begin with some fairly obvious possibilities: a review of a restaurant, film, book, piece of art, product, dramatic performance, television program, and so forth.

Before you rush out to the local video store, however, consider your own interests. What hobbies or outside interests do you have? What are you already an "expert" on? What jobs have you held, and what could you evaluate about your job?

Finally, check through the class notes for your current classes: What are you studying in other classes you could evaluate? You might choose a work of literature, a piece of art, a piece of equipment in your lab, a particularly good teacher, or even the course itself.

Collecting Examples and Criteria

For evaluative essays, use the observing, remembering, and investigating skills already practiced in chapters 3, 4, and 5. Collect information by *observing* your subject several times, taking careful notes. List, brainstorm, or freewrite on your *memories* associated with this subject. Check in *written sources* (books, articles, and newspapers) for evaluations, reviews, and consumer articles. *Interview* any friends, teachers, and businesspeople who might have relevant information or opinions. If appropriate, conduct an informal *survey* to determine the opinions of other people about your subject.

As you collect information, note possible *criteria* for evaluating your subject. You must have information to support your judgments about each criterion. If you are writing about a film, for example, and effective acting is one criterion, make sure you write down the names of principal actors, the characters they play, and details and bits of dialogue from scenes where their acting is particularly effective.

Use a three-column log to help you collect information on your topic. For a film review, two criteria might be as follows:

Subject : <u>Batman</u>

Criteria	Judgment	Evidence
Effective Acting	Michael Keaton & Jack Nicholson are usually excellent at hero and villain	The specific scenes of confrontation show the tension and drama, although Nicholson is too much a cartoon figure whose gags continue after his death.
Dramatic cinematography	Director Tim Burton & cinematographer Roger Pratt dramatically recreate Gotham City at night	The flights through the dark alleys of the city, the absence sunshine and greenery, the dark costume and mask of Batman, and the final, eerie moonlight encounter reinforce the nighttime drama.

Shaping Your Evaluating Essay

After you have collected some criteria and evidence, review the essays in this chapter. If you are evaluating a book, film, television show, commercial product, or an artistic performance, do the essays in this chapter suggest ways to organize your essay? Then test the following shaping strategies against your notes: Which of the following strategies will best organize and present your ideas for your audience?

Analysis by Criteria. Evaluations of consumer products are often organized by category or criteria. The writer states the criteria that are important for buyers of this particular item, gives a judgment in each area, and then supports each judgment with evidence.

Roy Liu's essay, "Four is Enough," is organized by a thesis sentence which previews the four main criteria. Liu devotes one well-developed paragraph to each criterion.

Overall Claim or Thesis: For its size, the Quad 4 engine is the most fuel efficient, powerful, quickest accelerating and reliable engine that I have encountered.

Body paragraph 1/criterion 1: fuel efficiency
   judgment: fuel efficiency excellent
   evidence: highest fuel efficiency of
             cars in its class, according to
             Car and Driver and writer's own experience

Body paragraph 2/criterion 2: high horsepower
   judgment: remarkable horsepower for its weight
   evidence: horsepower tests at 150 horsepower,
             compared to 98–105 for comparable engines;
             writer's personal experience

Body paragraph 3/criterion 3: quick acceleration
   judgment: great acceleration
   evidence: Time trials by *Car and Driver* and writer's
             personal experience

Body paragraph 4/criterion 4: high reliability
    judgment: requires minimal repairs
    evidence: engine has fewer parts to break; engine is
                virtually maintenance-free; writer's
                experience over two years

Comparison/Contrast. Frequently, writers of evaluations compare two products, performances, or works of art. Comparisons (and contrasts) can add evidence and support to the writer's judgments, but they can also help shape or organize the whole essay. In her review of *Batman*, Pauline Kael uses comparisons primarily to add additional evidence. Kael compares the film to the following: *The Mark of Zorro;* the 1930 mystery comedy, *The Bat Whispers;* Batman novels such as Frank Miller's *The Dark Night Returns* and Alan Moore's *The Killing Joke;* the 1927 film, *The Man Who Laughs; Blade Runner, Brazil,* Fritz Lang's *Metropolis,* and *Wings of Desire;* and the original Batman comic books.

In "Man, Bytes, Dog," however, James Gorman organizes his whole essay around his comparison of a Cairn terrier to a Macintosh computer. He begins with the basic comparison:

Macintosh:
Weight (without printer): 20 lbs.
Memory (RAM): 128 K
Price (with printer): $3,090

Cairn Terrier:
Weight (without printer): 14 lbs.
Memory (RAM): some
Price (without printer): $250

Gorman then combines comparison/contrast with criteria analysis: For most of his criteria, Gorman describes the features of both the Macintosh and the Cairn terrier:

Reliability: In five to ten years, I am sure, the Macintosh will be superseded by a new model, like the Delicious or the Granny Smith. The Cairn Terrier, on the other hand, has held its share of the market with only minor modifications for hundreds of years. In the short term, Cairns seldom need servicing, apart from shots and the odd worming, and most function without interruption during electrical storms.

Classification. Occasionally, a subject for evaluation contains several different types. An evaluation of the writing implements sold by most bookstores, for example, might classify (and then evaluate) each type: *mechanical pencils,* with their high-tech combination of metals and plastics and automatic lead-feed systems; *plastic ball-pen "pencils,"* with those rock-hard erasers that never erase anything; and the *multicolored ball pens,* with the outside plastic color matching the ink, in shades from yellow or aqua to lavender and burnt orange.

In "A Head Full of Bees," Merrill Markoe uses a system of classification to shape her evaluation of weekend daytime television. She classifies the television shows according to type and then devotes a few paragraphs to each kind of show:

PBS Shows

Shopping Shows

Fishin' Shows

Horror Shows

Shows with Names That Don't Sound Like Real Shows

Chronological Order. Writers of reviews of books, films, and performances often follow the chronological order of the plot or main events, giving their judgments (and supporting evidence) as they describe the main events. In "A Not So Special Effect," Richard Prieto weaves in his description, judgments, and evidence in a roughly chronological order. Opening sentences of each of the body paragraphs show how he reviews the plot of the film, working in his evaluation of the actors' performances, the story line, and special effects.

Overall claim: David Weinman, the director, concentrates

so much on the special effects that he forgets the plot and the acting.

Body paragraph 1: "In the beginning of the movie, Rollie Tyler (Bryan Brown) introduces himself as a master of his craft. . . ."

Body paragraph 2: "The story line seems simple enough, but the addition of Leo McCarthy (Brian Dennehy), a New York detective, confuses it."

Body paragraph 3: "Not knowing how deeply everyone is involved creates another problem."

Body paragraph 4: "Rollie's character is the heart of the problem with the acting."

Conclusion: " 'F/X: Murder by Illusion' has more glitter than gold. The chase scenes and murders are cleverly done, but this movie emphasizes special effects and does not satisfy a thinking audience."

Drafting your Evaluating Essay

You may simply start writing and see if a shape develops that will work for your particular subject and audience. Or you may prefer to outline your essay—using an appropriate shaping strategy—to see if all your evidence will fit before you start writing.

In either case, gather all your materials together. Reread your collecting and shaping notes. If you have an idea for a catchy title or lead-in, start there. Otherwise, start with the body of your paper and save your introduction for later. When you get stuck, reread what you have written so far or check your notes again, and keep writing.

Revising your Evaluating Essay

Use the following guidelines as you give feedback to your peers and revise your own drafts. Revising is more than fixing spelling or changing the wording of a sentence or two. Revision often requires substantial changes in the overall claim, organization, amount of evidence, or appeal to the audience.

Review the title and lead-in. Is the title just a label ("Road Test of the Mazda Miata") or does it describe creatively ("Man, Bytes, Dog")? Which strategy would be best for the intended audience? Do the opening sentences or lead-in get the reader's attention?

Check the overall claim or thesis. It should state an overall claim that *relates* to both the strengths and weaknesses discussed in the body of the essay.

Clarify the criteria for the audience. Remember that criteria are standards of value or the ideal against which the writer measures the particular case. Categories (shopping shows, fishing shows, horror shows) are not necessarily criteria. Criteria should be ideal attributes: effective acting, exciting story line, or realistic settings.

Reexamine the appropriateness of the criteria for the audience. Often evaluations do not use criteria appropriate for the subject and audience. Readers of *Time* magazine may check film reviews merely to see if a movie is entertaining and worth the price of admission; readers of *Film Quarterly* are much more interested in the craft and technical expertise of the director.

Check each criterion for judgment and supporting evidence. For each major criterion, the writer should make a judgment (good or bad, effective or ineffective) and have specific details, description, testimony, test data, or other information to support the judgment.

Review data and direct quotations for accuracy. Data, testimonies, or quotations from printed sources, interviews, or surveys must be *quoted accurately* and the sources must be referred to or cited in the essay.

Review transitions at the beginning of body paragraphs. At the beginning of body paragraphs, use key words and transitional phrases to *signal* the major divisions in the evaluation.

Revise and edit sentences to improve clarity and avoid errors. Use your peer readers' reactions and check your handbook to clarify sentences and correct errors in spelling, punctuation, or inappropriate usage.

Postscript For Your Evaluating Essay

When you have finished your essay, answer the following questions. Be sure to hand in this response with your essay.

1. What *sources* of information provided most of your evidence: remembering experiences, observing the subject directly, and/or reading about the subject or interviewing other people?

2. What was your original opinion of your subject? How did that evaluation change as you wrote your essay? Cite one specific judgment that you *changed* or *discovered* as you wrote the essay.

3. Which of the *shaping strategies* described in this chapter were most helpful as you wrote this essay?

4. Where in the essay did you adapt your criteria, judgments, or evidence for your *audience?* Where did you write in a style appropriate for your audience?

5. What do you like best about the essay? What problems did you have as you wrote? What would you work on if you had more time?

The Roadster Returns

PREREADING JOURNAL TOPIC

Assume that you have decided to buy a new sports car, a convertible. Beginning with price, what five criteria would you look for in this automobile? List them in order of importance to you, and describe specifically what characteristics you look for in each criterion.

STUDENT JOURNAL RESPONSES

First I'd look for a car with a price that represents its attributes, not just the name plate. I don't want to spend an extra ten thousand just to get a Porsche. Next would be the engine: I'd want a fuel injected V-8, a five speed, close-ratio transmission, and a proven rear/front end system to handle the horsepower. Sporty handling options are essential. I want sway bars, rack-and-pinion steering, anti-lock braking, and low-profile tires. Basically, I want to be able to drive like crazy and scare the heck out of myself. A plush interior would be the next criterion. I want leather seats, CD player, sound insulated interior so I can hear a pin drop at top speed. Finally, if I'm going to put down that much money, I want my first choice of color: bright yellow with a tan leather interior.

Wow! Look at that! I just inherited a cool $75,000. First thing I'm going to do is check out all the great sports cars under $70,000. I definitely want a gold car with lightning bolts painted on the roof. The sound system has to crank — I mean, if you can't hear me coming with the Violent Femmes cranked a mile away, it's not doing the job. After the price and the sound system, I want a car that zips to 130 m.p.h. in about 6.5 seconds. Inside, I want the leather with gold trim to show off the beads and fuzzy animals I hang on the rear view mirror. Last, I guess I'll go for those new flourescent green windshield wipers. Maybe I'll take the leftover five grand and drive down to Mexico.

Consumer Reports *magazine reviews consumer products ranging from cameras, kitchen knives, and contact lenses to hair mousse, sewing machines, and automobiles. They maintain their integrity by accepting no advertising in their monthly issues. Every spring, they devote an issue to informing consumers about new and used car models, frequency of repair records, and car-buying strategies. The magazine annually tests some three dozen new cars to distinguish between "sound engineering and advertising puffery."*

"The Roadster Returns," Consumer Reports' *review of a popular sport convertible, the* Mazda Miata, *appeared in the 1990 annual auto issue. The test drivers found that the car handled well but, like most sports cars, lacked space and creature comforts. As you read the article, notice how* CR's *editors organize their criteria, judgments, and evidence into four key categories.*

THE ROADSTER RETURNS

← *Who is the author of this article?*[1]

Clever lead-in

We don't often test convertibles or cars with only two seats. We figure buyers don't need testers to remind them that two seats can't hold two couples. Or that in most places most of the time it's too hot, too cold, too wet, or too smelly to put a convertible's top down. Or to pass judgments on whether a car is more cute, less cute, or cute as a bug.

(Puts down buyers who want a "cute car"

But we could hardly ignore the *Mazda MX-5 Miata.* Buyers have lined up, money in their teeth, to pay anywhere from $15,000 to $18,000 for *Miatas* that list for only $13,800. The enthusiast press has enthused. So who knows? Perhaps there was more to the *Miata* than nostalgia for the *Triumphs, Austin-Healeys, MGs,* and *Karmann-Ghias* of yesteryear. Perhaps Mazda had finally figured out how to make a little convertible two-seater that wasn't cramped, rough-riding, and noisy.

2

What does this mean?

[No such luck. The *Mazda* is very cramped. There's so little room for the driver's left foot that you must wedge it under the clutch pedal, making the first downshift awkward. The car is very rough riding. It bounces you up and down on smooth roads and rattles your teeth on rough ones. And it's very noisy. The roar of the engine and exhaust drowns conversation and compresses music to mere rhythm.

3

Overall claim

Still, Mazda has engineered out some of the worst failings of vintage sports cars. The top fits well and is easy to take down and put up. There are few rattles. After some 6000 miles of driving, we've lost any fear that something is about to go wrong. And Mazda has kept what's best in sports cars—responsive acceleration and fast, precise steering and handling.]

But don't sports car drivers want noise and road feel?

4

ENGINE AND DRIVETRAIN

The small, multivalve Four started and ran very well. The five-speed transmission shifted crisply. The punchy movement of the stubby shifter enhances the car's sporty feel.

5

Judgement

The *Miata*'s sporty acceleration didn't compromise fuel economy (expect about 30 mpg overall).

6

[HANDLING AND BRAKING]

← *Category*

[In normal driving, the rear-wheel-drive *Miata*'s quick, precise handling was a pleasure. The car

7

Criterion: Sports cars should handle quickly and precisely.

was responsive and predictable in our accident-avoidance tests and hard turns at our test track. When our drivers became too enthusiastic, the car's rear end moved out, but the *Miata* then responded instantly to steering corrections. The optional power steering (which most buyers will probably choose) didn't detract from road feel. Braking was faultless.]

8

COMFORT AND CONVENIENCE

The *Miata* has a [stiff, jerky, sports-car ride,] making long expressway trips [unpleasant.] On back roads, the car shared every [bump] in the road with its occupants.

Judgement: 9
stiff, jerky, bumpy.

Noise was as pronounced with the top up as it was with the top down. But the source was different. Obviously, wind was at fault when the top was down. [The exhaust was a tedious drone when the top was up. Road roar was ever present. (Measurements at 60 mph revealed the *Miata* to be 60 percent noisier inside than the *Ford Taurus*, 50 percent noisier than the *Geo Prism*.)]

10

Evidence:
" tedious drone"

The *Miata* is built for small to medium-sized adults. Tall occupants felt cramped with the top down, claustrophobic with it up. The bucket seats are sportingly low, firm, and enveloping. The seatbacks recline. But to accommodate a tall person's legs, the seat must be moved all the way back. Then the seat butts up against the bulkhead, limiting the reclining feature and, with it, support for the lower back. Drivers may feel too close to the steering wheel. Foot space around the operating pedals is so confined that you can hardly avoid catching your shoe on the underside of the clutch pedal.

11

X *Too bad.*
At 6'4",
I'd never
make it.

x *Dangerous!*

The *Miata* has a [capable climate-control system,] with Bilevel and Mix settings that provide useful air distribution. Heat was [generously supplied.] Defrosting was [effective.] Defogging was [mediocre] unless the air-conditioner was on.

12

Judgement:
good and
bad points

The plastic rear window has no defroster. It stayed cloudy for some time on damp days.

Most operating controls are easy to reach and convenient to operate. The ignition switch, however, is hard to see and awkward to get at. The trunk is tiny. Since there's little space behind the seats, a couple would be hard-put to take the *Miata* on a vacation trip. Inside the trunk, sharp edges on the exposed jack handle could scar luggage.

13

Sports car people don't carry luggage!

The battery is in the trunk. The close quarters make the engine-oil dipstick and filter hard to get at.

Right. 14
Like my VW Bug. 15

Mazda provides a bumper-to-bumper warranty for three years or 36,000 miles. Rust perforation coverage is for five years with no mileage limitation.

SAFETY AND RELIABILITY

Convertibles disappeared in the mid-1970s, deemed unsafe because they lacked rollover protection. With the exception of the $80,000 *Mercedes-Benz 300/500 SL,* the new generation of convertibles lacks rollbars too. Cars as low-slung as the *Miata* resist rollovers, of course. Indeed, the *Miata* hardly leaned at all in the hardest turns. But accidents are called accidents because they're unpredictable.

16

Huh? Didn't this magazine jump all over the Suzuki Samurai because it rolled over? 17

Both seats have conventional lap-and-shoulder belts. The driver has the added protection of an air bag. The belts were comfortable for most riders, a bit constraining for tall occupants. A locking clip is required to secure a child safety seat.

With the top up, all drivers had trouble seeing to the rear. The convertible top caused blind spots, and the plastic rear window caused distortion. Tall drivers found that the inside rear-view mirror and the windshield header interfered with their forward view.

18
? Is the top manual or electric?

Government crash tests indicate a potential

? In a rollover, 19 *too?*

for head injury to the driver. The passenger was well protected.

The curved plastic front and rear ends of the *Miata* look entirely bumperless, but there's strong stuff under the skin. Our series to tests with our bumper basher caused no visible damage.

20

Since the Miata made its debut only last summer, we have no reliability data. Other Mazdas have been quite good. We found only eight sample defects, all of them minor.

21

Why doesn't the writer have an overall conclusion here?

MAZDA MX-5 MIATA

[***Tested car.*** Two-door convertible, $13,800 list. Standard equipment includes 1.6 liter, 16-valve Four, five-speed manual transmission, power 4-wheel disc brakes, tinted glass, driver-side air bag, interval wipers, and performance tires. Major options in our car: air-conditioning, limited-slip differential, and Option Package A (alloy wheels, leather-wrapped steering wheel, power steering, and stereo cassette system). List price, as equipped, $16,294, including destination and port processing charge.]

22

Description of vehicle. (Shouldn't this come first?)

RATINGS

Interesting, because the Miata doesn't __have__ front bumpers

○ Better ← → Worse ●

Start/running	○	Front seating	○
Acceleration	○	Heating	○
Transmission	○	Ventilation	◐
Economy	◐	Air-conditioning	○
Routine handling	○	Controls	◐
Emergency handling	○	Displays	○
Braking	○	Trunk	○
Ride	●	Servicing	●
Noise	●	Bumpers	○
Driving position	○	Reliability	No data

Overall claim: Despite the Miata's rough ride, noise, and cramped interior, it is a quick and responsive sports car.

QUESTIONS ON MEANING

1. What is the writer's overall judgment of the *Mazda Miata?*
2. In each of the four main categories, what are the *Miata's* strengths and weaknesses?

QUESTIONS ON PURPOSE AND STRATEGY

1. What sentences in this article illustrate that the writer's purpose is to distinguish between "sound engineering and advertising puffery"?
2. Sometimes the writer uses human judgments as evidence ("The exhaust was a tedious drone when the top was up") and sometimes machine-measured data ("Measurements at 60 mph revealed the *Miata* to be 60 percent noisier inside than the *Ford Taurus*"). Where could or should the writer use more mechanical data or statistics as evidence?

QUESTIONS ON AUDIENCE AND LANGUAGE

1. Locate a copy of *Consumer Reports.* Scan through several articles. How is the writing different from another popular magazine you are familiar with—*Time* magazine, *Rolling Stone,* or *National Geographic?* Based on your comparison, describe characteristic features (subject matter, length, format, sentence style) of *Consumer Reports* articles.
2. Sentences in this article are often short, staccato bits of information. In what paragraphs is this style most apparent? Is this style appropriate for the intended audience?

QUESTIONS FOR DISCUSSION AND WRITING

1. Explain the difference between a category (such as "Engine and Drivetrain") and a criterion. Where does the writer refer to categories? Where does the writer state or imply the criterion for each of these categories?

2. Find one other review of the *Mazda Miata* in automobile magazines such as *Car and Driver* or *Road and Track.* Compare the two evaluations. Do the two writers use the same criteria? If not, what are the differences? Do the writers make the same judgments? If not, how is their evidence or data different?

3. Like the test car, the article's style handles crisply with its bold headings for each major criterion, but its sentences are abrupt and lack syntactic comfort. Choose one paragraph with four or more sentences. Rewrite the sentences to make them flow more smoothly. As necessary, combine sentences and add transitions to improve coherence.

4. Based on your reading of this article, revise the criteria from your Prewriting Journal Entry. Go to a local car dealer and test drive a new car. During your test drive, collect data to support your judgments about each criterion. Write your response in a format appropriate for *Consumer Reports.*

The City Gone Psycho

PAULINE KAEL

(1919–   )

PREREADING JOURNAL ENTRY

As a child, what was your favorite adventure film? Did you see it first in a theater or on video? Describe your initial reactions and responses. Have you seen this film more recently? What was your reaction on seeing it a second (or third) time?

Pauline Kael was born in California, majored in philosophy at the University of California at Berkeley, and wrote film scripts and essays before trying her hand at movie reviews. She has published essays in magazines such as Vogue, Film Quarterly, Harper's, *and* The New Republic. *Since 1968, she has reviewed films for* The New Yorker *and has published collections of her essays and reviews in* Kiss Kiss Bang Bang *(1968),* Reeling *(1976), and* When the Lights Go Down *(1980).*

As you read "The City Gone Psycho," consider Kael's own description of her movie reviews: "I try to use my initial responses (which I think are probably my deepest and most honest ones) to explore not only what a movie means to me, but what it may mean to others: to get at the many ways in which movies, by affecting us on sensual and primitive levels, are a supremely pleasurable—and dangerous—art form."

In "Batman," the movement of the camera gives us 1 the sensation of swerving (by radar) through the sinister nighttime canyons of Gotham City. We move swiftly among the forbidding, thickly clustered skyscrapers and dart around the girders and pillars of their cavelike underpinnings. This is the brutal city where crime festers—a city of alleys, not avenues. In one of these alleys, Bruce Wayne as a child watched, helpless, as his parents were mugged and senselessly shot down. Now a grown man and fabulously wealthy, Bruce (Michael Keaton) patrols the city from the rooftops. He has developed his physical strength to the utmost, and, disguised in body armor, a cowl, and a wide-winged cape, and with the aid of a high-tech arsenal, he scales buildings and swoops down on thugs and mobsters—Batman.

There's a primitive visual fascination in the idea of a 2 princeling obsessed with vengeance who turns himself into a creature of the night, and the director, Tim Burton, has given the movie a look, a tone, an eerie intensity. Burton, who's thirty, has a macabre sensibility, with a cheerfulness that's infectious; his three films ("Pee-wee's Big Adventure" and "Beetlejuice" are the other two) get you laughing at your own fear of death.

Seen straight on, the armored Batman is as stiff and 3 strong-jawed as a Wagnerian hero. His cowl-mask has straight-up sides that end in erect ears; he gives the impression of standing at attention all the time. (He's on guard duty.) But something else is going on, too. The eye slits reveal only the lower part of his eyes—you perceive strange, hooded flickers of anger. When Batman is in motion, what you see can recall the movies, such as "The Mark of Zorro" and the 1930 mystery comedy "The Bat Whispers," that the eighteen-year-old cartoonist Bob Kane had in mind when he concocted the comic-book hero, in 1939. Though the Tim Burton film is based on Kane's characters, it gets some of its funky, nihilistic charge from more recent "graphic novels" about Batman, like Frank Miller's 1986 "The Dark Knight Returns" and Alan Moore's 1988 "The Killing Joke." This powerfully glamorous new "Batman," with sets angled and lighted like film noir, goes beyond pulp; it gallops into the cocky unknown.

In the movie's absurdist vision, Batman's antagonist is 4 the sniggering mobster Jack Napier (Jack Nicholson), who turns into the leering madman the Joker. Clearly, Batman and the Joker are intended to represent good and evil counterparts, or, at least, twin freaks, locked together in combat; it was Jack Napier who made an orphan of Bruce Wayne, and it was Batman who dropped Jack into the vat of toxic chemicals that disfigured him. That's the basic plan. But last year's writers' strike started just as the movie was set to go into production, and the promising script, by Sam Hamm (it reads beautifully), never got its final shaping; the touching up that Warren Skaaren (and uncredited others) gave it didn't develop the characters or provide the turning points that were needed. With the young hipster Keaton and the aging hipster Nicholson cast opposite each other, we expect an unholy taunting camaraderie—or certainly some recognition on Batman's part that he and the Joker have a similarity. And we do get a tease now and then: when the two meet, their actions have the formality of Kabuki theatre. But the underwritten movie slides right over the central conflict: good and evil hardly know each other.

At times, it's as if pages of the script had drifted away. 5 The mob kingpin (Jack Palance, in a hearty, ripe performance) is toppled by Jack Napier, who moves to take control of the city, but we're not tipped to what new corruption he has in mind. We wait for the moment when the photojournalist Vicki Vale (Kim Basinger), who's in love with Bruce Wayne and is drawn to Batman, will learn they're the same person. She's just about to when the scene (it's in her apartment) is interrupted by the Joker, who barges in with his henchmen—we expect him to carry her away. The revelation of Batman's identity is suspended (we never get to see it), and the Joker trots off without his prize. After this double nonwhammy, a little air seems to leak out of the movie. And it's full of these missed moments; the director just lets them go. Vicki and Bruce, dining together, are seated at opposite ends of an immense banquet table in a baronial hall in Wayne Manor; two thousand years of show business have prepared us for a zinging payoff—we feel almost deprived when we don't get it. Yet these underplayed scenes have a pleasing suggestiveness. The dinner scene, for example, shows us that Bruce is flexible, despite his attraction to armor. (He collects it.) And Vicki quickly realizes that the Bruce Wayne-Batman identity is less important than the question Is he married only to his Batman compulsion or is he willing to share his life with her?

When Nicholson's Joker appears for the first time, the 6 movie lights up like a pinball machine: the devil has arrived. (Nicholson is playing the role Keaton played in "Beetlejuice.") The Joker is marvellously dandified—a fashion plate. The great bohemian chapeaus and the playing-card zoot suits, in purple, green, orange, and aqua, that Bob Ringwood has designed for him have a harlequin chic. They're very like the outfits the illustrator Brian Boland gave the character in "The Killing Joke," and Nicholson struts in them like a homicidal minstrel, dancing to hurdy-gurdy songs by Prince—the Joker's theme music. But the grin carved into the Joker's face doesn't have the horror of the one on Conrad Veidt's face in the 1927 "The Man Who Laughs" (where Bob Kane acknowledges he took it from). Veidt played a man who never forgot his mutilation. Nicholson's Jack Napier is too garish to suffer from having been turned into a clown; the mutilation doesn't cripple him, it fulfills him. And so his wanting to get back at Batman is just crazy spite.

The master flake Tim Burton understands what there 7 is about Batman that captures the moviegoer's imagination. The picture doesn't give us any help on the question of why Bruce Wayne, in creating an alternate identity, picked a pointy-eared, satanic-looking varmint. (Was it simply to gain a sense of menace and to intimidate his prey?) But Burton uses the fluttering Batman enigmatically, playfully. He provides potent, elusive images that draw us in (and our minds do the rest). There may be no more romantic flight of imagination in modern movies than the drive that Vicki and Batman take, by Batmobile, rocketing through a magical forest. Yet though we're watching a gothic variation of the lonely-superhero theme, we're never allowed to forget our hero's human limitations. He's a touchingly comic fellow. When he's all dressed up in his bat drag, he still thinks it necessary to identify himself by saying, in a confidential tone, "I'm Batman."

The movie's darkness is essential to its hold on us. 8 The whole conception of Batman and Gotham City is a nighttime vision—a childlike fantasy of the big city that the muggers took over. The caped crusader who can find his way around in the miasmal dark is the only one who can root out the hoods. The good boy Batman has his shiny-toy weapons (the spiked gauntlets, the utility belt equipped with projectile launcher, even the magnificent Batwing fighter plane), but he's alone. The bad boys travel in packs: the Joker and his troupe of sociopaths break into the Flugelheim Museum, merrily slashing and defiling the paintings—the Joker sees himself as an artist of destruction.

Batman and the Joker are fighting for the soul of the 9 city that spawned them. We see what shape things are in right from the opening scenes. Gotham City, with its jumble of buildings shooting miles and miles up into the dirty skies, is the product of uncontrolled greed. Without sunshine or greenery, the buildings look like derelicts. This is New York City deliberately taken just one step beyond the present; it's the city as you imagine it when you're really down on it. It's Manhattan gone psycho. But even when you're down on it you can get into your punk fantasies about how swollen it is, how blighted and yet horribly alive.

The designer, Anton Furst, seems to have got into 10 that kind of jangled delight, putting together domes and spires, elongated tenements, a drab city hall with statues bowed down in despair, and streets and factories with the coal-mine glow of the castles and battlements in "Chimes at Midnight." Gotham City has something of the sculptural fascination of the retro-future cities in "Blade Runner" and "Brazil"—it's like Fritz Lang's "Metropolis" corroded and cankered. If H.G. Wells' Time Machine took you there, you'd want to escape back to the present. Still, you revel in this scary Fascistic playground: the camera crawls voluptuously over the concrete and the sewers, and the city excites you—it has belly-laugh wit.

When Gotham City celebrates its two-hundredth birth- 11 day, the big parade balloons are filled with poison gas— an inspiration of the Joker's. (He rides on a float, jiggling to the music; his painted red grin has wing tips.) Paranoia and comic-book cheesiness don't defeat Tim Burton; he feels the kick in them—he likes their style. The cinematographer, Roger Pratt, brings theatrical artifice to just about every shot—a high gorgeousness, with purples and blacks that are like our dream of a terrific rock concert. The movie even has giant spotlights (and the Batsignal from the original comic books). This spectacle about an avenging angel trying to protect a city that's already an apocalyptic mess is an American variant of "Wings of Desire." It has a poetic quality, but it moves pop fast. The masked man in the swirling, windblown cape has become the hero of a comic opera that's mean and anarchic and blissful. It has so many unpredictable spins that what's missing doesn't seem to matter much. The images sing.

QUESTIONS ON MEANING

1. From Kael's article, identify the leading characters in *Batman,* the actors who play those roles, the director of the film, the costume and set designers, and the original author of the *Batman* comic book.

2. List key events in the plot of *Batman* that Kael reveals in her review.

QUESTIONS ON PURPOSE AND STRATEGY

1. Find one paragraph whose purpose is to provide basic information and description of the film. Find one paragraph whose purpose is to judge or evaluate some element of the film. Does Kael's review contain more description than evaluation? Explain.

2. In her review, Kael mixes shaping strategies. Where does her order seem most chronological, following the sequence of events in the film? Where does she compare or contrast *Batman* to other films? Where does she analyze the film into various parts: characters, plot, set design, cinematography, and costumes?

QUESTIONS ON AUDIENCE AND LANGUAGE

1. Describe Kael's intended audience for her review. Is she writing for teenagers who have just seen the film? For the average moviegoer? For the film historian? Explain your choice, referring to *specific sentences* from Kael's review.

2. As is appropriate for a *New Yorker* review, Kael occasionally uses sophisticated language ("miasmal dark") and complicated sentences ("He has developed his physical strength to the utmost, and, disguised in body armor, a cowl, and a wide-winged cape, and with the aid of a high-tech arsenal, he scales buildings and swoops down on thugs and mobsters—Batman"). Find other examples of Kael's sophisticated vocabulary and style.

QUESTIONS FOR DISCUSSION AND WRITING

1. Assume that Kael is revising her review for your college or local newspaper. First, read several reviews from your paper. Then reread Kael's review. What parts or paragraphs should she omit? What information might she add?

2. Kael says that the film "doesn't give us any help on the question of why Bruce Wayne, in creating an alternate identity, picked a pointy-eared, satanic-looking varmint." Do you agree?

3. From a local video store, borrow a film you have already seen at least once. Watch the film. Take notes on the parts of the film you like best/least. Decide on criteria you wish to emphasize. With a specific newspaper or magazine in mind, write your own review.

Man, Bytes, Dog

JAMES GORMAN

(1949–   )

PREREADING JOURNAL ENTRY

Evaluations often compare two similar people, products, or performances: two automobiles, two restaurants, two authors, two kinds of pets, two jobs, two hobbies, two teachers, two boyfriends, and so forth. Just for fun, make notes for your evaluation of two different subjects: an automobile and a pet, a home appliance and a boyfriend, or a fast-food restaurant and a film. Apply the criteria you use to evaluate one of these subjects to *both* subjects.

James Gorman is a free-lance writer who has published articles in magazines such as The Sciences *and* The New Yorker *and has written a humorous column (sometimes about science) in* Discover *magazine. In the introduction to his most recent book,* The Man with No Endorphins *(1988), Gorman concludes with a characteristically humorous thank-you to all the people who have helped him: "Of course, with all this help . . . there is still, as every writer (and every reader of introductions) knows, somebody who has sole and final responsibility for what goes down on paper . . . and it's not me. No sir. If I have to share responsibility for the good stuff, I'm not going to eat the errors. The funny parts are mine, all right, but if there's anything wrong with any of these pieces it's Richard Leibmann-Smith's fault."*

"Man, Bytes, Dog," which appeared originally in The New Yorker, *reveals James Gorman's comic approach to his scientific subjects. Instead of writing the predictable article evaluating the relative merits of the IBM and Macintosh computers, Gorman imaginatively compares two dissimilar "products": an Apple Macintosh and a dog, a Cairn terrier.*

Many people have asked me about the Cairn Terrier. 1
How about memory, they want to know. Is it I.B.M.-
compatible? Why didn't I get the I.B.M. itself, or a Kaypro,
Compaq, or Macintosh? I think the best way to answer
these questions is to look at the Macintosh and the Cairn
head on. I almost did buy the Macintosh. It has terrific
graphics, good word-processing capabilities, and the
mouse. But in the end I decided on the Cairn, and I think
I made the right decision.

Let's start out with the basics: 2

Macintosh:
Weight (without printer): 20 lbs.
Memory (RAM): 128 K
Price (with printer): $3,090

Cairn Terrier:
Weight (without printer): 14 lbs.
Memory (RAM): Some
Price (without printer): $250

Just on the basis of price and weight, the choice is 3
obvious. Another plus is that the Cairn Terrier comes in
one unit. No printer is necessary, or useful. And—this
was a big attraction to me—there is no user's manual.

Here are some of the other qualities I found put the 4
Cairn out ahead of the Macintosh:

Portability: To give you a better idea of size, Toto in "The 5
Wizard of Oz" was a Cairn Terrier. So you can see that if the
young Judy Garland was able to carry Toto around in that little
picnic basket, you will have no trouble at all moving your Cairn
from place to place. For short trips it will move under its own
power. The Macintosh will not.

Reliability: In five to ten years, I am sure, the Macintosh will 6
be superseded by a new model, like the Delicious or the Granny
Smith. The Cairn Terrier, on the other hand, has held its share
of the market with only minor modifications for hundreds of
years. In the short term, Cairns seldom need servicing, apart

from shots and the odd worming, and most function without interruption during electrical storms.

Compatibility: Cairn Terriers get along with everyone. And 7 for communications with any other dog, of any breed, within a radius of three miles, no additional hardware is necessary. All dogs share a common operating system.

Software: The Cairn will run three standard programs, SIT, 8 COME, and NO, and whatever else you create. It is true that, being microcanine, the Cairn is limited here, but it does load the programs instantaneously. No disk drives. No tapes.

Admittedly, these are peripheral advantages. The real 9 comparison has to be on the basis of capabilities. What can the Macintosh and the Cairn do? Let's start on the Macintosh's turf—income-tax preparation, recipe storage, graphics, and astrophysics problems:

	Taxes	Recipes	Graphics	Astrophysics
Macintosh	*yes*	*yes*	*yes*	*yes*
Cairn	*no*	*no*	*no*	*no*

At first glance it looks bad for the Cairn. But it's 10 important to look beneath the surface with this kind of chart. If you yourself are leaning toward the Macintosh, ask yourself these questions: Do you want to do your own income taxes? Do you want to type all your recipes into a computer? In your graph, what would you put on the *x* axis? The *y* axis? Do you have any astrophysics problems you want solved?

Then consider the Cairn's specialties: playing fetch 11 and tug-of-war, licking your face, and chasing foxes out of rock cairns (eponymously). Note that no software is necessary. All these functions are part of the operating system:

	Fetch	Tug-of-War	Face	Foxes
Cairn	*yes*	*yes*	*yes*	*yes*
Macintosh	*no*	*no*	*no*	*no*

Another point to keep in mind is that computers, even 12 the Macintosh, only do what you tell them to do. Cairns perform their functions all on their own. Here are some of the additional capabilities that I discovered once I got the Cairn home and housebroken:

Word Processing: Remarkably, the Cairn seems to understand 13 every word I say. He has a nice way of pricking up his ears at words like "out" or "ball." He also has highly tuned voice-recognition.

Education: The Cairn provides children with hands-on ex- 14 perience at an early age, contributing to social interaction, crawling ability, and language skills. At age one, my daughter could say "Sit," "Come," and "No."

Cleaning: This function was a pleasant surprise. But of 15 course cleaning up around the cave is one of the reasons dogs were developed in the first place. Users with young (below age two) children will still find this function useful. The Cairn Terrier cleans the floor, spoons, bib, and baby, and has an unerring ability to distinguish strained peas from ears, nose, and fingers.

Psychotherapy: Here the Cairn really shines. And remember, 16 therapy is something that computers have tried. There is a program that makes the computer ask you questions when you tell it your problems. You say, "I'm afraid of foxes." The computer says, "You're afraid of foxes?"

The Cairn won't give you that kind of echo. Like 17 Freudian analysts, Cairns are mercifully silent; unlike Freudians, they are infinitely sympathetic. I've found that the Cairn will share, in a nonjudgmental fashion, disappointments, joys, and frustrations. And you don't have to know BASIC.

This last capability is related to the Cairn's strongest 18 point, which was the final deciding factor in my decision against the Macintosh—user-friendliness. On this criterion, there is simply no comparison. The Cairn Terrier is the essence of user-friendliness. It has fur, it doesn't flicker when you look at it, and it wags its tail.

QUESTIONS ON MEANING

1. List the criteria that Gorman uses to evaluate the Macintosh against the Cairn terrier.
2. What advantages does the Macintosh have over the Cairn? What advantages does the Cairn have over the Macintosh? What is the Cairn's strongest point?

QUESTIONS ON PURPOSE AND STRATEGY

1. Is Gorman's purpose to entertain his readers? To evaluate the Macintosh versus the Cairn terrier? To argue that an ordinary dog might be better than a sophisticated computer? To satirize computer lovers and their jargon? Explain your choice(s).
2. Gorman uses comparison/contrast within each criterion to develop his essay. The criteria paragraph on "Reliability" illustrates this strategy: First Gorman says that the Macintosh will be superseded by a new model, and then he describes how the Cairn has held its market share for hundreds of years. Check the rest of the essay: Does Gorman discuss both the Cairn and the Macintosh in each section of his essay?
3. Reread Gorman's opening four sentences. Describe the strategy he uses to get his readers' attention. Do you think his lead-in is effective?

QUESTIONS ON AUDIENCE AND LANGUAGE

1. "Man, Bytes, Dog" was first published in *The New Yorker*. Which of the following magazines might also publish Gorman's essay: *Newsweek, Ms., Business Week, Sports Illustrated,*

Computer World, Esquire, The New Republic? Defend your choice(s).

2. Gorman generates much of his humor by applying computer terminology to his Cairn terrier: "The Cairn will run three standard programs, SIT, COME, and NO, and whatever else you create." Find two other places in the essay where Gorman uses this tactic to create humor.

QUESTIONS FOR DISCUSSION AND WRITING

1. In class, generate criteria that you would use to evaluate two kinds of dogs for use as family pets. Then, reversing Gorman's strategy, apply these criteria to a piece of machinery, appliance, or other inanimate object of your choice. What amusing or absurd comparisons or judgments might you reach?

2. In a serious vein, list criteria for the person, product, or performance you intend to write about. Then compare these standards to the criteria you generated in item 1 for a family pet. Does the comparison help you revise your original list? Does it help you think of new criteria?

A Head Full of Bees

MERRILL MARKOE

PREREADING JOURNAL ENTRY

Find a television set hooked up to cable. Flip through at least twenty channels, watching each one for twenty to thirty seconds. In your journal, jot down time of day, the channel number, and the titles or a few descriptive phrases for each program or advertisement you find on that channel. When you've finished your notes, write your overall impressions of what you saw.

"At my home in Los Angeles, Merrill Markoe says, "I can sometimes turn the dial and find three shopping shows on at the same time. A friend of mine says he gets seventeen." A former writer for "Late Night with David Letterman," Markoe scans the weekend shows for Rolling Stone, *searching for amusing—and sometimes horrifying—events on cable television.*

"A Head Full of Bees" is Markoe's humorous evaluation of weekend cable programs that range from the educational shows on PBS and C-SPAN to those fishing shows where full-grown men sweet-talk fish or the shopping shows where cohost Lisa Mendola "offers the world a chance to see the terrifying specter of what it would be like if Vanna White were allowed to babble on and on, endlessly, forever." Humor depends on a sharp sense of detail, so Markoe vividly describes these programs, gives the names of the TV stars, re-creates the absurd dialogue, and wonders aloud, "Who exactly is the audience for these shows?"

When I was a kid, there was nothing better than 1
weekend TV. You'd get up early on Saturday morning,
hit the on button and just watch, finally getting to do

what you would have done every morning if it hadn't been for scheduling conflicts like school. But there would come a point in the early afternoon when the sun was getting high in the sky and you'd suddenly realize you were still indoors in front of the tube, still wearing your pajamas. Then, without warning, the TV programming would change: the cheery music and the mouse voices gave way to somebody whispering, and—horror of horrors—a golf course filled the screen. And a white-hot boredom would start to set in, beginning behind the eyes and rapidly radiating outward until it set in motion a violent molecular spin at the core of your DNA that, if left unchecked, could actually cause your facial features to melt. (I'm pretty sure it happened to a kid who lived in our area.)

The only warning you get before this deadly chain 2 reaction is triggered is a low-pitched buzzing noise near the base of the skull. This noise, as it grows louder, makes you feel like you have a head full of bees. Scientists believe that exposure to the following weekend-afternoon-TV phenomena tends to induce this dangerous head-full-of-bees condition.

I. MEN IN GOATEES

For some reason, weekend-afternoon TV showcases a lot 3 of guys sporting nature's most offensive facial-hair configuration. And all of them have one important thing in common: they think they have something important to share with you. It may be cooking tips, home-repair tips, painting tips or legislative tips. (There are a lot of men with goatees on C-SPAN.) Whatever the topic, the presentation is not only boring but also full of awful, corny jokes, because men who wear goatees on weekend-afternoon TV shows are utterly convinced that everything they have to say is unbelievably charming.

II. PBS

PBS's deadly contribution here is shows that have *with* in 4 the title, like *Guitar with Frederick Noad, Calligraphy with Ken*

Brown or *Lap Quilting with Georgia Bonesteel.* These shows are all the more irritating because they make you feel guilty for not liking them. They mean well; they're only trying to be educational. Plus they frequently feature someone with a goatee (which in the case of Georgia Bonesteel can be a frightening thing).

III. AFTERNOON COMMERCIALS

Okay, everyone knows that most commercials are depress- 5 ing. But the commercials on weekend afternoons are depressing in a life-threatening way. They range from strangely disheartening membership pitches ("We all agree the $120 it costs to join the NRA is worth it, but if you call now you also get a discount on dismemberment insurance") to dazzlingly demoralizing insurance ads ("I can't tell you how much it means to Mickey and me to not have to worry about becoming a burden to our children," says a sweet, white-haired old man to the incandescently beaming Gavin MacLeod, who is so overcome that all he can say is, "That's terrific"). Monty Hall wants to know how you are planning to pick up the pieces after your loved ones are gone. Ed McMahon and Bob Barker both want to sell you insurance, and Ed promises, "No questions asked . . . no salesman will visit you." Certainly an effective tactic, but even more effective would be a promise that Ed McMahon and Bob Barker won't show up either.

IV. SHOPPING SHOWS

At my home in Los Angeles, I can sometimes turn the 6 dial and find three shopping shows on at the same time. A friend of mine says he gets seventeen. And sometimes all seventeen are selling nothing but various lengths of gold chain—treacherous head-full-of-bees territory.

On *TelShop* a woman hawks "satin sheets made of one- 7 hundred-percent Dacron polyester. . . . And they look for all the world like satin." On *QVC* (Quality Value Convenience) Rod Harter—a man who looks like a police artist's rendering of a white Caucasian male—and Maxine Shnall cohost a segment called "What's New to Make Your Life Easier." And what *is* new to make your life easier? Well, how about the Doze Alarm, for $10.25? It's a little gadget that attaches to your ears or glasses and sounds off whenever your head bobs into a sleep position. Rod describes it as an "ingenious device that is putting technology to use for the benefit of mankind."

QVC also features frequent live phone calls, designed 8 to showcase the verbal wit and style of its hosts. "Have you ordered anything from us before?" Maxine Shnall asks a caller named Suzanne.

"A sixteen-inch gold chain," says Suzanne.   9

"Good!" says Maxine. "Do you enjoy shopping at 10 home?"

"Yes," says Suzanne.   11

"Well, that's good, Suzanne," says Maxine.   12

But Maxine isn't the only one here with a flair for 13 conversation. All the shopping-show personalities are this good. Take Alan Stepp and Lisa LaMendola on *CDN* (Consumer Discount Network). Alan, a yuppie white boy with a slight Southern accent, likes to pepper his speech with foreign phrases. "These are gonna go *muy pronto*," he says of some stereo equipment. "Enjoy every *momento* of it."

His cohost, Lisa, offers the world a chance to see 14 firsthand the terrifying specter of what it would be like if *Wheel of Fortune* let Vanna White babble on and on, endlessly, ceaselessly, forever. "Like we used to say in basketball cheerleading, 'You can do it, you can do it, you *can*,'" she chirps just before launching into a personal plea for letters from "Tom Cruise . . . or Tom Cruise look-alikes. And Bo Derek look-alikes, write to Alan. . . . Write to us!"

V. FISHIN' SHOWS

Saturdays and Sundays are alive with fish. These shows 15
are all pretty much the same. They tend to focus on
selected examples of our fresh and saltwater friends in
the throes of painful, lingering death while big, goofy,
open-faced guys laugh and say things like "Hey, sports
fans, that's a good'n."

I'm the kind of hypocrite who would rather watch 16
hundreds of human beings pretend to bite the dust than
one perfectly nice fish get creamed just to fill up some
afternoon programming time. These shows make me edgy,
and so does the strange way their hosts talk to the fish.
"Come on, sugar, do something to me," says the host of
either *Fishing the West* (syndicated) or *Babe Winkelman's
Good Fishing* (USA Network). (Unless it was Orlando Wilson of *Fishin' with Orlando Wilson* [WTBS].)

"Boy, look at that fish fight," says the guy on *Fishin'* 17
Hole (ESPN) as his friends load up a lure the size and
shape of a shoe tree. By the way, never trust any show
that drops *g*s in its title. It's a basic rule of viewin'—excuse
me, viewing.

On Sunday there is the long-awaited *Lady Bass Classic*, 18
brought to you from Lake Chickamauga, in Chattanooga,
Tennessee. "These women are not here by accident," says
our narrator, putting my mind at rest. I believe we all
have quite enough to worry about without the fear of
accidentally winding up at the *Lady Bass Classic*.

On *Country Sportsman* (TNN), our fishing guest today 19
is Claude Akins. As we troll down the waterways in our
little boat, the conversation with Claude begins to grow
kind of intimate.

"This is a little bit easier than doing *Nashville*," host 20
Bobby Lord says to a clearly puzzled Claude Akins. "You
were in the movie *Nashville*, weren't you?"

"No," says Claude. 21

"Weren't you? I'm sorry," says Lord as he reels in a 22
fish, only to release it later because "we don't have a frying
pan." I am greatly relieved when the half-hour is over

and the only one clubbed and fried has been our very special fishing guest Claude Akins.

VI. HORROR SHOWS

In this category the accidental far outnumbers the inten- 23 tional. Most of the former can be identified by title alone. *Microwaves Are for Cooking* (PBS), for example, seems innocent enough at first. But it quickly turns terrifying as Rose Marie, in a black hair ribbon, appears onscreen peeling broccoli. "People love it this way," she explains, just before hissing at the chef, "How can I talk above the sound of that food processor?"

Also falling into the accidental-horror category are 24 religious and public-service morality plays characterized by no background music, drab actors and open weeping. Then, too, there's that old warhorse, William F. Buckley Jr.'s *Firing Line.* All those years of twitching and facial contortions have caused Buckley's face to slide into the waistband of his pants.

But perhaps the most frightening show of all is the 25 *Herbalife Communications Network* (USA Network), a self-congratulatory pep rally for working and potential Herbalife vitamin and health-food salesmen. The show stars the slickest man on the face of the planet, Herbalife president Mark Hughes, a cross between MTV's Mark Goodman and Engelbert Humperdinck. Nearly as scary is the ecstatic studio audience, made up entirely of Herbalife salespeople. It's like *Night of the Living Dead* starring Up with People.

VII. SHOWS WITH NAMES THAT DON'T SOUND LIKE REAL SHOWS

Real TV shows have names like *Growing Pains* or *Who's the* 26 *Boss?* or *Mr. Belvedere.* (Look, I said real shows. I didn't say good shows.) On Sunday afternoons, NBC has a program called *The Exciting World of Speed and Beauty.* Right away you know that something's up. If it is truly so exciting, fast and beautiful, why is it on in the middle of Sunday afternoon? Today's show features the owner of a hydroplane racing team. "Bernie Little," says the announcer, "is a lot like the rest of us. . . . The only difference is *he* is living the exciting world of speed and beauty *every day of his life.*" In other words, our lives are totally empty. Thanks a lot for reminding us, Bernie.

Who exactly is the audience for these shows? What 27 are the demographics? I think it's sweet of the networks to target all of their weekend-afternoon shows at one dazed, overweight couple that resides in a trailer park somewhere out there.

QUESTIONS ON MEANING

1. In your own words, state Merrill Markoe's overall judgment about weekend afternoon television programs.

2. What categories of shows does Markoe review? Which of her comments don't fit into these categories?

QUESTIONS ON PURPOSE AND STRATEGY

1. Is Markoe's purpose primarily to *evaluate* weekend afternoon television programming or to *entertain* us with strange people, events, and dialogue that occur on these shows? Explain.

2. Most evaluations use cause-and-effect reasoning to argue that something has a positive or negative value. What effect does afternoon television viewing have on the author? List the causes that contribute to this effect.

3. Markoe achieves coherence (smooth flow of ideas) in her essay partly by *repeating* ideas, references, or images. Where in the body of her essay does she echo or repeat her opening theme that afternoon television is like a comic "horror" show, that it is something weird, fearful, or frightening?

QUESTIONS ON AUDIENCE AND LANGUAGE

1. According to Markoe, who is the audience for these afternoon shows? Who is the audience for her *review* of these shows?

2. As a writer for the David Letterman show, Markoe knows how to use the language of humor. Reread her essay, looking for additional examples of *exaggeration* ("if Vanna White were allowed to babble on and on, endlessly, forever"), comic *comparisons* ("It's like *Night of the Living Dead* starring *Up with People*"), and *irony or sarcasm* ("But Maxine isn't the only one here with a flair for conversation").

3. Markoe writes informally, as though she were carrying on a conversation with the reader. Reread the essay, looking for places where she talks directly to the reader or where she uses informal language ("Okay," "a lot of guys," or "I'm pretty sure"). Is her colloquial (conversational) style appropriate for her purpose and audience?

QUESTIONS FOR DISCUSSION AND WRITING

1. Markoe has selected a few weekend shows to illustrate her argument. What shows or kinds of shows does she omit? Check a local TV guide.

2. If Markoe has attacked a particular kind of weekend afternoon television program that you like to watch, write a response to her. Watch your program carefully, gathering evidence of the program's virtues as well as its faults. Assume that your response will be published as a "Letter to the Editors" in *Rolling Stone*.

3. Choose a *category* of television programs (sports, sitcoms, old late-night movie reruns, cops and druggies, home improvement shows, good morning news/variety programs) or even a *segment* of a program (the weather, the sports, the local crimes) and write an evaluative essay about it. Look for both strengths and weaknesses. Gather specific evidence. Determine criteria and then argue for your overall evaluation.

The Civil Rights Movement: What Good Was It?

ALICE WALKER

(1944–   )

PREREADING JOURNAL ENTRY

Reread your remembering essay. Ask yourself, "What was the *value* of those events in your life?" What were the positive and negative aspects? State two criteria that you would use in judging those events. (A criterion might be, "Good events in our lives are those that disturb our familiar, self-satisfied view of the world" or "Good events allow us to attempt new activities, even if we fail.")

The daughter of a Georgia sharecropper, Alice Walker attended Sarah Lawrence College, was a voter registration worker, a staff member of the New York City welfare department, a worker in a Head Start program in Mississippi, and a writer-in-residence at several colleges and universities including Jackson State, Tougaloo, Wellesley, Brandeis, and the University of California at Berkeley. In 1983, Walker won the Pulitzer Prize for The Color Purple, *her third novel. Although the novel, and then the film, brought her immediate recognition, her career as a writer was already firmly established with three volumes of poetry, two collections of short stories,* In Love and Trouble: Stories of Black Women *(1973) and* You Can't Keep a Good Woman Down *(1981), and her novel about the Civil Rights Movement,* Meridian *(1976).*

"The Civil Rights Movement: What Good Was It?" originally appeared in the American Scholar *and was later reprinted in Walker's collection of "womanist" prose,* In Search of Our Mother's Gardens. *"I wrote the following essay," Walker explains, "in the winter of 1966– 67 while sharing one room above Washington Square Park in New York*

with a struggling young Jewish law student who became my husband. It was my first published essay and won the three-hundred-dollar first prize in the annual American Scholar *essay contest. The money was almost magically reassuring to us in those days of disaffected parents, outraged friends, and one-item meals, and kept us in tulips, peonies, daisies, and lamb chops for several months."*

Someone said recently to an old black lady from 1 Mississippi, whose legs had been badly mangled by local police who arrested her for "disturbing the peace," that the Civil Rights Movement was dead, and asked, since it was dead, what she thought about it. The old lady replied, hobbling out of his presence on her cane, that the Civil Rights Movement was like herself, "if it's dead, it shore ain't ready to lay down!"

This old lady is a legendary freedom fighter in her 2 small town in the Delta. She has been severely mistreated for insisting on her rights as an American citizen. She has been beaten for singing Movement songs, placed in solitary confinement in prisons for talking about freedom, and placed on bread and water for praying aloud to God for her jailers' deliverance. For such a woman the Civil Rights Movement will never be over as long as her skin is black. It also will never be over for twenty million others with the same "affliction," for whom the Movement can never "lay down," no matter how it is killed by the press and made dead and buried by the white American public. As long as one black American survives, the struggle for equality with other Americans must also survive. This is a debt we owe to those blameless hostages we leave to the future, our children.

Still, white liberals and deserting Civil Rights sponsors 3 are quick to justify their disaffection from the Movement by claiming that it is all over. "And since it is over," they will ask, "would someone kindly tell me what has been gained by it?" They then list statistics supposedly showing how much more advanced segregation is now than ten years ago—in schools, housing, jobs. They point to a gain in conservative politicians during the last few years. They speak of ghetto riots and of the survey that shows that most policemen are admittedly too anti-Negro to do their jobs in ghetto areas fairly and effectively. They speak of every area that has been touched by the Civil Rights Movement as somehow or other going to pieces.

They rarely talk, however, about human attitudes 4 among Negroes that have undergone terrific changes just during the past seven to ten years (not to mention all those years when there was a Movement and only the Negroes knew about it). They seldom speak of changes in personal lives because of the influence of people in the Movement. They see general failure and few, if any, individual gains.

They do not understand what it is that keeps the 5 Movement from "laying down" and Negroes from reverting to their former *silent* second-class status. They have apparently never stopped to wonder why it is always the white man—on his radio and in his newspaper and on his television—who says that the Movement is dead. If a Negro were audacious enough to make such a claim, his fellows might hanker to see him shot. The Movement is dead to the white man because it no longer interests him. And it no longer interests him because he can afford to be uninterested: he does not have to live by it, with it, or for it, as Negroes must. He can take a rest from the news of beatings, killings, and arrests that reach him from North and South—if his skin is white. Negroes cannot now and will never be able to take a rest from the injustices that plague them, for they—not the white man—are the target.

Perhaps it is naïve to be thankful that the Movement 6 "saved" a large number of individuals and gave them something to live for, even if it did not provide them with everything they wanted. (Materially, it provided them with precious little that they wanted.) When a movement awakens people to the possibilities of life, it seems unfair to frustrate them by then denying what they had thought was offered. But what was offered? What was promised?

What was it all about? What good did it do? Would it have been better, as some have suggested, to leave the Negro people as they were, unawakened, unallied with one another, unhopeful about what to expect for their children in some future world?

I do not think so. If knowledge of my condition is all 7 the freedom I get from a "freedom movement," it is better than unawareness, forgottenness, and hopelessness, the existence that is like the existence of a beast. Man only truly lives by knowing; otherwise he simply performs, copying the daily habits of others, but conceiving nothing of his creative possibilities as a man, and accepting someone else's superiority and his own misery.

When we are children, growing up in our parents' 8 care, we await the spark from the outside world. Sometimes our parents provide it—if we are lucky—sometimes it comes from another source far from home. We sit, paralyzed, surrounded by our anxiety and dread, hoping we will not have to grow up into the narrow world and ways we see about us. We are hungry for a life that turns us on; we yearn for a knowledge of living that will save us from our innocuous lives that resemble death. We look for signs in every strange event; we search for heroes in every unknown face.

It was just six years ago that I began to be alive. I had, 9 of course, been living before—for I am now twenty-three—but I did not really know it. And I did not know it because nobody told me that I—a pensive, yearning, typical high-school senior, but Negro—existed in the minds of others as I existed in my own. Until that time my mind was locked apart from the outer contours and complexion of my body as if it and the body were strangers. The mind possessed both thought and spirit—I wanted to be an author or a scientist—which the color of the body denied. I had never seen myself and existed as a statistic exists, or as a phantom. In the white world I walked, less real to them than a shadow; and being young and well hidden among the slums, among people who also did not exist—either in books or in films or in the government of their own lives—I waited to be called to life. And, by a miracle, I was called.

There was a commotion in our house that night in 10 1960. We had managed to buy our first television set. It was battered and overpriced, but my mother had gotten used to watching the afternoon soap operas at the house where she worked as maid, and nothing could satisfy her on days when she did not work but a continuation of her "stories." So she pinched pennies and bought a set.

I remained listless throughout her "stories," tales of 11 pregnancy, abortion, hypocrisy, infidelity, and alcoholism. All these men and women were white and lived in houses with servants, long staircases that they floated down, patios where liquor was served four times a day to "relax" them. But my mother, with her swollen feet eased out of her shoes, her heavy body relaxed in our only comfortable chair, watched each movement of the smartly coiffed women, heard each word, pounced upon each innuendo and inflection, and for the duration of these "stories" she saw herself as one of them. She placed herself in every scene she saw, with her braided hair turned blond, her two hundred pounds compressed into a sleek size-seven dress, her rough dark skin smooth and *white*. Her husband became "dark and handsome," talented, witty, urbane, charming. And when she turned to look at my father sitting near her in his sweat shirt with his smelly feet raised on the bed to "air," there was always a tragic look of surprise on her face. Then she would sigh and go out to the kitchen looking lost and unsure of herself. My mother, a truly great woman who raised eight children of her own and half a dozen of the neighbors' without a single complaint, was convinced that she did not exist compared to "them." She subordinated her soul to theirs and became a faithful and timid supporter of the "Beautiful White People." Once she asked me, in a moment of vicarious pride and despair, if I didn't think that "they" were "jest naturally smarter, prettier, better." My mother asked this: a woman who never got rid of any of her children, never cheated on my father, was never a hypocrite if she could help it, and never even tasted liquor. She could not even bring herself to blame "them" for making her believe what they wanted her to believe: that if she did not look like them, think like them, be sophisticated and corrupt-for-comfort's-sake like them, she was a nobody. Black was not a color on my mother; it was a shield that made her invisible.

Of course, the people who wrote the soap-opera scripts 12 always made the Negro maids in them steadfast, trusty, and wise in a home-remedial sort of way; but my mother, a maid for nearly forty years, never once identified herself with the scarcely glimpsed black servant's face beneath the ruffled cap. Like everyone else, in her daydreams at least, she thought she was free.

Six years ago, after half-heartedly watching my moth- 13 er's soap operas and wondering whether there wasn't something more to be asked of life, the Civil Rights Movement came into my life. Like a good omen for the future, the face of Dr. Martin Luther King, Jr., was the first black face I saw on our new television screen. And, as in a fairy tale, my soul was stirred by the meaning for me of his mission—at the time he was being rather ignominiously dumped into a police van for having led a protest march in Alabama—and I fell in love with the sober and determined face of the Movement. The singing of "We Shall Overcome"—that song betrayed by nonbelievers in it—rang for the first time in my ears. The influence that my mother's soap operas might have had on me became impossible. The life of Dr. King, seeming bigger and more miraculous than the man himself, because of all he had done and suffered, offered a pattern of strength and sincerity I felt I could trust. He had suffered much because of his simple belief in nonviolence, love, and brotherhood. Perhaps the majority of men could not be reached through these beliefs, but because Dr. King kept trying to reach them in spite of danger to himself and his family, I saw in him the hero for whom I had waited so long.

What Dr. King promised was not a ranch-style house 14
and an acre of manicured lawn for every black man, but
jail and finally freedom. He did not promise two cars for
every family, but the courage one day for all families
everywhere to walk without shame and unafraid on their
own feet. He did not say that one day it will be us chasing
prospective buyers out of our prosperous well-kept neighborhoods, or in other ways exhibiting our snobbery and
ignorance as all other ethnic groups before us have done;
what he said was that we had a right to live anywhere in
this country we chose, and a right to a meaningful well-
paying job to provide us with the upkeep of our homes.
He did not say we had to become carbon copies of the
white American middle class; but he did say we had the
right to become whatever we wanted to become.

Because of the Movement, because of an awakened 15
faith in the newness and imagination of the human spirit,
because of "black and white together"—for the first time
in our history in some human relationship on and off
TV—because of the beatings, the arrests, the hell of battle
during the past years, I have fought harder for my life
and for a chance to be myself, to be something more than
a shadow or a number, than I had ever done before in
my life. Before, there had seemed to be no real reason
for struggling beyond the effort for daily bread. Now
there was a chance at that other that Jesus meant when
He said we could not live by bread alone.

I have fought and kicked and fasted and prayed and 16
cursed and cried myself to the point of existing. It has
been like being born again, literally. Just "knowing" has
meant everything to me. Knowing has pushed me out into
the world, into college, into places, into people.

Part of what existence means to me is knowing the 17
difference between what I am now and what I was then.
It is being capable of looking after myself intellectually as
well as financially. It is being able to tell when I am being
wronged and by whom. It means being awake to protect

myself and the ones I love. It means being a part of the world community, and being *alert* to which part it is that I have joined, and knowing how to change to another part if that part does not suit me. To know is to exist: to exist is to be involved, to move about, to see the world with my own eyes. This, at least, the Movement has given me.

The hippies and other nihilists would have me believe 18 that it is all the same whether the people in Mississippi have a movement behind them or not. Once they have their rights, they say, they will run all over themselves trying to be just like everybody else. They will be well fed, complacent about things of the spirit, emotionless, and without that marvelous humanity and "soul" that the Movement has seen them practice time and time again. "What has the Movement done," they ask, "with the few people it has supposedly helped?" "Got them white-collar jobs, moved them into standardized ranch houses in white neighborhoods, given them nondescript gray flannel suits?" "What are these people now?" they ask. And then they answer themselves, "Nothings!"

I would find this reasoning—which I have heard many, 19 many times from hippies and nonhippies alike—amusing if I did not also consider it serious. For I think it is a delusion, a cop-out, an excuse to disassociate themselves from a world in which they feel too little has been changed or gained. The real question, however, it appears to me, is not whether poor people will adopt the middle-class mentality once they are well fed; rather, it is whether they will ever be well fed enough to be able to choose whatever mentality they think will suit them. The lack of a movement did not keep my mother from *wishing* herself bourgeois in her daydreams.

There is widespread starvation in Mississippi. In my 20 own state of Georgia there are more hungry families than Lester Maddox would like to admit—or even see fed. I went to school with children who ate red dirt. The

Movement has prodded and pushed some liberal senators into pressuring the government for food so that the hungry may eat. Food stamps that were two dollars and out of the reach of many families not long ago have been reduced to fifty cents. The price is still out of the reach of some families, and the government, it seems to a lot of people, could spare enough free food to feed its own people. It angers people in the Movement that it does not; they point to the billions in wheat we send free each year to countries abroad. Their government's slowness while people are hungry, its unwillingness to believe that there are Americans starving, its stingy cutting of the price of food stamps, make many Civil Rights workers throw up their hands in disgust. But they do not give up. They do not withdraw into the world of psychedelia. They apply what pressure they can to make the government give away food to hungry people. They do not plan so far ahead in their disillusionment with society that they can see these starving families buying identical ranch-style houses and sending their snobbish children to Bryn Mawr and Yale. They take first things first and try to get them fed.

They do not consider it their business, in any case, to 21 say what kind of life the people they help must lead. How one lives is, after all, one of the rights left to the individual—when and if he has opportunity to choose. It is not the prerogative of the middle class to determine what is worthy of aspiration. There is also every possibility that the middle-class people of tomorrow will turn out ever so much better than those of today. I even know some middle-class people of today who are not *all* bad.

I think there are so few Negro hippies because middle- 22 class Negroes, although well fed, are not careless. They are required by the treacherous world they live in to be clearly aware of whoever or whatever might be trying to do them in. They are middle class in money and position, but they cannot afford to be middle class in complacency. They distrust the hippie movement because they know that it can do nothing for Negroes as a group but "love" them, which is what all paternalists claim to do. And since the only way Negroes can survive (which they cannot do, unfortunately, on love alone) is with the support of the group, they are wisely wary and stay away.

A white writer tried recently to explain that the reason 23 for the relatively few Negro hippies is that Negroes have built up a "super-cool" that cracks under LSD and makes them have a "bad trip." What this writer doesn't guess at is that Negroes are needing drugs less than ever these days for any kind of trip. While the hippies are "tripping," Negroes are going after power, which is so much more important to their survival and their children's survival than LSD and pot.

Everyone would be surprised if the Israelis ignored 24 the Arabs and took up "tripping" and pot smoking. In this country we are the Israelis. Everybody who can do so would like to forget this, of course. But for us to forget it for a minute would be fatal. "We Shall Overcome" is just a song to most Americans, *but we must do it.* Or die.

What good was the Civil Rights Movement? If it had 25 just given this country Dr. King, a leader of conscience, for once in our lifetime, it would have been enough. If it had just taken black eyes off white television stories, it would have been enough. If it had fed one starving child, it would have been enough.

If the Civil Rights Movement is "dead," and if it gave 26 us nothing else, it gave us each other forever. It gave some of us bread, some of us shelter, some of us knowledge and pride, all of us comfort. It gave us our children, our husbands, our brothers, our fathers, as men reborn and with a purpose for living. It broke the pattern of black servitude in this country. It shattered the phony "promise" of white soap operas that sucked away so many pitiful lives. It gave us history and men far greater than Presidents. It gave us heroes, selfless men of courage and strength, for our little boys and girls to follow. It gave us hope for tomorrow. It called us to life.

Because we live, it can never die. 27

QUESTIONS ON MEANING

1. According to Alice Walker, what has the Civil Rights Movement given her? What is "good" about that gift?
2. What does Walker believe the Civil Rights Movement has given black people?
3. In paragraph nineteen, Walker says, "The real question, however, it appears to me, is not whether poor people will adopt the middle-class mentality once they are well fed; rather, it is whether they will ever be well fed enough to be able to choose whatever mentality they think will suit them." In your own words, explain what Walker means by this statement.

QUESTIONS ON PURPOSE AND STRATEGY

1. Walker's essay is, in part, a response to writers who claim that the Civil Rights Movement is dead. In what paragraph(s) does Walker present their viewpoint? What is their argument?
2. Walker uses a cause-and-effect strategy to develop her argument. The cause is Martin Luther King and the Civil Rights Movement, and the effects are the changes they produced in people's lives. List as many of the effects as you can find. Which of these changes were most beneficial?

QUESTIONS ON AUDIENCE AND LANGUAGE

1. Who is Walker's audience for this essay? The essay was originally published in 1967. If she were to revise it now, what parts might she omit? What might she add?
2. Martin Luther King's speech, "I Have a Dream," repeats the parallel sentence pattern, "I have a dream that one day. . . ." several times to create a dramatic effect. Reread the final three paragraphs of Walker's essay. Where does she use parallel sentence structures to create a similar dramatic effect?

QUESTIONS FOR DISCUSSION AND WRITING

1. Writing in the *Dictionary of Literary Biography*, critic Thadious M. Davis describes a theme that underlies all of Alice Walker's work: "At whatever cost, human beings have the capacity to live in spiritual health and beauty; they may be poor, black, and uneducated, but their inner selves can blossom." Where in Walker's essay is this theme most obvious?

2. Walker describes how her mother watched the white soap operas, identifying with every scene, "her braided hair turned blond, her two hundred pounds compressed into a sleek size-seven dress, her rough dark skin smooth and *white*." Do television soap operas and sitcoms in the 1990s portray blacks and minorities and women in realistic roles, in roles that offer the hope of "knowing" that Walker says pushed her "out into the world, into college, into places, into people," into life itself?

3. Martin Luther King Day, in most states, is a holiday declared in memory of the man and the Civil Rights Movement and is celebrated on the second Monday of each January. Find a local newspaper from last year's Martin Luther King Day. What events took place in your city or community? To what extent do they demonstrate Alice Walker's argument about the value of the Civil Rights Movement?

A Not So Special Effect

RICHARD PRIETO

(1971–   )

PREREADING JOURNAL ENTRY

Write for five minutes on the *worst* movie you've seen lately. First, describe the film—the title, director, actors, setting, and basic plot. Then explain why you thought this film was so disappointing.

Richard Prieto is a radio and television major at the University of Central Florida. Assigned an evaluating essay by his instructor, Janice Pratt, Prieto says he watched a videocassette of a "horrible" movie entitled, F/X: Murder By Illusion. *"After watching the video," Prieto says, "I began organizing my paper by taking the notes I took from the movie and making a cluster out of them." In his essay, Prieto argues that the film does have some interesting special effects, but it has little else to recommend it.*

F/X: Murder by Illusion is a hollow movie. The movie's 1 packaging, special effects, excites the viewer, but there is nothing inside the box. David Weinman, the director, concentrates so much on the special effects that he forgets the plot and the acting. A jumbled story line with chasing and murdering does not unravel until the very end, leaving the viewer asking, "What's going on?" and, "Where's the acting?"

In the beginning of the movie, Rollie Tyler (Bryan 2 Brown) introduces himself as a master of his craft, special effects, by staging a murder scene. The Justice Department takes great interest in his skills and hires him to work on a project for the Witness Protection Program. His job is to stage an assassination of a mafia leader, DeFranco (Jerry Orbach). The scene is so superbly done that it even fools Rollie. Little does Rollie know that the Justice Department tries to hide Rollie's participation permanently by killing him. What ensues is a storyline in which the head of the Justice Department, Murphy, works illegally to protect his mafia interests while Rollie tries to escape death.

The story line seems simple enough, but the addition 3 of Leo McCarthy (Brian Dennehy), a New York detective, confuses it. Leo arrives *in medias res*. He takes up the task of uncovering the illegal activity. In doing so, his entrance causes Rollie to disappear throughout a major portion of the film, so the audience ends up following a man who is never completely understood. There is a lack of understanding him because his morals in the end are questionable.

Not knowing how deeply everyone is involved creates 4 another problem. Is the head of the Justice Department, Murphy, and a few of his disciples involved or the entire department? There are even instances when members of the New York police force get involved. Illegal activity does not define itself clearly enough in this film, and it is not until the ending that the storyline unfolds.

Rollie's character is the heart of the problem with the 5 acting. Instead of understanding a man's struggle against an ominous force, we end up not believing his actions in the end. The problem with the ending lies in Rollie's vengeful attitude. "Forget why you hired me?" becomes his motto toward the unknown criminals. This attitude causes him to single-handedly take on about ten men and prevail. Such instances as his use of handy mirrors and gadgets hidden in his pockets fool all the men into thinking he is in one place when he is not. Rollie could not be that good to fool ten men unless their IQs were all below five.

F/X: Murder by Illusion has more glitter than gold. The 6 chase scenes and murders are cleverly done, but this movie emphasizes special effects and does not satisfy a thinking audience. Add some acting and a simpler storyline and it might work. If Rollie did not take a vengeful attitude, he would make himself more believeable if not more human. If you still want to see this movie, go to the theater as a child would go to see a cartoon. Picture yourself pointing at the screen saying, "Wow!" to all the special effects, because that is what this movie is all about.

QUESTIONS ON MEANING

1. State, in your own words, Prieto's overall claim about this film.

2. According to Prieto, what are the strengths and weaknesses of *F/X: Murder by Illusion?*

QUESTIONS ON PURPOSE AND STRATEGY

1. Prieto's primary purpose is to describe and evaluate this film, but in the process he also explains how to improve this film. What specific suggestions does Prieto make?

2. Film reviews typically intermix description of the film with judgments about the film. Reread body paragraphs two through five. Which sentences are primarily descriptive? Which sentences contain judgments?

QUESTIONS ON AUDIENCE AND LANGUAGE

1. Describe Prieto's intended audience for his review.

2. Based on Prieto's review, what kind of moviegoer might like *F/X: Murder by Illusion?*

3. If you have not seen this film, does Prieto sufficiently explain the plot so you can understand his criticism of the film? Cite one specific paragraph where Prieto does or does not give sufficient information.

QUESTIONS FOR DISCUSSION AND WRITING

1. Assume that you are helping Prieto revise his review to make it clearer to someone who has *not* seen this film. Where do you want more explanation? What sentences could be revised to improve clarity or conciseness?

2. Using your Prewriting Journal Entry, write a brief (200–250 words) review of that film to include in a campus or local newspaper.

Four is Enough

ROY LUI
(1970–   )

PREREADING JOURNAL ENTRY

What appliance, automobile, or consumer product are you
dissatisfied with? First, describe the primary features of
the ideal product. Then compare your product with that
ideal. Specifically, where does it meet your ideal and where
does it fall short?

*Roy Lui, a student in John Jordan's writing class at Colorado State
University, has driven a variety of automobiles from small imports to
larger domestic models. He decided to write his evaluating essay about
a four cylinder engine, the Quad 4, after driving his Oldsmobile for
several months. "When we were given the topic," Lui explains, "I figured
why not write about this stupendous engine that makes my car fly like
the wind!" In "Four is Enough," Lui claims that the Quad 4 is the most
powerful, reliable, and fuel efficient four-cylinder engine he's tested.*

Clustering and Criteria Grid

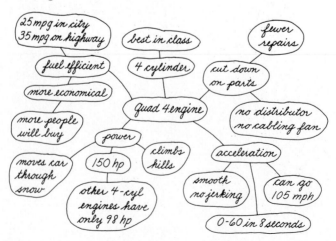

Criteria	Judgment	Evidence
Good fuel efficiency	Excellent	25 mpg city 35 mpg highway drive 250 miles on one tank (13 gallons)
Good power	Excellent for 4-cylinder	150 horsepower, compared to 98 for other engines in class Pulls out of snow & mud Climbs hills easily
Strong acceleration	Excellent	0-60 in less than 8 seconds Can go more than 105 mph. Smooth, steady acceleration No jerking

Notes and Rough Draft

Overall Claim: The Quad 4 engine is the most fuel efficient and most powerful engine in its class.

I have driven many types of cars in my life. Most of them happen to be small to mid-size cars but I have driven large cars also. I discovered one day the most powerful, fuel efficient 4-cylinder engine so far. The engine that I discovered was the Quad 4 engine. It's an engine produced by the Oldsmobile corporation and it was first used as a racing engine. Criteria I will use to support my claim will include the following: fuel efficiency, power, acceleration, and repairs.

Fuel efficiency seems to be a very important characteristic of life today. With fossil fuels being used to maximum height and depleting at a very scary rate, fuel economy is important to owners of car.

Since gasoline prices are rising sky high, many people want to find the most economical car on the market. The engine is an important aspect of this because it is the engine that burns the fuel. The Quad 4 is a 4-cylinder engine that can go 25 miles per gallon in the city and 35 miles per gallon on the highway. This is very economical and I can drive approximately 250 miles on one tank of gas which happens to be a 13 gallon tank.

Most 4-cylinder engines have only 98 horsepower, but the Quad 4 engine has 150 horsepower. Some evidence of the power is that I have packed my car to maximum capacity with luggage, a bike, one person, and a 20 lb. tool box. This probably totaled 500 pounds and with the weight of my car, the overall total is probably several thousand pounds. With all this weight, it still managed to climb hills with considerable ease. Whereas when I drove my cousin's Dodge Colt which has a 4-cylinder engine and about 98 horsepower, it took forever to climb a hill of about the same incline. The engine is also very dependable when stuck in snow or mud. It pulls the car out with ease.

My car can accelerate from rest to 60 mph in approximately 8 seconds. Even when climbing a hill, the engine has the capability of accelerating extremely fast also. Some evidence to support this is my friend. He is really into cars and enjoys reviewing and driving the latest models. In his own words, he said, "This engine has the best acceleration I have seen." Considering that this engine was originally a test and racing engine, it's still quite an accomplishment converting it into a consumer product. (Use Consumer Reports or Car and Driver for evidence.)

```
Repairs are decreased to a drastic
minimum because many of the parts aren't
there, such as the distributor, carburetor,
and engine cooling fan. As Consumer Reports
says, "What's not there can't break down."
They've engineered the engine to cut it
down to the most efficient, compact engine
possible. As far as repairs, according to
Car and Driver (give evidence &
statistics).
```

Final Version

<h2 style="text-align:center">Four is Enough</h2>

Do you have a car that requires refueling every 1 week from just driving to and from work? I have driven many types of cars in my life; most of them happen to be small to mid-size cars, but I have also driven large cars. Many people want to buy smaller cars because they're more economical with gasoline, and they seem to be more efficient than the bigger cars. But on the other hand, an equal number of people want the power of the bigger engine that smaller or mid-size cars don't provide. In the past year, the Oldsmobile corporation has produced a 4-cylinder engine that has the fuel efficiency of a 4-cylinder but the power of a V-8 or 8-cylinder. This remarkable invention is named the Quad 4 engine. It was first introduced as a racing engine but soon became a commercial product in the automobile market, and I am lucky enough to have this engine in my car. The Quad 4 engine is the most fuel efficient, powerful, quickest-accelerating engine that I have ever encountered, and it requires very little maintenance to keep running and functioning properly.

If you are tired of spending a fortune on a car 2 that guzzles gasoline as if it were dying of thirst, don't worry, you're not alone. I, as many others, do consider fuel efficiency to be an important factor to look for when buying a new car. With fossil fuels being used to the maximum and resources depleting at a very scary rate, gas prices are shooting sky high. For local consumers to live with these ridiculous prices, they have to buy a car that will burn less fuel. To buy a car that's fuel efficient, one has to look at the engine because it is that which burns the gasoline. According to *Car and Driver*'s Estimated Fuel Economy Test, the Quad 4 engine gets 25 mpg in the city and 36 mpg on the highway. This statistic wiped out the other cars in its class that were listed: the Volkswagen Jetta, which gets only 22 mpg in the city and 30 mpg on the highway, and the Chrysler LeBaron, which gets 20 mpg in the city and approximately 28 mpg on the highway. This is excellent because I can drive 250 miles to college on one tank of gas, which incidentally happens to be a 13-gallon tank. In addition, I have to buy gas only every three weeks when I use my vehicle for normal city driving. This greatly helps my pocketbook.

Even though most 4-cylinder engines produce only 3 about 98–105 horsepower, the Quad 4 engine generates a whopping 150 horsepower. This is very remarkable for a 4-cylinder engine. With this much power, one can haul quite a bit of weight in his car and still move and maneuver it with reasonable ease. For example, last fall I packed my car to the roof with luggage, a bike, one person, tool boxes, and boxes full of books I brought to college. I estimate the total weight was approximately 500 pounds, and with the weight of my car, the overall weight was probably several thousand pounds. With all this weight, this engine still managed to power my car up hills with considerable zip. My cousin's Dodge Colt, which also has a 4-cylinder, has a difficult time climbing a hill or just hauling two people and three bags of groceries from the grocery store. Not only is the Quad 4 reliable for hauling, it can get a 3,000-pound car out of the mud or snow easily. For example, one time last winter when the snow was a foot deep, my car got stuck, and all that was required to get it out was just a couple of gentle pushes of the accelerator.

For those of you who love to ride like the wind, 4 the acceleration is great in the Quad 4. My car can accelerate from 0 to 60mph in less than 8 seconds. *Car and Driver* measured the exact time at 7.8 seconds. Other engines in its class (the Chrysler LeBaron GTS Turbo, Volkswagen Jetta GLI 4-cyl., and the Nissan Maxima SE) accelerated to 60 in 8.2, 8.5, and 8.3 seconds, respectively. Some evidence other than these statistics is my friend's expert opinion. He really enjoys keeping up with the latest models. He reviews and drives new cars as a hobby, since he works in a Pontiac dealership. He actually said, "This engine has the best acceleration I have ever seen in a 4-cylinder." As soon as one pushes the accelerator, there is a sudden tug, the engine comes alive with a roar, and those horses work madly to accelerate the car to an amazing top speed of 115 mph. Considering that this engine was originally a test and racing engine, it's a real accomplishment in converting it to a consumer product.

Repairs are minimal in the Quad 4 because when 5 the Oldsmobile engineers designed this engine, they cut down on some major parts to make the engine less complicated and more efficient. These major parts include the distributor and cooling fan. The resulting decrease in repairs will thus lead to saving of hard-earned money. Engineers then rewired the electrical system to take electricity directly from the battery and placed the fuel injectors in front so it will cool easier. As a result, the cooling fan is not required. As *Consumer Reports* was quoted as saying, "What's not there can't break down." The engineers have reduced the engine to the most efficient, compact engine possible. Other than the basic oil changes, adding fluids, and just regular maintenance, the Quad 4 is virtually mainte-nance-free. To support this, in the two years that I've had the Quad 4 in my car, I've never had any problems whatsoever with it. It still runs as smoothly and reliably as when I first purchased it.

Overall, the Quad 4 engine is the most fuel effi- 6 cient, powerful, quickest-accelerating engine that I have ever encountered. It requires little maintenance, is exciting when it comes to speed, and more than produces enough power to haul a good-sized load of supplies. *Motor Trend* magazine claims the Quad 4 is "the most fuel efficient, normally aspirated, gasoline engine ever mass produced." All these essential elements I look for, as I'm sure you do, when buying a car. I have found them in the Quad 4, and I feel I have made a very wise decision in buying it. This engine is an extremely good investment, especially when one considers the high price of owning a car today.

QUESTIONS ON MEANING

1. What overall claim does Lui make for the Quad 4 engine?
2. What four criteria does Lui use to develop his overall claim?

QUESTIONS ON PURPOSE AND STRATEGY

1. Lui's purpose is to persuade his readers that the Quad 4 engine is one of the best 4-cylinder engines *that he has ever encountered.* How would he have to change his essay if he argued that the Quad 4 engine is the best 4-cylinder engine *on the market?*
2. Lui uses both personal experience and statistical evidence to support his judgment on each criteria. Which kind of support is more effective, in your judgment? Should he use both?
3. As a strategy, should Lui at least mention one deficiency of the Quad 4 engine? Why or why not? Explain.

QUESTIONS ON AUDIENCE AND LANGUAGE

1. Describe Lui's intended audience. Must his readers be experts on cars to understand his essay? How might expert automobile testers react to his judgments and evidence?

2. Rewrite the opening sentence of paragraph three to make a smoother transition between fuel efficiency and power. Rewrite the opening sentence of paragraph five to make a smoother transition between acceleration and repairs.

QUESTIONS FOR DISCUSSION AND WRITING

1. In an earlier draft, Lui's concluding sentence for the essay read, "This engine is an extremely good investment when one considers the high price for owning a car in these modern days in which a motor vehicle is a necessity." Why is Lui's revised version of this sentence better? Could it be still further revised?

2. Reread your Prereading Journal Entry. Following Lui's example, construct a criteria grid for your topic. Write out an overall claim you could make, based on your criteria grid.

8

PROBLEM SOLVING

We need to adopt that famous Noah principle: No more prizes for predicting rain. Prizes only for building arks.
—Louis V. Gerstner, President of American Express

Why do the bloody years keep rolling by without guns becoming subject to the kind of regulation we calmly apply to drugs, cars, boat trailers, CB radios and dogs?
—Lance Morrow, "It's Time to Ban Handguns"

[Students] must be jolted into believing in themselves as unique men and women who have the power to shape their own future.
—William Zinsser, "College Pressures"

We all complain about problems in the world around us. As armchair critics, however, few of us think about solutions to problems. And even fewer propose practical, workable solutions. An old saying goes, "If you're so smart, why aren't you rich?" Indeed. If we all know how to make money, why aren't we as rich as Donald Trump? If we can all recognize the problems we face, why can't we put solutions into action? Why is that so tough?

Writing proposals to solve problems is difficult primarily because we are asking readers to change both their *beliefs* and their *behavior*. Proposals usually demand action: Writers persuade readers to **do** something—to clean up the environment, reform television programming, reduce handgun deaths, eliminate racist and sexist behavior, improve our schools, or conduct a war on drugs. In business, proposals might request owners or management to make the workplace more efficient or more attractive for customers. Many proposals request funding for a project, to study the effects of earthquakes on buildings and bridges, or to study how learning disabilities affect college students. Solving even those "minor" problems in our personal lives requires difficult changes. Persuading someone to follow a diet or fix up a personal relationship requires demonstrating that it *should* be done and then arguing that it *can* be done—that it is possible, practical, and feasible.

Problem solving requires several critical thinking and writing skills. Writers must accurately *observe* and describe the problem so that the reader agrees that the problem is serious—and that it should be solved. Writers should *remember* and relate their own experiences to this problem. Writers must *evaluate* the problem or *explain how* it came about, or what its causes were. Writers then *investigate* possible solutions and *explain why* their proposal is better than other solutions. As support for their proposal, writers must show that the solution is feasible: It won't take too much time, use too many resources, or cost too much. The best proposals combine creativity with hard-headed, critical thinking.

STRATEGIES FOR READING AND WRITING ABOUT PROBLEM SOLVING

As you read the problem-solving essays in this chapter, watch for the following techniques or features. Note: Not *all* proposals have *all* of these features. Depending on the occasion or audience, they will place primary emphasis on the analysis of the problem, the proposed solution, or the analysis of alternative solutions.

Description of some event that calls attention to the problem. Writers of proposals often begin with some incident or event that dramatizes the problem or shows why the problem is so acute right now. If the writer is proposing a solution to violence caused by automatic weapons, the proposal may open with a description of a recent news item: School children in California were killed by an attacker wielding an assault rifle.

Demonstration that the problem exists and is serious. A proposal begins by describing exactly what the problem is. If the controversy is about automatic weapons, perhaps the weapons are only part of the problem: Drugs, early release of convicts, or psychological instability may be part of the problem, too. (Often, describing the problem in a new way or with a different perspective becomes the basis for a creative solution.)

Proposal of a solution (or solutions) that will solve the problem. A proposal clearly states the writer's solution(s). The solution states the combination of changes in belief and action that will remedy the situation. Usually, writers *limit* the problem and thus the solution: We cannot eliminate all gun-related violence, but we can reduce deaths of innocent bystanders by banning automatic weapon sales.

Support for the proposal. Writers use evidence and examples to show that their solution is more reasonable than alternative solutions and/or that it is practical and feasible. Since writers cannot support a possible future action with actual examples, they often draw comparisons (how reducing gun-related violence is like reducing dependency on drugs—it requires education as well as law enforcement), or they recall past events or precedents (how a solution did or did not work in a previous case or in another country).

READING A PROBLEM-SOLVING ESSAY

When you read the essays in this chapter, use the following strategies.

Prereading

Use the Prereading Journal Topic (or your own freewriting on the subject) to record what you already know about this problem and its possible solutions. Also think about the audience: Who is the author addressing? Who should the author address? What does the headnote about the author tell you about the occasion and the particular kind of proposal you are reading? Who is the writer? Is this a personal or business problem or a proposal advocating sweeping social reforms? Can you determine from the context whether this proposal is serious or humorous?

First Reading

As you read, assume the role of the intended audience. Read for information, analysis of the problem, and persuasiveness of the proposal. As you read, place a "?" next to a confusing or questionable passage, a "X" next to a passage you disagree with, and a "!" next to a surprising or striking passage. Highlight or place a wavy line under important passages. Underline any words or phrases you want to look up later. *When you finish, write in your own words the problem the writer describes and the proposed solution.*

Annotated Reading

As you read the essay a second time, write your own observations and reactions in the margin. "I think this is/ is not a serious problem." "I believe/don't believe that this solution will work." "The writer seems to ignore the idea that . . ." Also read from a writer's point of view. Note the key features of proposal writing. Place brackets [] around passages that illustrate the main features of proposals: introductory reference to current event; description of the problem; statement of the solution; and support for the proposal. Label each strategy in the margin near your brackets. If you see the writer using other strategies, label them. Note key features of style (Is the language about right or too difficult for the audience to understand?) or format that are appropriate or inappropriate for the audience and situation.

Collaborative Reading

In the class or your small group, read each other's Prereading Journal entries. What did other people in the class or your group think about this issue *before* reading the essay? (It's important to determine your various perspectives to decide whether the author successfully changed your beliefs or persuaded you to act.) Next, read each other's marginal annotations and compile a jointly annotated version of the essay. When you've finished an annotation that reflects a consensus (and also notes minority reactions to this essay), write one question or observation about this essay that you would like the class to discuss.

WRITING A PROBLEM-SOLVING ESSAY

Writing a problem-solving essay requires research, but if you think "I need to go to the library to write a research paper," you already have the wrong idea. Start your problem-solving essay by researching or "I-searching" your own *memory* and experiences. Write out specific experiences, set at a specific time and place, that demonstrated the problem for you. If these experiences made you aware of the problem, they will certainly make your readers see the problem.

You will, at some point, need to find a few articles and books in the library for *background information* on your problem. After all, you shouldn't be reinventing the wheel. You should see if other people know about your problem. You should know who has already attempted to solve your problem and how successful their efforts have been. Finding and photocopying written sources is important, but don't allow these sources to control your essay.

Don't forget to *interview* classmates, friends, and family members about this problem: What memorable experiences have they had? Then research the problem with your own legs, ears, and eyes. Where can you go to *observe* the problem firsthand? Finally, ask yourself: "Who is my audience? Who needs this information?" Use your remembering, interviewing, and observing strategies to re-create the problem for your readers. They should be able to see it, touch it, and feel it.

When you start investigating your *solution*, use your observing, remembering, and interviewing strategies. Is there some place where you can observe these solutions in action? Write down your best solutions, but then test them against your memory. Would those solutions work in your experience? What do other people think about your solutions? Finding an expert or two (a friend, a teacher, a businessperson, a doctor, a parent, or someone who works daily with your problem) is essential. You may quote these experts in your paper, you may use their advice to help you find a good written source in the library, or you may revise your solution based on their advice and experience.

In summary, write out your own experiences. Observe the problem firsthand. Talk to people. Think about your audience. Go to the library. But remember: Your purpose is not to summarize other people's solutions, but to synthesize all the information you gather into *your own proposal* to solve the problem.

Choosing a Subject for a Problem-Solving Essay

First brainstorm personal problems and then list public problems. Where your personal problems intersect with a larger social problem, you may have a workable topic.

Personal Topics. Brainstorm a "What's Bugging You" list: living space, mechanical objects, your environment, health, food, sleep, clothes, fitness, friends, music, sports, rules and regulations, courses, teachers, parents, social life, bosses, cars, parking, and jobs.

Public Topics. Brainstorm those aspects of the following large social problems that interest you: civil rights, the environment, health, treatment of minorities, education, automobiles, guns, government, computers, alcohol, drugs, traffic laws, taxes, health insurance, political campaigns, child care, sports, union labor, cities, military weapons, and sexist stereotypes.

Another strategy for public topics is the imaginative approach. If you were the President of the United States for a week, what one problem would you try to solve? If you were a millionaire, what local problem would you work on? If you had just $10,000 to improve one aspect of your campus, what would you do?

Collecting Ideas and Information

Focus. With a possible topic in mind, focus your subject by asking and answering the following "wh" questions:

Who, what, when, and where is the problem?

How or why does the problem exist?

Who, what, when, and where are the solutions?

What are the parts or steps in your solution?

Why will your solution work?

Who needs to know about this problem and its solution?

Who is the intended audience for the proposal?

Demonstrate That the Problem Exists. Use all of the following strategies to gather information:

Remember your own experiences with the problem.

Observe people, places, events connected with the problem.

Interview people who know about the problem.

Read and photocopy a few articles or parts of books on the problem.

Examine Alternative Solutions. Use the following strategies to investigate possible solutions:

Remember your own experiences with possible solutions.

Observe people, places, and events that illustrate a possible solution.

Interview experts for their ideas about feasible solutions.

Read and photocopy articles or parts of books that describe solutions.

Investigate Drawbacks or Objections. Reread your notes and photocopied sources for possible drawbacks, feasibility problems, or contradictions. Be sure to ask experts *why, when,* or *where* their recommended solution might *not* work.

Shaping Your Problem-Solving Essay

As you gather information and ideas for your essay, test your topic against each of the following shaping strategies. Which of the following ideas or patterns will help organize your presentation of the problem and solution for your particular audience?

Chronological Order. Sometimes writers discuss the *history* of their problem, showing how the problem developed over time. In "It's Time to Ban Handguns," Lance Morrow organizes his paragraph around a historical list of assassinations and shootings:

> After one more handgun made it into American history last week . . . a lot of Americans said to themselves, "Well maybe *this* will finally persuade them to do something about those damned guns." Nobody would lay a dime on it. The National Rifle Association battened down its hatches for a siege of rough editorial weather, but calculated that the antigun indignation would presently subside, just as it always does. After Kennedy. After King. After Kennedy. After Wallace. After Lennon. After Reagan.

Causal Analysis. Frequently, writers analyze the *causes* of a problem—and thus show how to solve the problem. In "The Warming of the World," Carl Sagan explains how carbon dioxide traps the earth's reflected heat and thus warms our world:

> Accordingly, if you add air to a world, you heat it: The surface now has difficulty when it tries to radiate back to space in the infrared. The atmosphere tends to absorb the infrared radiation, keeping heat near the surface and providing an infrared blanket for the world. . . .

Patterns for Problem Solving. The following patterns or brief outlines suggest four ways to organize your problem-solving essay. Perhaps one of these patterns will work for your topic.

Problem-Solution Pattern

   I.   Introduction

   II.   The problem: identify and demonstrate

   III.   The solution(s): evidence

   IV.   Answering possible objections, costs, drawbacks

   V.   Conclusion: implementation, call to action

Point-by-Point Pattern

I. Introduction

II. The overall problem: identify and demonstrate

III. One part of the problem, its solution, evidence, feasibility

IV. Second part of the problem, its solution, evidence, feasibility

V. Third part of the problem, its solution, evidence, feasibility

VI. Conclusion: implementation, call to action

Alternatives Pattern

I. Introduction

II. The problem: identify and demonstrate

III. Alternative solution one, why it's not satisfactory

IV. Alternative solution two, why it's not satisfactory

V. Alternative solution three, why it works best: evidence, feasibility

VI. Conclusion: implementation, call to action

Step-by-Step Pattern

I. Introduction

II. The problem: identify and demonstrate

III. Plan for implementing solution; how solution has worked in past
Step one: show why this step is necessary and feasible
Step two: show why this step is necessary and feasible
Step three: show why this step is necessary and feasible

IV. Conclusion

Drafting Your Problem-Solving Essay

Reread your collecting and shaping notes. Make sure your photocopies of articles are handy. If you prefer to write from a sketch outline, review your plan. Reconsider your audience—are you still comfortable writing to your selected audience? Once you begin drafting, write as much as you can. If you have to stop, write a few sections of the next paragraph so you know where to pick up again. Don't stop to check spelling or punctuation. If you are working on a computer, remember to save your file frequently and print out your draft when you finish.

Revising Your Problem-Solving Essay

Use the following strategies when revising your problem-solving essay:

Ask a reader to role-play your audience. Ask your reader to read your solutions critically. What have you left out? Why, when, or where might the solution *not* work? What problems with feasibility have you left out?

Check your introductory paragraphs. Do you have a *lead-in* that catches your reader's attention and dramatizes the problem? Do you have a clear *thesis* statement about your problem and your recommended solution?

Review your proposal for key elements. Have you stated the problem clearly, examined alternative solutions, proposed your solution, given evidence to show why it is feasible, answered objections to your proposal, and outlined steps for implementation? (Remember that not *all* proposals have all of these elements, but don't ignore one of these tactics if it is important for *your* proposal.)

Support your proposal with evidence. Use specific examples from your experience and observations, information from your interviews, and ideas and statistics from written sources.

Check your facts and quotations from sources for accuracy. Check your quotations for accuracy. Use accurate in-text citations and a "Works Cited" page.

Revise your essay for clarity. Check your sentences for unnecessary words, imprecise phrasing, vague language, and unnecessary padding. Use transitions between paragraphs to clarify your organization for your reader.

Edit your essay. Have a peer editor review your essay for problems in spelling, word choice, punctuation, usage, or mechanics.

Postscript for Your Problem-Solving Essay

Before you hand in your essay, answer the following questions. Hand in this postscript with your completed essay.

1. Which of the following strategies did you use in gathering information and ideas for this essay: *remembering* your own experiences, *observing* the problem (or solution) firsthand, *interviewing* friends and experts, and *reading* sources from the library? Which of these strategies was most useful?

2. What was the most difficult part of writing this essay: choosing a topic, collecting information and ideas, shaping and organizing, or revising and editing? How did you work through that difficult stage?

3. What are the best parts of your essay (the introduction, the demonstration of the problem, the proposal of your solution, the conclusion)? What parts still need more work?

4. If you had one more week to work on this paper, what would you do?

It's Time to Ban Handguns

LANCE MORROW

(1939–   )

PREREADING JOURNAL TOPIC

America definitely has a gun problem. Famous people such as John and Robert Kennedy, Martin Luther King, John Lennon, and Ronald Reagan have been shot. Clerks at small businesses are regularly gunned down. People disagree, however, about the solution. The National Rifle Association says that guns are a constitutional right and that "Guns don't kill people; people kill people." On the other side, people claim that outlawing handguns (not rifles) would reduce the killing. Write for five minutes, describing *your* position on this issue. If possible, refer to an actual shooting reported recently in your newspaper or on television.

STUDENT JOURNAL RESPONSES

I feel the same as the NRA — guns don't kill — it is the person who pulls the trigger who kills. I grew up with guns. I feel <u>safe</u> with a gun in the house. I feel that if a person enters my house, tries to hurt me, my boyfriend, my dog, my possessions, I would have no qualms in shooting that person. Yes, many of the "wrong people" have guns, but the drugs are illegal and look how many people have or do drugs. Even if guns are made illegal, the "wrong people" will be able to buy or steal them. I'd prefer to make the odds even and have my own weapon.

501

Personally I hate handguns. My mother was killed because of the easy access of handguns, and so have too many innocent people (like my friend Jerry Ward who was shot in the back of the head trying to calm a fight). I absolutely agree that handguns and people kill, not one or the other. Therefore, banning or outlawing handguns would reduce the shooting incidents but probably wouldn't cure it. (It is worth a try, though!) I don't see how the NRA can argue that guns are a constitutional right if innocent deaths occur. What about the constitutional right to life!

Lance Morrow is a senior writer for Time *magazine who has contributed to nearly a hundred cover stories. He was born in Lewisburg, Pennsylvania, and graduated from Harvard before starting with* Time *magazine in 1965. He has written about his relationship with his father, Hugh Morrow, in* The Chief: A Memoir of Fathers and Sons *(1984) and about his travels in* America: A Rediscovery *(1987). Many of his articles and essays are collected in* Fishing in the Tiber *(1988).*

"It's Time to Ban Handguns" appeared in Time *magazine shortly after an assassination attempt on President Ronald Reagan. In this essay, Morrow examines the multiple causes of handgun violence in America and then proposes his solution. Morrow's remedy, however, involves more than just advocating new gun laws or enforcing the ones already on the books: He offers his understanding of guns and motives for violence as part of the solution.*

IT'S TIME TO BAN HANDGUNS

By a curiosity of evolution, every human skull harbors a prehistoric vestige: a reptilian brain. This atavism, like a hand grenade cushioned in the more civilized surrounding cortex, is the dark hive where many of mankind's primitive impulses originate. To go partners with that throwback, Americans have carried out of their own history another curiosity that evolution forgot to discard as the country

1

! neat image

? Paragraph has too many complex words/ideas.

502

changed from a sparsely populated, underpoliced agrarian society to a modern industrial civilization. That vestige is the gun—most notoriously the handgun, an anachronistic tool still much in use.[Since 1963 guns have finished off more Americans (400,000) than World War II did.]

Scary statistic.

[After one more handgun made it into American history last week (another nastily poignant little "Saturday night" .22 that lay like an orphan in a Dallas pawnshop until another of those clammy losers took it back to his rented room to dream on), a lot of Americans said to themselves, "Well, maybe *this* will finally persuade them to do something about those damned guns."]Nobody would lay a dime on it. The National Rifle Association[battened down its hatches for a siege of rough editorial weather,] but calculated that the antigun indignation would presently subside, just as it always does. [After Kennedy. After King. After Kennedy. After Wallace. After Lennon. After Reagan.] After . . . the nation will be left twitching and flinching as before to the pops of its 55 million pistols and the highest rate of murder by guns in the world.

2

Event that calls attention to the problem.

Clever image

! Effective list !

The rest of the planet is both appalled and puzzled by the spectacle of a superpower so politically stable and internally violent.[Countries like Britain and Japan, which have low murder rates and virtual prohibitions on handguns, are astonished by the over-the-counter ease with which Americans can buy firearms.]

3

Comparison with other countries (what are their rates and laws?)

Americans themselves are profoundly discouraged by the handguns that seem to breed uncontrollably among them like roaches. For years the majority of them have favored restrictions on handguns.[In 1938 a Gallup poll discovered that 84% wanted gun controls. The latest Gallup finds that 62% want stricter laws governing handgun sales. Yet Americans go on buying handguns at the rate of one every 13

4

! Image

Statistics demonstrate that problem is serious

seconds. The murder rate keeps rising.] It is both a cause and an effect of gun sales. And every few years—or months—[some charismatic public character takes a slug from an itinerant mental case caressing a bizarre fantasy in his brain and the sick, secret weight of a pistol in his pocket.]

Emotional!

Why do the bloody years keep rolling by without guns becoming subject to the kind of regulation we calmly apply to drugs, cars, boat trailers, CB radios and dogs? The answer is only partly that the National Rifle Association is, by some Senators' estimate, the most effective lobbying organization in Washington and the deadliest at targeting its congressional enemies at election time. The nation now has laws, all right—a patchwork of some 25,000 gun regulations, federal, state and local, that are so scattered and inconsistent as to be preposterously ineffectual.

5

*Comparison:
Pets must
be regulated
so why not
guns?*

Firearms have achieved in the U.S. a strange sort of inevitability—the nation's gun-ridden frontier heritage getting smokily mingled now with a terror of accelerating criminal violence and a sense that as the social contract tatters, the good guys must have their guns to defend themselves against the rising tribes of bad guys. It is very hard to persuade the good guys that all those guns in their hands wind up doing more lethal harm to their own kind than to the animals they fear; that good guys sometimes get drunk and shoot other good guys in a rage, or blow their own heads off (by design or accident) or hit their own children by mistake. Most murders are done on impulse, and handguns are perfectly responsive to the purpose: a blind red rage flashes in the brain and fires a signal through the nerves to the trigger finger— BLAM! Guns do not require much work. You do not have to get your hands bloody, as you would with a knife, or make the strenuous and intimately dangerous effort required to kill with

6

*People should
be required
to take
courses in
gun safety.*

Very true

bare hands. The space between gun and victim somehow purifies the relationship—at least for the person at the trigger—and makes it so much easier to perform the deed. The bullet goes invisibly across space to flesh. An essential disconnection, almost an abstraction, is maintained. That's why it is so easy—convenient, really—to kill with one of the things.

Effective description

The post-assassination sermon, an earnest lamentation about the "sickness of American society," has become a notably fatuous genre that blames everyone and then, after 15 minutes of earnestly empty regret, absolves everyone. It is true that there is a good deal of evil in the American air; television and the sheer repetitiousness of violence have made a lot of the country morally weary and dull and difficult to shock. Much of the violence, however, results not from the sickness of the society but the stupidity and inadequacy of its laws. [The nation needs new laws to put at least some guns out of business.] Mandatory additional punishments for anyone using a gun in a crime—the approach that Ronald Reagan favors—would help. But a great deal more is necessary. Because of the mobility of guns, only federal laws can have any effect upon them. Rifles and shotguns— long guns—are not the problem; they make the best weapons for defending the house anyway, and they are hard for criminals to conceal. Most handguns are made to fire at people, not at targets or game. [Such guns should be banned. The freedoms of an American individualism bristling with small arms must yield to the larger communal claim to sanity and safety—the "pursuit of happiness."]

7

makes much more sense to ban TV!

Morrow's solution

Clear statement of Morrow's thesis and proposal

That would, of course, still leave millions of handguns illegally in circulation; the penalties for possessing such weapons, and especially for using them in crime, would have to be severe. Even at that, [it would take years to start cleansing the nation of handguns.] Whatever its content,

8

He is not ? optimistic about his own proposal?

no substantive program for controlling guns probably stands any chance of getting through Congress unless Ronald Reagan supports it. He ought to do so, not because he has been shot in the chest but because it should be done.

thesis: Morrow claims that because handguns are a major cause of violence 9 and death in america, federal laws should regulate their possesion and require punishments for those who use handguns to commit a crime.

The indiscriminate mass consumption of guns has finally come to disgrace Americans abroad and depress them at home. It has been almost 90 years since the historian Frederick Jackson Turner propounded his famous thesis about the end of the American frontier. But the worst part of the frontier never did vanish. Its violence, once tolerable in the vast spaces, has simply backed up into modern America, where it goes on blazing away.

QUESTIONS ON MEANING

1. Find one sentence from Morrow's essay to answer each of the following questions: What is the problem? Who wants to solve the problem? Why hasn't the problem already been solved? What are Morrow's solutions?

2. What, according to Morrow, are solutions that don't work? Why, according to Morrow, is the gun such a convenient method of killing?

QUESTIONS ON PURPOSE AND STRATEGY

1. Which sentences in Morrow's essay most clearly express his position on gun control?

2. Where does Morrow use each of the following kinds of evidence: statistics, examples from history, and comparisons with other countries or regulations?

QUESTIONS ON AUDIENCE AND LANGUAGE

1. Who is Morrow's intended audience?

2. Define the following words from the first paragraph: "atavism," "cortex," "agrarian," and "anachronistic." How might

this relatively sophisticated language affect Morrow's audience? How did it affect you?

3. Morrow frequently uses words "loaded" with emotional meaning: "clammy losers," "nation left twitching and flinching," and "charismatic public character takes a slug from an itinerant mental case." Does this language help Morrow achieve his purpose for his intended audience?

QUESTIONS FOR DISCUSSION AND WRITING

1. What are potential problems with Morrow's solution?

2. Reread your Prereading Journal Entry. What would you change about your entry after reading Morrow's essay?

3. From the perspective of a gun owner and member of the NRA, write a short editorial responding to Morrow's essay.

I Want a Wife

JUDY SYFERS

(1937–   )

PREREADING JOURNAL ENTRY

What do you look for in an ideal mate? Describe the characteristics of your ideal man or woman. What talents, interests, or background do you find most appealing?

Judy Syfers was born in San Francisco, California, and received her B.F.A. degree from the University of Iowa. After her male university professors discouraged her from pursuing a graduate education, she became a wife and mother of two children. Syfers has published numerous other essays on unions, abortion, and the role of women in society.

"I Want a Wife" was originally published in Ms. *magazine in 1971 and has become a classic satire of the stereotyped image many men still have about women. The problem Syfers addresses is faced by a divorced male friend of hers: Who can he find who will support him through school, take care of his children, do the housework and shopping and cooking and cleaning without complaint? The solution? A wife, of course.*

I belong to that classification of people known as wives. 1 I am A Wife. And, not altogether incidentally, I am a mother.

Not too long ago a male friend of mine appeared on 2 the scene fresh from a recent divorce. He had one child, who is, of course, with his ex-wife. He is looking for another wife. As I thought about him while I was ironing one evening, it suddenly occurred to me that I, too, would like to have a wife. Why do I want a wife?

I would like to go back to school so that I can become 3
economically independent, support myself, and, if need
be, support those dependent upon me. I want a wife who
will work and send me to school. And while I am going
to school I want a wife to take care of my children. I want
a wife to keep track of the children's doctor and dentist
appointments. And to keep track of mine, too. I want a
wife to make sure my children eat properly and are kept
clean. I want a wife who will wash the children's clothes
and keep them mended. I want a wife who is a good
nurturant attendant to my children, who arranges for
their schooling, makes sure that they have an adequate
social life with their peers, takes them to the park, the
zoo, etc. I want a wife who takes care of the children when
they are sick, a wife who arranges to be around when the
children need special care, because, of course, I cannot
miss classes at school. My wife must arrange to lose time
at work and not lose the job. It may mean a small cut in
my wife's income from time to time, but I guess I can
tolerate that. Needless to say, my wife will arrange and
pay for the care of the children while my wife is working.

I want a wife who will take care of *my* physical needs. 4
I want a wife who will keep my house clean. A wife who
will pick up after my children, a wife who will pick up
after me. I want a wife who will keep my clothes clean,
ironed, mended, replaced when need be, and who will see
to it that my personal things are kept in their proper place
so that I can find what I need the minute I need it. I
want a wife who cooks the meals, a wife who is a *good*
cook. I want a wife who will plan the menus, do the
necessary grocery shopping, prepare the meals, serve them
pleasantly, and then do the cleaning up while I do my
studying. I want a wife who will care for me when I am
sick and sympathize with my pain and loss of time from
school. I want a wife to go along when our family takes a
vacation so that someone can continue to care for me and
my children when I need a rest and change of scene.

I want a wife who will not bother me with rambling 5
complaints about a wife's duties. But I want a wife who

will listen to me when I feel the need to explain a rather difficult point I have come across in my course of studies. And I want a wife who will type my papers for me when I have written them.

I want a wife who will take care of the details of my 6 social life. When my wife and I are invited out by my friends, I want a wife who will take care of the babysitting arrangements. When I meet people at school that I like and want to entertain, I want a wife who will have the house clean, will prepare a special meal, serve it to me and my friends, and not interrupt when I talk about things that interest me and my friends. I want a wife who will have arranged that the children are fed and ready for bed before my guests arrive so that the children do not bother us. I want a wife who takes care of the needs of my guests so that they feel comfortable, who makes sure that they have an ashtray, that they are passed the hors d'oeuvres, that they are offered a second helping of the food, that their wine glasses are replenished when necessary, that their coffee is served to them as they like it. And I want a wife who knows that sometimes I need a night out by myself.

I want a wife who is sensitive to my sexual needs, a 7 wife who makes love passionately and eagerly when I feel like it, a wife who makes sure that I am satisfied. And, of course, I want a wife who will not demand sexual attention when I am not in the mood for it. I want a wife who assumes the complete responsibility for birth control, because I do not want more children. I want a wife who will remain sexually faithful to me so that I do not have to clutter up my intellectual life with jealousies. And I want a wife who understands that *my* sexual needs may entail more than strict adherence to monogamy. I must, after all, be able to relate to people as fully as possible.

If, by chance, I find another person more suitable as 8 a wife than the wife I already have, I want the liberty to replace my present wife with another one. Naturally, I will expect a fresh, new life; my wife will take the children and be solely responsible for them so that I am left free.

When I am through with school and have a job, I want my wife to quit working and remain at home so that my wife can more fully and completely take care of a wife's duties. 9

My God, who *wouldn't* want a wife? 10

QUESTIONS ON MEANING

1. Who is the speaker, the "I" in paragraphs one and two? Who is the speaker beginning in paragraph 3?

2. In the body paragraphs of the essay (paragraphs three through nine), what seven expectations does this speaker have of a wife?

QUESTIONS ON PURPOSE AND STRATEGY

1. Satire is the art of ridiculing foolishness or pride in order to expose and correct it. What attitudes or behavior is Syfers ridiculing? Does or will her essay succeed in its satiric purpose to expose or correct these follies?

2. Does Syfers exaggerate the duties of a wife in this essay? (Is it fair to use exaggeration in a satire?)

QUESTIONS ON AUDIENCE AND LANGUAGE

1. Who is Syfer's audience? Why is it appropriate that the essay was published in *Ms.* magazine?

2. In paragraph four, count the number of sentences that begin with "I want. . . ." What is the effect of this repetition?

3. Describe the personality of the character or voice that speaks in paragraphs three through nine. Is he a likeable person? Is he a despicable person?

QUESTIONS FOR DISCUSSION AND WRITING

1. Using Syfers's definition, is your own mother a "wife"?

2. Imagine that Syfers had decided to write about this problem and its solution in a straightforward way, without satire.

Write the opening paragraph or two for a "straight" version of this essay.

3. Write an essay explaining *your* solution to the "wife" problem described in this essay. How should couples avoid exploiting either the man or the woman in a relationship?

College Pressures

WILLIAM ZINSSER

(1922–   )

PREREADING JOURNAL ENTRY

Which of the following college *goals* is uppermost in your mind: pleasing your parents, finding yourself, learning about your major, getting good grades, getting a job, or some other goal? In reaching this goal or goals, which college *pressures* bother you the most: pressure from parents, from teachers, from friends, from yourself, from lack of money, or some other pressure?

William Zinsser was born in New York City, has taught in the English department at Yale University, and is the author of the bestselling book, On Writing Well: An Informal Guide to Writing Nonfiction *(1976).*

In "College Pressures," Zinsser investigates the problems that college students face—particularly the pressures that they put on themselves. Zinsser explains that he wishes he could reduce that pressure, by telling students that "there will be plenty of time to change jobs, change careers, change whole attitudes and approaches." The solution, Zinsser argues, is to be willing to take chances and not be so concerned about predetermined goals.

Dear Carlos: I desperately need a dean's excuse for 1 my chem midterm which will begin in about 1 hour. All I can say is that I totally blew it this week. I've fallen incredibly, inconceivably behind.

Carlos: Help! I'm anxious to hear from you. I'll be in 2 my room and won't leave it until I hear from you. Tomorrow is the last day for . . .

Carlos: I left town because I started bugging out again. 3
I stayed up all night to finish a take home make-up exam
& am typing it to hand in on the 10th. It was due on the
5th. P.S. I'm going to the dentist. Pain is pretty bad.

Carlos: Probably by Friday I'll be able to get back to 4
my studies. Right now I'm going to take a long walk. This
whole thing has taken a lot out of me.

Carlos: I'm really up the proverbial creek. The prob- 5
lem is I really *bombed* the history final. Since I need that
course for my major . . .

Carlos: Here follows a tale of woe. I went home this 6
weekend, had to help my Mom, & caught a fever so didn't
have much time to study. My professor . . .

Carlos: Aargh! Nothing original but everything's piling 7
up at once. To be brief, my job interview . . .

Hey Carlos, good news! I've got mononucleosis. 8

Who are these wretched supplicants, scribbling notes 9
so laden with anxiety, seeking such miracles of postponement and balm? They are men and women who belong
to Branford College, one of the twelve residential colleges
at Yale University, and the messages are just a few of the
hundreds that they left for their dean, Carlos Hortas—
often slipped under his door at 4 A.M.—last year.

But students like the ones who wrote those notes can 10
also be found on campuses from coast to coast—especially
in New England and at many other private colleges across
the country that have high academic standards and highly
motivated students. Nobody could doubt that the notes
are real. In their urgency and their gallows humor they
are authentic voices of a generation that is panicky to
succeed.

My own connection with the message writers is that I 11
am master of Branford College. I live in its Gothic
quadrangle and know the students well. (We have 485 of
them.) I am privy to their hopes and fears—and also to
their stereo music and their piercing cries in the dead of
night ("Does anybody *ca-a-are?*"). If they went to Carlos
to ask how to get through tomorrow, they come to me to
ask how to get through the rest of their lives.

Mainly I try to remind them that the road ahead is a 12
long one and that it will have more unexpected turns than
they think. There will be plenty of time to change jobs,
change careers, change whole attitudes and approaches.
They don't want to hear such liberating news. They want
a map—right now—that they can follow unswervingly to
career security, financial security, Social Security and,
presumably, a prepaid grave.

What I wish for all students is some release from the 13
clammy grip of the future. I wish them a chance to savor
each segment of their education as an experience in itself
and not as a grim preparation for the next step. I wish
them the right to experiment, to trip and fall, to learn
that defeat is as instructive as victory and is not the end
of the world.

My wish, of course, is naive. One of the few rights 14
that America does not proclaim is the right to fail. Achievement is the national god, venerated in our media—the
million-dollar athlete, the wealthy executive—and glori-
fied in our praise of possessions. In the presence of such
a potent state religion, the young are growing up old.

I see four kinds of pressure working on college stu- 15
dents today; economic pressure, parental pressure, peer
pressure, and self-induced pressure. It is easy to look
around for villains—to blame the colleges for charging
too much money, the professors for assigning too much
work, the parents for pushing their children too far, the
students for driving themselves too hard. But there are
no villains; only victims.

"In the late 1960s," one dean told me, "the typical 16
question that I got from students was 'Why is there so
much suffering in the world?' or 'How can I make a
contribution?' Today it's 'Do you think it would look better
for getting into law school if I did a double major in
history and political science, or just majored in one of
them?' " Many other deans confirmed this pattern. One
said: "They're trying to find an edge—the intangible
something that will look better on paper if two students
are about equal."

Note the emphasis on looking better. The transcript 17
has become a sacred document, the passport to security.
How one appears on paper is more important than how
one appears in person. *A* is for Admirable and *B* is for
Borderline, even though, in Yale's official system of grad-
ing, *A* means "excellent" and *B* means "very good." Today,
looking very good is no longer good enough, especially
for students who hope to go on to law school or medical
school. They know that entrance into the better schools
will be an entrance into the better law firms and better
medical practices where they will make a lot of money.
They also know that the odds are harsh. Yale Law School,
for instance, matriculates 170 students from an applicant
pool of 3,700; Harvard enrolls 550 from a pool of 7,000.

It's all very well for those of us who write letters of 18
recommendation for our students to stress the qualities
of humanity that will make them good lawyers or doctors.
And it's nice to think that admission officers are really
reading our letters and looking for the extra dimension
of commitment or concern. Still, it would be hard for a
student not to visualize these officers shuffling so many
transcripts studded with *A*s that they regard a *B* as
positively shameful.

The pressure is almost as heavy on students who just 19
want to graduate and get a job. Long gone are the days
of the "gentleman's C," when students journeyed through
college with a certain relaxation, sampling a wide variety
of courses—music, art, philosophy, classics, anthropology,
poetry, religion—that would send them out as liberally
educated men and women. If I were an employer I would
rather employ graduates who have this range and curiosity
than those who narrowly pursued safe subjects and high
grades. I know countless students whose inquiring minds
exhilarate me. I like to hear the play of their ideas. I don't
know if they are getting *A*s or *C*s, and I don't care. I also
like them as people. The country needs them, and they
will find satisfying jobs. I tell them to relax. They can't.

Nor can I blame them. They live in a brutal economy. 20
Tuition, room, and board at most private colleges now

comes to at least $7,000, not counting books and fees. This might seem to suggest that the colleges are getting rich. But they are equally battered by inflation. Tuition covers only 60 percent of what it costs to educate a student, and ordinarily the remainder comes from what colleges receive in endowments, grants, and gifts. Now the remainder keeps being swallowed by the cruel costs—higher every year—of just opening the doors. Heating oil is up. Insurance is up. Postage is up. Health-premium costs are up. Everything is up. Deficits are up. We are witnessing in America the creation of a brotherhood of paupers— colleges, parents, and students, joined by the common bond of debt.

Today it is not unusual for a student, even if he works 21 part time at college and full time during the summer, to accrue $5,000 in loans after four years—loans that he must start to repay within one year after graduation. Exhorted at commencement to go forth into the world, he is already behind as he goes forth. How could he not feel under pressure throughout college to prepare for this day of reckoning? I have used "he," incidentally, only for brevity. Women at Yale are under no less pressure to justify their expensive education to themselves, their parents, and society. In fact, they are probably under more pressure. For although they leave college superbly equipped to bring fresh leadership to traditionally male jobs, society hasn't yet caught up with this fact.

Along with economic pressure goes parental pressure. 22 Inevitably, the two are deeply intertwined.

I see many students taking premedical courses with 23 joyless tenacity. They go off to their labs as if they were going to the dentist. It saddens me because I know them in other corners of their life as cheerful people.

"Do you want to go to medical school?" I ask them.   24

"I guess so," they say, without conviction, or "Not 25 really."

"Then why are you going?"   26

"Well, my parents want me to be a doctor. They're 27 paying all this money and . . ."

Poor students, poor parents. They are caught in one 28
of the oldest webs of love and duty and guilt. The parents
mean well; they are trying to steer their sons and daughters
toward a secure future. But the sons and daughters want
to major in history or classics or philosophy—subjects with
no "practical" value. Where's the payoff on the humanities? It's not easy to persuade such loving parents that the
humanities do indeed pay off. The intellectual faculties
developed by studying subjects like history and classics—
an ability to synthesize and relate, to weight cause and
effect, to see events in perspective—are just the faculties
that make creative leaders in business or almost any
general field. Still, many fathers would rather put their
money on courses that point toward a specific profession—
courses that are prelaw, premedical, prebusiness, or, as
I sometimes heard it put, "prerich."

But the pressure on students is severe. They are truly 29
torn. One part of them feels obligated to fulfill their
parents' expectations; after all, their parents are older and
presumably wiser. Another part tells them that the expectations that are right for their parents are not right for
them.

I know a student who wants to be an artist. She is very 30
obviously an artist and will be a good one—she has already
had several modest local exhibits. Meanwhile she is growing as a well-rounded person and taking humanistic
subjects that will enrich the inner resources out of which
her art will grow. But her father is strongly opposed. He
thinks that an artist is a "dumb" thing to be. The student
vacillates and tries to please everybody. She keeps up with
her art somewhat furtively and takes some of the "dumb"
courses her father wants her to take—at least they are
dumb courses for her. She is a free spirit on a campus of
tense students—no small achievement in itself—and she
deserves to follow her muse.

Peer pressure and self-induced pressure are also in- 31
tertwined, and they begin almost at the beginning of
freshman year.

"I had a freshman student I'll call Linda," one dean 32

told me, "who came in and said she was under terrible pressure because her roommate, Barbara, was much brighter and studied all the time. I couldn't tell her that Barbara had come in two hours earlier to say the same thing about Linda."

The story is almost funny—except that it's not. It's 33 symptomatic of all the pressures put together. When every student thinks every other student is working harder and doing better, the only solution is to study harder still. I see students going off to the library every night after dinner and coming back when it closes at midnight. I wish they could sometimes forget about their peers and go to a movie. I hear the clacking of typewriters in the hours before dawn. I see the tension in their eyes when exams are approaching and papers are due: *Will I get everything done?*

Probably they won't. They will get sick. They will get 34 "blocked." They will sleep. They will oversleep. They will bug out. *Hey Carlos, help!*

Part of the problem is that they do more than they 35 are expected to do. A professor will assign five-page papers. Several students will start writing ten-page papers to impress him. Then more students will write ten-page papers, and a few will raise the ante to fifteen. Pity the poor student who is still just doing the assignment.

"Once you have twenty or thirty percent of the student 36 population deliberately overexerting," one dean points out, "it's bad for everybody. When a teacher gets more and more effort from his class, the student who is doing normal work can be perceived as not doing well. The tactic works, psychologically."

Why can't the professor just cut back and not accept 37 longer papers? He can, and he probably will. But by then the term will be half over and the damage done. Grade fever is highly contagious and not easily reversed. Besides, the professor's main concern is with his course. He knows his students only in relation to the course and doesn't know that they are also overexerting in their other courses. Nor is it really his business. He didn't sign up for dealing with the student as a whole person and with all the emotional baggage the student brought along from home. That's what deans, masters, chaplains, and psychiatrists are for.

To some extent this is nothing new: a certain number 38 of professors have always been self-contained islands of scholarship and shyness, more comfortable with books than with people. But the new pauperism has widened the gap still further, for professors who actually like to spend time with students don't have as much time to spend. They also are overexerting. If they are young, they are busy trying to publish in order not to perish, hanging by their fingernails onto a shrinking profession. If they are old and tenured, they are buried under the duties of administering departments—as departmental chairmen or members of committees—that have been thinned out by the budgetary axe.

Ultimately it will be the students' own business to break 39 the circles in which they are trapped. They are too young to be prisoners of their parents' dreams and their class-mates' fears. They must be jolted into believing in them-selves as unique men and women who have the power to shape their own future.

"Violence is being done to the undergraduate expe- 40 rience," says Carlos Hortas. "College should be open-ended: at the end it should open many, many roads. Instead, students are choosing their goal in advance, and their choices narrow as they go along. It's almost as if they think that the country has been codified in the type of jobs that exist—that they've got to fit into certain slots. Therefore, fit into the best-paying slot.

"They ought to take chances. Not taking chances will 41 lead to a life of colorless mediocrity. They'll be comfort-able. But something in the spirit will be missing."

I have painted too drab a portrait of today's students, 42 making them seem a solemn lot. That is only half of their story; if they were so dreary I wouldn't so thoroughly enjoy their company. The other half is that they are easy to like. They are quick to laugh and to offer friendship.

They are not introverts. They are usually kind and are more considerate of one another than any student generation I have known.

Nor are they so obsessed with their studies that they 43 avoid sports and extracurricular activities. On the contrary, they juggle their crowded hours to play on a variety of teams, perform with musical and dramatic groups, and write for campus publications. But this in turn is one more cause of anxiety. There are too many choices. Academically, they have 1,300 courses to select from; outside class they have to decide how much spare time they can spare and how to spend it.

This means that they engage in fewer extracurricular 44 pursuits than their predecessors did. If they want to row on the crew and play in the symphony they will eliminate one; in the '60s they would have done both. They also tend to choose activities that are self-limiting. Drama, for instance, is flourishing in all twelve of Yale's residential colleges as it never has before. Students hurl themselves into these productions—as actors, directors, carpenters, and technicians—with a dedication to create the best possible play, knowing that the day will come when the run will end and they can get back to their studies.

They also can't afford to be the willing slave of 45 organizations like the *Yale Daily News.* Last spring at the one-hundredth anniversary banquet of that paper—whose past chairmen include such once and future kings as Potter Stewart, Kingman Brewster, and William F. Buckley, Jr.[1]—much was made of the fact that the editorial staff used to be small and totally committed and that "newsies" routinely worked fifty hours a week. In effect they belonged to a club; Newsies is how they defined themselves at Yale. Today's student will write one or two articles a week, when he can, and he defines himself as a

---

[1] Stewart is a retired Justice of the U.S. Supreme Court; Brewster is a former president of Yale; and Buckley is a writer and the host of *Firing Line.*

student. I've never heard the word Newsie except at the banquet.

If I have described the modern undergraduate pri- 46 marily as a driven creature who is largely ignoring the blithe spirit inside who keeps trying to come out and play, it's because that's where the crunch is, not only at Yale but throughout American education. It's why I think we should all be worried about the values that are nurturing a generation so fearful of risk and so goal-obsessed at such an early age.

I tell students that there is no one "right" way to get 47 ahead—that each of them is a different person, starting from a different point and bound for a different destination. I tell them that change is a tonic and that all the slots are not codified nor the frontiers closed. One of my ways of telling them is to invite men and women who have achieved success outside the academic world to come and talk informally with my students during the year. They are heads of companies or ad agencies, editors of magazines, politicians, public officials, television magnates, labor leaders, business executives, Broadway producers, artists, writers, economists, photographers, scientists, historians— a mixed bag of achievers.

I ask them to say a few words about how they got 48 started. The students assume that they started in their present profession and knew all along that it was what they wanted to do. Luckily for me, most of them got into their field by a circuitous route, to their surprise, after many detours. The students are startled. They can hardly conceive of a career that was not preplanned. They can hardly imagine allowing the hand of God or chance to nudge them down some unforeseen trail.

QUESTIONS ON MEANING

1. What four kinds of college pressures does Zinsser describe? How are these pressures intertwined?
2. What sentences best express Zinsser's solution to the problem of college pressures?

QUESTIONS ON PURPOSE AND STRATEGY

1. What is Zinsser's basic purpose in this essay? To explain that students are under pressure? To reassure his audience that these pressures normal? To offer a solution to their pressure?

2. Reread paragraph fifteen. What do you *expect* Zinsser to discuss, based on the essay map in this paragraph? Where does the rest of the essay *not* meet your expectations?

3. Rank the four pressures Zinsser cites in order of their importance for you. Then rank them according to the amount of support Zinsser devotes to each. Does Zinsser give the most support to the most important causes? Should he?

4. Zinsser begins his essay by citing notes from actual students. Does this lead-in get your interest? If Zinsser began his essay as Mike Rose does in "Writing around the Rules," would it still be effective? How might Zinsser write his lead-in if he imitated Norman Atkins's opening paragraph of "Fast Food for Thought"?

QUESTIONS ON AUDIENCE AND LANGUAGE

1. Who is Zinsser's audience? Students who work under pressure? Parents of students who are experiencing pressure? Professors who contribute to the pressure? Counselors who advise students under pressure?

2. What words might best describe Zinsser's tone (his attitude toward his subject): *matter-of-fact, angry, sympathetic, satiric, condescending,* or some other word? Find three sentences which clearly express this tone.

QUESTIONS FOR DISCUSSION AND WRITING

1. Zinsser wrote this essay about students at Yale University. In what ways are the students and the pressures similar at your school? In what ways are the students and the pressures different?

2. Zinsser quotes Dean Carlos Hortas as saying that students

"ought to take chances. Not taking chances will lead to a life of colorless mediocrity. They'll be comfortable. But something in the spirit will be missing." Discuss whether you agree with this advice.

3. Choose a problem you face in college. Describe the problem using specific examples from your experience. Interview your classmates to see how they have solved or tried to solve that particular problem. Write an essay explaining your problem and proposing a solution that you believe should work.

The Warming of the World

CARL SAGAN

(1934–   )

PREREADING JOURNAL ENTRY

Explain what you know about the greenhouse effect. What
is it? Why is it called the greenhouse effect? What predic-
tions about planetary warming have you heard recently?
What recent environmental changes might reduce the
effect?

---

*"The public is a lot brighter and more interested in science than
they're given credit for. . . . They're not numbskulls."* Astronomer Carl
Sagan's respect for his audience and his high enthusiasm about the wonders of the universe have sparked the imaginations of the millions of
readers of **The Dragons of Eden** *(1977) and* **Cosmos** *(1980) and
watchers of his television series, "Cosmos." The son of a textile worker
in New York City, Sagan received his undergraduate and graduate
degrees from the University of Chicago. He has taught at dozens of
universities, including Stanford, the University of California at Berkeley, Cornell, and Harvard.*

*In "The Warming of the World," Sagan explains the causes of the
greenhouse effect, describes the problems that global warming might
cause, and sets forth his solutions. Because increases in carbon dioxide
emissions in one part of the world affect the entire planet, Sagan argues
that any technological solutions must have long-term objectives and must
be applied worldwide—on every continent and in every country.*

When humans first evolved—in the savannahs of East 1
Africa a few million years ago—our numbers were few
and our powers feeble. We knew almost nothing about
controlling our environment—even clothing had yet to be

invented. We were creatures of the climate, utterly dependent upon it.

A few degrees hotter or colder on average, and our 2 ancestors were in trouble. The toll taken much later by the ice ages, in which average land temperatures dropped some 8°C (centigrade, or Celsius), must have been horrific. And yet, it is exactly such climatic change that pushed our ancestors to develop tools and technology, science and civilization. Certainly, skills in hunting, skinning, tanning, building shelters and refurbishing caves must owe much to the terrors of the deep ice age.

Today, we live in a balmy epoch, 10,000 years after 3 the last major glaciation. In this climatic spring, our species has flourished; we now cover the entire planet and are altering the very appearance of our world. Lately—within the last century or so—humans have acquired, in more ways than one, the ability to make major changes in that climate upon which we are so dependent. The Nuclear Winter findings are one dramatic indication that we can change the climate—in this case, in the spasm of nuclear war. But I wish here to describe a different kind of climatic danger, this one slower, more subtle and arising from intentions that are wholly benign.

It is warm down here on Earth because the Sun shines. 4 If the Sun were somehow turned off, the Earth would rapidly cool. The oceans would freeze, eventually the atmosphere itself would condense out and our planet would be covered everywhere by snowbanks of solid oxygen and nitrogen 10 meters (about 30 feet) high. Only the tiny trickle of heat from the Earth's interior and the faint starlight would save our world from a temperature of absolute zero.

We know how bright the Sun is; we know how far 5 from it we are; and we know what fraction of the sunlight reaching the Earth is reflected back to space (about 30 percent). So we can calculate—with a simple mathematical equation—what the average temperature of the Earth should be. But when we do the calculation, we find that the Earth's temperature should be about 20°C below the freezing point of water, in stark contradiction to our everyday experience. What have we done wrong?

As in many such cases in science, what we've done 6 wrong is to forget something—in this case, the atmosphere. Every object in the universe radiates some kind of light to space; the colder the object, the longer the wavelength of radiation it emits. The Earth—much colder than the Sun—radiates to space mainly in the infrared part of the spectrum, not the visible. Were the Sun turned off, the Earth would soon be indetectable in ordinary visible light, though it would be brilliantly illuminated in infrared light.

When sunlight strikes the Earth, part is reflected back 7 into the sky; much of the rest is absorbed by the ground and heats it—the darker the ground, the greater the heating. The ground radiates back upward in the infrared. Thus, for an airless Earth, the temperature would be set solely by a balance between the incoming sunlight absorbed by the surface and the infrared radiation that the surface emits back to space.

When you put air on a planet, the situation changes. 8 The Earth's atmosphere is, generally, still transparent to visible light. That's why we can see each other when we talk, glimpse distant mountains and view the stars.

But in the infrared, all that is different. While the 9 oxygen and nitrogen in the air are transparent in both the infrared and the visible, minor constituents such as water vapor (H_2O) and carbon dioxide (CO_2) tend to be much more opaque in the infrared. It would be useless for us to have eyes that could see at a wavelength, say, of 15 microns in the infrared, because the air is murky black there.

Accordingly, if you add air to a world, you heat it: 10 The surface now has difficulty when it tries to radiate back to space in the infrared. The atmosphere tends to absorb the infrared radiation, keeping heat near the surface and providing an infrared blanket for the world. There is very little CO_2 in the Earth's atmosphere—only 0.03 percent. But that small amount is enough to make the Earth's atmosphere opaque in important regions of the infrared spectrum. CO_2 and H_2O are the reason the global temperature is not well below freezing. We owe our comfort—indeed, our very existence—to the fact that these gases are present and are much more transparent in the visible than in the infrared. Our lives depend on a delicate balance of invisible gases. Too much blanket, or too little, and we're in trouble.

This property of many gases to absorb strongly in the 11 infrared but not in the visible, and thereby to heat their surroundings, is called the "greenhouse effect." A florist's greenhouse keeps its planty inhabitants warm. The phrase "greenhouse effect" is widely used and has an instructive ring to it, reminding us that we live in a planetary-scale greenhouse and recalling the admonition about living in glass houses and throwing stones. But, in fact, florists' greenhouses do not keep warm by the greenhouse effect; they work mainly by inhibiting the movement of air inside, another matter altogether.

We need look only as far as the nearest planet to see 12 an example of an atmospheric greenhouse effect gone wild. Venus has in its atmosphere an enormous quantity of carbon dioxide (roughly as much as is buried as carbonates in all the rocks of the Earth's crust). There is an atmosphere of CO_2 on Venus 90 times thicker than the atmosphere of the Earth and containing some 200,000 times more CO_2 than in our air. With water vapor and other minor atmospheric constituents, this is enough to make a greenhouse effect that keeps the surface of Venus around 470°C (900°F)—enough to melt tin or lead.

When humans burn wood or "fossil fuels" (coal, oil, 13 natural gas, etc.), they put carbon dioxide into the air. One carbon atom (C) combines with a molecule of oxygen (O_2) to produce CO_2. The development of agriculture, the conversion of dense forest to comparatively sparsely vegetated farms, has moved carbon atoms from plants on the ground to carbon dioxide in the air. About half of this new CO_2 is removed by plants or by the layering down of carbonates in the oceans. On human time-scales, these changes are irreversible: Once the CO_2 is in the atmosphere, human technology is helpless to remove it. So the overall amount of CO_2 in the air has been growing— at least since the industrial revolution. If no other factors operate, and if enough CO_2 is put into the atmosphere, eventually the average surface temperature will increase perceptibly.

There are other greenhouse gases that are increasingly 14 abundant in the Earth's atmosphere—halocarbons, such as the freon used in refrigerator cooling systems; or nitrous oxide (N_2O), produced by automobile exhausts and nitrogenous fertilizers; or methane (CH_4), produced partly in the intestines of cows and other ruminants.

But let's for the moment concentrate on carbon diox- 15 ide: How long, at the present rates of burning wood and fossil fuels, before the global climate becomes significantly warmer? And what would the consequences be?

It is relatively simple to calculate the immediate warm- 16 ing from a given increase in the CO_2 abundance, and all competent calculations seem to be in good agreement. More difficult to estimate are (1) the rate at which carbon dioxide will continue to be put into the atmosphere (it depends on population growth rates, economic styles, alternative energy sources and the like) and (2) feed-backs—ways in which a slight warming might produce other, more drastic, effects.

The recent increase in atmospheric CO_2 is well docu- 17 mented. Over the last century, this CO_2 buildup should have resulted in a few tenths of a degree of global warming, and there is some evidence that such a warming has occurred.

The National Academy of Sciences estimates that the 18 present atmospheric abundance of CO_2 is likely to double by the year 2065, although experts at the academy predict a one-in-20 chance that it will double before 2035—when an infant born today becomes 50 years old. Such a doubling would warm the air near the surface of the Earth by 2°C or 3°C—maybe by as much as 4°C. These are average temperature values; there would naturally be considerable local variation. High latitudes would be warmed much more, although a baked Alaska will be some time coming.

There would be precipitation changes. The annual 19 discharge of rivers would be altered. Some scientists believe that central North America—including much of the area that is now the breadbasket of the world—would be parched in summer if the global temperature increases by a few degrees. There would be some mitigating effects; for example, where plant growth is not otherwise limited, more CO_2 should aid photosynthesis and make more luxuriant growth (of weeds as well as crops). If the present CO_2 injection into the atmosphere continued over a few centuries, the warming would be greater than from all other causes over the last 100,000 years.

As the climate warms, glacial ice melts. Over the last 20 100 years, the level of the world's oceans has risen by 15 centimeters (6 inches). A global warming of 3°C or 4°C over the next century is likely to bring a further rise in the average sea level of about 70 centimeters (28 inches). An increase of this magnitude could produce major damage to ports all over the world and induce fundamental changes in the patterns of land development. A serious speculation is that greenhouse temperature increases of 3°C or 4°C could, in addition, trigger the disintegration of the West Antarctic Ice Sheet, with huge quantities of polar ice falling into the ocean. This would raise sea level by some 6 meters (20 feet) over a period of centuries, with the eventual inundation of all coastal cities on the planet.

There are many other possibilities that are poorly 21 understood, including the release of other greenhouse gases (for example, methane from peat bogs) accelerated by the warming climate. The circulation of the oceans might be an important aspect of the problem. The scientific community is attempting to make an environmental-impact statement for the entire planet on the consequences of continued burning of fossil fuels. Despite the uncertainties, a kind of consensus is in: Over the next century or more, with projected rates of burning of coal, oil and gas, there is trouble ahead.

The problem is difficult for at least three different 22 reasons:

(1) We do not yet fully understand how severe the 23 greenhouse consequences will be.

(2) Although the effects are not yet strikingly notice- 24 able in everyday life, to deal with the problem, the present generation might have to make sacrifices for the next.

(3) The problem cannot be solved except on an inter- 25 national scale: The atmosphere is ignorant of national boundaries. South African carbon dioxide warms Taiwan, and Soviet coal-burning practices affect productivity in America. The largest coal resources in the world are found in the Soviet Union, the United States and China, in that order. What incentives are there for a nation such as China, with vast coal reserves and a commitment to rapid economic development, to hold back on the burning of fossil fuels because the result might, decades later, be a parched American sunbelt or still more ghastly starvation in sub-Saharan Africa? Would countries that might benefit from a warmer climate be as vigorous in restraining the burning of fossil fuels as nations likely to suffer greatly?

Fortunately, we have a little time. A great deal can be 26 done in decades. Some argue that government subsidies lower the price of fossil fuels, inviting waste; more efficient usage, besides its economic advantage, could greatly ameliorate the CO_2 greenhouse problem. Parts of the solution might involve alternative energy sources, where appropriate: solar power, for example, or safer nuclear fission reactors, which, whatever their other dangers, produce no greenhouse gases of importance. Conceivably, the long-awaited advent of commercial nuclear fusion power might happen before the middle of the next century.

However, any technological solution to the looming 27 greenhouse problem must be worldwide. It would not be sufficient for the United States or the Soviet Union, say, to develop safe and commercially feasible fusion power plants: That technology would have to be diffused worldwide, on terms of cost and reliability that would be more attractive to developing nations than a reliance on fossil fuel reserves or imports. A serious, very high-level look at patterns of U.S. and world energy development in light of the greenhouse problem seems overdue.

During the last few million years, human technology, 28 spurred in part by climatic change, has made our species a force to be reckoned with on a planetary scale. We now find, to our astonishment, that we pose a danger to ourselves. The present world order is, unfortunately, not designed to deal with global-scale dangers. Nations tend to be concerned about themselves, not about the planet; they tend to have short-term rather than long-term objectives. In problems such as the increasing greenhouse effect, one nation or region might benefit while another suffers. In other global environmental issues, such as nuclear war, all nations lose. The problems are connected: Constructive international efforts to understand and resolve one will benefit the others.

Further study and better public understanding are 29 needed, of course. But what is essential is a global consciousness—a view that transcends our exclusive identification with the generational and political groupings into which, by accident, we have been born. The solution to these problems requires a perspective that embraces the planet and the future. We are all in this greenhouse together.

QUESTIONS ON MEANING

1. Why is the popular name, "greenhouse effect," not literally accurate?

2. How, according to Sagan, does the warming of our planet actually occur?

3. What are Sagan's solutions? What changes in technology and lifestyle might slow down global warming? What changes in international politics need to occur?

QUESTIONS ON PURPOSE AND STRATEGY

1. Is Sagan's purpose to explain the causes and effects of greenhouse warming? To show how serious the problem can become? To propose workable solutions to the problem of global warming?

2. How many paragraphs does Sagan devote to explaining *causes* of the greenhouse effect? How many paragraphs focus on the possible *effects* of global warming? How many paragraphs does Sagan give to his *solutions*? Based on your findings, is Sagan more interested in explaining the problem or in detailing his solution?

3. Describe Sagan's *voice* and *tone*. What personality does he project through his essay? What is his attitude toward his subject? Is he angry, concerned, or apathetic? Is he excited and emotional or calm and reasonable? What effect does his use of "we" in the opening and closing paragraphs have on the reader?

QUESTIONS ON AUDIENCE AND LANGUAGE

1. Describe Sagan's intended audience. Sagan's essay originally appeared in *Parade* magazine. Would you read this essay if you saw it printed there? Could a ninth grader in a science class understand this essay?

2. Sagan uses scientific language throughout his article. Is Sagan correct in assuming that you know the meanings of his scientific terms? To understand his article, which of the following words should you check in your dictionary: *Celsius, epoch, glaciation, wavelength, radiation, infrared, spectrum, oxygen, nitrogen, opaque, carbon dioxide, nitrous oxide, microns, halocarbons, photosynthesis,* or *carbonates*?

QUESTIONS FOR DISCUSSION AND WRITING

1. Sagan's essay was written in 1985. What information or ideas in this essay might be revised, based on more recent findings? Which of Sagan's solutions are currently being applied, either locally or worldwide?

2. Write an essay describing the problems caused by carbon dioxide emissions in your community. What local programs promise to reduce greenhouse gasses? How effective are these efforts? What else needs to be done?

3. Global warming is just one of the harmful effects of progress. What are other negative effects of technological progress? Focus on *one* such effect (chemical or radioactive wastes, diaper disposal, automobile tire dumps, insecticide spraying, oil spills, landfill shortages, or traffic gridlock) that you notice around you. Describe the problem and offer your solution(s).

Even the Bad Guys Wear White Hats

EDWARD ABBEY

(1927–1989)

PREREADING JOURNAL ENTRY

Based on your impressions from the news, television, or the movies, what do you imagine life on a farm or cattle ranch would be like? If you have any experience with farming or cattle ranching, how is the reality different from the media's version?

Most Americans first met Edward Abbey dressed as an Arches National Park Ranger in Desert Solitaire *(1968). In that collection of essays, Abbey alternately celebrates the Utah canyonlands and attacks the industrial tourists who arrive like hoards of locusts in their cars and Winnebagos. Although his subject is usually nature, his agenda is always aggressively political: Abbey likes nothing better than kicking the shins of road-builders, dam-builders, strip-miners, or public-lands abusers.*

Born in Pennsylvania, Abbey was educated at the University of New Mexico and lived in the West as a park ranger, lecturer, and writer. His publications include The Monkey Wrench Gang *(1975),* Abbey's Road *(1979),* Down the River *(1982), and a selections from his works in* Slumgullion Stew *(1984).*

In "Even the Bad Guys Wear White Hats," Abbey argues that Western ranchers who graze their cattle on public lands are subsidized by the government while their cows overgraze and destroy the land. Although Abbey playfully suggests that we should solve the problem by opening a hunting season on range cattle, by repopulating federal lands with elk, buffalo, antelope, wolves, and eagles, and by stocking desert water holes with alligators, his real solution is simply to get cows off our public lands.

In the process of recommending his solution, Abbey takes potshots at the "sacred" American myth of the cowboy.

When I first came West in 1948, a student at the 1 University of New Mexico, I was only twenty years old and just out of the Army. I thought, like most simple-minded Easterners, that a cowboy was a kind of mythic hero. I idolized those scrawny little red-nosed hired hands in their tight jeans, funny boots, and comical hats.

Like other new arrivals in the West, I could imagine 2 nothing more romantic than becoming a cowboy. Nothing more glorious than owning my own little genuine working cattle outfit. About the only thing better, I thought, was to be a big league baseball player. I never dreamed that I'd eventually sink to writing books for a living. Unluckily for me—coming from an Appalachian hillbilly background and with a poor choice of parents—I didn't have much money. My father was a small-time logger. He ran a one-man sawmill and a submarginal side-hill farm. There wasn't any money in our family, no inheritance you could run 10,000 cattle on. I had no trust fund to back me up. No Hollywood movie deals to finance a land acquisition program. I lived on what in those days was called the G.I. Bill, which paid about $150 a month while I went to school. I made that last as long as I could—five or six years. I couldn't afford a horse. The best I could do in 1947 and '48 was buy a thirdhand Chevy sedan and roam the West, mostly the Southwest, on holidays and weekends.

I had a roommate at the University of New Mexico. 3 I'll just call him Mac. I don't want him to come looking for me. Mac came from a little town in southwest New Mexico where his father ran a feed store. Mackie was a fair bronc rider, eager to get into the cattle-growing business. And he had some money, enough to buy a little cinder-block house and about forty acres in the Sandia Mountains east of Albuquerque, near a town we called Landfill. Mackie fenced those forty acres, built a corral, and kept a few horses there, including an occasional genuine bronco for fun and practice.

I don't remember exactly how Mackie and I became 4 friends in the first place. I was majoring in classical philosophy. He was majoring in screwworm management. But we got to know each other through the mutual pursuit of a pair of nearly inseparable Kappa Kappa Gamma girls. I lived with him in his little cinder-block house. Helped him meet the mortgage payments. Helped him meet the girls. We were both crude, shy, ugly, obnoxious—like most college boys.

My friend Mac also owned a 1947 black Lincoln 5 convertible, the kind with the big grille in front, like a cowcatcher on a locomotive, chrome plated. We used to race to classes in the morning, driving the twenty miles from his house to the campus in never more than fifteen minutes. Usually Mac was too hung over to drive, so I'd operate the car, clutching the wheel while Mac sat beside me waving his big .44, taking potshots at jackrabbits and road signs and billboards and beer bottles. Trying to wake up in time for his ten o'clock class in brand inspection.

I'm sorry to say that my friend Mac was a little bit 6 gun-happy. Most of his forty acres was in tumbleweed. He fenced in about half an acre with chicken wire and stocked that little pasture with white rabbits. He used it as a target range. Not what you'd call sporting, I suppose, but we did eat the rabbits. Sometimes we even went deer hunting with handguns. Mackie with his revolver, and me with a chrome-plated Colt .45 automatic I had liberated from the U.S. Army over in Italy. Surplus government property.

On one of our deer hunting expeditions, I was sitting 7 on a log in a big clearing in the woods, thinking about Plato and Aristotle and the Kappa Kappa Gamma girls. I didn't really care whether we got a deer that day or not. It was a couple of days before opening, anyway. The whole procedure was probably illegal as hell. Mac was out in the woods somewhere looking for deer around the clearing. I was sitting on the log, thinking, when I saw a chip of bark fly away from the log all by itself, about a foot from my left hand. Then I heard the blast of Mac's revolver—that big old .44 he'd probably liberated from his father. Then I heard him laugh.

"That's not very funny, Mackie," I said.   8

"Now, don't whine and complain, Ed," he said. "You 9 want to be a real hunter like me, you gotta learn to stay awake."

We never did get a deer with handguns. But that's 10 when I had my first little doubts about Mackie, and about the cowboy type in general. But I still loved him. Worshiped him, in fact. I was caught in the grip of the Western myth. Anybody said a word to me against cowboys, I'd jump down his throat with my spurs on. Especially if Mac was standing nearby.

Sometimes I'd try to ride those broncs that he brought 11 in, trying to prove that I could be a cowboy too. Trying to prove it more to myself than to him. I'd be on this crazy, crackpot horse, going up, down, left, right, and inside out. Hanging on to the saddle horn with both hands. And Mac would sit on the corral fence, throwing beer bottles at us and laughing. Every time I got thrown off, Mac would say, "Now get right back on there, Ed. Quick, quick. Don't spoil 'im."

It took me a long time to realize I didn't have to do 12 that kind of work. And it took me another thirty years to realize that there's something wrong at the heart of our most popular American myth—the cowboy and his cow.

You may have guessed by now that I'm thinking of 13 criticizing the livestock industry. And you are correct. I've been thinking about cows and sheep for many years. Getting more and more disgusted with the whole business. There are some Western cattlemen who are nothing more than welfare parasites. They've been getting a free ride on the public lands for over a century, and I think it's time we phased it out. I'm in favor of putting the public lands livestock grazers out of business.

First of all, we don't need the public lands beef 14 industry. Even beef lovers don't need it. According to most government reports (Bureau of Land Management, Forest Service), only about 2 percent of our beef, our red

meat, comes from the eleven Western states. By those
eleven I mean Montana, Nevada, Utah, Colorado, New
Mexico, Arizona, Idaho, Wyoming, Oregon, Washington,
and California. Most of our beef, aside from imports,
comes from the Midwest and the East, especially the
Southeast—Georgia, Alabama, Florida—and from other
private lands across the nation. More than twice as many
beef cattle are raised in the state of Georgia than in the
sagebrush empire of Nevada. And for a very good reason:
back East, you can support a cow on maybe half an acre.
Out here, it takes anywhere from twenty-five to fifty acres.
In the red rock country of Utah, the rule of thumb is one
section—a square mile—per cow.

Since such a small percentage of the cows are produced 15
on public lands in the West, eliminating that industry
should not raise supermarket beef prices very much.
Furthermore, we'd save money in the taxes we now pay
for various subsidies to these public lands cattlemen.
Subsidies for things like "range improvement"—tree
chaining, sagebrush clearing, mesquite poisoning, disease
control, predator trapping, fencing, wells, stock ponds,
roads. Then there are the salaries of those who work for
government agencies like the BLM and the Forest Service.
You could probably also count in a big part of the salaries
of the overpaid professors engaged in range-management
research at the Western land-grant colleges.

Moreover, the cattle have done, and are doing, intol- 16
erable damage to our public lands—our national forests,
state lands, BLM-administered lands, wildlife preserves,
even some of our national parks and monuments. In
Utah's Capital Reef National Park, for example, grazing
is still allowed. In fact, it's recently been extended for
another ten years, and Utah politicians are trying to make
the arrangement permanent. They probably won't get
away with it. But there we have at least one case where
cattle are still tramping about in a national park, trans-
forming soil and grass into dust and weeds.

Overgrazing is much too weak a term. Most of the 17
public lands in the West, and especially in the Southwest,

are what you might call "cowburnt." Almost anywhere and everywhere you go in the American West you find hordes of these ugly, clumsy, stupid, bawling, stinking, fly-covered, disease-spreading brutes. They are a pest and a plague. They pollute our springs and streams and rivers. They infest our canyons, valleys, meadows, and forests. They graze off the native bluestem and grama and bunch grasses, leaving behind jungles of prickly pear. They trample down the native forbs and shrubs and cactus. They spread the exotic cheat grass, the Russian thistle, and the crested wheat grass. *Weeds.*

Even when the cattle are not physically present, you'll 18 see the dung and the flies and the mud and the dust and the general destruction. If you don't see it, you'll smell it. The whole American West stinks of cattle. Along every flowing stream, around every seep and spring and water hole and well, you'll find acres and acres of what range-management specialists call "sacrifice areas"—another understatement. These are places denuded of forage, except for some cactus or a little tumbleweed or maybe a few mutilated trees like mesquite, juniper, or hackberry.

I'm not going to bombard you with graphs and statis- 19 tics, which don't make much of an impression on intelligent people anyway. Anyone who goes beyond the city limits of almost any Western town can see for himself that the land is overgrazed. There are too many cows and horses and sheep out there. Of course, cattlemen would never publicly confess to overgrazing, any more than Dracula would publicly confess to a fondness for blood. Cattlemen are interested parties. Many of them will not give reliable testimony. Some have too much at stake: their Cadillacs and their airplanes, their ranch resale profits and their capital gains. (I'm talking about the corporation ranchers, the land-and-cattle companies, the investment syndicates.) Others, those ranchers who have only a small base property, flood the public lands with their cows. About 8 percent of the federal land permittees have cattle that consume approximately 45 percent of the forage on the government rangelands.

Beef ranchers like to claim that their cows do not 20 compete with deer. Deer are browsers, cows are grazers. That's true. But when a range is overgrazed, when the grass is gone (as it often is for seasons at a time), then cattle become browsers too, out of necessity. In the Southwest, cattle commonly feed on mesquite, cliff rose, cactus, acacia, or any other shrub or tree they find biodegradable. To that extent, they compete with deer. And they tend to drive out other and better wildlife. Like elk, or bighorn sheep, or pronghorn antelope.

How much damage have cattle done to the Western 21 rangelands? Large-scale beef ranching has been going on since the 1870s. There's plenty of documentation of the effects of this massive cattle grazing on the erosion of the land, the character of the land, the character of the vegetation. Streams and rivers that used to flow on the surface all year round are now intermittent, or underground, because of overgrazing and rapid runoff.

Our public lands have been overgrazed for a century. 22 The BLM knows it; the Forest Service knows it. The Government Accounting Office knows it. And overgrazing means eventual ruin, just like strip mining or clear-cutting or the damming of rivers. Much of the Southwest already looks like Mexico or southern Italy or North Africa: a cow-burnt wasteland. As we destroy our land, we destroy our agricultural economy and the basis of modern society. If we keep it up, we'll gradually degrade American life to the status of life in places like Mexico or southern Italy or Libya or Egypt.

In 1984 the Bureau of Land Management, which was 23 required by Congress to report on its stewardship of our rangelands—the property of all Americans, remember— confessed that 31 percent of the land it administered was in "good condition," 42 percent in "fair condition," and 18 percent in "poor condition." And it reported that only 18 percent of the rangelands were improving, while 68 percent were "stable" and 14 percent were getting worse. If the BLM said that, we can safely assume that range conditions are actually much worse.

What can we do about this situation? This is the fun 24
part—this is the part I like. It's not too easy to argue that
we should do away with cattle ranching. The cowboy myth
gets in the way. But I do have some solutions to overgrazing.

I'd begin by reducing the number of cattle on public 25
lands. Not that range managers would go along with it,
of course. In their eyes, and in the eyes of the livestock
associations they work for, cutting down on the number
of cattle is the worst possible solution—an impossible
solution. So they propose all kinds of gimmicks. More
cross-fencing. More wells and ponds so that more land
can be exploited. These proposals are basically a maneuver
by the Forest Service and the BLM to appease their critics
without offending their real bosses in the beef industry.

I also suggest that we open a hunting season on range 26
cattle. I realize that beef cattle will not make very sporting
prey at first. Like all domesticated animals (including most
humans), beef cattle are slow, stupid, and awkward. But
the breed will improve if hunted regularly. And as the
number of cattle is reduced, other and far more useful,
beautiful, and interesting animals will return to the rangelands and will increase.

Suppose, by some miracle of Hollywood or inheritance 27
or good luck, I should acquire a respectable-sized working
cattle outfit. What would I do with it? First, I'd get rid of
the stinking, filthy cattle. Every single animal. Shoot them
all, and stock the place with real animals, real game, real
protein: elk, buffalo, pronghorn antelope, bighorn sheep,
moose. And some purely decorative animals, like eagles.
We need more eagles. And wolves. We need more wolves.
Mountain lions and bears. Especially, of course, grizzly
bears. Down in the desert, I would stock every water tank,
every water hole, every stock pond, with alligators.

You may note that I have said little about coyotes or 28
deer. Coyotes seem to be doing all right on their own.
They're smarter than their enemies. I've never heard of
a coyote as dumb as a sheepman. As for deer, especially
mule deer, they, too, are surviving—maybe even thriving,

as some game and fish departments claim, though nobody claims there are as many deer now as there were before the cattle industry was introduced in the West. In any case, compared to elk the deer is a second-rate game animal, nothing but a giant rodent—a rat with antlers.

I've suggested that the beef industry's abuse of our 29 Western lands is based on the old mythology of the cowboy as natural nobleman. I'd like to conclude this diatribe with a few remarks about this most cherished and fanciful of American fairy tales. In truth, the cowboy is only a hired hand. A farm boy in leather britches and a comical hat. A herdsman who gets on a horse to do part of his work. Some ranchers are also cowboys, but many are not. There is a difference. There are many ranchers out there who are bigtime farmers of the public lands—our property. As such, they do not merit any special consideration or special privileges. There are only about 31,000 ranchers in the whole American West who use the public lands. That's less than the population of Missoula, Montana.

The rancher (with a few honorable exceptions) is a 30 man who strings barbed wire all over the range; drills wells and bulldozes stock ponds; drives off elk and antelope and bighorn sheep; poisons coyotes and prairie dogs; shoots eagles, bears, and cougars on sight; supplants the native grasses with tumbleweed, snakeweed, povertyweed, anthills, mud, dust, and flies. And then leans back and grins at the TV cameras and talks about how much he loves the American West. Cowboys are also greatly overrated. Consider the nature of their work. Suppose you had to spend most of your working hours sitting on a horse, contemplating the hind end of a cow. How would that affect your imagination? . . .

Do cowboys work hard? Sometimes. But most ranchers 31 don't work very hard. They have a lot of leisure time for politics and bellyaching. Anytime you go into a small Western town you'll find them at the nearest drugstore, sitting around all morning drinking coffee, talking about their tax breaks.

Is a cowboy's work socially useful? No. As I've already 32

pointed out, subsidized Western range beef is a trivial item in the national beef economy. If all of our 31,000 Western public land ranchers quit tomorrow, we'd never miss them. Any public school teacher does harder work, more difficult work, more dangerous work, and far more valuable work than any cowboy or rancher. The same thing applies to registered nurses and nurses' aides, garbage collectors, and traffic cops. Harder work, tougher work, more necessary work. We need those people in our complicated society. We do not need cowboys or ranchers. We've carried them on our backs long enough.

"This Abbey," the cowboys and their lovers will say, 33 "this Abbey is a wimp. A chicken-hearted sentimentalist with no feel for the hard realities of practical life." Especially critical of my attitude will be the Easterners and Midwesterners newly arrived here from their Upper West Side apartments, their rustic lodges in upper Michigan. Our nouveau Westerners with their toy ranches, their pickup trucks with the gun racks, their pointy-toed boots with the undershot heels, their gigantic hats. And, of course, their pet horses. The *instant rednecks*.

To those who might accuse me of wimpery and sen- 34 timentality, I'd like to say this in reply. I respect real men. I admire true manliness. But I despise arrogance and brutality and bullies. So let me close with some nice remarks about cowboys and cattle ranchers. They are a mixed lot, like the rest of us. As individuals, they range from the bad to the ordinary to the good. A rancher, after all, is only a farmer, cropping the public rangelands with his four-legged lawnmowers, stashing our grass into his bank account. A cowboy is a hired hand trying to make an honest living. Nothing special.

I have no quarrel with these people as fellow humans. 35 All I want to do is get their cows off our property. Let those cowboys and ranchers find some harder way to make a living, like the rest of us have to do. There's no good reason why we should subsidize them forever. They've had their free ride. It's time they learned to support themselves.

In the meantime, I'm going to say goodbye to all you 36 cowboys and cowgirls. I love the legend, too—but keep your sacred cows and your dead horses off of my elk pastures.

QUESTIONS ON MEANING

1. In your own words, state the problem that Abbey addresses. Then state Abbey's solution. What parts of both the problem and the solution involve *actions*? What parts of the problem and solution involve people's *attitudes*?

2. What *reasons* or arguments does Abbey cite for removing cattle from public lands?

QUESTIONS ON PURPOSE AND STRATEGY

1. Early in his essay, Abbey reasonably proposes his solution to a problem ("I'm in favor of putting the public lands livestock grazers out of business"). Later on, he says his essay is a "diatribe" (a bitter or abusive denunciation). Is his purpose to propose a workable solution to a real problem, to stir up everyone's emotions, or to achieve some other goal?

2. Abbey spends over two pages narrating personal experiences. If he cut out this introduction and began immediately with his proposal, what would the essay lose?

3. Although Abbey says he is not going to "bombard you with graphs and statistics, which don't make much of an impression on intelligent people anyway," he gives several sets of statistics in the following paragraphs. Did you find these statistics effective? Is his strategy for introducing them effective? Explain.

QUESTIONS ON AUDIENCE AND LANGUAGE

1. Abbey delivered an original version of this speech at the University of Montana. Where does Abbey appeal to this audience? Where does he deliberately provoke them? Con-

sidering Abbey's purpose, is his "appeal" to his audience effective?

2. Describe Abbey's voice—the personality he reveals through his language. Some readers have called him reasonable and sensible, while others find him outlandish, passionate, absurd, and cantankerous. Find at least five examples of sentences that illustrate Abbey's voice or voices.

3. Abbey is noted for his colorful language. He describes overgrazed pastures as a "cow-burnt wasteland." He calls a deer a "rat with antlers." He describes himself and Mac as "crude, shy, ugly, obnoxious—like most college boys." Find three other examples of Abbey's colorful language. Does this language make his essay—and his proposal—more effective?

QUESTIONS FOR DISCUSSION AND WRITING

1. Describe Abbey's attitude toward the cowboy myth. Is he attracted to it? Is he irritated by it? Abbey says that the "beef industry's abuse of our Western lands is based on the old mythology of the cowboy as natural nobleman." Explain what Abbey means by this statement.

2. Assume that you are the editor of *Reader's Digest*. Your task is to edit Abbey's essay for your middle-class family audience. What words, sentences, or paragraphs would you cut for your abridged version? Explain your choices.

3. Write an essay on some form of government subsidy that should (or should not) be eliminated: oil research and drilling on public lands, government subsidies for school lunch programs, mining or logging practices in national or state forests, or government-subsidized student loans. What is the problem? What solution do you recommend? Who is your intended audience?

Where Will Kids Go Tomorrow?

KIMBERLY COX

(1971–   )

PREREADING JOURNAL ENTRY

Call your parents and interview them about the child care arrangements they made in your family. If one of your parents was able to stay home full time, how did their friends manage child care? Do they think that employers should offer child care for their employees? Write down their answers.

Kimberly Cox is a math education major at the University of Central Florida. According to her instructor, Catherine Schutz, Cox wrote her essay following class discussions of social problems that people will face in the 1990s. Although the class focused on the justice system and animal experimentation, Cox says she chose to write about child daycare "because more and more children spend their after-school hours at a daycare center. I think it's important for those hours to be spent wisely, and mothers should know the options they have to choose from." In her essay, Cox investigates child-care systems currently available in the United States, discusses current problems, and then describes two solutions: increased subsidies for child-care systems and federally mandated support by employers.

The day is Wednesday, and the time is 7:45 A.M. Mrs. 1 Johnson drops off her two young children at the local day-care center for the hundredth time. From the day-care center, they will be transported to their elementary school, and then after school they will be picked up again and returned to the day-care center. Mrs. Johnson will pick them up at approximately 6:00 P.M. after work. What will happen to Mrs. Johnson and her children if she can no longer afford to keep them there before and after school? Where will her children stay for six hours by themselves? This problem has affected many working mothers, especially in the last few years. What can be done to help working mothers and their children? Although the day-care system may seem to be working, the problem is actually getting worse because of the high day-care center fees and the lack of government support.

According to Janet Swenson in *Alternatives in Quality* 2 *Child Care,* the three types of child-care systems are the family day-care home, the group day-care home, and the day-care center (9). All three have common characteristics such as insurance premiums, building ordinances, and fees. But each one of these systems is different. In the family day-care home, a mother takes care of as many children as she can accommodate in her home. Before being allowed to stay in such a home, the children must have a physical examination and all of their required shots. A disadvantage of the family day-care home occurs when the children run out of activities to keep them occupied. Many times television is the only available "toy" for the children since there is a limited number of games (Swenson 10).

The group day-care home is much like the family day- 3 care home. The difference is that the mother hires helpers to give the children more individual attention, and the house may have extra rooms added to give more space. The day-care home is ideal for children who need before- and after-school care, but who do not require much individual mothering. Even so, this system lacks in individual loving attention and exciting and stimulating activities for the children (Swenson 10).

The day-care center is the most popular situation. The 4 center can serve twelve or more children and it offers good facilities and a staff that is usually trained in the area of child care. Many day-care centers can also handle infants if the care the infant will receive is much like that of a mother. There are also many activities besides television for the children such as a playground, books, movies, and time for "show and tell." The amount of individual attention is greater in a day-care center because there are many people working to keep the children occupied.

The obvious problem, however, is that each of these 5 types of day-care systems requires money. Michelle Seligson explains in her book, *School-Age Child Care: A Policy Report,* that a child is the fourth largest expense for parents behind shelter, food, and taxes, and usually parents cannot afford to pay more than 10 percent of their total income on their children. This means that sources must be found to help fund agencies and institutions that care for children, and that each individual program must minimize its expenses so that the care can be affordable (30). Because of government spending cuts on day-care institutions, the child-care programs are being forced to go to another area of government funding to get money. This is making it harder to serve low-income families where the financial burden is greatest.

The government, in turn, seems very unwilling to 6 cooperate with parents. In "Child Care: All Talk, No Action," Peggy Simpson described two bills that were voted down in December of 1988. These bills, valued at $2.5 billion, and known as the Act for Better Child Care and the Medical Leave Act, would have enabled parents to get child care easier and would have required "employers to offer ten weeks of unpaid leave for parents of newborn, newly adopted, or seriously ill children" (81). These bills will be reintroduced at the end of 1989, and if needed, will be introduced again in 1990. Before the 1988 elections, Bob Dole was quoted as saying, "I do hope we can move on to matters of importance and stop playing games with this parental leave and child care bill" (Simpson 82). But hopes do not pay bills.

On a more positive note, businesses are starting to 7

realize the importance of child care, and the significance of allowing substantial time off for maternity leave. Many employers are starting to offer day-care services through their companies and are more lenient with problems such as doctor appointments and sick leaves. If the government would realize the importance of quality child care and time off after giving birth or adopting a newborn baby, and act on these realizations, then the problem could be eliminated.

But for now, Mrs. Johnson will continue taking her 8 children to the nearby day-care center, and hoping that she will be able to afford the fees. Whether or not Mrs. Johnson will be able to afford even the most basic day care remains to be seen. What is certain is that without the organized support from politicians such as Mr. Dole, Mrs. Johnson's children are unlikely to receive the care they deserve during the six hours their mother is working. If that turns out to be the case, then many of our children will be forced to turn from day-care centers to a life on the streets.

Works Cited

Seligson, Michelle. *School-Age Child Care: A Policy Report.* Wellesley, Massachusetts: School-Age Child Care Project, 1983.

Simpson, Peggy. "Child Care: All Talk, No Action." *Ms.* December 1988: 81–82.

Swenson, Janet P. *Alternatives in Quality Child Care.* Washington, D.C.: Day Care and Child Care Development Council of America, 1972.

QUESTIONS ON MEANING

1. What problems in child-care systems does Cox describe?
2. What solutions does Cox recommend?

QUESTIONS ON PURPOSE AND STRATEGY

1. Describe Cox's purpose(s) in her essay. Is her information on types of available child care relevant to her purpose?
2. Cox reserves her specific example (about Mrs. Johnson) for

the introduction and conclusion. In what paragraphs might she add other specific examples? Which of the following specific examples might be most effective: an example of a specific child's activity schedule in a day-care center; an example of a parent who is coping without child-care support; or an example of a local business that provides child care?

QUESTIONS ON AUDIENCE AND LANGUAGE

1. Describe Cox's intended audience.

2. Describe Cox's voice in her essay. Is she personal and involved? Is she distant or detached from her subject? Should she modify her voice to better achieve her purpose for her readers?

3. In the rough draft version, Cox originally introduced the quotation by Bob Dole as follows: "To show the ignorance of politicians on the issue of child care is this ridiculous statement that Bob Dole was quoted as saying before the 1988 elections. . . ." Next to this statement, one editor wrote, "This is you thinking; keep this out of final draft." Why did the editor write this comment? Did Cox improve this sentence in her final version?

QUESTIONS FOR DISCUSSION AND WRITING

1. Brainstorm solutions to the child-care system that Cox does *not* discuss. Which solutions don't require congressional legislation? What can individuals or local agencies do?

2. What child-care legislation has passed Congress since Cox wrote her essay? What companies currently have model child-care programs?

3. In small groups, discuss how your parents' full-time jobs did or did not negatively affect your childhood. If both parents worked, how did you spend your time before and after school? Do you wish one parent had been home full time? If one of your parents was at home, did you still feel

neglected? Imagine that you were six years old again. What advice would you give your parents?

4. Reread your Prereading Journal Entry. Look in your college directory and local phone book for child-care information. What services does your school provide to college students with children? What information about child-care programs is available locally? Have child-care opportunities improved or worsened since your parents coped with this problem?

Freshman Roommate Fiasco

GEORGE ABATE
(1971–   )

PREREADING JOURNAL ENTRY

If you have a roommate, describe the problems you have.
What does your roommate do that drives you crazy? What
do *you* do that irritates your roommate? What changes
might help reduce the tensions?

*A journalism major at Ohio University, George Abate was a student
in Jennifer Beard's composition class. "Although I told the students,"
Beard explains, "that they could do research and write about more global
problems, I emphasized that the key to success was personal involvement
with the topic." Abate follows this advice by writing about a problem
that is right in front of his nose: his roommate. Can an organized, orderly
type A neatnik, Abate asks, find happiness with a disorganized, hyperactive party animal? Abate first explains some of the causes behind the
typical nerve wracking personality conflicts, gives specific examples to
show his problem, and then leads the reader through the steps he and
his roommate Dave took to resolve their differences.*

Brainstorming and Planning Notes

<u>Roommate Problems</u>
Some obvious problems, especially for freshmen, are there are
so many cultural shocks and things to get used to → being
away from home for the first time → all the responsibilities
→ laundry, cafeteria food, on top of the fact of moving into
a new room.

Reasons for Problems with New Room
1. Not home → don't have space and luxuries
2. Quarters generally small
3. Have to cope with other people's habits, and work out agreements that fit each person's own traits and idiosyncracies → No two people are exactly alike. Ex. Some people are early morning risers while others are out till 1, 2 every night. ALSO likes of music, etc.

Solving Problems
1. Be patient, and understanding, and flexible
2. If the problem continues, contact an R.A. or R.D.
3. If the situation just won't work out, switch out of room.

Survey of People in Biddle
1. What was biggest problem : Roommate and room
                             Leaving home
                             Study habits
2. What kinds of roommate problems did you have : Organization
                             Sleeping
                             Music
                             Other
3. How did you solve these problems ? Friends
                             R.A. or D.A.
                             Other
4. What qualties do you think are most important in a roommate ?
5. How much time do you spend in your room ?

Rough Draft

When any person mentions freshman year
in college, many images are brought to
mind. But one of the most common is that of
those first few months when family and
friends are left behind for the first time.
With this, probably the word that captures
it all is "culture shock" from just the
newness of many responsibilities so long
taken for granted—laundry, cafeteria food,
totally new surroundings and a redefinition
of certain words: acceptance, security,
friendship, work, and fun. One of the major
problems almost all college students face
is adjusting to a roommate. These can be
some of the most nerve wracking experiences
for a number of reasons, and there are
simple solutions to these complex problems.

The "newness" of college is most
apparent in the struggling relationships of
the roommates. One of the major reasons why
it's so tough to cope is that the college
dorm really doesn't start out as "home."
The luxuries of space and not worrying
about the fact that the room is trashed,
are finished with the "close" cohabitation.
The dorm rooms are generally extremely
small, and one person shouldn't overrun
their bounds of space. Of course, tension
increases when a roommate has to climb over
the stinky clothes, old pizza boxes, shoes,
and books to get to his own "area." Most of
the tension and problems arise from the
fact that every person is extremely
different due to their backgrounds, needs,
and wants. Coping with an early morning
riser when one roommate has gone to bed
only a few hours before, or hard metal rock
when another is a fan of classical (rap,
etc.).

For the problems with roommates I will

gladly use my roommate and myself as an
example. My roommate Dave Marshall and I
live in Biddle Hall, a serious study dorm.
Dave and I have many similarities but we
have just as many differences. Our
differences were at their starkest one
early Sunday morning when we were working
on Dave's bed. Dave always said he hated
the loft because he'd conk his head on the
ceiling every time he'd wake up, because it
was so high up, and he was always
complaining about how hot he was up there.
Dave came in at 4:00 A.M. after partying
all night, slept for an hour and a half and
then zipped off on his motorcycle to get
supplies. At 9:00 he dashed into the room,
very hyper, and started to take out the
bolts. Now we sort of need to back up a
little here; I had been up for a half an
hour, with a number of things on my mind,
and when he dashed into the room he just
started right into his work. He didn't
clear any area around the bed, didn't move
stuff around so he'd have room to work,
nothing. I on the other hand am a very
meticulous person, who likes to think
through all the steps before beginning
working. This was not the way I wanted to
work, but as his roommate I felt obligated
to help. He didn't have all the equipment,
enough wrenches or bolts, so in a crazy
whirlwind, he left again on his motorcycle
after tearing down the bed and putting the
mattress in the middle of the room with
screws and tools hidden and lying
everywhere. I didn't know what to do. All
this really bothered me: how he was
working, the fact that I wasn't helping
him, and I also really worried about his
safety on this bitterly cold Sunday morning
knowing the hyper state of mind he was in.
Well, after pacing back and forth, I

decided to let Chip, our R.A. know what was going on, and ask about what should be done. At the time I talked to him, I woke him out of a sleep. He listened quietly to me, and then calmly and basically this in a few words. "Don't worry, you've done what you can to help. He is working out the problems his way. Relax now, you can offer to help but he has got to solve the problem and don't worry, just let him know that you worried and care about his safety." Well, I took his advice and Dave worked it out.

So how can the problems between roommates be solved? The first point to remember are patience and understanding. My worrying about the problems, or even confronting him and telling him he was doing the job "the wrong way" would not have helped. After I told Dave that I worried about him, he told me I shouldn't have and then we moved on to the next step: communication. He and I then talked about the best way to position the bed and dressers. This led to the final key to working out our disagreements: compromise. We both gave up some, in order to solve the problem of the bed. I followed Chip's suggestion and let Dave work it out on his own.

This set of solutions may seem far too simplistic, but from the feedback of some fellow dorm members and my R.A., patience, understanding, and compromise were the most common words. Now an astute reader may be saying, well what if this doesn't actually solve the problems, what should be done? The next step would be, with your roommate, to go and talk to the R.A. and try and talk out some of the problems. The last resort after talking to the Resident Director, if things still weren't working out, would be to switch out of the room.

The universal conflicts in roommate
relationships can be solved through
patience and compromise.

Final Draft

When the words "culture shock" are mentioned 1
what images come to mind? Probably some of the most
vivid pictures are of those first few months of the
freshman year in college: the disorientation after family and friends are left behind, and the "newness" of
the totally different surroundings. With the responsibilities of laundry, eating habits, and many minute
points taken for granted for so long, it's easy to feel
overwhelmed. Some of the most nerve wracking problems are concentrated in the universal struggles of
adjusting to a roommate. In Lee Upcraft's *The Freshman
Year Experience: Helping Students Survive and Succeed in
College,* the mundane conflict of roommates was raised
to a higher level when he stated "that roommates
challenge each other's confidence and self-understand-
ing, force each other to become more tolerant and
accepting, force each other to express themselves more
clearly, and affect each other's attitudes" (144). Most
roommates don't start out with these complex ideas in
mind when they come to college, however; they are
just interested in their own personal needs and wants.
Living in Biddle Hall, my roommate Dave Marshall
and I are prime examples of freshmen who have
roommate problems and the broad, but effective methods for resolving them.

Many of our struggles came from differences in 2
our lifestyles. One of the major reasons why problems
occur is that the college dorm really doesn't start out
as "home". Tension increased in our room from the
very beginning because I'd have to climb over stinky
clothes, old pizza boxes, shoes and books left behind
by Dave; in such close quarters this put a strain on
everything. In addition, I didn't even have a desk of

my own to work at: Dave's stereo system was on top of it, and he put the refrigerator where my chair to my desk was supposed to slide. Another problem we had was I'm an early morning riser and I would wake only a few hours after Dave had gone to bed.

Our differences came to a head early one Sunday 3 morning when we were working on Dave's bed. Dave's loft bed had his dresser and desk underneath it and was extremely high. He was always complaining about how hot he was up there and that he'd conk his head on the ceiling every time he'd wake up! This particular Sunday morning Dave decided he had had enough: he was taking the bed down. After partying all night Dave came in at 4:00 A.M., slept for an hour and a half, and then zipped off on his motorcycle to get supplies. At 9:00 he dashed into the room and instantly started to take out the bolts. I had been up for a half an hour with a number of things on my mind, and feeling obligated as his roommate I offered to help him. I am a very meticulous person who likes to get everything totally organized before beginning. Well, when he said he'd be glad to have me help him, I, in a sleepy state, began thinking about how I'd work out the problem.

I said, "Come on Dave let's talk through the steps 4 we're going to take." This I thought would let him know first of all I didn't like how he was working and that if I was going to be a good helper I wanted and needed to know a general outline.

Dave ignored me. 5

He didn't clear any area around the bed so he'd 6 have room to work or even set up a place to put tools and bolts. After he tore down the bed and put the mattress in the middle of the room with screws and tools hidden and lying everywhere, I kept on nagging him to see if I could help. In response to my nagging he started bossing me around, making me contort and strain my body in the corner to lift and move the frame. The whole time the same thought ran angrily through my head, "This is not the way to work. I hate this."

With the whole room turned upside-down, Dave 7 realized he needed some more screws and a wrench. With eyes flashing he dashed out of the room to zoom off on his motorcycle with his destination some faraway store. A minute later he rushed back and asked me if I knew where his glasses and leather jacket were because it was such an abnormally cold morning. The jacket and glasses were of course hidden underneath a pair of shorts lying on his mattress, which had the bed frame and a number of bolts on it.

After he left, I just paced back and forth, wonder- 8 ing what to do with this mess and angry at the whole situation. So I figured, "Well, one thing I can do is sweep the floor." While sweeping, I felt an overwhelming feeling of guilt that I wasn't really helping him, and that I wasn't a good roommate. I started to worry about his safety because I realized he was in a very hyper, frantic mood. After nearly forty-five minutes, I began believing that he was wrapped around a tree somewhere, and I worried about who I'd call and what I'd do if he didn't show up.

In this state of mind I decided to let Chip, our 9 Resident Assistant, know what was going on. He listened quietly to me, and then calmly and basically said, "Don't worry, you've done what you can to help; Dave's working out the problems his way. Relax now. You can offer to help but he's got to solve the problem. Just let him know that you worried and care about his safety."

So how can the problems between roommates be 10 solved? How did Dave and I work this bed fiasco out? The first points to remember are patience and understanding. My worrying about the problems, or even confronting Dave and telling him he was doing the job "the wrong way," would not have helped. After I told Dave that I worried about him, he told me I shouldn't have, and then we moved onto the next step:

communication. He and I then talked about the best way to position the bed and dressers in the room. This included the final key to our working out our disagreements with the bed: compromise. I followed Chip's suggestion and let Dave work it out on his own, and he positioned the dresser and bed so it was suitable for both of us.

An astute reader may be saying, "Well, what if all 11 this doesn't solve the problem, what should be done?" The next step would be to iron out some of the major disagreements between the two roommates by talking with the R.A. If the tension and strife still aren't solved, the Resident Director could be contacted and a psychologist could even be employed to discuss ways of coping with the differences. Some roommates, no matter what they do, cannot be compatible with each other. The last resort then would be switching out of the room.

Even though patience, understanding, communi- 12 cation, and compromise may seem simplistic and abstract, these points were the key to resolving the problems between Dave and me. I now have my own desk, Dave no longer complains about the bed, and he is even beginning to take better care so his stuff doesn't clutter up the whole room. The system that we now use to cope with problems is stating our views and complaints, and then working out a solution that is agreeable to both of us. After talking to my fellow dorm members, some upper-class friends, and my R.A., these basic coping skills were reinforced even more. The main points that I found from listening to them were that disagreements can be worked out in the long run, and that differences in personality and lifestyle can be smoothed over so that the cramped dorm prison cell eventually becomes "home."

Works Cited

Upcraft, M. Lee, et al. *The Freshman Year Experience: Helping Students Survive and Succeed in College.* San Francisco: Jossey-Bass, 1989.

QUESTIONS ON MEANING

1. In your own words, state the major problem that George Abate and his roommate Dave Marshall faced.
2. What are the four steps in Abate's recommended solution?

QUESTIONS ON PURPOSE AND STRATEGY

1. Does Abate concentrate more on explaining the problem or describing the solution? Which part of his essay's purpose (demonstrating the problem or explaining the solution) does he more effectively achieve?
2. In his introduction, Abate uses a quotation from his source. Explain which other introductory or attention-getting strategies would also be effective: a personal example, an example from another pair of roommates in his hall, a statistic about the number of roommates who split after one semester, or a description of his expectations (before he arrived at school) about his roommate?

QUESTIONS ON AUDIENCE AND LANGUAGE

1. Describe Abate's intended audience. Where does his essay most effectively address this audience? Where is he least effective in appealing to this audience?
2. Choose one paragraph from Abate's rough draft and compare it with the same paragraph in the final draft. What changes in specific sentences did he make? What changes in word choice did he make? Explain why the revised version does or does not more effectively achieve his purpose for his intended audience.

QUESTIONS FOR DISCUSSION AND WRITING

1. Abate clearly *shows* the bed episode that led to the problems, but he only *tells* about the solution. Write an example that *shows,* using more specific and vivid detail, how the two roommates solved their problem.

2. The fourth step in Abate's solution is to "compromise." Did Abate just do what his roommate wanted? Did his roommate just do what Abate wanted? Did they actually compromise?

3. From the quotation Abate cites from Upcraft's book, choose *one* of the four ideas and then describe an experience with your roommate that shows how you "challenge each other's confidence," or "force each other to become more tolerant," or "force each other to express themselves more clearly," or "affect each other's attitudes."

9

ARGUING

Mere knowledge of the truth will not give you the art of persuasion.
— Plato, *Phaedrus*

The distinction between active and passive euthanasia is thought to be crucial for medical ethics. The idea is that it is permissible, at least in some cases, to withhold treatment and allow a patient to die, but it is never permissible to take any direct action designed to kill the patient. . . . However, a strong case can be made against this doctrine. In what follows I will set out some of the relevant arguments, and urge doctors to reconsider their views on this matter.
— James Rachels, "Active and Passive Euthanasia"

My friends, I must say to you that we have not made a single gain in civil rights without determined legal and nonviolent pressure. Lamentably, it is an historical fact that privileged groups seldom give up their privileges voluntarily.
— Martin Luther King, Jr., "Letter from Birmingham Jail"

We have all had arguments with friends, casual acquaintances, or even strangers about politics, sports, diets, classes, or music. We usually enjoy hearing their viewpoints and expressing our own beliefs. At the end of some discussions, however, we feel frustrated at our inability to convince others. Sometimes we wish we had been quick enough to think of a better response. And sometimes we realize that we simply don't know enough to argue the issue intelligently. Written argument, however, gives us a second chance to learn about the issue, to list the pro and con arguments, to think of good examples for our arguments, and to arrange our argument effectively for our audience.

Written argument is a formalized, written debate in which we play both sides, imagining the opposing arguments and then countering them with our best ideas and evidence. Role-playing is therefore essential for effective argumentative writing. We cannot merely assert our belief in the "truth" and expect to change our readers' minds. The art of persuasion requires imagining how the opposition will react to our position, and then tailoring our arguments and evidence specifically for our readers.

Like a formal debate, written argument has specific rules and regulations. Participants in this game play to win—to persuade their readers—but their argument must follow certain rules of "fair play." Writers must use appeals to logic to persuade their readers. Writers also use appeals to their own good character to bolster the argument. And finally, writers may use emotional appeals, but only if those appeals do not unfairly distort the issue.

Although written argument has clear rules, writers do not always know if they are "winning." Referees do not blow a whistle and shout: "Unsportsmanlike conduct! You have unfairly characterized the opposing argument," or "Illegal Procedure! You have no evidence to support your claim." In actual practice, every reader is a silent referee who, instead of blowing a whistle, simply remains unconvinced by a poor argument. When writers do represent the opposing positions and argue fairly, however, they can increase the chances of persuading their audience.

It is no secret that argument is the most important kind of writing practiced in colleges and universities. As the most public of all forms of writing, argument is a cornerstone of democracy. Our political, social, and individual freedoms depend on our ability to articulate multiple points of view, on our skill at arguing fairly for a position, and on our willingness to reach a consensus or compromise position. As you read the essays in this chapter, notice how the authors not only argue their positions but also invite you to participate in the ongoing public debate.

STRATEGIES FOR READING AND WRITING ABOUT ARGUING

As you read the argumentative essays in this chapter, look for the following arguing strategies.

Introduction that sets the context for the argument. Argumentative essays often begin with a description or an example that shows *who* is for this issue, *how* or *when* the argument developed, and *why* the whole controversy is important. An argumentative essay about unnecessary violence or injury in sports, for example, might begin with a single, memorable incident.

Statement of a debatable thesis or claim. Early in the essay, the writer states a *claim* usually involving a cause and effect, a statement of value, or a proposal to solve a problem. The claim must be debatable: Both sides of the argument must have some merit. If the writer argues that professional hockey is too violent, there must be a reasonable argument that says that some controlled violence is a legitimate part of the game.

Representation of the opposing arguments. Writers of argument describe the important opposing arguments fairly. Usually writers will represent and then attempt to refute the opposing arguments as they develop their own arguments.

Use of evidence to refute the opposition and support the claim. Mere assertions of belief or disagreement will not persuade readers. Effective arguments refute the opposing arguments and support the writer's claim with evidence: specific examples, detailed description, quotations from authorities, facts, or statistics.

Writing in a reasonable tone. Writers of argument treat their opponents—and their readers—with respect. They argue reasonably and avoid illogical statements or inflammatory language.

READING AN ARGUING ESSAY

Prereading

Before you read each essay, write out your position on that issue in the Prereading Journal Entry. Then read the headnote to determine the background and context for the controversy. Does the writer have some relevant experience with this issue? Does any of the biographical information—or the title of the essay—lead you to expect the writer to be either pro or con on this topic?

First Reading

First, analyze yourself as the audience for this topic. Are you sympathetic to the writer's stance? Are you indifferent or just uninformed? Do you disagree with the writer's claim? As you read, decide whether the writer is intending the essay for someone who agrees, is undecided, or disagrees. In the margin, place an "X" next to a statement you disagree with; place a "?" next to a passage that has questionable logic or support. Use an "!" for a striking passage or passage you agree with. Highlight or place a wavy line under key sentences. Underline any words you want to look up later. When you finish, write in your own words the writer's claim.

Annotated Reading

As you read the essay a second time, write your own reactions in the margin. What is the writer's best argument? The best piece of evidence? Where is the writer's argument weakest? What opposing argument is omitted? Reread the "Strategies for Reading and Writing about Arguing." Place brackets [] around passages that illustrate the main features of argumentative essays. In the margin, label at least one passage illustrating each feature, and outline the essay by noting the thesis and the major arguments against and for the writer's claim. Finally, note features of style: sentences or vocabulary that are effective, too simple, or too difficult. Where was the writing clear, and where was it difficult to track? Where was the language appropriate or inappropriate for the writer's intended audience?

Collaborative Reading

In class or in a small group, share your journal entries and annotations. What did your group or the class think about this essay before you read it? How many agreed, disagreed, or were uninformed or undecided? Did the article change any readers' minds? Share and then compile a jointly annotated version of the essay. At the end of the essay, write out the writer's claim or thesis. Finally, write one question about this essay for the class to discuss in more detail.

WRITING AN ARGUING ESSAY

Your first question should be, "How is an arguing essay different from the essays I have already written?"

First, you must write an essay that responds to opposing arguments. You should argue your side, the pro side, but you must counter or refute the arguments on the opposing or con side. That requires writing a claim that is debatable. **Your claim or thesis must have reasonable arguments on both sides.** "Although smoking cigarettes is still legal, our public health demands that we ban all smoking on the job."

Second, you may choose to argue a claim of fact, of cause and effect, of value, or of policy—or some combination. A **claim of fact** distinguishes between myths or false perceptions and the reality: "Although abusive men often think their actions are justified and abused women sometimes think they deserve punishment, both are in reality emotionally disturbed." A **claim of cause and effect** says that something has caused, is causing, or will cause a particular effect: "Although Americans support democracy around the world, our foreign policy in Nicaragua clearly influenced the outcome of their "free" election." A **claim of value** leads, obviously, to an evaluating essay that examines both sides of the argument: *Out of Africa* is a great film not because of its beautiful shots of Africa but because it portrays the spirit of an indomitable woman." A **claim of policy** leads to a problem-solving essay that examines both sides of the argument: "Although some Americans claim that seat belt laws infringe on their privacy, the safety of the public demands tougher, nationwide legislation." For each of these claims, you must present **both sides** of the issue.

Third, you will still collect evidence to support your claim, but pay attention to *how* this evidence will affect or appeal to your reader. Most of your evidence will support an **appeal to reason:** By giving facts, statistics, citations from authorities, quotations, examples, and personal experience, you demonstrate that A logically causes B, that movie A is great because it meets clearly defined criteria, or that tougher seat belt legislation is the best policy.

Your evidence, your reasonable tone, and your personal experience will also support an **appeal to character.** Readers are often persuaded by the good character of the writer. If your readers see that you have some experience with the issue, have worked hard to discover the truth, and have treated your opponents fairly, your good character will help convince them.

Your examples, personal experience, or choice of evidence may lead also to an **appeal to emotion.** Evoking emotions of anger, pity, or fear through your evidence will help your argument as long as your emotional appeals do not obviously distort or manipulate the truth. If your readers feel you are too emotional, however, your emotional appeal may dissuade your audience.

Choosing a Subject for Your Arguing Essay

The ideal topic is one that has generated public debate and controversy, but one that connects to your own experience. Try listing controversial topics in one column, and your authority list or experiences in the other. Where they match, you may have a workable topic.

Brainstorm additional topics for the left-hand column. Then list your own interests, hobbies, or important experiences in the right-hand column. Where both topics match or intersect, you may have a workable topic.

Controversial Topics	Authority List/Personal Experience
High college tuition	
DWI laws	
Insurance rates for cars	
Day-care legislation	
Drug testing for jobs	
Emission regulations for cars	
Living together as marriage alternative	
Balance of trade with Japan	
Labels for rock music	

Controversial Topics	Authority List/Personal Experience
Disposable diapers	
Required computer literacy classes	
Nutrition labels on food	
Reducing hospital costs	
Prejudice in the workplace	
Smoking regulations on airplanes	
Regulating handguns	

Collecting Arguments and Examples

For this essay, you will need information from books and articles in your library, but don't forget your field research. Whom can you interview on your topic? Would an informal survey of reactions of your friends, family, or classmates give you ideas or information? Be sure to make photocopies of the important sources you uncover in the library. If you interview an authority, take along a tape recorder.

As you gather information, keep thinking about the pros and cons of your topic. Which arguments that you discover will support your claim and which are arguments that you must counter? If you are arguing that parents should use cloth diapers to reduce deforestation and the landfill crisis, look for all the arguments on both sides.

Claim: Parents should use cloth diapers instead of disposable diapers.

Pro	Con
Evidence shows that disposable diapers are creating a landfill crisis.	Disposable diapers are more convenient.

Pro	Con
Disposable diapers encourage the "throw-away" attitude toward all consumer products.	Disposable diapers are actually more sanitary for the child.
Cloth diapers are less expensive.	Disposable diapers do not require washing and using water supplies.
Cloth diapers do not require chopping down trees.	New disposable diapers are biodegradable.
The new so-called biodegradable diapers will not decompose without sunlight.	

Shaping Your Arguing Essay

One of the oldest outlines for argumentative essays comes from classical rhetoric. Use the following outline as a **guide** rather than a rigid plan for your own topic.

    I. Introduction: Announces the subject; gets your audience's interest and attention; creates positive appeal to your good character

    II. Narration: Gives background, context, statement of problem, or definition of key terms

    III. Partition: States your claim or thesis; outlines or maps out your arguments

    IV. Argument: Presents the arguments and evidence for your claim

    V. Refutation: Counters the arguments of your opposition

VI. Conclusion: Summarizes arguments, suggests your solution if appropriate, or ties back into the introduction

Most argumentative essays have these six parts or features, but they do not necessarily occur in this order. Some writers refute the opposing arguments before giving their own reasons and evidence. Since most short argumentative essays combine the introduction, narration, and partition in a few short introductory paragraphs, use the following abbreviated outlines as possible patterns for your own topic.

Outline 1 Intro (attention getter, background, claim, and map)

Your arguments .

Refute opposing arguments

Conclusion

Outline 2 Intro

Refute opposing arguments

Your arguments

Conclusion

Outline 3 Intro

Refute first opposing argument which leads to your first argument

Refute second opposing argument which leads to your second argument

Refute third opposing argument which leads to your third argument, etc.

Your additional arguments

Conclusion

Test each of these patterns against your topic. Which will work best for your claim, your evidence, and your audience?

Drafting Your Arguing Essay

Especially if you are doing extended research for this essay, start writing your ideas as soon as possible in your journal. Don't think you need to do all of your research and then start writing. Whenever you get an idea, start writing, and then leave a blank space or draw a line in your draft where you need more evidence. Your goal is not to patch together seventeen quotations from articles in books and articles. Your goal is to use your research to learn what has already been said about your topic and then decide what you think. Write your own ideas and arguments as soon as you decide what you believe.

When you have gathered sufficient evidence, collect all your photocopies of sources, your notes from interviews, your prewriting, and notes. If you've tested one of the argumentative outlines, use that to sketch out a plan. If you prefer to start writing first and organize later, then get started. If you have a good example, description, set of facts, or statistics for your lead-in, start there. If not, start with your claim and worry about your lead-in later. If you have to quit drafting temporarily, stop in the middle of a paragraph where you know what is coming next. Then write a note to yourself about what you will say next.

Revising Your Arguing Essay

Use the following guidelines as you revise and then edit your essay.

Reconsider your audience. Ask a friend or classmate to role-play your audience. What additional arguments can they imagine? Where is you argument or evidence the weakest? Do you address your arguments to your intended audience?

Review your introduction. Do you catch your reader's attention with a startling example or statistic, a vivid description, a quotation, or a specific example from your own experience? Do you state your claim clearly by the end of your opening paragraphs?

Establish the background for your claim. Have you defined key terms? Have you explained the problem? Have you described the subject you are evaluating?

Respond to opposing arguments. If you have only given your side, you haven't really written an argumentative essay. Make sure that you represent and then respond to key opposing arguments.

Give supporting evidence for each reason. Make sure that every assertion you make is supported by facts, statistics, observations, quotations from authorities, examples, or your own personal experience.

Make clear transitions between paragraphs. Signal the major arguments or counterarguments in your essay. Your reader should be able to follow your argument just by reading the first sentence or two in each paragraph.

Check in-text citations for accuracy. Quote directly when the writer's original words are more exact or more persuasive than your paraphrase might be. Use ellipsis points (. . .) to omit unimportant words from a long direct quotation. When you use a writer's exact words, when you paraphrase, or when you use facts or statistics, cite the source in your text at the end of the sentence (see sample student essays for MLA format). Failure to cite your sources properly constitutes plagiarism.

Revise and edit your essay. Revise sentences to improve conciseness and clarity and reduce wordiness and clutter. Review for problems in grammar, usage, spelling, and mechanics.

Postscript for Your Arguing Essay

When you have finished your essay, answer the following questions. Hand in this postscript with your essay.

1. What did you *learn* about your subject as you researched it? On what points did you change your mind? What was the most surprising bit of evidence you found?

2. Which of the opposing arguments is the strongest? Which of your arguments is the strongest? Where is your evidence strongest and where weakest?

3. Describe how you think a reader who totally *disagrees* with your position will react to your essay.

4. If you had two more days to gather evidence, which of the following would you do: Find more articles or books in the library? Interview another authority? Observe a place, action, or person? Use more of your own experience? Explain.

Active and Passive Euthanasia

JAMES RACHELS

(1941–)

PREREADING JOURNAL ENTRY

A person lies in a hospital bed, dying of cancer. Several physicians agree the illness is terminal. The patient wishes to die. The family and the doctor disagree, however, about how this person should die. The choice is to withdraw means of support and let the patient die (passive euthanasia) or have the doctor give the patient a lethal injection (active euthanasia). What choice should the family and the doctor make? Explain your decision.

STUDENT JOURNAL RESPONSES

If the patient wishes to die, I feel that active euthanasia should be used. Many of the injections are quick and painless. In comparison with a lingering illness, the injection is immediate and cost-effective. I feel that the active injection will save the family money and will open the hospital space and facilities for another cancer victim that may have a better chance. That may be a cold attitude to bring in economics, but if the space and medical technology could be used for another patient, active euthanasia should be the choice.

Basically, I think we should let the patient die, rather than actively kill him. My swim coach Pete had a cerebral hemorrhage causing brain damage. He was in a coma. There was nothing that could be done, so they let him die. But he was in a coma — I don't *think it was painful for him. I think it just comes down to individual questions. Is the patient suffering? How long has the patient been ill? Would passive euthanasia be painful? Is the patient really aware of what is going on? I don't think we should use active euthanasia, but every case is different.*

Should doctors use extraordinary means to sustain life when a patient has a terminal illness? Do patients have a "right to die?" Should people be able to choose death with dignity? As a philosopher, James Rachels challenges the traditionally held idea that "withdrawing support and letting a person die (passive euthanasia)" is a better choice, morally, than actively ending a person's life. Rachels was born in Columbus, Georgia, was educated at Mercer University and the University of California, and has taught at the University of Miami, Coral Gables. He has edited a collection of essays, **Moral Problems** (1979), focusing on contemporary ethics.

"Active and Passive Euthanasia" urges doctors—particularly those American Medical Association delegates responsible for writing policy statements—to reconsider their views on active euthanasia. Is killing someone, Rachels asks, "morally worse" in all cases than letting that person die? Rather than allow a terminally ill patient to die slowly, to suffer needlessly for days and even weeks, shouldn't doctors (with the consent of the patient and/or the family) give a painless lethal injection?

ACTIVE AND PASSIVE EUTHANASIA

The distinction between active and passive euthanasia is thought to be crucial for medical ethics. The idea is that it is permissible, at least in some cases, to withhold treatment and allow a patient to die, but it is never permissible to take any direct action designed to kill the patient. This doctrine seems to be accepted by most doctors, and it is endorsed in a statement adopted by the House of Delegates of the American Medical Association on December 4, 1973: 1

But if the patient is going to die, a lethal injection should be used.

The intentional termination of the life of one human being by another—mercy killing—is contrary to that for which the medical profession stands and is contrary to the policy of the American Medical Association.

The cessation of the employment of extraordinary means to prolong the life of the body when there is irrefutable evidence that biological death is imminent is the decision of the patient and/or his immediate family. The advice and judgment of the physician should be freely available to the patient and/or his immediate family.

Opposing position

[However, a strong case can be made against this doctrine. In what follows I will set out some of the relevant arguments, and urge doctors to reconsider their views on this matter.]

Rachel's thesis

To begin with a familiar type of situation, a patient who is dying of incurable cancer of the throat is in terrible pain, which can no longer be satisfactorily alleviated. He is certain to die within a few days, even if present treatment is continued, but he does not want to go on living for those days since the pain is unbearable. So he asks the doctor for an end to it, and his family joins in the request.

2

Suppose the doctor agrees to withhold treatment, as the conventional doctrine says he may. The justification for his doing so is that the patient is in terrible agony, and since he is going to die anyway, it would be wrong to prolong his suffering needlessly. But now notice this. If one simply withholds treatment, it may take the patient longer to die, and so he may suffer more than he would if more direct action were taken and a lethal injection given. This fact provides strong reason for thinking that, once the initial decision not to prolong his agony has been made, active euthanasia is actually preferable to passive euthanasia, rather than the reverse. To say otherwise is to endorse the option that leads to more suffering rather than less, and is con-

3

? How about just giving patient a pain killer so he doesn't suffer?

! Right

trary to the humanitarian impulse that prompts
the decision not to prolong his life in the first
place.

Part of my point is that the process of being
"allowed to die" can be relatively slow and
painful, whereas being given a lethal injection
is relatively quick and painless.[Let me give a
different sort of example. In the United States
about one in 600 babies is born with Down's
syndrome.] Most of these babies are otherwise
healthy—that is, with only the usual pediatric
care, they will proceed to an otherwise normal
infancy. Some, however, are born with congen-
ital defects such as intestinal obstructions that
require operations if they are to live. Sometimes,
the parents and the doctor will decide not to
operate, and let the infant die. Anthony Shaw
describes what happens then:

Uses statistics here

4

> When surgery is denied [the doctor]
> must try to keep the infant from suffering
> while natural forces sap the baby's life away.
> As a surgeon whose natural inclination is to
> use the scalpel to fight off death, standing
> by and watching a salvageable baby die is
> the most emotionally exhausting experience
> I know. It is easy at a conference, in a
> theoretical discussion, to decide that such
> infants should be allowed to die. It is alto-
> gether different to stand by in the nursery
> and watch as dehydration and infection
> wither a tiny being over hours and days.
> This is a terrible ordeal for me and the
> hospital staff—much more so than for the
> parents who never set foot in the nursery.[1]

Example: Down's syndrome

Appeal to emotion

[I can understand why some people are opposed
to all euthanasia, and insist that such infants

[1] A. Shaw, "Doctor, Do We Have a Choice?" *The New York Times
Magazine,* January 30, 1972, p. 54. (Author's note.)

must be allowed to live. I think I can also understand why other people favor destroying these babies quickly and painlessly.] But why should anyone favor letting "dehydration and infection wither a tiny being over hours and days?" The doctrine that says that a baby may be allowed to dehydrate and wither, but may not be given an injection that would end its life without suffering, seems so patently cruel as to require no further refutation. The strong language is not intended to offend, but only to put the point in the clearest possible way.

tone: argues reasonably with doctors

Emotional appeal

My second argument is that the conventional doctrine leads to decisions concerning life and death made on irrelevant grounds.

5

Consider again the case of the infants with Down's syndrome who need operations for <u>congenital</u> defects unrelated to the syndrome to live. Sometimes, there is no operation, and the baby dies, but when there is no such defect, the baby lives on. Now, an operation such as that to remove an intestinal obstruction is not prohibitively difficult. The reason why such operations are not performed in these cases is, clearly, that the child has Down's syndrome and the parents and doctor judge that because of that fact it is better for the child to die.

6

? How often does this happen?

But notice that this situation is absurd, no matter what view one takes of the lives and potentials of such babies. If the life of such an infant is worth preserving, what does it matter if it needs a simple operation? Or, if one thinks it better that such a baby should not live on, what difference does it make that it happens to have an unobstructed intestinal tract? In either case, the matter of life and death is being decided on irrelevant grounds. It is the <u>Down's syndrome</u>, and not the intestines, that is the issue. The matter should be decided, if at all, on that basis, and not be allowed to depend on the essentially irrelevant question of whether the intestinal tract is blocked.

7

What exactly is Down's syndrome?

What makes this situation possible, of course, is the idea that when there is an intestinal blockage, one can "let the baby die," but when there is no such defect there is nothing that can be done, for one must not "kill" it. The fact that this idea leads to such results as deciding life or death on irrelevant grounds is another good reason why the doctrine should be rejected.

8

[One reason why so many people think that there is an important moral difference between active and passive euthanasia is that they think killing someone is morally worse than letting someone die.] But is it? Is killing, in itself, worse than letting die? To investigate this issue, two cases may be considered that are exactly alike except that one involves killing whereas the other involves letting someone die. Then, it can be asked whether this difference makes any difference to the moral assessments. It is important that the cases be exactly alike, except for this one difference, since otherwise one cannot be confident that it is this difference and not some other that accounts for any variation in the assessments of the two cases. So, let us consider this pair of cases:

Opposing argument 9

Sets up his example

In the first, Smith stands to gain a large inheritance if anything should happen to his six-year-old cousin. One evening while the child is taking his bath, Smith sneaks into the bathroom and drowns the child, and then arranges things so that it will look like an accident.

10

?This example is not believable

In the second, Jones also stands to gain if anything should happen to his six-year-old cousin. Like Smith, Jones sneaks in planning to drown the child in his bath. However, just as he enters the bathroom Jones sees the child slip and hit his head, and fall face down in the water. Jones is delighted; he stands by, ready to push the child's head back under if it is necessary, but it is not necessary. With only a little thrashing about, the child drowns all by

11

This example is X about murder, not euthenasia!

!!

himself, "accidentally," as Jones watches and does nothing.

Now Smith killed the child, whereas Jones "merely" let the child die. That is the only difference between them. <u>Did either man behave better, from a moral point of view?</u> If the difference between killing and letting die were in itself a morally important matter, one should say that Jones's behavior was less reprehensible than Smith's. But does one really want to say that? I think not. In the first place, both men acted from the same motive, personal gain, and both had exactly the same end in view when they acted. It may be inferred from Smith's conduct that he is a bad man, although that judgment may be withdrawn or modified if certain further facts are learned about him— for example, that he is mentally deranged. But would not the very same thing be inferred about Jones from his conduct? And would not the same further considerations also be relevant to any modification of this judgment? Moreover, suppose Jones pleaded, in his own defense, "After all, I didn't do anything except just stand there and watch the child drown. I didn't kill him; I only let him die." Again, if letting die were in itself less bad than killing, this defense should have at least some weight. But it does not. Such a "defense" can only be regarded as a grotesque perversion of moral reasoning. Morally speaking, it is no defense at all.

[Now, it may be pointed out, quite properly, that the cases of euthanasia with which doctors are concerned are not like this at all.] They do not involve personal gain or the destruction of normal healthy children. Doctors are concerned only with cases in which the patient's life is of no further use to him, or in which the patient's life has become or will soon become a terrible burden. However, the point is the same in these cases: the bare difference between killing and

[Margin notes, handwritten:]
12
good question!

Here is where Rachels shows he is a philosopher. This is confusing.

13
Keeps in touch with opposing arguments.

letting die does not, in itself, make a moral difference. If a doctor lets a patient die, for humane reasons, he is in the same moral position as if he had given the patient a lethal injection for humane reasons. If his decision was wrong—if, for example, the patient's illness was in fact curable—the decision would be equally regrettable no matter which method was used to carry it out. And if the doctor's decision was the right one, the method used is not in itself important.

Says action. ? and inaction are the same thing — are they?

The AMA policy statement isolates the crucial issue very well; the crucial issue is ["the intentional termination of the life of one human being by another."] But after identifying this issue, and forbidding "mercy killing," the statement goes on to deny that the cessation of treatment is the intentional termination of a life. This is where the mistake comes in, for what is the cessation of treatment, in these circumstances, if it is not "the intentional termination of the life of one human being by another"? Of course it is exactly that, and if it were not, there would be no point to it.

14

Quotes directly from statement for his argument.

[Many people will find this judgment hard to accept.] One reason, I think, is that it is very easy to conflate the question of whether killing is, in itself, worse than letting die, with the very different question of whether most actual cases of killing are more reprehensible than most actual cases of letting die. Most actual cases of killing are clearly terrible (think, for example, of all the murders reported in the newspapers), and one hears of such cases every day. On the other hand, one hardly ever hears of a case of letting die, except for the actions of doctors who are motivated by humanitarian reasons. So one learns to think of killing in a much worse light than of letting die. But this does not mean that there is something about killing that makes it in itself worse than letting die, for it is not the

Represents 15 opposition's questions. and objections, again.

Comes back to his argument.

bare difference between killing and letting die
that makes the difference in these cases. Rather,
the other factors—the murderer's motive of
personal gain, for example, contrasted with the
doctor's humanitarian motivation—account for
different reactions to the different cases.

[I have argued that killing is not in itself any
worse than letting die; if my contention is right,
it follows that active euthanasia is not any worse
than passive euthanasia.] What arguments can
be given on the other side? The most common,
I believe, is the following:

Repeats his thesis 16

["The important difference between active
and passive euthanasia is that, in passive euthanasia, the doctor does not do anything to
bring about the patient's death. The doctor does
nothing, and the patient dies of whatever ills
already afflict him. In active euthanasia, however, the doctor does something to bring about
the patient's death: he kills him. The doctor
who gives the patient with cancer a lethal injection has himself caused his patient's death;
whereas if he merely ceases treatment, the cancer is the cause of the death."]

Opposing argument 17

A number of points need to be made here.
The first is that it is not exactly correct to say
that in passive euthanasia the doctor does nothing, for he does do one thing that is very
important: he lets the patient die. "Letting someone die" is certainly different, in some respects,
from other types of action—mainly in that it is
a kind of action that one may perform by way
of not performing certain other actions. For
example, one may let a patient die by way of
not giving medication, just as one may insult
someone by way of not shaking his hand. But
for any purpose of moral assessment, it is a type
of action nonetheless. The decision to let a
patient die is subject to moral appraisal in the
same way that a decision to kill him would be
subject to moral appraisal: it may be assessed as
wise or unwise, compassionate or sadistic, right

18

? Sounds like a philosopher again

Philosopher's language.

or wrong. If a doctor deliberately let a patient die who was suffering from a routinely curable illness, the doctor would certainly be to blame for what he had done, just as he would be to blame if he had needlessly killed the patient. Charges against him would then be appropriate. If so, it would be no defense at all for him to insist that he didn't "do anything." He would have done something very serious indeed, for he let his patient die.

action vs. inaction again.

Fixing the cause of death may be very important from a legal point of view, for it may determine whether criminal charges are brought against the doctor. But I do not think that this notion can be used to show a moral difference between active and passive euthanasia. The reason why it is considered bad to be the cause of someone's death is that death is regarded as a great evil—and so it is. However, if it has been decided that euthanasia—even passive euthanasia—is desirable in a given case, it has also been decided that in this instance death is no greater an evil than the patient's continued existence. And if this is true, the usual reason for not wanting to be the cause of someone's death simply does not apply.

19

An important difference, especially if the patient wishes to die.

Finally, doctors may think that all of this is only of academic interest—the sort of thing that philosophers may worry about but that has no practical bearing on their own work. After all, doctors must be concerned about the legal consequences of what they do, and active euthanasia is clearly forbidden by the law. But even so, doctors should also be concerned with the fact that the law is forcing upon them a moral doctrine that may well be indefensible, and has a considerable effect on their practices. Of course, most doctors are not now in the position of being coerced in this matter, for they do not regard themselves as merely going along with what the law requires. Rather, in statements such as the AMA policy statement that I have

20

Audience : Philosopher talking to doctor.

quoted, they are endorsing this doctrine as a central point of medical ethics. In that statement, active euthanasia is condemned not merely as illegal but as "contrary to that for which the medical profession stands," whereas passive euthanasia is approved. However, the preceding considerations suggest that there is really no moral difference between the two, considered in themselves (there may be important moral differences in some cases in their *consequences,* but, as I pointed out, these differences may make active euthanasia, and not passive euthanasia, the morally preferable option). So, whereas doctors may have to discriminate between active and passive euthanasia to *Closes by* satisfy the law, they should not do any more *returning to* than that. <u>In particular, they should not give</u> *Claim by* <u>the distinction any added authority and weight</u> *doctors.* <u>by writing it into official statements of medical</u> <u>ethics.</u> *Claim: Doctors should reconsider their ethical views and allow active euthanasia in certain circumstances.*

QUESTIONS ON MEANING

1. What sentence(s) best express Rachels's thesis?

2. List the opposing or con arguments that Rachels addresses. What is his answer to each opposing argument?

3. What is Rachels's "call to action" in his conclusion?

QUESTIONS ON PURPOSE AND STRATEGY

1. Does Rachels hope to change his readers' beliefs or attitudes? Does he hope to persuade his readers to take some action? Explain.

2. Rachels uses hypothetical examples to argue his points. What examples does he give? Which examples did you find most or least effective?

QUESTIONS ON AUDIENCE AND LANGUAGE

1. Who is Rachels's immediate audience? In what paragraphs does he address this audience most directly? Who else might be interested in Rachels's argument?

2. Rachels is a philosopher. Even if you did not know that, however, what specific *words* and *sentences* reveal that he is a philosopher—not a doctor, or a lawyer, or a person whose family member is terminally ill?

QUESTIONS FOR DISCUSSION AND WRITING

1. In paragraph eighteen, Rachels says, "For example, one may let a patient die by way of not giving medication, just as one may insult someone by way of not shaking his hand. But for the purpose of moral assessment, it is a type of action nonetheless." Do you agree that a crime of "inaction" is as morally serious as a crime of direct "action?" Use an example of another kind of crime to illustrate your answer.

2. Rachels's example of Smith and Jones is interesting, but actual circumstances are not always like hypothetical cases. How is the reality different from this example? Should those differences affect the conclusion that Rachels draws?

3. Reread your Prereading Journal Entry. After reading Rachels's essay, how would you modify your response? If you disagree with Rachels, how would you counter his arguments?

4. Imagine a scenario where you might wish for active euthanasia. Would active euthanasia, in this case, be equivalent to suicide? Does a human being's "right" to death with dignity overrule your moral sense that suicide is wrong?

Why Are Americans Afraid of Dragons?

URSULA K. LE GUIN

(1929–   )

PREREADING JOURNAL ENTRY

If you have read any fantasy fiction—including fairy
tales such as "Cinderella," "Little Red Riding Hood," or
"Alice in Wonderland"—describe your memory of these
tales. Did you like or dislike reading them? Explain *why*
people should or should not read these stories.

*"As great scientists have said and all children know, it is above all
by the imagination that we achieve perception, and compassion, and
hope." The virtues of fantasy should need no defense, but Ursula Le
Guin argues in her speeches, essays, poems, and novels that imagination
is the "one thing needful" in the lives of both children and adults. Her
most famous science fiction and fantasy novels include* The Earthsea
Trilogy *(1968–1972) and* The Left Hand of Darkness *(1969),
works which have taken their place besides J. R. R. Tolkien's* Lord of
the Rings *and C. S. Lewis's "Narnia" series. Le Guin was born in
Berkeley, California, received degrees from Radcliffe College and Columbia University, and calls Portland, Oregon, her home.*

*"Why Are Americans Afraid of Dragons" takes a slightly different
approach to argument. Instead of abstractly arguing the pros and cons
of fantasy literature, she frames the heart of her essay as a dialogue
between herself and the practical, profit-and-loss businessman of America
who sees no practical value in fantasy literature. "Did you ever notice,"
she asks, "how very gloomy billionaires look in their photographs? They
have this strange, pinched look, as if they were hungry." Hungry, Le
Guin claims, for their lost childhood.*

This was to be a talk about fantasy. But I have not 1
been feeling very fanciful lately, and could not decide
what to say; so I have been going about picking people's
brains for ideas. "What about fantasy? Tell me something
about fantasy." And one friend of mine said, "All right,
I'll tell you something fantastic. Ten years ago, I went to
the children's room of the library of such-and-such a city,
and asked for *The Hobbit;* and the librarian told me, 'Oh,
we keep that only in the adult collection; we don't feel
that escapism is good for children.' "

My friend and I had a good laugh and shudder over 2
that, and we agreed that things have changed a great deal
in these past ten years. That kind of moralistic censorship
of works of fantasy is very uncommon now, in the children's libraries. But the fact that the children's libraries
have become oases in the desert doesn't mean that there
isn't still a desert. The point of view from which that
librarian spoke still exists. She was merely reflecting, in
perfect good faith, something that goes very deep in the
American character: a moral disapproval of fantasy, a
disapproval so intense, and often so aggressive, that I
cannot help but see it as arising, fundamentally, from
fear.

So: Why are Americans afraid of dragons?   3

Before I try to answer my question, let me say that it 4
isn't only Americans who are afraid of dragons. I suspect
that almost all very highly technological peoples are more
or less antifantasy. There are several national literatures
which, like ours, have had no tradition of adult fantasy
for the past several hundred years: the French, for instance. But then you have the Germans, who have a good
deal; and the English, who have it, and love it, and do it
better than anyone else. So this fear of dragons is not
merely a Western, or a technological, phenomenon. But
I do not want to get into these vast historical questions; I
will speak of modern Americans, the only people I know
well enough to talk about.

In wondering why Americans are afraid of dragons, 5
I began to realize that a great many Americans are not
only antifantasy, but altogether antifiction. We tend, as a
people, to look upon all works of the imagination either
as suspect, or as contemptible.

"My wife reads novels. I haven't got the time." 6
"I used to read that science fiction stuff when I was a 7
teenager, but of course I don't now."
"Fairy stories are for kids. I live in the real world." 8
Who speaks so? Who is it that dismisses *War and Peace,* 9
The Time Machine, and *A Midsummer Night's Dream* with this
perfect self-assurance?[1] It is, I fear, the man in the street—
the hardworking, over-thirty American male—the men
who run this country.

Such a rejection of the entire art of fiction is related 10
to several American characteristics: our Puritanism, our
work ethic, our profit-mindedness, and even our sexual
mores.

To read *War and Peace* or *The Lord of the Rings* plainly 11
is not "work"[2]—you do it for pleasure. And if it cannot
be justified as "educational" or as "self-improvement,"
then, in the Puritan value system, it can only be self-
indulgence or escapism. For pleasure is not a value, to the
Puritan; on the contrary, it is a sin.

Equally, in the businessman's value system, if an act 12
does not bring in an immediate, tangible profit, it has no
justification at all. Thus the only person who has an excuse
to read Tolstoy or Tolkien is the English teacher, because
he gets paid for it. But our businessman might allow
himself to read a best-seller now and then: not because it
is a good book, but because it is a best-seller—it is a
success, it has made money. To the strangely mystical
mind of the money-changer, this justifies its existence;
and by reading it he may participate, a little, in the power

---

[1] *War and Peace, The Time Machine,* and *A Midsummer Night's Dream:* by
Leo Tolstoy, H. G. Wells, and William Shakespeare, respectively. [Eds.]
[2] *The Lord of the Rings:* the trilogy by J. R. R. Tolkien. [Eds.]

and mana of its success. If this is not magic, by the way,
I don't know what is.

The last element, the sexual one, is more complex. I 13
hope I will not be understood as being sexist if I say that,
within our culture, I believe that this antifiction attitude
is basically a male one. The American boy and man is very
commonly forced to define his maleness by rejecting
certain traits, certain human gifts and potentialities, which
our culture defines as "womanish" or "childish." And one
of these traits or potentialities is, in cold sober fact, the
absolutely essential human faculty of imagination.

Having got this far, I went quickly to the dictionary. 14

The *Shorter Oxford Dictionary* says: "Imagination. 1. The 15
action of imagining, or forming a mental concept of what
is not actually present to the senses; 2. The mental
consideration of actions or events not yet in existence."

Very well; I certainly can let "absolutely essential 16
human faculty" stand. But I must narrow the definition
to fit our present subject. By "imagination," then, I
personally mean the free play of the mind, both intellectual
and sensory. By "play" I mean recreation, re-creation, the
recombination of what is known into what is new. By
"free" I mean that the action is done without an immediate
object of profit—spontaneously. That does not mean,
however, that there may not be a purpose behind the free
play of the mind, a goal; and the goal may be a very
serious object indeed. Children's imaginative play is clearly
a practicing at the acts and emotions of adulthood; a child
who did not play would not become mature. As for the
free play of an adult mind, its result may be *War and
Peace,* or the theory of relativity.

To be free, after all, is not to be undisciplined. I should 17
say that the discipline of the imagination may in fact be
the essential method or technique of both art and science.
It is our Puritanism, insisting that discipline means repres-
sion or punishment, which confuses the subject. To discipline something, in the proper sense of the word, does
not mean to repress it, but to train it—to encourage it to

grow, and act, and be fruitful, whether it is a peach tree or a human mind.

I think that a great many American men have been 18 taught just the opposite. They have learned to repress their imagination, to reject it as something childish or effeminate, unprofitable, and probably sinful.

They have learned to fear it. But they have never 19 learned to discipline it at all.

Now, I doubt that the imagination can be suppressed. 20 If you truly eradicated it in a child, he would grow up to be an eggplant. Like all our evil propensities, the imagination will out. But if it is rejected and despised, it will grow into wild and weedy shapes; it will be deformed. At its best, it will be mere ego-centered daydreaming; at its worst, it will be wishful thinking, which is a very dangerous occupation when it is taken seriously. Where literature is concerned, in the old, truly Puritan days, the only permitted reading was the Bible. Nowadays, with our secular Puritanism, the man who refuses to read novels because it's unmanly to do so, or because they aren't true, will most likely end up watching bloody detective thrillers on the television, or reading hack Westerns or sports stories, or going in for pornography, from *Playboy* on down. It is his starved imagination, craving nourishment, that forces him to do so. But he can rationalize such entertainment by saying that it is realistic—after all, sex exists, and there are criminals, and there are baseball players, and there used to be cowboys—and also by saying that it is virile, by which he means that it doesn't interest most women.

That all these genres are sterile, hopelessly sterile, is 21 a reassurance to him, rather than a defect. If they were genuinely realistic, which is to say genuinely imagined and imaginative, he would be afraid of them. Fake realism is the escapist literature of our time. And probably the ultimate escapist reading is that masterpiece of total unreality, the daily stock market report.

Now what about our man's wife? She probably wasn't 22 required to squelch her private imagination in order to play her expected role in life, but she hasn't been trained to discipline it, either. She is allowed to read novels, and even fantasies. But, lacking training and encouragement, her fancy is likely to glom on to very sickly fodder, such things as soap operas, and "true romances," and nursy novels, and historico-sentimental novels, and all the rest of the baloney ground out to replace genuine imaginative works by the artistic sweatshops of a society that is profoundly distrustful of the uses of the imagination.

What, then, are the uses of the imagination? 23

You see, I think we have a terrible thing here: a 24 hardworking, upright, responsible citizen, a full-grown, educated person, who is afraid of dragons, and afraid of hobbits, and scared to death of fairies. It's funny, but it's also terrible. Something has gone very wrong. I don't know what to do about it but to try and give an honest answer to that person's question, even though he often asks it in an aggressive and contemptuous tone of voice. "What's the good of it all?" he says. "Dragons and hobbits and little green men—what's the *use* of it?"

The truest answer, unfortunately, he won't even listen 25 to. He won't hear it. The truest answer is, "The use of it is to give you pleasure and delight."

"I haven't got the time," he snaps, swallowing a Maalox 26 pill for his ulcer and rushing off to the golf course.

So we try the next-to-truest answer. It probably won't 27 go down much better, but it must be said: "The use of imaginative fiction is to deepen your understanding of your world, and your fellow men, and your own feelings, and your destiny."

To which I fear he will retort, "Look, I got a raise last 28 year, and I'm giving my family the best of everything, we've got two cars and a color TV. I understand enough of the world!"

And he is right, unanswerably right, if that is what he 29 wants, and all he wants.

The kind of thing you learn from reading about the 30 problems of a hobbit who is trying to drop a magic ring into an imaginary volcano has very little to do with your social status, or material success, or income. Indeed, if there is any relationship, it is a negative one. There is an inverse correlation between fantasy and money. That is a law, known to economists as Le Guin's Law. If you want a striking example of Le Guin's Law, just give a lift to one of those people along the roads who own nothing but a backpack, a guitar, a fine head of hair, a smile, and a thumb. Time and again, you will find that these waifs have read *The Lord of the Rings*—some of them can practically recite it. But now take Aristotle Onassis, or J. Paul Getty: could you believe that those men ever had anything to do, at any age, under any circumstances, with a hobbit?

But, to carry my example a little further, and out of 31 the realm of economics, did you ever notice how very gloomy Mr. Onassis and Mr. Getty and all those billionaires look in their photographs? They have this strange, pinched look, as if they were hungry. As if they were hungry for something, as if they had lost something and were trying to think where it could be, or perhaps what it could be, what it was they've lost.

Could it be their childhood? 32

So I arrive at my personal defense of the uses of the 33 imagination, especially in fiction, and most especially in fairy tale, legend, fantasy, science fiction, and the rest of the lunatic fringe. I believe that maturity is not an outgrowing, but a growing up: that an adult is not a dead child, but a child who survived. I believe that all the best faculties of a mature human being exist in the child, and that if these faculties are encouraged in youth they will act well and wisely in the adult, but if they are repressed and denied in the child they will stunt and cripple the adult personality. And finally, I believe that one of the most deeply human, and humane, of these faculties is the power of imagination: so that it is our pleasant duty, as librarians, or teachers, or parents, or writers, or simply as grownups, to encourage that faculty of imagination in our children, to encourage it to grow freely, to flourish like the green bay tree, by giving it the best, absolutely the best and purest, nourishment that it can absorb. And never, under any circumstances, to squelch it, or sneer at it, or imply that it is childish, or unmanly, or untrue.

For fantasy is true, of course. It isn't factual, but it is 34 true. Children know that. Adults know it too, and that is precisely why many of them are afraid of fantasy. They know that its truth challenges, even threatens, all that is false, all that is phony, unnecessary, and trivial in the life they have let themselves be forced into living. They are afraid of dragons, because they are afraid of freedom.

So I believe that we should trust our children. Normal 35 children do not confuse reality and fantasy—they confuse them much less often than we adults do (as a certain great fantasist pointed out in a story called "The Emperor's New Clothes"). Children know perfectly well that unicorns aren't real, but they also know that books about unicorns, if they are good books, are true books. All too often, that's more than Mummy and Daddy know; for, in denying their childhood, the adults have denied half their knowledge, and are left with the sad, sterile little fact: "Unicorns aren't real." And that fact is one that never got anybody anywhere (except in the story "The Unicorn in the Garden," by another great fantasist, in which it is shown that a devotion to the unreality of unicorns may get you straight into the loony bin). It is by such statements as, "Once upon a time there was a dragon," or "In a hole in the ground there lived a hobbit"—it is by such beautiful non-facts that we fantastic human beings may arrive, in our peculiar fashion, at the truth.

QUESTIONS ON MEANING

1. Explain, in your own words, Le Guin's thesis or claim. Find three sentences from the essay that support your paraphrase.

2. What characteristics of American culture help explain why Le Guin's hypothetical "man in the street" rejects fiction and fantasy?

3. According to Le Guin, what does "imagination" mean and what are the primary *uses* of the imagination?

QUESTIONS ON PURPOSE AND STRATEGY

1. Le Guin *explains* what the imagination is and what the uses of imagination are, she *evaluates* the businessman's opinion that "Fairy stories are for kids," and she *argues* that imagination is vital to the growth of every human being. Find the paragraphs that support each of these purposes in the essay. Which purpose dominates the essay?

2. Le Guin repeatedly puts the opposing arguments in the form of questions asked or statements made by men. Identify places in this essay where she uses this strategy. In those paragraphs, is she attacking the men themselves, their beliefs, or both?

3. Find three paragraphs where Le Guin uses sufficient evidence (facts, examples of fantasy works, quotations, details from her experience, images and comparisons, examples from history) to support her opinions. Find one paragraph where she needs more evidence. What evidence could she use?

QUESTIONS ON AUDIENCE AND LANGUAGE

1. This essay was originally delivered as a speech at a Pacific Northwest Library Association conference in Portland, Oregon. Where in the essay does Le Guin refer to or appeal to this audience? How would her speech be received at the Portland Kiwanis Club or the local Chamber of Commerce?

2. Le Guin writes with a distinctive voice and tone. Which of the following words best describes her voice or personality as revealed in her writing: *self-assured, wishy-washy, opinionated, assertive,* or some other word? Which of the following words best describes Le Guin's tone or attitude toward her subject: *serious, indifferent, angry, philosophical, ironic, humorous,* or some other word?

QUESTIONS FOR DISCUSSION AND WRITING

1. In paragraph twenty-one, Le Guin says that "the ultimate escapist reading is that masterpiece of total unreality, the daily stock market report." Explain why you agree or disagree with that statement.

2. Using a work of fantasy such as "Cinderella," "Little Red Riding Hood," or "The Emperor's New Clothes," explain what Le Guin means when she says, "For fantasy is true, of course. It isn't factual, but it is true."

3. Imagine that you are a businessperson in Portland who has been asked to speak immediately following Le Guin. Your job is to present the other side of this argument—to disagree with Le Guin's stereotyped view of American men and women, to defend realistic fiction, or to argue against the practical value of works such as *The Lord of the Rings*. You have this copy of her speech. Write out your response.

Kill 'Em, Crush 'Em, Eat 'Em Raw!

JOHN MCMURTRY

(1939–   )

PREREADING JOURNAL ENTRY

What sport do you enjoy playing or watching? Describe incidents in that sport that you would call violent. In your opinion, is the violence necessary to this sport? Should the rules of the game or the equipment be changed to better protect the players?

"Indeed, it is arguable that body shattering is the very point *of football, as killing and maiming are of war." John McMurtry, a philosophy teacher and author of* The Structure of Marx's World View *(1978), played professional football with the Calgary Stampeders. A veteran of the high school, college, and professional football "wars," McMurtry's first injury, torn knee ligaments, occurred at age thirteen. Following a succession of broken noses, ripped knee ligaments, fractured ankles and ribs, dislocated shoulders, and injuries to his spinal cord, McMurtry finally left the playing field and returned to the library to read his favorite philosophers: Hegel, Marx, and Plato. He received his Ph.D. in philosophy at the University of London and taught at the University of Guelph in Canada.*

In "Kill 'Em, Crush 'Em, Eat 'Em Raw!" McMurtry remembers his own experiences in football and then describes in detail the similarities between football and war. If the "very point*" of football is for players to "kill" each other for the entertainment of spectators, McMurtry argues, how can we defend the sport? McMurtry examines the opposing arguments and concludes that football's organized violence benefits neither fans nor players. His own experience is the most persuasive evidence:*

After injuring his ribs one more time while throwing a crushing block, McMurtry elects to retire from professional football.

A few months ago my neck got a hard crick in it. I 1 couldn't turn my head; to look left or right I'd have to turn my whole body. But I'd had cricks in my neck since I started playing grade-school football and hockey, so I just ignored it. Then I began to notice that when I reached for any sort of large book (which I do pretty often as a philosophy teacher at the University of Guelph) I had trouble lifting it with one hand. I was losing the strength in my left arm, and I had such a steady pain in my back I often had to stretch out on the floor of the room I was in to relieve the pressure.

A few weeks later I mentioned to my brother, an 2 orthopedic surgeon, that I'd lost the power in my arm since my neck began to hurt. Twenty-four hours later I was in a Toronto hospital not sure whether I might end up with a wasted upper limb. Apparently the steady pounding I had received playing college and professional football in the late Fifties and early Sixties had driven my head into my backbone so that the discs had crumpled together at the neck—"acute herniation"—and had cut the nerves to my left arm like a pinched telephone wire (without nerve stimulation, of course, the muscles atrophy, leaving the arm crippled). So I spent my Christmas holidays in the hospital in heavy traction and much of the next three months with my neck in a brace. Today most of the pain has gone, and I've recovered most of the strength in my arm. But from time to time I still have to don the brace, and surgery remains a possibility.

Not much of this will surprise anyone who knows 3 football. It is a sport in which body wreckage is one of the leading conventions. A few days after I went into the hospital for that crick in my neck, another brother, an outstanding football player in college, was undergoing spinal surgery in the same hospital two floors above me. In his case it was a lower, more massive herniation, which every now and again buckled him so that he was unable to lift himself off his back for days at a time. By the time he entered the hospital for surgery he had already spent several months in bed. The operation was successful, but, as in all such cases, it will take him a year to recover fully.

These aren't isolated experiences. Just about anybody 4 who has ever played football for any length of time, in high school, college or one of the professional leagues, has suffered for it later physically.

Indeed, it is arguable that body shattering is the very 5 *point* of football, as killing and maiming are of war. (In the United States, for example, the game results in 15 to 20 deaths a year and about 50,000 major operations on knees alone.) To grasp some of the more conspicuous similarities between football and war, it is instructive to listen to the imperatives most frequently issued to the players by their coaches, teammates and fans. "Hurt 'em!" "Level 'em!" "Kill 'em!" "Take 'em apart!" Or watch for the plays that are most enthusiastically applauded by the fans. Where someone is "smeared," "knocked silly," "creamed," "nailed," "broken in two," or even "crucified." (One of my coaches when I played corner linebacker with the Calgary Stampeders in 1961 elaborated, often very inventively, on this language of destruction: admonishing us to "unjoin" the opponent, "make 'im remember you" and "stomp 'im like a bug.") Just as in hockey, where a fight will bring fans to their feet more often than a skillful play, so in football the mouth waters most of all for the really crippling block or tackle. For the kill. Thus the good teams are "hungry," the best players are "mean," and "casualties" are as much a part of the game as they are of a war.

The family resemblance between football and war is, 6 indeed, striking. Their languages are similar: "field general," "long bomb," "blitz," "take a shot," "front line," "pursuit," "good hit," "the draft" and so on. Their principles and practices are alike: mass hysteria, the art of intimidation, absolute command and total obedience, territorial aggression, censorship, inflated insignia and propaganda, blackboard maneuvers and strategies, drills, uniforms, formations, marching bands and training camps. And the virtues they celebrate are almost identical: hyperaggressiveness, coolness under fire and suicidal bravery. All this has been implicitly recognized by such jock-loving Americans as media stars General Patton and President Nixon, who have talked about war as a football game. Patton wanted to make his Second World War tank men look like football players. And Nixon, as we know, was fond of comparing attacks on Vietnam to football plays and drawing coachly diagrams on a blackboard for TV war fans.

One difference between war and football, though, is 7 that there is little or no protest against football. Perhaps the most extraordinary thing about the game is that the systematic infliction of injuries excites in people not concern, as would be the case if they were sustained at, say, a rock festival, but a collective rejoicing and euphoria. Players and fans alike revel in the spectacle of a combatant felled into semiconsciousness, "blindsided," "clotheslined" or "decapitated." I can remember, in fact, being chided by a coach in pro ball for not "getting my hat" injuriously into a player who was already lying helpless on the ground. (On another occasion, after the Stampeders had traded the celebrated Joe Kapp to BC, we were playing the Lions in Vancouver and Kapp was forced on one play to run with the ball. He was coming "down the chute," his bad knee wobbling uncertainly, so I simply dropped on him like a blanket. After I returned to the bench I was reproved for not exploiting the opportunity to unhinge his bad knee.)

After every game, of course, the papers are full of 8 reports on the day's injuries, a sort of post-battle "body count," and the respective teams go to work with doctors and trainers, tape, whirlpool baths, cortisone and morphine to patch and deaden the wounds before the next game. Then the whole drama is reenacted—injured athletes held together by adhesive, braces and drugs—and the days following it are filled with even more feverish activity to put on the show yet again at the end of the next week. (I remember being so taped up in college that I earned the nickname "mummy.") The team that survives this merry-go-round spectacle of skilled masochism with the fewest incapacitating injuries usually wins. It is a sort of victory by ordeal: "We hurt them more than they hurt us."

My own initiation into this brutal circus was typical. I 9 loved the game from the moment I could run with a ball. Played shoeless on a green open field with no one keeping score and in a spirit of reckless abandon and laughter, it's a very different sport. Almost no one gets hurt and it's rugged, open and exciting (it still is for me). But then, like everything else, it starts to be regulated and institutionalized by adult authorities. And the fun is over.

So it was as I began the long march through organized 10 football. Now there was a coach and elders to make it clear by their behavior that beating other people was the only thing to celebrate and that trying to shake someone up every play was the only thing to be really proud of. Now there were severe rule enforcers, audiences, formally recorded victors and losers, and heavy equipment to permit crippling bodily moves and collisions (according to one American survey, more than 80% of all football injuries occur to fully equipped players). And now there was the official "given" that the only way to keep playing was to wear suffocating armor, to play to defeat, to follow orders silently and to renounce spontaneity for joyless drill. The game had been, in short, ruined. But because I loved to play and play skillfully, I stayed. And progressively and inexorably, as I moved through high school, college and pro leagues, my body was dismantled. Piece by piece.

I started off with torn ligaments in my knee at 13. 11 Then, as the organization and the competition increased, the injuries came faster and harder. Broken nose (three times), broken jaw (fractured in the first half and dismissed as a "bad wisdom tooth," so I played with it for the rest of the game), ripped knee ligaments again. Torn ligaments in one ankle and a fracture in the other (which I remember feeling relieved about because it meant I could honorably stop drill-blocking a 270-pound defensive end). Repeated rib fractures and cartilage tears (usually carried, again, through the remainder of the game). More dislocations of the left shoulder than I can remember (the last one I played with because, as the Calgary Stampeder doctor said, it "couldn't be damaged any more"). Occasional broken or dislocated fingers and toes. Chronically hurt lower back (I still can't lift with it or change a tire without worrying about folding). Separated right shoulder (as with many other injuries, like badly bruised hips and legs, needled with morphine for the games). And so on. The last pro game I played—against Winnipeg Blue Bombers in the Western finals in 1961—I had a recently dislocated left shoulder, a more recently wrenched right shoulder and a chronic pain centre in one leg. I was so tied up with soreness I couldn't drive my car to the airport. But it never occurred to me or anyone else that I miss a play as a corner linebacker.

By the end of my football career, I had learned that 12 physical injury—giving it and taking it—is the real currency of the sport. And that in the final analysis the "winner" is the man who can hit to kill even if only half his limbs are working. In brief, a warrior game with a warrior ethos into which (like almost everyone else I played with) my original boyish enthusiasm had been relentlessly taunted and conditioned.

In thinking back on how all this happened, though, I 13 can pick out no villains. As with the social system as a whole, the game has a life of its own. Everyone grows up inside it, accepts it and fulfills its dictates as obediently as helots. Far from ever questioning the principles of the activity, people simply concentrate on executing these principles more aggressively than anybody around them. The result is a group of people who, as the leagues become of a higher and higher class, are progressively insensitive to the possibility that things could be otherwise. Thus, in football, anyone who might question the wisdom or enjoyment of putting on heavy equipment on a hot day and running full speed at someone else with the intention of knocking him senseless would be regarded simply as not really a devoted athlete and probably "chicken." The choice is made straightforward. Either you, too, do your very utmost to efficiently smash and be smashed, or you admit incompetence or cowardice and quit. Since neither of these admissions is very pleasant, people generally keep any doubts they have to themselves and carry on.

Of course, it would be a mistake to suppose that there 14 is more blind acceptance of brutal practices in organized football than elsewhere. On the contrary, a recent Harvard study has approvingly argued that football's characteristics of "impersonal acceptance of inflicted injury," an overriding "organization goal," the "ability to turn oneself on and off" and being, above all, "out to win" are of "inestimable value" to big corporations. Clearly, our sort of football is no sicker than the rest of our society. Even its organized destruction of physical well-being is not anomalous. A very large part of our wealth, work and time is, after all, spent in systematically destroying and harming human life. Manufacturing, selling and using weapons that tear opponents to pieces. Making ever bigger and faster predator-named cars with which to kill and injure one another by the million every year. And devoting our very lives to outgunning one another for power in an ever more destructive rat race. Yet all these practices are accepted without question by most people, even zealously defended and honored. Competitive, organized injuring is integral to our way of life, and football is simply one of the more intelligible mirrors of the whole process: a sort of colorful morality play showing us how exciting and rewarding it is to Smash Thy Neighbor.

Now it is fashionable to rationalize our collaboration 15 in all this by arguing that, well, man *likes* to fight and injure his fellows and such games as football should be encouraged to discharge this original-sin urge into less harmful channels than, say, war. Public-show football, this line goes, plays the same sort of cathartic role as Aristotle said stage tragedy does: without real blood (or not much), it releases players and audience from unhealthy feelings stored up inside them.

As an ex-player in this seasonal coast-to-coast drama, 16 I see little to recommend such a view. What organized football did to me was make me *suppress* my natural urges and re-express them in an alienating, vicious form. Spontaneous desires for free bodily exuberance and fraternization with competitors were shamed and forced under ("If it ain't hurtin' it ain't helpin' ") and in their place were demanded armored mechanical moves and cool hatred of all opposition. Endless authoritarian drill and dressing-room harangues (ever wonder why competing teams can't prepare for a game in the same dressing room?) were the kinds of mechanisms employed to reconstruct joyful energies into mean and alien shapes. I am quite certain that everyone else around me was being similarly forced into this heavily equipped military precision and angry antagonism, because there was always a mutinous attitude about full-dress practices, and everybody (the pros included) had to concentrate incredibly hard for days to whip themselves into just one hour's hostility a week against another club. The players never speak of these things, of course, because everyone is so anxious to appear tough.

The claim that men like seriously to battle one another 17 to some sort of finish is a myth. It only endures because it wears one of the oldest and most propagandized of masks—the romantic combatant. I sometimes wonder whether the violence all around us doesn't depend for its survival on the existence and preservation of this tough-guy disguise.

As for the effect of organized football on the spectator, 18 the fan is not released from supposed feelings of violent aggression by watching his athletic heroes perform it so much as encouraged in the view that people-smashing is an admirable mode of self-expression. The most savage attackers, after all, are, by general agreement, the most efficient and worthy players of all (the biggest applause I ever received as a football player occurred when I ran over people or slammed them so hard they couldn't get up). Such circumstances can hardly be said to lessen the spectators' martial tendencies. Indeed it seems likely that the whole show just further develops and titillates the North American addiction for violent self-assertion. . . . Perhaps, as well, it helps explain why the greater the zeal of U.S. political leaders as football fans (Johnson, Nixon, Agnew), the more enthusiastic the commitment to hardline politics. At any rate there seems to be a strong correlation between people who relish tough football and people who relish intimidating and beating the hell out of commies, hippies, protest marchers and other opposition groups.

Watching well-advertised strong men knock other peo- 19 ple around, make them hurt, is in the end like other tastes. It does not weaken with feeding and variation in form. It grows.

I got out of football in 1962. I had asked to be traded 20 after Calgary had offered me a $25-a-week-plus-commissions off-season job as a clothing-store salesman. ("Dear Mr. Finks:" I wrote. [Jim Finks was then the Stampeders' general manager.] "Somehow I do not think the dialectical subtleties of Hegel, Marx and Plato would be suitably oriented amidst the environmental stimuli of jockey shorts and herringbone suits. I hope you make a profitable sale or trade of my contract to the East.") So the Stampeders traded me to Montreal. In a preseason intersquad game with the Alouettes I ripped the cartilages in my ribs on the hardest block I'd ever thrown. I had trouble breathing and I had to shufflewalk with my torso on a tilt. The doctor in the local hospital said three weeks rest, the coach said scrimmage in two days. Three days later I was back home reading philosophy.

QUESTIONS ON MEANING

1. According to McMurtry, what are the similarities between football and war?

2. What claim does McMurtry make about football? What sentences in his essay most clearly express this claim?

3. What opposing arguments does McMurtry present and then refute in his essay?

QUESTIONS ON PURPOSE AND STRATEGY

1. Which of the following describe McMurtry's primary purpose: To recall his own injuries? To explain how football is like war? To show how football causes injuries and promotes violence? To modify the rules of football? To propose that football be abolished?

2. McMurtry's essay was first published in 1971, during the height of the Vietnam War protests. In your own words, describe McMurtry's political purpose in his essay.

3. In how many of McMurtry's twenty paragraphs does he write about his personal experience with football? Is his personal experience effective at supporting his argument? Should he use more statistics about football injuries? Should he interview his football player friends for their experiences? Should he quote coaches, doctors, owners, or other authorities?

QUESTIONS ON AUDIENCE AND LANGUAGE

1. Who is McMurtry's intended audience? Players who are thinking about their football careers? Football fans? Coaches? Politicians? Business people? Find specific lines in the essay that appeal to each audience.

2. In paragraphs five and six, McMurtry describes how the language of football is like the language of war. In what other paragraphs does McMurtry use war language to describe football? List the war-like phrases from those paragraphs.

QUESTIONS FOR DISCUSSION AND WRITING

1. According to McMurtry, who is to blame for the violence in football? If you think the violence in football or basketball or hockey is too extreme, what or whom do you blame? How would you propose remedying the situation?

2. If you disagree with McMurtry, what arguments and supporting evidence could you cite? Decide how you would respond to McMurtry's arguments, think of evidence you could use, and draft a letter to McMurtry, arguing against his claim.

3. Explain the relationship between McMurtry's attitude toward football and Marx's belief that capitalism exploits its workers. Despite their six-figure salaries, are professional football players exploited by management?

4. Choose a game or sport that does not usually have violent physical contact, such as chess, ping pong, Monopoly, poker, jogging, fishing, or skiing. Then explain that sport using an analogy: Compare your sport to some other activity in order to explain an essential feature of your sport. For example, fishing is like teasing a younger brother or sister: It combines elements of play with an edge of cruelty.

Should Couples Live Together First?

JOYCE BROTHERS

(1929–   )

PREREADING JOURNAL ENTRY

Would you live with a man or woman before marriage or
instead of marriage? What conditions would have to exist?
What would be (or are) the advantages and disadvantages?
In your opinion, does marriage help or harm a relationship? Explain.

According to New York Times *critic Susan Bolotin, Joyce Brothers
"brings the lessons of psychology, for better or for worse, to millions of
Americans. . . . If we want to discover what the majority of American
women feel about men, she can tell us." Joyce Brothers is the author of
several popular love and marriage books, including* The Brothers
System for Liberated Love and Marriage *(1974) and* What Every
Woman Should Know about Men *(1982). Brothers was born in
New York, graduated from Cornell University, and earned her M.A.
and Ph.D. at Columbia University.*

"Should Couples Live Together First?" appeared originally in Parade *magazine in 1985. In this essay, Brothers argues that living together is not a good test for marriage. As you read her essay, however,
you may think that she's not arguing her case at all. She appears to be
describing current research studies and then allowing you to make up
your own mind. Instead of arguing directly, Brothers uses several studies
of married and unmarried couples to argue her claim indirectly for her.
She poses the questions and then interweaves her views as she describes
the results of each study.*

My third year of college, one of my sorority sisters 1
was "so in love" she just couldn't wait. Throwing caution
to the proverbial winds, she confided to us that she was
setting up housekeeping with a young man. She would
report to classes, as would he, but they would live off
campus. And if their friends were "really good pals," no
one else would ever know.

At the sorority house, we covered for her, signing her 2
in at night. The risk was worth it, because she promised
to report back—and, my God, the knowledge we'd gain!

In the late '40s and early '50s, few young women lived 3
with a boyfriend. Most lived at home or, if at college, in
segregated dorms or in sorority houses, where the house-
mother was as strict as a nun. Of course, there were a
few liberated souls who couldn't accept the double standards and rigid sexual codes of the time. My sorority sister
fit into this category. What she elected to do was shocking
but fascinating to almost all of her relatively timid classmates. So when she suddenly appeared back at the sorority
house, we waited, wide-eyed and open-mouthed, for the
full report.

"Wasn't it the most wonderful thing that ever hap- 4
pened?" a pretty sophomore gushed. "Tell. Tell. Do you
have a ring? When's the wedding?"

Our friend looked grim. "I'm here to stay," she said, 5
somewhat bitterly. "Between the dishes and the hygiene,
I'm up to here with water. I've had it. It's over! That's it."

Our friend didn't know then what studies have re- 6
vealed over the last few years: If a couple are really in
love, then sex deepens it. But if they're not, sex doesn't
make real love happen.

Mother always said: If you go too far with a fellow, 7
he won't respect you. I guess I believed her, because I
never tried. Most women in those days (including myself)
dated a number of guys. Then, when that magic someone
came along, you progressed to going steady; you were
"pinned" (as I was) or, if in high school, given some kind
of insignia to let others know about your good fortune.
You progressed to being engaged and then, if things went

well, you married (as I did—I've been married to Milton since 1949).

Is living together a good test for marriage? "I wouldn't 8 dream of marrying someone I hadn't lived with," young people frequently say today. "That's like buying a pair of shoes you haven't tried on."

Sounds logical, doesn't it? A couple have a trial period 9 of cohabitation. If they find they are compatible, they get married. If not, they go their separate ways. They find out *before* they marry whether they'll get along. And that should cut down on the divorce rate. Right?

Wrong, say sociologists Jeffrey Jacques and Karen 10 Chason of Florida A&M University. They studied two groups of students married for at least 13 months. In one, the couples had lived together before their marriage; in the other, they had not. The researchers say they could find few differences between the couples. Satisfaction with the marriage was no higher (or lower) if the couple had cohabited. Neither was dissatisfaction—as many couples in one group as in the other seemed headed for conflict or divorce. Both groups reported that they still found their partners sexually attractive and rated their sex lives as highly satisfactory.

The researchers suggest, based on their findings, that 11 the types of learning that occur during cohabitation aren't as related to marriage as we usually assume. They don't work *against* a successful marriage, but they don't work *for* one either. Cohabitation as a testing ground for marriage hasn't really met the test.

Why doesn't a trial period of living together alter the 12 marriage experience? For one thing, both people know that it's a trial period. Either can walk out the next time the lease is up for renewal. The cohabiting woman doesn't have to put up with a man who mistreats her; the man doesn't have to put up with a moody mate. Both may tend to be on their best behavior. And, since it is a trial, both may find it easier to put up with traits in the other that would be unbearable if a shared lifetime stretched ahead.

Then there's the matter of money. In a live-in arrange- 13

ment, money tends to be "his" or "hers." Expenses may be shared, but the future isn't jeopardized if she spends more than she can afford on clothes or if he continually loses on the horses. It's different after they're wed and saving for a house and children. Then each can resent the other's extravagances.

In-laws are rarely a factor in a live-in arrangement— 14 they often disapprove and stay aloof from the couple. Only after marriage do in-laws intrude and cause disagreements, tears, and divided loyalties. Nor does a live-in arrangement usually have to adapt to children, who require adjustments in a marriage that some relationships can't accommodate.

Living together, it seems, prepares one for a future 15 living-together arrangement with someone else. It appears to have little correlation with happiness in marriage.

Why they do it. According to the U.S. Census Bureau, 16 the number of men and women living together without the benefits of wedlock has more than tripled since 1970. That's close to 2 million, compared to 523,000 in 1970. Why this increase? The Census Bureau report says: "A number of factors may be contributing to the change in the living arrangements of young men and women, including the postponement of marriage, rise in divorce, emphasis on advanced education, employment problems and high housing costs."

In citing "postponement of marriage," the bureau 17 seems to be saying that the couples eventually will get married, that cohabitation is merely a prelude to wedlock. But live-in couples don't necessarily share that view.

Prof. George Thorman, while at the Graduate School 18 of Social Work at the University of Texas, decided to find out why young people chose cohabitation instead of marriage. He surveyed 431 students at the university's campus in Austin and found that more than one-third were living intimately with a member of the opposite sex or had done so in the past. Only cohabitation lasting at least three months was counted.

Then he interviewed 30 long-term live-in couples— 19

almost half had lived together longer than a year. They ranged from 18 to 30 years of age, from sophomores to graduate students.

His interviews revealed that, in most cases, the couples 20 did not decide lightly to live together. Three-fourths had strong ties of affection and commitment before they moved in together, though only two couples had plans to marry. Many were afraid of marriage; they had lived with unhappily married parents or had watched the relationships of live-in couples deteriorate after marriage. They spoke of marriage as a "duty" relationship, "a dead end," "a drag" and "giving up something wonderful which would only lead to taking a partner for granted."

Most of Thorman's couples denied that sex was the 21 reason for living together. Sex is freely available outside such arrangements, they explained. The intimacy they sought—and claimed to find—through cohabitation was emotional and intellectual as well as physical. Most saw their relationship as a more honest, growth-promoting interaction than the usual dating and courtship. Most were sexually faithful to each other, just as they would be expected to be if they were married. The difference seemed to be that they felt they had freely chosen this commitment to the live-in partner—it wasn't demanded of them by parents or society. Perhaps, for them, marriage had been pushed too much as a moral duty, too little praised and not shown to be a meaningful lifestyle.

All of this prompted Thorman to conclude that the 22 live-in couples had a lifestyle similar to that of married couples—though his subjects didn't see it that way.

An alternative to marriage? Joe and Kathy are living 23 together. John and Mary are dating steadily. Which pair is more likely to split up? To marry? Dr. Judith Lyness Fischer, while at Pennsylvania State University, interviewed 23 couples who had been dating and 15 who had been living together for at least eight months. All were middle class, in their early 20s. All indicated that they felt themselves in serious relationships.

They were questioned eight months later. Two-thirds 24

(16) of the dating couples either had split up or married. Only two of the live-in couples had married—the rest still were living together. Dr. Lyness Fischer suggests that we must begin to look at the relatively new living-together phenomenon not as a step toward marriage but as an alternative.

Couples who cohabit may not marry each other, as 25 dating couples are more apt to do. But it still is possible that they will learn important lessons about living with one another—sharing, cooperating, meeting one another's needs. These may be carried on into a more mature relationship—a marriage—or they may not. Cohabiting couples are now a part of our society. Lyness Fischer feels that society will benefit if their place in it is examined without prejudice.

A rip-off for women? While lecturing at colleges around 26 the country, I have noticed that a growing number of liberated women—many of whom once would have favored living-together arrangements—have concluded that sharing bed and board with a male is just another rip-off. Even when there is full equality in the rooms where a couple live, once they step outside the front door, women are realizing, the myth is shattered, and the odds are tipped in the men's favor. How can you divide equally the payment of rent, the cost of food and other daily necessities when the disparity of earning power between a male and female of similar talents and backgrounds increases rather than decreases? When the romance fades and the household is broken up, is a 50-50 split of property fair when the woman has contributed three-fourths of her salary while the man has contributed only one-fourth of his? If the woman doesn't work and the man pays all the bills, does he then take everything, even though the woman has given her time and energy to making the relationship of free love seem really free?

Emotionally, many women seem to want and need 27 more commitment than do many men, and some become disillusioned by the disposable quality of sex and love that too often seems thoughtless and without continuity. Many are finding that, just as they become adjusted to a living arrangement and press for more commitment, the man becomes vague. When they want to have a child, they are faced with the prospect of having one out of wedlock or none at all. And some find that they eventually lose out to a woman who hasn't become quite so familiar on a day-to-day basis.

Hiding from each other. Shelly and Scott finally had set 28 their wedding date. "At least we know this is one marriage that will work," said Scott's mother, whose three marriages hadn't worked: After all, Shelly and Scott had lived together like a pair of lovebirds for five years. Surely that had given them a chance to iron out all their differences.

Or had it? Even before the ceremony, they were 29 arguing about where to spend the honeymoon. Shelly wanted to go skiing; Scott wanted to cruise on an exotic beach and soak up the sun. They compromised on Palm Springs.

Before the honeymoon was over, they were having 30 sexual difficulties. Scott found himself getting bored with their sexual routine. Always before, he had been able to dream about the beauties he saw around the pool. ("Maybe I'll make love to her one day after Shelly and I break up," he would fantasize.) But now he was a married man. It would be Shelly and the same routine forever.

It turned out that Shelly wasn't happy with their love 31 life either. "I've never been satisfied," Shelly admitted on the last night of the honeymoon. "I've pretended to be in order to please you, but I'm tired of pretending while you have all the fun. I think we need to see a sex therapist." This, after they'd lived together for five years! Hadn't their years together counted for anything?

They frequently don't, says Dr. Matti Gershenfeld of 32 Rydal, Pa. "To maintain their living-together relationship, couples often hide from each other important aspects of their true selves."

Dr. Gershenfeld surveyed 100 couples who were living 33 together and planning marriage. "I found that they had never discussed such important matters as sex, whether or not they wanted children, finances, careers, leisure activities," says the psychologist. "Or, if they had discussed them, it was in only the most general terms." They were reluctant to explore these areas before marriage because they were afraid differences might mar the relationship, she explains.

Living together, the couples spoke and behaved cau- 34 tiously, avoided criticizing each other and repressed true feelings and anger. But after marriage, all the hostile feelings come out. Each gets busy trying to redo the other into a more acceptable partner.

Counseling—not just for the married. It used to be as- 35 sumed that live-in unmarried couples who were dissatisfied would simply split and try again with someone new. But that's not the way it is today. Increasing numbers of such couples are going to marital counselors with their problems. Today, an estimated 10 percent of marriage counselors' caseloads are unwed couples.

Why don't they just break up? Or, if they are so 36 committed to the relationship, why don't they legalize it? Frequently, the couple combine these two questions when they go to a counselor. "Should we get married or break up?" they ask. The counselor helps them define their relationship and their problems within it. After that, they can answer their own question.

Once both partners have committed themselves to 37 counseling, they feel freer to air grievances and work out differences. They learn about themselves and the ways they relate to an intimate partner. Outcomes vary, from marriage to continuing the relationship to breaking up. But counselors and those they have counseled both believe that the experience provides strengths and skills that will help create happier, better-grounded future relationships—including marriage.

The forces that drive them to it. Is your son or daughter 38 living with a lover without the benefit of marriage? And are you blaming them—or yourself—for this situation? Why did they go wrong? Where did you go wrong?

The blame is possibly misplaced and probably belongs 39

in a nature/culture gap for which neither you nor your children are responsible.

Once puberty was the line dividing childhood and 40 adulthood. Shortly thereafter, young people married and started rearing families. They shouldered the responsibilities and the privileges of adults.

Not so anymore. Modern industry isn't geared to 41 taking 13- and 15-year-olds into the work force. So, after puberty, most young people go on to high school, and half go on to college. That's a long wait between a sexual maturing, conferred by nature, and cultural maturity, conferred by society. An estimated one-third of college students are making their own compromise: cohabiting without the benefit of legal marriage.

Are live-ins different? Do these young people differ from 42 the two-thirds who aren't living with someone of the opposite sex? Not much, says psychologist Eleanor Macklin of Syracuse University. She conducted a study of college students and found that those cohabiting had very similar backgrounds to those who weren't. The same proportion of both groups came from two-parent homes with parents of like education and income. Religion was the outstanding difference. Those without a religion that they were still practicing were four times as likely to cohabit as those with a viable faith.

Students in both groups desired eventually to contract 43 a conventional marriage. Less than 10 percent of those who abstained from cohabiting felt it was morally wrong— most said they had not yet found the right partner. Seventy percent of the live-ins felt that their emotional attachment to the partner was more important than sexual fulfillment. Nearly 10 percent had lived together for some months before engaging in intimate relations. In all, observers at several universities found that cohabitants are normal, healthy kids trying to make the best of a nature/culture bind of which most parents are unaware.

Not just college students. Some parents hesitate to send 44 their off-spring to college because that seems to be where most of the cohabitation outside wedlock takes place.

That isn't really the case, say psychologists Michael 45 Newcomb and Peter Bentler of UCLA. It's just that cohabitation in college populations has been more often researched than cohabitation in the larger community.

When their research on 159 nonstudent couples ap- 46 plying for marriage licenses in Los Angeles is compared with research on college campuses, it would appear that working couples are almost twice as likely to cohabit as are students. Researchers have found that 18 percent to 20 percent of the college population is cohabiting. Newcomb and Bentler found that 47 percent of their nonstudent sample had lived together before marriage. They came from all walks of life, all levels of education and varied backgrounds (though only 6 percent were nonwhite). Some had cohabited for a month or two, most for about six months, and the rest for at least a year—some for more than three years.

But they all applied for that marriage license. Most 47 couples who cohabit do eventually marry. They don't always marry each other, but 90 percent marry. Marriage is still the accepted, and expected, way of life even for those who try alternatives, the researchers say.

I never discussed my dating days with my daughter, 48 Lisa. There were always so many other things to chat about when she was a little girl. Perhaps because of this, I was especially delighted when Lisa and I were asked to be the guests on a talk show in St. Louis on the subject of mothers and daughters. Lisa was asked about my attitudes on premarital sex and how our discussions had influenced her own dating behavior. I was very interested in her reply.

She said she couldn't recall any precise words from 49 me on this matter, but she did feel strongly that, whatever lifestyle she elected to follow, she could count on my support. Her own feeling was that, if she really loved the man enough to want to marry him, there would be no point in living together, because this didn't really "test" anything. Therefore, she chose not to live with anyone until her marriage.

Lisa married a fellow ophthalmologist in 1976. They 50 work together as well as live together, and it's a good, rewarding marriage.

There are now 7.3 million more marriageable women 51 than marriageable men in the U.S. Men are the blue-chip stock, and they're getting *very* spoiled.

Things that used to push men into marriage aren't 52 there anymore. As we all know, they don't need to get married to have sex. The old idea that married men are more stable and better bets for employers also is passing. So is the notion that society expects them to marry. There's even less need to get married for such services as good food and clean laundry. Many men now pride themselves on being good cooks, and there's usually a Laundromat close by. The external pressures to marry are gone.

No doubt about it—when a woman is living with a 53 man, giving him all the advantages and none of the disadvantages of marriage, his urge to get married is much less than when the woman is less available, less like "an old shoe."

Mother warned a long time ago: If you give him 54 everything, you're going to lose something. And *we have.* We may have "come a long way," but a lot of women are beginning to discover that, on this particular issue, Mother was probably right.

QUESTIONS ON MEANING

1. In her essay, Brothers asks and then answers a series of questions. In the title, she asks, "Should Couples Live Together First?" In paragraph eight, she asks, "Is living together a good test for marriage?" What other questions does she pose? What is her answer to each question?

2. Brothers cites six research studies in her essay. For each study, identify the researcher(s) and the results or conclusions that Brothers cites.

3. What is the "nature/culture bind" that Brothers discusses in paragraph forty-three?

QUESTIONS ON PURPOSE AND STRATEGY

1. In your own words, state Brothers's thesis or claim. Then find three sentences from her essay that state or rephrase her thesis.

2. Which opposing or con arguments does Brothers give? How does she refute these arguments?

3. Where does Brothers use personal experience to support her argument? Do these examples effectively support her claim?

4. Rather than directly stating her own opinion or argument, Brothers often quotes or paraphrases statements from researchers to clarify her position. In paragraph six, for example, she says, "Our friend didn't know then what studies have revealed over the last few years: If a couple are really in love, then sex deepens it. But if they're not, sex doesn't make real love happen." Find three other examples of this strategy. Is it effective for her purpose and audience?

QUESTIONS ON AUDIENCE AND LANGUAGE

1. Who is Brothers's audience? Parents? Mothers? Women in their twenties? Men? Brothers's essay was published in *Parade* magazine. Examine a copy of that magazine. Profile the typical reader.

2. Examine sentences in which Brothers uses the words *marry* or *marriage*. Are the terms presented in a positive or negative manner? How does her use of these words support her thesis?

QUESTIONS FOR DISCUSSION AND WRITING

1. Reread the six examples of research studies that Brothers cites. Then compare the conclusions that the researchers draw (as summarized by Brothers) and Brothers's own conclusions about these studies. Are Brothers's conclusions justified by the studies? Would your conclusions from these studies differ from Brothers's conclusions?

2. Reread paragraphs twenty-six and twenty-seven. Does Brothers stereotype men or women by assigning typical roles and attitudes? Reread the final paragraph of the essay. Is this conclusion justified by the research presented in the essay? Is Brothers's statement sexist and stereotyped or only realistic?

3. Conduct your own study on attitudes toward marriage by asking four or five people to read and respond to the ideas in Brothers's essay. Choose your respondents from couples you know who are living together and from married couples and/or your parents. Give each person a copy of this essay and ask them to explain in writing how their own personal experience agrees or disagrees with the research studies or with Brothers's conclusions. In your essay, explain how this additional information has modified your original position on this subject (as described in your Prereading Journal Entry).

Letter from Birmingham Jail

MARTIN LUTHER KING, JR.

(1929–1968)

PREREADING JOURNAL ENTRY

Without reading the following headnote, write in your journal what you know about Martin Luther King. What do you know about his life or death? What did he mean by "civil disobedience" or nonviolent protest? How is Martin Luther King Day celebrated in your town or city? What current public figure is most active in nonviolent protest for civil rights of minorities?

In 1955, an unknown Baptist minister named Martin Luther King organized a Negro boycott of the segregated bus system in Montgomery, Alabama. To the dismay of the white citizens, the boycott lasted 381 days. From 1955 until his assassination in 1968, King was the acknowledged leader of the American Civil Rights Movement. Born the son of a Baptist minister, King earned degrees from Morehouse College, Crozer Theological Seminary, Boston University, and Chicago Theological Seminary. King's writings include Why We Can't Wait *(1964) and* Where Do We Go from Here: Chaos or Community? *(1967). Although King's most dramatic moment was the delivery of his "I Have a Dream" speech to 200,000 civil rights protesters at the Lincoln Memorial, his legacy to America is the defense of civil disobedience in "Letter from Birmingham Jail," a document that echoes Plato's* Apology, *Henry David Thoreau's "Civil Disobedience," and Mahatma Gandhi's Nonviolent Resistance.*

"Letter from Birmingham Jail" was written in April 1963, while King was in jail in Birmingham, Alabama, for acts of civil disobedience. King is responding to a letter signed by eight Jewish, Catholic, and Protestant clergymen appealing for "Law and Order and Common Sense." In their statement, the clergymen express concern about "unwise

and untimely" demonstrations "led in part by outsiders." They call for "honest and open negotiation of racial issues" and deplore the "extreme measures" that, though technically peaceful, might incite "hatred and violence." They then praise law enforcement officials for their "calm manner" and request that "our own Negro community" withdraw from the demonstrations. "When rights are consistently denied," the clergymen conclude, "a cause should be pressed in the courts and in negotiations among local leaders, and not in the streets." In his letter, King replies to each of these statements.

MY DEAR FELLOW CLERGYMEN:

While confined here in the Birmingham city jail, I 1 came across your recent statement calling my present activities "unwise and untimely." Seldom do I pause to answer criticism of my work and ideas. If I sought to answer all the criticisms that cross my desk, my secretaries would have little time for anything other than such correspondence in the course of the day, and I would have no time for constructive work. But since I feel that you are men of genuine good will and that your criticisms are sincerely set forth, I want to try to answer your statement in what I hope will be patient and reasonable terms.

I think I should indicate why I am here in Birmingham, 2 since you have been influenced by the view which argues against "outsiders coming in." I have the honor of serving as president of the Southern Christian Leadership Conference, an organization operating in every southern state, with headquarters in Atlanta, Georgia. We have some eighty-five affiliated organizations across the South, and one of them is the Alabama Christian Movement for Human Rights. Frequently we share staff, educational, and financial resources with our affiliates. Several months ago the affiliate here in Birmingham asked us to be on call to engage in a nonviolent direct-action program if such were deemed necessary. We readily consented, and when the hour came we lived up to our promise. So I, along with several members of my staff, am here because

I was invited here. I am here because I have organizational ties here.

But more basically, I am in Birmingham because 3 injustice is here. Just as the prophets of the eighth century B.C. left their villages and carried their "thus saith the Lord" far beyond the boundaries of their home towns, and just as the Apostle Paul left his village of Tarsus and carried the gospel of Jesus Christ to the far corners of the Greco-Roman world, so am I compelled to carry the gospel of freedom beyond my own home town. Like Paul, I must constantly respond to the Macedonian call for aid.

Moreover, I am cognizant of the interrelatedness of 4 all communities and states. I cannot sit idly by in Atlanta and not be concerned about what happens in Birmingham. Injustice anywhere is a threat to justice everywhere. We are caught in an inescapable network of mutuality, tied in a single garment of destiny. Whatever affects one directly, affects all indirectly. Never again can we afford to live with the narrow, provincial "outside agitator" idea. Anyone who lives inside the United States can never be considered an outsider anywhere within its bounds.

You deplore the demonstrations taking place in Bir- 5 mingham. But your statement, I am sorry to say, fails to express a similar concern for the conditions that brought about the demonstrations. I am sure that none of you would want to rest content with the superficial kind of social analysis that deals merely with effects and does not grapple with underlying causes. It is unfortunate that demonstrations are taking place in Birmingham, but it is even more unfortunate that the city's white power structure left the Negro community with no alternative.

In any nonviolent campaign there are four basic steps: 6 collection of the facts to determine whether injustices exist; negotiation; self-purification; and direct action. We have gone through all these steps in Birmingham. There can be no gainsaying the fact that racial injustice engulfs this community. Birmingham is probably the most thoroughly segregated city in the United States. Its ugly record of brutality is widely known. Negroes have experienced grossly unjust treatment in the courts. There have been more unsolved bombings of Negro homes and churches in Birmingham than in any other city in the nation. These are the hard, brutal facts of the case. On the basis of these conditions, Negro leaders sought to negotiate with the city fathers. But the latter consistently refused to engage in good-faith negotiation.

Then, last September, came the opportunity to talk 7 with leaders of Birmingham's economic community. In the course of the negotiations, certain promises were made by the merchants—for example, to remove the stores' humiliating racial signs. On the basis of these promises, the Reverend Fred Shuttlesworth and the leaders of the Alabama Christian Movement for Human Rights agreed to a moratorium on all demonstrations. As the weeks and months went by, we realized that we were the victims of a broken promise. A few signs, briefly removed, returned; the others remained.

As in so many past experiences, our hopes had been 8 blasted, and the shadow of deep disappointment settled upon us. We had no alternative except to prepare for direct action, whereby we would present our very bodies as a means of laying our case before the conscience of the local and the national community. Mindful of the difficulties involved, we decided to undertake a process of self-purification. We began a series of workshops on nonviolence, and we repeatedly asked ourselves: "Are you able to accept blows without retaliating?" "Are you able to endure the ordeal of jail?" We decided to schedule our direct-action program for the Easter season, realizing that except for Christmas, this is the main shopping period of the year. Knowing that a strong economic-withdrawal program would be the by-product of direct action, we felt that this would be the best time to bring pressure to bear on the merchants for the needed change.

Then it occurred to us that Birmingham's mayoral 9 election was coming up in March, and we speedily decided to postpone action until after election day. When we discovered that the Commissioner of Public Safety, Eugene

"Bull" Connor, had piled up enough votes to be in the run-off, we decided again to postpone action until the day after the run-off so that the demonstrations could not be used to cloud the issues. Like many others, we wanted to see Mr. Connor defeated, and to this end we endured postponement after postponement. Having aided in this community need, we felt that our direct-action program could be delayed no longer.

You may well ask, "Why direct action? Why sit-ins, 10 marches, and so forth? Isn't negotiation a better path?" You are quite right in calling for negotiation. Indeed, this is the very purpose of direct action. Nonviolent direct action seeks to create such a crisis and foster such a tension that a community which has constantly refused to negotiate is forced to confront the issue. It seeks so to dramatize the issue that it can no longer be ignored. My citing the creation of tension as part of the work of the nonviolent-resister may sound rather shocking. But I must confess that I am not afraid of the word "tension." I have earnestly opposed violent tension, but there is a type of constructive, nonviolent tension which is necessary for growth. Just as Socrates felt that it was necessary to create a tension in the mind so that individuals could rise from the bondage of myths and half-truths to the unfettered realm of creative analysis and objective appraisal, so must we see the need for nonviolent gadflies to create the kind of tension in society that will help men rise from the dark depths of prejudice and racism to the majestic heights of under-standing and brotherhood.

The purpose of our direct-action program is to create 11 a situation so crisis-packed that it will inevitably open the door to negotiation. I therefore concur with you in your call for negotiation. Too long has our beloved Southland been bogged down in a tragic effort to live in monologue rather than dialogue.

One of the basic points in your statement is that the 12 action that I and my associates have taken in Birmingham is untimely. Some have asked: "Why didn't you give the new city administration time to act?" The only answer that

I can give to this query is that the new Birmingham administration must be prodded about as much as the outgoing one, before it will act. We are sadly mistaken if we feel that the election of Albert Boutwell as mayor will bring the millennium to Birmingham. While Mr. Boutwell is a much more gentle person than Mr. Connor, they are both segregationists, dedicated to maintenance of the status quo. I have hoped that Mr. Boutwell will be reasonable enough to see the futility of massive resistance to desegregation. But he will not see this without pressure from devotees of civil rights. My friends, I must say to you that we have not made a single gain in civil rights without determined legal and nonviolent pressure. Lamentably, it is an historical fact that privileged groups seldom give up their privileges voluntarily. Individuals may see the moral light and voluntarily give up their unjust posture; but, as Reinhold Niebuhr has reminded us, groups tend to be more immoral than individuals.

We know through painful experience that freedom is 13 never voluntarily given by the oppressor; it must be demanded by the oppressed. Frankly, I have yet to engage in a direct-action campaign that was "well timed" in the view of those who have not suffered unduly from the disease of segregation. For years now I have heard the word "Wait!" It rings in the ear of every Negro with piercing familiarity. This "Wait" has almost always meant "Never." We must come to see, with one of our distinguished jurists, that "justice too long delayed is justice denied."

We have waited for more than 340 years for our 14 constitutional and God-given rights. The nations of Asia and Africa are moving with jetlike speed toward gaining political independence, but we still creep at horse-and-buggy pace toward gaining a cup of coffee at a lunch counter. Perhaps it is easy for those who have never felt the stinging darts of segregation to say, "Wait." But when you have seen vicious mobs lynch your mothers and fathers at will and drown your sisters and brothers at whim; when you have seen hate-filled policemen curse, kick, and even kill your black brothers and sisters; when you see the vast majority of your twenty million Negro brothers smothering in an airtight cage of poverty in the midst of an affluent society; when you suddenly find your tongue twisted and your speech stammering as you seek to explain to your six-year-old daughter why she can't go to the public amusement park that has just been advertised on television, and see tears welling up in her eyes when she is told that Funtown is closed to colored children, and see ominous clouds of inferiority beginning to form in her little mental sky, and see her beginning to distort her personality by developing an unconscious bitterness toward white people; when you have to concoct an answer for a five-year-old son who is asking, "Daddy, why do white people treat colored people so mean?"; when you take a cross-country drive and find it necessary to sleep night after night in the uncomfortable corners of your automobile because no motel will accept you; when you are humiliated day in and day out by nagging signs reading "white" and "colored"; when your first name becomes "nigger," your middle name becomes "boy" (however old you are) and your last name becomes "John," and your wife and mother are never given the respected title "Mrs."; when you are harried by day and haunted by night by the fact that you are a Negro, living constantly at tiptoe stance, never quite knowing what to expect next, and are plagued with inner fears and outer resentments; when you are forever fighting a degenerating sense of "nobodiness"—then you will understand why we find it difficult to wait. There comes a time when the cup of endurance runs over, and men are no longer willing to be plunged into the abyss of despair. I hope, sirs, you can understand our legitimate and unavoidable impatience.

You express a great deal of anxiety over our willingness 15 to break laws. This is certainly a legitimate concern. Since we so diligently urge people to obey the Supreme Court's decision of 1954 outlawing segregation in the public schools, at first glance it may seem rather paradoxical for us consciously to break laws. One may well ask: "How can you advocate breaking some laws and obeying others?" The answer lies in the fact that there are two types of laws: just and unjust. I would be the first to advocate obeying just laws. One has not only a legal but a moral responsibility to obey just laws. Conversely, one has a moral responsibility to disobey unjust laws. I would agree with St. Augustine that "an unjust law is no law at all."

Now, what is the difference between the two? How 16 does one determine whether a law is just or unjust? A just law is a man-made code that squares with the moral law or the law of God. An unjust law is a code that is out of harmony with the moral law. To put it in the terms of St. Thomas Aquinas: An unjust law is a human law that is not rooted in eternal law and natural law. Any law that uplifts human personality is just. Any law that degrades human personality is unjust. All segregation statutes are unjust because segregation distorts the soul and damages the personality. It gives the segregator a false sense of superiority and the segregated a false sense of inferiority. Segregation, to use the terminology of the Jewish philosopher Martin Buber, substitutes an "I-it" relationship for an "I-thou" relationship and ends up relegating persons to the status of things. Hence segregation is not only politically, economically, and sociologically unsound, it is morally wrong and sinful. Paul Tillich has said that sin is separation. Is not segregation an existential expression of man's tragic separation, his awful estrangement, his terrible sinfulness? Thus it is that I can urge men to obey the 1954 decision of the Supreme Court, for it is morally right; and I can urge them to disobey segregation ordinances, for they are morally wrong.

Let us consider a more concrete example of just and 17 unjust laws. An unjust law is a code that a numerical or power majority group compels a minority group to obey but does not make binding on itself. This is *difference* made legal. By the same token, a just law is a code that a majority compels a minority to follow and that it is willing to follow itself. This is *sameness* made legal.

Let me give another explanation. A law is unjust if it 18

is inflicted on a minority that, as a result of being denied the right to vote, had no part in enacting or devising the law. Who can say that the legislature of Alabama which set up that state's segregation laws was democratically elected? Throughout Alabama all sorts of devious methods are used to prevent Negroes from becoming registered voters, and there are some counties in which, even though Negroes constitute a majority of the population, not a single Negro is registered. Can any law enacted under such circumstances be considered democratically structured?

Sometimes a law is just on its face and unjust in its 19 application. For instance, I have been arrested on a charge of parading without a permit. Now, there is nothing wrong in having an ordinance which requires a permit for a parade. But such an ordinance becomes unjust when it is used to maintain segregation and to deny citizens the First-Amendment privilege of peaceful assembly and protest.

I hope you are able to see the distinction I am trying 20 to point out. In no sense do I advocate evading or defying the law, as would the rabid segregationist. That would lead to anarchy. One who breaks an unjust law must do so openly, lovingly, and with a willingness to accept the penalty. I submit that an individual who breaks a law that conscience tells him is unjust, and who willingly accepts the penalty of imprisonment in order to arouse the conscience of the community over its injustice, is in reality expressing the highest respect for law.

Of course, there is nothing new about this kind of civil 21 disobedience. It was evidenced sublimely in the refusal of Shadrach, Meshach, and Abednego to obey the laws of Nebuchadnezzar, on the ground that a higher moral law was at stake. It was practiced superbly by the early Christians, who were willing to face hungry lions and the excruciating pain of chopping blocks rather than submit to certain unjust laws of the Roman Empire. To a degree, academic freedom is a reality today because Socrates practiced civil disobedience. In our own nation, the Boston Tea Party represented a massive act of civil disobedience.

We should never forget that everything Adolf Hitler 22 did in Germany was "legal" and everything the Hungarian freedom fighters did in Hungary was "illegal." It was "illegal" to aid and comfort a Jew in Hitler's Germany. Even so, I am sure that, had I lived in Germany at the time, I would have aided and comforted my Jewish brothers. If today I lived in a Communist country where certain principles dear to the Christian faith are suppressed, I would openly advocate disobeying that country's antireligious laws.

I must make two honest confessions to you, my Chris- 23 tian and Jewish brothers. First, I must confess that over the past few years I have been gravely disappointed with the white moderate. I have almost reached the regrettable conclusion that the Negro's great stumbling block in his stride toward freedom is not the White Citizen's Counciler or the Ku Klux Klanner, but the white moderate, who is more devoted to "order" than to justice; who prefers a negative peace which is the absence of tension to a positive peace which is the presence of justice; who constantly says, "I agree with you in the goal you seek, but I cannot agree with your methods of direct action"; who paternalistically believes he can set the timetable for another man's freedom; who lives by a mythical concept of time and who constantly advises the Negro to wait for a "more convenient season." Shallow understanding from people of good will is more frustrating than absolute misunderstanding from people of ill will. Lukewarm acceptance is much more bewildering than outright rejection.

I had hoped that the white moderate would under- 24 stand that law and order exist for the purpose of establishing justice and that when they fail in this purpose they become the dangerously structured dams that block the flow of social progress. I had hoped that the white moderate would understand that the present tension in the South is a necessary phase of the transition from an obnoxious negative peace, in which the Negro passively accepted his unjust plight, to a substantive and positive peace, in which all men will respect the dignity and worth of human personality. Actually, we who engage in non-violent direct action are not the creators of tension. We merely bring to the surface the hidden tension that is already alive. We bring it out in the open, where it can be seen and dealt with. Like a boil that can never be cured so long as it is covered up but must be opened with all its ugliness to the natural medicines of air and light, injustice must be exposed, with all the tension its exposure creates, to the light of human conscience and the air of national opinion, before it can be cured.

In your statement you assert that our actions, even 25 though peaceful, must be condemned because they precipitate violence. But is this a logical assertion? Isn't this like condemning a robbed man because his possession of money precipitated the evil act of robbery? Isn't this like condemning Socrates because his unswerving commitment to truth and his philosophical inquiries precipitated the act by the misguided populace in which they made him drink hemlock? Isn't this like condemning Jesus because his unique God-consciousness and never-ceasing devotion to God's will precipitated the evil act of crucifixion? We must come to see that, as the federal courts have consistently affirmed, it is wrong to urge an individual to cease his efforts to gain his basic constitutional rights because the quest may precipitate violence. Society must protect the robbed and punish the robber.

I had also hoped that the white moderate would reject 26 the myth concerning time in relation to the struggle for freedom. I have just received a letter from a white brother in Texas. He writes: "All Christians know that the colored people will receive equal rights eventually, but it is possible that you are in too great a religious hurry. It has taken Christianity almost two thousand years to accomplish what it has. The teachings of Christ take time to come to earth." Such an attitude stems from a tragic misconception of time, from the strangely irrational notion that there is something in the very flow of time that will inevitably cure all ills. Actually, time itself is neutral; it can be used either destructively or constructively. More and more I feel that the people of ill will have used time much more effectively than have the people of good will. We will have to repent in this generation not merely for the hateful words and actions of the bad people, but for the appalling silence of the good people. Human progress never rolls in on wheels of inevitability; it comes through the tireless efforts of men willing to be co-workers with God, and without this hard work, time itself becomes an ally of the forces of social stagnation. We must use time creatively, in the knowledge that the time is always ripe to do right. Now is the time to make real the promise of democracy and transform our pending national elegy into a creative psalm of brotherhood. Now is the time to lift our national policy from the quicksand of racial injustice to the solid rock of human dignity.

You speak of our activity in Birmingham as extreme. [27] At first I was rather disappointed that fellow clergymen would see my nonviolent efforts as those of an extremist. I began thinking about the fact that I stand in the middle of two opposing forces in the Negro community. One is a force of complacency, made up in part of Negroes who, as a result of long years of oppression, are so drained of self-respect and a sense of "somebodiness" that they have adjusted to segregation; and in part of a few middle-class Negroes who, because of a degree of academic and economic security and because in some ways they profit by segregation, have become insensitive to the problems of the masses. The other force is one of bitterness and hatred, and it comes perilously close to advocating vio-lence. It is expressed in the various black nationalist groups that are springing up across the nation, the largest and best-known being Elijah Muhammad's Muslim movement. Nourished by the Negro's frustration over the continued existence of racial discrimination, this movement is made up of people who have lost faith in America, who have absolutely repudiated Christianity, and who have con-cluded that the white man is an incorrigible "devil."

I have tried to stand between these two forces, saying 28 that we need emulate neither the "do-nothingism" of the complacent nor the hatred and despair of the black nationalist. For there is the more excellent way of love and nonviolent protest. I am grateful to God that, through the influence of the Negro church, the way of nonviolence became an integral part of our struggle.

If this philosophy had not emerged, by now many 29 streets of the South would, I am convinced, be flowing with blood. And I am further convinced that if our white brothers dismiss as "rabblerousers" and "outside agitators" those of us who employ nonviolent direct action, and if they refuse to support our nonviolent efforts, millions of Negroes will, out of frustration and despair, seek solace and security in black-nationalist ideologies—a development that would inevitably lead to a frightening racial nightmare.

Oppressed people cannot remain oppressed forever. 30 The yearning for freedom eventually manifests itself, and that is what has happened to the American Negro. Something within has reminded him of his birthright of freedom, and something without has reminded him that it can be gained. Consciously or unconsciously, he has been caught up by the *Zeitgeist,* and with his black brothers of Africa and his brown and yellow brothers of Asia, South America, and the Caribbean, the United States Negro is moving with a sense of great urgency toward the promised land of racial justice. If one recognizes this vital urge that has engulfed the Negro community, one should readily understand why public demonstrations are taking place. The Negro has many pent-up resentments and latent frustrations, and he must release them. So let him march; let him make prayer pilgrimages to the city hall; let him go on freedom rides—and try to understand why he must do so. If his repressed emotions are not released in nonviolent ways, they will seek expression through violence; this is not a threat but a fact of history. So I have not said to my people, "Get rid of your discontent." Rather, I have tried to say that this normal and healthy discontent can be channeled into the creative outlet of nonviolent direct action. And now this approach is being termed extremist.

But though I was initially disappointed at being cate- 31 gorized as an extremist, as I continued to think about the matter I gradually gained a measure of satisfaction from the label. Was not Jesus an extremist for love: "Love your enemies, bless them that curse you, do good to them that hate you, and pray for them which despitefully use you, and persecute you." Was not Amos an extremist for justice: "Let justice roll down like waters and righteousness like an ever-flowing stream." Was not Paul an extremist for the Christian gospel: "I bear in my body the marks of the Lord Jesus." Was not Martin Luther an extremist: "Here I stand; I cannot do otherwise, so help me God." And John Bunyan: "I will stay in jail to the end of my days before I make a butchery of my conscience." And Abraham Lincoln: "This nation cannot survive half slave and half free." And Thomas Jefferson: "We hold these truths to be self-evident, that all men are created equal. . . ." So the question is not whether we will be extremists, but what kind of extremists we will be. Will we be extremists for hate or for love? Will we be extremists for the preservation of injustice or for the extension of justice? In that dramatic scene on Calvary's hill three men were crucified. We must never forget that all three were crucified for the same crime—the crime of extremism. Two were extremists for immorality, and thus fell below their environment. The other, Jesus Christ, was an extremist for love, truth, and goodness, and thereby rose above his environment. Perhaps the South, the nation, and the world are in dire need of creative extremists.

I had hoped that the white moderate would see this 32 need. Perhaps I was too optimistic; perhaps I expected too much. I suppose I should have realized that few members of the oppressor race can understand the deep groans and passionate yearnings of the oppressed race, and still fewer have the vision to see that injustice must be rooted out by strong, persistent, and determined action.

I am thankful, however, that some of our white brothers in the South have grasped the meaning of this social revolution and committed themselves to it. They are still all too few in quantity, but they are big in quality. Some— such as Ralph McGill, Lillian Smith, Harry Golden, James McBride Dabbs, Ann Braden, and Sarah Patton Boyle— have written about our struggle in eloquent and prophetic terms. Others have marched with us down nameless streets of the South. They have languished in filthy, roach-infested jails, suffering the abuse and brutality of police-men who view them as "dirty nigger-lovers." Unlike so many of their moderate brothers and sisters, they have recognized the urgency of the moment and sensed the need for powerful "action" antidotes to combat the disease of segregation.

Let me take note of my other major disappointment. 33 I have been so greatly disappointed with the white church and its leadership. Of course, there are some notable exceptions. I am not unmindful of the fact that each of you has taken some significant stands on this issue. I commend you, Reverend Stallings, for your Christian stand on this past Sunday, in welcoming Negroes to your worship service on a nonsegregated basis. I commend the Catholic leaders of this state for integrating Spring Hill College several years ago.

But despite these notable exceptions, I must honestly 34 reiterate that I have been disappointed with the church. I do not say this as one of those negative critics who can always find something wrong with the church. I say this as a minister of the gospel, who loves the church; who was nurtured in its bosom; who has been sustained by its spiritual blessings and who will remain true to it as long as the cord of life shall lengthen.

When I was suddenly catapulted into the leadership 35 of the bus protest in Montgomery, Alabama, a few years ago, I felt we would be supported by the white church. I felt that the white ministers, priests, and rabbis of the South would be among our strongest allies. Instead, some have been outright opponents, refusing to understand the freedom movement and misrepresenting its leaders; all too many others have been more cautious than courageous and have remained silent behind the anesthetizing security of stained glass windows.

In spite of my shattered dreams, I came to Birmingham 36 with the hope that the white religious leadership of this community would see the justice of our cause and, with deep moral concern, would serve as the channel through which our just grievances could reach the power structure. I had hoped that each of you would understand. But again I have been disappointed.

I have heard numerous southern religious leaders 37 admonish their worshipers to comply with a desegregation decision because it is the law, but I have longed to hear white ministers declare: "Follow this decree because integration is morally right and because the Negro is your brother." In the midst of blatant injustices inflicted upon the Negro, I have watched white churchmen stand on the sideline and mouth pious irrelevancies and sanctimonious trivialities. In the midst of a mighty struggle to rid our nation of racial and economic injustice, I have heard many ministers say: "Those are social issues, with which the gospel has no real concern." And I have watched many churches commit themselves to a completely otherworldly religion which makes a strange, un-Biblical distinction between body and soul, between the sacred and the secular.

I have traveled the length and breadth of Alabama, 38 Mississippi, and all the other southern states. On sweltering summer days and crisp autumn mornings I have looked at the South's beautiful churches with their lofty spires pointing heavenward. I have beheld the impressive outlines of her massive religious-education buildings. Over and over I have found myself asking: "What kind of people worship here? Who is their God? Where were their voices when the lips of Governor Barnett dripped with words of interposition and nullification? Where were they when Governor Wallace gave a clarion call for defiance and hatred? Where were their voices of support when bruised and weary Negro men and women decided to rise from the dark dungeons of complacency to the bright hills of creative protest?"

Yes, these questions are still in my mind. In deep 39 disappointment I have wept over the laxity of the church. But be assured that my tears have been tears of love. There can be no deep disappointment where there is not deep love. Yes, I love the church. How could I do otherwise? I am in the rather unique position of being the son, the grandson, and the great-grandson of preachers. Yes, I see the church as the body of Christ. But, oh! How we have blemished and scarred that body through social neglect and through fear of being nonconformists.

There was a time when the church was very powerful— 40 in the time when the early Christians rejoiced at being deemed worthy to suffer for what they believed. In those days the church was not merely a thermometer that recorded the ideas and principles of popular opinion; it was a thermostat that transformed the mores of society. Whenever the early Christians entered a town, the people in power became disturbed and immediately sought to convict the Christians for being "disturbers of the peace" and "outside agitators." But the Christians pressed on, in the conviction that they were "a colony of heaven," called to obey God rather than man. Small in number, they were big in commitment. They were too God-intoxicated to be "astronomically intimidated." By their effort and example they brought an end to such ancient evils as infanticide and gladiatorial contests.

Things are different now. So often the contemporary 41 church is a weak, ineffectual voice with an uncertain sound. So often it is an archdefender of the status quo. Far from being disturbed by the presence of the church, the power structure of the average community is consoled by the church's silent—and often even vocal—sanction of things as they are.

But the judgment of God is upon the church as never 42 before. If today's church does not recapture the sacrificial spirit of the early church, it will lose its authenticity, forfeit the loyalty of millions, and be dismissed as an irrelevant social club with no meaning for the twentieth century. Every day I meet young people whose disappointment with the church has turned into outright disgust.

Perhaps I have once again been too optimistic. Is 43 organized religion too inextricably bound to the status quo to save our nation and the world? Perhaps I must turn my faith to the inner spiritual church, the church within the church, as the true *ekklesia* and the hope of the world. But again I am thankful to God that some noble souls from the ranks of organized religion have broken loose from the paralyzing chains of conformity and joined us as active partners in the struggle for freedom. They have left their secure congregations and walked the streets of Albany, Georgia, with us. They have gone down the highways of the South on tortuous rides for freedom. Yes, they have gone to jail with us. Some have been dismissed from their churches, have lost the support of their bishops and fellow ministers. But they have acted in the faith that right defeated is stronger than evil triumphant. Their witness has been the spiritual salt that has preserved the true meaning of the gospel in these troubled times. They have carved a tunnel of hope through the dark mountain of disappointment.

I hope the church as a whole will meet the challenge 44 of this decisive hour. But even if the church does not come to the aid of justice, I have no despair about the future. I have no fear about the outcome of our struggle in Birmingham, even if our motives are at present misunderstood. We will reach the goal of freedom in Birmingham and all over the nation, because the goal of America is freedom. Abused and scorned though we may be, our destiny is tied up with America's destiny. Before the pilgrims landed at Plymouth, we were here. Before the pen of Jefferson etched the majestic words of the Declaration of Independence across the pages of history, we were here. For more than two centuries our forebears labored in this country without wages; they made cotton king; they built the homes of their masters while suffering gross injustice and shameful humiliation—and yet out of a bottomless vitality they continued to thrive and develop. If the inexpressible cruelties of slavery could not stop us, the opposition we now face will surely fail. We will win our freedom because the sacred heritage of our nation and the eternal will of God are embodied in our echoing demands.

Before closing I feel impelled to mention one other 45 point in your statement that has troubled me profoundly. You warmly commended the Birmingham police force for keeping "order" and "preventing violence." I doubt that you would have so warmly commended the police force if you had seen its dogs sinking their teeth into unarmed, nonviolent Negroes. I doubt that you would so quickly commend the policemen if you were to observe their ugly and inhumane treatment of Negroes here in the city jail; if you were to watch them push and curse old Negro women and young Negro girls; if you were to see them slap and kick old Negro men and young boys; if you were to observe them, as they did on two occasions, refuse to give us food because we wanted to sing our grace together. I cannot join you in your praise of the Birmingham police department.

It is true that the police have exercised a degree of 46 discipline in handling the demonstrators. In this sense they have conducted themselves rather "nonviolently" in public. But for what purpose? To preserve the evil system of segregation. Over the past few years I have consistently preached that nonviolence demands that the means we use must be as pure as the ends we seek. I have tried to make clear that it is wrong to use immoral means to attain moral ends. But now I must affirm that it is just as wrong, or perhaps even more so, to use moral means to preserve immoral ends. Perhaps Mr. Connor and his policemen have been rather nonviolent in public, as was Chief Pritchett in Albany, Georgia, but they have used the moral means of nonviolence to maintain the immoral end of racial injustice. As T. S. Eliot has said, "The last temptation is the greatest treason: To do the right deed for the wrong reason."

I wish you had commended the Negro sit-inners and 47 demonstrators of Birmingham for their sublime courage, their willingness to suffer, and their amazing discipline in the midst of great provocation. One day the South will recognize its real heroes. They will be the James Merediths, with the noble sense of purpose that enables them to face jeering and hostile mobs, and with the agonizing loneliness that characterizes the life of the pioneer. They will be old, oppressed, battered Negro women, symbolized in a seventy-two-year-old woman in Montgomery, Alabama, who rose up with a sense of dignity and with her people decided not to ride segregated buses, and who responded with ungrammatical profundity to one who inquired about her weariness: "My feets is tired, but my soul is at rest." They will be the young high school and college students, the young ministers of the gospel and a host of their elders, courageously and nonviolently sitting in at lunch counters and willingly going to jail for conscience' sake. One day the South will know that when these disinherited children of God sat down at lunch counters, they were in reality standing up for what is best in the American dream and for the most sacred values in our Judaeo-Christian heritage, thereby bringing our nation back to those great wells of democracy which were dug deep by the founding fathers in their formulation of the Constitution and the Declaration of Independence.

Never before have I written so long a letter. I'm afraid 48 it is much too long to take your precious time. I can assure you that it would have been much shorter if I had been writing from a comfortable desk, but what else can one do when he is alone in a narrow jail cell, other than write long letters, think long thoughts, and pray long prayers?

If I have said anything in this letter that overstates the 49 truth and indicates an unreasonable impatience, I beg you to forgive me. If I have said anything that understates the truth and indicates my having a patience that allows me to settle for anything less than brotherhood, I beg God to forgive me.

I hope this letter finds you strong in the faith. I also 50

hope that circumstances will soon make it possible for me to meet each of you, not as an integrationist or a civil-rights leader but as a fellow clergyman and a Christian brother. Let us all hope that the dark clouds of racial prejudice will soon pass away and the deep fog of mis-understanding will be lifted from our fear-drenched com-munities, and in some not too distant tomorrow the radiant stars of love and brotherhood will shine over our great nation with all their scintillating beauty.

Yours for the cause of Peace and Brotherhood,
MARTIN LUTHER KING, JR.

QUESTIONS ON MEANING

1. King's letter replies to the charges made by eight clergymen. How many of their points does he respond to? Identify the paragraphs containing his response.

2. Two of King's most important arguments answer the charge that his actions are "untimely" and "unlawful." What argu-ments and evidence does he use to answer these two charges?

3. King says he is disappointed with the "white moderate." Who is the white moderate? Why is King disappointed? Why does he mention this issue in his letter to the clergymen?

QUESTIONS ON PURPOSE AND STRATEGY

1. In your own words, describe King's purpose.

2. Reread King's essay. Concentrate on only the first sentence of each paragraph. What do these sentences tell you about the organization or the argumentative strategy of King's letter?

3. In his essay, King supports his argument with facts, personal experience, quotations by authorities, and biblical references. Which of these kinds of evidence does he use most fre-quently? Which is most effective?

4. King is firm in his position, but his tone is often courteous and accommodating in his replies to the clergy. Find three

examples where his tone is courteous or respectful. Does this moderate, reasonable tone make his argument more effective?

QUESTIONS ON AUDIENCE AND LANGUAGE

1. King's immediate audience is the eight clergymen, but his larger audience includes members of the Southern Christian Leadership Conference, the people who participated in the demonstrations, the white moderate, other members of "the church," and the public at large. Where does King refer to or appeal to each of these groups?

2. The title of this essay is "Letter from Birmingham Jail," but is it really a letter? Would it be more accurate to call it an essay, an article, a political treatise, or an editorial? Explain your choice.

3. In which paragraphs does King use appeals to reason, to character, and to emotion? Which of these appeals did you find most effective?

4. In paragraph fourteen, locate examples of images or figurative language. Which of these did you find most effective? In paragraphs fourteen, twenty-four, and twenty-five King uses parallel sentence structures to add emphasis to his points. In what other paragraphs does he use parallelism? Which of these did you find most effective?

QUESTIONS FOR DISCUSSION AND WRITING

1. In paragraph forty-six, King says, "I have consistently preached that nonviolence demands that the means we use must be as pure as the ends we seek." In fact, though, hasn't King broken laws and caused some violence in seeking his ends? To what extent does King let his ends justify the means?

2. Reread Alice Walker's essay, "The Civil Rights Movement: What Good Was It?". Write a letter to Alice Walker describing how King's methods and legacy have improved one aspect of your life.

3. In the library, find out about recent actions of political or environmental protest groups. Focus on one group that has made recent headlines. Compare their tactics to the "four basic steps" for nonviolent civil disobedience King outlines in paragraphs six through nine. Has this group followed King's procedure? In your opinion, are their methods timely, just, and nonviolent? Are their methods effective?

No Smoking

TERESA SCHMIDT

(1971–   )

PREREADING JOURNAL ENTRY

Everyone knows that smoking is a legal activity, and most people agree that we have a right to smoke if we do not interfere with other people's rights. We also know that smoking causes eye and throat irritation, loss of appetite, emphysema, stroke, and cancer. Based on this and other information, explain why you think smoking should or should not be banned from the workplace.

A student in Emily Golson's composition class at Colorado State University, Teresa Schmidt decided to write her argumentative essay about smoking in the workplace. "Smoking in our breakroom at work seemed completely unnecessary," she explains, "so I chose a smoking ban as my topic. During my research I found that smoking really is a problem as it causes health and productivity problems." Her argumentative essay, "No Smoking," makes a rather radical proposal: Ban all smoking on the job. Just ten years ago, such proposals would have seemed far-fetched. However, with smoking not permitted in many public buildings or on most airplane flights and with nonsmoking areas available in many restaurants, banning smoking from the workplace seems just around the corner. Does Schmidt convince you that the employee's right to a workplace free from health hazards is more important than the right to smoke a legal substance?

Helen McCarthy worked for the Department of 1
Social and Health Services for the state of Washington
for over ten years. At work she was regularly exposed
to tobacco smoke. A nonsmoker, Helen complained to

her superiors about the smoke, but no arrangements were made to help her. Eventually, Helen developed obstructive lung cancer. (Scott 13)

At first, one may think that Helen's is a rare and unusual case. However, there is an increasing number of non-smokers throughout the country who suffer illnesses from or are simply tired of being exposed to tobacco smoke on the job. There is, in addition, an increased recognition of the right of employees to work in a smoke-free environment. Due to the awareness of nonsmokers' rights, some companies have implemented smoking policies in an effort to provide a more healthy and more productive workplace. While no-smoking policies offer a good start to an improved work environment, there should be a ban on smoking in the workplace to ultimately get rid of all smoking on the job.

On-the-job smoking is a hot issue for both smokers 2 and nonsmokers, and many managers now see smoking as a productivity problem. Although opponents question whether smoking affects one's productivity, it has, in fact, been proven that a smoker costs a company, both medically and in productivity, more than a nonsmoker. According to William Weis, an associate professor in the Albers School of Business at Seattle University, a "smoking employee costs his or her employer an estimated $5,740 more annually than a non-smoking employee" (Collison 80). These costs include absenteeism (which is 50 percent greater for smokers), medical care, lost earnings, insurance, damages, and the health impact (Collison 80). Absenteeism, and absence due to smoking breaks, is but one of the productivity problems, yet it accounts for a great deal of employer costs. Marvin Kristein, associate professor of Economics at the State University of New York at Stony Brook states:

> There's a whole range of productivity losses (associated with smoking) that are well documented, not so much in research literature as such, but in discussions about all the time wasted in smoking rituals and smoking breaks. (Cain 3)

Obviously, when a smoker leaves his or her work station for a cigarette, it costs the company money and lost productivity. These, no doubt, are costs that can and need to be eliminated. It is senseless for an employer to have to pay these costs for a habit, smoking, that can easily be banned. William Weiss says, "It doesn't make good sense to invest your money in a smoker" (Cain 3). Put simply, it doesn't make sense to allow smoking at the workplace when it cannot benefit the company and only causes increased costs to the employers.

In addition to the factor of productivity, the legal 3 aspect of a smoking ban must be considered. Opponents to a smoking ban insist that it infringes on their right to smoke. However, on the part of the nonsmoker, the right to a smoke-free workplace is greater. In addition, employers must provide a safe workplace for all employees. Jim Collison, President, Independent Small Business Employers, explains: "Employers should remember that from a strictly legal standpoint, they are obligated under common law to provide a safe and healthy working environment for employees" (81). It can easily be seen that if smoking is allowed, a safe environment cannot be provided. In some instances, "Nonsmokers have sued successfully under the common law . . . and have won workers compensation cases, unemployment compensation and disability insurance payments and other benefits" (Fisher 54). Such cases of nonsmokers suing their employers successfully are not uncommon. As nonsmokers assert their right to breathe clean air, more cases occur, and it is becoming obvious that there needs to be a smoking ban to protect all employees. Only where there is a ban on smoking can there be a safe and healthy working environment.

When discussing the issue of smoking at the workplace, 4 perhaps the most important aspect is the health risk smoking causes to both smokers and nonsmokers. It was proven in 1964 that smoking is, in fact, linked to lung cancer, and in 1986 Surgeon General C. Everett Koop warned further that involuntary smoking can cause lung cancer and other illnesses in healthy nonsmokers (Involuntary Risk 64). Involuntary smoking can be defined as simply breathing in the vicinity of people with lit cigarettes in enclosed areas (Involuntary Risk 64). Anyone who has been with a smoker indeed knows that in addition to lung cancer, their smoke can also cause eye irritation, coughing, headaches, and throat soreness. While eye irritation may seem trivial to some smokers, it nonetheless is a problem that occurs on a daily basis in offices and break rooms and can, eventually, lead to greater health problems. Employees who do not smoke should not be subjected to the risks of involuntary smoking and need to be able to work in a safe environment. Surgeon General Koop states that "the right of the smoker stops at the point where his or her smoking increases the disease risk of those occupying the same environment "(Involuntary Risk" 64). Ultimately, the only way to ensure a risk-free environment for workers is to ban smoking completely at the workplace. By doing so, the health of many people can be preserved, and the number of those who suffer from the tragedies of smoking-related illnesses will decrease.

Many opponents of a smoking ban at the workplace 5 believe that smoking simply isn't a problem. One manager stated that "smoking is not a problem because a small percentage of our employees are smokers and these people are considerate, careful smokers" (McKendrick 12). What needs to be understood is that any smoking cannot be considerate or careful. The fact is, smoking is a health risk and can cause serious illnesses. Those who feel smoking isn't a problem are simply closing their eyes to the rights of those who don't smoke. In addition, they are ignoring the statistics that prove that smoking is a health risk.

The most serious argument of the opponents is that 6 banning smoking at the workplace is a form of discrimination. Opponents charge that it is a personal choice if an individual chooses to smoke, and by banning smoking, employers discriminate against smokers. However, employers do have the legal right to discriminate against smokers. William Weis explains that "workers have no rights to smoke or sing or whistle or play the piano in the workplace" (Collison 81). Ultimately, employees have no right to do anything that might cause harm to another employee, and this includes smoking. Smoking is indeed a personal choice, but where it endangers another, at the workplace, it needs to be banned.

After working at a small retail store for over two years 7 where there was only one break room for both smokers and nonsmokers, I can attest that smoking is simply unacceptable in the workplace. It seemed that the majority of the employees where I worked smoked, and there was not a day when I didn't come home from work smelling of tobacco smoke. A nonsmoker, I often chose to skip my breaks because I could not stand sitting in a smoke-filled room. My eyes constantly watered, itched, and reddened from the tobacco smoke. For those of us who did not smoke, the break room, instead of being a place to relax for a bit, was a disgusting, ash-filled room. The manager insisted she could do nothing. However, this is not true. With a smoking ban, break rooms like mine and offices and break rooms everywhere can become clean, safe, healthy, and more productive. The choice to smoke is indeed a personal one. However, at the workplace, where it endangers the health of others and hinders productivity, smoking needs to be banned. Perhaps if there had been a smoking ban, Helen McCarthy would not have developed lung cancer, and I might have enjoyed my job more. With the support of a ban on smoking at the workplace, employees can enjoy cleaner, healthier, and more productive lives and careers.

Works Cited

Cain, Carol. "No Smoking. Employers Say Restrictions Can Cut Costs." *Business Insurance* 17 Jan. 1983: 3, 22.

Collison, Jim. "Workplace Smoking Policies: 16 Questions and Answers." *Personnel Journal* April 1988: 80–82.

Fisher, Karen J. "Smoke Free or Free to Smoke?" *American City and County* Feb. 1989: 53–56.

"Involuntary Risk." *Time* 29 Dec. 1986: 64.

McKendrick, Joseph E. "Smoking Policies Take Off." *Management World* Jan./Feb. 1988: 12–13.

Scott, R. Craig. "The Smoking Controversy Goes to Court." *Management World* Jan./Feb. 1988: 13–14.

QUESTIONS ON MEANING

1. What sentence(s) best express Schmidt's thesis or claim?

2. In which paragraphs does Schmidt counter her opponents' arguments that smoking does not affect productivity, that smoking is legal, and that banning smoking at the workplace is a form of discrimination?

QUESTIONS ON PURPOSE AND STRATEGY

1. Does Schmidt make a claim of fact, cause and effect, value, policy, or some combination of all four? Referring to specific sentences, explain your choice(s).

2. Schmidt elects to write about her own personal experience in the closing paragraph. Should she have included her experience in her essay? Should she have discussed it in the introduction or in earlier paragraphs? Explain your recommendation.

3. Is Schmidt proposing that each company should ban smoking from its workplace, or is she recommending national legislation *requiring* that all companies ban smoking?

QUESTIONS ON AUDIENCE AND LANGUAGE

1. After reading Schmidt's essay, one student commented, "I don't get the feeling that Schmidt is talking to me, but I don't know who her audience really is." Explain why you agree or disagree with this reaction. What advice would you give to Schmidt?

2. Reread the second sentence in paragraph two and the first

sentence in paragraph four. How could these sentences be revised to make the language more concise or the meaning clearer?

3. In which body paragraphs does Schmidt use an effective transition in the opening sentence to signal a new idea to her reader? Which paragraph could use a clearer transition? Write a new opening sentence for that paragraph.

QUESTIONS FOR DISCUSSION AND WRITING

1. Are the opposition's arguments that banning smoking infringes on a smoker's rights and that banning smoking is a form of discrimination essentially the same argument? How are these two arguments similar? How are they different?

2. Writers of argumentative essays often put their strongest or most convincing arguments last. What is Schmidt's best argument? Where does it occur in the essay? Explain why she should or should not change its placement.

3. Write a letter to Schmidt, arguing that smoking should *not* be banned from the workplace.

4. Write an essay investigating the smoking regulations in your school, workplace, or community. Is there a controversy about banning smoking in any of these places? After investigating conditions, write your own argumentative essay proposing a solution to your local problems.

Battered

KIMBERLY S. FREEMAN

(1969–   )

PREREADING JOURNAL ENTRY

In your judgment, what kinds of physical discipline should parents use on their children? Is physical punishment (spanking or slapping) necessary in some cases? In relationships between men and women, is physical discipline necessary? Explain.

A student at Oklahoma State University, Kimberly S. Freeman wrote an argumentative essay for her instructor, James Yates, on abusive relationships between men and women. In reading the research, she discovered that abusive men and battered women form a curious symbiotic relationship: Men who suffer from low self-esteem or men who were neglected or even abused as children become abusers. In turn, women with low self-esteem sometimes think they actually deserve the battering they receive. As Freeman argues in her essay, often both individuals are, in fact, emotionally disturbed, and the results are often tragic.

Pro and Con List

Subject: Abusive relationships between men and women

Claim: Although abusive men often think their actions are justified and abused women sometimes think they deserve punishment, both are in reality emotionally disturbed.

Pro (the reality)	*Con (their perceptions)*
Research shows that the root of the problem often lies in the family or in drugs or alcohol.	Abusive men think that slapping a woman is not a problem.
Men express their insecurity by taking control through violence.	Abusive men may think that the problem is just "personal" between the man and woman.
No man or woman really likes to be beaten or abused.	Some abusive men think that women like to be beaten. If they don't fight back, they like it.
Women do feel responsible for the man's behavior.	Abused women think they can change the man's behavior.
Low self-esteem plays a part in both men and women in abusive relationship.	Abused women sometimes think they deserve punishment.

First Draft of Opening Paragraphs

Her upper eyelid grotesquely protruded from its proper place, swelling to become one with the eyebrow. Blackish-grey and yellow hues penetrated the tender skin. Red, tan, and bleeding, the lower eyelid refused to function properly upon her blinking. The eye socket continuously oozed an opaque, sticky substance in an attempt to soothe the injury. No more than a slit, the white of the eye exhibited an abundance of tiny broken capillaries. The left side of her mouth was disguised beneath a deformed swollen mass of bruised skin. She held her left arm stable with her right hand. It was just a sprain. If only she had not made him angry. He did not mean to hurt her. He would change. The prevalence of

abuse by a male in a relationship is
frightening, and the number of women who
remain with their abuser is even more
disturbing.

The scenario is terribly familiar: a
battered woman who refuses to leave her
abuser. The obvious question is "Why?" Why
does the man abuse, and why does the woman
accept the harsh and inhumane treatment?
Abuse is a complex and intriguing behavior.
The roots come from the male's desire to
control. Men are not necessarily
consciously aware of their need to
dominate. Rather, they are socialized to
feel uncomfortable when not in control
(Schecter 219). This need to dominate
displays itself through verbal, emotional,
and physical abuse toward a woman with whom
he is in a relationship.

Final Draft

The room finally stops spinning. Her upper eyelid 1
grotesquely protrudes from its proper place, swelling
and becoming one with the eyebrow. Blackish-grey
and yellow hues penetrate the tender, surrounding
skin. Red, torn, and bleeding, the lower eyelid refuses
to function properly when she tries to blink. The eye
socket steadily oozes an opaque, sticky substance, in
an effort to soothe the raw injury. The left side of her
mouth is disguised beneath a deformed and swollen
mass of bruised skin. Numbness begins engulfing not
only her face, but also her soul. She holds her left arm
in her lap. It is just a sprain and is beginning to throb.

Abuse is a complex and intriguing behavior. To 2
abuse is to misuse or injure another being through
verbal, emotional, or physical means. Abuse is common. It is so common that an estimated 13 million
couples experience this horrifying form of domestic
violence each year (Sonkin et al. 34). A more specific

form of abuse is that of battering. To batter is to strike continuously, and this action is usually carried out by the male in the relationship. Such abusive behavior is frightening, and the number of women who remain with their abuser is eerie. Although men may think that their physical abuse is not a problem and women may think that they deserve abuse, both points of view are wrong. Men who batter and abuse women are emotionally disturbed, as are the women who allow the abuse to occur.

"Hey," a burly man mumbles, "I ain't got no [3] problem. It's that woman who gots the problem. She thinks she's as good as a man. A couple of slaps quickly reminds her who the boss is." Perhaps "a few slaps" does get results, but this is clearly a twisted action for a man to take toward a woman. The fact that the desired results are achieved in no way justifies his abusive actions. This mentality of needing to control is vital in abusive relationships. As Susan Schechter states in *Women and Male Violence*, "Men are not necessarily consciously aware of their need to dominate. Rather, they are socialized to feel uncomfortable when not in control" (219). The need to dominate exhibits itself through verbal, emotional, and physical abuse toward a woman with whom he is in a relationship. A domineering persona has been shown to be evident in most male abusers of women. Nevertheless, there are no cut-and-dry indications of a man who is abusive. Men who batter come from all socioeconomic backgrounds, races, religions, and walks of life (Sonkin et al. 41).

"So maybe I shove my girlfriend around a bit," a [4] well-tanned man in shorts and a tank admits through a slight grin, "It's not a problem. It's personal; just between her and me." Reality provides us with a different picture in that abuse does not affect just the woman and man involved. It often is a family problem, and a deeply rooted one. Recent studies have shown that 45 percent of abusers saw their own mothers being abused by their fathers, and 62 percent were under the influence of alcohol or other drugs during the beating incident (Sonkin et al. 35). Abusive behavior is often learned by the male in childhood. The harmful actions he observed are engrained into his mind. His "harmless shoves" are not harmless. The fact that the woman may not be physically injured is not truly relevant. The crux of the matter is that the man is dealing with his problems through dominance and physical force when he deems it "necessary."

"She knows I don't like her talking to that man- 5 friend of hers. All he wants is one thing, and I'm just trying to protect her. Sometimes she just doesn't listen, and I have to make her listen," declares a man in a Pierre Cardin suit. Perhaps the woman's male friend is a louse, and maybe he is not concerned with her best interests. Nonetheless, for the man involved with her to use abuse as a means to "protect" her is a sorry excuse. The problem is with the husband, not the friend. In *The Abusive Partner,* Maria Roy claims, "Battering is violence disguised as a form of power, for at its very essence is an extremely small and very frail self-image that is desperately yearning to be recognized, acknowledged, and fortified; a self-image so negative that it seeks to destroy itself by destroying others" (4).

Low self-esteem plays an important part for both 6 the male and female in an abusive relationship. Low self-esteem seems to be particularly important in regard to the female and her actions. Typically thought of as being the more passive and submissive of the sexes, the female with a low self-image places herself in a possibly dangerous situation.

"She likes it. She wants to know that I'm a real 7 man, and if that means an occasional blow to the jaw to remind her, that's life. I've got no problem with it. She's got no problem with it," he says coyly. Clearly though, the female does have a problem in much the same way as the male does. A female's failure to fight back does not mean that she "enjoys it." The abused woman's mentality set is so disturbed that it brings about confused and absurd beliefs. In a study of wife abuse, Jennifer Fleming says that the extremely low levels of self-esteem found among battered women allows them to conclude that although they may not be worthy of much, at least they merit the attention of a beating (85). These women believe that they somehow deserve to be abused. Their thought process should send chills up our spines! No human being deserves to be physically or verbally abused. It is a barbaric action, and one that needs to be stopped.

The burning question is why the woman does not 8 remove herself from the abusive relationship. From an outsider's viewpoint, to leave is the obvious answer to her dilemma. However, from the abused woman's view, the answer is hidden in a sea of confusion and emotion. These women do not remain in the relationship because they basically like being beaten. They have difficulty leaving because of complex psychosocial reasons (Walker 43). The woman often feels completely responsible for her partner's violent actions. She may believe that the batterer would change his behavior if only she could change her own (Walker 33). Abuse is a psychological game: one of control and dominance, and one of pain.

The abusive relationship is tragic. A union that is 9 meant to exude love and respect becomes one of hatred and abuse. The story becomes even more freakish in that the two individuals remain in such a twisted situation. Lenore E. Walker states the phenomenon rather concisely: "Both the batterer and battered woman fear they cannot survive alone, and so continue to maintain a bizarre symbiotic relationship from which they cannot extricate themselves" (43). The woman is at fault, and the man is at fault. Nevertheless, the burden of change lies heavily upon the woman. She must remove herself from the abusive situation. A church or community center can provide temporary lodging and beneficial counseling for a woman with no place to turn. An abusive lifestyle is not living. It is simply existing, and no person deserves this form of empty existence. Both the man and the woman need help. Until such aid is sought, however, the silent cries of battered women will continue to fill the blackest of nights in our troubled society.

Works Cited

Fleming, Jennifer Baker. *Stopping Wife Abuse.* New York: Anchor Press, 1979.

Roy, Maria. *The Abusive Partner: An Analysis of Domestic Battering.* New York: Van Nostrand Reinhold, 1982.

Schechter, Susan. *Women and Male Violence.* Boston: South End Press, 1982.

Sonkin, Daniel Jay, Del Martin, and Lenore E. Walker, *The Male Batterer: A Treatment Approach.* New York: Springer Publishing Co., 1985.

Walker, Lenore E., *The Battered Woman.* New York: Harper and Row, 1979.

---. *The Battered Woman Syndrome.* New York: Springer Publishing Co., 1984.

QUESTIONS ON MEANING

1. According to Freeman, how do some men rationalize their behavior? What are the real causes of their behavior?

2. How do women sometimes rationalize their beatings? Why, according to Freeman, do they sometimes stay in abusive relationships?

QUESTIONS ON PURPOSE AND STRATEGY

1. Is Freeman making a claim of fact, cause and effect, value, or policy? Does it contain some elements of each? Find specific sentences that support your choice(s).

2. Freeman chooses to represent the "opposing arguments" through the quotations from a hypothetical abusive male. In

which paragraphs does she use this strategy? In which paragraphs is it most or least effective?

3. Freeman does not use personal experience in her essay. If you were giving her advice on her essay, what experience might she use? If she had suffered some physical abuse, should she use that experience in her essay? If she has not been personally abused, should she interview friends or acquaintances for their experiences?

QUESTIONS ON AUDIENCE AND LANGUAGE

1. Describe Freeman's intended audience.

2. What kind of lead-in does Freeman use to get her reader's attention? How does Freeman revise her lead-in for her final version? Does her added detail improve her description? Does her change to present tense improve her description? Explain.

QUESTIONS FOR DISCUSSION AND WRITING

1. Do you agree with Freeman when she says, "The burden of change lies heavily upon the woman. She must remove herself from the abusive situation"?

2. What parts of Freeman's essay (lead-in, statement of claim, definition, arguments and evidence, presentation of opposing arguments, conclusion) are the most effective? Which could be revised and improved?

3. Reread one or more of the following essays and write an essay explaining how each is or is not relevant to Freeman's essay:

John McMurtry, "Kill 'Em, Crush 'Em, Eat 'Em Raw!"

Judy Syfers, "I Want a Wife"

Robin Lakoff, "You Are What You Say"

William F. Buckley, Jr., "Why Don't We Complain?

Dick Gregory, "Shame"

Nancy Friday, "Competition"

4. Reread your Prewriting Journal Entry. Explain how Freeman's essay did or did not change your initial ideas on this subject. At what points do you agree or disagree with Freeman's essay?

THEMATIC
TABLE OF CONTENTS

Contemporary Issues

The Environment

Popular Culture

The Woman's Perspective

Cultural Diversity

Friends and Family

Education

College Life

Reading

NORMAN ATKINS *Fast Food for Thought* 305
URSULA K. LE GUIN *Why Are Americans Afraid of Dragons?* 590
JOHN HOLT *How Teachers Make Children Hate Reading* 25
EILEEN SIMPSON *Dyslexia* 55
MARIE WINN *Television and Reading* 46
RICHARD WRIGHT *The Library Card* 33

Writing

JOAN DIDION *On Keeping a Notebook* 105
NORA EPHRON *Revision and Life: Take It from the Top* 135
GERALD FORD *There Is a Whole Lot of Shaking Going On!* 331
GEORGE ORWELL *Why I Write* 95
MIKE ROSE *Writing Around Rules* 126
WILLIAM ZINSSER *The Act Of Writing: One Man's Method* 116

CREDITS

INDEX